Rethinking Society for the 21ˢᵗ Century

Report of the International Panel on Social Progress

Volume 3: Transformations in Values, Norms, Cultures

This is the third of three volumes containing a report from the International Panel on Social Progress (IPSP). The IPSP is an independent association of top research scholars with the goal of assessing methods for improving the main institutions of modern societies. Written in accessible language by scholars across the social sciences and humanities, these volumes assess the achievements of world societies in past centuries, the current trends, the dangers that we are now facing, and the possible futures in the twenty-first century. It covers the main socio-economic, political, and cultural dimensions of social progress, global as well as regional issues, and the diversity of challenges and their interplay around the world. This particular volume covers topics such as world cultures and religions, families, global health, education, and the contributions of social sciences to institutional change.

The International Panel on Social Progress brings together more than 300 scholars from all disciplines of social sciences and the humanities, and from all continents. Since 2014, the mission of the Panel has been to gather expertise and disseminate knowledge on the perspectives for social progress around the world in the coming decades. The Panel is an independent initiative supported by more than 30 scientific or academic institutions and international foundations. With Amartya Sen as President and Nancy Fraser, Ravi Kanbur, and Helga Nowotny as co-chairs of the Scientific Council, the Panel has been co-directed by Olivier Bouin and Marc Fleurbaey.

Rethinking Society for the 21st Century

Report of the International Panel on Social Progress

Volume 3: Transformations in Values, Norms, Cultures

CAMBRIDGE
UNIVERSITY PRESS

CAMBRIDGE
UNIVERSITY PRESS

University Printing House, Cambridge CB2 8BS, United Kingdom

One Liberty Plaza, 20th Floor, New York, NY 10006, USA

477 Williamstown Road, Port Melbourne, VIC 3207, Australia

314–321, 3rd Floor, Plot 3, Splendor Forum, Jasola District Centre, New Delhi – 110025, India

79 Anson Road, #06-04/06, Singapore 079906

Cambridge University Press is part of the University of Cambridge.

It furthers the University's mission by disseminating knowledge in the pursuit of
education, learning, and research at the highest international levels of excellence.

www.cambridge.org
Information on this title: www.cambridge.org/9781108423144
DOI: 10.1017/9781108399661

First published 2018

Printed in the United Kingdom by TJ International Ltd. Padstow Cornwall

A catalogue record for this publication is available from the British Library.

Library of Congress Cataloging-in-Publication Data
Names: International Panel on Social Progress, author.
Title: Rethinking society for the 21st century : report of the International Panel on Social Progress. Other titles: Socio-economic
transformations. | Political regulation, governance, and societal transformations. | Transformations in values, norms, cultures.
Description: Cambridge, United Kingdom ; New York, NY : Cambridge University Press, 2018. | Includes index. |
Volume 1. Socio-economic transformations – Volume 2. Political regulation, governance, and
societal transformations – Volume 3. Transformations in values, norms, cultures.
Identifiers: LCCN 2018003514 | ISBN 9781108399593 (Set of 3 hardback volumes) | ISBN 9781108423120 (vol. 1 : hardback) |
ISBN 9781108423137 (vol. 2 : hardback) | ISBN 9781108423144 (vol. 3 : hardback) | ISBN 9781108399579 (Set of 3 paperback volumes) |
ISBN 9781108436328 (vol. 1 : paperback) | ISBN 9781108436335 (vol. 2 : paperback) | ISBN 9781108436342 (vol. 3 : paperback)
Subjects: LCSH: Social change. | Progress. | Political science. | Civilization–21st century.
Classification: LCC HN18.3 .I568 2018 | DDC 306–dc23
LC record available at https://lccn.loc.gov/2018003514

ISBN 978-1-108-39959-3 Set of 3 hardback volumes
ISBN 978-1-108-42312-0 Volume 1 Hardback
ISBN 978-1-108-42313-7 Volume 2 Hardback
ISBN 978-1-108-42314-4 Volume 3 Hardback
ISBN 978-1-108-39957-9 Set of 3 paperback volumes
ISBN 978-1-108-43632-8 Volume 1 Paperback
ISBN 978-1-108-43633-5 Volume 2 Paperback
ISBN 978-1-108-43634-2 Volume 3 Paperback

Contents

Concluding Chapters

Introduction to Volume 3

Authors:[1]
Olivier Bouin, Marie-Laure Djelic, Marc Fleurbaey, Ravi Kanbur, Elisa Reis

---

[1] Affiliations: OB: RFIEA; MLD: Sciences Po; MF: Princeton University; RK: Cornell University; ER: Federal University of Rio de Janeiro.

0.1 The IPSP Report: Aims and Method

This section briefly recalls elements which are presented in more detail in the Introduction to Volume 1, and is identical to the first section of the Introduction to Volume 2.

The International Panel on Social Progress (IPSP) is an academic, bottom-up initiative, aiming to assess the perspectives for social progress in the coming decades, in the world. Mobilizing large numbers of social scientists and humanities scholars, the IPSP project is complementary to many ongoing efforts by various groups and organizations with which it is collaborating, such as the United Nations and its Agenda 2030, the OECD and its multiple initiatives for a "better life" and "inclusive growth," the World Bank and its work against poverty and inequality, the ILO and its "decent work" agenda, the Social Progress Imperative and its measurement initiative supplementing economic indicators, and many others.

The IPSP distinguishes itself from other initiatives by examining not just policy issues for the medium term but also structural and systemic issues for the long term, by mobilizing a uniquely wide set of perspectives, from all relevant disciplines as well as from all continents, and by speaking to actors who are or will be the "change-makers" of society. The Panel mobilizes the notion of "social progress" to emphasize that social change is not a neutral matter and that a compass is needed to parse the options that actors and decision-makers face. The message of this Panel is a message of hope: we can improve our institutions, curb inequalities, expand democracy, and secure sustainability. Importantly, there is not a unique direction of progress but multiple possibilities and many ideas that can and should be experimented.

The Report presented has 22 chapters spread over three volumes. Every chapter is co-signed by a multidisciplinary team of authors and represents the views of this team. In total, more than 260 authors have been involved, with about 60 percent of contributions coming, in roughly equal proportions, from economics, sociology, and political science. Each chapter starts with a long summary of its contents, so as to help readers navigate the Report.

Every chapter is meant to be a critical assessment of the state of the art in the topic covered in the chapter, acknowledging ongoing debates and suggesting emerging points of consensus. Most chapters contain recommendations for action and reform, with an effort to make the underlying values explicit. This Report provides the reader with a unique overview of the state of society and possible futures, with a wealth of ideas and suggestions for possible reforms and actions. For scholars and students, it also offers an exceptional guide to the literature in the relevant academic disciplines of social sciences and the humanities. Readers are invited to take this Report as a resource, as a mine for ideas and arguments, as a tool for their own thought and action. They are also invited to engage with Panel members and share their views and experiences.

0.2 Outline of the Report and of Volume 3

The Report is divided into three parts, with two introductory and two concluding chapters. The introductory chapters lay out the main social trends that form the background of this Report (Chapter 1), and the main values and principles that form a "compass" for those who seek social progress (Chapter 2).

The first part of the Report deals with socio-economic transformations, and focuses on economic inequalities (Chapter 3), growth and environmental issues (Chapter 4), urbanization (Chapter 5), capitalist institutions of markets, corporations and finance (Chapter 6), and labor (Chapter 7), concluding with a reflection on how economic organization determines wellbeing and social justice (Chapter 8).

The second part of the Report scrutinizes political issues, analyzing the ongoing complex trends in democracy and the rule of law (Chapter 9), the forms and resolutions of situations of violence and conflicts (Chapter 10), and the mixed efficacy of supranational institutions and organizations (Chapter 11), as well as the multiple forms of global governance (Chapter 12), and the important role for democracy of media and communications (Chapter 13). It concludes with a chapter on the challenges to democracy raised by inequalities, and the various ways in which democracy can be rejuvenated (Chapter 14).

The third part of the Report is devoted to transformations in cultures and values, with analyses of cultural trends linked to "modernization" and its pitfalls, as well as globalization (Chapter 15), a study of the complex relation between religions and social progress (Chapter 16), an examination of the promises and challenges in ongoing transformations in family structures and norms (Chapter 17), a focus on trends and policy issues regarding health and life-death issues (Chapter 18), a study of the ways in which education can contribute to social progress (Chapter 19), and finally, a chapter on the important values of solidarity and belonging (Chapter 20).

The two concluding chapters include a synthesis on the various innovative ways in which social progress can go forward (Chapter 21) and a reflection on how the various disciplines of social science can play a role in the evolution of society and the design of policy (Chapter 22).

The present volume (Volume 3) contains the third part of the report and the two concluding chapters. The fact that culture is relegated to the last part of the Report should not suggest that its role is limited in the pursuit of social progress. Actually, every chapter in this volume gives the strong impression that neglecting the cultural dimension is a recipe for catastrophe. As Chapter 15 argues, "human beings are not only social beings, as the IPSP emphasizes, but also cultural beings. We are meaning-making beings, who evaluate options (including visions of social progress) by how they fit into our 'cultural scripts' and 'collective imaginaries,' and whether they recognize and respect our collective identities, loyalties, and sense of belonging." The time in which social reformers thought, after Marx, that the economy was the base and that ideas were only a derivative "superstructure" is over, and one can even argue that many unfair structures of economic organization owe their stability not just to the strength of powerful vested interests but also to cultural frames that assign various agents to their situations, often with their consent.

Chapter 15 explains the importance of culture as the broad set of "the everyday social norms, ideas and identities that define the meaningfulness of social interactions of individuals and societies." This chapter underscores the pitfalls of the view of "modernization" and "individualization" which has accompanied the self-perception of the dominant culture in the West, pointing instead to a multiplicity of modernities emerging across the world. Chapter 16 considers the religious phenomenon from the perspective of social relations and makes a vigorous plea for a more complex apprehension of the relation between religion and social progress than typically found among both critics and apologists. Chapter 17 scrutinizes the evolutions observed in the domain of family life, with contradictory trends toward equality and dignity within the family. Indeed, this chapter documents a multiplication of legitimate forms of families, while simultaneously observing a persistent division of tasks in the household as well as the emergence of ideological backlash and resistance to evolution. It emphasizes the efficacy of official norms and legal regulations in a domain that is often considered strictly private. Chapter 18 deals with health and the important life stages, from cradle to grave, that shape people's opportunities to make use of their bodies. It highlights how health is both a matter of public policy and a domain in which ethical issues and cultural norms remain central. Health and demography appear also in other chapters (in particular Chapter 1 for long-run trends, 3 for inequalities, and 11 for global public health governance) and Chapter 18 provides a useful and thorough synthesis. Chapter 19 studies the essential domain of education, which concentrates the hopes of many reformists (including the UN Agenda 2030) due to its crucial role not just of training the workforce but also of forming responsible and critical citizens. It argues that education as a system requires a comprehensive approach that encompasses access issues, contents issues, and internal governance issues. This part is concluded by Chapter 20, which sheds light on the importance of social relations through dimensions of solidarity and belonging. It argues that, far from being a secondary concern, these dimensions should become central in the search for social progress,

and can help give a new (less narrow and less individualistic) life to classical values of equality and freedom. It provides many examples of how these notions play out in different parts of the world.

Finally, the two concluding chapters open the Report to new horizons. Chapter 21 argues, through general argument but also a good number of concrete examples, that social progress can be explored in multiple directions. This is an essential point of this Report, which both argues for the usefulness of the notion of progress in an era which needs to recover a notion of the direction the world should be going, while simultaneously strongly rejecting the old view that progress follows only one line. Many ideas deserve to be researched and experimented with, and various societal arrangements can open up promising paths. Chapter 22 presents a discussion on the contribution of social sciences to policy-making and societal transformations. This chapter can be particularly useful for students and scholars who wonder about their potential role and place in society. In their 2013 "Manifest for the Social Sciences," Craig Calhoun and Michel Wieviorka challenged their peers: "If social sciences exist, is it not, precisely, because analyzing action, institutions, social relations, structures, can help to build a better world?" This challenge contributed to motivating the creation of this Panel. Chapter 22, itself, does not examine the question of the usefulness of this Panel. This question will be answered by the readers of this Report.

Acknowledgments

The preparation of this Report has benefited from support by many individuals and organizations. Please refer to the Introduction to Volume I for details.

Introduction

Transformations in Values, Norms, Cultures

15

Social Progress and Cultural Change

Coordinating Lead Authors:[1]
John Bowen, Will Kymlicka

Lead Authors:[2]
Martin Hopenhayn, Takyiwaa Manuh, Abdul Raufu Mustapha

Contributing Authors:[3]
Faisal Garba, Jan Willem Duyvendak

[1]   Affiliations: JB: Anthropology, Washington University in St. Louis, USA; WK: Philosophy, Queen's University, Kingston, Canada.
[2]   Affiliations: MH: Instituto de Humanidades, Universidad Diego Portales, Chile; TM: United Nations Economic Commission for Africa, Ethiopia; ARM: Centre for African Studies, University of Oxford, UK.
[3]   Affiliations: FG: Sociology, University of Cape Town, South Africa; JWD: Sociology, University of Amsterdam, Netherlands.

611

Summary

In this chapter, we take on the challenge of how to assess social progress while taking full account of the particularities that characterize cultures (and religions, ethnicities, national belonging). Drawing on the example of modernization theory in the post-war period, we discuss some common pitfalls in the ways in which culture and processes of cultural change are perceived and understood. We focus on two issues that are of particular relevance to the IPSP: the need to nurture an ethos of solidarity and citizenship; and the need to address risks of cultural exclusions and stigmatization.

One important obstacle to taking adequate account of culture lies in the persistent, if not always explicit, influence of "modernization theory" in the social sciences. According to this theory, modernization is characterized by a series of social processes – such as education, literacy, urbanization, legal codification, and bureaucratization – which disembedded people from their traditional ways of life. People no longer simply inherit ascribed roles and relationships within a traditional culture, but are exposed to different ways of life, and (to varying degrees) have options for the kind of person they want to be, and the kind of life they want to lead. The inevitable result, according to modernization theory, is a kind of *individualization,* and this kind of individualization is indeed a marker of "progress."

Instead, we argue that (1) individuals by their very nature draw on social ties and cultural orientations to create fulfilling lives, however individualistically they may see themselves; (2) the disembedding of individuals from inherited social roles and communities can take both emancipatory and pathological forms; and, conversely, (3) the embedding of individuals within strong community identities can also take multiple forms, some progressive and some pathological. As a result, it is a mistake to equate social progress with the withering of traditional identities or the disembedding of individuals from community. Social justice requires a set of social relationships and cultural repertoires that sustain human capacities in an inclusive way, and radical individualism is as much a threat to this as sectarian communalism or authoritarian traditionalism.

We also argue that modernization theory's core assumptions about the decline of traditions and the rise of new, rationalized forms of sociability can operate to exclude wide segments of humanity from the categories of modern, reflexive, or cosmopolitan social actors. We explore how non-elite actors draw on their seemingly "parochial" or "traditional" identities to help develop new forms of solidarity, including transnational ties. While claims to protect cultural integrity or religious orthodoxy can be invoked to block social progress, we must take our analyses below surface-level rhetoric, and examine the ways in which religious, political, and legal actors actually engage in the (re)interpretation of traditions, such as the ways that Islamic jurisprudence is being reinterpreted to favor more gender-equal forms of practice. Cultural resources may be particularly important when they draw on deep-seated senses of obligation and orientation to garner support for change; the challenge is to bring about convergences on broadly recognized desiderata of bettering human welfare.

"Traditional" or "primordial" attachments are not unconditionally regressive or backward. The persistence of such attachments, and their political mobilization, is not always to be regretted, but rather can, under some circumstances, serve as a vehicle for progressive politics and cultural change. We need a more fine-grained way of assessing the mobilization of groups to protect their "cultures" and "identities." We illustrate these dynamics through a series of cases and debates, including case studies of intercultural health initiatives in Latin America and evolving identities in Sub-Saharan Africa, as well as debates over the new spatial dynamics of culture, and over Islamic family law – all of which offer lessons for how to identify (and to render productive) the ambivalences inherent in both individualization and traditionalism, and thereby offer new ways to think about social progress.

Drawing on these examples, we believe that modernity can be realized through distinct cultural and religious traditions. Indeed, we see culture as a historical quarry from which social imaginations extract creative and substantial framing of modernization in local meaningful ways, and culture may be a powerful source for synergies between identity dynamics and socially inclusive forms of individualization.

In public and academic discussion, this idea is sometimes discussed under the heading of "multiple modernities." According to one simplistic version of this idea, modernization does not necessarily lead societies to converge on particular economic or political forms (such as secular liberal democracies), but rather can take very different forms shaped by different cultural or religious traditions, such as Muslim or Evangelical conceptions of modernity, or modernity as developed in a more authoritarian direction in Singapore or Qatar. In our view, when the idea of multiple modernities is interpreted in this way – as a clash between monolithic civilizational models of modernity – it too often operates to suppress

15

both intercultural learning and internal dissent and critique. However, the idea of multiple modernities can help clarify the normative stakes in evaluating different models or trajectories of social progress. We find that many of today's intellectual and political struggles concern the tension between universalistic political ideas, on the one hand, and particular sets of norms and values that are generated and reproduced in specific political contexts, on the other. Adopting the idea of a plurality of viable and attractive trajectories toward social progress directs us to examine at a more detailed level the mechanisms that can and do move institutions and societies toward broadly acceptable goals and at the same time draw on (often disparate) elements of cultural and religious traditions and convictions. *Put simply, there may be effective convergence toward broadly held ideals about equality and justice, but where these ideas are framed in terms of distinct cultural and religious views and resources.*

The challenge then becomes: given profound differences across cultural and religious convictions – which do not reduce to "societies," "regions," or "civilizations" – what mechanisms can be said to both develop consistently with those convictions and aim to achieve social progress, as all might be able to recognize it? To take one broadly held aspiration, do we find distinct pathways toward gender equality that also preserve key elements of, say, Evangelical, or East Asian, or Amazonian ideas and practices? We explore this question through an extended case study of reforms of Islamic family law that move toward greater gender equality while preserving local Islamic understandings. These reforms are carried out through new legal codes and court decisions, without directly challenging the validity of long-standing understandings transmitted by scholars of Islam. In this way, they preserve the space between religious authorities and legal authorities that allows for the trading of concepts across different registers, different understandings of law. We explore this idea of "practical convergences," and how it can contribute to a richer understanding of the prospects for social progress in our diverse world.

15

15.1 Culture in the Study of Social Progress

Any project of social progress is likely to involve significant cultural change, transforming people's identities, aspirations, loyalties, horizons, perceptual and cognitive regimes, norms, and values. Drawing on the example of modernization theory in the post-war period, we discuss some common pitfalls in the ways in which culture and processes of cultural change are perceived and understood. We focus on two issues that are of particular relevance to the IPSP: the need to nurture an ethos of solidarity and citizenship; and the need to address risks of cultural exclusions and stigmatization. Although these issues were acknowledged within post-war modernization theory, it lacked the tools to analyze them, and to address them today requires a more sophisticated understanding of the politics of cultural inclusion and exclusion. This requires both a refinement of our general theoretical concepts, and also a comparative and historically nuanced perspective on culture that takes into account regional differences, asymmetric developments, and social specificities.

We define "culture" broadly, to refer not primarily to "the arts" or so-called high and low culture, but to culture in the anthropological sense of the everyday social norms, ideas, and identities that define the meaningfulness of social interactions of individuals and societies. Culture in this broad sense is invoked for political purposes in a bewildering array of contexts. In some contexts, it is used to justify claims for the legal recognition or political protection of particular practices, on the grounds that these are "essential" to a group's culture. In other contexts, it is used to explain inequalities between groups or societies, as when people say that Roma poverty is due to their "culture," or that failed democratization in Arab countries is due to Arab/Islamic "culture." In all of these contexts, and further heightened by the invocation of the "return of religion," culture appears as an essentialized and fixed imperative, tied to a specific bounded and clearly identifiable group, ignoring the reality that cultures are always evolving, contested, and interacting as social practices, and that individuals can and do take a critical perspective, explicitly and implicitly, toward cultural inheritances.

In response to these problems, some commentators have proposed that we abandon references to culture, in both academic analysis and public discourse.[4] But this is neither feasible nor desirable. Human beings are not only social beings, as the IPSP emphasizes, but also cultural beings. We are meaning-making beings, who evaluate options (including visions of social progress) by how they fit into our "cultural scripts" and "collective imaginaries," and whether they recognize and respect our collective identities, loyalties, and sense of belonging. Struggles for social and political change are therefore also cultural contestations. Recent manifestations of political protest (for example the Arab Spring, Pussy riot, Iranian protest culture) make conscious use of forms of cultural representation to articulate new visions of life and social engagement.[5] We need to find a way to constructively engage with these cultural frames, and we ignore them at our peril, as we will see in the case of modernization theory.

15.2 Post-War Modernization Theory

One important obstacle to taking adequate account of culture lies in the persistent, if not always explicit, influence of "modernization theory" in the social sciences: a legacy which obscures rather than illuminates the challenges involved in cultural change. Even though modernization theory today has few explicit advocates, its influence remains pervasive, shaping the background assumptions behind many academic and public conversations about cultural change. In this section, therefore, we attempt to unpack these background assumptions, and identify their problematic effects.

To begin, it may be useful to recall the main tenets of post-war modernization theory. Ideas about "modernity" and "modernization" have taken many different forms over the past decades and centuries,[6] but our focus here is a specific school of thought known as "modernization theory" that emerged in the US in the 1950s, and dominated Western social science (and Western foreign policy) from the 1950s to 1970s. Its academic proponents included W.W. Rostow in economics, David Apter in political science, S.M. Lipset in sociology, and Alex Inkeles and David McClelland in social psychology. But it was much more than just an academic fashion: it emerged in close collaboration with policy-makers, and shaped the work of governments, international agencies, and philanthropic organizations. This was the time of decolonization, when social scientists were seeking the right formulas for creating new states out of old (mainly colonized) societies.[7]

According to this theory, modernization is characterized by a series of social processes – such as education, literacy, urbanization, legal codification, and bureaucratization – which disembedded people from their traditional ways of life. People no longer simply inherit ascribed roles and relationships within a traditional culture, but are exposed to different ways of life, and (to varying degrees) have options for the kind of person they want to be, and the kind of life they want to lead. The inevitable result, according to modernization theory, is a kind of *individualization*. People's horizons are no longer bound to a particular tribe or village, and this in turn leads at an individual level to the privileging of individually chosen goals over ascribed group norms, and at the political level to the privileging of civic identities over primordial ethnic or religious identities. As modernization proceeds, individuals come to orient themselves politically toward modern public institutions, and to define themselves as citizens of the society as a whole.

It is important to note that this process of individualization had a double movement: in the first instance, it involved emancipating or *disembedding* individuals from their traditional ways of life, so that

---

4   For example, see Ahmad 1992; Al-Azmeh 1996; Mamdani 2000; Appiah 2005; Sen 2007.
5   On cultural representations as the means to articulate visions of social engagement, see the foundational works of Georg Simmel, Pierre Bourdieu, or Raymond Williams.
6   For an overview, see Delanty 2007.
7   See Latham (2000) and Gilman (2003) for these dense interconnections between academia, governments and philanthropic foundations. Modernization theory was in many ways a precursor to the IPSP in its attempt to offer policy-makers an international model of social progress based on the findings of social science.

they could become autonomous and achievement-oriented individuals;[8] in the second moment, it involved *re-embedding* these autonomous individuals within larger civil societies and public institutions.[9] Individuals' solidarities and loyalties would thereby shift from primordial kinship/tribal groups to the civic nation. In this way, the account of individualization as a cultural process was linked to, and helped generate, an account of the cultural foundations of the modern state, with its distinctively modern and secular modes of authority.

Viewed this way, modernization theory is not just about particular social reforms or institutional processes, such as urbanization or bureaucratization, but is also fundamentally about *cultural change*: about creating new kinds of individual subjectivities, with new values of individual choice, individual achievement, and civic commitment. Modernization theory sought to create the very autonomous individuals and civic-minded citizens who in turn would sustain and support modernizing public institutions. Modernization theory was, in the title of one of its most famous works, about "making men modern" (Inkeles 1969). It was not just institutions that needed to be made modern, but the individuals themselves.

As this brief summary makes clear, modernization theory rests on a basic dichotomy between "tradition" and "modernity," and defines social progress in terms of how far individuals and societies have moved from the former to the latter:

> According to modernization theorists, modern society was cosmopolitan, mobile, controlling of the environment, secular, welcoming of change, and characterized by a complex division of labour. Traditional society, by contrast, was inward looking, inert, passive toward nature, superstitious, fearful of change, and economically simple. (Gilman 2003: 5)

Like other grand narratives of history and progress, this narrative of "from tradition to modernity" is now widely discredited. Indeed, it suffered a "shockingly rapid collapse in the late 1960s and early 1970s" (Gilman 2003: 23). This is partly because so many modernization projects in the developing world failed miserably, leading not to stable and prosperous civic societies, but to unstable authoritarian regimes. Defenders of modernization theory often blamed these failures on people's irrational attachment to their traditional culture, but most observers concluded that modernization theory itself was

partly to blame, with its "hopelessly reductionist" account of cultural change.[10]

Why is it reductionist? To oversimplify, culture appears in modernization theory in two ways. First, it acts as an *obstacle* to social progress. When modernization projects failed, the common explanation was that people were too attached to their traditional ways of life. Processes of cultural transmission and cultural affiliation had therefore to be ruptured or dissolved in order to reduce cultural obstacles to modernization.[11] Second, culture is treated as an *outcome* or dependent variable on the individual level, allowing development to be measured in terms of whether people had indeed become "individualized" (that is, had come to have civic identities in place of traditional ethnic/tribal loyalties, and "achievement-oriented" values in place of passive or fatalistic traditional attitudes and values).[12]

What modernization theory lacked was any account of how people's inherited identities and ways of life could be a source of creativity and capability in addressing the challenges of development. While appeal to "tradition" can certainly be invoked to block progress, it is equally true that people often turn to inherited practices and solidarities to help make sense of change, to organize collectively to manage the risks of change, and to take advantage of the opportunities that come with change. Indeed, tradition is never just mechanically reproduced. Tradition is always subject to both creative and strategic reinterpretation, just as creativity and strategic innovation always takes place in reference to inherited practices. Categorizing cultural practices as either "tradition" or "modernity" thus obscures rather than reveals the actual dynamics involved: it ignores the ways tradition is always being creatively reinterpreted, and it ignores the way modernity is always dependent on inherited cultural forms and processes.[13]

This reductionist view of culture is now widely discredited among anthropologists and cultural sociologists, and few social scientists today take the "traditional versus modern" dichotomy as the starting point for analysis.[14] Yet many commentators argue that the tropes of modernization theory continue to inform public debates. Brohman argues that its reductionist views resurfaced in the Washington Consensus and other market-based visions of international development which "share a disregard for indigenous knowledge and popular participation," and which blame failed development on dysfunctional cultures (Brohman 1995).[15] More generally, modernization theory has

---

[8] See, for example, McClelland's (1961) account of "the achievement motive," which he contrasted with the passivity and fatalism of traditional cultures, and which he attempted to formalize and measure cross-culturally as "N-Ach."

[9] This was central to the Lipset (1959) and Almond and Verba (1963) accounts of "civic culture," conceptualized as the transcending and displacing of ethnic/tribal/sectarian loyalties.

[10] In Gilman's (2003) words, it was exposed as "hopelessly reductionist in its conception of change abroad, fundamentally conservative in its politics, and blindly reflective of the political and social prejudices of the mid-century American Establishment" (3).

[11] "Within modernization theory, cultural factors such as ethnicity typically represented obstacles to development that were rooted in traditional societies and that were destined to disappear in the course of development. The neglect of culture and 'ethnodevelopment' is not merely an oversight of mainstream theories, but should be seen as a paradigmatic blind spot" (Brohman 1995). A similar blind spot can be found in the "anthropology of poverty" tradition which developed in the late fifties and early sixties in Latin America, with its analysis of the half-modern-half-anomic culture of poor populations in the urban-marginal periphery (e.g. Lewis 1961).

[12] For this diagnosis of the way modernization theory conceived of culture as either obstacle or outcome, see Gilman 2003: 262.

[13] In Jeffrey Alexander's words, the "practice-oriented" view of culture "suggests that reflexivity, whether modern, late modern or postmodern, can be understood only within the context of cultural tradition, not outside of it. Typification, invention and strategization are simultaneous moments of every social action; they cannot be separated and compartmentalized" into either tradition or modernity (Alexander 1996: 136).

[14] "The years after 1970 witnessed a steady abatement of the conceptual tension between modernity and tradition" (Gilman 2003: 253).

[15] The Washington Consensus refers to a set of ten policy prescriptions for developing countries first discussed in 1989.

arguably become the kind of default "common sense" when explaining progress or its lack:

> In the collective view of most Americans (including intellectuals) poor countries and their peoples remained irrational, corrupt, inefficient, excessively fecund, technologically inadequate, incompetent, disease-ridden, superstitious, mired in age-old ways of doing things, and so on. (Gilman 2003: 266–267)

In effect, modernization theory operates as a kind of zombie category: officially dead, but surprisingly alive and well, continuing to shape public views of what progress is, and how to achieve it.[16]

And not surprisingly, the supposed beneficiaries of "progress" are often keenly sensitive to this legacy. When progress is defined in antithesis to inherited identities and practices, individuals are put in the impossible position of having to choose between their culture and progress, a choice they resent and reject. A recent study of development projects in Ecuador illustrates the problem (Radcliffe 2015). Some international organizations started from the premise that indigenous women were disadvantaged by their traditional culture, and so framed development projects as encouraging and enabling women to challenge their community's identity and culture through training in non-indigenous ideas of modern citizenship. Other projects, however, started from the premise that "indigenous women must not be urged to choose between their culture and their rights," and that women can find sources for empowerment through engaging with their culture, not distancing themselves from it (Walsh, forthcoming). Whereas the former projects collapsed in failure, the latter projects were more successful.

The same tendency has been observed within Europe. Some European feminist organizations start from the premise that Muslim women are inherently oppressed by their traditional culture, and this assumption persists even when the Muslim women themselves dispute it, because "once a conflict narrative has been forged … policy actors only hear Muslim women if they confirm cultural oppression" (Bassel and Emejulu 2010). The net result has been to render invisible the efforts of Muslim women who find sources of strength and empowerment within their inherited cultures and identities, who are told instead that they must choose between their culture and their rights.[17] (We return to this example in Section 15.8.) For all those who understand agency, self-recognition, and self-development within the context of what is culturally meaningful for them, the emancipatory promise of modernization theory rings hollow.

Defining progress in antithesis to inherited cultural identities is not only alienating for the supposed beneficiaries of progress, but also risks exacerbating social exclusion. Defenders of modernization theory may have seen themselves as inviting everyone to participate in an inclusive civic life, but when this civic life in defined as the antithesis of a group's culture, affected social groups are not just culturally excluded, but become socially "othered." This social othering occurs at the level of institutional ethos (e.g. in schools and the media) as well as the everyday interactions of social life, in which group members are marked out and subjected to stigmatizing stereotypes, paternalistic expectations, and constant monitoring.[18] Such exclusion also deprives societies of the multiple sources of cultural vitality necessary for social progress. To address the massive challenges we face, domestically and globally, we cannot rely solely on hegemonic Western paradigms of modernization and rationalization. We need to learn from the insights of diverse cultural and civilizational heritages, and from the new ways of being together that can emerge when these diverse traditions interact. In this sense, modernization must be reframed, not as "resolving" cultural difference through a predetermined logic of rationalization,[19] but as the often unpredictable crossroads of cultural change (Touraine 1997; Touraine and Khosrokhavar 2010).

In these and other ways, the core assumption of modernization theory that progress requires disavowing tradition sets up false choices, exacerbates social exclusion, and closes down possibilities for progressive cultural change. If we are to truly overcome the legacy of modernization theory, we need to be aware of these pitfalls, and to expand our ideas about the complex relationships between social progress and cultural change.

In the rest of this chapter, we hope to take some steps in this direction. We begin by focusing on the core idea of modernization theory: namely, individualization, which as we saw earlier is understood as a dual process of "disembedding" from traditional cultures and "re-embedding" in modern civic societies. While individualization is certainly a very real phenomenon,[20] modernization theory mischaracterizes both moments. In Section 15.3, we argue that modernization theory had no account of how or why disembedded individuals would "re-embed" – that is, why they would develop civic loyalties or solidarities, rather than simply becoming egoistical, apathetic, or consumerist, or "hunkering down" (in Putnam's terminology).[21] Indeed, Beck and Beck-Gernsheim argue that this sort of "disembedding without re-embedding" is precisely what defines the contemporary world, as distinct from the early modern era "in which the disembedding of individuals from traditional feudal structures was followed by a relatively fast re-embedding in new social structures of capitalist society (nation, class, and core family)" (Beck and Beck-Gernsheim 2002). Similarly, Zygmunt Bauman (2000) finds no "mechanisms of re-embedding" in the era of "liquid modernity." For Beck, Beck-Gernsheim, Bauman, and other sociologists

---

[16] "As a formal theory, modernization had been discredited in nearly all quarters by the late 1970s," but "modernist ideas about development are still (inescapably?) with us" (Gilman 2003: 266). For an interesting example, see Aboderin's (2004) discussion of how the assumptions of modernization theory about the nature of "traditional" and "modern" families make it impossible to understand changes in family support for aging parents in Africa.

[17] For a similar analysis in the African context of the dangers of asking women to choose between their culture and their rights, see Tamale 2008.

[18] See Bowen et al. 2014 on the difference institutions make in framing and shaping Western European state interactions with Muslim citizens.

[19] Modernization paradigms in Latin America typically assumed that cultural identities would be "resolved" through convergent rationalization (see Bartra 1987; Calderón, Hopenhayn, and Ottone 1997; Hopenhayn 2015).

[20] For example, the repeated iterations of the World Values Survey show a steady and global trend toward "post-materialist" values. See also studies of the rise of individualism in school textbooks around the world (Lerch et al. 2017).

[21] See Putnam 2007. As discussed in Section 15.6, another possible outcome is that disembedded individuals attach themselves not to civic institutions, but to uncivil forms of extremism.

of modernity, such as Richard Sennett, "radicalized individualization has not resulted in more freedom for the individual but rather in a disembedding and a feeling of rootlessness" (Juul 2013).[22]

In our view, these assessments may be too bleak, and underestimate the extent to which individuals continue to generate civic loyalties and solidarities. However, this clearly cannot be taken for granted, as modernization theory tended to do. Indeed, we can see the costs of this indifference to the "mechanisms of re-embedding" in the destructive effects of neoliberal reforms that expanded the scope of markets at the expense of public provision (discussed in Section 15.4). So, the first point to note is that "individualization" is not inherently or unconditionally a marker of social progress, and the task of building solidarities remains pressing, for which a richer account of culture can help.

In the following sections, we explore the flip side: just as individualization is not an unconditional good, so too "traditional" or "primordial" attachments are not unconditionally regressive or backward. The persistence of such attachments, and their political mobilization, is not always to be regretted, but rather can, under some circumstances, serve as a vehicle for progressive politics and cultural change. We need a more fine-grained way of assessing the mobilization of groups to protect their "cultures" and "identities." We illustrate these dynamics through a case study of evolving identities in Sub-Saharan Africa (Section 15.6), and through debates over the new spatial dynamics of culture (Section 15.7) and the idea of "multiple modernities" (Section 15.8), all of which offer lessons for how to identify (and to render productive) the ambivalences inherent in both individualization and traditionalism, and thereby offer new ways to think about social progress.

15.3 Paradoxes of Individualization and Social Progress

As we noted earlier, processes of modernization are in large part processes of individualization, disembedding people from ascribed social roles and requiring them to make their own way as individuals in the world. This is a dramatic historical evolution, but deeply ambiguous and paradoxical in its effects on human wellbeing and human freedom, with many different possible trajectories. Modernization theory failed to identify these ambiguities, in part because it had an overly simple view of the relationship between "modernization" as a *process* and "modernity" as a *value* or *goal*. Modernization as a process can be understood as the ongoing reconstruction of society based on multiple forms of rationalization: economic, productive, organizational, bureaucratic, political, demographic, and of human capital. These processes of modernization are supposed to lead to "modernity," understood as a particular sort of moral and political order built around values such as equality, individual liberties, and pluralism (Touraine 1992). In the

minds of modernization theorists, modernity in this sense was usually understood along the lines of a Western liberal democratic nation-state, committed to individual rights and material opportunities guaranteed to all on the basis of their universal citizenship status (rather than on the basis of particularistic relationships of kinship, ethnicity, or religion). This vision relied on the assumption of a virtuous circle between modernization (the rationalization of economics and politics) and modernity as a political culture of freedom and equality.

In reality, however, the link between modernization and modernity has proven to be anything but direct. In many cases, on every continent, modernization unfolded without modernity, and indeed even repressed or inhibited modernity. From fascist Germany to the communist Soviet Union to the military dictatorships of Latin America, intense modernization processes were put in place, promoting bureaucratic modernization and industrial productivity and the expansion of human capital, but suppressing human rights and individual freedom.[23] Modernization can lead to authoritarian if not totalitarian political orders as much as to democracy.

Moreover, even where political authoritarianism has been avoided, modernization processes have not necessarily generated a humanistic ethic of respect for subjectivity and diversity. Instead, all too often, we find an instrumentalization both of social life and of the natural world. The current crises of global warming, the extinction of species, the exhaustion of natural resources, and the pollution of water, soil, and air can be seen as the manifestation of a "depredation culture," made possible by an unprecedented capacity to transform nature. Attitudes toward immigrants, children, the poor, the elderly, or those with disabilities are often governed by instrumental calculations of economic returns, not by a sense of solidarity or shared fate. Here again, modernization-as-rationalization does not by itself guarantee that we have an ethically meaningful or sustainable image of development or progress, and we may end up instead with an instrumental reification, treating other humans, other species, and nature as simply resources to be manipulated or exploited in the name of bureaucratic or economic efficiency.

To combat this, we need to denaturalize our ideas of modernization, and rethink our metrics of individualization, modernity, and progress. Social progress has too often been conceived according to what can be statistically observed; that is, the "ratio mensura" has determined what is considered relevant for policies and politics. Thus, social progress has been fitted into a positivistic-instrumental view with an elaborate system of aggregate indicators of welfare and capacity development (from poverty indicators to sector indicators in health, education, social security, housing, etc.). Constant self-reflexivity, informed by diverse cultural voices, is required to denaturalize the embedded mono-rationality of economic or bureaucratic rationalization.[24]

---

[22] For a related diagnosis of how modernization undermines all forms of solidarity, not just traditional forms, see Etzioni 1996: "after the forces of modernity rolled back the forces of traditionalism, these forces did not come to a halt: instead in the last generation (roughly from 1960 onwards), they pushed ahead relentlessly, eroding the much weakened foundations of social virtue." Etzioni is himself a former proponent of modernization theory, but now emphasizes the necessity of a "communitarian" counterweight to the forces of individualization.

[23] See Marcuse (1964); Adorno and Horkheimer (2002).

[24] On self-reflexivity as a key component of late modernity see Giddens (1991) and Beck, Giddens, and Lash (1994).

Doing so requires a wide research agenda to explore how we can put together what has typically been kept separate or even considered contradictory: economic growth and a sense of belonging; productive time and free time; material production and spirituality; the relation between building human capital and educating for meaningful lives and active citizenship; responding to urgent needs and ensuring long-term intergenerational solidarity.

This is a big task, partly addressed already in Chapter 2 on the metrics of progress, but we will focus here on one dimension of the task: namely, how to rethink individualization. As we have seen, modernization processes entail individualization, but individualization has not always led to "modernity" as a moral and political order based on values of respect for individual freedom and civic equality. Instead, modernization has produced divergent and ambivalent forms of individualization, both emancipatory and harmful, and a central task for any project of social progress is to think about how to enable the former and contain the latter.

Let us begin with the more negative forms of individualization that have promoted instrumental attitudes toward others, and undermined a sense of belonging and solidarity. One is what C.B. Macpherson called *possessive individualism* (Macpherson 1962), a view he dates back to the seventeenth-century liberal philosopher John Locke, with his emphasis on the centrality of appropriating private property to a fully human life. Another is what has been called *postmodern narcissism* or the reinforcement of narcissistic behaviors in late capitalism (Lasch 1991; Beck and Beck-Gernsheim 2002; Lipovetsky 2003).

Postmodern narcissism emerges as a will to individual gratification and self-realization, where the Other is absent or instrumental to personal attainment (the Other here may be the community, society, those in need, or those far away).[25] Combined with the use of information flows for building pathways to personal achievement and gratification, postmodern narcissism strongly correlates individualization with *self-management*. Individualization along these lines is progressively "cabled" on a system of provisional affinities, mutual usefulness, and goal-oriented relations with others where such others are viewed as instrumental. Individualization moves through short-term relations, with the rapid obsolescence both of projects and bonds, as goods, contents, discourses, events, and relations all become disposable.

Many commentators view postmodern narcissism as a pervasive ideology of the contemporary world. According to Jameson and others, it is a cultural expression of late capitalism or consumer capitalism, where individualization is more and more dependent on consumption and the search for immediate gratification at an individual level; on self-image in a world centered on image exchange; on low compromise and provisional identification with self-centered projects (Jameson 1998; Maffesoli 2000; Bauman 2007). Individualization in this form makes society overloaded with anxiety, due to the need to move on,

to rotate through the use of objects and services, and to see the world and others as potential objects for consumption and disposal.

Needless to say, this sort of narcissism is not promoted on moral grounds. On the contrary, it is routinely denounced by educators, commentators, and indeed everyday citizens, who bemoan its impact on individual lives and on social cohesion. Nevertheless, it is more and more "normalized" when it comes to individual aspirations, self-management, interpersonal relations, network communication, and life projects. Both postmodern narcissism and possessive individualism spread virally throughout society in everyday market operations, speculative economics, competitiveness, the self-management boom, consumerism as the basis for personal gratification, self-image idolatry in the pervasive circulation of images, and so on. Postmodern narcissism has arguably acquired an unprecedented cultural and psychological drive. It has its own efficacy in building a prevailing personality, modeling expectations and goals, determining family life and forms of love, transforming the relation with work, the disposition to share or not to share, and the nature and scope of commitments. Narcissism operates as a "molecular" mechanism (in the words of Deleuze and Guattari). It privileges personal gratification over social welfare and privileges self-management over collective projects; it tends to instrumental and aesthetic bonds more than to family or community bonds; and it values immediacy over long-term projects. It nurtures an intensive and diversified interaction with symbolic and material goods that are replaced faster and faster, providing combustion to an economic order based on rapid obsolescence.

These forms of individualization are clearly problematic from the perspective of social progress. At the best of times, they lead to difficulty in sustaining long-term significant bonds with others. But at this historical moment, they leave us radically ill-equipped to deal with growing global challenges, including the intergenerational solidarity needed to address global warming and other catastrophic scenarios; or the sense of social justice needed to address growing wealth concentration or rising populism; or the sense of international justice and humanitarian concern needed to address violent conflicts, migration flows, worldwide social fragmentation and anomie, and rising threats to democratic stability.

In one sense, none of this is particularly new. Since World War II, there have been repeated warning by academics, artists, and intellectuals of the dangers that modernization-as-rationalization is leading not to a humane society but to the dominance of instrumental rationality.[26] In Jürgen Habermas's influential formulation, modern society needs to prevent the "systems logic" of bureaucratic and market rationality, with its requirements of efficiency, calculability, predictability, and control, from "colonizing" the "life world," with its focus on shared understandings of ethical visions. Other authors have discussed this in terms of the conflict between rationalization and subjectivity (Alain Touraine), or between formal and substantial rationality (Max

---

[25]   We use the label "postmodern narcissism" to denote a form of individualism that neglects a sense of solidarity, responds exclusively to personal interests, and does not hesitate to manipulate others for self-accomplishments. It is in part produced by cultural changes associated with the rise of a "market society" (discussed in Section 15.4) and the resulting weakening of social cohesion, but also operates to reproduce and strengthen these trends.

[26]   Indeed, this anxiety about the rise of egoism and consumerism is a long-standing complaint of both conservatives and radicals, although conservatives are more likely to blame the ideology of liberalism or secular humanism, whereas radicals blame the ideology of capitalism.

Weber, Max Horkheimer, Agnes Heller), or between rationalization and meaning (Edgar Morin, Gianni Vattimo). In all of these accounts, modernization has the tendency, if unchecked, of creating a society in which social relationships are instrumentalized, with nothing (and nobody) seen as having intrinsic value or worthy of enduring allegiance.

However, we should not reduce individualization to possessive individualism and postmodern narcissism. There are also emancipatory forms of individualization that challenge inherited social relationships, not in the name of consumerism and narcissism, but in the name of equality and justice. Individualization "denaturalizes" inherited social hierarchies, and thereby contributes to critical awareness regarding discrimination, social justice gaps, the invisibility of particular groups in public debate, and forms of alienation and domination in modernization processes. This critical awareness in turn often leads to new forms of collective action, social solidarities, and democratic agency, leading to new capabilities for meaningful freedom and valuable livelihoods (Sen 1984, 1999; Alkire 2002).

Feminist struggles for equal rights and non-discrimination are an example of such collectively mobilized individualization aimed at expanding autonomy and recognition, and reframing justice and redistributive politics. The goal is not primarily to give women an equal opportunity to be narcissists or consumers, but rather to deconstruct patriarchal ideologies about what sorts of lives and activities are worthy of respect. Similarly the struggles of sexual minorities today illustrate how individualization involves claims for public visibility, and articulates new ways of being human and of experiencing and valuing body, desire, love, and pleasure.

These forms of individualization generate a repertoire of pro-identity and pro-recognition actions that converge into claims for more equality and justice. Individualization can thus be understood as a mechanism of horizontal differentiation that fosters visibility for diverse groups and generates struggles for recognition. In this sense, individualization can be related to the "subaltern speaking" (in the words of Spivak). Individualization is visible in those acts or moments in which a subject who has been historically subordinated or discriminated on the basis of gender, race, or caste, and who has lacked both power and recognition, stands for his/her dignity and rights, and by so doing changes (or makes no longer unquestionable) a relation of radical asymmetry in power.

Individualization here supports both autonomous action and claims to be treated as an equal. It can install a relation of resistance, opening a gap or a hiatus in the midst of a relation where domination was the norm. Thus, individualization implies self-affirmation in a relation where prevailing patterns of asymmetry in rights and power appear as what they are (unmasked) and, at the same time, as what cannot continue prevailing if self-affirmation is to be considered a genuine claim for dignity and reciprocity.[27]

In this way, individualization is deepening our idea of equality, which is an evolving concept and value (CEPAL 2010). It moves with history and enriches its semantics with both old and new meanings. Today, these include the redistributive struggle (not only between social classes but also in the spheres of gender, ethnicity, generation); access to an expanding spectrum of public goods and public services as part of the rights of the citizen; recognition and visibility of groups defined by their difference; the right of every citizen to fair treatment and fair access to justice; new ways of political participation that go beyond the boundaries of electoral democracy so as to give space to a diversity of actors who have no access to the mechanisms of liberal representation or who are skeptical about their efficacy or legitimacy; and the imperative of global and intergenerational solidarity vis-à-vis planetary economic and environmental challenges. The claiming and defending of equality in these forms not only builds solidarity among mobilized groups, but also helps build a broader sense of social membership that unites all citizens. The civil, political, and social rights of citizenship provide a powerful basis for individuals to develop a sense of belonging and affiliation to society as a whole (Rawls 1971; CEPAL 2007).

Individualization has the potential to revive and strengthen democracy, not only by opening up the political process to previously marginalized groups, but also by demanding greater accountability in the pursuit of public goods and the common interest. Individualization delegitimizes older structures of political authority based on paternalism and deference, as individuals demand the right to judge for themselves, and seek the information needed to make these judgments. Transparency and accountability become more and more a democratic demand, a possibility made feasible by information and communication technologies (ICTs). The creative use of ICTs to expose and share information is both a source of power and a means of controlling power, including modern versions of Robin Hood who steal information from the powerful to give to the people. While "bad" hackers damage your computers, use your credit cards, or invade your private information, "good" hackers are the new heroes of the information society. They hold a critical stance toward the status quo and their deeds may show a deep sense of service to the community in ways that are still hard to grasp.

Hackers are not the only examples of such "emancipatory individualization," understood here as the will to "make a difference." Activists around the world are sharing capacities and knowledge, putting together initiatives aiming at the democratization of power throughout networks and communities, denouncing spurious proceedings and abuse of power in the corporate and political spheres, promoting alternatives for sustainable life at a personal and local level, spreading tolerance and openness vis-à-vis cultural diversity and creative options for living meaningful lives. ICTs allow these forms of individualization to gain visibility and support, and become viral even when activists lack traditional forms of power or material resources. They may enter the big house of global debate through the small window of a house in a suburb.[28]

---

[27] An emblematic case is the one posed by the African American civil rights activist Rosa Parks, when on December 1, 1955, she refused to give her seat in the bus to a white passenger.

[28] Instead of a logic of "aggregation through standardization," of the sort that characterized the rationalization processes of modernization theory, people are pursuing "synergy through diversification." In doing so, new and unpredictable cultural forms of individualization arise.

In short, emancipatory individualism makes possible new forms of horizontal solidarity among co-citizens as well as new forms of democratic agency and accountability vis-à-vis state institutions and other institutions of power. At their best, these forms of individualization offer the possibility of embedding democracy down to the roots of the social fabric, employing new discourses and new communication processes to create new understandings of what a global community should and could be, triggering new patterns of belonging and sharing, and more democratic relations of power.

In our view, these emancipatory forms of individualization are as much a part of the contemporary landscape as the possessive individualism and postmodern narcissism discussed earlier. It is a mistake, therefore, to assume that individualization is inherently inconsistent with social solidarity or civic-mindedness. Indeed, the psychological evidence suggests that the "individualism-collectivism dimension is unrelated to the egoism-civicness dimension" (Rothstein 2017: 307).[29] Some countries with high levels of individualization (as measured, for example, by support for rights to dissent, to choice, and to self-expression) are among the most solidaristic (as measured by redistribution). There is, in short, such a thing as "solidaristic individualism" which involves a robust ethos and practice of citizenship. Individualization here operates at a "higher level," that is, with an integrative vocation and not as a mechanism that deepens fragmentation, social injustice, and "bowling alone" (Sennet 1998, 2005; Putnam 2000; Bauman 2004, 2011).

However, it is equally clear that this sort of emancipatory or solidaristic individualism is always at risk of degenerating into narcissistic or possessive individualism. Both are prevalent in contemporary societies, and indeed are intermingled in complex ways. Different figures of individualism – *homo economicus*, user of public services, beneficiary of social policies, narcissistic consumer, equal-rights-bearing citizen, autonomous subject – circulate globally. The new global order is permeated by the paradoxical coexistence of growing claims for equal justice and the globalized culture of possessive individualism and postmodern narcissism. Narcissism and equality live together, one as a naturalized everyday practice and the other as a consecrated value subject to political struggle and part of policy agendas.

The challenge is to turn vicious circles of individualization – in which postmodern narcissism feeds into a culture of depredation – into virtuous circles of emancipatory individualization, in which demands for equality and recognition generate new forms of living well together. In our view, we may be at a historical threshold where such a turn is possible, where individualization becomes a source of empowerment for social movements, of capillarity in resistance strategies, of democratization of voice and visibility, and of regrouping according to new collective identities.

However, this is by no means guaranteed, and deliberate efforts will be needed to move individualization from the axis of possessive and competitive individualism to the axis of social citizenship, equality, and cross-cultural non-hierarchical identities. Addressing these complex relations between individualization and belonging, individualization and solidarity, and individualization and social justice should be a central focus of any account of the relationship between cultural change and social progress.

In the past, this challenge has often been discussed solely within a Western liberal framework, but today it must be broadened to include a more global flow of ideas and identities (see also Section 15.7). Western experiences of individualization are not the only possible starting points or endpoints. When informed and nurtured by different cultural traditions, individualization processes may evolve new ways of being together and new senses of belonging.[30]

Consider, in this respect, the idea of "buen vivir" or "sumak kawsay" that has been incorporated into the Constitution of Ecuador. "Sumak kawsay" is an ancient Quechua concept, also present among the Aymará in Bolivia as "suma qamaña," and has been adopted officially into the new Bolivian Constitution as well. This vision considers humans as part of Mother Earth (in the Andean culture, related to the idea of "Pachamama"). "Buen vivir" ("living well") stresses a sense of belonging of the individual to the community and to nature. It entails a strong sense of balance between human welfare and respect for the natural environment, and views economic growth and productive development not as an end in itself but rather as a means to living well.

These ideas may be unfamiliar to Western ears, but they are directly relevant to the challenge of ensuring that modernization (as rationalization processes) lead to modernity (as values of freedom and equality). They offer a new way of ensuring that modernization-as-rationalization leads to empowerment and not to the colonization of social life. And indeed the Ecuadorian and Bolivian constitutions invoke buen vivir not in opposition to modern ideas of equal citizenship, but precisely as a principle for interpreting ideas of equal citizenship.[31] The result is a novel cultural creation, a hybrid synthesis of diverse cultural sources, emerging to deal with the specifically modern social, economic, political, and environmental challenges of Andean society.

This suggests that we need to rethink the modernization paradigm as the crossroads of cultural exchanges (Touraine 1997; Touraine and Khosrokhavar 2010). Once we acknowledge that progress does not have a singular (Western) starting point or endpoint, the very idea of modernity must be rescripted through the active acknowledgment of the heterogeneity of cultural worlds, civilization heritages, and future aspirations. This will entail seeing modernization as a process that every society confronts: not as an external influence with a singular (Western) origin, but as a set of processes that have local and extralocal sources and entanglements (García Canclini 1990; Appadurai 1996), and which require novel forms of cultural hybridizations (Castells 2010).

---

29   See also Welzel 2010.
30   For paradigmatic reflections on this in the Latin American context, see Paz (1950), Martín Barbero (1987), and García Canclini (1990).
31   The Preamble to the Ecuador constitution states "We decided to construct a new form of citizen co-existence, in diversity and harmony with nature, to reach 'el buen vivir, el sumak kawsay.' " Related discourses include "Ecological Swaraj" in India or "Eco-Ubuntu" in South Africa. See Salazar (2015).

15

Box 15.1 | Intercultural Health Policies in Latin America: Harmonizing Cultural Recognition with Greater Access to Social Welfare

After centuries of viewing indigenous peoples' culture as an obstacle to (Western-defined) social progress, Latin American countries have recently started to accept that social progress must be "intercultural." This process is most advanced in the fields of education and health. In education, intercultural education policies have addressed capacity-building, with special emphasis on bilingualism in areas with high concentrations of indigenous populations with a mother tongue other than Spanish. Intercultural bilingual education, in addition to using an indigenous language and Spanish, includes a curriculum drawing on both cultures' contents and worldviews. Intercultural health, in turn, as a concept and policy, seeks to reconcile indigenous cultures' knowledge and traditions with general public health care systems. Even if most programs have up to now targeted indigenous peoples, options are increasingly opening for indigenous and non-indigenous peoples to choose, in a free and informed manner, different approaches to health care that draw on different cultural traditions.

In line with more "emancipatory" forms of individualization set forth in this chapter, intercultural health seeks to reconcile diversity promotion and social welfare. It embodies social solidarity by investing public resources in improving health conditions in more vulnerable health populations, within a context of advocating and promoting diversity in collective practices and worldviews. This opens up alternatives in terms of the available forms of self-care, in ways of understanding the body-mind system, and in medical care delivery format and pharmacological options, all within a broad framework for understanding health. In this light, intercultural health reinforces the idea that cultural change should not necessarily follow a linear path leading to Western welfare standards, and seeks to go beyond unilinear and homogeneous development views.

In the past two decades in Latin America, intercultural health public policy has moved forward in two different and complementary directions. First, it operates as a "dynamic and ongoing process of relations, communication and learning among cultures, under conditions of mutual legitimacy and equality," which is built "among individuals and groups with culturally different knowledge and practices," understanding interculturality as a cross-cutting strategy that incorporates and promotes "knowledge and practices related to the health, illness and care process, both in official medicine and indigenous medicines" (CEPAL 2014: 215). Second, it has "expanded to include the promotion of change in structural exclusion factors, as well as in the organization and supply of health services" (CEPAL 2014: 215). This has thus given rise both to divergence and complementarity between two different emphases: expanding the range of health benefits for the entire population by including indigenous traditions; and using public health policy to address the structural exclusion of indigenous populations.

In this context, intercultural health incorporates indigenous peoples' knowledge and health practices as part of the "cultural mediation" required to optimize the impact of health programs and benefits. According to a recent extensive study by CEPAL (2014), the combination of Western and indigenous health has contributed to improving the health care and living conditions of indigenous peoples. Important progress has been achieved in areas such as mother and child health, nutrition, primary care, and infectious disease control.

Intercultural health dissemination has followed a "bottom-up" rationale based on small-scale programs at community and local levels, which over time have acquired greater institutional status in intercultural health policy. According to CEPAL research, by 2014, 14 Latin American countries had in place a state agency with a specific mandate to address intercultural health,[32] even if their focuses and modes of implementation vary from one country to another.

---

[32] According to information from CEPAL, PAHO, and health ministries in the region's countries, these countries include Argentina, Bolivia, Brazil, Chile, Colombia, Ecuador, Guatemala, Honduras, Mexico, Nicaragua, Panama, Paraguay, Peru, and Venezuela (CEPAL 2014: 216).

How does this cultural mediation work in practice? It may involve having traditional and "modern" medicine specialists in the same facilities (so that the patient may choose, or make the best use of different expertise in integrated care). It may also involve the possibility of referrals from one system to another. It may involve the inclusion within the pharmacological repertoire of traditional indigenous natural products, and the inclusion within mental health care of not only psychologists and psychiatrists but also spiritual guides for indigenous groups and peoples. As CEPAL's systematic study has shown, intercultural health policies and programs in the region have been developed in three directions, namely: the use of indigenous medicine elements in health care or management; the joint delivery of Western and indigenous medicine in the same health facilities; and the creation of horizontal coordination mechanisms between indigenous and Western health systems, while preserving their own spaces (CEPAL 2014: 221).

An increasingly widespread practice, with successful experiences in Bolivia, Chile, Ecuador, and Mexico, is offering Western and indigenous health services in the same health care center. In these centers, patients may choose between the two systems that share the same health infrastructure, with cross-referrals within a same health care unit. These practices are a clear example of how the expansion of services can be compatible in a more pluralistic social progress framework. In this joint modality, endorsed by CEPAL, intercultural health aims "to articulate indigenous and western medicine as a response to indigenous and non-indigenous populations; provide health services according to the worldview of the various peoples, and retrieve and enhance indigenous medicine and the role of their representatives and knowledge holders" (CEPAL 2014: 221).

In the case of Bolivia, in December 2013, an Ancestral Traditional Medicine Law was passed to regulate the "exercise, practice and articulation of Bolivian ancestral traditional medicine in the National Health System" (Art. 92), for which purpose the Vice-Ministry of Traditional Medicine and Intercultural Affairs "will promote the implementation of intersectoral actions for the design, implementation and evaluation of intersectoral standards and health indicators" (Art. 14). In Brazil, the National Health Care Policy for Indigenous Peoples of Brazil undertakes to guarantee indigenous peoples' access to comprehensive health care in accordance with the principles and standards of the Single Health System (SUS in Portuguese), taking into account social, cultural, geographical, historical, and political diversity. In Paraguay, the 2010 National Indigenous Health Policy aims to incorporate indigenous medicine in the implementation of health programs and plans included in the National Health Policy.

It is important to emphasize that within these models of intercultural health, the aim is not simply to recognize discrete indigenous traditions, let alone to freeze them in perpetuity, but to enable transformative social change and mutual learning. In Brazil, for example, the Human Resources Training Program for Action in Intercultural Contexts "aims to foster indigenous peoples' appropriation of western medicine knowledge and technical resources, so that this knowledge may enhance their heritage of therapies or other cultural practices" (CEPAL 2014: 218). This sort of intercultural mediation is not seen as a threat to the purity of cultural traditions, but as a way of strengthening the capabilities of all citizens.

The extent to which these models of intercultural health have penetrated and transformed the public health system varies across countries, and indeed across different fields of public health practice. According to CEPAL's overview of regional experiences, "most countries have introduced intercultural activities in the context of strategies on primary health care, sexual health and reproductive rights, as well as in the framework of mother and child programs as well as those aimed at mental health and infectious diseases" (CEPAL 2014: 219). CEPAL highlights positive-impact actions on HIV/AIDS in Brazil, Ecuador, and Panama, tuberculosis and malaria in Colombia and Panama, Chagas disease in Argentina, and diarrhea in Costa Rica; and also highlights effective health human resource training activities using a multicultural approach in Argentina, Bolivia, Chile, Costa Rica, Ecuador, Honduras, Mexico, and Peru, aimed to promote traditional medicines (CEPAL 2014: 219).

In sum intercultural health programs have shown positive results in terms of advancing social progress through respect for indigenous peoples' rights and cultural diversity. However, these impacts should not be overestimated. Health gaps persist when comparing the situation of indigenous populations with that of the rest of the population in all the region's countries. This new paradigm of intercultural health policy has brought important benefits, but cannot by itself address all the social determinants of health, where ethnic and racial gaps are evident. Thus, indigenous populations in Latin America continue to face higher incidences of extreme poverty, and less access to drinking water and decent housing, which in turn leads to higher levels of malnutrition and child mortality. Furthermore, progress in intercultural health initiatives is slow and uneven, partly because entrenched institutional practices are often refractory to their inclusion, and partly because creating successful mechanisms of coordination and mediation that allow citizens to benefit from (and to move between) diverse approaches is a challenge.

These limitations indicate that while intercultural health policies have had positive effects, they are clearly not a panacea. They need to be situated within a broader social progress framework, with fairer distribution of wealth and income, and a sustained reduction of gaps in human development capabilities and opportunities. [33]

15.4   From Market Economy to Market Society

So far, we have argued that individualization can take diverse forms, with very different implications for social progress. At its best, modern individuals see themselves as belonging to a community of shared fate, embracing an ethos of citizenship and mutual obligation. This is the sort of "re-embedded" individualism that modernization theory assumed was the natural outcome of modernization processes. In reality, however, this civic-minded and solidaristic form of individualization is always competing with, and in danger of degenerating into, a more possessive and narcissistic form, in which disembedded individuals are not re-embedded in broader social solidarities. Deliberate political efforts are required to promote civic-minded forms of individualization, and we have suggested some of the cultural resources that are available for such efforts, including new forms of political awareness, collective mobilization, and cross-cultural interactions.

Unfortunately, there are powerful trends operating in the other direction, not least the profound influence of the neoliberal era, which in many ways has operated to tip individualization processes in the wrong direction. The term "neoliberalism" is notoriously vague, but we follow Evans and Sewell in distinguishing four facets of what they call the "neoliberal phenomenon": (1) neoliberal economic theory (stressing the welfare-maximizing consequences of market exchanges); (2) neoliberalism as political ideology (stressing the superiority of market allocation over public provision, and advocating for lower taxes, more personal responsibility, and the weakening of unions); (3) neoliberalism as policy paradigm (stressing privatization of public enterprises, free-trade agreements, and deregulating labor and capital markets); and (4) neoliberalism as "social imaginary" (extolling entrepreneurship, self-reliance, consumerism, and volunteerism while associating government programs with inefficiency and corruption) (Evans and Sewell 2013). As Evans and Sewell emphasize, these four dimensions do not stand or fall together: many states that never embraced neoliberal political ideology (such as Germany or Sweden) have nonetheless adopted aspects of the neoliberal policy paradigm, and the neoliberal social imaginary evolves in response to transnational cultural influences that are not directly tied to policy choices. Nonetheless, as they document, there was a confluence of these four trends in what they call the "neoliberal era," dating roughly from the election of Thatcher and Reagan in 1980 to the late 1990s, when several major international organizations including the OECD, World Bank, and UNICEF sounded the alarm bell about the costs of neoliberal policy reforms, and called instead for "social investment" (Jenson and Levi 2013: 84). Neoliberal political ideology and policy paradigms no longer have the hegemony they possessed in this neoliberal era, and must now struggle against a range of competing ideologies and policy paradigms. Nonetheless, they remain powerful, not least in shaping our evolving ideas of individualization and modernization.

The economic and political dimensions of the neoliberal era are described in other chapters; our concern here is with their cultural implications. The neoliberal era not only changed the distribution of economic resources and political power, but also changed people's subjectivities and identities: their sense of membership and belonging, and their views of what we owe each other as members of society.[34] Indeed, it changed these in ways that modernization theory did not predict, and probably would not have endorsed.

Modernization theory operated within a framework that John Ruggie calls "embedded liberalism," which dominated Western thinking from the end of World War II into the 1980s. This framework embraced the need for markets and international trade, but assumed that markets had to be embedded in (and regulated by) a larger social context that was not itself founded on market norms, including a substantial role for a national welfare state.[35] On this view, markets can serve to advance human wellbeing, but only if they are embedded within a political community that rests on norms of citizenship.

---

[33]   Based on: *Los pueblos indígenas en América Latina: avances en el último decenio y retos pendientes para la garantía de sus derechos* (CEPAL 2014). English summary version: *Guaranteeing Indigenous People's Rights in Latin America: Progress in the Past Decade and Remaining Challenges.*

[34]   For reflections on this, see Hall and Lamont (2013).

[35]   See Ruggie (1982). The idea that markets need to be continually (re-)embedded in society was central to Karl Polanyi's (1957) work on the "double movement" of markets and society.

This framework was radically disrupted by neoliberal policy reforms in the 1980s, in two different ways. First, social functions that were once the province of the state were handed over to the market (e.g. through privatization, deregulation, and commodification). As a result, spheres of social life that were once regulated by a logic of citizenship are now regulated by a logic of market exchanges. Second, even where functions have been retained by public institutions, the operation of these institutions has been reconceived using market metaphors and concepts. Public institutions of education or health care, for example, have been subjected to new management philosophies that emphasize ideas of competition, incentives, the return on investment, and "responsibilization." As a result, even in their relation to public institutions, individuals are treated more as "consumers" or "clients" than as "citizens."

The net effect has been a substantial change in the everyday metabolism of social life, as markets have become disembedded from society (Latcher 1999). Some commentators describe this as a form of "market fundamentalism" (Somers 2008), but we might also describe it as a shift from a "market economy" to a "market society," in the sense that market norms have come to characterize ever-wider domains of society, at the expense of norms of civic responsibility (Sandel 2012).

Modernization theory did not foresee this change, since it took embedded liberalism as the natural endpoint of modernization. This blind spot parallels its blind spot about individualization: just as modernization theory assumed that disembedded individuals would naturally be re-embedded in civic institutions, so too it assumed that markets would naturally be embedded in a larger framework of democratic citizenship. In reality, the embedding of both individuals and markets within society is a fragile achievement that needs to be continually fostered.

The negative effects of market fundamentalism on economic inequality and democracy are discussed elsewhere in this Report. Our focus here is on its implications for cultural change, on how individuals understand their own identity and construct the meaning of their social relationships. In one sense, the influence of market relations on people's cognitive maps and moral values is a long-standing phenomenon, dating back to the origins of commercial capitalism in the fifteenth and sixteenth centuries, and has been a staple topic in the classics of social science (Marx, Weber, Simmel).[36] However, the neoliberal era has arguably defined a new "common sense," operating through the media, universities, policy-making networks, and other spaces to advance not only a particular set of economic rules, but also a world vision aiming at re-educating subjectivities and identities in various ways. Neoliberalism as a social imaginary or cultural repertoire has deepened a one-dimensional form of individualization as the private quest for personal benefit and profit, within the framework of a "naturalized" ethics of possessive individualism. These ideas are no longer restricted to the sphere of market competition, but increasingly shape all of social life.

As a result, we are encouraged to think of ourselves as a "company of one," with the responsibility to manage our life and our relationships as an economic asset (Lane 2011). Productivity becomes an issue not just of corporate strategy or national planning, but of self-management. We are expected to acquire the knowledge, information, and social connections needed not just for a particular job, but to adapt in a world where skills are subject to rapid obsolescence and where forms of organization ceaselessly change. As Korean philosopher Byung-Chul Han (2012) has pointed out, productivity goes well beyond economics and permeates a new superego where self-regulation becomes a pervasive mechanism in the reproduction of (increasingly unequal) social relations.

We can identify a number of perverse effects of this cultural shift. One is the gradual erosion of ideas of social citizenship. The idea of the citizen is being reinvented as one of a client and consumer, thus eroding the sense of solidarity and of entitlement to social rights that underlies the welfare state. The result is not only to diminish public support for the disadvantaged or vulnerable, but also to make receipt of this support a source of shame and stigma, since it is seen as a failure of self-management. In some cases, this may even lead citizens to forego the support they need rather than face the stigma that attaches to public support in a neoliberal era (see Box 15.2 on recent welfare reforms in the Netherlands).

A second effect concerns the growing centrality of consumption to self-identity and social status. This has been fostered by many different factors, including the globalization of markets, low-cost economies, and access to credit and easy financing. Whatever the causes, *homo economicus* appears at full peak in the neoliberal era. The worldwide access to an expanding spectrum of goods and services, both material and symbolic, is at the same time a powerful means of status differentiation. The highly developed consumer world centers communication and self-esteem in consumption patterns and consumption talk.

A third effect is the decline of public space: The most eloquent expression of the commoditization of social life is the substitution of the public square by the shopping center as a place of social encounter and social exchange. The global mall, with its endlessly diverse and constantly updated merchandise, is an icon of the "life of the city" today, the new version of what Baudelaire, Simmel, and Walter Benjamin saw in the illuminated streets of Paris or Berlin in the turn from the nineteenth to the twentieth century. But whereas earlier liberals celebrated the urban public sphere as a space for public discussion and the formation of shared understandings (Habermas's "communicative action"), commercial spaces are now celebrated as shrines for private consumption.

These cultural effects of the neoliberal era are sometimes said to be offset by certain positive cultural trends, such as the rise of a more multicultural or cosmopolitan ethos. Neoliberal policy reforms included economic globalization, and in the process brought people into contact with a much wider array of cultural products. Late capitalism may encourage consumerism, but it encourages us to consume and enjoy the products of many different cultures, including the food, music, and

---

[36] The relation between ethics, religion, and modern economic rationality is examined in the classical study by Max Weber (1952). See also Marx's analysis of how the pervasiveness of commodity exchange restructures human relations in a fetishist form (Marx 1968); and Simmel's analysis of the cultural and social influence of money in modern society (1999). It is a suggestive coincidence that the texts by Weber and Simmel were both published for the first time when the twentieth century arrived, in the year 1900.

Box 15.2 | Fear of Shame: Citizens Facing Restricted Access to State Support for Long-Term Care in the Netherlands[37]

As in many other countries, citizens in the Netherlands are encouraged to mobilize their private networks to arrange for long-term care (LTC) before seeking state support. Recent policies summoning such "active citizenship" posit that public goods, such as the provision of care, are best arranged at the lowest feasible level of organization, such as the family and community. Against the background of an aging population and financial and economic crises, neoliberal policy-makers deem cutbacks to health care both desirable and necessary: necessary because LTC costs have increased over the past decades, and desirable because the services-led model is said to have disengaged citizens from informal caregiving. To contain costs and to encourage citizens to take a greater role in informal caregiving, care under the Dutch Social Support Act (Wet Maatschappelijke Ondersteuning, WMO) is no longer a legal right of citizenship. Recent legislation restricts access to LTC to the most severely disabled. The rhetoric furthermore suggests that there are "welfare queens" receiving excessive care, at times fraudulently. Implicitly, the rhetoric also suggests that those who are not "genuinely disabled" should feel guilty about using publicly financed care.

The current redistribution of care rights builds on the distinction between relatively mild and critical care needs and preserves rights only for "those who really need it." To enact this divide, around 230,000 LTC clients in the Netherlands were re-assessed. Sixty thousand people lost their entitlements to care entirely, while even more individuals, most often the elderly and people with psychiatric or cognitive disabilities, had their entitlements reduced. Many affected individuals reported increased dependence on their private networks, reduced psychological wellbeing, and less time spent outdoors. Still, only a minority made use of the available opportunity to appeal against the decision of the independent needs assessment center (the CIZ).

Emotions were central in our respondents' decisions not to appeal; none mentioned that they lacked the ability to do so. Those who did not appeal were, broadly speaking, too ashamed to do so, going to great lengths to avoid the risk of (further) stigmatization, of depriving other fellow citizens of care, or of showing distrust and disloyalty toward authorities. In contrast to the common perception that not making use of the right to appeal is a "failure" on the part of dissatisfied clients, clients resisted appealing so as to manage their reputations and to avoid shame.

The fear of shame follows from seeing oneself in the eyes of others and prompts people to adjust their conduct and emotions accordingly. Older and chronically ill people did not want to risk potential shame by appealing. The shame of social stigma was evident as they did not want to be perceived as "begging." They refrained from identifying with people receiving more care as this would imply that they were among the "most severely disabled." They would rather become isolated than admit inability to manage their daily lives. With the right to care distributed on the basis of the severity of need, claiming it today is a different matter than when these clients entered public care, then seen as a right of citizenship. They thus preserved their dignity by not asking for more than they were judged entitled to by the needs assessment center.

Affected clients also distanced themselves from other, perhaps needier persons. In this way, they could see themselves as relatively independent and loyal to the authorities. When clients compared themselves with needier individuals, they actively downplayed their anger, feeling ashamed to claim their rights. At least they had "a roof over their heads." Avoiding shame proved a crucial concern for disabled and elderly persons who already felt that they had to defend their dignity. If policy states that only the "truly needy" deserve publicly financed care, this raises significant emotional hurdles for individuals who, against the evidence, resist identifying themselves as "truly needy."[38]

---

[37] Written by Jan Willem Duyvendak.
[38] This text heavily draws on Ellen Grootegoed, Christian Broer, and Jan Willem Duyvendak (2013).

clothing of diverse societies. Commentators have called this a form of "neoliberal multiculturalism," or "Benetton multiculturalism," after one of the many global corporations that has specialized in celebrating the savvy consumer who relishes the opportunity to sample this cultural smorgasbord. Can we not see this as a positive cultural consequence of the market society?[39]

Perhaps, but it is important to note that the neoliberal era was characterized by a dualistic approach to globalization. It is a striking feature of the neoliberal era that global mobility was extended much more to capital than to human beings.[40] Capital is actively sought and encouraged to move across borders; indeed, the few barriers that limited the movement of capital were done away with as part of neoliberal policy reforms (Gosh and Chandrasekhar 2004; Harvey 2007). By contrast, there is often strong opposition to the mobility of certain kinds of bodies. Members of the global elite, irrespective of their group designation, traverse the globe with increasing ease. But non-white poor and working-class persons face mounting barriers in their attempts to move into this supposedly global village that is sold to them through all kinds of advertising media, cultivated through desires for a better life, and heightened by the relative affluence of those who have successfully migrated. Unlike capital, bodies carry and mark culture, and these cultures are often seen as "out of place" in the societies into which migrants move (see Section 15.7). While some groups and individuals adopt new names and patterns of speech in order to meld into the places not meant for them, others resist melding in. They insist on, and oftentimes openly display, their "other" identities, sometimes at risk to their bodily integrity. They live their cultures, and in the process, reconfigure the cultural maps of the world, threatening inherited assumptions about where cultures "A," "B," and "C" belong.

The celebration of multicultural consumption coexists with increasing efforts to restrict the mobility of these Others, and with attempts to impose increasingly restrictive "integration" conditions on those who are permitted to enter or stay. As a result, the neoliberal era is characterized by a deep cultural cleavage between a cosmopolitan elite that makes everywhere home,[41] and the "Other" working class and poor from the South who are largely unwelcome, especially in times of economic crisis. Xenophobia, Islamophobia, and a racism coded in the language of cultural difference are the reaction in the North to the presence of this latter category, resulting in cultural othering, social exclusion, and economic and political marginalization. This dualistic approach to globalization – celebrating mobile capital while policing mobile bodies, particularly those seen as "Other" in class or culture – is

as much a part of the neoliberal era's social imaginary as the celebration of consumerism.[42]

In these and other respects, the neoliberal era has exacerbated the challenge of ensuring that individualization takes emancipatory and civic forms rather than narcissistic or anti-social forms. Where markets are disembedded from society, it is harder to ensure that individuals too are not disembedded.

Many commentators argue that the heyday of neoliberal political ideology and policy paradigms is over, having lost its hegemony in the late 1990s, and further delegitimized by the global crisis of 2008. However, memory is short, and the perception of the market as the dorsal spine of social life remains strong. In any event, the cultural effects of the neoliberal era have already penetrated both institutional practices and individual subjectivities. A central task is to repair this damage, and to rebuild the cultural foundations of civility and solidarity.

15.5   The Politics of Primordial Identities: Emancipatory or Regressive?

So far, we have argued that both the real-world *processes* of individualization and modernization theory's *assumptions* about the disembedding of persons leave us with challenges of building solidarities, that these challenges remain pressing, and that to meet them a richer account of culture and progress is necessary.[43] The remainder of this chapter addresses this necessity, beginning with some observations on the role that inherited ethnic and religious identities can play in this process.

As discussed in Section 15.2, modernization theorists expected inherited ethnic and religious identities to weaken under modernization, or at least for their "groupness" to diminish. This has not occurred. To be sure, modernization has radically transformed traditional ways of life, but as Barth noted, ethnic group members may retain a strong sense of identity, despite or indeed because of radical changes in the content of their ways of life (Barth 1969).[44] And as Brubaker notes, the "groupness" associated with these ethnic categories may increase if people find themselves in institutions favoring collective action or if they encounter threats to shared interests (Brubaker et al. 2008).

While post-war modernization theorists tended to discount (or denounce) the persistence of these ethnic identities, scholarly attitudes have evolved. The "modern vs. traditional" dichotomy no

---

[39]   For debates on neoliberal multiculturalism, see Kymlicka (2013).

[40]   This is another example of the need to distinguish neoliberal economic theory from neoliberalism as political ideology. Most neoliberal economic theorists would happily agree that people should be able to move freely from the global South to the global North, and that the freer movement of labor would promote efficiency as much as the mobility of capital. Key champions of neoliberal political ideology, by contrast, such as Reagan and Thatcher, were adamant defenders of the need to restrict immigration.

[41]   Although elites are united by their class interests, they are also differentiated by race and gender. Non-white members of these classes find themselves at the receiving end of crude racism. Elite women are not necessarily shielded from sexism by their wealth.

[42]   On the links between neoliberalism and racist populism, see Lentin and Titley (2011).

[43]   See the related discussion in Chapter 16, which notes the need for new research on how religion relates to social progress, coming to "a field that long assumed either that religion would disappear and need not be considered or that religious beliefs and practices represented the vestiges of underdevelopment to be overcome."

[44]   This focus on the persistence of group boundaries despite changes in substantive norms and practices remains a central feature of the sociological study of race and ethnicity – see, for example, Lamont and Molnár (2002).

longer provides the master-frame for social science,[45] and ideas of respect for "diversity" and "pluralism" have become part of the lexicon of "world culture."[46] Yet it is testament to the ongoing influence of modernization theory that many commentators today still express surprise at the persistence of ethnic and religious identities, inevitably described as the "revival" of ethnicity or the "return" of religion (Smith 1981; Brown 1989; Ebaugh 2002; Robertson 2011)[47] as if these are pre-modern irruptions into modernity, and deviations from the straight path to modernity. And while a diversity of ethnic and religious lifestyles is often acknowledged and even celebrated, attitudes become much more ambivalent, if not hostile, when these identity groups become politically mobilized and make claims for rights and recognition. Even today, 50 years after the heyday of modernization theory, we still struggle to make sense of the politics of primordial identities.

Part of the difficulty is the sheer heterogeneity of such politics, spanning the spectrum in their ideologies and goals. Cases of fratricidal ethnic and sectarian civil wars tend to receive the most news coverage, but it is important to remember the far larger number of cases where the political mobilization of ethnic and religious groups is peaceful, benign, and indeed progressive. A prominent example is the political mobilization of indigenous peoples in Latin America, demanding (and in part achieving) the adoption of what Donna Lee Van Cott calls "multicultural constitutionalism" throughout the region, with the constitutional recognition of the distinct legal status of indigenous groups, including rights to self-government, land claims, and recognition of customary law in many countries, reversing centuries of economic dispossession, political marginalization, and cultural denigration (Van Cott 2000; Sieder 2002; Yashar 2005).

There are vibrant debates in Latin America about how well these reforms are actually working in practice. Some critics argue that they involve merely symbolic changes. Indeed, some argue that these policies were designed by elites precisely to deflect political attention away from underlying power structures (Hale 2002). Others argue that while providing tangible benefits to indigenous peoples, multicultural reforms are creating new ethnic hierarchies in the process – for example, by excluding Black (Afro-Latino) groups who are not typically considered as "indigenous peoples" (Hooker 2005). Yet others argue that they are imprisoning people in cultural scripts, and jeopardizing individual freedom. In order to qualify for new multicultural rights, members of indigenous communities are expected to "act Indian" (Tilley 2002) – i.e., to follow "authentic" cultural practices – an expectation that strengthens the hand of conservative or patriarchal leaders within the community who assert the authority to determine what is "authentic" (Sieder 2001).

Most commentators, however, while acknowledging these risks, argue that the rise of indigenist politics in Latin America has been a positive force, and not just for indigenous peoples but for society generally.

It has helped to enhance democratic participation among previously excluded groups, to reduce the danger of a return to authoritarian rule, to build legitimacy for the process of democratic consolidation, and indeed to serve as a laboratory for innovative experiments in citizenship (Yashar 2005). In this sense, at its best, the new minority politics has been truly transformative, not just in the sense of transforming the lives of minorities, but more generally in transforming national politics in a more progressive, inclusive, democratic, tolerant, and peaceful direction. Based on these and other examples of transformative minority politics from around the world,[48] important international reports have strongly endorsed the idea of a "multicultural democracy," including the UNDP's ground-breaking 2004 Human Development Report on "Cultural Liberty in Today's Diverse World," and UNESCO's 2008 "World Report on Cultural Diversity."

Yet these ideas face strong resistance, including within the international community, in part because for every example of progressive ethnic politics, we can find contrary examples with very different results. Consider indigenist politics in West Africa. In this context, claims of indigeneity or autochthony are often used not to challenge inherited forms of hierarchy and exclusion, but rather to consolidate them: to permanently relegate "outsiders" from other parts of the country to a second-class status, thereby perpetuating relations of enmity and exclusion, rather than building more inclusive relations of democratic citizenship (Bowen 2005; Geschiere 2005, 2009). What look, on the surface, to constitute similar claims to indigenous rights turn out, in practice, to generate very different political results. And of course, at the far end of the political spectrum, we have even more violent and intolerant forms of identity politics, grounded in what Appadurai calls "predatory identities" whose "social construction and mobilization require the extinction of other, proximate social categories, defined as threats to the very existence of some group" (Appadurai 2006: 51). This is the sort of identity politics that leads to segregation, ethnic cleansing, or even genocide.

It is one of the central challenges of our age to figure out why identity politics sometimes takes a more progressive and emancipatory form and sometimes takes a more exclusionary or even predatory form. We are far from having a systematic theory or scientific consensus on this question. The factors at work are complex, operating at multiple levels. For example, the prospects for inclusive identity politics depend in part on the larger regional and global context. Minorities have often been used as pawns in inter-state conflicts or to justify intervention by imperial powers. Where minorities are seen (however wrongly) as fifth columns for neighboring enemies or distant imperial powers, state–minority relations tend to become heavily "securitized," reducing the space for democratic politics. In this context, international factors can often undermine the prospects for progressive identity politics.[49] Yet international actors can also have a constructive impact, as indeed they did in Latin America, where international human rights organizations and global indigenous advocacy networks helped

---

45   On the rise and fall of "tradition vs. modernity" as the master concept of social science, see Jameson (1991).

46   See, for example, Terra and Bromley (2012). The authors situate the spread of multicultural education within the "world culture" framework.

47   See also Chapter 16 on the inaccuracy of the "return" metaphor in relation to religion.

48   We take the term "transformative minority politics" from Mundy (2010).

49   This is a particular concern in the Middle East. See the discussion in Kymlicka and Pföstl (2014).

promote inclusive citizenship (Brysk 2000).[50] We discuss further examples of these linkages in Section 15.7.

Similarly, national-level factors can either facilitate or impede progressive identity politics. Many nation-states have defined their identity and citizenship in homogenizing and "unanimist" ways that pathologize diversity and dissent, but other states have put diversity and dissent as defining features of their society and democracy.[51] And of course minorities themselves have their own traditions of authority, accountability, debate, and tolerance, which may affect whether and how they take up the opportunities made available by international networks or domestic political structures, as we discuss further in Section 15.8. How these different transnational, national, and local factors interact to determine the direction of identity politics is an open question requiring further research.

We cannot even begin to unpack these dynamics, however, unless we explicitly set aside the legacies of modernization theory, with its knee-jerk assumption that primordial identities, and identity politics, are a priori outdated obstacles to social progress. In reality, political mobilizations along lines of race, ethnicity, religion, or indigeneity are often struggles against exclusionary features of the dominant conceptions of social progress. Modernization theorists typically assumed that the "public institutions" and "civic identities" they were defending were accessible to all. But we know that these institutions and identities are almost always marked by various cultural hierarchies, valorizing certain groups as advanced, civilized, and responsible, while denigrating others as backward and unruly. Social progress was presented by these institutions as the natural outcome of the history, language, and culture of certain groups, while the history, language, and culture of other groups were presented as obstacles to progress. In order to participate in "public" and "civic" life, members of these stigmatized groups were required to hide or suppress their distinct identities, and to constantly address prejudices about their worth and belonging. Even when the institutional rules do not formally discriminate on a racial or religious basis, they still may reproduce these hierarchies of status and recognition. Insofar as mobilization around subaltern group identities is intended to challenge these (implicit or explicit) hierarchies, they may be seen, not as evidence of uncivil sectarianism and tribalism, or as a futile rejection of cultural change or cultural influences, but as struggles for more inclusive and effective forms of democracy, citizenship, and social progress. We need to be alive to these possibilities.

Of course, this is not to deny that uncivil sectarianism and tribalism also exist, but the challenge is precisely how to differentiate the more emancipatory from the more regressive forms of "primordial" politics. Because of its knee-jerk dismissal of all such identity politics, modernization theory leaves us unable to either understand, or constructively respond to, the reality of, and indeed the *modernity* of, identity-group politics.

15.6   A Case Study of Shifting African Identities

To better understand how these changes in identity and values operate, it may be useful to consider a case study, one that brings together the dynamics of individualization, ethnic loyalties, and transformations in the nature of authority, in this case the fragmentation of authority in parts of Islamic West Africa. As mentioned in Section 15.3, the tensions between individualization and belonging, individualization and solidarity, and individualization and social justice take different forms in different regions, with important consequences for social progress. In West Africa, individualization has often taken place within the context of collectivities framed by social understandings based on the sacred and the clan. These entities are part of the very fabric of modernization in these societies, and not just "primordial" leftovers from the past. The very process of individualization calls forth new rationalizations of the social world on which are then erected new sociabilities, all the while retaining the sacred and the clan as the basic format of society. This is a social process characterized by the corrosion of existing social orders, but the process of disruption is paralleled by other processes suggestive of the reconstitution of individual and collective being in new ways.

To start with the example of the sacred, we can trace how Islam has, over the millennia, shaped the processes of collective identity formation in parts of Africa stretching from Senegal to Ethiopia; and how individualization has happened in these societies. In this zone of Africa, the processes of Islamization and state formation intersected in a complex web which can be analyzed in three distinct stages: containment, mixing, and reform.

> In the first stage, African kings contained Muslim influence by segregating Muslim communities, in the second stage African rulers blended Islam with local traditions as the population selectively appropriated Islamic practices, and finally in the third stage, African Muslims pressed for reforms in an effort to rid their societies of mixed practices and implement Shariah. This three-phase framework sheds light on the historical development of the medieval empires of Ghana, Mali, and Songhay and the 19th century jihads that led to the establishment of the Sokoto Caliphate in Hausaland and the Umarian state in Senegambia. (Hill 2009: 1)

In the Sokoto Caliphate, the emergence of a theocracy was preceded by the rise of the Sufi brotherhoods within the framework of Maliki Sunni Islam:

> During the eighteenth century, there was a meaningful shift in Sufi brotherhoods away from the old patterns of decentralized and diffusive affiliations toward larger-scale and more coherent forms of organization. In the process of restructuring, the role of the shaykh was expanded and brotherhoods became centralized, disciplined organizations that included networks of deputies. (Levtzion and Pouwels 2010)

---

[50]   For a more general discussion of these international factors, see Boulden and Kymlicka (2015).

[51]   On Middle Eastern and North African (MENA) states as "unanimist," and the negative implications of this for minorities, see Picard (2012). See also Khaddar's (2012) contrast between "anti-colonial nationalisms" that were broad-based inclusive movements of resistance and "state nationalisms" that (in either their secular or Islamist versions) have been authoritarian and homogenizing. As the MENA context shows, secular/civic nationalisms can be as authoritarian and homogenizing as "ethnic" or religiously defined nationalisms.

15

This can be seen as a process of modernization – bureaucratization and rationalization – but still within the realm of the sacred. Qadiriyya brotherhood identity was central to the jihad of 1804 that led to the creation of the Sokoto Caliphate: the Arabic verse, *qasidaa jamiyya qadiriyya*, penned by the leader of the jihad, Shaykh Uthman dan Fodio, was alleged to have "had a hypnotic effect upon devotees on the eve of the jihad." Shaykh dan Fodio was also reported to have said: "I belong to the Qadiriyya and everyone who follows me belongs to it" (Loimeier 1997: 21). Furthermore, followers of the jihad were frequently referred to by ordinary people as "*qadirawa*" or followers of the Qadiriyya brotherhood.

However, this fairly homogeneous Qadiriyya community started to change by the 1830s. Fragmentation of religious authority took place, as well as the disembedding of individuals from the dominant Qadiriyya template. This process of individualization would ultimately lead to the rise of new, radical groups such as Boko Haram. Central to this process of the fragmentation of sacred authority was the process of individualization. The process of Islamization was closely tied to the process of state formation. The consolidation of the Caliphate that resulted from the 1804 jihad was soon to lead to tensions in the management of political authority. The jockeying for dynastic privileges created factions within the jihadi aristocracies. These were made worse by pressure from the encroaching British colonial forces which were felt from about the 1860s.

Other brotherhoods arose within the Caliphate, starting with the Tijaniyya brotherhood in the 1830s. Though still within the Sunni fold, the Tijaniyya were rivals to the Qadiriyya (Mustapha 2014). Indeed, by 2009 the Caliphate community had become so fragmented that a survey conducted by the Pew Foundation found that across modern Nigeria, only 38 percent of Muslims identified themselves as Sunni, 12 percent identified as Shia (a religious orientation introduced after the Iranian Revolution of 1978), 3 percent as Ahmadiyya (an allegedly "heretical" import from colonial Pakistan), and 44 percent as "just Muslim," thereby eschewing any brotherhood affiliation. Only 9 percent of the sample explicitly identified with the Qadiriyya, with the Tijaniyya having overtaken the Qadiriyya with 19 percent of the Muslim population (Pew Forum on Religion and Public Life 2010; Ostien, forthcoming).

We must therefore recognize the sacred as constantly changing, some modernizing, others reaching back to the past. The sacred spaces are not immune to the forces of individualization, rationalization, and bureaucratization. From about the 1830s, therefore, the perfect identity match of belonging to the Caliphate and to the Qadiriyya began to be undermined. Individual and dynastic interests soon led some to remove themselves from the claims of the Qadiriyya and change their religious affiliation, thereby reshaping the framework of individual and collective sociability. Being Muslim was no longer identical with being Qadiriyya. And the first to benefit from this process was the rival Tijaniyya brotherhood which began to emerge from around 1830.

For much of the nineteenth century, this process of individualization and the resulting fragmentation of sacred authority involved only a relatively small circle of religious scholars and Caliphate aristocrats. From the 1940s, however, the process accelerated, fueled by economic and political developments associated with colonialism and the founding of the modern Nigerian state. Increased opportunities within the colonial world fueled the process of individualization, often expressed in the religious or economic spheres. Indeed, it is important to emphasize that religion remained the most powerful idiom for expressing political and social change, making it difficult to establish a clean separation between the sacred and the temporal. Tijaniyya affiliation became pronounced in regions of market expansion, in which new mercantile classes resisted the old largely Qadiriyya aristocracies. After the 1970s, further rapid social and economic change intensified this process of the dissolution of older collective religious identities and the individualization of the process of religious belief and affiliation. In northern Nigeria, this remains a highly problematic process of disembedding without re-embedding, as noted by Clarke and Linden:

> People are now "role performers" in isolation so that their moral beliefs and values have had to be privately contrived and constructed. The arbitrary quality of behavior that results from this privatization of morals and values is profoundly disturbing, and is worsened by the pressured and frenetic character of urban life, corruption and near social breakdown in large cities. (Clarke and Linden 1984: 92)

While the old Sufi brotherhoods were based on hierarchies and networks which maintained some semblance of order within the religious and social spheres, the reformist Islam that challenged them from the 1970s emphasized a reformist rationality which privileged the autodidact. This do-it-yourself character of millenarian, and later reformist, Islam, faced with the crisis of postcolonial states, opened the gates for the emergence of violent groups such as Maitatsine and Boko Haram, bent on pushing their idiosyncratic versions of Islam (Mustapha 2014). Paradoxically, while individualization might have weakened old Sufi Qadiriyya notions of belonging, solidarity, and social justice, it has also provided the basis for the emergence of competing "footloose" millenarian, Salafi, and jihadi groups who claim to have the panacea for society's ills, but are oriented toward different notions of belonging, solidarity, and social justice. In this particular example, while individualization might have increased individual freedom of affiliation, it is questionable if there has been any step forward in social progress and social justice as these groups lack widespread social support and seek to impose themselves on society by authoritarian, militaristic means.

Although this example of the impact of individualization on sacred authority is based on the case of northern Nigeria, the general principles are applicable across much of Africa where large populations of Muslims are to be found. Other factors, like the capacity of state institutions to regulate religious life, dictate the specific expressions of this general tendency. In Africa, just because groups are religious by definition, we cannot assume that they are caught in the web of the "primordial," outside the realm of individualization and modernization.

More common across West Africa, however, are clans based on kinship systems, which constitute our second example of the process of ongoing individualization in this part of the world. These kinship systems are quite distinct from the ideology of "tribes" and "tribalism" through which incorrect, cultural primordialist assumptions are often made about African social dynamics (Mafeje 1971; Ekeh 1975). As the anthropologist Archie Mafeje (1991) noted, these clans and kinship groups are the real building blocks of many societies in Africa. Furthermore, Ekeh (1990) suggests that in the history of these groups and clans there is a close connection between transatlantic slavery, the strength and resilience of the clans, and the more modern phenomenon of ethnicity. In the times of slavery, he suggests, the individual sought refuge in "corporate kinship groups" as a defense against the oppressive slaving local state. Under colonialism, Ekeh argues, these kinship groups were conceptually expanded "into the construction of ethnic groups." The ethnic is therefore a dynamic construct, and not a primordial given.

Despite the strength of ethnicity in modern African social and political life, the corrosive forces of individualization are beginning to weaken the fabric of these kinship groups. Migration, urbanization, and demographic growth have all contributed to undermining the notion of a corporate kinship group, tied together by co-residence. As co-residence becomes difficult or impossible to sustain, more and more individuals are breaking away from the common compound and reconstituting their households elsewhere, away from the kinship group. Residential patterns in many African cities increasingly reflect social class status instead of the previous lineage ties. In many instances, ceremonies like marriages and burials become sites for re-enacting and re-affirming kinship solidarity, weakened by increasing dispersal and individualization. Among the Yoruba of southwestern Nigeria, for example, the *asoebi*, the clan "uniforms" worn by all members of the clan at such ceremonies, are used to indicate the social closeness of the clan and its distinction from others. Though modern technologies like mobile telephony and social media are also increasingly used to overcome some of the consequences of physical dispersion, and sustain some form of sociability among kin groups, there is no doubt that the forces of individualization are also beginning to corrode clan solidarity, an important pillar of African social life. How this disembedding process works out – whether in a new progressive re-embedding within solidarity groups, or in new class-infused residential hierarchies – will determine the pattern and future of social progress in Africa.

15.7 Global Flows and Transnational Identities

The historical experience of West Africa shows that religious and kinship groups are always evolving, often in response to transnational factors, such as the broad spatial reach of Islamic movements over several centuries. But we are arguably witnessing today a qualitative change in the spatial dynamics of cultural change, due to the increasing globalization of identities, networks, and social movements.

Countless examples could be given, but youth culture and protest movements are particularly striking manifestations of these global flows and transnational identities. Aided by the globalization of material and immaterial goods, youth of all social locations in terms of class and geography share a lot in common: they listen to similar music genres, support football teams in the same leagues, and put on the latest clothing. Although youth culture follows the reality of

the unequal global distribution of capital, with most of the items of fashion, music, and sporting icons coming from the West, it is not simply a foreign injection into an otherwise static local culture. Youth culture is a fusion of the local and the received in ways that reflect a core feature of all human culture – influences from without infused with local inventions (Steinberg, Parmar, and Richard 2006).

The diachronic development (not spread) of the hip-hop genre of music can be used to illustrate this point. In Ghana, for instance, there has been an ongoing fusion of a localized syncretic music genre called "high-life" with hip-hop, to form a novel musical form called "hip-life." In this way, youth have come to navigate entertainment in a world where they have varied access to 24-hour global music channels, in close competition with a long history of syncretic local musical traditions. Growing collaborations between hip-life artists and musicians across West Africa and those from Southern Africa, and indeed between musicians in Africa and others from the Americas, facilitate cultural sharing, leading to the recognition, acknowledgment, respect, and localization of the cultural outputs of others, which they begin to see as theirs as well. Through a shared music, youth become interested in other parts of the world, over time investing an emotional and intellectual interest in what they can learn from afar. Socially conscious songs create groups of young people who become interested in understanding and working to undo injustice, as they are aware of its dimensions near and far from them. Facebook, Twitter, and WhatsApp operate as sources of information and debating platforms keeping youth abreast of developments across every part of the world.[52]

Like youth culture, protest movements are also increasingly globalized. Global protest movements have gone beyond international working-class solidarity united by the status of "worker" to encompass groups of people sharing similar cultural worlds although inhabiting distant locales. Today we can speak of a global LGBTIQ (lesbian, gay, bisexual, transexual, intersex, and queer) movement, the anti-war movement, or the student movement against educational injustices, encompassing African-American students under the banner of #BlackLivesMatter, Dalit students in India, or French students fighting changes to labor laws. All these groups are involved in international causes through their local struggles.

Global protest movements are both the result of the changed geography of culture and accelerators of such changes. In the first instance, global protest movements come to exist by the expansion and convergence of desires, conditions, and ways of being by people separated by distance. The virtual world of the internet makes it possible for queer activists to share experiences of stigmatization and to imagine strategies to globalize their localized struggles. This in turn expands the spatial base of cultures. A group of Dalits in Maharashtra, India, whose experience puts them in conversation with shack dwellers in Durban, South Africa, come to imagine who they are and their destiny as intricately tied to what happens in the USA or South Africa (Hardtmann 2009). Thus, beyond the actual physical movement of people into new spaces, the shared concerns and aspirations of social groups place

---

52 Increasingly, authoritarian regimes from Asia to Africa are clamping down on youth access to these media as a means of controlling dissent and the development of solidarities.

them in situations where their conception of who they are begins to involve others that they might never have seen.

These and other examples of transnational identities and global cultural flows provide ample proof – if any more were needed – that "culture" cannot be understood as defined by, or enclosed within, national boundaries. While we do not subscribe to apocalyptic notions of the end of history or the end of the nation-state, the massive flows of persons and cultures across territories render untenable the assumption of the nation-state as a container that delimits the cultural world of a person. The nation-state continues to confer an important civic identity but it does not delimit the range of cultural identification. Chinatowns, the global Sikh community, or Ashanti Unions[53] across Europe and North America, have roots traceable to particular nation-states, yet are not reducible to any nation-state. A Ghanaian hip-life musician and an Indian LGBTIQ activist can draw on their respective local resources and the struggles of Hijra transgender persons in their interactions with American hip-hop artists and Swiss gender activists.

These global cultural dynamics not only challenge nation-centric views of culture, they also challenge prevalent ideas about the link between "culture" and "place." As we noted in Section 15.4, there remains a persistent tendency to equate cultures and places. The living reality of cultural intermeshing is sidelined in favor of a view of cultures and space as identical (Usman 2006). On this view, each culture naturally belongs in one place, and it is therefore "out of place" for people from one place to carry their culture to other places. Cultures belong in particular places, and particular places belong to particular cultures. This tendency to identify each territory with a timeless ethnic group or groups appears in different guises and traditions, from Orientalist traditions of scholarship to "blood and soil" nationalist ideologies.

In one sense, this equation of place and culture was always deeply distorting. As we have seen in Section 15.6, cultural identities in West Africa have been shaped by transnational trends for centuries. Indeed, historical research has shown that cultural and religious groups in Africa and Asia that have been thought of as localized and organic are actually trans-local in origin and orientation (Vail 1989; Hamilton 1998).[54] And the intensification of transnational flows made by possible by information and communication technologies makes the equation of place and culture today even less plausible.

Nonetheless, this equation of culture and place remains stubbornly resilient, and continues to operate as a major obstacle to social progress. As we discussed in Section 15.4, while cultural flows are increasingly global, they remain strongly marked by class and racial hierarchies. While capital and members of the global elite traverse the globe with increasing ease, non-white poor and working-class persons face mounting barriers in their attempts to move, in part because they are seen as carriers of cultures that are "out of place" in the societies into which they might move.

Even those middle- and upper-middle-class persons who are able to move find themselves limited by their race and cultural otherness. An example is the Afropolitan movement which revolves around highly educated Africans of middle-class origins who move between a number of global cities and Africa (Bwesigye 2013). They bemoan the treatment they receive from the West, including the failure to be properly recognized for their personal achievements.[55]

This suggests that the globalization of cultures and the cosmopolitanisms that it engenders have not yet displaced inherited ideas about which cultures belong in which spaces. Indeed, there is disturbing evidence that these global flows are often met with a politics of exclusion that aggressively reasserts these old equations of place and cultures, and insists that people and cultures be left in their assumed natural places. Xenophobic populism is once again mainstream in today's world, not only in the West but in many parts of the global South as well.[56] The declaration in many European countries that multiculturalism eats at the fabric of society and thereby erases the uniqueness of Englishness or Germanness (Sarrazin 2010) is the culmination of this long-held view that each people has a *lebensraum* (living space) where they incubate their cultures.

What is the alternative to this politics of exclusion in the age of global cultural flows? We would argue for the creation of a political community based on residency, cultural inclusion, and civic responsibilities, irrespective of origin, while respecting historical association. This could be described as a rejection of the unitary dictates of assimilation in favor of a more "multicultural" approach. However, paradoxically, multiculturalism in its own way can sometimes operate to reproduce the equation of culture and place. Multiculturalism's insurgent egalitarianism is conceptually and practically limited insofar as its departing assumption is the relationship (albeit a mutually respecting one) between a natural culture of place and the assumed outside cultures that deserve respect. In this way, multiculturalism too often concedes to a culture-place association instead of a culture-in-constant-making-and-unmaking. Instead of separate cultures – the foreign ones accommodated by the natural one – the culture of a place should be seen as tributaries that wash into a cultural river that is not given but continually constituted.

The promotion of a residential form of political belonging is not incompatible with the need to recognize and valorize cultural difference. Nor

---

[53] Ashanti Unions are cultural and welfare organizations of Ghanaians of Asante origin, a major ethnic group in Ghana. They are found in many cities across the word where there are a sizable population of people who identify as Asante (Manuh 1998).

[54] For every group that claims a primordial connection to its current territory, there are other groups for whom the awareness of a continuous distance of cultural spread is central to their myths of origin.

[55] Afropolitanism differs in this respect from counter-systemic movements like pan-Africanism. Pan-Africanism is a global movement whose central objective is the restoration of the humanity of people of African descent wherever they may find themselves. Many of the leaders of the independence struggle in Africa returned to Africa after encountering pan-Africanism as students in Europe and North America (James 2012). Whereas pan-Africanism addresses the question of imperialism in its economic and cultural dimensions, Afropolitanism settles for personal advancement and the performance and commodification of Africanity. It therefore does not address the intersecting relations between class, cultural otherness, and exclusion which keep so many people on the margins of the global village.

[56] Recall our discussion of the exclusionary nature of the politics of autochthony in West Africa in Section 15.5.

does it mean seeing cultures as floating objects with no spatial base, as some insist (Mbembe 2002). Cultural invention is always anchored in some history and a sense of continuity, and cultural practices are often rooted in particular material and spatial configurations.[57] We can reject "culture talk" when it is used as the basis for exclusion – when it is used to say that only culture A belongs in place A – without rejecting claims for the recognition of the cultural rights of minorities and indigenous peoples and the celebration of cultures as the handiwork of human interventions.[58] The cosmopolitanism that mobility facilitates is therefore not rootless. It is tied to a history that people often trace to a given place. But it is not contained in and/or immobilized by one given place. In India, for example, the resurgence of majoritarian politics in the form of a Hindutva movement which equates Bharat Mata (Mother India) with a single Hindu history and language is already challenged by civic movements that proffer an alternative view of India, one premised on a long history of heterogeneity, cultural difference, and linguistic multiplicity (Pande, Garba, and Chaturvedi 2016).

We believe this alternative to the politics of exclusion is already implicit in the UN Sustainable Development Goals (SDGs), which arguably serve as a minimal, widely shared vision of how to overcome some of the ills of today's world, at least at the state level. Goals 4 and 5 set out to eliminate gender inequality and ensure social inclusion and human rights for all. The underlying premise is the intricate connection between social exclusion and material disadvantage. Where groups are unable to safely express their cultural difference, this is invariably linked to a curtailment of the rights of such groups to pursue economic opportunities in ways that makes them socially whole, as subjectively defined. Social exclusion through cultural alienation often compounds the disadvantage that women suffer. Social inclusion as envisaged by the SDGs will require the fundamental opening up of a totality of social arrangements from the economic to the political, anchored in cultural plurality and mutual respect for various of ways of being, irrespective of origin. (See the discussion of "multiple modernities" in Section 15.8.)

In sum, the cumulative result of developments in information and communications technology, the acceleration of intra- and inter-place inequalities, civil conflicts, and ecological changes, and the transmission of desires and aspirations across all corners of the globe have meant that cultures and places that were previously considered separate and isolated are now in close and intense interaction. What has been termed the "Age of Migration" (Castles et al. 2014) has drastically changed the configuration of cultural and human demographics across the world. Chinese small-scale miners and tuck-shop operators are common features of villages in South Africa and England. African traders are visible on the streets of Mumbai just as Syrian refugees can be seen in every part of Europe today. The new possibilities this opens up are reflected in the syncretic nature of youth culture and protest movements: their use of symbols, accoutrements of mobilization, and causes and sources of struggles and inspiration. The centrality of migration in the new waves of the peopling of the world, and the

intractable presence of the ethnic question in all corners of the globe, rule out any homogenizing conception of modernization. People are not losing their identities as they move from one place to the other. They reconstruct their identities and the self-perceptions of the (new) places (in)to which they move.

To take advantage of these new possibilities, however, we need to overcome the *centro-centrism* of modernization theory (Sitas 2014). There is still much work to do in undoing the hierarchy – implicit and explicit – that ranks cultures from simple to high, primitive to sophisticated, and/or traditional to modern – and in undoing the exclusionary equation of culture and place. Cultures must be understood for what they truly are – human creations in the face of the social and natural environment. If so understood, the dynamism and learning that makes cultures possible in the first place will be recognized as the destiny of all cultures (Harrison and Kagan 2006).

15.8 Social Progress and Cultural Change: Multiple Modernities?

15.8.1 Multiple Cultural Pathways for Modernization

As we have seen, modernization theory and its descendants consider cultural identity and cultural minorities more a problem than an asset for the promotion of individualization, and they set a prescriptive agenda for social change aiming (explicitly or implicitly) at transitioning "backward" societies into "civilized" states through the process of modernization. Modernity was understood as anchored in demands for rights and struggles for social progress, in aspirations and trajectories of social emancipation and self-realization, and in the expansions of liberties and civic commitment, all of which were seen as requiring the rupturing or at least weakening of inherited cultural bonds.

Against this vision, we believe that modernity can be realized through distinct cultural and religious traditions. Indeed, we see culture as a historical quarry from which social imaginations extract creative and substantial framings of modernization in locally meaningful ways, and culture may be a powerful source for synergies between identity dynamics and socially inclusive forms of individualization. We earlier cited the example of "buen vivir" as an illustration of this potential, in which modernization processes are being reframed based on values that are not limited to the Western experience, and instead take account of other ways of knowing and being.

15.8.2 Progress and Particularity

In much public and academic discussion, this idea is sometimes discussed under the heading of "multiple modernities." According to

---

[57]   As the United Nations Commission on Human Rights has discussed in depth, the right of minorities and indigenous peoples to enjoy their culture (as specified in Article 27 of the 1966 International Covenant on Civil and Political Rights) often has implications for land use, whether in relation to sacred sites or other land-based cultural practices. These rights are further elaborated in the 2007 UN Declaration on the Rights of Indigenous Peoples (Wiessner 2011).

[58]   As Sylvia Tamale (2008) argues, culture is an important site of struggle over economic and social resources for women. To advocate the avoidance of culture talk (as recommended by Mamdani 2000) could potentially amount to denying subordinated groups the resources to assert and affirm themselves.

this idea, modernization does not necessarily lead societies to converge on particular economic or political forms (such as capitalism or secularism), but rather can take very different forms shaped by different cultural or religious traditions, such as Muslim or Evangelical conceptions of modernity, or modernity as developed in a more authoritarian direction in Singapore or Qatar. Of course, even in the era of modernization theory there was a profound clash between capitalist and communist conceptions of modernity. But during the Cold War both sides shared the assumption that modernization would displace traditional religious and cultural frameworks: the idea of an "Islamic" or "Confucian" modernity was as inconceivable to Soviet as to Western modernizers.

Since its emergence in the 1990s, the idea of multiple modernities has been subject to critical discussion, in particular about its heuristic rigor and its possible political implications. For one, it is unclear whether "modernity" can be defined in a clear way. Eisenstadt's (2000) classical formulation emphasized the antinomies and conflicts unleashed by the loss of a taken-for-granted cosmic ordering. Of particular importance regarding religious change is recognizing that processes of rationalization and standardization have been accompanied by their opposite, explosions of sectarian and dissident movements (Hefner 1998). This perspective suggests that modernity is a world condition in which disparate movements and orientations compete and clash (compare Schmidt 2006). But is there, then, any value-orientation common to various flavors of "modernity"? Once one proposes any one core concept or value, whether secularism, equality, or individual autonomy, then the concept points toward liberal ideal types or "promissory notes" (Wittrock 2000), leaving as a subsequent task the reconciling of those ideal types with particular Islamic, or Confucian, or more locally specific multiple modernities (Fourie 2012). However, one can adopt the historical perspective, set out by Max Weber and more recently by Charles Taylor (2007) in his conception of our "secular age," that modernity came with the disenchantment of the world and makes it no longer possible to take for granted a uniform or universal social order or belief system. All who live in the modern world are then modern, whether they use, ignore, or reject words similar to "modernity." In that case an exploration of the modern condition, rather than a set of modern values, becomes the object of study.

Some critics also argue that, while seeming to recognize the validity of non-Western conceptions of modernity, the "multiple modernities" perspective allows Western states to evade the postcolonial critique of Western modernity. This critique applies in particular to the "civilizational" versions of multiple modernities (Wittrock 2012), which involve tracing disparate contemporary forms of modernity to their Axial Age origins. These versions acknowledge non-Western trajectories but do not integrate into their analyses either the histories of colonialism and imperialism that subtend Western modernity, or the particular assumptions about individualism and capitalism that lie at the center of triumphalist narratives (Chakrabarty 2002). From this critical perspective, the spread of "modernity" was not an innocent transmission of ideas but the result of Western efforts to win control over trade, to exploit natural resources, and to exercise political domination.

If Indonesian political and legal institutions look like French ones, it is because of a combination of French expansion within Europe and Dutch imperialism in Asia, and not because of parallel genealogies of concepts and institutions.

One finds also the opposite fear, namely, that ideas of "multiple modernities" allow authoritarian states to evade internal critique of their rule, enabling authoritarian rulers to discount critics and dissidents as tainted by "foreign" ideals. Some of these critiques are embedded in and resonate with deeper controversies about the nature of knowledge production between the global North and global South. Appeals to "multiple modernities" may appear to reflect a more inclusive or expansive conception of ways of knowing the world, but in reality, they may reproduce, rather than overcome, long-standing debates about who is empowered to define modernity. Moreover, the idea of "modernity" itself is embedded in historical processes and struggles and thus is not completely neutral. For example, the term "modernity" has been explicitly opposed, in particular moments over the past century, by currents within the Catholic Church and within US Protestantism.

In our view, the idea of multiple modernities can be useful, not if it operates to essentialize or naturalize different "civilizational" models of modernity (e.g. "Western" versus "Confucian" modernity), but rather it if helps to clarify the normative stakes in evaluating different trajectories of social progress. Many of today's intellectual and political struggles concern the tension between universalistic political ideas, on the one hand, and particular sets of norms and values that are generated and reproduced in specific political contexts, on the other. Adopting the idea of a plurality of viable and attractive trajectories toward social progress directs us to examine at a more detailed level the mechanisms that can and do move institutions and societies toward broadly acceptable goals and at the same time draw on (often disparate) elements of cultural and religious traditions and convictions. *Put simply, there may be effective convergence toward broadly held ideals about equality and justice, even though these ideas are framed in terms of distinct cultural and religious views and resources.*

The issue is: given profound differences across cultural and religious convictions – which do not reduce to "civilizations," "societies," or "regions" – what mechanisms can be said to both develop consistently with those convictions and aim to achieve social progress, as all might be able to recognize it? To take one broadly held aspiration, do we find distinct pathways toward gender equality that also preserve key elements of, say, Evangelical, or East Asian, or Amazonian ideas and practices?

As Wittrock (2000: 55) puts it, modernity may be seen as "a set of hopes and expectations that entail some minimal conditions of adequacy that may be demanded of macrosocietal institutions no matter how much these institutions may differ in other respects." This stricture emphasizes that different framings would nonetheless be susceptible to comparisons in terms of directions of substantive change.[59] Applied to the gender case, we would make the question more precise: do distinct trajectories regarding gender roles and relations

---

[59] On similar lines see Schmidt (2006), drawing on a parallel with the "varieties of capitalism" literature.

across different traditions tend in the same direction, i.e., toward promoting better conditions for women in everyday life? We would consider evidence of such convergences to indicate the pertinence of the multiple modernity perspective, as reformulated here, to discussions of social progress.

Regarding the specific mechanisms that could lead to such multiple trajectories, and looking at a meso or micro level, Göle (2000: 114) refers to "processes of cohabitation, hybridization, and reciprocal borrowing" across traditions. This direction of research helps avoid the assumption that trajectories and convergences stem from entirely endogenous factors. Legal changes may be enacted by individual states, but they also may reflect global or transnational shifts and outlooks, via cross-readings of international legal literature, new religious interpretations, or shifts in ideas of fairness and justice.

These formulations offer not solutions but pertinent questions. What role for social progress can be found in these borrowings? Can consensus be reached regarding "minimal conditions of adequacy"? What is meant by "consensus"? Does it require explicit agreement, as when representatives of different traditions, groups, or societies cosign a text or treaty? Or can it also involve implicit, though measurable, progress toward achieving such "minimal conditions"? Those speaking for traditions may feel constrained to declare complete fidelity and coherence (i.e., without the acknowledgment of hybridity), even when analysts can discern such changes.

What emerges from this discussion is that *if* the overriding question is the degree to which social progress can occur within distinct and disparate frameworks, *then* we should not be primarily interested in whether people claim the label "modernity" for themselves, interesting though such a study might be in answering other questions. Accordingly, we do not here seek to survey various ideas associated with the word "modernity" in different times and places, but to develop the specific ideas put forth above, namely, that social progress can proceed on multiple tracks and with disparate framings, that it may be observed through the study of changes in practical circumstances, and that such changes may or may not be made explicit in enunciated models of society, culture, or religion – indeed that such progress may in some cases require *not* formulating explicit models of "modernity" but rather framing change as the development of tradition.

In order to offer a concrete example as a basis for further theoretical reflections, we consider the question of the social progress made (or not made) by women in Muslim-majority countries.

15.8.3   Women in Islam: A Case Study

This case study lends itself well to the principal challenge we have set out, namely, to discern evidence for practical movement of practices and welfare toward broadly accepted value horizons. Studying mechanisms of practical convergence as an empirical phenomenon obviates the need to define explicit and abstract principles, such as, in this case, "gender equality," a phrase that has encountered resistance on many fronts. The very term "gender," often used in English across different language communities, is contested – in France some have taken "gender theory" to signal an attempt to dissolve male/female distinctions; in Indonesia, as the point of entry for Western imperialist thinking about family forms (see Oyewumi 1997 for the case of Nigeria). A history of debates and arguments about Western domination, secularism, and the rightful autonomy of different religious and cultural traditions colors any discussion that begins with demands to renounce elements of traditions (for example, Catholic, Evangelical, or Islamic) if they violate a principle of "gender equality."

We consider Islam in greater depth here (although parallel arguments could be made about social progress in other religious traditions). We can discern areas of measurable movement toward fairness and equality in the legal treatment of Muslim women and men regarding family matters, including marriage, divorce, inheritance, physical violence, and the rights of children (Al-Sharmani 2013). This is "practical convergence" from distinct starting points. For example, Indonesia, with the world's largest Muslim population, has an Islamic legal code that deals with family matters and that is applied in the country's Islamic court system and in some other settings. The code is based on broadly recognized elements from Islamic law, particularly from the Shafi'i legal school dominant in Southeast Asia. The code preserves certain elements of formal gender asymmetry: for example, men have the power to divorce, whereas women must ask a judge to dissolve their marriage. But the code also stipulates that both men and women approach a court in order to divorce, and that they prove one or more of the same list of accepted grounds for divorce. Most divorces are justified as due to the marriage's breakdown. Thus, the formal asymmetry of Islamic divorce is preserved but substantively equal possibilities for divorce are achieved. The complete divorce picture is far from symmetric, in that post-divorce payments differ for men and women (as has been the case for most of recent Western history); the example is apposite but partial.

More generally, reforms of Islamic divorce law carried out by countries with Islamic legal systems have sought to preserve local Islamic understandings but to place conditions on their exercise: men have the right to divorce their wives, but only with a judge's permission; daughters need their fathers' consent to marry, but fathers cannot compel their daughters to marry. These reforms are carried out through new legal codes and court decisions, without directly challenging the validity of long-standing understandings transmitted by scholars of Islam. In this way, they preserve the space between religious authorities and legal authorities that allows for trading concepts across different registers, different understandings of law (Tucker 2008).

At the same time, divorce in the West has changed even more radically. Legally and religiously recognized divorce is a very recent phenomenon in Western Europe. Divorce rights also index the relative capacities of women and men, and since the 1960s, Europe and North America have witnessed both a reframing of marriage and divorce in contractual terms and an enhancement of women's legal and economic autonomy during and after marriage. In some respects, (post-)Christian regimes of marriage and divorce have become closer to Islamic ones.

Viewed in this way, these convergences are not matters of Muslims adopting Western ideas, but distinct trajectories that allow substantive progress while preserving distinct starting points in different cultural or religious frameworks. By contrast, demanding agreement to universal, secular propositions would preformat the field of acceptable responses in a way that privileges some over others, as well as hindering efforts to preserve distinct starting points. Universal propositions no longer bear the trace of their derivation from cultural or religious traditions; they cannot. Such propositions thereby lose legitimacy for some practitioners of the tradition. This outcome can be, we believe, deleterious for encouraging shared social lives.

15.8.3.1   Judges' Interpretations

Along with statutory changes in Muslim countries, progress toward gender equality has also come from changes in legal practices themselves. Let us take a more micro-level look at the mechanisms at work in shaping outcomes in Islamic courts. In most of the cases already referred to, statutes or codes are supposed to guide judges' work. But judges also respond (more or less) to extra-legal forces, which can include views on Islamic law that diverge from those contained in such codes. In addition, litigants may use courts as arenas for bargaining about family dynamics and resources. Studies in diverse countries shed light on one or more of these mechanisms.[60]

First, judges have tended to interpret the legal framework (which retains its gender-unequal formulations) in such a way as to favor women when possible, for example by using wide definitions of "harm" (darar) done to a woman and narrow definitions of her "disobedience" (nushûz), which is the basis of counterclaims sometimes made by husbands. Tunisia provides one example. Judges on the Tunis family court (where almost all judges are women) have generally applied the norm that to abandon the marital home without good cause would indeed count as nushûz, and that in a divorce case such behavior could lead a judge to award the husband damages. But they also hold that if a wife claimed that she did so for good reason, she should be believed unless the husband can prove otherwise. Furthermore, in practice, even when the judges found that a wife had committed nushûz, they refrained from awarding damages (Voorhoeve 2014: 166–172).

Across many countries, Islamic judges tend to grant women divorces when asked to do so. The available evidence indicates that women usually win their divorce if they pursue the case. In some countries a major reason for this is the gradual acceptance of marital discord as grounds for dissolution. In Morocco, for example, legal reforms passed in 2004 led to a sharp rise in divorce suits, most brought by, and won by, women, and almost all women who brought suit on grounds of discord, notably easy to prove, won. Women's suits based on the husband's absence or failure to adequately support his wife also were granted most of the time: in a Cairo sample from 1972–1982, women won 95.5 percent of their cases on these grounds or on other grounds involving the husband's failure to adequately fill his role. In 2000, new laws were passed in Egypt explicitly allowing khul` divorces, and a Cairo study done in the early 2000s found that 67 of 69 women bringing khul` divorce suits obtained their divorces (Rosen 2017). When Lawrence Rosen analyzed historical and contemporary

data regarding Islamic courts, he concluded that "Women commonly 'win' their law suits in the family courts of the Muslim world roughly 65–95 percent of the time" (Rosen 2017).

15.8.3.2   Judges' Governance of Courtroom Bargaining

Procedures are also an important part of legal practice. In Iran, Mir-Hosseini (1993) documents ways in which a sympathetic judge allows a divorce proceeding to stretch out, allowing the wife to bargain for her consent. Even though the husband's right to unilaterally divorce his wife is clear, a judge can schedule a series of reconciliation sessions involving diverse relatives in order to push the husband toward a settlement. Wives may hold out for custody of children or favorable monetary settlements in exchange for agreeing to the divorce. In these cases, despite the husband's divorce rights, the judge's mandate to attempt reconciliation can tip the bargaining scale in favor of the wife.

What leads judges to act in ways that seem to ally with women? Courts may favor women to the extent that they see them as the weaker party. The favoring may be by way of placing the burden of proof on the husband. Such is often the case with regard to husbands' claims of disobedience, for example, or, in a related move, by stipulating, either explicitly or implicitly, that the very fact that the wife brought a divorce suit is evidence of marital discord and thus grounds for divorce. National laws also may do this: Indonesian and Malaysian laws both require that husbands wishing to take a second wife prove they are capable of financing two households and treating both women equally. That such equality of treatment is both broad and difficult opens the door to discretionary denials of polygamy requests. It also is important that the judges making these decisions increasingly include women. For example, in 2005, 28 percent of all Tunisian judges were women, but in the Tunis city child and family court, 88 percent of judges were women (Voorhoeve 2014: 13).

15.8.3.3   Changes in Women's and Men's Legal Consciousness

In some cases reforms in divorce law have also changed the idea of the gendered power balance in negotiating marriage and divorce. Sonneveld (2010) points out that in the Egyptian case, the legislative reform transformed the idea of khul` divorce, initiated by the wife, from a transaction requiring the husband's consent, to an empowering of women to take unilateral action. Furthermore, sometimes khul` reform took place as part of a package that also increased women's rights to work. Hassani-Nezhad and Sjögren (2014) conclude that in Middle Eastern countries, making divorce easier for women to initiate has also increased women's labor force participation, especially for younger women.

Reporting from Iran, Osanloo (2009: 129–134) shows how women's claims to be rights-bearers are nourished by the codification of Iranian civil law, which makes explicit individual rights; the framing is thus in terms of multiple pathways to asserting rights rather than the strategic

---

[60]   The following draws on the fuller analysis in Bowen (2017).

manipulation of references in the courtrooms. Women become adept at formulating their cases in legal terms precisely because they have to go through the courts to obtain a divorce, whereas men, possessed of the right of unilateral divorce, remain relatively ill-equipped to speak the language of the law.

15.8.3.4   Practical Convergences versus Explicit Translation

This case study suggests that we look for evidence of social progress in "practical convergences," or instances of reasoning toward a shared horizon from distinct starting points, and the concomitant changes in institutional arrangements. The material presented in this section is not intended to provide an overall assessment of how Muslim women are faring in the many domains of their social lives, but to provide examples of pertinent evidence that, in an exhaustive study, would be drawn from across those domains.

More generally, the case study indicates a crucial category of mechanisms that can provide social progress while not requiring explicit renunciations of religious and cultural traditions. These mechanisms involve reinterpretations of texts, creative use of procedural rules, and statutory supplements to authoritative (including religiously revealed) canons.

We close this section by noting the difference between what we are calling "practical convergences" of disparate traditions and what Jürgen Habermas calls the "translation" of culturally particular tenets into universal ones (2006). The translation approach asks how, in the political arena, to construct equivalence relations between religious justifications (e.g. "God said so") and public justifications presumed to be accessible to all ("it preserves life"). Habermas (2006: 11) argues that when citizens bring religious reasons to public debates, they and others share a responsibility for translating those reasons into "generally accessible arguments."

Habermas makes his argument with respect to justifications of the sort citizens might advance in debates over public policy: about abortion restrictions, or taxation, or foreign policy. It is relatively easy to imagine citizens arriving at these "translations," even if they have derived the same-sounding justification from different sources. Citizens might oppose abortion on grounds that one should not kill, but one might derive that position from Catholic teachings, from the Qur'an, or from a moral stand that has no explicitly religious derivation. Framing the problem as one of translation implies that the issue concerns propositions about the world that can be detached from distinct social and evaluative frameworks. It then appears as if the issue is neither epistemic nor social but one of pure form: by *p*, the Muslims mean *q*, and that is also what the Calvinists mean by *r*.

But the issues that arouse dispute and debate about the compatibility of different religious traditions with "modernity" are not of this order. They concern entire ways of organizing life, where gender relations, ways of dress, patterns of socializing, ideas about education and faith,

artistic practices, and pronouncements about marriage and divorce coexist in varyingly weighted combinations – something more like a culture or a way of life than a cognitive stance. They concern how distinct orientations can coexist, or whether their perceived incommensurability renders one intolerable to the other – whether, for example, gender asymmetry renders conservative Islam unacceptable for some secularists, or unregulated sexuality makes secularism unacceptable to some Muslims. We have sought here to raise the possibility that there are multiple ways to look for progress toward gender equality and other potential indicators of social progress, and that the distinction between practical convergence and translation raises one important area of methodological multiplicity.

Working toward shared outcomes requires practices of derivation and justification, which are processes of reasoning, carried out in public ways. Focusing on these takes us away from the assumption that secular ways of thinking are rational and religious ones are only defectively so because they are grounded in revelation. Both ways of thinking can involve highly developed processes of inference and argumentation – and both have starting points that must be posited – the social contract, the moment of revelation. Once we shift focus from the starting points to shared horizons, we may start to see signs of social progress where before we saw civilizational incompatibilities.[61]

15.9   Conclusion

Throughout this chapter we have approached from several different angles the basic challenge of how to assess social progress while taking full account of the particularities that characterize cultures (and religions, ethnicities, national belonging). Post-war modernization theory failed to do so because it saw the goal of history in terms of the disembedding of individuals from their traditions. Against that approach we have argued that (1) individuals by their very nature draw on social ties and cultural orientations in order to create fulfilling lives, however individualistic their self-conception; (2) individualization or disembedding can take multiple forms, some of which are hospitable to the pursuit of social justice, but others quite antithetical; (3) the maintaining and mobilizing of inherited ethnic and religious identities also can take many different forms, some hospitable and others antithetical to social progress. The politics of cultural change is therefore complicated, and cannot be captured by simple slogans about modernity versus tradition, or individualism versus the group.

We have also argued that modernization theory's core assumptions about the decline of traditions and the rise of new rationalized forms of sociability is exclusionary: these assumptions define the categories of modern, reflexive, or cosmopolitan social actors in a way that excludes large segments of humanity. Drawing on examples from Latin America, Africa, and the Middle East, we have explored how individuals can creatively draw on their traditions to develop new forms of inclusive citizenship and horizontal solidarity, challenging and transcending old hierarchies and exclusions. We have also argued that to assess social progress we must take our analyses well beyond surface-level

---

[61]   There are obvious links here to studies of the multiple ways in which policy proposals can be framed, thereby attracting distinct constituencies. See for example Skocpol (1994) on the politics of US social security.

rhetoric, and examine the ways in which religious, political, and legal actors reinterpret traditions so as to achieve "practical convergence" on widely recognized values, such as more gender-equal forms of jurisprudence. Cultural resources may be particularly important when they draw on deep-seated senses of obligation and orientation to garner support for change; the challenge is to bring about convergences on broadly recognized desiderata of social progress and human welfare.

References

Aboderin, I. 2004. "Modernization and Ageing Theory Revisited: Current Explanations of Recent Developing World and Historical Western Shifts in Material Family Support for Older People." *Ageing and Society* 24: 29–50.

Adorno, Theodor, and Max Horkheimer. 2002. *Dialectic of Enlightenment*. Palo Alto, CA: Stanford University Press.

Ahmad, A. 1992. "Three Worlds Theory: End of a Debate," in *In Theory. Classes, Nations, Literature*. London: Verso.

Al-Azmeh, Aziz. 1996. *Islams and Modernities*. London: Verso.

Alexander, Jeffrey C. 1996. "Critical Reflections on Reflexive Modernization." *Theory, Culture & Society* 13/4: 133–138.

Alkire, Sabina. 2002. *Valuing Freedoms: Sen's Capability Approach and Poverty Reduction*. New York: Oxford University Press.

Almond, Gabriel, and Sidney Verba. 1963. *The Civic Culture: Political Attitudes and Democracy in Five Nations*. Princeton, NJ: Princeton University Press.

Al-Sharmani, Mulki. (ed.) 2013. *Feminist Activism, Women's Rights and Legal Reform*. London: Zed Books.

Appadurai, Arjun. 1996. *Modernity at Large: Cultural Dimensions of Gobalization*. Minneapolis: University of Minnesota Press.

Appadurai, Arjun. 2006. *Fear of Small Numbers: An Essay on the Geography of Anger*. Durham, NC: Duke University Press. ✈

Appiah, Kwame Anthony. 2005. *The Ethics of Identity*. Princeton, NJ: Princeton University Press.

Barth, Fredrik. 1969. *Ethnic Groups and Boundaries*. Boston: Little Brown.

Bartra, Roger. 1987. *La jaula de la melancholia: identidad y metamorfosis del mexicano*. México: Grijalbo.

Bassel, Leah, and Akwugo Emejulu. 2010. "Struggles for Institutional Space in France and the United Kingdom: Intersectionality and the Politics of Policy." *Politics & Gender* 6/4: 517–544.

Bauman, Zygmunt. 2000. *Liquid Modernity*. Cambridge: Polity Press.

Bauman, Zygmunt. 2004. *Wasted Lives, Modernity and Its Outcasts*. Cambridge: Cambridge University Press.

Bauman, Zygmunt. 2007. *Vida de consumo*. Buenos Aires: Fondo de Cultura Económica.

Bauman, Zygmunt. 2011. *Collateral Damage: Social Inequalities in a Global Age*. Cambridge: Cambridge University Press.

Beck, Ulrich, and Elisabeth Beck-Gernsheim. 2002. *Individualization: Institutionalized Individualism and Its Social and Political Consequences*. London: SAGE.

Beck, Ulrich, Anthony Giddens, and Scott Lash. 1994. *Reflexive Modernization: Politics, Tradition and Aesthetics in the Modern Social Order*. Stanford, CA: Stanford University Press.

Boulden, Jane, and Will Kymlicka. 2015. *International Approaches to Governing Ethnic Diversity*. Oxford: Oxford University Press.

Bowen, John R. 2005. "Normative Pluralism in Indonesia: Regions, Religions, and Ethnicities," in Will Kymlicka and Boagang He (eds.), *Multiculturalism in Asia: Theoretical Perspectives*. Oxford: Oxford University Press.

Bowen, John R. 2017. "Gender, Islam, and Law," WIDER Working Paper 2017/152. United Nations University, July 2017. www.wider.unu.edu/publication/gender-islam-and-law.

Bowen, John R., Christophe Bertossi, Jan Willem Duyvendak, and Mona Lena Krook. (eds.) 2014. *European States and Their Muslim Citizens: The Impact of Institutions on Perceptions and Boundaries*. Cambridge: Cambridge University Press.

Brohman, John. 1995. "Universalism, Eurocentrism, and Ideological Bias in Development Studies: From Modernisation to Neoliberalism." *Third World Quarterly* 16/1: 121–40.

Brown, David. 1989. "Ethnic Revival: Perspectives on State and Society." *Third World Quarterly* 11/4: 1–17.

Brubaker, Rogers, et al. 2008. *Nationalist Politics and Everyday Ethnicity in a Transylvanian Town*. Princeton, NJ: Princeton University Press.

Brysk, Alison. 2000. *From Tribal Village to Global Village: Indian Rights and International Relations in Latin America*. Stanford, CA: Stanford University Press.

Bwesigye, B. 2013. "Is Afropolitanism Africa's new single story?" *ASTER(IX): A Journal of Literature, Art, Criticism*, November.

Byung-Chul Han. 2012. *La sociedad del cansancio*, Spanish transl. Arantzazu Saratxaga Arregi. Barcelona: Herder.

Calderón, Fernando, Martín Hopenhayn, and Ernesto Ottone. 1997. *Esa esquiva modernidad: desarrollo, ciudadanía y cultura en América Latina y el Caribe*. Edit. Caracas: Nueva Sociedad-UNESCO.

Castells, Manuel. 2010. *The Information Age: Economy, Society and Culture*, second edition. Oxford: Wiley-Blackwell.

Castles, S., J., Miller, H.G. de Haas, and H. de Haas. 2014. *The Age of Migration: International Population Movements in the Modern World*, fifth edition. London: Palgrave McMillan.

CEPAL (Economic Commission for Latin America and the Caribbean). 2007. *Social Cohesion: Inclusion and a Sense of Belonging in Latina America and the Caribbean*. Santiago: CEPAL.

CEPAL. 2010. *Time for Equality: Closing Gaps, Opening Trails*. Santiago: CEPAL.

CEPAL. 2014. *Los pueblos indígenas en América Latina: avances en el último decenio y retos pendientes para la garantía de sus derechos*. Santiago: CEPAL.

Chakrabarty, Dipesh. 2002. *Habitations of Modernity*. Chicago: University of Chicago Press.

Clarke, I., and Peter Linden. 1984. *Islam in Modern Nigeria: A Study of a Muslim Community in a Post-Independent State (1960–80)*. Mainz: Gruenewald.

Delanty, Gerard. 2007. "Modernity," in George Ritzer (ed.), *Blackwell Encyclopedia of Sociology*, vol. 6. Oxford: Blackwell.

Ebaugh, Helen Rose. 2002. "Return of the Sacred: Reintegrating Religion in the Social Sciences." *Journal for the Scientific Study of Religion* 41/3: 385–395.

Eisenstadt, Shmuel Noah. 2000. "Multiple Modernities." *Daedalus* 129: 1–29.

Ekeh, Peter. 1975. "Colonialism and the Two Publics in Africa: A Theoretical Statement." *Comparative Studies in Society and History*, 17/1: 91–112.

Ekeh, Peter. 1990. "Social Anthropology and Two Contrasting Uses of Tribalism in Africa." *Comparative Studies in Society and History*, 32/4: 660–700.

Etzioni, Amitai. 1996. *The New Golden Rule: Community and Morality in a Democratic Society*. New York: Basic Books.

Evans, Peter, and William Sewell. 2013. "Neoliberalism: Policy Regimes, International Regimes and Social Effects," in Peter A. Hall and Michèle Lamont (eds.), *Social Resilience in the Neoliberal Era*. Cambridge: Cambridge University Press.

Fourie, Elsje. 2012. "A Future for the Theory of Multiple Modernities: Insights from the New Modernization Theory." *Social Science Information* 51/1: 52–69.

García Canclini, Néstor. 1990. *Culturas híbridas. Estrategias para etrar y salir de la modernidad*. México: Grijalbo.

Geschiere, Peter. 2005. "Autochthony and Citizenship: New Modes in the Struggle over Belonging and Exclusion in Africa." *Forum for Development Studies* 32/2: 371–384.

Geschiere, Peter. 2009. *The Perils of Belonging: Autochthony, Citizenship, and Exclusion in Africa and Europe*. Chicago: University of Chicago Press.

Giddens, Anthony. 1991. *Modernity and Self-Identity: Self and Society in the Late Modern Age*. Cambridge: Policy Press.

Gilman, Nils. 2003. *Mandarins of the Future: Modernization Theory in Cold War America*. Baltimore, MD: Johns Hopkins University Press.

Göle, Nilüfer. 2000. "Snapshots of Islamic Modernities." *Daedalus* 129: 91–117.

Gosh, Jayitri, and C.P. Chandrasekhar. 2004. *The Market that Failed: Neoliberal Economic Reforms in India*. New Delhi: Leftward Books.

Grootegoed, Ellen, Christian Broer, and Jan Willem Duyvendak. 2013. "Too Ashamed to Complain: Cuts to Publicly Financed Care and Clients' Waiving of their Right to Appeal." *Social Policy and Society* 12: 475–483.

Habermas, Jürgen. 2006. "Religion in the Public Sphere." *European Journal of Philosophy* 14/1: 1–25.

Hale, Charles. 2002. "Does Multiculturalism Menace? Governance, Cultural Rights, and the Politics of Identity in Guatemala." *Journal of Latin American Studies* 34: 485–524.

15

Hall, Peter, and Michèle Lamont. (eds.) 2013. *Social Resilience in the Neoliberal Era*. New York: Cambridge University Press.

Hamilton, C. 1998. *Terrific Majesty: The Powers of Shaka Zulu and the Limits of Historical Invention*. Cambridge, MA: Harvard University Press.

Hardtmann, E.M. 2009. *The Dalit Movement in India: Local Practices, Global Connections*. Delhi: Oxford University Press.

Harrison, L.E., and J. Kagan. 2006. *Developing Cultures: Essays on Cultural Change*. New York: Routledge.

Harvey, David. 2007. "Neoliberalism as Creative Destruction." *Annals of the American Academy of Political and Social Science* 610 (*NAFTA and beyond: Alternative Perspectives in the Study of Global Trade and Development*): 22–44.

Hassani-Nezhad, Lena, and Anna Sjögren. 2014. "Unilateral Divorce for Women and Labor Supply in the Middle East and North Africa: The Effect of Khul Reform." *Feminist Economics*, 20/4: 113–137.

Hefner, W.R. 1998. "Multiple Modernities: Christianity, Islam and Hinduism in a Globalizing Age." *Annual Review of Anthropology* 27: 83–104.

Hill, Margari. 2009. "The Spread of Islam in West Africa: Containment, Mixing, and Reform from the Eighth to the Twentieth Century." *Spice Digest Africa* [Stanford Program on International and Cross-cultural Education], Spring.

Hooker, Juliet. 2005. "Indigenous Inclusion/Black Exclusion: Race, Ethnicity and Multicultural Citizenship in Contemporary Latin America." *Journal of Latin American Studies* 37/2: 285–310.

Hopenhayn, Martín. 2015. *América Latina desigual y descentrada*. Buenos Aires: Norma.

Inkeles, Alex. 1969. "Making Men Modern: On the Causes and Consequences of Individual Change in Six Developing Countries." *American Journal of Sociology* 75/2: 208–225.

James, C.L.R. 2012. *A History of Pan-Africanist Revolt*. Oakland, CA: PM Press.

Jameson, Fredric. 1991. *Postmodernism, or, the Cultural Logic of Late Capitalism*. Durham, NC: Duke University Press.

Jameson, Fredric. 1998. "Culture and Finance Capital," in *The Cultural Turn: Selected Writings on the Postmodern, 1983–1998*. London: Verso.

Jenson, Jane, and Ron Levi. 2013. "Narratives and Regimes of Social and Human Rights: The Jack Pines of the Neoliberal Era," in Peter A. Hall and Michèle Lamont (eds.), *Social Resilience in the Neoliberal Era*. Cambridge: Cambridge University Press.

Juul, Sorren. 2013. *Solidarity in Individualized Societies: Recognition, Justice and good judgement*. Abingdon, Oxfordshire: Routledge. ✗

Khaddar, Moncfel. 2012. "Nationalist Ruling Parties, National Governments Ideologies, Partisans and Statesmen." *Journal of North African Studies* 17/1: 67–96.

Kymlicka, Will. 2013. "Neoliberal Multiculturalism?" in Peter A. Hall and Michèle Lamont (eds.), *Social Resilience in the Neoliberal Era*. Cambridge: Cambridge University Press.

Kymlicka, Will, and Eva Pföstl. 2014. *Multiculturalism and Minority Rights in the Arab World*. Oxford: Oxford University Press.

Lacher, Hannes. 1999. "Embedded l Liberalism, Disembedded Markets." *New Political Economy* 4/3: 343–360.

Lamont, Michèle, and Virág Molnár. 2002. "The Study of Boundaries in the Social Sciences." *Annual Review of Sociology* 28/1: 167–195.

Lane, Carrie M. 2011. *A Company of One: Insecurity, Independence, and the New World of White-Collar Unemployment*. Ithaca, NY: Cornell University Press.

Lasch, Christopher. 1991. *The Culture of Narcissism: American Life in an Age of Diminishing Expectations*. New York: W.W. Norton.

Latham, Michael. 2000. *Modernization as Ideology: American Social Science and "Nation Building" in the Kennedy Era*. Chapel Hill: University of North Carolina Press.

Lentin, Alana, and Gavin Titley. 2011. *The Crises of Multiculturalism: Racism in a Neoliberal Age*. London: Zed Books.

Lerch, Julia, Patricia Bromley, Francisco Ramirez, and John Meyer. 2017. "The Rise of Individual Agency in Conceptions of Society: Textbooks Worldwide, 1950–2011." *International Sociology* 32/1: 38–60.

Levtzion, Nehemia, and Randall L. Pouwels. (eds.) 2010. *History of Islam in Africa*. Oxford: James Currey.

Lewis, Oscar. 1961. *The Children of Sanchez: Autobiography of a Mexican Family*. New York: Random House.

Lipovetsky, Gilles. 2003. *La era del vacío: ensayo sobre el individualismo contemporáneo*. Barcelona: Anagrama.

Lipset, Seymour Martin. 1959. "Some Social Requisites of Democracy: Economic Development and Political Legitimacy." *American Political Science Review* 53/1: 69–105.

Loimeier, R. 1997. *Islamic Reform and Political Change in Northern Nigeria*. Evanston, IL: Northwestern University Press.

Macpherson, C.B. 1962. *The Political Theory of Possessive Individualism (Hobbes to Locke)*. Oxford: Oxford University Press.

Mafeje, Archie. 1971. "The Ideology of 'Tribalism.'" *Journal of Modern African Studies*, 9/2: 253–261.

Mafeje, Archie. 1991. *The Theory and Ethnography of African Social Formations: the Case of the Interlacustrine Kingdoms*. Dakar: CODESRIA.

Maffesoli, Michel. 2000. *L'instant éternel*. Paris : Denoel.

Mamdani, Mahmood. 2000. *Beyond Rights Talk and Culture Talk*. New York: St. Martin's Press.

Manuh, T. 1998. "Ghanaians, Ghanaian Canadians, and Asantes: Citizenship and identity among migrants in Toronto." *Africa Today*. 45/3: 481–493.

Marcuse, Herbert. 1964. *One-Dimensional Man*. Boston, MA: Beacon Press.

Martín Barbero, Jesús. 1987. *De los medios a las mediaciones: comunicación, cultura y hegemonía*. México: Ediciones G. Gili.

Marx, Karl. 1968. *El Capital*, Spanish transl. Wenceslao Roces. México: Fondo de Cultura Económica.

Mbembe, A. 2002. "African Modes of Self-Writing." *Public Culture* 14/1: 239–273.

McClelland, David. 1961. *The Achieving Society*. New York: Free Press.

Mir-Hosseini, Ziba. 1993. *Marriage on Trial: A Study of Islamic Family Law*, revised edition. London: I.B. Tauris.

Mundy, Jacob. 2010. "The Failure of Transformative Minority Politics in Algeria: The Kabyli Citizens" Movement and the State," in Michael Mbanaso and Chima Korieh (eds.), *Minorities and the State in Africa*, Amherst, NY: Cambria.

Mustapha, A.R. (ed.) 2014. *Sects and Social Disorder: Muslim Identities & Conflict in Northern Nigeria*. Woodbridge, Suffolk: James Currey.

Osanloo, Arzoo. 2009. *The Politics of Women's Rights in Iran*. Princeton, NJ: Princeton University Press.

Ostien, Philip. Forthcoming. "The Muslim Majority in Northern Nigeria: Sects and Trends," in A.R. Mustapha and D. Ehrhardt (eds.), *Creed and Grievance: Muslims, Christians and Society in Northern Nigeria*. Woodbridge, Suffolk: James Currey.

Oyewumi, Oyeronke. 1997. *The Invention of Women: Making an African Sense of Western Gender Discourses*. Minneapolis: University of Minnesota Press.

Pande, A., F. Garba, and R. Chaturvedi. 2016. "Displacing hierarchies: nation and universities in India and Africa." *Review of African Political Economy* brief. http://roape.net/2016/04/01/displacing-hierarchies-nation-and-universities-in-india-and-africa/#'.

Paz, Octavio. 1950. *El laberinto de la soledad*. México: Cuadernos Americanos.

Pew Forum on Religion and Public Life. 2010. *Tolerance and Tension: Islam and Christianity in Sub-Saharan Africa*. Washington, DC: Pew Research Center.

Picard, Elizabeth. 2012. "Nation-Building and Minority Rights in the Middle East," in A. Longva and A. Roald (eds.), *Religious Minorities in the Middle East: Domination, Self-Empowerment, Accommodation*. Leiden: Brill.

Polanyi, Karl. 1957. *The Great Transformation: The Political and Economic Origin of Our Time*. Boston: Beacon Press.

Putnam, Robert. 2000. *Bowling Alone: The Collapse and Revival of American Community*. New York, Simon & Schuster.

Putnam, R.D. 2007. "E Pluribus Unum: Diversity and Community in the Twenty-First Century." 2006 Johan Skytte Prize Lecture. *Scandinavian Political Studies*, 30/2, 137–174.

Radcliffe, Sarah. 2015. *Dilemmas of Difference: Indigenous Women and the Limits of Postcolonial Development Policy*. Durham, NC: Duke University Press.

Rawls, John. 1971. *A Theory of Justice*. Cambridge, MA: Harvard University Press.

Robertson, Roland. 2011. "The 'Return' of Religion and the Conflicted Condition of World Order." *Journal of Globalization Studies* 2/1: 35–36.

Rosen, Lawrence. 2017. *Islam and the Rule of Justice*, Chicago: University of Chicago Press.

Rothstein, Bo. 2017. "Solidarity, Diversity and the Quality of Government," in Keith Banting and Will Kymlicka (eds.), *The Strains of Commitment: the Political Sources of Solidarity in Diverse Societies*. Oxford: Oxford University Press.

Ruggie, John. 1982. "International Regimes, Transactions, and Change: Embedded Liberalism in the Postwar Economic Order," *International organization* 36/2: 379–415.

15

Salazar, Juan Francisco. 2015. "Buen Vivir: South America's Rethinking of the Future We Want." *The Conversation* July 23, 2015. http://theconversation.com/buen-vivir-south-americas-rethinking-of-the-future-we-want-44507.

Sandel, Michael. 2012. *What Money Can't Buy: The Moral Limits of Markets*. New York: Farrar, Straus, and Giroux.

Sarrazin, T. 2010. *Deutschland Schafft Sich Ab. Wie Wir Unser Land aufs Spiel Setzen*. Berlin: DVA.

Schmidt, Volker H. 2006. "Multiple Modernities or Varieties of Modernity?" *Current Sociology* 54/1: 77–97.

Sen, Amartya. 1984. "Rights and Capabilities," in *Resources, Values and Development*. Cambridge, MA: Harvard University Press.

Sen, Amartya. 1999. *Development as Freedom*. Cambridge, MA: Harvard University Press.

Sen, Amartya. 2007. *Identity and Violence*. London: Penguin.

Sennet, Richard. 1998. *The Corrosion of Character: The Personal Consequences of Work in the New Capitalism*. New York: W.W. Norton.

Sennet, Richard. 2005. *The Culture of the New Capitalism*. New Haven, CT: Yale University Press.

Sieder, Rachel. 2001. "Advancing Indigenous Claims through the Law," in Jane Cowan, Marie-Bénédicte Dembour, and Richard Wilson (eds.), *Culture and Rights: Anthropological Perspectives*. Cambridge: Cambridge University Press.

Sieder, Rachel. (ed.) 2002. *Multiculturalism in Latin America: Indigenous Rights, Diversity and Democracy*. New York: Palgrave.

Simmel, Georg. 1999. *The Philosophy of Money*, transl. Tom Bottomore and David Frisby. London: Routledge.

Sitas, A. 2014. "Rethinking Africa's Sociological Project." *Current Sociology* 62: 457.

Skocpol, Theda. 1994. "From Social Security to Health Security?" *Journal of Health Politics, Policy and Law* 19/1: 239–242.

Smith, Anthony. 1981. *The Ethnic Revival*. New York: Cambridge University Press.

Somers, Margaret. 2008. *Genealogies of Citizenship: Markets, Statelessness, and the Right to Have Rights*. New York: Cambridge University Press.

Sonneveld, Nadia. 2010. "Khul` Divorce in Egypt: How Family Courts Are Providing a 'Dialogue' between Husband and Wife." *Anthropology of the Middle East* 5/2: 100–120.

Steinberg, S., P. Parmar, and B. Richard. (eds.) 2006. *Contemporary Youth Culture: An International Encyclopaedia*, vol. 1. London: Greenwood Press. ✗

Tamale, Sylvia. 2008. "The Right to Culture and the Culture of Rights: A Critical Perspective on Women's Sexual Rights in Africa." *Feminist Legal Studies* 16/1: 47–69.

Taylor, Charles. 2007. *A Secular Age*. Cambridge, MA: Harvard University Press.

Terra, Luke, and Patricia Bromley. 2012. "The Globalization of Multicultural Education in Social Science Textbooks: Cross-National Analyses, 1950–2010." *Multicultural Perspectives* 14/3: 136–143.

Tilley, Virginia. 2002. "New Help or New Hegemony? The Transnational Indigenous Peoples" Movement and `Being Indian" in El Salvador." *Journal of Latin American Studies* 34/3: 525–554.

Touraine, Alain. 1992. *Critique de la modernité*. Paris: Fayard.

Touraine, Alain. 1997. *Pourrons-nous vivre ensemble?* Paris: Fayard.

Touraine, Alain, with Farhad Khosrokhavar. 2010. *La recherche de soi*. Paris: Fayard.

Tucker, Judith. 2008. *Women, Family, and Gender in Islamic Law*. Cambridge: Cambridge University Press.

Usman, Y.B. 2006. *Beyond Fairy Tales: Selected Historical Writings of Yusufu Bala Usman*. Zaria: Abdulahi Smith Centre for Historical Research.

Vail, L. 1989. *The Creation of Tribalism in Southern Africa*. Berkeley: Currey University of California Press.

Van Cott, Donna Lee. 2000. *The Friendly Liquidation of the Past: The Politics of Diversity in Latin America*. Pittsburgh: University of Pittsburgh Press.

Voorhoeve, Maaika. 2014. *Gender and Divorce Law in North Africa*. London: I.B. Tauris.

Walsh, Denise. Forthcoming. "Multiculturalism and Women's Rights," in Chris Brown and Robyn Eckersley (eds.), *The Oxford Handbook on International Political Theory*. Oxford University Press.

Weber, Max. 1952. *The Protestant Ethic and the Spirit of Capitalism*. London: George Allen and Unwin.

Welzel, Christian. 2010. "How Selfish Are Self-Expression Values? A Civicness Test." *Journal of Cross-Cultural Psychology* 41/2: 152–174.

Wiessner, Siegfried. 2011. "The Cultural Rights of Indigenous Peoples: Achievements and Continuing Challenges." *European Journal of International Law* 22/1: 121–140.

Wittrock, Björn. 2000. "Modernity: One, None or Many? European Origins and Modernity as a Global Condition." *Daedalus* 129/1: 31–60.

Wittrock, Björn. 2012. "The Axial Age in Global History: Cultural Crystallizations and Societal Transformations," in N. Bellah Robert and Joas Hans (eds.), *The Axial Age and Its Consequences*. Cambridge, MA: Harvard University Press.

Yashar, Deborah. 2005. *Contesting Citizenship in Latin America: The Rise of Indigenous Movements and the Post-Liberal Challenge*. Cambridge: Cambridge University Press.

15

16

Religions and Social Progress: Critical Assessments and Creative Partnerships

Coordinating Lead Authors:[1]
Grace Davie, Nancy T. Ammerman

Lead Authors:[2]
Samia Huq, Lucian N. Leustean, Tarek Masoud, Suzanne Moon, Jacob K. Olupona, Vineeta Sinha, David A. Smilde, Linda Woodhead, Fenggang Yang

Contributing Author:[3]
Gina Zurlo

---

[1] Affiliations: GD: University of Exeter, UK; NA: Boston University, USA.
[2] Affiliations: SH: BRAC University, Dhaka, Bangladesh; LL: Aston University, UK; TM: Harvard University, Kennedy School of Government, USA; SM: University of Oklahoma, USA; JO: Harvard Divinity School, USA; VS: National University of Singapore; DS: Tulane University, USA; LW: Lancaster University, UK; FY: Purdue University, USA.
[3] Affiliation: GZ: Boston University, USA.

Summary

This chapter starts from the premise that some 80 percent of the world's population affirms some kind of religious identification, a percentage that is growing rather than declining. Emphasizing the significance of belief and practice in everyday lives and local contexts, we analyze the impact of religion and its relevance to social progress in a wide variety of fields: family, gender, and sexuality; diversity and democracy; conflict and peace; everyday wellbeing; and care for the earth. We also identify a series of cross-cutting themes that establish a foundation for policy-making.[4]

In the Introduction, we set out our overall goal, which is to provide ways to assess the nature and significance of religion in the specific local contexts in which social progress is pursued. Careful assessment includes attention to everyday practices, not just official doctrines. We demonstrate that religion – as identity, practice, belief, and membership – is integral to the social lives of a vast portion of the world's population. Religion is in itself a cultural good; thus, social progress must include nurturing spaces in which individuals and collectivities can pursue religious ends.

Section 16.2 on "Family, Gender, and Sexuality" affirms that domestic and gendered relationships have always been shaped by religious rules, rituals, and prohibitions. Here we offer tools for assessing both religious obstacles and the potential for partnership in the quest for progress in these most basic of social locations. Setting aside a lingering binary between secular progress and religious reaction is the first step. A burgeoning literature reveals a strong defense of the nuclear family on the part of some religious organizations, but also progressive reinterpretations and tactical uses of existing tradition on the part of others.

Section 16.3 deals with "Religion, Diversity, and Democracy," demonstrating the range of religious ecologies that arise from population movement and media connections. As multiple religious communities encounter each other, the goal remains constant: to discover how religiously diverse people learn to flourish in each other's company. This implies the development of governing structures that are accountable to, and representative of, their citizens. We consider different understandings of multiculturalism and secularism, in addition to democracy itself, noting that religious traditions themselves have capacities to promote democratic governance. Not least, "street-level ecumenism" (pragmatic cooperative activity) is often more effective than a dialogue between religious or secular elites.

Section 16.4 is concerned with "Religion, Conflict, and Peace." A clear conclusion emerges: religion is neither inherently violent nor inherently peaceful, but includes practices, beliefs, values, and institutions that can lead in either direction. A careful assessment of the particular context and the particular religions in play is likely to enhance social progress. Close attention is paid to sites – geographical, political, and social – of potential destructive violence and effective peace-making. The sometimes tense relations between human rights and religion are central to the discussion.

Section 16.5 turns in a different direction to examine the many dimensions of "Everyday Wellbeing: Economy, Education, Health, and Development." We argue that economic wellbeing, education, and health care are goals shared by religious groups and are often woven into religious worldviews. That said, there are many places where religious ideas and practices are at odds with secular norms. Finding common ground is difficult, but well-chosen partnerships can vastly extend the reach of programs that enhance wellbeing. States, non-governmental organizations (NGOs), faith communities, and religiously infused local cultures all have a role to play.

Section 16.6 is concerned with "Care for the Earth" itself, recognizing that religious understandings of the earth and faith-based activism on behalf of the environment share much with secular groups. Effective partnerships enhance the capacities of the diverse players in this field. More profoundly, at least some faith communities assert a moral stance which contests the very framing of "environment-as-resource" in global capitalist society, challenging thereby entrenched systems of power, knowledge, and technology.

Section 16.7, entitled "Themes and Implications: An Action Toolkit," captures the essence of the chapter. It starts by drawing the threads of the chapter together in five interconnected themes: the persistence of religion in the twenty-first century; the importance of context in discerning outcomes – underlining the role of social science in this; the urgent need for enhanced cultural competence and improved religious literacy; the

---

4   We wish to thank Kira Ganga Kieffer, Boston University, for constructing our bibliography, Caleb South, Princeton University, for a very helpful early reading, and Adam Westbrook, Boston University, for his careful proofreading, along with Cécile Laborde and Gerrie ter Haar for especially helpful comments.

significance of religion in initiating change; and – especially – the benefits of well-judged partnerships. Each of these themes concludes with an action toolkit.

In sum, we argue that researchers and policy-makers pursuing social progress will benefit from careful attention to the power of religious ideas to motivate, of religious practices to shape ways of life, of religious communities to mobilize and extend the reach of social change, and of religious leaders and symbols to legitimate calls to action. The continuing need for critical but appreciative assessment and the demonstrable benefits of creative partnerships are our stand-out findings.

16

16.1　Introduction

The pursuit of social progress and human flourishing is inevitably intertwined with religion. Well over 80 percent of the world's population is connected to some sort of religion, a percentage that is growing rather than declining.[5] The consequences of those connections and commitments are, however, enormously varied, at least in part because the connections themselves are widely different in intensity and character. This chapter provides a guide to that variation and impact.

Most religious adherents, even nominal ones, see their religious traditions as a basic good, providing blessings to themselves and others. In the very places where social and political life is most precarious, religious communities can provide key protections and forms of self-help; and in the most comfortable of places, religious communities often become sites of celebration and solidarity. At the same time, religious movements, communities, and leaders can present important obstacles to progressive change. Understanding the variety of contributions and challenges presented by religion is essential to work for social progress. Neither good nor ill can be assumed at the outset. Analyzing existing evidence regarding the conditions and consequences of specific religious configurations will be a primary task of this chapter.

We will argue that religions can play a distinctive role in reaching and mobilizing portions of the population not always well supported by governmental or economic institutions. Thus, the pervasive grassroots presence of religious leaders and collectivities is a critical resource for those seeking change. This observation is paired with a second theme that will run through this chapter. The goals and methods of secular change agents may not always match perfectly with the goals and methods of religious organizations, a fact that must be recognized from the start. But in most contexts there are areas where creative partnerships are possible, many of which can be highly productive.

We begin this introductory section by thinking carefully about the nature of religion itself and its relation to things deemed secular. A narrow focus on official doctrines and memberships is not sufficient for current religious circumstances, especially beyond Europe and North America. That broader scope – looking seriously at everyday religious life across the globe – will call into question the modern assumptions both that secularization is inevitable and that it is a necessary path to progress. Indeed, as Chapter 15 has made clear, assumptions based in a modernization narrative are often obstacles that blind scientists to the agency and creativity of social actors.

These assumptions are not easily shed, however. Social science itself was birthed with ideas about religion and secularization at its core, and as the modern social sciences developed in post-Enlightenment Europe it seemed natural to speak of religion and secularity as occupying separate – and competing – domains. Religions were primarily understood as systems of belief based on supernatural assumptions and organized into major systems of authority and power. These were seen as standing in natural opposition to empirical, scientific, and political ways of understanding and ordering the world. This opposition and the gradual triumph of science and expertise were theorized as secularization. In Peter Berger's (1969) influential statement of the theory, the forces of the modern world would eventually remove the necessity for supernatural explanations, and those who still believed in forces beyond this world could either hold those beliefs as privatized opinions or gather in "sheltering enclaves" with fellow believers. Religion itself would lose its ability to be a powerful force shaping the secular public world.

Even Berger himself has renounced much of the theory that bore his imprint, noting not only the robust presence of religious affiliation around the world and the visibility of religiously inspired political movements, but also the persistence of the most dramatically supernatural forms of religion *alongside* modern ways of knowing (Berger 2014). While some would describe this as a "resurgence" of religion, we prefer to argue that the old modernization narratives never captured the religious realities of the larger world in which questions of social progress must be addressed today.

16.1.1　Defining Religion and Its Relation to Social Progress

One of the most challenging tasks in addressing the question of religion and social progress is establishing the terms of the conversation. Social progress, as previous chapters have argued, must be disentangled from its Enlightenment presumptions in order to encompass a broader understanding of movements toward freedom, dignity, and relationships of solidarity and mutual wellbeing. Once we leave aside the premise that every part of the world will develop along universal lines set out by Western Europe's history, we also have to disentangle ideas about progress from ideas about secularity. That task begins with a careful reassessment of how religion is defined and identified.

16.1.1.1　Expanding Definitions of Religion

The existing social science literature depends to a large extent on research methods developed in North America and Europe. At their best, these encompass some of the complexity that characterizes the religious dimensions of society. Sophisticated survey-based measures are often very useful for producing a broad snapshot; but as Figure 16.1 demonstrates, surveys can produce widely varying pictures of the same place, depending on which aspect of religion is taken to be most critical.

In this chapter, when we say "religion," we will have in mind both the very broad range of institutions, beliefs, and practices that social

---

[5]　The peak year for non-religious populations is 1970. Since then, religions of all kinds have been growing, including Christianity in Eastern Europe and Sub-Saharan Africa, Buddhism and other religions in China, and Islam in the Middle East and Africa. These trends are driven in part by non-religious people converting, but mostly they are a consequence of standard demographic forces such as births and deaths. Despite shrinking populations of Christian believers in Western Europe and North America, these forces are likely to result in sustained religious growth globally through 2050 (Johnson, Grim, and Zurlo 2016).

Measuring Religion Quantitatively

Different strategies of measurement can provide very different assessments on which to base an understanding of the role of religion in a society.

(1) Affiliation. Religious affiliation refers to membership in or attachment to a particular organized religion, typically by means of having one's name on an official record or indicating membership on a census or survey. This may indicate a measure of religious social identification.

(2) Attendance. This is a popular survey measure for analyzing the strength of religion in a particular country. Usually the question is worded something similar to, "Aside from weddings and funerals, how often do you attend religious services?". This may indicate social interaction with a religious group.

(3) Salience. This construct attempts to measure how important religion is in the lives of respondents, usually on a scale from "not at all important" to "very important". Sometimes the question is presented to respondents as how "religious" a person they perceive themselves to be, on a scale from "extremely religious" to "extremely non-religious".

(4) Belief. There are a range of specific beliefs that survey respondents can be asked about, but since each tradition's beliefs vary, these measures are hard to compare. Belief in God or a higher power is perhaps the most widely used, but religious people in some traditions would not answer "yes".

(5) Practice. Like belief, there are many different ways of measuring religious practice, such as giving money, praying, attendance at activities besides regular services, private devotion, scripture reading, holiday observance, and obeying dietary restrictions.

Case Study: New Zealand

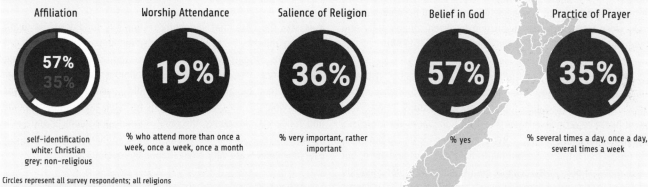

Affiliation	Worship Attendance	Salience of Religion	Belief in God	Practice of Prayer
57% / 35%	19%	36%	57%	35%
self-identification white: Christian grey: non-religious	% who attend more than once a week, once a week, once a month	% very important, rather important	% yes	% several times a day, once a day, several times a week

Circles represent all survey respondents; all religions

Case Study: Jordan

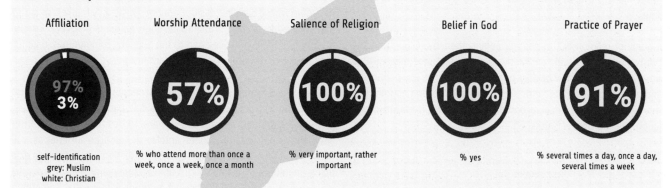

Affiliation	Worship Attendance	Salience of Religion	Belief in God	Practice of Prayer
97% / 3%	57%	100%	100%	91%
self-identification grey: Muslim white: Christian	% who attend more than once a week, once a week, once a month	% very important, rather important	% yes	% several times a day, once a day, several times a week

Circles represent all survey respondents; all religions

Data sources: Todd M. Johnson, Brian J. Grim, & Gina A. Zurlo, eds. World Religion Database. Leiden/Boston: Brill, accessed April 2017; World Values Survey Wave 6: 2010–2014.

Figure 16.1 | Measuring religion.

scientists have typically thought of as religion *and* the much larger domain of everyday beliefs and practices that constitute lived religion. This means that the particular contexts and the particular challenges of people's lived experience matter. Religions have their impact as a part of the life projects of individuals and groups. This has several effects on how we look at religion. First, we expect ordinary practice to diverge from the ideas of religious professionals, in that we expect ordinary practitioners and religious professionals each to appropriate beliefs and practices that help them respond to the demands of their particular personal and institutional context (McGuire 2008). Religious ideas and practices are *situated*, meaning (among other things) that every religious tradition is internally diverse. They are also active and constantly *changing*. As new people enter a context through migration or new ideas are encountered through media, ordinary practitioners and theologians alike engage religion in active ways. They are not simply enacting established beliefs and rituals, but through their action, they are contributing to the ongoing creation and re-creation of them (Bender 2010).

Religion as it is lived is also a very *practical and material* thing, not simply an otherworldly preoccupation. It may address this-worldly goals ranging from overcoming substance abuse to seeking justice, from socializing children to escaping violence (Smilde 2007). Daniel Levine captures well this sense of religious practice. "The lived experience of religion," he writes, "is closely linked to ways of managing ordinary life." As a result, "it is not just that religious beliefs spill over from neatly confined church spaces to infuse action in other parts of life. On close inspection, the distinction between otherworldly and this-worldly … does not hold up very well" (Levine 2012: 8).

Religion is intertwined not only with everyday activities but also with ordinary places and things. In Singapore, for instance, Thai Buddhist talismans are simultaneously objects of supernatural power and items of lucrative economic trade (Yee 1996). In places like Malaysia, Vietnam, Thailand, and Indonesia, religion is often located in the midst of the global marketplace. Sacred things hold blessings and merit, but are also material objects that can be bought and sold; indeed religion itself can be subjected to commodifying tactics (Kitiasa 2008). People do not just live their religion by thinking and believing or by joining an official religious organization. An embodied, practical perspective on religion includes rituals, spaces, and emotions as well (Vasquez 2010; Brenneman 2012).

Our study of religion in this chapter begins, then, by recognizing the pervasiveness of spiritual sensibilities and the fact that this spiritual realm is, for much of the world, as real and powerful as any political or economic force. In turn, its forms are in constant flux and negotiation, interacting with the political, economic, social, and cultural structures through which progress is pursued.

16.1.1.2   Understanding Secularity

To understand religion properly, we also need to reflect on our understandings of "secularity." Throughout the world, governments, agencies, and ordinary people may assert the necessity for domains where religious presence and authority are excluded. The shape of that territory is highly variable, defined by a given society, not by something inherent in the activities themselves (Burchardt and Wohlrab-Sahr 2013). Both secularity – a perceived state of affairs – and secularism – a desired state of affairs – can be thought of as orientations emerging from Western modernity but with variations elsewhere. The secular is descriptive of domains of life in which there are no perceived religious dimensions. For example, advanced Western countries usually define economic transactions as quintessentially secular, but in many other cultures they have important religious significance. National constitutions often attempt to set legal boundaries between secular and religious domains, but such boundaries vary widely, both in law and in practice. And of course, there can be great variation between individuals and between groups even within a given culture regarding what is treated as religious and what is secular. We should expect to find variation from one context to another in whether it makes sense to talk about a secular world at all, and where the line between secular and sacred should or could be drawn, a point made well by Talal Asad (2003).

In short, neither secularity nor religion has a natural domain or function. Religion should rather be understood as beliefs and practices oriented to transcendent realities. Virtually anything humans confront, create, or do can be given religious meaning. Conversely, since anything can potentially be religious, there is nothing that is inherently and always secular. This does not mean that everything *is* religious (or secular), only that many things *can* be.

It is still the case that humanity's "limiting conditions" – death, suffering, injustice – are likely to be explained and confronted in religious terms. Progressive efforts to reduce the rate of death, suffering, and injustice frequently draw on religious traditions. Religious practices may be aimed at this-worldly challenges, including survival in violent contexts and demands for basic rights (Rubin, Smilde, and Junge 2014). Equally, the most ordinary biographical and social achievements – family formation, birth, community celebration, and everyday work – are very often shaped by religious ritual.

Discarding assumptions about an inherent religious/secular divide is especially important for scholars who aim to understand cultures outside "the West." Scholars from the North Atlantic region are often too quick to dismiss as instrumental, insincere, or "backward" the religions of people whose basic necessities are not satisfied by markets or states and who address their problems through religious practices. Careful attention to those practices, and to the religious communities in which they are lived, can often yield important insights.

Nor are the spiritual sources to which people turn just a phenomenon of the less-developed world. A widely popular range of rituals, pilgrimages, shrines, and practices characterizes a milieu of "spirituality" that is present in European and North American societies as well (Heelas and Woodhead 2004). Some of those who participate are also active members of established religions, but many seek to connect with something beyond themselves without naming that something in theistic terms.

The relationship between religion and social progress must be approached, then, with full cognizance of both the presence and the

16

variability of religious beliefs, communities, practices, and leaders. No universal boundary defines the religious and the secular, nor is there any clear justification for regarding some societies as religious and some not.

16.1.2   Religion and Social Progress

As set out in Chapter 2, for many humans, religion is in itself a cultural good, and in that sense, social progress must include nurturing spaces in which individuals and collectivities can be free to pursue religious ends. Establishing societies in which diverse religious expressions can be freely pursued should be seen as a fundamental aim of social progress; and we will examine the evidence that such religious freedom enhances prospects for other social goods. The chapter will go on to argue that religious communities can be spaces of valued solidarity and mutual esteem, another of the fundamental goods toward which social progress aims. In addition, we will assess the circumstances under which religious communities can be partners in providing for the wellbeing of the community.

We will also examine the ways in which religions can be impediments to basic principles of equal dignity, for example when they stand in the way of women or limit freedom of expression or block participation in democratic governing. Indeed, the same mechanisms that create religious solidarities can also limit toleration, restrict educational exploration, or lead to violent conflict. We will examine the various ways religious power may be allied with political projects to diminish wellbeing for denigrated populations. Throughout, we will assess religions in their local, embodied particularity in order to evaluate the possible ways they may or may not enable human flourishing.

Religion that seems especially incompatible with social progress is often designated "fundamentalist." This implicit contrast to mainstream or more established religion is misleading. The term is best used to refer to a type of highly salient religious identity and practice that claims to be based on inerrant "fundamentals" in a religious tradition (Marty and Appleby 1991).[6] While fundamentalist religion clearly poses a challenge to liberal modernity, it also provides forms of self-help or political mobilization in dire and oppressive contexts that mainstream religion and other secular ideologies either ignore or simply conform to.

This points to another important way in which religion is implicated in social progress. We will provide evidence for the utility of religious communities as critical spaces in which the very parameters of progress can be discussed, debated, and given moral grounding. As the authors of Chapter 22 tell us, social progress requires the ability to think about how "it could be different." It requires that a society engage in moral deliberation and moral judgments. Progress is not simply a matter of finding the right technological formulas. Imagining what a society could become requires reaching beyond oneself, beyond the everyday world as it is. Progress implies a sense of meaning and purpose that has, even if unstated, moral valence. There are many ways

such deliberations and transcendent imagination can be fostered, but for much of the world's population religious communities and religious rituals are the spaces in which humans do the work of envisioning this-worldly transformation.

This can be illustrated by thinking about social progress in African contexts (Olupona 2012, 2014). At the center of many African cosmologies is the lifelong quest for a good life that is engaged in by individuals and communities. From birth to death, the blessings of health and long life, wealth, and children are intended to strengthen and support communal structures, and seeking to acquire such blessings without embedding them within the larger society is condemned. Spiritual belief and ritual undergird ways of pursuing peace and tranquility among neighbors, participation in a community of respect, fairness, and accountability, and being in healthy harmony with the earth itself. Religion and social progress are mutually implicated.

The basic framework that informs this chapter, then, is the assertion that progress and religious tradition are not *of necessity* antithetical. Even when the religious and cultural context sounds alien to the ears of Western-educated experts, assessing likely benefits and partnerships – as well as likely resistance or danger – requires critical grounded knowledge. Religious traditions and religious authorities can and do block needed changes that would increase the larger flourishing of a community. This chapter will assess both those blockages and the often-overlooked ways in which religious institutions, beliefs, and practices are partners and facilitators of the work of social progress. We begin that task by examining the many issues that link religion with the most intimate areas of social life, moving in subsequent sections to the larger arenas of political, economic, and ecological concerns.

16.2   Family, Gender, and Sexuality

As Chapter 17 on the "Pluralization of Families" points out, the vast majority of the world's population lives the majority of life within family units, of varying shapes and sizes. And as *this* chapter demonstrates, a large majority of the world's population is also religious. Intimate human relationships have always been shaped and surrounded by religious rules, rituals, and prohibitions. If anything, religions' concern with family, gender, and sexuality has increased in the modern period. This shift coincides with the pluralization of family forms, more fluid gender identities, the drive to achieve equality between the sexes, and other changes documented in Chapter 17. Inevitably, this has generated internal tensions and debate within many religious traditions and has affected their adherents. Understanding the ever-changing intersections among religions, gender, sexuality, and family life is central to making the sort of progress envisaged in that chapter.

Advances in this field have, however, been hampered by the modernist theory criticized in Chapter 15, with its lingering binary between secular progress and religious reaction – the former considered automatically positive for the wellbeing of women, children, and gay people, the latter negative. Our approach takes advantage of the recent and

16

---

[6]   Equating "fundamentalism" with political radicalism or violent extremism is especially misleading. On the relationship between religion and violence, see Section 16.4.

647

burgeoning multidisciplinary research on religion and gender which considers not only male-led, hierarchically organized forms of "official" religion, but also everyday lived religion, in which women, men, and young people seek to change or reform religion, make tactical uses of it, or bypass its official forms altogether (Ammerman 2007; McGuire 2008; Woodhead 2014). This enables us to offer a critical assessment of religion's past, present, and future social impact.

16.2.1   Religion and the Modern Family

Historically, religion has been associated with every form of family and almost every imaginable form of sexual and gendered relation. The Bible, for example, variously supports concubinage, polygamy, monogamy, singleness and celibacy, and even discusses child sacrifice and murder.

In the modern period, however, the heterosexual nuclear family came to dominate the religious as well as the secular imagination (see Chapter 17). Official forms of religion and their male leaders played an important role in shaping the ideal. In the West, the Protestant Reformers of the sixteenth century led the way by criticizing celibacy – including all-female religious orders – and sacralizing the patriarchal family unit (Roper 1992). In modern industrial societies many religious leaders endorsed the male breadwinner model, exalting women's domestic responsibilities, and affirming strong parental authority over children. By the late twentieth century, most male-led official religions had come to accept the permissibility of women's paid work outside the home, but many continued to endorse in some form a doctrine of the "complementary" but essentially different roles of men and women.

The defense of the so-called "traditional" family was strongest in fundamentalism (originally a movement within Christianity dating from the start of the twentieth century, but with manifestations in most of the other world religions since then). Although it is most often associated with the Abrahamic religions of Judaism, Christianity, and Islam, the sacralized nuclear-family model finds religious defenders worldwide. It has also been linked with colonial and postcolonial nation-building projects – both secular and religious – where women have been relegated to the "domestic and spiritual realm" (Chatterjee 1989: 239; see also Sarkar 2001; Menon 2010). The family unit is presented as a God-given norm with clear boundaries which must be vigorously defended by the faithful. It is attributed a sacred status, with anything which threatens it categorized as profane – including sexual infidelity, "secular" state policies, egalitarian gender ideologies, feminism, and homosexuality.

Away from official religious teachings and pronouncements, however, the lived realities of religious families allow for a great deal of negotiation, even circumvention of strictures. For example, in the face of changes that have led to the pluralization of family forms, ordinary Catholics often ignore the Catholic Church's condemnation of contraception, homosexual relations, and remarriage after divorce (Clague

2014). There are LGBTQ movements in most religions, as well as liberal religious wings, which disagree with "official" teachings on topics such as women's roles and same-sex marriage. Sometimes this pluralization of family forms within religions has gained official sanction, as, for example, in the development of plural forms of Muslim "marriage."[7]

Religious clashes over different family ideals have become potent sites of political mobilization. They can spill over national boundaries and give rise to unexpected alliances, such as coalitions in defense of the traditional family which cross previously sharp religious and theological boundaries. In addition, the politics of sexuality and gender can become entangled with other political fissures. In contemporary East Africa, for example, homosexuality is often linked to the perceived ills and injustices of Western colonial societies, and to threats against religion, nationhood, and African masculinity (Ward 2002).

There are currently many "hot" conflict points where family and gender-related ideals clash violently. They include abortion clinics, reproductive health legislation, legalization of same-sex marriage, and women's dress. The clash is most vivid when fundamentalist forms of religion oppose what they see as modern forms of sexual "decadence." The results can be murderous, as in forms of Islamic terrorism targeted at gay clubs and "decadent" Western cultural venues.

16.2.2   Religion and Gender

Questions about family relations are intertwined with questions about the nature of gender, and here too religion plays a role. Women are not universally more religious than men, but expressions of religion often vary by gender. In each tradition and context, religious practice and piety figure somewhat differently in the lives of women and men, with the "gender gap" (with women more actively religious than men) greatest in Christianity (Pew Research Center 2016).

16.2.2.1   Conservative Religion

Studies of women in conservative religious groups have challenged many assumptions. Researchers have discovered a variety of ways in which women both benefit from and sometimes subvert masculine-dominated forms of religion. In her study of a North American fundamentalist Christian community, Nancy Ammerman discovered that "most women learn to influence family decision-making while still deferring to their husband's authority" and "find ways to live with the tension between fundamentalist norms for family structure and modern norms of individuality and equality" (Ammerman 1987: 146). Other studies, like those of Elizabeth Brusco (1986) or Bernice Martin (2001) in Latin America, find that women can benefit by appealing to religious norms to tame machismo and domesticate their menfolk, turning them into better fathers and husbands. Lynn Davidman (1991), looking at women in Orthodox Judaism, finds that women benefit from the way in which the tradition sacralizes women's roles as wives and mothers in stable family units, a conclusion also supported by

---

7   See the "Muslim Marriages Project" directed by Annelies Moors: http://religionresearch.org/musmar2014/project-information/.

studies of the burgeoning ultra-orthodox movement in Judaism (e.g. Heilman 1999).

Recent anthropological studies on the postcolonial situation in Egypt and the Middle East assess women's engagement with conservative Islam to understand how they respond to liberal assumptions (one could say blind spots) on modernity, piety, femininity, and agency. For example Saba Mahmood's (2005) study of women in Egypt's piety movement highlights how women learn to inhabit conservative norms as a way of forming the self as worthy and responsible. In doing so women are not only able to claim a place in previously male-only spaces such as the mosque, but become agents of change in their households and communities. Lara Deeb's (2006) work on women in the suburbs of Beirut discusses similar engagements to argue that such religiosity is to be understood as a re-enchantment of modernity, where the "Western woman" is invoked both as foil and impetus to create an authentically Islamic and modern way of life in which pious selves are fashioned.[8] Samia Huq's (2011) study of the cultivation of piety among educated, urban Bangladeshis shows that while women remain attached to traditional families headed by men, they exercise greater individualistic reflection, in relation both to the domestic sphere and to the cultural and economic conditions which have historically used sexual appeal to render women and wives subservient.

The "bargains" struck with official pious and conservative modes of femininity and family (Kandiyoti 1988) do not, however, eliminate risks, costs, and violence for women. R. Marie Griffith's (1997) study of the Charismatic-Evangelical Christian "Women's Aglow" movement concludes: "If, in certain ways, prayer and testimony seem to create possibilities for the liberation and transformation worshippers claim to experience, they may just as readily work to opposite ends, further institutionalizing the roles and boundaries that constrict women's space" (1997: 210). Although it provided a safe space in which some women could speak to one another about violence and abuse within the pious household, the remedy was limited.

Gender-based violence does not seem to be especially linked to particular religions or strands within them. No large-scale systematic study exists, but work on domestic violence in Christian groups in North America (e.g. Sevcik et al. 2015) suggests that rates are not significantly higher than outside such contexts.[9] Studies of clerical abuse in Ireland (e.g. Keenan 2012) reveal an interlocking system of inequalities in which religion is just one factor. The extreme example of religiously legitimated male domination and violence against women in fundamentalist groups like ISIS and Boko Haram is now beginning to be studied (e.g. Stern and Berger 2016), but larger patterns and processes are not yet well understood.

Thus, even when they can be subverted and used tactically, and though secular solutions may be worse than what they replace, conservative religious legitimations of difference and inequality between men, women, and children often stand as blocks in the way of progress.

16.2.2.2   Liberal and Reform Movements

Internal religious critiques of sexism date back at least to the nineteenth century. Worldwide, effective calls for equal human dignity have sometimes taken religious as well as secular forms. Fresh energy was poured into religious movements for progressive change from the 1970s onward. In the wake of the Iranian revolution of 1979, for example, an epistemological and theoretical shift took place in Islamic thought which involved the historical contextualization of Islam and women's roles and responsibilities in Muslim societies (e.g. Mernissi 1991; Ahmed 1992). This fed into an ongoing attempt to dissociate Islam from structural inequalities and cultural practices sanctioning discrimination against women (Barlas 2002; Moghadem 2005; Najmabadi 2005).

In Christianity, a great deal of effort was injected into campaigns for women's ordination as priests, which proved successful in most Protestant denominations between the 1920s and 1990s, but not in the Roman Catholic or Orthodox Churches (Chaves 1997). These campaigns were accompanied by the development of "feminist theology," in which Christian doctrines, ethics, and liturgy were read and reinterpreted through an explicitly feminist lens (Parsons 2010). In Buddhism, there were successful efforts to revive orders of Buddhist nuns (Mohr and Tsedroen 2009; Kawanami 2013). Female religious orders remain important in several religions, including Roman Catholic Christianity, where they focus women's collective energy and often work actively for greater equality – sometimes against the wishes of male authority.

In Islam, recent reform movements include Musawah, initiated in Kuala Lumpur and currently headquartered in Rabat. Musawah aims to reform Muslim family law, working with legal experts, Islamic clergy and scholars, and anthropologists and historians. By highlighting the diversity of legitimate Islamic juristic opinion and by engaging in research on the ground, it seeks to shift the construction of marriage and gender relations from one in which women are obedient and subjugated to one more compatible with scriptural injunctions to show love, mercy, and equal respect for both genders (Anwar 2009; Mir-Hosseini, al-Sharmani, and Rumminger 2015). Musawah continues to advocate reform in family laws in many parts of the world and has had some notable successes, for example in legal reform in Morocco.

Such initiatives are not without critique from other Muslims, however. Lila Abu-Lughod (2015) argues that movements such as Musawah and the Global Muslim Women's Shura Council resort to a human rights model that separates Muslim women from their own cultures and obscures the structural, political, and economic factors – played out at a global level and in the everyday – that contribute to women's suffering. And Saba Mahmood (2006) points out that an imperialist logic is at play when Islamic cultural practices such as veiling or "honor killings" are declared in need of remedy, thereby justifying Western military and other kinds of intervention in Muslim societies.

---

[8]   In a recent experiment involving approximately 2,500 adult subjects in Egypt, Masoud, Jamal, and Nugent (2016) found that individuals were more likely to favor women's leadership when they were shown that it was consistent with Qur'anic teachings.

[9]   This study helpfully points out that responses to domestic violence are best when they draw on the particular religious or secular beliefs of the community.

Outside agents seeking progressive change would do well to listen carefully to the everyday narratives of women's lives, mindful that faith-based organizations themselves are often sites where progressive change begins.

Internal movements for religious reform have generally focused on women and femininities, and less attention has been paid to men, masculinities, and gender relations in a broader sense. Where there has been explicit attention to masculinity, it has often been in order to defend a patriarchal family model. In the wake of feminism, such defense in conservative Christian circles is often couched in terms of the support of strong but "responsible" forms of male headship. Van Klinken's (2013) study of African Christian masculinities in the context of AIDS reveals a strongly heterosexual, masculinist Protestant Christian mode of male headship, and a gentler Catholic one which is "queered" by devotion to Mary and the general use of more feminine imaginary. Gender never means just women, and religious effects on the gender order cover a wide spectrum.

16.2.3 Sexuality

Religious leaders and teachings have often been prescriptive about both sex and sexual identity. Many religions continue to frown upon sex outside of marriage, but most have abandoned the enforcement of sexual prescriptions within marriage. That said, the Roman Catholic Church's insistence on "natural" rather than artificial forms of birth control remains an important exception.

Growing diversity and fluidity in relation to gender and sexual identity and practice has called forth a more vocal response. Opposition to homosexuality is by no means confined to religion, but it is a feature of all fundamentalisms and a great deal of mainstream religious opinion as well. But there are also dissenting voices, who reread traditional religious sources to problematize "homophobic" readings. For example, the story of the Prophet Lut/Lot and the City of Sodom which is present in the Qur'an as well as the Bible can and has been read not as a condemnation of "sodomy," but as a story of oppressive power, miserliness, inhospitality, and arrogance where male sex acts are vilified for the abuse of power they represent in that particular context. In his study of *Homosexuality in Islam*, Kugle (2003) begins with the Qur'an's injunction that humanity should respect and celebrate diversity, going on to show how later commentaries highlighted the existence of hermaphrodites (a third gender). The Sunna (sayings and examples of the Prophet Muhammad) also mention men who are akin to women and men who are not attracted to women, without elaborating on the reason for their lack of desire. Resources such as these, from within religious traditions, can provide a bridge between religious populations and secular reformers.

There are bridges in everyday practice, as well. LGBTQ movements are now found within all religious traditions, sometimes pressing for reform of official religion, and sometimes setting up alternative religious communities and networks. A recent study of the religious and sexual identities of young people across many religious traditions (Yip

and Page 2013) found that those in conservative religious groups generally found their faith a support in helping them defend their identity in wider society, claiming, "If God made me like this, this is who I am meant to be."

Such movements and the issues they represent are often major conflict points within religions, as well as in secular societies. The global Anglican communion of churches, for example, has become internally riven over the legitimacy of homosexual practice and same-sex marriage (Hassett 2007). In Islam, organizations like the UK-based Imaan and the Safra Project for women, along with the US-origin Al-Fatiha Foundation, are similarly controversial. The latter, founded in 1998, offers a platform for believing and practicing LGBTQ Muslims transnationally, with several chapters in the United States and offices in Canada, the UK, Spain, and South Africa. However, an international Islamic group called Al-Mouhajiroun, which seeks an Islamic Caliphate, declared in 2001 that members of Al-Fatiha were apostates. In spite of these pressures, a handful of mosques in the United States and South Africa have openly gay imams. They remain marginal, however, and are strongly opposed by many well-respected contemporary voices of Islamic authority.[10]

16.2.4 Alternative Religions and Spiritualities

Alternative religious movements can serve as incubators for social change, and over the course of history there have been religious communities which have experimented with various forms of sexual, gender, and family relations – including promiscuity, polygamy, polygyny, communal childrearing, and of course, various forms of celibacy.

Religions run chiefly by women – and often for women – have been rare (Sered 1994), but their relative weight and importance in the religious landscape has increased in modern times. Some are self-consciously new, but most involve at least a partial revival of indigenous traditions. Today they include goddess movements, Wicca, various forms of ecologically oriented "holistic" spirituality, and movements focused on healing of the earth and of "body, mind, and spirit" (e.g. Reiki, yoga, religious forms of mindfulness, neo-paganism, and other revived forms of indigenous religion and "nature religion"). Some are focused on individual wellbeing; others combine this with political and ecological activism.

This second wave, starting with Wicca in the 1940s, expanded on nineteenth-century movements such as Theosophy and Christian Science which were founded and dominated by women. More recent charismatic figures like Starhawk (1979), the feminist activist and witch, offered new rituals and practices which women and men could adapt to their own lives, relationships, and socio-sexual situations. A study of alternative spiritualities in Britain in the early twenty-first century found that 80 percent of their leaders and participants were women (Heelas and Woodhead 2004).

From being counter-cultural in the first half of the twentieth century, the "alternative" spiritual milieu has expanded its influence to

---

10   See for example Henking (2012) and Jama (2015).

become increasingly mainstream in many countries. Its spread has been assisted by its easy relations with new media, old and new healing and wellbeing practices, and the opportunities opened by entrepreneurial consumer capitalism (Lofton 2010). "Spirituality" is now found in everyday education, health care, and popular culture throughout Europe and North America and more widely. It involves a quiet but effective shift away from male religious authorities and official forms of religion to authority located in the conscience of each individual, in connections with one another, and in tapping the "energy" of the cosmos. Typically, but not necessarily, such spirituality takes an appreciative and affirming view of equal gender relations and is relaxed about the pluralization of family forms and intimate relations.

16.2.5   Conclusion

Study of the lived realities of religion reveals that in spite of official teachings of many male-dominated "world religions," religious communities and people very often arrive at pragmatic compromises surrounding family, sexuality, and gender relations. Broadly speaking, the main religious stances and orientations may be summarized as "Consolidating" (legitimating existing inequality), "Tactical" (working within existing constraints to subvert them), "Questing" (seeking alternatives for personal benefit rather than structural change), and "Counter-cultural" (working for progressive structural change) (Woodhead 2007). Assessing a local group's particular religious orientation(s) to gender, family, and sexuality is essential to any effort at social reform, and essential to finding points where values converge and where religious organizations have needed capacities. That means recognizing that the most important differences run not just between but *within* different religious traditions (including all the "world religions"), and even within a family unit itself.

16.3   Religion, Diversity, and Democracy

In this section and the one to follow, we address the complex connections between religion, politics, and social progress. We begin with a focus on religious diversity, looking first at the reasons for this and then at the shifts in religious realities across the globe. Following this, we turn to the ways in which diversity is managed in different parts of the world, paying particular attention to "multiculturalism" and "secularism," recognizing that both are various. That discussion leads in turn to the relationship between religion(s) and democracy itself – an issue already touched on in Chapter 14. Then in Section 16.4, we elaborate on questions of human rights, violent conflicts, and peace-making.

In the course of this section, the reader's attention is drawn to a longer version of this chapter placed on the IPSP website in which concrete situations are developed in sidebars to illustrate particular points. The links are supplied in footnotes.

16.3.1   Diversity, Mobility, and Migration

The mobility and migration of people constitutes a major theme running through the work of the IPSP – unsurprisingly in that the presence of migrants and the tensions surrounding them have become critical flashpoints at the beginning of the twenty-first century, challenging societies to develop effective modes of political and social governance. Religion must be considered a significant factor in this process. Just as migration can be propelled by a faltering economy or civil unrest, it can be spurred by political and cultural persecution of a religious group. And just as migration can remake families and cultures, it also remakes religious traditions and political processes.

A distinguished body of research now exists on the multifaceted relationship between religion and migration (Warner and Wittner 1998; Beckford 2016). One theme stands out: the effects constitute a two-way flow, often mediated by the communication technologies that link communities across territory. Religions inspire, manage, and benefit from the migration process, but at the same time beliefs, identities, and practices are reshaped by the associated dislocating of populations. Take, for example, the evolution of religions that are "traditionally" linked to particular global regions or national contexts. What happens when members of a religious majority learn to live as a minority in a new place, in which culture and religion are no longer interrelated? It is important to look in detail at the ways in which organizational forms and leadership styles adapt. Equally significant are the currents that feed back into the country of origin and their effects on the home community.[11]

The role of religion in the reception of migrants is the subject of Part V of Beckford's (2016) first volume, and a particularly instructive example can be found in Margarita Mooney's (2013) study of Haitian immigrants in three very different places: Miami, Montreal, and Paris. Mooney notes that the differentiation between religion and the state in the United States (a structural variable) allows faith-based organizations to assist and advocate for Haitians in Miami. In contrast, both Quebec (characterized by secular nationalism) and France (dominated by a more assertive secularism) discourage community organizations based on religious or ethnic identifications. The greater scope for action allowed to the primarily religious mediating organizations established by the Haitian community in Miami more effectively assisted the reception of newcomers. Thus, macro, meso, and micro levels are brought together in the understanding of religion as a crucial variable in the successful resettlement of migrants.

A further point is important: diversity does not always depend on physical contact between people. Religious differences can exist "virtually" as well as on the ground. Modern means of communication make us aware of previously unfamiliar religious practices and populations. Where citizens have little personal knowledge or experience of religions, media representations – dominated by what commands immediate attention – shape attitudes (Knott and Poole 2013). The growing use of media technologies in the portrayal of and the communication between religions is a vital element in the management of religious differences. It also plays a role in the constant reconfigurations of the religious field per se.

---

[11]   An extensive body of material examines these mutual influences. Stoeckl (2014) explores Orthodox communities; Sinha (forthcoming) introduces a wide literature on diaspora Hinduism. Warner and Wittner (1998) and Yang and Ebaugh (2001a, 2001b) offer valuable insights regarding new immigrant communities in the United States.

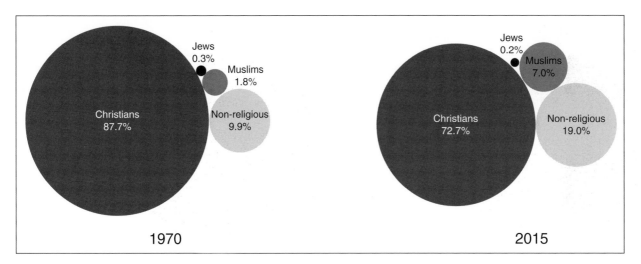

Figure 16.2 | Religious diversity in southern, western, and northern Europe, 1970 and 2015.

Note: Historically Europe (39 countries) has been the most Christian continent in the world. However, the region experienced a sharp decline in its Christian affiliation between 1970 and 2015, resulting in a rise of non-religious self-identification (atheist and/or agnostic). That said, large numbers of Europeans still identify with their churches depite the fact that they neither believe nor practice their religion. There has also been a significant growth in the Muslim population due to immigration. The Jewish population continues to decline.

Source: Todd M. Johnson, Brian J. Grim, & Gina A. Zurlo, eds. *World Religion Database.* Leiden/Boston: Brill, accessed April 2017.

16.3.2   The Many Faces of Religious Diversity

The presence of religious diversity is far from uniform (Grim 2015). In most parts of the world diversity is growing, in others declining, and in still others it remains relatively stable. The following examples illustrate these patterns, articulating the wide variety of reasons for both growth and decline during the period 1970–2015.[12]

At one end of the spectrum are those societies that were relatively stable for a long period of time, but which are now becoming more religiously diverse. Western Europe is an obvious and high-profile example (see Figure 16.2). Here there has been economically motivated in-migration since the mid-twentieth century, bringing not only substantial numbers of Christians from the global South but a growing Muslim presence (Roy 2007). The political consequences are considerable, but are experienced differently in different nation-states.[13]

Coterminous with this transformation, though much less noticed until the late twentieth century, has been the diversification of Latin American Christianity. Here a solidly Catholic global region is now experiencing the rapid growth of Protestantism, mostly in its Pentecostal forms (see Figure 16.3). Once again there is variation from country to country, but

the changing nature of the continent overall – including the effects on Catholicism itself – reflects a wider global shift.[14]

Aspects of these changes can be seen in a second set of examples: those parts of the world which were sites of aggressive and politically motivated secularization for most of the twentieth century but which are now experiencing religious restoration and growth. Since 1989, formerly hegemonic Orthodox churches have reasserted themselves strongly in Russia and Eastern Europe, but at the expense very often of minority religions (see Figure 16.4). In China, the process is more complex. Not only does the Communist Party in China remain resolutely atheist, but its attitudes toward religions deemed "foreign" are different from its dealings with Confucianism, Daoism, or Buddhism (Yang 2012).[15] That said, China is a part of the world where Christianity is growing noticeably not least in its Pentecostal forms (see Figure 16.5).[16]

A third set of cases is located in parts of the world where religious diversity most certainly exists but is nothing new. In Southeast Asia, for example, there has been little overall change over this period (see Figure 16.6). That said, what might be called "constitutive" diversity continues to evolve as migration – at times propelled by

---

[12] These draw on the material brought together in Johnson, Grim, and Zurlo (2016). Additional religious demographic data can be gleaned from the Association of Religion Data Archives (ARDA), Pennsylvania State University (www.thearda.com/); Economic and Social Data Service (ESDS) (www.esds.ac.uk/); Integrated Public Use Microdata Series International (IPUMS), Minnesota Population Center, University of Minnesota (https://international.ipums.org/international/); and ZACAT Data Archive for the Social Sciences (GESIS), Leibniz Institute for the Social Sciences (http://zacat.gesis.org/).

[13] These connections are spelled out in sidebar 16.1, "Post-war Changes in Europe," by Grace Davie, at www.ipsp.org/downloads. For a comparison of European approaches to the United States, see Casanova (2007).

[14] The implications of these shifts can be seen in Venezuela's democratic struggles. See Section 16.3.4, as well as sidebar 16.6, "Religious Diversity and Democratic Challenges in Venezuela" by David Smilde and Isabella Chojnacki, at www.ipsp.org/downloads.

[15] The history of Chinese religious diversity and regulation is explored in more depth in sidebar 16.2, "Accommodating New Forms of Religion: Chinese Dilemmas" by Fenggang Yang, at www.ipsp.org/downloads.

[16] It is notoriously difficult to estimate the number of Christians in China and figures range widely. Although there are multiple disputes surrounding the Chinese numbers, we rely on the World Religion Database (Johnson, Grim, and Zurlo 2016). The WRD takes into consideration both registered and unregistered Christian affiliation. Further, the WRD places Christianity in China in the context of other religions, thereby serving as the most uniformly reliable source.

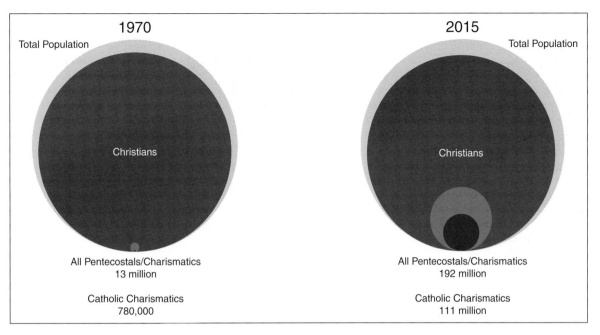

Figure 16.3 | The growth of Pentecostalism in Latin America, 1970 and 2015.
Note: Pentecostal and Charismatic Christianity grew substantially in Latin America between 1970 and 2015, from 13 million to 192 million. Some of this growth occurred in Protestant and Independent denominations such as the Assemblies of God and the Universal Church of the Kingdom of God. However, most Charismatics in Latin America are Roman Catholic. Brazil is an important center of Pentecostal and Charismatic Christianity both in Latin America and globally. It is home to the largest branch of the Assemblies of God as well as the largest Catholic Charismatic community in the world.
Source: Todd M. Johnson, Brian J. Grim, & Gina A. Zurlo, eds. *World Religion Database.* Leiden/Boston: Brill, accessed April 2017.

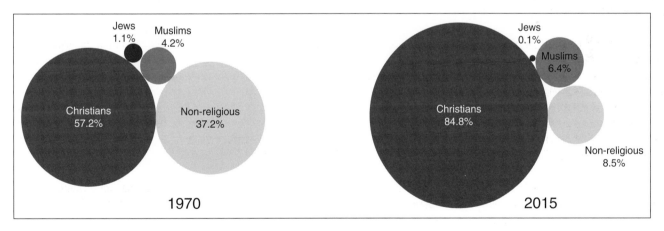

Figure 16.4 | Religious diversity in Russia and Eastern Europe, 1970 and 2015.
Note: Patterns of religious affiliation in Eastern Europe (Belarus, Bulgaria, Czech Republic, Hungary, Moldova, Poland, Romania, Russia, Slovakia, Ukraine) differ markedly from the rest of the continent. The year 1970 marked the height of identification as non-religious, as large sections of Eastern Europe were then dominated by state-imposed atheism. In the early 1990s, non-religion began a gradual decline as Christianity, primarily Orthodoxy, grew, offsetting secularizing trends in other parts of the continent. Judaism has also declined partly as a result of anti-Semitism.
Source: Todd M. Johnson, Brian J. Grim, & Gina A. Zurlo, eds. *World Religion Database.* Leiden/Boston: Brill, accessed April 2017.

repression – moves religious traditions along with people. It is equally clear that colonialism altered the religious ecology in this part of the world (and elsewhere) in ways that can still be seen.[17]

The United States is very different, but it too is a society built on diversity, as wave after wave of migrants found their way there – initially across the Atlantic and more recently from very different parts

---

[17] Singapore's postcolonial religious diversity is explored in sidebar 16.3, "'Religious Education' in a Southeast Asian Context: Insights from Singapore" by Vineeta Sinha, at www.ipsp.org/downloads.

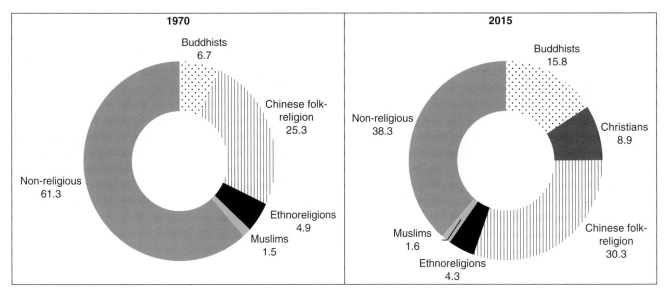

Figure 16.5 | The growth of religion in China, 1970 and 2015.

Note: Religious adherence of all kinds in China has been steadily increasing since 1970. The practice of more "traditional" Chinese religions like Buddhism, Chinese folk-religion, and Confucianism has increased. Christianity grew dramatically in China from 1970 to 2015, from under 1% of the population (876,000) to nearly 9% (123 million). The Chinese constitution states that citizens have "freedom of religious belief" but limits protections for religious practice to "normal religious activities." Religious groups must register with the government and belong to one of five state-sanctioned "patriotic religious associations": Buddhist, Taoist, Muslim, Catholic, or Protestant.

Source: Todd M. Johnson, Brian J. Grim, & Gina A. Zurlo, eds. *World Religion Database*. Leiden/Boston: Brill, accessed April 2017.

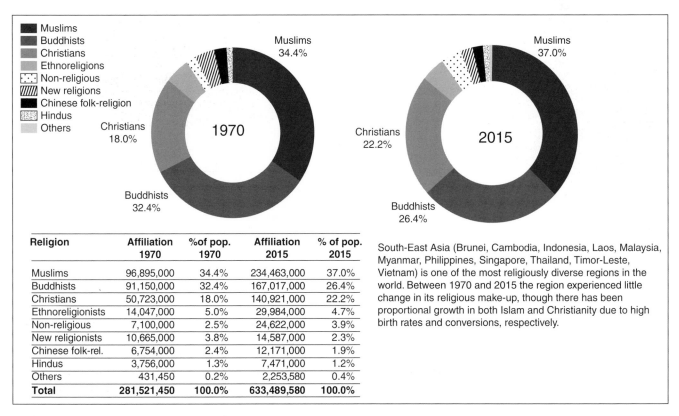

Religion	Affiliation 1970	%of pop. 1970	Affiliation 2015	% of pop. 2015
Muslims	96,895,000	34.4%	234,463,000	37.0%
Buddhists	91,150,000	32.4%	167,017,000	26.4%
Christians	50,723,000	18.0%	140,921,000	22.2%
Ethnoreligionists	14,047,000	5.0%	29,984,000	4.7%
Non-religious	7,100,000	2.5%	24,622,000	3.9%
New religionists	10,665,000	3.8%	14,587,000	2.3%
Chinese folk-rel.	6,754,000	2.4%	12,171,000	1.9%
Hindus	3,756,000	1.3%	7,471,000	1.2%
Others	431,450	0.2%	2,253,580	0.4%
Total	**281,521,450**	**100.0%**	**633,489,580**	**100.0%**

South-East Asia (Brunei, Cambodia, Indonesia, Laos, Malaysia, Myanmar, Philippines, Singapore, Thailand, Timor-Leste, Vietnam) is one of the most religiously diverse regions in the world. Between 1970 and 2015 the region experienced little change in its religious make-up, though there has been proportional growth in both Islam and Christianity due to high birth rates and conversions, respectively.

Figure 16.6 | Religious diversity in Southeast Asia, 1970 and 2015.

Source: Todd M. Johnson, Brian J. Grim, & Gina A. Zurlo, eds. *World Religion Database*. Leiden/Boston: Brill, accessed April 2017.

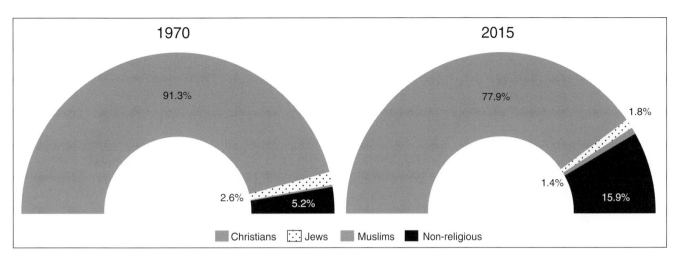

Figure 16.7 | The changing diversity of the United States, 1970 and 2015.

Note: Despite a gradual decline of its Christian population, the United States remained the country with the most Christians in 2015 at nearly 251 million. Many mainline denominations (Methodists, Baptists, Lutherans, etc.) are losing members, while Pentecostal/Charismatic and Evangelical denominations are growing, such as the Assemblies of God and smaller, Independent churches. Losses from Christianity resulted in gains for atheists and agnostics, who in 2015 represented nearly 16% of the population. The United States has also experienced an increase of its Buddhist, Hindu, Sikh, Baha'i, and Jain populations, though these each represent 1% or less of the population.

Source: Todd M. Johnson, Brian J. Grim, & Gina A. Zurlo, eds. *World Religion Database*. Leiden/Boston: Brill, accessed April 2017.

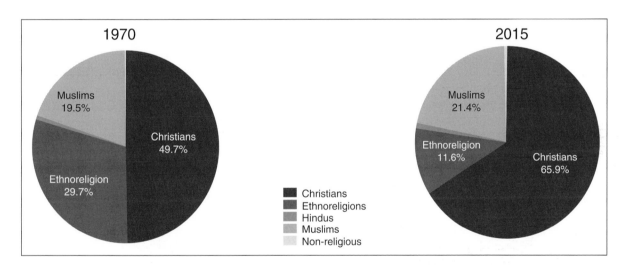

Figure 16.8 | Religious diversity in East Africa, 1970 and 2015.

Note: Eastern Africa (Burundi, Comoros, Djibouti, Eritrea, Ethiopia, Kenya, Madagascar, Malawi, Mauritius, Mayotte, Mozambique, Reunion, Rwanda, Seychelles, Somalia, South Sudan, Tanzania, Uganda, Zambia, Zimbabwe) has experienced a decrease in religious diversity through the continued growth of Christianity and Islam, each of which have received converts from traditional religionists (ethnoreligionists). However, the range of diversity varies within the region, as some countries are Muslim-majority (Somalia, Comoros), some are Christian-majority (Burundi, Kenya), and some have large populations of both (Eritrea).

Source: Todd M. Johnson, Brian J. Grim, & Gina A. Zurlo, eds. *World Religion Database*. Leiden/Boston: Brill, accessed April 2017.

of the world (see Figure 16.7). Diversity is part of American self-understanding: individually, collectively, and constitutionally.[18] In recent years, the challenges have included the accommodation of faiths other than Christian, especially Islam – a problematic step for some Americans.

The final group of cases reminds us that increasing diversity is not uniformly the case; the reverse process also occurs, but once again for

widely differing reasons. In large swathes of Africa, for instance, there is decreasing diversity due to a "modernizing" process that encourages adherence to "world" religions rather than to a plethora of local traditional faiths (see Figure 16.8). That said, careful attention should be paid to the details of each country – they are far from uniform.

The Middle East, conversely, is characterized by decreasing diversity because of conflict and dispersion. The displacement of historic

---

[18]   The US case is elaborated in more detail in sidebar 16.4, "Managing Religious Diversity in the United States" by Nancy Ammerman, at www.ipsp.org/downloads.

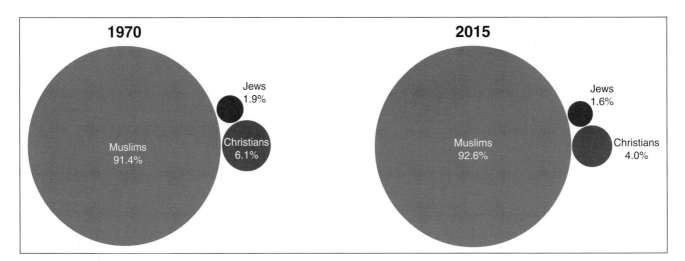

Figure 16.9 | Religious diversity in the Middle East, 1970 and 2015.
Note: The political situation of the Middle East (Bahrain, Cyprus, Egypt, Iran, Iraq, Israel, Jordan, Kuwait, Lebanon, Oman, Palestine, Qatar, Saudi Arabia, Syria, Turkey, United Arab Emirates, Yemen) has significantly influenced its religious composition. Historic communities of religious minorities – particularly Christians, Jews, and Baha'is – have emigrated from the region in large numbers after centuries of relative stability. It is likely that the Middle East will continue to become less religiously diverse over time.
Source: Todd M. Johnson, Brian J. Grim, & Gina A. Zurlo, eds. *World Religion Database*. Leiden/Boston: Brill, accessed April 2017.

religious communities, long at home in the region, is a recent and tragic phenomenon (see Figure 16.9).[19]

What emerges from all these examples is the constantly generative nature of religious diversity in the twenty-first century. As political, social, economic, and natural forces push populations from one place to another, some parts of the world will become more religiously diverse, while others will become more homogeneous. Equally important in any given society are the shifts produced by changes internal to the population. Individuals in new contexts have new religious options, keeping in mind that changing or leaving one's religion is a possibility understood differently in different parts of the world and can by no means be taken for granted (Martin 2013: 185).

In short, religion is a crucially important factor in understanding diversity but it never stands alone. It is part of a bigger picture which must be approached contextually. That said, religious diversity is distinctive, for which reason it is inadvisable to think of religious identities simply as one among other cultural preferences. Differences in religious belief and practice are likely to strike more foundational chords than differences in taste or style. Diversities, moreover, can be found within as well as between faiths. Indeed "liberals" from various faiths may well have more in common with each other than they do with their respective, rather more "conservative" co-religionists.

James Beckford (2003) underlines an additional point: religious diversity (a state of affairs) is to be distinguished from religious pluralism (a normative term implying the acceptance or otherwise of diversity). The descriptive and the normative are all too often confused in the literature. Beckford also separates out societal, organizational, and individual levels of understanding, reflecting the fact that religious

diversity presents differently in different domains: state, politics, civil society, culture, interpersonal relations, and so on.[20] It follows that *individuals* may welcome diversity within societies or polities that do not, and vice versa. Some groups may, in fact, advocate for societal toleration so as to protect their own exclusivist beliefs (Yang 2014).

16.3.3   The Governance of Religious Diversity

As set out in Chapter 2 of this Report, social progress depends on establishing civil societies where people of diverse heritage can not only work and live together, but also flourish in each other's company. Each society, moreover, must find a way forward within the parameters set by its past. For this reason, "progress" will look different in different places. Here we look at two ways of achieving this goal: sets of ideas captured by the terms "multiculturalism" and "secularism."

16.3.3.1   Understanding Multiculturalism

The idea of multiculturalism has been introduced in Chapter 15. It is a term with multiple meanings. At one level it is part of an expanding cultural market, allowing the discerning consumer to pick and choose from an increasing range of cultural goods (food, clothing, art, music, and so on). Very different in valance is the notion of multiculturalism as an inherently divisive process that damages – necessarily – the dominant or host culture.

Tariq Modood, a prominent British scholar, captures these dilemmas in a summary article published in *The Guardian* (Modood 2011). In this, Modood notes that the growing assertion of strongly held religious

---

[19]   There is a developed discussion on recent developments in the Middle East in Chapter 20.
[20]   For additional discussions of the politics of religious diversity, see Demerath (2001), Wuthnow (2004), Banchoff (2008), and Finucane and Feener (2014).

identities struck many as "too multicultural," not at all the friendly differences in music or food previously celebrated. The timing is important. The article came in the context of a high-profile statement by the then UK Prime Minister indicating that multiculturalism had failed. Similar misgivings were felt in France and Germany – a trend that continues. Indeed it is sentiments such as these that encourage the far-right movements that are currently gaining purchase in many parts of Europe, exacerbated by the unexpected influx of migrants arriving in Europe from the Middle East. The flow peaked in 2015; the political consequences began to unfold in 2016.[21]

The authors of Chapter 15 offer a solution – or more accurately a way of thinking – which, once again, is echoed by Modood: that is, to see the building of a multicultural society as a process in which new ideas and new ways of doing things are constantly drawn into the mainstream, which is itself reconstituted – continually so. Many different actors have a part to play in this demanding task. Among them are religious organizations at every level of society and the myriad ordinary individuals that inhabit them. Public communication and mutual education, along with "street-level ecumenism" (working side by side) are often more effective than dialogue between elites, both religious and secular, in securing positive outcomes.[22]

16.3.3.2   Secularism and the Liberal State

Secularism is a similarly flexible concept, and it too is contentious. A complex terminology has evolved in this field to distinguish forms of secularism that seek to accommodate difference from their more radical counterparts which exclude the presence of religion on principle from the public square. Rowan Williams (2012) terms the former "procedural" secularism and the latter "programmatic" secularism. Modood (2013) prefers "moderate" and "radical," but the distinction is similar.

In her path-breaking work in this field, Cécile Laborde (2017) opens up the debate in new ways. She starts from the following question: should the liberal state necessarily be secular? In her response, she argues that there is indeed a minimal secularism – or separation between state and religion – that is required by the liberal state, but that secularism is more complex than is often thought. Specifically, it is incorrect to assume that liberal democracy requires the strict separation of state and religion that is found in the French or the US model.

In reaching this conclusion, Laborde follows the argument of this chapter in that she underlines that religion is more – much more – than a statement of belief about what is true, or a code of moral and ethical conduct. Religion refers equally to ways of living, to political theories of justice, to modes of voluntary association, and to vulnerable collective identities. Thus, Laborde disaggregates religion into its various dimensions, and in so doing dispenses with the Western,

Christian-inflected conception of religion that liberal political theory relies on, particularly with reference to the separation between religion and state. As a result, there is considerably more variation in permissible state–religion arrangements than either secular liberals or religiously minded liberals have often assumed – a flexibility that can be extended to non-Western societies.[23]

It is with this flexibility in mind that we turn to democracy itself.

16.3.4   Religion and Democratic Governance

Inequalities across religious groups, like other inequalities, can pose challenges to democracy. Chapter 14 develops this theme in detail and concludes by advocating a "principled distance" between the state and religion. As Section 16.3.3 makes clear, there are various models for that relationship. In what follows the argument is turned in a slightly different direction in order to ask what the social-scientific literature tells us about the role of different forms of religion in the development and maintenance of participatory democracy (see Chapter 9). It begins with a historical perspective.

Different religious traditions have at different times been identified as either providing the foundations for democratic governance or constituting impediments to it. For instance, Alexis de Tocqueville wrote that Catholics "constitute the most republican and the most democratic class of citizens which exists in the United States." The reason for this, he argued, was Catholicism's emphasis on equality:

> [T]he Catholic faith places all human capacities upon the same level; it subjects the wise and ignorant, the man of genius and the vulgar crowd, to the details of the same creed; it imposes the same observances upon the rich and needy, it inflicts the same austerities upon the strong and the weak, it listens to no compromise with mortal man, but, reducing all the human race to the same standard, it confounds all the distinctions of society at the foot of the same altar. (de Tocqueville 1898: 384)

More than 100 years later, sociologist Seymour Martin Lipset came to a diametrically opposed conclusion regarding the compatibility of Catholicism and democracy (Lipset 1959: 93). Lipset argued that democracy requires a political belief system that accommodates competition among ideas, while the Catholic Church claims that it alone has the truth. Catholic countries, he contended, were particularly prone to instability and were inhospitable to the kind of compromise and pluralism that lie at the heart of democracy.

Temporal and spatial variation in the democratic fortunes of Catholic-majority countries in Latin America, Southeast Asia, Sub-Saharan Africa, and southern Europe demonstrate that both de Tocqueville and Lipset were wrong in assigning either democratic or anti-democratic

---

[21]   See Section 16.3.2, as well as sidebar 16.1, "Post-war Changes in Europe" by Grace Davie, at www.ipsp.org/downloads for further detail.

[22]   Singapore provides an instructive example of religious and state actors working together in a multicultural society. See sidebar 16.3, " 'Religious Education' in a Southeast Asian Context: Insights from Singapore" by Vineeta Sinha, at www.ipsp.org/downloads.

[23]   The Indian case offers an important and much-discussed example of the application of secularism to a non-Western society. It is expanded in detail in sidebar 16.5, "India: The World's Largest Democracy" by Vineeta Sinha, at www.ipsp.org/downloads.

16

essences to the Catholic faith. However, similar arguments continue to be invoked with respect to other religions – most notably, Islam. Here the record is primarily a negative one, with thinkers over several generations arguing that Islam is inherently inhospitable to democratic government. For instance, Montesquieu declared that "The moderate government is better suited to the Christian religion, and despotic government to Mohammedanism," on account of the "gentleness so recommended in the gospel," which he contrasted to the "despotic fury" that allegedly characterized the behavior of "Mohammedan princes" (Montesquieu 1748 [2001]: 468).

More recently, political historian Elie Kedourie wrote that, "[T]he ideas of the secularity of the state, of society being composed of a multitude of self-activating, autonomous groups and associations – all these are profoundly alien to the Muslim political tradition" (Kedourie 1992: 6). Similarly, Samuel P. Huntington invoked Islam itself to explain why few Muslim-majority countries transitioned to democracy during the so-called "Third Wave" of democratization that began in the 1970s. "To the extent that governmental legitimacy and policy flow from religious doctrine and religious expertise," he wrote, "Islamic concepts of politics differ from and contradict the premises of democratic politics" (Huntington 1991: 28).

Although several Muslim countries have been able to construct and sustain democracy – including Indonesia, Senegal, Turkey, and most recently, Tunisia – arguments about the incompatibility of Islam and democracy continue to carry influence. Here the evidence requires careful scrutiny. Cross-national, country-level statistical analyses continue to reveal a positive correlation between the proportion of a country's population that is Muslim and its propensity toward authoritarianism (see for example Fish 2002; Donno and Russet 2004); however more fine-grained studies carried out at the individual level have failed to validate the skepticism toward Islam's democratic prospects.

For instance, in a study of mass attitudes toward religion and democracy in Algeria, Egypt, Morocco, and the Palestinian territories in the 1980s and 1990s, Marc Tessler (2002: 350) found that "Islam is not the obstacle to democratization that some western and other scholars allege it to be." And in a thorough analysis of cross-national data from the World Values Survey, Pippa Norris and Ronald Inglehart (2011: 134) find that "surprisingly similar attitudes toward democracy are found in the West and the Islamic world." Similarly, Amaney Jamal (2006: 59), analyzing a subset of these survey data from Egypt and Jordan, argues that "the dichotomization of Islam and democracy is a false construct," as evidenced by the fact that "the vast majority of respondents in both Egypt and Jordan demonstrate simultaneous support for both Islam and democracy." More recently, a study of attitudes toward democracy in ten Muslim-majority countries conducted by Sabri Ciftci (2010: 1460) found that greater adherence to Islamic precepts is unrelated to support for democracy, which "is remarkably high, and … independent of 'sectarian' or theological traditions across the Muslim world." Similar findings have been recorded by Stepan and Robertson (2003) and Hoffman (2004). In short, individual-level support for democracy is widespread among the world's Muslims.

Moving beyond specific religious traditions, scholars have attempted to explore whether religion itself is conducive or unconducive to democracy. On the one side are scholars who believe that religions inculcate intolerance toward alternative *Weltanschauungs* and instill in their followers norms of obedience and deference to authority, rendering them inhospitable to democracy and individual liberty. We have seen variants of this view above in arguments about Islam and Catholicism. On the other side are scholars who identify religious social institutions as schools for the "the development of civic skills and norms that can have a positive effect on support for democracy" (Bloom and Arikan 2013). Political scholarship in the American context has revealed how religious organizations can channel individuals into democratic politics (R.L. Wood 2002; Schlozman et al. 2012).

In a study of more than 60,000 survey respondents in 54 countries, Bloom and Arikan (2013) try to adjudicate between these two views and instead find support for both of them. Certain religious values appear to instill unfavorable attitudes toward democracy, while participation in religious social networks appears to be *positively* associated with some forms of support for democracy. As we argue throughout this chapter, "religion" has multiple dimensions, and attention to ground-level practices may reveal a different picture from the view at the level of ideas and theologies.

This suggests that it is important to move beyond the level of individual values and examine the role that religious *groups* play in enabling or inhibiting the emergence of democratic political orders. For example, Toft, Philpott, and Shah (2011) have argued that democracy is more likely to emerge and survive when religious actors are included in transition processes, instead of being viewed as hostile forces to be contained. In the Arab context, recent scholarship has shown that so-called Islamist parties – previously thought to be opposed to democracy and individual liberty – have emerged as some of the region's foremost exponents of democratic political arrangements (Wickham 2013), even as the space for such arrangements has constricted in recent years.

In the Latin American case, the Catholic Church's development of "liberation theology" was accompanied by the practice of organizing "base Christian communities" in which local citizens articulated their daily life concerns and organized to advocate for change (Roelofs 1988; Gill 1998; Smilde 2003). A further point should, however, be noted. In the democratic conflicts of Latin America, the involvement of religion is many-sided. In Venezuela, for example, the Catholic hierarchy has been a key actor opposing the socialist project of Chavismo. Yet clerics influenced by liberation theology have provided significant support to that project. Similarly Neo-Pentecostal Protestants have supported Chavismo, while traditional Protestant groups have not.[24]

Thus, the overwhelming impression conveyed by these and other cases is that religions (or religion in general) are neither inherently pronor anti-democratic, left nor right, or even for religious freedom nor against it. Each situation must be examined on its own terms.

---

[24]   These complexities are expanded in sidebar 16.6, "Religious Diversity and Democratic Challenges in Venezuela" by David Smilde and Isabella Chojnacki, at www.ipsp.org/downloads.

16.3.5 Conclusion

The careful management of religious diversity and the need to build just and effective systems of government in which different forms of religion can not only find a place but flourish are central to social progress. In both respects, the challenges are considerable and the rewards great, but the cost of failure is high. The following section continues this story, paying close attention to the circumstances in which religious conflict and violence are likely to ensue. Such situations include insensitive approaches to diversity and the discriminatory policies of repressive (often secular) states.

16.4   Religion, Conflict, and Peace

Social progress is all too often halted by violence and aggression that deprive individuals and communities of the necessary conditions for seeking just, equitable, and peaceful ways of life. Conflicts over resources and power are often intertwined with conflicts over values and identity, and religions are often visibly implicated, exacerbating the difficulties. The rise of brutal violence both in the Middle East and on the streets of Western capitals is but the most recent evidence. At the same time, religious groups are themselves victims of violence and persecution.

The relationship between religion and violence runs in multiple directions. Religious leaders and institutions are not just combatants, but are often key players in negotiating terms of post-conflict reconciliation, transitional justice, and even gang intervention. All world religions encompass representations and rituals of both peace-making and violence. As Christian Smith (1996a: 1) argues, religion has a "disruptive, defiant [and] unruly face." It can break with existing social configurations and alter existing equilibriums. We should expect therefore that just as religion can often be a key factor in turning social and political tensions into violent struggle, it can also facilitate negotiation and coexistence in seemingly hopeless situations. Critical assessment of the potential for both good and ill can lay the foundation for fruitful collaborations.

In what follows we look first at religion as a source of conflict and violence, scrutinizing complex evidence and paying particular attention to sites and conditions in which a negative outcome is likely. We then consider the very real ways in which religions and religious organizations contribute to reconciliation and peace-making both formally and less formally. The section concludes with an overview of international institutions advancing religion, peace, and human rights.

16.4.1   Religion As a Source of Conflict and Violence

Following the Cold War, an intrinsic link between religion and violence was hypothesized as one of the main factors affecting the international world order. Samuel Huntington's *The Clash of Civilizations* (1996) argued that the "fault-lines" between civilizations indicated future lines of conflict. The ideological conflict of the communist period would be replaced, he predicted, by religious and ethnic differences which drew on long-standing animosities accumulated during previous centuries. Religion, in this view, was prone to inducing violent conflicts due to both historical tensions and the emergence of new international identities. Mark Juergensmeyer made a prediction similar to Huntington's, but in a somewhat different direction. He argued that the post-1989 period would see "A New Cold War" pitting religious nationalism against the secular state. Furthermore, "Even though virtually all religions preach the virtues of non-violence, it is their ability to sanction violence that gives them political power" (1993: 164).

These relatively recent speculations about religion and violence have emerged in the midst of vast global and political change, but have their roots much earlier. Scott Montgomery and Daniel Chirot (2015: 6) claim that the circulation of ideas after the Enlightenment forms a constitutive part of the ways in which societies engage with violence. Specifically, "If earlier upheavals of the social order sought their legitimacy in theology, law, and tradition, from the eighteenth century onward such changes were powered by ideas that were secular and that looked to found society and its institutions on concepts presumably anchored in an evidence-based, reason-led 'scientific' understanding of man and the universe." Michael Barnett et al. (2015: 19) take a similar view: namely that the Western social science literature has systematically built on the assumption that "religion is a principal source of violence and instability." The post-Westphalian world system is assumed to be secular at the expense of religion, which has been regarded as the root of state violence (Juergensmeyer 2011). Barnett et al. (2015: 26) go on to note the Enlightenment belief that liberalism would tame "the religious beast."

Religious violence – it seems – stands out because it does not have the same claim to legitimacy that secular violence appears to have. Indeed, the dominant social-scientific narratives regarding religion and violence are Eurocentric insofar as they give states the benefit of the doubt while regarding religious groups guilty until proven innocent. The international system which emerged after the 1648 Peace of Westphalia endorsed the state as the main actor. As a result, the use of violence has been interpreted differently for religions than for secular states as they interact in the international arena.

The reality, however, is that secular states and ideologies have carried out as much violence as the "religious beast" in recent centuries, if not more. Analyses of state conflicts since 1900 demonstrate that political (secular) ideologies and modern nationalisms have been more widely implicated in violent conflicts than have religions. The situation, however, is nuanced. Jonathan Fox used the State Failure Dataset to examine 161 countries and their involvement in religious conflicts between 1950 and 1996. He demonstrated that although they "[occurred] less often than other types of conflicts, religious conflicts have increased [during this period], and are more intense than nonreligious conflicts" (Fox 2004). A similar conclusion was reached by Susanna Pearce (2005), who examined 278 "territorial conflict phases" between 1946 and 2001 documented in the Armed Conflict Dataset available at the International Peace Research Institute in Oslo. Pearce pointed out that "religious conflicts are more intense than other types of conflicts," but only "under specific conditions," suggesting that education, eschatological perceptions of the world (expecting an imminent cataclysmic end), and identity crises could all affect levels of violence. Taken together, this evidence indicates that religious passions are often mobilized in situations of violent conflict, but careful assessment is necessary in order to discern exactly how religions are involved.

Analysis should not begin with assumptions that any one religion has more capacity for violence than others. The employment of violence either symbolically or physically has been present in all world religions and across many historical periods (Girard 1979; Cavanaugh 2009; Ross 2011; Ghassem-Fachandi 2012; Juergensmeyer, Kitts, and Jerryson 2013; Leustean 2014). In some cases – such as anti-Muslim violence by Hindus in India or Buddhists in Myanmar – religious majorities foment violence against rival religious groups. In many other cases – for example the Lord's Resistance Army (a quasi-Christian cult in northern Uganda and surrounding states) or Boko Haram (an Islamist group in northern Nigeria and the Lake Chad Basin) – radical offshoots take up arms in ways deemed heretical by more mainstream religious adherents. But in using their own powerful mix of ritual and ideology they wreak havoc in the name of their god. The range of religious combatants and victims is broad indeed.

A more systematic assessment of this range of religious conflict has led Jonathan Fox (2000: 15) to declare that "there is little evidence here to support the argument that Islam, or any religion for that matter, makes ethnoreligious minorities more conflict prone." Using T.R. Gurr's Minorities at Risk Phase 3 Dataset, Fox identifies 105 "ethnoreligious minorities," namely ethnic communities which embrace a particular religion. The data indicate that the widespread perception that some religions (especially Islam) always endorse violence is incorrect.

The stand-out form of violence in recent decades is perhaps religious terrorism – that is, religiously motivated efforts to undermine legitimate authorities and advance political goals through fear and intimidation. Based on their analysis of the Global Terrorism Database, Toft, Philpott, and Shah (2011) note that since the 1980s, terrorism itself has been on the rise, with religious motivations at the fore and Islam involved in the large majority of the attacks around the world. Still, civil wars are no less prevalent or destructive, and they are less dominated by religious motives. For the period 1940–2000, Toft (2006) counted 133 such struggles (where at least 1,000 people died, with casualties on both sides). Only 42 of these involved religion, and in 17 of those, religion was a peripheral rather than a central element. Religions can be implicated in different forms of violence in distinct and varied ways.

16.4.1.1   Sites of Potential Religious Tension

If violence is not an inherent consequence of religion, it becomes important to ask about the particular sites in which destructive violence may arise. Contestation over the built environment and sacred spaces is one of these. It can involve multiple layers of religious and secular conflict, often with deep historical roots. Long histories of physical segregation can divide communities along lines of faith, class, or ethnicity, increasing the likelihood of mutual distrust. Consider, for example, attacks on Christian churches in Indonesia, most recently in the region of Aceh. In 2015 Muslim opponents threatened to

burn down a church because, they argued, these churches were built without legal permits. The threat of violence (and it is worth noting that the threat itself is violent, even if the purported cause seems drily legalistic) has been consequential in many places in Indonesia, causing numerous churches to be shut down. Such strategies have also been used to marginalize Christians in the Middle East.

In the Indonesian case, there are clear connections to recent religious politics, but there is a deeper context to keep in mind, reflecting a colonial history of religious segregation. Dutch authorities, acting as secular powers, designated areas according to religion, and most importantly forbade Christian proselytization in Muslim areas (Birchok 2016). Thus, the appearance of Christian churches outside their "permitted" areas fuels a sense of righteous indignation among Muslims that for some justifies threats of violence. Similarly, the desecration and reappropriation of religious spaces in the Middle East indicates that the symbolism of centuries-old churches and monasteries remains a potent flashpoint. Saint Elijah's Monastery in Iraq, founded in the sixth century by the Church of the East, was looted during the 2003 war, occupied by American forces, and then destroyed in 2014 by ISIS.

Likewise, nationalist politics were deeply intertwined in the reconstruction of religious spaces in Herzegovina. Incompatible nationalist views clashed: one promoting the equality of all traditional faiths in the region, and the other asserting a form of Catholic nationalism through aggressive claims on sacred spaces (Sells 2003). In other cases, relatively recent processes of religious or ethnoreligious segregation (often pursued by secular national authorities) disrupt access by some to previously shared resources like water, physical space, health care, or political representation (Appadurai 2000; Baird 2009; Parks 2012). In these cases, sacred spaces become material representations not only of religious difference but also of wider social inequities predicated on that difference, and thus develop into flashpoints for violent action.

The regulation of religious diversity is yet another political sector where conflict can become violent. Grim and Finke (2011: 222) suggest that, as a general pattern, countries which suppress religious freedom have witnessed an increase in conflict, persecution, and organized violence, whereas states which encourage freedom of religious expression are most successful in addressing organized violence. These authors analyzed patterns of religious persecution across the world, using data provided by the International Religious Freedom Reports issued by the US State Department. Their review shows that religious persecution is on the increase. Contrary to the widespread perception that only a minority of countries engage in suppressing religious freedom, they found religious persecution in 86 percent of the cases. Between 2000 and 2007, 123 out of 143 countries had at least one documented case of a person "physically abused or displaced from their homes because of a lack of religious freedom" (Grim and Finke 2011: 18).

All of this suggests that high levels of violence in a society are likely to involve an interaction of political and religious forces. Fox (2000) argues that it is not militant "Islam" but autocratic governments (which are disproportionately present in Islamic countries) that complicate the picture of Islam's relationship to violent conflict. Saba Mahmood points to similar political and religious processes in postcolonial Egypt: here "secular governance has contributed to the exacerbation of religious tensions … hardening interfaith boundaries and polarizing religious differences" (2016: 1).

Situations of autocratic governance and religious repression are seedbeds for religious tension, but so are secular states that fail to provide practical and cultural foundations for viable everyday life. Scholars have long argued that faith-based organizations are likely players in filling the gap left by states that do not provide for their citizens. In many cases that provision is beneficent, but it can also be brutally violent, as the examples of ISIS and Boko Haram make clear. When secular projects fail, some of the alternatives that appear will inevitably be religious (Wood 2015). With a monopoly on the use of force and no competition for means of governing, a violent religious movement can establish itself in territory otherwise neglected.

16.4.1.2   Evaluating the Evidence

The general perception within the academic and policy-making world is that politics is rational while religion draws on the irrational and, thus, is "prone to violence" (Martin 2011, 2014). This is not helpful; nor is the tendency to place all forms of religious violence under the same umbrella. As we have seen, there are ample symbolic resources within all religions to justify violence, and there is ample historic and contemporary evidence that violence can have a religious dimension. The question is not "Does religion cause violence?" but under what circumstances, and in what ways. Religion is not an outside force that impinges upon secular social dynamics. Rather it is integrally and historically implicated in existing social configurations and their changes over time.

A careful assessment of the particular religious ideas, symbols, rituals, and collectivities in play will help to identify particular points of danger. As we have seen, contestation over physical spaces is one such point, as is the repressive management of diverse religious populations. An excess of regulation can easily spill over into the kind of social and cultural conflict that erupts into violence either by or against religious minorities. At the same time state-centered efforts at protecting religious rights can turn religious differences into legal categories (Shakman Hurd 2015). Finally, situations of weak or failed secular states leave the door open for violent, religious, and authoritarian efforts to establish order. Thus, assessing both vulnerable sites and the particular religious ideas and leaders arising from them is a critical preventive practice with respect to social progress.

16.4.2   Religion as a Resource for Peace and Reconciliation

Religion has an important role in processes of conflict and violence, but it also plays a role in peace and reconciliation. Marc Gopin (1997) suggests that religion can often bring together conflictual parties by drawing on widely shared religious values that provide the starting point toward peace negotiation. Religion is a prime marker not only in group identity but also in legitimating the pursuit of peace (Appleby 2000). Concepts of "justice," "righteousness," and "tolerance" are shared by many religions either at institutional or individual levels (Torrance 2006; Llewellyn and Philpott 2014).

A wide range of religious and secular organizations are involved in organized peace and reconciliation programs (Little 2007), with deep expertise residing in the World Council of Churches; the Interfaith Dialogue and Peacebuilding Program at the United States Institute of Peace; the Bureau of Conflict and Stabilization Operations at the US State Department; the International Center for Religion and Diplomacy in Washington, DC; and the Iraq Inter-Religious Congress, a faith-based initiative for national reconciliation. The engagement of religious actors ranges from participating in group discussion to a more visible public presence in conflict zones. In the 1980s, faith-based communities built transnational networks to work for peace in Central America (Smith 1996b). During the 1989 violent demonstrations against the communist regime in Romania, religious symbols displayed in both private and public spaces supported the demonstrators; and during the 2013 Euromaidan demonstrations in Kiev, both priests and hierarchs placed themselves between the police and protesters.

Religious contributions to peace-building are often quite local and concrete. And just as sacred spaces can be sites of conflict, they can also become powerful sites for peaceful interaction. Shrines and pilgrimage sites can be shared by multiple faith communities (Emmett 1997; Albera and Couroucli 2012), even if that peaceful sharing may not always reflect perfectly harmonious relationships. Negotiating cultural differences about the appropriate use of sacred space requires considerable effort, but it can produce what DeBernardi (2009) calls "syncretic amity," including the co-celebration of religious events. The visibility of sacred spaces in multi-religious environments over the long term can do much to counter social division and fears by making religion and its practices comprehensible to those outside the spiritual community itself. Similarly, sacred spaces can become sites of interfaith solidarity in response to terrorism. In 2011, for example, Muslims made a human chain around a Coptic Christian church to protect worshippers during Christmas Mass, and Egyptian Christians took similar action to protect Muslims at prayer. Flourishing societies in the future must take lessons from these public and visible opportunities to honor sacred spaces and communities across lines of difference.

In post-conflict situations, religious actors have played a similar role in transitional justice efforts. As civil society and political actors come together to deal with past violations of human rights, faith-based organizations have played significant roles in Chile (the Christian Churches' Foundation for Social Assistance) (Ferrara 2015: 171) and in South Africa's Truth and Reconciliation Commission (Sitze 2013). Likewise, a wide range of local religious actors participated in Northern Ireland (Wells 2010), and a third-party religious community, Sant'Egidio, brokered the 1992 peace accord in Mozambique (Anouilh 2005). Peace-building processes can draw on religious discourses and practices and the authority of local religious organizations, as evident in the reconstruction of war-torn societies in Sierra Leone (Martin 2016) and Libya (Lamont 2016) and the long-term struggle against authoritarianism and violence in Latin America (Wilde 2016).

The role of religion in reconciliation can be seen in much more micro contexts as well. In Latin America, where an unabated crime wave has resulted in levels of violence as high as those of countries in civil war, religion has become one of the principal means by which people confront the associated challenges. Much of Latin America's violence

16

now takes the form of street crime, with young men involved in small-scale drug dealing and gang activity. Escaping the complex of substance abuse, crime, and violence is one of the most important factors generating the growth of Evangelical Protestantism in the region. Evangelicalism provides young men with a cultural logic of transformation that allows them to side-step the alternative logic of vendetta and navigate contexts of extreme violence (Burdick 1993; Smilde 2007). More recent research has demonstrated the direct involvement of Evangelical groups in gang exit in Central America. In Guatemala, Honduras, and El Salvador, gangs are almost impossible to exit alive. Those who try are hunted down and killed by gang members. But a convincing religious conversion is one of the few mechanisms that allow young men to find a way out. Some Evangelical ministries also provide tangible services such as tattoo removal and relocation for former gang members in order to facilitate exit (Brenneman 2012).

The effectiveness of Evangelical groups in gang prevention has, of course, been noticed by states and other actors charged with ensuring citizen security – and has therefore spurred multiple forms of "faith-based" initiatives. These have been criticized by some scholars who suggest that Pentecostal rehabilitation practices "ultimately silence structural forces while laying blame on individual action," thereby justifying neoliberal reforms (O'Neill and Fogarty-Valenzuela 2015: 75; see also Pine 2009). These tensions between micro-level changes and the need for macro-level transformation are echoed in the range of religious organizations and practices themselves. In Central America, Catholic organizations focus more on gang prevention than exit, and see conversion and personal regeneration as relatively superficial compared with structural changes, such as access to education and jobs (Brenneman 2012). Nor is religious practice always benign. "Our Lady of the Holy Death" or *La Santa Muerte* in Mexico is venerated to give strength and faith to those who seek it to carry out crimes and violence, just as much as by those who seek to confront the chaos (Roush 2014). The same has been shown of Evangelicalism in contexts such as Jamaica and Brazil. In all of these cases, religious practices can provide strength to confront danger, whichever side of it you are on (Arias 2014).

Religious practices, ideas, and organizations can, then, be valuable resources in seeking more peaceful societies, but careful and critical assessment remains key. While religious values can be brought into strategies of conflict resolution, understanding either peace-making or the conflicts themselves through the lens of religion is a culture-driven process that demands extensive local knowledge. Each group will see gestures of goodwill through its own system of symbols, which may be at odds with each other (Gopin 2003). Nor can religious symbols and practices overcome the absence of adequate economic structures and a trustworthy state. A generalized reliance on external peace-building formulas, whether or not they involve religious actors, will falter in local contexts such as Congo, Kosovo, Sudan, and Rwanda (Autesserre 2014). Just as "religion" is not a generalized cause of violence, neither is it a universal panacea.

16.4.3   Religion and Human Rights

Running through our discussions of religion's role in political and social life have been questions of human rights and how they are to be understood and implemented. "Human rights" is a defining

discourse in the management of diversity, in the self-understanding of democracy, in the resolution of conflict, and in the fair distribution of resources. Across these domains, the relationship between human rights activists and religious groups runs the spectrum from active advocacy to open hostility.

Foremost among international statements on the ways in which human beings should be treated at individual and community levels is the United Nations Universal Declaration of Human Rights, adopted in 1948, which includes Article 18: "Everyone has the right to freedom of thought, conscience and religion; this right includes freedom to change his religion or belief, and freedom, either alone or in community with others and in public or private, to manifest his religion or belief in teaching, practice, worship and observance." Thus, freedom of religion and belief, in its current historical form, is seen as a fundamental and universally applicable right. Individuals (i.e. all human beings everywhere in the world) are the primary holders and beneficiaries of this right; states, conversely, are the primary holders of the correlative obligations (Lindholm et al. 2004: xxxvii).

The establishment of a UN Special Rapporteur on Freedom of Religion or Belief implies recognition of both the importance and the difficulty of finding ways forward in places where diverse religious and secular norms are valued, and in situations where they may come into conflict – gender-specific abuses being among the most common. As an independent expert appointed by the UN Human Rights Council, the Rapporteur's role is to identify existing (and emerging) obstacles to the right to freedom of religion or belief and to present recommendations on the ways in which such obstacles might be overcome. Similarly, the Organization for Security and Cooperation in Europe has addressed issues related to the freedom of religion and belief in its Warsaw-based Office for Democratic Institutions and Human Rights; and in May 2016, the European Commission appointed Former European Commissioner Ján Figel' as the first Special Envoy for the promotion of freedom of religion or belief outside the European Union. Such institutional arrangements allow a forum for adjudicating the complex relationships between religious freedom and other human rights (Leustean and Madeley 2009; Haynes 2012).

Here as elsewhere, social progress is facilitated by the kind of critical assessment an expert can provide. It is also facilitated by the imagination of human rights advocates who are willing to seek creative partnerships with faith-based organizations and religious leaders who share – and can translate – their goals.

16.4.4   Conclusion

At Rice University in April 2016, John Kerry, the US Secretary of State, summarized the contemporary tension between religion, conflict, and peace:

> Religion today remains deeply consequential, affecting the values, the actions, the choices, the worldview of people in every walk of life on every continent … It is a part of what drives some to initiate war, others to pursue peace; some to organize for change, others to cling desperately to old ways, resist modernity; some to reach eagerly

across the borders of nation and creed, and others to build higher and higher walls separating one group from the next. (Kerry 2016)

His words resonate with the research reported in this chapter. Religion is an aspect of human society that is not going to disappear anytime soon. It is neither inherently violent nor inherently peaceful, but includes practices, beliefs, values, and institutions that can lead in either direction. Assessment of the particular context and the particular religions in play is the first step toward social progress. Our evidence-based review of the relationship between religion and violence reveals the inherent complexity of any attempt to move past religious violence and engage religious strengths toward building a more peaceful world. An increasing number of international institutions have incorporated the interplay between religion and conflict resolution by emphasizing the universality of human rights as a common element spanning the world religions and other faith expressions.

16.5 Everyday Wellbeing: Economy, Education, Health, and Development

Structures of just and effective governance, along with the absence of violent conflict, are essential to social progress. Among the intended fruits of such structural change is the everyday wellbeing of populations – food and shelter, health and education, and the capacity to produce and share in economic goods in order to live in ways that are individually and communally valued (Sen 1999). These broader questions are explored in depth in other chapters in these volumes, but here we turn our attention to religion's multifaceted role in this sphere. The wellbeing of persons and communities lies at the heart of much religious practice and teaching. Along with governments, philanthropic actors, and NGOs, religious institutions have a widespread grassroots presence in health care, education, and welfare provision. They are well placed to be critical partners in the pursuit of social progress.

This is an area of rapidly evolving research that has emerged as assumptions linking secularization with economic development have receded (Rakodi 2015). Some researchers have added standardized indicators of religion to statistical models that analyze economic capacity and wellbeing (Barro and McCleary 2003). Because religious belief and practice is especially difficult to standardize, however, a more local and institutional approach holds greater promise. Much of our current knowledge comes, in fact, from relatively small case studies, findings from which are now being published in a clutch of excellent edited collections.[25] While case studies pose challenges for generalization, they reflect the reality of the range of particularities relevant to the relationship between religion and material wellbeing.

16.5.1 Religion and Economic Progress in Less-Developed Countries

A century ago, Max Weber introduced the possibility that specific religious beliefs lead to ways of life with often unintended,

but nevertheless important, economic consequences. He famously associated Protestant Christianity with the establishment of capitalist economies (Weber 1905[1958]). He expected, however, that as science and technology took hold in the capitalist West, the sense of divine imperative would disappear. However, in the West, as well as in many societies around the world, economic and technological pragmatism continues to exist in more or less comfortable coexistence with holistic spiritual concerns. Social development seems not – or not necessarily – to require secularization.

When secular social change agents encounter a society seemingly dominated by belief in supernatural powers, it can appear an insurmountable obstacle, but as part of the social landscape, spiritual beliefs must be taken into account. From creation myths to harvest prayers and fertility rituals, human spirituality has long linked human flourishing to the supernatural. Throughout the world, spirits are understood to inhabit people's everyday lives at least as powerfully as the forces of the market. While such beliefs can diminish the sense of personal and social agency, they can just as easily contain cultural resources that shape the everyday wellbeing of populations.

Outside of advanced industrialized contexts, religious practice is especially likely to be oriented toward this-worldly concerns of social life. Among the most rapidly growing religious groups, for example, are those that espouse a "prosperity gospel" that links spiritual and material blessings (Miller, Sargeant, and Flory 2013). Part of the larger family of groups dubbed Pentecostal, their emphasis on spiritual gifts and otherworldly rewards would seem to predict the opposite of economic or social activism in this world. Rather than channeling followers toward progress, they may merely assuage the pains of the neoliberal market with otherworldly promises. Like Barro and McCleary (2003), Woodberry (2006) suggests that the emphasis on attending multiple religious services and giving significant sums to the work of the church are opportunity costs that may weigh against more productive forms of time and money investment and diminish wealth accumulation.

Other observers have pointed to a more Weberian interpretation, looking for the indirect effects of participation in such groups. They claim that the "born-again" experience introduces a sense of rupture with the past that often allows a range of new behaviors and relationships to emerge (Droogers 2001). Individuals who choose a new religious loyalty are exercising the kind of agency and independence from traditional communities required in modern economies. In the multiple African case studies Freeman (2012) has collected, it is apparent that NGOs may provide needed technical training, but it is Pentecostal religion that can move a smallholder farmer from a life entangled in close-knit family and community and traditional politico-ritual structures to values and practices conducive to becoming an individualist, strategic, profit-maximizing agent. Economic success may also be facilitated by the lifestyle practices often encouraged in Pentecostal communities – abstaining from alcohol, devotion to a monogamous family, hard work, financial planning, and the like (Martin 1990; Brusco 1995). Similar patterns of individual ethical transformation can also be seen in Islamic spiritual reform programs in Indonesia (Rudnyckyj 2015). These

---

[25] See especially ter Haar (2011a), Clarke and Jennings (2008), and Tomalin (2015).

reported effects have drawn widespread skepticism, and Woodberry (2006) suggests that they may be most demonstrable among those initially escaping poverty and in places with the lowest education rates and highest levels of corruption.

Whatever the indirect connections to economic progress, religious communities and religious practices are very often directly involved in providing material assistance – from food aid to job referrals – both to their participants and to the surrounding community. Such practices are misunderstood by social scientists as an "instrumentalization" of religion, but in contexts in which people cannot count on their basic necessities being satisfied, "salvation" refers to being saved from struggles in this world. Rubin, Smilde, and Junge (2014), for example, describe the many roles of religion in Latin America's "zones of crisis," which they define as, "spaces of material deprivation, exclusion, violence, and environmental destruction" (9). The empirical studies they examine show how religious beliefs, practices, leaders, and institutions have become part of the life strategies that people construct. From dealing with violence, oppression, and sickness, to strategies for forming social movements or reforming patriarchal gender relations, religion is implicated in the tactics individuals and collectivities deploy to confront the difficulties of their everyday lives.

Still, we need to avoid reifying the "global South" as something essentially different from the industrialized North. Global markets and global communication link both material challenges and religious strategies across all regions of the world. New and energetic religious expressions developed in Asia, Africa, and Latin America are now part of the religious landscapes of Europe and North America, carried there by migrants, missionaries, and media (Corten and Marshall-Fratani 2001; Martin 2002; Olupona and Gemignani 2007). Advanced industrialized countries have their own extensive zones of crisis, not only in global cities like New York and London, but in forgotten rural areas such as Appalachia and the Canadian Maritime Provinces. Ethnographic research in the United States, moreover, reveals many of the same strategies linking spiritual life to material wellbeing and health, not only among impoverished communities (Sullivan 2011), but also among well-educated and privileged populations (McGuire 1988; Ammerman 2013).

Religious phenomena, then, may be linked to Weberian-style disciplined economic behavior and to the strategies of comfort and coping that Marx would have predicted, but also to concrete and direct material support. Each local context may include all of the above. For example, in her study of Pentecostal groups in Tanzania, Hasu (2012) describes two very different but equally relevant relations between economic and religious life. At Glory of Christ Tanzania Church, the poorest of the rural migrants to the city bear testimony to the Spirit's ability to resurrect them from the bewitching spells cast by powerful older kin in the communities they left behind. They find in this church both meaningful explanations of their lives and means of coping in a bruising economic world. At Efatha Church, also in Dar es Salaam, a "prosperity" version of Pentecostalism appeals to, and helps to create more middle-class followers. They hear about positive thinking, African pride, empowerment, education, hard work, and planning; and they see the vast business and institutional enterprises supported by church leaders as evidence and inspiration. Even within similar religious belief

systems, then, the spiritual world is intertwined in economic lives in different ways – patterns that must be understood if the wellbeing of those communities is to be addressed.

The same careful analysis must accompany attempts to understand the role of religion in women's educational and economic activities. As we have argued in Section 16.2 of this chapter, conservative beliefs in virtually all religious traditions can be mobilized to keep women in subservient positions, and tragedies such as the shooting of Malala Yousafzai reinforce the reality of the threats that women face in many parts of the world. Economic and social progress is unlikely when women are kept from education, health care, and productive contributions to their communities. Thus, movements to advance the rights of women have often existed in adversarial relationships with conservative religious movements and leaders (e.g. Bradley and Kirmani 2015). Those same women, however, frequently see the efforts of largely secular development organizations as irrelevant at best or colonial impositions at worst (Chowdhury 2009). Misunderstandings abound.

What rights movements hear and reject is the patriarchal rhetoric of conservative religions, but there is sometimes a different reality beyond the words. For example, Gooren's research in Guatemala demonstrates that Evangelical churches often provide women with opportunities for leadership, new networks of support for entrepreneurship, and more economically productive and attentive husbands (Gooren 2011). Other research shows that in practice women can use seemingly patriarchal religious beliefs as a way to gain authority over men and consolidate their commitment to the household (Griffith 1997; Smilde 1997). This suggests that progress requires attention both to the specific religious beliefs in question and to the religious networks in which they are embedded. Theological arguments and religious officials may be important, but it is often religion-in-practice that provides significant points of convergence with human rights and economic assistance agendas (ter Haar 2011b). Building bridges across that cultural and religious divide is a necessary task if outside support is to be effective in enabling women (and men) to participate in building the economic strength of their communities. Local religious leaders can, in fact, be development allies – even interpreting and translating new technologies – if they are included in the conversation (Bompani and Smith 2013).

Access to finance requires equally careful assessment and an eye toward pragmatic compromise. Finance is critical to participation in the global economy, and religious beliefs are sometimes at the root of self-exclusion from this form of economic activity. Mohseni-Cheraghlou (2015) shows, for example, that Muslim-dominant countries in the Middle East and North Africa have the highest rates (10 percent) of citing religious reasons for avoiding formal banking institutions. What his research also shows, however, is that higher concentrations of sharia-compliant financial services increase overall participation in banking. A religious obstacle may also have a religious solution.

16.5.2   Religion and NGOs: Pathways to Partnerships

Critical reflection on the relationship between less-developed and economically dominant parts of the world inevitably raises the ongoing realities of colonialism. It has often been noted that the colonial sword was accompanied by the cross, with today's postcolonial world still bearing the religious imprint of that earlier era. As "development" and "aid" programs emerged in the second half of the twentieth century, the religious missionary impulse was explicitly rejected by most agents of progress. Religion was relegated to the realm of private individual preferences and seen as irrelevant to economic and political agendas (Tomalin 2013). As a result, Marshall claims, in spite of "much overlap and many synergies, the two worlds (development and faith) have largely operated in separate universes" (Marshall 2012: 193). The result is a de facto secularizing agenda that accompanies the work of most of the world's agencies of economic development, an agenda that is often experienced as alien to the lives of the people whose wellbeing is at stake. Without genuine embeddedness in local cultures, including the religious ways of those cultures, efforts at changes in economic, health, and educational patterns have often proved short-lived (Jones 2012; Watkins and Swidler 2013).

Still, the role of faith-based organizations (FBOs) in health and development is difficult to ignore. Organizations from every faith tradition have entered relief and development work and are among the largest donor entities (Clarke 2008; Deacon and Tomalin 2015). Such work is hardly new, as religious traditions have long enshrined practices such as zakat (one of Islam's five "pillars") that institutionalize support by religious practitioners for the material wellbeing of their communities. In some cases that humanitarian support is limited to fellow believers, but Gooren (2011) found otherwise: among development groups in Guatemala aid freely crossed sectarian (and non-religious) lines.

Inevitably, this humanitarian impulse has come with political strings attached. State aid agencies are frequently assumed to be acting with foreign policy goals in mind. FBOs, as well, often mix humanitarian assistance and political change, both repressive and progressive. Janine Clark (2008) has examined the role of the Islamic Center Charity Society, the semi-autonomous charitable arm of the Muslim Brotherhood and one of the largest NGOs in Jordan. Its work includes establishing schools, colleges, clinics, and training centers (that serve a mostly middle-class clientele), along with providing direct aid to people in poverty. Its ability to engage issues of women's rights is more limited, a restriction that results from both its conservative religious milieu and the authoritarian state context in which it works. Assessing or working alongside such faith-based development organizations requires careful questions about the populations to which they have access and the practical assistance they can provide, along with a clear-sighted assessment of the political and religious constraints that may limit the work. The effects of religion on economic wellbeing involve both the spiritual beliefs and practices of the groups in question and the religious and political infrastructure.

16.5.3   Religion and Education

Nowhere is this clearer than in education. As the authors of Chapter 19 argue, education is central to pursuing individual wellbeing and social progress, and religions throughout the world – not just in developing countries – are significant providers of education at all levels.[26] Protestants everywhere, with their emphasis on individual reading of scripture, have been especially vigorous in establishing schools that extend education beyond the elites (Woodberry 2012). Until the mid-twentieth century, education in British colonies was largely in the hands of missionaries (Smyth 2004), and postcolonial regimes in Africa and the Middle East often simply nationalized the existing religious schools (Sharkey 2012). The effects of this infrastructure remain significant.

Different religious traditions are involved in establishing schools. In Indonesia in 2007, 13 percent of all students were enrolled in Islamic schools. These include both pesantren (traditionalist boarding schools) and madrasas (modernist day schools). Since the 1970s, state initiatives to modernize and standardize the general curriculum at madrasas and pesantren have produced a thriving, mostly privately financed infrastructure of religious schools which feeds students to higher education as well as training them for a variety of vocations (Lukens-Bull 2001; Azyumardi, Afrianty, and Hefner 2007). They have long integrated religious education and general education, and are generally more affordable for rural and poor students than national schools. Interestingly they weathered the Asian financial crisis between 1997 and 2001 without the drop in enrollment experienced by other schools (Azyumardi, Afrianty, and Hefner 2007).

Some religious schools can be sites of resistance to progressive change, and careful assessments are always in order. On balance, however, religious schools are likely partners in increasing the economic and civic skills of a population and reaching its most disadvantaged citizens. For example, rigorous case comparisons across Latin America, Africa, and Asia demonstrate both higher accessibility and equal or higher test performance for students in faith-based schools (Barrera-Osorio, Patrinos, and Wodon 2009).

16.5.4   Religion and Health

Religious capacity is also present in the realm of health promotion and care, but is often surrounded by controversy, raising difficult issues ranging from family planning, to immunization, to female genital mutilation, and end-of-life issues. Public health providers are frequently horrified by the harm that they see – harm that must not be ignored. As Duff and Buckingham point out, "Though public sector and faith-linked entities bring distinctive assets that help achieve health goals, ideological challenges present barriers to collaboration and need careful negotiation on both sides" (2015: 1787). Confronting the seeming impasse between secular health professionals and faith-based providers, a series of essays in The Lancet (July 2015) has offered an evidence-based way forward, based on identifying common goals and values. Tomkins and her co-authors (2015: 1782) argue that clarifying areas of real disagreement can allow cooperation elsewhere. Not all partnerships will be advisable, but if advancing health goals is critical to poverty reduction, the full range of available health care providers is needed to meet the challenge.

---

[26]   The World Bank, among others, attempts to provide comprehensive data on the educational capacities of the world's nations. While it is usually possible to track "private" providers, religious providers are not tracked as a separate category.

An accurate assessment of overall religious capacity and impact is difficult, however, since religious organizations are generally not distinguished as a separate category in NGO reporting. The "Religious Health Assets" project represents a pioneering effort to integrate religion into the study of health systems, identifying all the organizations and resources that are seeking to improve the health of a population (Olivier et al. 2015). Olivier and her colleagues concluded that the extent of health care provision provided by faith-based groups in Africa is often overstated, with estimates ranging from 5 to 45 percent. However, they did find some evidence that faith-based health care providers take care of a slightly higher percentage of the poor compared with their public and private equivalents (Olivier et al. 2015: 1770–1771). Religious providers seem to excel in mobilizing and supporting volunteers, in prioritizing poor, marginalized, and hard-to-reach populations, and in developing innovative progressive fee structures that require the poor to pay little.

Responses to HIV offer a case study of the complexity of the relationship between religion and health. In the early days of the epidemic, religious leaders in Africa painted HIV/AIDS as God's anger and not a matter for either compassion or education. However, as serious campaigns began on the continent, churches joined others, particularly the state, to lend support to AIDS victims. Many churches established programs of home support and took on the care of orphans. They also developed both local health care delivery systems and informal modes of mutual education aimed at prevention (Trinitapoli and Weinreb 2012).

That experience helped to inform responses to the Ebola crisis. A team of medical anthropologists contributed their findings on the cultural significance of burial practices, and religious leaders in affected countries were asked to define what is meant by "dignified burial." The result was a new World Health Organization burial protocol[27] that Marshall and Smith (2015: e25) describe as "vital in halting spread of the disease and laying foundations for community trust. In many respects, the protocol was a game-changer in the overall trajectory of crisis response." Careful local assessment and consultation led to a life-saving partnership between public health providers and communities at risk.

Similar patterns have been evident in Latin America. Seffner et al. (2011) looked closely at a health service engagement between the Brazilian Catholic Church and the Brazilian National STD/AIDS Program – at first glance not a likely collaboration. The National STD/AIDS Program established condom use as its principal measure of prevention, while the official stance of Brazil's Catholic Church is to oppose condom use, which it sees as promoting sexual promiscuity. However, the Catholic Church is hardly monolithic – indeed one Brazilian Catholic theologian has written a "theology of prevention" which has been widely used to support care for people with HIV or AIDS. In practice, the Casa Fonte Colombo, a Catholic organization, provides medical and psychological attention, spiritual guidance, massage therapy, donated clothing, bathrooms, and spaces for rest. Their services aid predominantly poor, HIV-positive patients, and are an important source of

education on how to live with the disease, including a prominently displayed and artfully decorated bowl of condoms for the taking. Here a local Catholic institution is able to work with secular governmental institutions by developing a grassroots working arrangement enacted without explicit public statements.

As in many other instances, religion as lived in everyday practice may not follow the lines apparent in official pronouncements. It is also the case that health goes far beyond what happens in medical institutions. Throughout the world, definitions of health and of health promotion are often not only physical but spiritual. This parallels an increasing recognition that "alternative" forms of healing can and do exist alongside highly developed forms of scientific medicine. Both states and insurers have recognized the advantages of broad-based pragmatic partnerships.

16.5.5 Religion, Welfare, and Health Care in Europe and the United States

Economic, physical, and social wellbeing are not simply matters of concern in the "global South." Across the developed world, markets do not always treat vulnerable people well. It is true that states have attempted to fill the gaps, even the playing field, and regulate markets, but neither states nor markets have yet succeeded in providing an equitable and comprehensive set of provisions that allow all their citizens to flourish. Among the providers filling the gaps are religiously affiliated voluntary organizations.

This is as true in Europe as it is in the United States, but the division of labor is different. In (then) Western Europe, the post-war settlement led to the development of the welfare state – or more accurately welfare states – a shift in which the state assumed the primary role for the education, social protection, welfare, and health care of its citizens. Post-war aspirations were high and lasted until the 1970s, when the effects of the oil crisis and shifting demographics (notably a rise in the number of older people) led to retrenchment.

Multiple voluntary agencies emerged to fill the gaps, among them a series of religious providers – modestly in those parts of Europe where the welfare state was relatively well funded, and more comprehensively further south (in the Mediterranean countries) where it was rudimentary right from the start. Bäckström and associates (Bäckström and Davie 2010; Bäckström et al. 2011) map these changes and the questions that emerge in consequence. The latter include the appropriateness and effectiveness of religious providers in this field (see also Beaumont and Cloke 2012). The response of the populations themselves was clearly articulated. Europeans would prefer a comprehensive and publicly funded welfare state. They know, however, that this is not realizable in the present economic climate, and it is better that the churches and related organizations fill the gaps than to have nothing at all. The situation, moreover, is becoming more rather than less acute as growing migrant populations provoke difficult questions of entitlement alongside problems of scarcity.

---

[27] For more information see www.who.int/csr/resources/publications/ebola/safe-burial-protocol/en/. Consultation with religious and community leaders provided the basis for changes in practice that would increase safety while honoring tradition.

In the United States, the welfare state is much less comprehensive than in Europe and there is no state church. The resulting system of voluntary religious organizing means that each religious group is responsible both for its own maintenance and for whatever beneficent activities it may choose to undertake; and a remarkable consensus exists that religious congregations should voluntarily contribute to the common good (Ammerman 2005: ch. 7). In the Evangelical Protestant culture of the United States, providing assistance to a "deserving" needy person is a personal virtue, and the state has no special place in the enactment of this sacred duty (Chaves 1999; Ebaugh, Chafetz, and Pipes 2006; Quadagno and Rohlinger 2009). The result is a weak welfare state and a strong charitable sector.

The resulting contributions by faith-based organizations are impressive. In 2006, it was estimated that $50 billion was spent on basic welfare provision by faith-based organizations, with government expenditures on similar services amounting to only $138 billion (Stritt 2008). In other sectors of the welfare state – housing, education, health – the state is a much more dominant player. Social welfare in the United States, then, has long been delivered through a complicated mix of explicitly religious resources (money, volunteers, and space), secular voluntary contributions, and state-funded programmatic effort (Bane, Coffin, and Thiemann 2000).

16.5.6   Strategic Partnerships for Wellbeing

Economic wellbeing, health, and education are goals of social progress that are shared by most religious groups, even as there are many places where religious ideas and practices are at odds with secular norms. States, NGOs, and faith communities all have a role to play. Establishing effective partnerships requires a holistic approach. In practical terms strategic disagreements are best approached at the local level, to encourage both mutual understanding and pragmatic solutions, as in the case of the Ebola crisis. Faith-linked organizations are pervasive throughout the world and are especially effective in reaching the most vulnerable populations. The health, education, and economic wellbeing of societies depend on every sector of society being positively engaged. Faith-linked organizations are neither the sole solution nor irrelevant to progress.

16.6   Care for the Earth

Most spiritual belief systems address the relationship between humans and the world around them, including non-humans of all kinds. Religious beliefs and practices are therefore expressed both within and through the physical spaces in which they are embedded – whether these be local places of worship or the earth itself. For this reason, diverse religious thinkers and religious communities have addressed the spiritual significance of human (material) action – whether routine or globally consequential.

Environmental concerns, including pollution, public health, and decreasing biodiversity, have inspired religious commentary since the late 1960s. More recently, religious leaders have begun to address climate change. Despite the disparity of religious beliefs and traditions,

a common theme is clear: concern for the environment involves fundamental principles that implicate not merely human relationships with non-humans, but human relationships with each other. It follows that concrete activities (such as recycling, or replanting forests) can be defined as necessary spiritual acts.

Prominent figures in the major world faiths are well placed to articulate environmental ethics for global audiences. Indigenous leaders, as well, speak with authority granted by long-standing connections to particular locations. All share a conviction that secular laws, science, and markets are insufficient to bring about lasting change. Instead, they advocate a personal and collective reconsideration of human obligations to each other and to the earth itself. Religious communities can therefore become key organizing centers and potent locations for reimagining how people can live differently on the earth – or, as Chapter 22 puts it, how society could be otherwise.

16.6.1   The Intrinsic Spiritual Significance of the Environment

Religious engagement with the environment – sometimes called eco-theology – involves a re-evaluation of sacred literature and/or oral traditions that speak to the spiritual significance of the natural world. To understand the difference between religious environmental activism and more secular approaches, it is vital to understand the ways that different religious organizations frame environmental activism within their own faith traditions and sacred texts.

In 1967, Lynn White Jr. hypothesized that: "[B]y destroying pagan animism, Christianity made it possible to exploit nature in a mood of indifference to the feelings of natural objects" (White 1967: 1205). By suggesting a direct relationship between Christian belief and harmful environmental practices, White argued that Christianity itself was implicated in environmental crises. The link between Christian beliefs and anti-environmentalism has been most visible in the skepticism of American Evangelicals to climate science. Many such critics are motivated by "end-times theology," arguing that no environmental action is necessary because the world is witnessing the "end times" prophesied in the Bible (Barker and Bearce 2013). Other groups link climate science with scientific work that they find unacceptable, such as evolution, or unethical, such as stem cell research.

These conservative Christian voices should not, however, be taken for the whole. Even within Evangelicalism there are significant differences. At the grassroots, Evangelicals' ideas differ only slightly from other white middle-class religious groups in the United States, and younger generations are increasingly likely to voice pro-environmental views (Smith and Johnson 2010; Funk and Alper 2016). Furthermore, Evangelicals outside the US may differ sharply on this point; the *Cape Town Commitment*, a document created by the international Evangelical Christian community, recognizes environmental activists as having a "missional calling" (Lausanne Movement 2011: 14).

Engaging and interpreting sacred texts in light of contemporary concerns is for many faith leaders a necessary foundation for action. For Christians and Muslims, an important focus has been a re-evaluation of scriptural claims that humans are given "dominion over the earth" by a creator. The Ecumenical Patriarch Bartholomew, in one of the earliest Christian writings on this subject, offered the following assessment:

> Human beings and the environment form a seamless garment of existence, a complex fabric that we believe is fashioned by God. It follows that to commit a crime against the natural world is a sin … How we treat the earth and all of creation defines the relationship that each of us has with God. (Bartholomew 1998: 4)

Similarly, in the papal encyclical *Laudato Si'*, Pope Francis stresses that the gift of creation requires a strong sense of responsibility toward both humans and non-humans. "Dominion over nature," he argues, is not free rein to indulge in exploitation but instead a responsibility to protect divine creation which Christians understand as a gift to all humans, including future generations (Francis 2015: 160–161). For other commentators, metaphors such as "Christian stewardship" offer effective models of virtuous behavior (Bartholomew 1998; Moody and Achenbaum 2014).

Islamic thinkers compare the special obligations of the wealthy toward the rest of human society to human obligations toward the natural world to argue for better care of the environment. Just as people with superior gifts (which are assumed to derive from God) are obliged within Islam to support the less prosperous, so are spiritually superior humans obligated to protect non-humans. Protecting creation is thus understood as a spiritually important act (Amery 2001; Haq 2001; Islamic Foundation for Ecology and Environmental Sciences 2015). It is worth noting, however, that both Christians and Muslims endorse a special role for humans, in contrast to biocentrism, which does not (Haq 2001: 154; Francis 2015: 88).

Islamic, Christian, and Jewish traditions also find environmental problems of spiritual importance because such problems are understood to be symptomatic of breakdowns in healthy human relationships and ways of life. Environmental justice makes care for the environment a necessary dimension of caring for the poor, since environmental problems disproportionately harm the poorest and most vulnerable members of society (Haq 2001: 152–153; Francis 2015: 116–120). Intergenerational equity, or the requirement that present generations have a duty to make sure that future generations thrive, is a dimension of environmental justice that resonates widely. Pope Francis, for example, urges Catholics to "extend the boundaries of solidarity through time and across species" (Francis 2015: 103–120). Numerous Christian Evangelical groups evoke intergenerational justice as the basis for re-evaluating dismissive attitudes toward the environment.[28] Both faith-based and secular groups can find a foundation for action in orientations toward intergenerational justice.

Other traditions (including Buddhism and many indigenous spiritualities) base environmental behavior on their belief that humans and non-humans exist in meaningful relationships with one another (Dalai Lama 1995; Kawagley 2006; Swearer 2006; Mavhunga 2014; Carroll 2015). Many indigenous cosmologies define expansive kinship networks between humans and non-humans, which are grounded in reciprocal responsibilities and feelings of gratitude toward non-human agents (Kawharu 2000; Mavhunga 2014; Carroll 2015). Such kinship networks strongly shape interactions with the wider environment. For example, among Maori, responsibilities for what non-Maori might call environmental resources are deeply embedded in kinship relations between human groups. No decisions bearing on one can be taken without reference to the other (Kawharu 2000: 352). In this holistic worldview extended relationships and shared understandings of accountability and reciprocal responsibilities motivate Maori to balance the needs of humans and non-humans, and thus provide for the spiritual and physical wellbeing of all.

Despite significant differences in spiritual belief systems, many religious groups share important fundamental beliefs that make collaboration on environmental issues both with each other and with secular groups entirely feasible. They each see environmental problems as directly connected to problematic social relationships, and they call for environmental action as part of an ethical obligation to maintain balanced interdependence. The common frame of reference is holism, which offers a foundation for shared perspectives that bridge secular and spiritual orientations, allowing for common, mutually beneficial, and mutually respectful action. As Chapter 4 has demonstrated, pursuit of a sustainable planet will require not only the best thinking of ethicists and philosophers about the common good, but also ideas grounded in the world's religious traditions.

16.6.2 Virtuous Behavior and the Challenge of Climate Change

For most religious and spiritual leaders, solving environmental problems requires collective and individual transformation. Calls for changed attitudes and ways of thinking are significant elements in this discourse, and are aimed at activating changed behavior. Taking a verse from the Qur'an, the "Islamic Declaration on Global Climate Change" enjoins Muslims not to "strut arrogantly on the earth" (Islamic Foundation for Ecology and Environmental Sciences 2015: 8). The *Cape Town Commitment* calls for a spirit of repentance for the "destruction, waste and pollution of the earth's resources and our collusion in the toxic idolatry of consumerism" (Lausanne Movement 2011: 14). Pope Francis encourages hopefulness and commitment as an antidote to despair or fatalism (Francis 2015: 44). These religious communities have made the fight against climate change integral to their views of a more satisfying spiritual life. They contrast such changes with conventional tools of environmental action such as law and regulation. Pope Francis argues that, lacking deeper convictions, regulation becomes something individuals seek to obstruct, remove, or avoid (Francis 2015: 91).

There is some evidence to support the idea that spiritual foundations for environmental activism can be particularly effective. For example, in a forest rehabilitation and watershed protection project in West Sumatra, local religious leaders were educated by visiting Islamic

---

[28] The Evangelical Environmental Network is one such, in an initiative known as "creation care." For more information see www.creationcare.org/.

teachers on the place of environment in Islam, and Islamic scholars, or *ulama*, were invited to deliver sermons about water conservation. The project team found that religious education noticeably increased interest in water issues, especially among women, who particularly embraced Islamic principles of environmental care. Secular organizers argued that the combination of religious and environmental education provided a stronger social foundation for sustainable change than environmental education alone (McKay 2013: 85). Such cooperative efforts have become widespread.

One group, Interfaith Power and Light, has been notably successful in reaching North American communities who might otherwise have been indifferent to environmental issues.[29] The collective efforts of their 18,000 American congregations help to generate broad religious support for environmental, especially climate, activism. Simple projects like providing energy-efficient appliances to churches, temples, and mosques are rendered simultaneously religious and pragmatic (Bingham 2016). In Latin America, the implications of climate change for social justice have increased collaborations between secular and faith-based organizations.[30] Cooperation on climate between indigenous organizations and Catholic and Protestant groups (an example of "street-level ecumenism") has even eased long-standing tensions between religious groups, a welcome by-product.

Indigenous peoples, many of whom live on the front lines of climate change, have gone further. They demanded representation at the Framework Convention on Climate Change and participated in the development of the UN's Sustainable Development Goals in 2015. The First Nations organization Idle No More protested the Keystone XL pipeline in Canada and the United States in order to gain sovereignty over their lands, and protect the environment from both the immediate threat of oil spills and the longer-term threat of climate damage.[31]

16.6.3   Epistemic Challenges and New Ways of Living

For many indigenous peoples, the very framing of environment and resources as something separate from humans constitutes the core problem. Such questioning of the philosophical basis on which the material world has been built is a central plank of spiritual environmental action. In many faith traditions, individuals are encouraged to turn their backs on the materialism that grounds the global economic system. Such radical calls for change are tempered by the recognition that consumption practices are conditioned by entrenched economic systems, scientific aims, and technological infrastructures, which may be difficult to dispense with or change (Francis 2015: 75–85). Human embeddedness in complex technical systems, for example electrical grids, constrains individual action (Pritchard 2011). More deeply, environmental planning is clearly rooted in complex political relationships (Jasanoff 2005). Thus, spiritual leaders are left with a thorny question: how can human societies go about making significant change?

Pope Francis encourages critical understanding of technology and materialism, explicitly rejecting a "technological fix" mentality for environmental problems (e.g. geoengineering). Applying more technology, he argues, is insufficient for grappling with integrated social, environmental, and spiritual problems. Indeed such fixes may exacerbate the impulse to dominate and fail to tackle the social problems at the core of climate change (Francis 2015: 75–85).[32] Islamic thinkers such as Seyyed Hossein Nasr have called for comprehensive rethinking of the science and technology enterprise by rebuilding the epistemological foundation of science in a way guided by Islamic belief (Nasr 1991, 2010). Although Nasr's thinking is controversial, many Muslim scientists and engineers have argued that belief has the power to change the character of technoscience (Razak and Majeed 1997; Amery 2001; Lotfalian 2004). Religious thinkers therefore may embrace more "revolutionary" change (Jasanoff and Kim 2015) than some might expect. As advocates seek progress in sustainability and environmental justice, revolutionary questioning such as this can constitute common ground for secular and faith-based communities.

The efforts of indigenous activists to remove damaging technologies such as dams or mines from their traditional lands has also raised awareness of the power relations embedded in these technologies (Simpson 2008; Voyles 2015). Such projects harm extended kinship relationships, and alienate indigenous peoples from sacred spaces. Furthermore, the tendency of megaprojects to benefit distant rather than local populations belies justifications based on "the common good" (Groenveldt 2003; Swainson and McGregor 2008; Hall and Branford 2012). Activists have pointed out that economic and health problems in indigenous communities are significantly exacerbated when the institutions and philosophical frameworks of dominant political authorities are the only ways such problems are addressed (Smith 2012). Implementing alternatives to prevailing models, however, can be politically difficult to achieve (Kawharu 2000; Carroll 2015).

Legal scholar Rebecca Tsosie, drawing on the work of Miranda Fricker, has highlighted the importance of epistemic injustice, the failure of legal systems to give weight to indigenous knowledge and cosmological belief systems (Tsosie 2012: 12). She highlights the injustices that result when US courts fail to recognize tribal members as valid culture experts, as for example when they found no cultural harm to Native Alaskan tribes from the Exxon Valdez oil spill, which made indigenous ways of life effectively impossible, or when the Hopi and Navajo were not permitted to stop the pumping of treated sewage onto a sacred mountain (Tsosie 2012: 12). Tribal understandings of meaningful human/non-human relationships were legally rejected on the basis that "true belief" was a purely mental construct, and thus no change in the material world could threaten it. Fighting for epistemological justice is therefore central to maintaining holistic ways of life.

By challenging the character and not just the consequences of human materialism, religious actors again may find common ground with

---

29   For more information, see www.interfaithpowerandlight.org.
30   See www.wola.org/es/node/5557.
31   For more information see http://idlenomore.ca.
32   There is an interesting resonance here with Ulrich Beck's *Risk Society* (1992).

secular groups who also push for reassessments of the way that humans live.

16.6.4   Conclusion

Commentators such as George Rupp (2001) insist that religious beliefs are too diverse and internally inconsistent to offer sufficient intellectual resources on which to ground environmental action. Evidence suggests otherwise. Religious interpretations of the earth and faith-based environmental activism share much with secular groups, including techniques for raising consciousness, concerns with environmental justice, and challenges to foundational ways of thinking that contribute to environmental and human harm. Religious leaders are mining their traditions to inspire changes in behavior and thinking that are harmonious with, if philosophically distinct from, purely secular work. Successful challenges to entrenched systems of power, knowledge, and technology can gain direction and legitimacy in cooperation with faith communities.

16.7   Themes and Implications: An Action Toolkit

Progress toward the flourishing of persons, households, societies, and the planet requires progress in religion and in its capacities to contribute social and cultural goods. It also requires better understanding of the place of religion in the late modern world. Encouraging such advances has been the primary goal of this chapter. Five interconnected themes have run through the previous sections: the persistence of religion in the twenty-first century; the importance of context in discerning outcomes; the need for improved cultural competence and religious literacy; the significance of religion in initiating change; and the benefits of well-judged partnerships. Each of these themes carries implications for action, which are spelled out in this section.

16.7.1   The Persistence of Religion

At the outset of this chapter we laid out evidence of the continuing significance of religion in the modern world. Specifically, a very high percentage of the global population claims some sort of identification with a religion, a percentage that is growing rather than declining overall. From this evidence, we argue that religion is persistent – a term chosen with care to signify that it is neither vanishing nor resurgent. And as a pervasive aspect of human cultures, religion is to be understood and respected. Social scientists, newly sensitized to a phenomenon that had been ignored for much of the twentieth century, are prone to "discover" religion where it has always been, but careful attention to religious demography in different parts of the world reveals a constantly changing array of presence and absence. Religion also takes new forms in late modernity – as indeed does everything else. Keeping this in mind and starting from observations of religion in everyday lives and local contexts, we have attempted here to analyze the impact of religion and its relevance to social progress in a wide variety of fields.

16.7.1.1   Implications for Action

Researchers, policy-makers, and activists should

- Start from the assumption that the presence of religious belief and practice is to be expected and that it is often a significant factor in whatever changes take place in a society.
- Support freedom for religious (and non-religious) identification, belief, and practice as a fundamental human right.
- Reject a simplistic distinction between progressive secularism and reactive religion, which has the effect of reinforcing precisely the reactionary reflex it sets out to condemn (Juergensmeyer 2015).

16.7.2   The Importance of Context

Throughout this chapter, a consistent conclusion emerges: the dangers of generalization. There is no single phenomenon – "religion" – that can be said to act in uniform ways across contexts. Whether it be in terms of households, of diversity, of democracy, of conflict, of peace-making, of welfare, of health care, or of the earth itself, the role of religion must be examined on its own terms and in local cultural context. In each and every case, religious beliefs, practices, and communities must be understood in particular historical, economic, political, and cultural trajectories. Careful attention to *religion as practiced*, not just to religion as doctrine or proclamation, is essential to achieving this level of local understanding. It is also critical to identifying potential partners for action on the one hand, and signs of potentially destructive conflict on the other. In short, the detail matters. The social sciences lend themselves to this task. It is the rigorous, but nonetheless sensitive, inquiry into the myriad aspects of religion and religiousness which leads first to critical appraisals and then to effective recommendations for policy.

16.7.2.1   Implications for Action

Researchers, policy-makers, and activists should

- Engage in careful and thorough investigations to determine religion's diverse forms in any given situation. Trusted local informants, along with scholarly experts, can be critical partners in interpretation, as can broad surveys that tap the full range of belief and practice, not just the loudest voices.
- Assess the degree to which religious factors may or may not be significant in a given context.
- Recognize the internal diversity of all religious traditions, thereby avoiding generalizations that may alienate potential allies and inhibit the search for pragmatic solutions.
- Be aware that "official" authorities and teachings may protect existing powers and hide important sites of innovation. This implies looking past formal pronouncements to everyday practices, especially in indigenous and other marginalized groups.

16.7.3   The Need for Cultural Competence and Religious Literacy

Both secular experts and religious leaders lack sufficient knowledge of each other's goals and resources. Community workers, politicians, policy-makers, and analysts need new kinds of knowledge to make the necessary judgments in this field. Knowledge of religion that comes only from media accounts is not sufficient. Within the social sciences, research on religion must not be restricted to a specialized subfield. We (all of us) need broad and deep pools of expertise to help identify the situations in which religious ideas and practices have become dangerous, as well as the places where creative synergies are possible. *Basic religious literacy* is a minimum standard for civic discourse and collective decision-making. Responsibility for that literacy will be allocated variously in different societies to educational systems, public programs, professional schools, and religious groups themselves. It is, however, an essential starting point. That said, the mutual knowledge that will make the most difference is likely to be gained in specific local contexts as diverse parties work together on concrete issues.

16.7.3.1   Implications for Action

Researchers, policy-makers, and activists should

- Insist that professional education in all fields establish basic religious literacy as a standard for cultural competence.
- Cultivate ongoing ties with religion scholars who can bring the necessary expertise to bear in any given situation. No single expert – secular or religious – should be expected to have all the knowledge required.
- Encourage funders and reviewers of social science research to be alert to opportunities to expand existing research programs, in order to include attention to the role of religions in political, economic, and household life.
- Take advantage of common projects to expand mutual knowledge and understanding and report on those findings to larger professional audiences.

16.7.4   The Significance of Religion in Initiating Change

Religions have – and always have had – powerful potential as initiators of progressive social change. Think for example of the initiatives to condemn slavery both in Europe and the United States. That impulse remains. It is true that religion's inherent potential for disrupting the status quo can lead to destructive movements; this should not be minimized. But by the same token, we need to recognize creative interventions by religious activists – initiatives that span democratization, peace-building, and ecology, among others. Religions encourage their participants to imagine the world as it could be and to act in ways that can make it so. When this happens, it arises from the power of religious ideas to motivate, of religious practices to offer transformative ways of life, of religious communities to mobilize, and of religious leaders and symbols to embody transcendent calls to action. All of that can be put to either good or ill. Attention to the *specific social mechanisms of religious life* has revealed, for instance, both the everyday structures of patriarchy that restrict women's freedom and the religious ideas and practices women can employ to resist. And attention to religious organizations and networks has pointed not only toward different points of departure but to tremendously expanded capacity and reach for health care and development in Africa.

16.7.4.1   Implications for Action

Researchers, policy-makers, and activists should

- Make room for the specific contributions that religious traditions may bring to pursuing social progress, ranging from religious stories and symbols, to everyday ritual practices, to recognized local leaders and organizational capacity. Each aspect has its own dynamic and potential.
- Be able to discern the likely value – or at times potential danger – of existing religious initiatives in any given area.
- Assess the degree to which practices may be separable from beliefs. Where beliefs seem promising for furthering progress, practices may imply the opposite – and vice versa. Cooperation may be possible without full agreement, and resistance to detrimental practices may be possible without attacking beliefs.

16.7.5   The Benefits of Well-Judged Partnerships

A stand-out finding running through this chapter is the strategic benefit in well-judged partnerships between religious and secular actors. Agencies of many different kinds benefit when religion is taken into account, and – where appropriate – when the considerable *resources of religions* are harnessed. Social progress depends on every sector of society – state, market, civil society, and more. Religion is particularly important in those parts of the world where secular agencies, both state and non-state, are for whatever reason eroded, at times seriously. In Brazil, for example, a Catholic community center became an ironic ally in government efforts to confront HIV/AIDS. In Indonesia, environmental restoration is gaining greater reach and effectiveness through collaboration with Muslim groups. In the United States and Europe, religious charities remain important to the social safety net. And throughout the world, efforts toward conflict transformation frequently depend on faith-based leadership. Whether pursuing human rights or democracy, economic development or women's empowerment, religious partners can bring value to the table.

It is important, however, to sound a note of caution: well-judged partnerships benefit all the parties involved; ill-judged partnerships are potentially dangerous. Political and social science research is essential to discern the precise conditions under which toxic forms of religion can join with toxic forms of political life, leading to harmful consequences for all concerned. Religion can encourage – indeed legitimate – destructive violence at every level of society, from the intimate to the global. But that is not the whole story. As the preceding sections of this chapter make clear, at times religion is the only force that can break through a stalemate, or offer a more hopeful vision of the future. And more immediately it is very often religious agencies – along with their secular counterparts – that bring aid to the excluded, support to the victims, and encouragement to the peacemakers.

16.7.5.1   Implications for Action

Researchers, policy-makers, and activists should

- Support the efforts of religious leaders, groups, and movements which are working to end discrimination and engender greater wellbeing, equality, and opportunity for more people.

16

- Support initiatives aimed at exposing and countering abuses both within religious communities and beyond.
- Look for overlapping goals, without expecting full agreement.
- Look for complementary organizational capacities that can be brought to bear on the issues in question.
- Engage with religious partners in debating and evaluating policy initiatives.
- Bring the expertise of social science to bear on the critical analyses necessary to discern both the dangers and the potential of partnerships with religious agencies.

In short, we underline the continuing need for research and action that give attention to religion. The social progress toward which these volumes point must encompass individual and social life as a whole, recognizing religious sensibilities as part of that whole. Critical but appreciative assessment is the first step in establishing creative partnerships that include religious individuals, organizations, and communities as key players in mobilizing for action and in debates about the future. They have much to offer – rich resources, significant skills, and sites for discussion. Imagining that society might indeed be "other" is a calling shared by religious and secular visionaries alike.

References

Abu-Lughod, L. 2015. *Do Muslim Women Need Saving?* Cambridge, MA: Harvard University Press.

Ahmed, L. 1992. *Women and Gender in Islam: Historical Roots of a Modern Debate.* New Haven, CT: Yale University Press.

Albera, D., and M. Couroucli. (eds.) 2012. *Sharing Sacred Spaces in the Mediterranean: Christians, Muslims, and Jews at Shrines and Sanctuaries.* Bloomington: Indiana University Press.

Amery, H.A. 2001. "Islamic Water Management." *Water International* 26/4: 481–489.

Ammerman, N.T. 1987. *Bible Believers.* Edison, NJ: Rutgers University Press.

Ammerman, N.T. 2005. *Pillars of Faith: American Congregations and Their Partners.* Berkeley: University of California Press.

Ammerman, N.T. (ed.) 2007. *Everyday Religion: Observing Modern Religious Lives.* New York: Oxford University Press.

Ammerman, N.T. 2013. *Sacred Stories, Spiritual Tribes: Finding Religion in Everyday Life.* New York: Oxford University Press.

Anouilh, P. 2005. "Sant'Egidio au Mozambique: De la charité à la fabrique de la paix." *Revue Internationale et Stratégique* 3/59: 9–20.

Anwar, Z. 2009. *Wanted: Equality and Justice in the Muslim Family.* Kuala Lumpur: SIS Forum.

Appadurai, A. 2000. "Spectral Housing and Urban Cleansing: Notes on Millennial Mumbai." *Public Culture* 12/3: 627–651.

Appleby, R.S. 2000. *The Ambivalence of the Sacred: Religion, Violence, and Reconciliation.* New York: Littlefield Publishers.

Arias, E.D. 2014. "Violence, Citizenship and Religion in a Rio de Janeiro Favela." *Latin American Research Review* 49: 149–167.

Asad, T. 2003. *Formations of the Secular: Christianity, Islam, Modernity.* Palo Alto, CA: Stanford University Press.

Autesserre, S. 2014. *Peaceland: Conflict Resolution and the Everyday Politics of International Intervention.* Cambridge: Cambridge University Press.

Azyumardi, A., D. Afrianty, and R. Hefner. 2007. "Pesantren and Madrasa: Muslim Schools and National Ideals in Indonesia," in R. Hefner and M.Q. Zaman (eds.), *Schooling Islam: The Culture and Politics of Modern Muslim Education.* Princeton, NJ: Princeton University Press.

Bäckström, A., and G. Davie (with N. Edgardh and P. Pettersson). (eds.) 2010. *Welfare and Religion in 21st Century Europe: Configuring the Connections.* Farnham, Surrey: Ashgate.

Bäckström, A., G. Davie, N. Edgardh, and P. Pettersson. (eds.) 2011. *Welfare and Religion in 21st Century Europe: Gendered Religious and Social Change.* Farnham, Surrey: Ashgate.

Baird, I.G. 2009. "Identities and Space: The Geographies of Religious Change amongst the Brao in Northeastern Cambodia." *Anthropos* 104/2: 457–468.

Banchoff, T.F. (ed.) 2008. *Religious Pluralism, Globalization, and World Politics.* New York: Oxford University Press.

Bane, M.J., B. Coffin, and R.F. Thiemann. (eds.) 2000. *Who Will Provide? The Changing Role of Religion in American Social Welfare.* Boulder, CO: Westview Press.

Barker, D.C., and D.H. Bearce. 2013. "End-Times Theology, the Shadow of the Future, and Public Resistance to Addressing Global Climate Change." *Political Research Quarterly* 66/2: 267–279.

Barlas, A. 2002. *"Believing Women" in Islam: Unreading Patriarchal Interpretations of the Qur'an.* Austin: University of Texas Press.

Barnett, M., C. Bob, N.F. Onar, A. Jenichen, M. Leigh, and L. Leustean. 2015. *Faith, Freedom, and Foreign Policy: Challenges for the Transatlantic Community.* Washington, DC: Transatlantic Academy. www.transatlanticacademy.org/sites/default/files/publications/TA %202015 %20report_Apr15_web.pdf.

Barrera-Osorio, F., H.A. Patrinos, and Q. Wodon. (eds.) 2009. *Emerging Evidence on Vouchers and Faith-Based Providers in Education: Case Studies from Africa, Latin America, and Asia.* Herndon, VA: World Bank Publications.

Barro, R.J., and R.M. McCleary. 2003. "Religion and Economic Growth across Countries." *American Sociological Review* 68/5: 760–781.

Bartholomew I, Ecumenical Patriarch. 1998. "From behind the Cyrillic Curtain: the Green Patriarch Speaks." *New Perspectives Quarterly* 15/1: 4–8.

Beaumont, J., and P. Cloke. 2012. *Faith-Based Organisations and Exclusion in European Cities.* Bristol: Policy Press.

Beck, U. 1992. *Risk Society: Towards a New Modernity.* London: SAGE.

Beckford, J. 2003. *Social Theory and Religion.* Cambridge: Cambridge University Press.

Beckford, J. (ed.) 2016. *Migration and Religion.* Cheltenham, Gloucestershire: Edward Elgar.

Bender, C. 2010. *The New Metaphysicals: Spirituality and the American Religious Imagination.* Chicago: University of Chicago Press.

Berger, P.L. 1969. *The Sacred Canopy.* New York: Anchor Doubleday.

Berger, P.L. 2014. *The Many Altars of Modernity: Toward a Paradigm for Religion in a Pluralist Age.* Boston: Walter De Gruyter.

Birchok, D.A. 2016. "Imagining a Nation Divided – Inside Indonesia." *Inside Indonesia* 124 (April–June).

Bloom, P.B.N., and G. Arikan. 2013. "Religion and Support for Democracy: A Cross-National Test of the Mediating Mechanisms." *British Journal of Political Science* 43/2: 375–397.

Bompani, B., and J. Smith. 2013. "Bananas and the Bible: Biotechnology, the Catholic Church, and Rural Development in Kenya." *International Journal of Religion and Society* 4/1–2): 17–32.

Bradley, T., and N. Kirmani. 2015. "Religion, Gender and Development in South Asia," in E. Tomalin (ed.), *The Routledge Handbook of Religions and Global Development.* London: Routledge.

Brenneman, R. 2012. *Homies and Hermanos: God and Gangs in Central America.* New York: Oxford University Press.

Brusco, E. 1986. "Colombian Evangelicalism as a Strategic Form of Women's Collective Action." *Feminist Issues* 6/2: 3–13.

Brusco, E. 1995. *The Reformation of Machismo.* Austin: University of Texas Press.

Burchardt, M., and M. Wohlrab-Sahr. 2013. "Multiple Secularities: Religion and Modernity in the Global Age – Introduction." *International Sociology* 28/6: 605–611.

Burdick, J. 1993. *Looking for God in Brazil: The Progressive Catholic Church in Urban Brazil's Religious Arena.* Berkeley: University of California Press.

Carroll, C. 2015. *Roots of Our Renewal: Ethnobotany and Cherokee Environmental Governance.* Minneapolis: University of Minnesota Press.

Casanova, J. 2007. "Immigration and the New Religious Pluralism: A European Union/United States Comparison," in T. Banchoff (ed.), *Democracy and the New Religious Pluralism.* New York: Oxford University Press.

Cavanaugh, W.T. 2009. *The Myth of Religious Violence: Secular Ideology and the Roots of Modern Conflict.* New York: Oxford University Press.

Chatterjee, P. 1989. "The Nationalist Resolution of the Woman Question," in K. Sanghari and S. Vaid (eds.), *Recasting Women.* New Delhi: Kali for Women.

Chaves, M. 1997. *Ordaining Women: Culture and Conflict in Religious Organizations.* Cambridge, MA: Havard University Press.

Chaves, M. 1999. "Religious Congregations and Welfare Reform: Who Will Take Advantage of 'Charitable Choice'?" *American Sociological Review* 64/6: 836–846.

Chowdhury, E.H. 2009. "Transnationalism Reversed: Engaging Religion, Development and Women's Organizing in Bangladesh." *Women's Studies International Forum* 32/6: 414–423.

Ciftci, S. 2010. "Modernization, Islam, or Social Capital: What Explains Attitudes toward Democracy in the Muslim World?" *Comparative Political Studies* 43/11: 1442–1470.

Clague, J. 2014. "Catholics, Families and the Synod of Bishops: Views from the Pews." *The Heythrop Journal* 55/6: 985–1008.

Clark, J.A. 2008. "FBOs and Change in the Context of Authoritarianism: The Islamic Center Charity Society in Jordan," in G. Clarke and M. Jennings (eds.), *Development, Civil Society and Faith-Based Organizations: Bridging the Sacred and the Secular*. Houndmills, Hampshire: Palgrave Macmillan.

Clarke, G. 2008. "Faith-Based Organizations and International Development: An Overview," in G. Clarke and M. Jennings (eds.), *Development, Civil Society and Faith-Based Organizations: Bridging the Sacred and the Secular*. Houndmills, Hampshire: Palgrave Macmillan.

Clarke G., and M. Jennings. (eds.) 2008. *Development, Civil Society and Faith-Based Organizations: Bridging the Sacred and the Secular*. Houndmills, Hampshire: Palgrave Macmillan.

Corten, A., and R. Marshall-Fratani. (eds.) 2001. *Between Babel and Pentecost: Transnational Pentecostalism in Africa and Latin America*. Bloomington: Indiana University Press.

Dalai Lama. 1995. *Ecology and the Human Heart*. www.dalailama.com/messages/environment/ecology-and-the-human-heart.

Davidman, L. 1991. *Tradition in a Rootless World: Women Turn to Orthodox Judaism*. Berkeley: University of California Press.

de Tocqueville, A. 1898. *Democracy in America*, transl. H. Reeve. New York: The Century Co. https://play.google.com/books/reader?id=cC8TAAAAYAAJ.

Deacon, G., and E. Tomalin. (eds.) 2015. *A History of Faith-Based Aid and Development*. London: Routledge.

DeBernardi, J. 2009. "Wudang Mountain and Mount Zion in Taiwan: Syncretic Processes in Space, Ritual Performance, and Imagination." *Asian Journal of Social Science* 37/1: 138–162.

Deeb, L. 2006. *An Enchanted Modern: Gender and Public Piety in Shi'i Lebanon*. Princeton, NJ: Princeton University Press.

Demerath, N.J. 2001. *Crossing the Gods: World Religions and Worldly Politics*. New Brunswick, NJ: Rutgers University Press.

Donno, D., and B. Russett. 2004. "Islam, Authoritarianism, and Female Empowerment: What Are the Linkages?" *World Politics* 56/4: 582–607.

Droogers, A. 2001. "Globalisation and Pentecostal Success," in A. Corten and R. Marshall-Fratani (eds.), *Between Babel and Pentecost: Transnational Pentecostalism in Africa and Latin America*. Bloomington: Indiana University Press.

Duff, J.F., and W.W. Buckingham. 2015. "Strengthening Partnerships between the Public Sector and Faith-Based Groups." *The Lancet* 386/10005: 1786–1794.

Ebaugh, H.R., J.S. Chafetz, and P.F. Pipes. 2006. "The Influence of Evangelicalism on Government Funding of Faith-Based Social Service Organizations." *Review of Religious Research* 47/4: 380–392.

Emmett, C.F. 1997. "The Status Quo for Jerusalem." *Journal of Palestine Studies* 26/2: 16–28.

Ferrara, A. 2015. *Assessing the Long-Term Impact of Truth Commissions: The Chilean Truth and Reconciliation Commission in Historical Perspective*. London: Routledge.

Finucane, J., and R.M. Feener. (eds.) 2014. *Proselytizing and the Limits of Religious Pluralism in Contemporary Asia*. Singapore: Springer.

Fish, S.M. 2002. "Islam and Authoritarianism." *World Politics* 55/1: 4–37.

Fox, J. 2000. "Is Islam More Conflict Prone Than Other Religions? A Cross-Sectional Study of Ethnoreligious Conflict." *Nationalism and Ethnic Politics* 6/2: 1–24.

Fox, J. 2004. "Religion and State Failure: An Examination of the Extent and Magnitude of Religious Conflict from 1950–1996." *International Political Science Review* 25/1: 55–76.

Francis (Pope 2013–). 2015. *Encyclical Letter Laudato Si' of the Holy Father Francis on Care for Our Common Home*. http://w2.vatican.va/content/dam/francesco/pdf/encyclicals/documents/papa-francesco_20150524_enciclica-laudato-si_en.pdf.

Freeman, D. 2012. *Pentecostalism and Development: Churches, NGOs and Social Change in Africa*. Houndmills, Hampshire: Palgrave Macmillan.

Funk, C., and B.A. Alper. 2016. *Religion and Views on Climate and Energy Issues*. Pew Research Center. www.pewinternet.org/2015/10/22/religion-and-views-on-climate-and-energy-issues/.

Ghassem-Fachandi, P. 2012. *Pogrom in Gujarat: Hindu Nationalism and Anti-Muslim Violence in India*. Princeton, NJ: Princeton University Press.

Gill, A. 1998. *Rendering unto Caesar: The Catholic Church and the State in Latin America*. Chicago: University of Chicago Press.

Girard, R. 1979. *La violence et le sacré*. Paris: Bernard Grasset.

Gooren, H. 2011. "Religion and Development Revisited: Some Lessons from Guatemalan Micro-Entrepreneurs," in G. ter Haar (ed.), *Religion and Development: Ways of Transforming the World*. New York: Columbia University Press.

Gopin, M. 1997. "Religion, Violence and Conflict Resolution." *Peace and Change* 22/1: 1–31.

Gopin, M. 2003. *Holy War, Holy Peace: How Religion Can Bring Peace to the Middle East*. Oxford: Oxford University Press.

Griffith, R.M. 1997. *God's Daughters: Evangelical Women and the Power of Submission*. Berkeley: University of California Press.

Grim, B.J. 2015. "Global Religious Diversity," in B. Grim, T. Johnson, V. Skirbekk and G. Zurlo (eds.), *Yearbook of International Religious Demography 2015*. Leiden: Brill.

Grim, B.J., and R. Finke. 2011. *The Price of Freedom Denied: Religious Persecution and Conflict in the Twenty-First Century*. Cambridge: Cambridge University Press.

Groenveldt, D. 2003. "The Future of Indigenous Values: Cultural Relativism in the Face of Economic Development." *Futures* 35: 917–929.

Hall, A., and S. Branford. 2012. "Development, Dams and Dilma: The Saga of Belo Monte." *Critical Sociology* 38/6: 851–862.

Haq, S.N. 2001. "Islam and Ecology: Toward Retrieval and Reconstruction." *Daedalus* 130/4: 141–177.

Hassett, M. 2007. *The Anglican Communion Crisis: How Episcopal Dissidents and Their African Allies Are Reshaping Anglicanism*. Princeton, NJ: Princeton University Press.

Hasu, P. 2012. "Prosperity Gospels and Enchanted Worldviews: Two Responses to Socio-Economic Transformation in Tanzanian Pentecostal Christianity," in D. Freeman (ed.), *Pentecostalism and Development: Churches, NGOs and Social Change in Africa*. Houndmills, Hampshire: Palgrave Macmillan.

Haynes, J. 2012. *Religious Transnational Actors and Soft Power*. Farnham, Surrey: Ashgate.

Heelas, P., and L. Woodhead. 2004. *The Spiritual Revolution: Why Religion Is Giving Way to Spirituality*. Oxford: Blackwell.

Heilman, S. 1999. *Defenders of the Faith: Inside Ultra-Orthodox Jewry*. Berkeley: University of California Press.

Henking, S. 2012. *Coming Out Twice: Sexuality and Gender in Islam*. http://religiondispatches.org/coming-out-twice-sexuality-and-gender-in-islam/.

Hoffman, S.R. 2004. "Islam and Democracy: Micro-Level Indications of Compatibility." *Comparative Political Studies* 37/6: 652–676.

Huntington, S.P. 1991. "Democracy's Third Wave." *Journal of Democracy* 2/2: 12–34.

Huq, S. (2011). "Piety, Music and Gender Transformation: Reconfiguring Women as Culture-Bearing Markers of Modernity and Nationalism in Urban Bangladesh." *Inter-Asia Cultural Studies* 12/2: 225–239.

Islamic Foundation for Ecology and Environmental Sciences. 2015. "Islamic Declaration on Global Climate Change." www.ifees.org.uk/wp-content/uploads/2016/10/climate_declarationmMWB.pdf.

Jama, A. 2015. *5 Imams Who Are Openly Gay*. http://islamandhomosexuality.com/5-imams-openly-gay/.

Jamal, A.A. 2006. "Reassessing Support for Islam and Democracy in the Arab World? Evidence from Egypt and Jordan." *World Affairs* 169/2: 51–63.

Jasanoff, S. 2005. *Designs on Nature: Science and Democracy in Europe and the United States*. Princeton, NJ: Princeton University Press.

Jasanoff, S., and S.H. Kim. (eds.) 2015. *Dreamscapes of Modernity: Sociotechnical Imaginaries and the Fabrication of Power*. Chicago: University of Chicago Press.

Johnson, T., B.J. Grim, and G. Zurlo. (eds.) 2016. *World Religion Database*. Leiden: Brill.

Jones, B. 2012. "Pentecostalism, Development NGOs and Meaning in Eastern Uganda," in D. Freeman (ed.), *Pentecostalism and Development: Churches, NGOs and Social Change in Africa*. Houndmills, Hampshire: Palgrave Macmillan.

Juergensmeyer, M. 1993. *The New Cold War? Religious Nationalism Confronts the Secular State*. Berkeley: University of California Press.

Juergensmeyer, M. 2011. "Rethinking the Secular and Religious Aspects of Violence," in C. Calhoun, M. Juergensmeyer, and J. Van Antwerpen (eds.), *Rethinking Secularism*. New York: Oxford University Press.

Juergensmeyer, M., M. Kitts, and M. Jerryson. (eds.) 2013. *The Oxford Handbook of Religion and Violence*. New York: Oxford University Press.

Kandiyoti, D. 1988. "Bargaining with Patriarchy." *Gender and Society* 2/3: 274–290.

Kawagley, A.O. 2006. *A Yupiaq Worldview: A Pathway to Ecology and Spirit*, second edition. Long Grove, IL: Waveland Press.

Kawanami, H. 2013. *Renunciation and Empowerment of Buddhist Nuns in Myanmar-Burma: Building a Community of Female Faithful*. Leiden: Brill.

Kawharu, M. 2000. "Kaitiakitanga: A Maori Anthropological Perspective of the Maori Socio-Environmental Ethic of Resource Management." *The Journal of Polynesian Society* 109/4: 349–370.

Kedourie, E. 1992. *Democracy and Arab Political Culture*. London: Routledge.

Keenan, M. 2012. *Child Sexual Abuse and the Catholic Church: Gender, Power and Organizational Culture*. New York: Oxford University Press.

Kerry, J. 2016. *Remarks at Rice University's Baker Institute for Public Policy*. https://2009-2017.state.gov/secretary/remarks/2016/04/256618.htm.

Kitiasa, P. 2008. *Religious Commodifications in Asia: Marketing Gods*. London: Routledge.

Knott, K.E., and T.T. Poole. 2013. *Media Portrayals of Religion and the Secular Sacred*. Farnham, Surrey: Ashgate.

Kugle, S.S.H. 2003. "Sexuality, Diversity and Ethics in the Agenda of the Progressive Muslims," in O. Safi (ed.), *Progressive Muslims: On Justice, Gender and Pluralism*. Oxford: OneWorld.

Laborde, C. 2017. *Liberalism's Religion*. Cambridge, MA: Harvard University Press.

Lamont, C.K. 2016. "Contested Governance: Understanding Justice Interventions in Post-Qadhafi Libya." *Journal of Intervention and State Building* 10/3: 382–399.

Lausanne Movement. 2011. *The Cape Town Commitment*. www.lausanne.org/content/ctc/ctcommitment.

Leustean, L. (ed.) 2014. *Eastern Christianity and Politics in the Twenty-First Century*. London: Routledge.

Leustean, L., and J. Madeley. (eds.) 2009. *Religion, Politics and Law in the European Union*. London: Routledge.

Levine, D.H. 2012. *Politics, Religion, and Society in Latin America*. Boulder, CO: Lynne Rienner.

Lindholm, T., W.C. Durham Jr., B.H. Tahzib-Le, and N. Ghanea. 2004. "Introduction," in T. Lindholm, W.C. Durham Jr., and B.H. Tahzib-Le (eds.), *Facilitating Freedom of Religion or Belief: A Deskbook*. Leiden: Martin Nijhoff Publishers.

Lipset, S.M. 1959. "Some Social Requisites of Democracy: Economic Development and Political Legitimacy." *American Political Science Review* 53/1: 69–105.

Little, D. (ed.) 2007. *Peacemakers in Action: Profiles of Religion in Conflict Resolution*. Cambridge: Cambridge University Press.

Llewellyn, J.J., and D. Philpott. (eds.) 2014. *Restorative Justice, Reconciliation and Peacebuilding*. New York: Oxford University Press.

Lofton, K. 2010. *Oprah: The Gospel of an Icon*. Berkeley: University of California Press.

Lotfalian, M. 2004. *Islam, Technoscientific Identities, and the Culture of Curiosity*. Lanham, MD: University Press of America.

Lukens-Bull, R.A. 2001. "Two Sides of the Same Coin: Modernity and Tradition in Islamic Education in Indonesia." *Anthropology and Education Quarterly* 32/3: 350–372.

Mahmood, S. 2005. *Politics of Piety: Islamic Revival and the Feminist Subject*. Princeton, NJ: Princeton University Press.

Mahmood, S. 2006. "Secularism, Hermeneutics and Empire: The Politics of Islamic Reformation." *Public Culture* 18/2: 323–347.

Mahmood, S. 2016. *Religious Difference in a Secular Age: A Minority Report*. Princeton, NJ: Princeton University Press.

Marshall, C. 2012. "Religion and Development," In T.S. Shah, A. Stepan, and M.D. Toft (eds.), *Rethinking Religion and World Affairs*. New York: Oxford University Press.

Marshall, K., and S. Smith. 2015. "Religion and Ebola: Learning from Experience." *The Lancet* 386/10005: 24–25.

Martin, B. 2001. "The Pentecostal Gender Paradox: A Cautionary Tale for the Sociology of Religion," in R. Fenn (ed.), *The Blackwell Companion to Sociology of Religion*. Oxford: Blackwell.

Martin, D. 1990. *Tongues of Fire: The Explosion of Protestantism in Latin America*. Oxford: Blackwell.

Martin, D. 2002. *Pentecostalism: The World Their Parish*. Oxford: Blackwell.

Martin, D. 2011. *The Future of Christianity: Violence and Democracy, Secularization and Religion*. Farnham, Surrey: Ashgate.

Martin, D. 2013. "Niche Markets Created by a Fissile Transnational Faith," in R.W. Hefner, J. Hutchinson, S. Mels, and C. Zimmerman (eds.), *Religions in Movement: The Local and the Global in Contemporary Faith Traditions*. New York: Routledge.

Martin, D. 2014. *Religion and Power: No Logos without Mythos*. Farnham, Surrey: Ashgate.

Martin, L.S. 2016. "Practicing Normality: An Examination of Unrecognizable Transitional Justice Mechanisms in Post-Conflict Sierra Leone." *Journal of Intervention and State Building* 10/3: 400–418.

Marty, M., and S. Appleby. (eds.) 1991. *Fundamentalisms Observed*, vol. 1. Chicago: University of Chicago Press.

Masoud, T., A. Jamal, and E. Nugent. (2016). "Using the Qur'ān to Empower Arab Women? Theory and Experimental Evidence from Egypt." *Comparative Political Studies* 49/12: 1555–1598.

Mavhunga, C.C. 2014. *Transient Workspaces: Technologies of Everyday Innovation in Zimbabwe*. Cambridge, MA: The MIT Press.

McGuire, M.B. 1988. *Ritual Healing in Suburban America*. New Brunswick, NJ: Rutgers University Press.

McGuire, M.B. 2008. *Lived Religion: Faith and Practice in Everyday Life*. New York: Oxford University Press.

McKay, J. 2013. "Lessons Learned from a Faith-Based Approach to Conservation in West Sumatra." *Asian Journal of Conservation Biology* 2/1: 84–85.

Menon, K. 2010. *Everyday Nationalism: Women of the Hindu Right in India*. Philadelphia: University of Pennsylvania Press.

Mernissi, F. 1991. *The Veil and the Male Elite: A Feminist Interpretation of Women's Rights in Islam*. New York: Basic Books.

Miller, D.E., K.H. Sargeant, and R.W. Flory. (eds.) 2013. *Spirit and Power: The Growth and Global Impact of Pentecostalism*. New York: Oxford University Press.

Mir-Hosseini, Z., M. al-Sharmani, and J. Rumminger. 2015. "Introduction," in Z. Mir-Hosseini, M. al-Sharmani, and J. Rumminger (eds.), *Men in Charge: Rethinking Authority in Muslim Legal Tradition*. Oxford: OneWorld.

Modood, T. 2011. "Multiculturalism: Not a Minority Problem." *The Guardian*: February 7.

Modood, T. 2013. *Multiculturalism*, second edition. Cambridge: Polity Press.

Moghadam, V. 2005. *Globalizing Women: Transnational Feminist Networks*. Baltimore, MD: Johns Hopkins University Press.

Mohr, T., and J. Tsedroen. 2009. *Dignity and Discipline: The Evolving Role of Women in Buddhism*. Somerville, MA: Wisdom Publications.

Mohseni-Cheraghlou, A. 2015. "Islamic Finance, Financial Inclusion and Poverty Reduction in MENA," in E. Tomalin (ed.), *The Routledge Handbook of Religions and Global Development*. London: Routledge.

Montesquieu, C. de S. 1748 [2001]. *The Spirit of Laws*, part 5, chapter 3. Kitchener, Ontario: Batoche Books.

Montgomery, S.L., and D. Chirot. 2015. *The Shape of the New: Four Big Ideas and How They Made the Modern World*. Princeton, NJ: Princeton University Press.

Moody, H.R., and W.A. Achenbaum. 2014. "Solidarity, Sustainability, Stewardship: Ethics across Generations." *Interpretation: A Journal of Bible and Theology* 68/2: 63–74.

Mooney, M. 2013. "Religion as a Context of Reception: The Case of Haitian Immigrants in Miami, Montreal and Paris." *International Migration* 51/3: 99–112.

Najmabadi, A. 2005. *Women with Mustaches and Men without Beards: Gender and Sexual Anxieties of Iranian Modernity*. Berkeley: University of California Press.

Nasr, S.H. 1991. "Islamization of Knowledge: A Critical Overview." *Islamic Studies* 30/3: 387–400.

Norris, P., and R. Ingelhart. 2011. *Sacred and Secular: Religion and Politics Worldwide*, second edition. Cambridge: Cambridge University Press.

Olivier, J., C. Tsimpo, R. Gemignani, et al. 2015. "Understanding the Roles of Faith-Based Healthcare Providers in Africa: Review of the Evidence with a Focus on Magnitude, Reach, Cost, and Satisfaction." *The Lancet* 386/10005: 1765–1775.

Olupona, J.K. 2012. *City of 201 Gods: Ilé-Ifè in Time, Space, and the Imagination*. Berkeley: University of California Press.

16

Olupona, J.K. 2014. *African Religions: A Short Introduction.* New York: Oxford University Press.

Olupona, J.K., and R. Gemignani. (eds.) 2007. *African Immigrant Religions in America.* New York: New York University Press.

O'Neill, K.L., and B. Fogarty-Valenzuela. 2015. "On the Importance of Having a Positive Attitude," in J. Auyero, P. Bourgois, and N. Scheper-Hughes (eds.), *Violence at the Urban Margins.* Oxford: Oxford University Press.

Parks, R. 2012. *Hygiene, Regeneration, and Citizenship: Jews in the Tunisian Protectorate.* Minneapolis: University of Minnesota Press.

Parsons, S. 2010. *The Cambridge Companion to Feminist Theology.* Cambridge: Cambridge University Press.

Pearce, S. 2005. "Religious Rage: A Quantitative Analysis of the Intensity of Religious Conflicts." *Terrorism and Political Violence* 17/3: 333–352.

Pew Research Center 2016. *The Gender Gap in Religion around the World.* www.pewforum.org/2016/03/22/the-gender-gap-in-religion-around-the-world/.

Pine, D. 2009. *Working Hard, Drinking Hard: On Violence and Survival in Honduras.* Berkeley: University of California Press.

Pritchard, S.B. 2011. *Confluence: The Nature of Technology and the Remaking of the Rhône.* Cambridge, MA: Harvard University Press.

Quadagno, J., and D. Rohlinger. 2009. "The Religious Factor in U.S. Welfare State Politics," in K. van Kersbergen and P. Manow (eds.), *Religion, Class Coalitions and Welfare State Regimes.* Cambridge: Cambridge University Press.

Rakodi, C. 2015. "Development, Religion and Modernity," in E. Tomalin (ed.), *The Routledge Handbook of Religions and Global Development.* London: Routledge.

Razak, A.A., and A.B.A. Majeed. (eds.) 1997. *Islam, Science, and Technology.* Kuala Lumpur: Institute of Islamic Understanding.

Roelofs, H. 1988. "Liberation Theology: The Recovery of Biblical Radicalism." *American Political Science Review* 82/2: 549–566.

Roper, L. 1992. *The Holy Household: Women and Morals in Reformation Augsburg.* Oxford: Oxford University Press.

Ross, J.I. 2011. *Religion and Violence: An Encyclopedia of Faith and Conflict from Antiquity to the Present.* New York: M.E. Sharpe.

Roush, L. 2014. "Santa Muerte, Protection and Desamparo: A View from a Mexico City Altar." *Latin American Research Review* 49: 129–148.

Roy, O. 2007. *Secularism Confronts Islam,* transl. G. Holoch. New York: Columbia University Press.

Rubin, J., D. Smilde, and B., Junge. 2014. "Lived Religion and Lived Citizenship in Latin America's Zones of Crisis." *Latin American Research Review* 49: 7–26.

Rudnyckyj, D. 2015. "Religion and Economic Development," in E. Tomalin (ed.), *The Routledge Handbook of Religions and Global Development.* London: Routledge.

Rupp, G. 2001. "Religion, Modern Secular Culture, and Ecology." *Daedalus* 130/4: 23–30.

Sarkar, T. 2001. *Hindu Nation: Community, Nation and Cultural Nationalism.* New Delhi: Permanent Black.

Schlozman, K.L., S. Verba, and H.E. Brady. 2012. *The Unheavenly Chorus: Unequal Political Voice and the Broken Promise of American Democracy.* Princeton, NJ: Princeton University Press.

Seffner, F., J. Garcia, M. Muñoz-Laboy, and R. Parker. 2011. "A Time for Dogma, a Time for the Bible, a Time for Condoms: Building a Catholic Theology of Prevention in the Face of Public Health at Casa Fonte Colombo in Porto Alegre, Brazil." *Global Public Health* 6: Supplement 2.

Sells, M. 2003. "Crosses of Blood: Sacred Space, Religion, and Violence in Bosnia-Herzegovina." *Sociology of Religion* 64/3: 309–331.

Sen, A. 1999. *Commodities and Capabilities.* New Delhi: Oxford University Press.

Sered, S.S. 1994. *Priestess, Mother, Sacred Sister: Religions Dominated by Women.* New York: Oxford University Press.

Sevcik, I., M. Rothery, N. Nason-Clark, and R. Pynn. 2015. *Overcoming Conflicting Loyalties: Intimate Partner Violence, Community Resources and Faith.* Edmonton: University of Alberta Press.

Shakman Hurd, E. 2015. *Beyond Religious Freedom: The New Global Politics of Religion.* Princeton, NJ: Princeton University Press.

Sharkey, H.J. 2012. "Middle Eastern and North African Christianity: Persisting in the Lands of Islam," in C.E. Farhadian (ed.), *Introducing World Christianity.* Malden, MA: Wiley Blackwell.

Simpson, L. (ed.) 2008. *Lighting the Eighth Fire: The Liberation, Resurgence, and Protection of Indigenous Nations.* Winnipeg, Manitoba: Arbeiter Ring Publishing.

Sinha, V. Forthcoming. "The Modern Hindu Diaspora," in T. Brekke (ed.), *Modern Hinduism.* Oxford: Oxford University Press.

Sitze, A. 2013. *The Impossible Machine: A Genealogy of South Africa's Truth and Reconciliation Commission.* Ann Arbor: The University of Michigan Press.

Smilde, D. 1997. "The Fundamental Unity of the Conservative and Revolutionary Tendencies in Venezuelan Evangelicalism: The Case of Conjugal Relations." *Religion* 27/4: 343–359.

Smilde, D. 2003. "Skirting the Instrumental Paradox: Intentional Belief through Narrative in Latin American Pentecostalism." *Qualitative Sociology* 26/3: 313–329.

Smilde, D. 2007. *Reason to Believe: Cultural Agency in Latin American Evangelicalism.* Berkeley: University of California Press.

Smith, B.G., and B. Johnson. 2010. "The Liberalization of Young Evangelicals: A Research Note." *Journal for the Scientific Study of Religion* 49/2: 351–360.

Smith, C. (ed.) 1996a. *Disruptive Religion: The Force of Faith in Social Movement Activism.* New York: Routledge.

Smith, C. 1996b. *Resisting Reagan: The U.S. Central America Peace Movement.* Chicago: University of Chicago Press.

Smith, L.T. 2012. *Decolonizing Methodologies: Research and Indigenous Peoples.* London: Zed Books.

Smyth, R. 2004. "The Roots of Community Development in Colonial Office Policy and Practice in Africa." *Social Policy and Administration* 38/4: 418–436.

Starhawk, M. 1979. *The Spiral Dance: A Rebirth of the Ancient Religion of the Great Goddess.* San Francisco: Harper and Row.

Stepan, A., and G. Robertson. 2003. "An 'Arab' More Than a 'Muslim' Electoral Gap." *Journal of Democracy* 14/3: 30–44.

Stern, J., and J. Berger. 2016. *ISIS: The State of Terror.* New York: Harper Collins.

Stoeckl, K. 2014. "Orthodox Churches and Migration," in L. Leustean (ed.), *Eastern Christianity and Politics in the Twenty-First Century.* London: Routledge.

Sullivan, S.C. 2011. *Living Faith: Everyday Religion and Mothers in Poverty.* Chicago: University of Chicago Press.

Swainson, L., and A. McGregor. 2008. "Compensating for Development: Orang Asli Experiences of Malaysia's Sungai Selangor Dam." *Asia Pacific Viewpoint* 49/2: 155–167.

Swearer, D.K. 2006. "Assessment of Buddhist Eco-Philosophy." *Harvard Theological Review* 99/2: 123–137.

ter Haar, G. (ed.) 2011a. *Religion and Development: Ways of Transforming the World.* New York: Columbia University Press.

ter Haar, G. 2011b. "Religion and Human Rights: Searching for Common Ground," in G. ter Haar (ed.), *Religion and Development: Ways of Transforming the World.* New York: Columbia University Press.

Tessler, M. 2002. "Islam and Democracy in the Middle East: The Impact of Religious Orientations on Attitudes toward Democracy in Four Arab Countries." *Comparative Politics* 34/3: 337–354.

Toft, M.D. 2006. "Religion, Civil War, and International Order." *BCSIA discussion paper.* Cambridge, MA: Kennedy School of Government.

Toft, M.D., D. Philpott, and T.S. Shah. 2011. *God's Century: Resurgent Religion and Global Politics.* New York: W.W. Norton.

Tomalin, E. 2013. "Religion and Rights-Based Approach to Development." *International Journal of Religion and Society* 4/1–2: 53–68.

Tomkins, A., J.F. Duff, A. Fitzgibbon, et al. 2015. "Controversies in Faith and Health Care." *The Lancet* 386/10005: 1776–1785.

Torrance, A.J. 2006. "The Theological Grounds for Advocating Forgiveness and Reconciliation in the Sociopolitical Realm," in D. Philpott (ed.), *The Politics of Past Evil: Religion, Reconciliation, and the Dilemmas of Transitional Justice.* Notre Dame, IN: University of Notre Dame Press.

Trinitapoli, J., and A. Weinreb. 2012. *Religion and AIDS in Africa.* New York: Oxford University Press.

Tsosie, R. 2012. "Indigenous Peoples and Epistemic Injustice: Science, Ethics, and Human Rights." *Washington Law Review* 87/4: 1133–1201.

Van Klinken, A. 2013. *Transforming Masculinities in African Christianity: Gender Controversies in the Time of AIDS.* Farnham, Surrey: Ashgate.

Vasquez, M.A. 2010. *More than Belief: A Materialist Theory of Religion.* New York: Oxford University Press.

Voyles, T.B. 2015. *Wastelanding: Legacies of Uranium Mining in Navajo Country.* Minneapolis: University of Minnesota Press.

16

Ward, K. 2002. "Same-Sex Relations in Africa and the Debate on Homosexuality in East African Anglicanism." *Anglican Theological Review* 84/1: 89–102.

Warner, R.S., and J. Wittner. 1998. *Gatherings in Diaspora: Religious Communities and the New Immigration.* Philadelphia, PA: Temple University Press.

Watkins, S.C., and A. Swidler. 2013. "Working Misunderstandings: Donors, Brokers, and Villagers in Africa's AIDS Industry." *Population and Development Review* 38: 197–218.

Weber, M. 1905 [1958]. *The Protestant Ethic and the Spirit of Capitalism*, transl. T. Parsons. New York: Scribner.

Wells, R. 2010. *Hope and Reconciliation in Northern Ireland: The Role of Faith-Based Organisations.* Dublin: Liffey Press.

White, L. 1967. "The Historical Roots of Our Ecological Crisis." *Science* 155/3767: 1203–1207.

Wickham, C.R. 2013. *The Muslim Brotherhood: Evolution of an Islamist Movement.* Princeton, NJ: Princeton University Press.

Wilde, A. (ed.) 2016. *Religious Responses to Violence: Human Rights in Latin America Past and Present.* Notre Dame, IN: University of Notre Dame Press.

Williams, R. 2012. *Faith in the Public Square.* London: Bloomsbury/Continuum.

Wood, G. 2015. "What ISIS Really Wants." *The Atlantic*, March.

Wood, R.L. 2002. *Faith in Action: Religion, Race, and Democratic Organizing in America.* Chicago: University of Chicago Press.

Woodberry, R.D. 2006. "The Economic Consequence of Pentecostal Belief." *Society* 44/1: 29–35.

Woodberry, R.D. 2012. "The Missionary Roots of Liberal Democracy." *American Political Science Review* 106/2: 244–274.

Woodhead, L. 2007. "Gender Differences in Religious Practice and Significance," in J. Beckford and N.J. Demerath (eds.), *The SAGE Handbook of the Sociology of Religion.* London: SAGE.

Woodhead, L. 2014. "Tactical and Strategic Religion," in N. Dessing, N. Jeldtoft and L. Woodhead (eds.), *Everyday Lived Islam in Europe.* Farnham, Surrey: Ashgate.

Wuthnow, R. 2004. "Presidential Address 2003: The Challenge of Diversity." *Journal for the Scientific Study of Religion* 43/2: 159–170.

Yang, F. 2012. *Religion in China: Survival and Revival under Communist Rule.* New York: Oxford University Press.

Yang, F. 2014. "Oligopoly Is Not Pluralism," in G. Giordan and E. Pace (eds.), *Religious Pluralism: Framing Religious Diversity in the Contemporary World.* Berlin: Springer.

Yang, F., and H.R. Ebaugh. 2001a. "Religion and Ethnicity among the New Immigrants: The Impact of Majority/Minority Status in Home and Host Countries." *Journal for the Scientific Study of Religion* 40/3: 367–378.

Yang, F. and H.R. Ebaugh. 2001b. "Transformations in New Immigrant Religions and Their Global Implications." *American Sociological Review* 66/2: 269–288.

Yee, S. 1996. "Material Interests and Morality in the Trade of Thai Talismans." *Southeast Asian Journal of Social Sciences* 24/2: 1–21.

Yip, A., and S. Page. 2013. *Religious and Sexual Identities: A Multi-Faith Exploration of Young Adults.* Farnham, Surrey: Ashgate.

16

17

Pluralization of Families

Coordinating Lead Authors:[1]
Merike Blofield, Fernando Filgueira

Lead Authors:[2]
Carmen Diana Deere, Maxine Eichner, Guðný Björk Eydal, Rhacel Parreñas, Neetha Pillai, Frances Rosenbluth, Tine Rostgaard, Lynn Welchman

Contributing Authors:[3]
Annabelle Hutchinson, William McGrew, Tee Zhuo

[1] Affiliations: MB: University of Miami, USA; FF: CIESU, Uruguay.
[2] Affiliations: CDD: University of Florida, USA; ME: University of North Carolina, USA; GBE: University of Iceland; RP: University of South California, USA; NP: Centre for Women's Development Studies, India; FR: Yale University, USA; TR: KORA, Denmark; LW: University of London, UK.
[3] Affiliations: AH, WM, TZ: Yale University, USA.

Summary

The family is an institution central to individual wellbeing because it provides caretaking, human development, economic interdependency, and affiliation. This chapter defines families as closely knit social groups bounded by relations of locally recognized kinship that are based on expectations of reciprocity, obligation, and obedience, usually but not always based on blood lineage and/or stable bonding and a shared dwelling.

The vast majority of the world's population live the majority of their lives within family units, of all shapes and sizes. Regardless of the tremendous diversity in family type and composition, and their socio-economic, political, and cultural contexts, all families have certain commonalities. They all must confront the need to balance production and reproduction, or, in other words, ensure income and care. Most families at some point raise children, and all age, if they are lucky enough not to die young. At best, families also provide their members with love, and a sense of meaning and belonging. At worst, families may grapple with severe material deprivation or be settings for neglect, abuse, and inequality in power relations, stunting the ability of their members to flourish as human beings. Families are also a site of potential struggle and conflict.

The driving question of the chapter is how societies can support conditions for the twenty-first century that allow families to flourish, and at the same time promote individual agency, equality, and dignity. Two interlocking questions follow from this: first, how can societies support families' important functions – caregiving, human development, and belonging – in order to promote the dignity, life opportunities, and risk protection of family members? Second, as they support these functions, how can societies minimize socio-economic and other inequalities and domination that families often reproduce, within and between them?

This chapter is divided into three parts. The first part provides a broad context for discussing families. It identifies boundaries between families and other spheres or institutions; summarizes contemporary challenges; discusses the legal recognition of families, both regarding partners and offspring; and finally, situates the socio-economic context of families. Part two focuses on relations within families. The discussion is divided into four sections: relations between partners; adult–child relations; aging family members; and other adults. Part three provides policy recommendations.

The empirical evidence shows a broad trend toward legal acceptance of consensual adult partnerships, although with regional variation. On partner relations, the evidence shows an overall tendency toward more gender-equitable family law and greater gender equality in education, labor force participation, and asset ownership, and that these are associated with improvements in women's bodily integrity and more shared decision-making, as well as enhanced wellbeing of the family as a whole. At the same time, these links are not automatic, and require concerted efforts by the state to both provide and enforce a legal framework in support of gender equality. On adult–child relations, the evidence shows that a state role in ensuring income floors for families with children is essential for children's physical and material wellbeing. Beyond this, ensuring a healthy balance of family (including paternal) care and good-quality institutional care allows children and their families to flourish. Finally, state efforts to protect children are most successful when they routinely support families in preventive ways. Care for older people around the world remains centered in the family. The challenge for aging societies is to ensure access to care services to relieve the burden on families, especially already overburdened women, and to ensure the dignity of older people.

The policy recommendations include, on family recognition, the view that the goal of state policy should be to support the broader range of relationships in which people are organizing their family lives, consistent with promoting human dignity and fairness within and outside of these relationships. For rights and regulations within families, laws should uphold equality and dignity between partners (and other adults), and respect and protection for children.

Given the massive transformations that families have undergone over the past half century, to deal with twenty-first-century challenges we recommend a strong, twofold role for the state (beyond legal regulations) to ensure flourishing families: first, transfers that guarantee a minimum income floor for all families with dependents (children, disabled, elderly); and second, publicly funded health, education, and care services with

17

universal principles, to allow families to maintain a healthy balance between the twin responsibilities of production and reproduction. While some of these investments pay for themselves over the medium and long term, we also make a call for progressive taxation, including a strong inheritance tax, to alleviate inequalities between families. In sum, families based on egalitarian principles, with supportive state policies that allow families to flourish, provide the most conducive setting to do what families can do at their best: provide a space where persons are loved and nurtured, love and nurture back, and are able to flourish to their fullest potential.

17.1   Introduction

The family is an institution central to individual wellbeing because it provides caretaking, human development, economic interdependency, and affiliation. The boundaries of which groups constitute families are conceptually murky, in part because family forms have varied enormously over time and location. We take as a simple conceptual definition that families are closely knit social groups bounded by relations of locally recognized kinship that are based on expectations of reciprocity, obligation, and obedience.[4] Families are usually, but not always, based on forms of blood lineage and/or stable bonding and a shared dwelling, often intergenerational and often, albeit not always, involving reproduction and caring for offspring at some point in the life-cycle. At best, families may provide their members with a space where persons are loved and nurtured, love and nurture back, and are able to flourish to their fullest potential. At worst, families may grapple with severe material deprivation or be settings for neglect, abuse, and inequality in power relations, stunting the ability of their members to flourish as human beings. Families are also a site of potential struggle and conflict.

This leads to the key question of this chapter: how can societies support conditions that allow families to flourish and at the same time promote individual agency, equality, and dignity?[5] Two interlocking questions follow from this: First, how can societies support families' important functions – caregiving, human development, and belonging – in order to promote the dignity, life opportunities, and risk protection of family members? Second, as they support these important functions of families, how can societies minimize the socio-economic and other forms of inequality and domination that are often reproduced, both within and between families? The quest in this chapter is to assess the empirical evidence in support of the best ways to achieve these goals. The chapter is divided into three parts. The first part provides a broad context for discussing families. First, it identifies boundaries between families and other spheres or institutions; second, it outlines contemporary challenges (which will then be discussed in depth later in the chapter); third, it discusses the legal recognition(s) of families, regarding both partners and offspring; and fourth, it discusses the socio-economic context of families. Part two focuses on relations within families. The discussion is divided into four sections: first, relations between partners; second, adult–child relations; third, aging family members; and fourth, other adults within families. Part three provides policy recommendations.

17.2   Conceptual Boundaries: Families, Markets, Communities, and States

17.2.1   Introduction

The ways that families function are deeply and importantly affected by their interaction with other societal spheres/institutions and practices.[6]

The most important of these are markets, the state, and the community (encompassing religious organizations, charities, trade unions, NGOs, and so forth). The ways in which the interactions between families and these other spheres/institutions are structured affect families' ability to perform their critical functions in a manner that supports equity and human dignity (Eichner 2010). These interactions in turn affect the distribution of social risks and opportunities among men and women; rich and poor; educated and non-educated; children, adults, and older people; and able-bodied and disabled.

In general, it is accepted in Western mainstream literature that these spheres are governed by different norms. Interactions within families are governed by norms of reciprocity and obligation, and often with children, obedience. Interactions in the market, in contrast, are governed by principles of competition, self-interest, and free exchange. Of course, this distinction between market, family, and state logics does not mean either that agents in families lack self-interest or that bargaining does not take place in families, but rather that the explicit rules of the game regarding how this bargaining and these conflicting interests are resolved are different from those governing the market and other spheres. Religious and charitable organizations, on the other hand, also embody distinct norms (addressed in Chapter 16).

The state, with legally binding and authoritative actions, has a special role to play in how the relationship between families and other institutions is organized (Przeworski 2003; Eichner 2010). The state performs three basic tasks, all of which affect families: regulating the behavior of individuals and institutions; the collection of resources from individuals, families, and organizations through taxation; and the distribution and allocation of resources in the community (Filgueira 2007). First, how the state recognizes and regulates families – including marriage and divorce laws, reproductive rights, child custody laws, and inheritance laws – profoundly affects how families are structured and the ways that they accomplish their tasks. This includes laws that limit (or conversely link) religious canons to family life and behavior (like permitting civil marriage or, conversely, sharia law). Second, state taxation limits the degree to which individuals can pool their assets and resources within families and pass them along to the next generation. Furthermore, whether and how the state distributes a broad range of goods and services deeply affects how families function. These three tasks and how they interact with families form the basis of much of our discussion in the next sections.

We have seen massive advances in material wellbeing and human development across the world over the past decades. Global GDP per capita has doubled in just 15 years, and infant mortality rates have declined by almost half in the past 25 years, from 63 deaths per 1,000 live births in 1990 to 32 deaths per 1,000 live births in 2015 (WHO 2015a). At the same time, socio-economic inequalities within societies

---

4   The authors of the chapter debated these conceptual distinctions, and some were critical of the implied public/private boundary between states, markets, and family, rather seeing the family, market, and state as mutually constitutive.

5   The authors debated about which words to use here. Initially the choice of the team was "autonomy" and "dignity," but some authors felt the first term reflected Western values.

6   Authors debated whether to use "institutions" or "spheres" in this context. Noting both allows for different perspectives.

have increased worldwide in the last 30 years,[7] and the benefits of the massive advances have been very unequally distributed, both across countries and regions, and across socio-economic classes, ethnic groups, and family types within countries. Usually we think of states and markets as the critical drivers of distributional inequalities. Yet, families also play a large role – one that is often neglected. We tend to see families as on the receiving end of inequality trends, rather than in the driver's seat. Of course families are affected by these inequalities (physical and financial assets, educational achievement, social capital), but it is also important to bear in mind that they strongly shape them, also affecting inequalities between and within families.

One key feature of state regulation relating to families deserves special consideration: how states respond to the social opportunities and social risks that recur across all human societies, and for which families are often on the front lines. The growth of the welfare state in the twentieth century, most expansively in advanced industrialized countries, but to varying extents also in developing countries, is, of course, related to the challenges represented by these social risks that befall individuals and families, including illness, disability, maternity, unemployment, and old age and death of the breadwinner(s), all important to the material security of families. With the expansion of welfare states in the second half of the twentieth century, combined with the gradual democratization of family relations, state transfers, tax policies, and services have also sought to implicitly or explicitly shape families, and in doing so have reinforced certain kinds of families over others; influenced socio-economic differences between families; and influenced the division of paid and unpaid labor between family members, especially mothers and fathers.

In the remainder of this section, we provide an overview of current trends. We then review two critical areas where families are changing because of market, state, and community transformations: first, the recognition and regulation of the changing landscape of family forms; and second, the dynamics that shape relations among family units.

17.2.2   Challenges in the Pluralization of Families Today

Families in most of the world must be understood in the context of the gender inequality that has historically sustained and regulated family relationships and regimes, in which adult males dominated and held the levers of political, economic, and social power over their children and spouses. This was the case in the codified traditions derived from Anglo-American common law, Roman law, classical Islamic law, and the customary law of many sub-Saharan and Asian societies.

From the 1960s onwards especially, increasing pressures have eroded the strength of male domination in Western states and in parts of Asia. Five major shifts have driven the transformation of family regimes in

this era: (a) the withering of most civil and political legal discrimination against women in both the marketplace and state structure/public and private spheres; (b) the increasing control of women over their reproductive capacity led by technological and cultural change; (c) legal and policy transformations and change in social practices and social structure which brought about radical changes in patterns of fertility, divorce, and family arrangements; (d) the incorporation of a growing share of women into the paid wage labor market; and (e) the rising belief that women should be treated equally with men. Prominent scholars have made the case that a "stalled" or "incomplete" revolution (Hochschild and Machung 1989; Esping-Andersen 2009) has occurred in this era regarding gender, work, and the family, essentially because while most women changed, most men and the state have not fully adapted to these changes.

Midway into the second decade of the twenty-first century it is possible to identify new trends and features that, to differing degrees, question the previous hierarchical arrangements:

- New family arrangements have emerged that depart from the heterosexual nuclear family that dominated the past century. In many countries, cohabitation, same-sex conjugal relations, single-female-headed households, and other family forms have gained cultural and legal acceptance. Yet, in most countries, legal recognition of these different family forms still lags behind the pace of change and negatively affects their viability and stability. This is addressed in Section 17.2.4.
- Rates of conjugal relationships have decreased, and significant numbers of those that develop have become less stable. This is particularly true for lower-income families. The breakdown of conjugal relationships negatively affects children by reducing stability, lessening adults' ability and opportunity to engage in caregiving to them, and decreasing adults' financial resources to invest in them. This breakdown also decreases the benefits of caregiving and affiliation among adults. We address this throughout the chapter.
- Fertility rates have been reduced and fertility has been postponed by the combined effects of access to technology, laws, and mores that give women and girls increased control over reproduction. Yet financial obstacles to reproductive autonomy remain in many countries, and access to abortion continues to be legally restricted. Further, inequality in fertility patterns across classes, and far below replacement-level fertility rates in some countries, illustrate the double challenge of democratizing reproductive control and allowing for a better balance between productive and reproductive behavior. This is addressed in Section 17.3.1.
- Within families, conjugal relations in the Western and in much of the non-Western world have become more gender-egalitarian and flexible, with broader entry and exit options and a more equal distribution of rights regarding asset control, lineage recognition, and power. This is addressed in Section 17.3.1. The sexual

---

[7]   Whether inequality has increased on a global level is contested; however, there is no doubt that it has increased at the country level. The apparent paradox is because lower-income countries have been closing the wealth gap with developed countries, especially when we consider China and India. Thus overall inequality might have decreased, since the average Chinese person is today closer in terms of income to, say, the average European. But within their borders Europeans, Americans, and Chinese people are more unequal.

division of paid and unpaid labor in families is characterized by the following trends:

- Overall, women have made clear gains in labor market participation and economic autonomy during the last half century. Yet women in many regions have been left behind on these measures, and even the advances hide significant inequalities along socio-economic lines.
- In industrialized Western societies, the gap in the distribution of non-paid labor and care work between men and women has decreased considerably, although significantly more in some countries than others. In no country, though, has it been eliminated. In most of the developing world, care and housework remain heavily the responsibility of women, limiting their ability to enter the labor force.

- Within families, intimate partner or familial violence has around the world become problematized, due especially to efforts by women's movements, although progress has been spotty overall and completely absent in some countries. This is addressed in Section 17.3.1.4b.
- The legal regulation of the parent–child relationship has in most countries shifted from a model of parental, especially paternal, control, to a model largely directed at the "best interests" of the child. At the same time, parent–child relationships are marked by increasing efforts to prepare both boys and girls for success in the market as adults. This is addressed in Section 17.3.2.
- There is a worldwide trend toward aging societies, produced by the confluence of reduced mortality and fertility together with life expectancy increases. The proportion of the world's population aged 60 years or over is expected to double from about 11 percent to 22 percent between 2000 and 2050 (UN 2002; WHO 2016b). While most developed nations have had decades to adjust to shifting age structures, the aging of the respective populations in many other regions is taking place very rapidly, often within a single generation. This is addressed in Section 17.3.3.
- Extended households (horizontal and vertical) remain an important part of the family landscape in the developing world, but are slowly being eroded. This is addressed in Section 17.3.4. Transnational families are also becoming more prominent (addressed throughout).

In sum, the changes taking place are providing more opportunities than ever before for relations based on mutual respect and dignity among family members. At the same time, civil and political remnants of gender-inegalitarian orders remain in many countries, affecting reproductive rights, marriage and divorce regulations, and the ability to protect oneself from violence. In light of our driving question – how can societies support conditions that allow families to flourish and at the same time promote individual autonomy, equality, and dignity? – we turn to examining family recognition and relations among family units.

17.2.3   Legal Recognition(s) of Families

Globally, the large majority of adults marry or live in a consensual union at some point in their lives. According to UN data covering the

decade of the 2000s for 159 countries, in the overwhelming majority of countries, 80 percent of women and men had been married or in a consensual union by the time they reached their late forties (UNDESA 2011: 2).

In the middle of the twentieth century, the dominant family form worldwide was the heterosexual marital family, in some regions supplemented by extended families. The legal regulation of families both responded to and enforced this dominance by granting married couples legal rights. In contrast, other family forms remained outside the scope of legal protections and were often criminalized.

At the end of the twentieth and beginning of the twenty-first centuries, other family forms have increased. Some of this phenomenon has been driven by rising rates of marital dissolution. While divorce and separation are still relatively rare statistically, according to UN data, globally they have increased from 2 percent of adults aged 35 to 39 in the 1970s to 4 percent in the 2000s, being much more common in developed than in developing countries (UNDESA 2011).

Meanwhile, the incidence of cohabitation without marriage has mushroomed in many Western countries, including several northern European countries, the United States, some Latin American countries, and the Caribbean. It has increased to a lesser extent in Africa and is still relatively unusual in Asia (UNDESA 2011). In addition, same-sex couples have become increasingly visible in the West, although less so in most countries in the Middle East, Africa, and Asia, many of which continue to criminalize same-sex relationships.[8]

In North America, Latin America, Western Europe, and South Africa, among others, there has been a steady increase in the share of households headed by a sole adult (because they are either never-married, separated, divorced, or widowed), and particularly, female-headed households (Vespa, Lewis, and Kreider 2013; Cienfuegos 2014; Euromonitor International 2014). Remarriage rates, nonetheless, tend to be high for both men and women. Data for 15 OECD countries for 2006–08 reveals that between 20 percent and 28 percent of all marriages are remarriages (UNDESA 2011: 3).

Globally, the large majority of adults also have children, although the number of children per parents – that is, the fertility rate – has declined (Agrillo and Nelini 2008; UN Population Division 2012). Combined with the increase in households headed by a sole adult and by remarried adults, developments in DNA testing and reproductive technology have made distinctions between social and biological parenthood both increasingly possible and increasingly visible. Therefore, deciding on what standards to use to determine parentage has become increasingly important.

The available data suggest that adults do better on a number of measures of wellbeing when they have supportive family relationships (Wyke and Ford 1992; Hewitt, Turrell, and Giskes 2010). Further, in general children do better when raised in a stable home with two parents (see Section 17.4). This said, a variety of relationships can

---

8   Variations exist in non-Western countries, with increasing recognition in South Africa, Taiwan, and Japan.

contribute to adults' and children's wellbeing. For example, a recent study found that couples in stable cohabiting relationships experience many of the benefits that married couples experience (Mernitz and Dush 2016). While marriage itself to a modest extent appears to contribute to the stability of the relationship (Brown and Booth 1996), and stronger feelings of subjective wellbeing (Dush and Amato 2005), non-marital relationships in some countries are more stable than marital relationships in others (Cherlin 2010). Additionally, differences in societal norms among countries have been shown to contribute to the varying levels of wellbeing between unmarried and married cohabitants. Cross-national studies indicate that the gap in wellbeing between unmarried cohabitants and married cohabitants (dubbed the "cohabitation gap") is greater in countries where cohabitation between unmarried people is less accepted and less common (Soons and Kalmijn 2009), as well as countries with more traditional gender and religious beliefs (Lee and Ono 2012).

Some countries have made significant headway in supporting families as they exist, rather than families as they continue to be imagined. Progress in this area has been patchy. Some legal systems remain exclusively focused on the heterosexual marital family. Others have broadened their definition of family in some respects but still inadequately recognize some types of families. This section considers the legal recognition of these emerging family forms, with respect to both relationships between adults and parent–child relationships.

17.2.3.1   Relationships among Adults

As relationships among adults have increasingly diverged from the model of heterosexual marriage, especially in Western countries, cohabiting couples have increasingly been recognized with distinct rights, while marriage rights have been extended to same-sex couples. This section considers the legal recognition of both forms of relationships, as well as the continuing issues raised by polygamous marriage.

17.2.3.1a   Unmarried Cohabiting Couples

Since the 1980s the marriage rate (for formal unions) has been declining globally.[9] Especially Western countries have seen a high rise in the rates of couples cohabiting without marriage as the practice has become more acceptable as both a step and an alternative to legal marriage (Mintz 2015). Indeed, in Latin American countries, South Africa, and Sweden, more children are born outside of marriage than within it (The Social Trends Institute 2016).

Until the late twentieth century, many countries, including the United States, criminalized non-marital cohabitation and refused to enforce claims between unmarried cohabitants after the relationship ended (Garrison 2008; Sutherland 2012).

In most of the Western world, albeit not in the East or Middle East, states have eased bans on cohabitation and gradually increased rights

and protections for unmarried couples during the last two generations. This change in policy recognized several facts. First, ignoring such relationships legally did little to reduce the escalating rates of non-marital cohabitation. Furthermore, this approach failed to support important caretaking and affiliation functions that these families could otherwise provide, and often unfairly advantaged one member of the couple if the relationship ended. Finally, with marriage increasingly concentrated among wealthier couples in Western countries, laws benefiting only marriage risked funneling benefits to those who needed them least.

In some Western countries, private rights have been accorded to couples based on their living together for a particular length of time. For example, many Western countries at the relationship's dissolution now give non-marital cohabitants some rights to property accumulated by either partner during the relationship. In New Zealand, Croatia, and much of Latin America, non-marital cohabitants who live together for several years have the same property rights as married couples, although sometimes the relationship has to be registered before they can receive them (Jakovac-Lozic 2000; Deere and León 2001; Akin 2003). These laws have been spurred in large part by the recognition that the financial costs of such break-ups are not equally shared by both members of the couple; instead the partners who perform more caretaking – generally women – tend to be disproportionately harmed financially at the relationship's end (Blumberg 2001).

Fewer Western countries have thus far provided public rights and benefits to unmarried couples during the relationship, although this appears to be changing. Canada now provides for parity of some federal benefits between married and cohabiting couples. It has also revised both tax and old-age pension rules so that the same standards apply to married and "common-law" partners (Bala and Goyal 2000). Further, most Western states now protect non-marital cohabitants under domestic violence statutes. This protection is particularly important in light of research that reveals that unmarried women are sometimes at greater risk of abuse by intimate partners than are married women (Tjaden and Thoennes 2000).

Other countries allow unmarried couples to enter into alternative formal statuses. Domestic partnership statuses, which were often developed as a marriage alternative for same-sex couples, now serve as an alternative status for opposite-sex couples as well, with similar or lesser rights than marriage. For example, France adopted civil unions in 1999, granting a broad range of benefits. Unlike marriage, this status is easy to both enter and exit – no marriage ceremony or divorce required. Today, there are two such civil unions for every three marriages (Sayare and Boem 2010).

In Latin America, the incidence of consensual unions has been on the rise in concert with their growing legal recognition, so that in most countries they mostly have the same rights as legal marriages (García and de Oliveira 2011). Many, perhaps most, Muslim-majority states allow for a form of ex post facto recognition of marriages that complies with the requirements of Islamic law in establishing marriage, even if

---

[9]   According to Mintz (2015: 169), the marriage rate has fallen since the 1980s in countries accounting for 87 percent of the world's population.

accompanying such measures with the prospect of penal sanctions for the avoidance of legal procedures. In regard to "unofficial" (unregistered) marriages in the United Arab Emirates and Egypt, public disquiet appears to have centered not so much around people marrying without the knowledge of the state, but on young persons (mostly females) marrying without the knowledge of their families – "secret marriages" that are perceived to violate sharia and state law (Hasso 2011).

17.2.3.1b   Same-Sex Relationships

The regulation of same-sex relationships has also been transformed in Western countries during the last half century. Until the mid-twentieth century, most countries criminalized same-sex behavior. These criminal prohibitions were largely rescinded in Western countries in the latter half of the twentieth century, or early in the twenty-first. Currently, no criminal prohibitions remain in Europe, North America, and Latin America. Further, a growing number of these countries have also allowed same-sex couples to enter domestic partnerships, and then in many countries to get married. The Netherlands became the first country to recognize same-sex marriage in 2001, and today, most developed countries and several Latin American countries recognize it (Pew Research Center 2013). Studies have shown that same-sex marriage stabilizes relationships, and increases the wellbeing of both adults and children in these families (Badgett 2011; Wight et al. 2013).

A number of the countries that do not allow same-sex couples to marry offer an alternative domestic partnership status only for same-sex couples (Pew Research Center 2013). Studies show that same-sex couples enter these alternative statuses at far lower rates than they enter into marriage.

These trends are not uniform. Currently, according to the UN Office of the High Commissioner, 70 countries continue to imprison citizens because of their sexual orientation, and five others – Iran, Mauritania, Saudi Arabia, Sudan, and Yemen – punish homosexuality with the death penalty (BBC World News 2014). South Africa is the only country outside of the West that allows same-sex marriage.

A few countries are even increasing prohibitions on same-sex relations. In 2013, India's Supreme Court reversed a 2009 order decriminalizing homosexual acts and reinstated a 153-year-old colonial-era law deeming a same-sex relationship an "unnatural offense" punishable by a ten-year jail term (*Koushal* v. *NAZ Foundation* 2013). In 2014 Nigeria passed the Same Sex Marriage (Prohibition) Act, which criminalized all forms of same-sex unions regardless of where the union was entered, with strong support from the Nigerian people (Adebanjo 2015).

17.2.3.1c   Polygamous Marriage

Polygamy (commonly practiced as polygyny, the marriage of one man to multiple women) is banned in many regions of the world. However, at the national level, it is still legal or generally accepted in 33 countries,

25 in Africa and 7 in Asia. Further, polygamy is accepted or legal for some groups in 18 additional countries in Africa and 21 in Asia. In a study of 26 countries that permitted polygamy, between 10 percent and 53 percent of women aged 15–49 had co-wives (UNDESA 2011: 4). The vast majority of the countries in which it is permitted are Muslim-majority.

Protecting the autonomy and equality of women in polygamous marriages has proven so challenging that several human rights organizations, including the United Nations Human Rights Committee, have declared polygamy a form of human rights abuse, and a number of African countries have declared polygamy illegal in recent years. Yet some critics of polygamy advocate an incremental restrictive approach to encourage the social and economic decline of the institution (WLUML 2003). The African Protocol of Women's Rights takes a middle position, endorsing monogamy but also protecting the rights of wives in polygynous marriage (Banda 2014). A minority of states in which polygamy is allowed accord wives some limited protections through requiring the consent of existing wives to new marriages, and providing some property and support rights to wives.

17.2.3.2   Parent–Child Relationships

During the last half century, legal regimes have also transformed the way they regulate parent–child relationships. At the middle of the twentieth century, laws determining paternity were largely governed by the marital presumption, which conferred paternity on the husband of the mother. With the advent of DNA testing toward the end of the twentieth century, laws have reckoned with how to weigh claims to paternity based on biology against paternity claims based on marriage to the mother.[10] Because of the higher rates of nonmarital births, countries have increasingly provided routes to establish paternity for children born outside of marriage. For example, the 1978 European Convention on the Legal Status of Children Born out of Wedlock mandates the establishment of voluntary paternal affiliation procedures. Further, with the advent of Assisted Reproductive Technologies, countries have grappled increasingly with how to determine parentage in an age where social and biological parenthood can diverge.

One parentage issue that has engendered much debate concerns the parenting rights of gays and lesbians. Until fairly recently, openly gay and lesbian couples were penalized in child custody determinations and were prohibited from adopting. Accumulated research now establishes that children raised by same-sex parents do as well as children raised by opposite-sex parents on relevant measures of wellbeing (see Perrin and Siegel 2013). Based on this evidence, most Western countries have repealed or at least rolled back these laws in recent years. All countries that recognize same-sex marriage allow adoption by married same-sex couples. However, some countries that do not allow same-sex marriage continue to deny full joint or step-child adoption to same-sex couples. Most Asian and African countries still prohibit such adoptions, with the prominent exception of South Africa.

---

[10]   In the US case, see for example *Michael H.* v. *Gerald D* (1989).

Another important change in recent decades is the emphasis on providing children the right to care from both parents. While children born out of wedlock traditionally did not have the same rights to support and care from their father that children born within a marriage were given, during the last half century most countries have firmly decreed that such children be treated equally with children born to married couples.[11] When it comes to the significant number of non-marital children who are born to parents in an existing, cohabiting relationship (McLanahan and Pettit 2003), most countries have moved to a legal model in which the parents are accorded the same parenting rights and duties as married couples. The current challenges center instead on how to ensure that children whose parents are not in intact relationships are accorded the same opportunities for relationships, financial support, and stability that married parents offer. We discuss the details of adult–child relations in Section 17.3.3.

17.2.4   The Socio-Economic Context of Families

Families enclose resources within their boundaries. They do so because family membership implies both legitimate claims over other family members' resources and obligations to transfer resources to other family members. These claims and obligations are both legally and culturally enshrined, through norms and customs.[12]

Resources can include material (money and property) as well as non-material resources (human capital, social capital, time devoted to care and service). Laws of inheritance, the obligation to care for offspring (both in terms of material welfare and non-material wellbeing), obligatory transfers among spouses, in some societies the obligation to care for the elderly, and in many societies the legal or de facto pooling of resources among spouses, legally enshrine these principles of family solidarity, reciprocity, and obligation.

These laws and cultural norms that bind families together can confront or moderate socio-economic inequalities insofar as they distribute resources to household members who have no other sources of income, protection, and services. Family solidarity, reciprocity, and obligation can provide both material wellbeing and meaning to the lives of family members. In the absence of state or communal systems of protection, family solidarity and resource distribution can provide protection and resources to individuals who might otherwise be devoid of any means of subsistence. Very importantly, however, these laws and cultural norms also imply that families are a central institution in the intergenerational and intra-generational reproduction of inequality.

Families transfer resources both intra- and intergenerationally. Within generations, families reproduce inequality because they pool assets and resources (property, money, time, social capital) and enclose them among their members (be it at household level or between households of the same lineage or family). Intergenerationally they do so also

through inheritance and family transfers between households. Since in most societies people with high socio-economic status tend to marry each other, families not only reproduce but can also increase socio-economic inequalities (Esping-Andersen 2009; Mintz 2015).

Family formation and dissolution, as well as variations in family arrangements, are strongly correlated with social class through income and/or education differentials. In general, the poor marry less and earlier and have less conjugal stability, and a larger proportion are in female-headed households. Within and across countries in Latin America, the mean age is much lower and the prevalence of consensual unions is much higher among lower-income groups and those with less education (García and de Oliveira 2011; Cienfuegos 2014).

Given these trends, the poor are usually less able to benefit from resource pooling. They also have higher rates of fertility in almost every society in the world (Skirbekk 2008). Thus, poorer families, while contributing more to the reproduction of a given society, are also the ones facing the starkest choices in terms of how to distribute scarce resources among family members. The result is that they often under-invest in their children's education, which in turn contributes to the intergenerational reproduction of inequality.

Besides the transfer of resources in daily life from parents to off-spring, the key mechanism in the transmission of inequality is inheritance. Family members tend to leave their life savings, properties, and other assets to their offspring (or to other family members or friends). State regulations – especially taxes – on inheritance are thus a central instrument to curtail – or ensure – the transmission of intergenerational inequalities. Yet, there is a trend toward reducing or eliminating inheritance or estate taxes; indeed, 13 countries or tax jurisdictions have repealed these since 2000, from Sweden and Norway to Portugal, Macau, Russia, Hong Kong, Singapore, the Czech Republic, Lichtenstein, Brunei, Austria, Hungary, and the Slovak Republic (Cole 2015). In the United States, the estate tax exemption grew from under US$1 million in 2001 to almost US$5.5 million in 2015 (Cole 2015) and was further increased in the 2017 tax reform.

According to Piketty (2014), the rise in the level of economic inequality in developed countries since 1980, particularly the US, is strongly associated with policy changes on taxation and finance as well as the underlying mechanisms of capital accumulation which promote wealth divergence rather than convergence. In the context of slower economic growth, private capital accumulates faster through inheritance than savings, worsening further the distribution of income and wealth.

As mentioned earlier, state policies that counteract these mechanisms and provide protections from social risks for families have been essential in promoting family wellbeing. For example, without the provision of public or subsidized transfers and health and care services, the birth of a severely disabled child into a poor family portends not only exacerbated hardship for the child but potential financial ruin for the family as well.

---

[11]   For the United States, see for example *Levy* v. *Louisiana* (1968). Chile was among the last countries in Latin America, in 1998, to equalize the rights of children born in and out of wedlock.

[12]   This said, it should be kept in mind that in any specific society, who or what counts as family can change depending on what is being mobilized or negotiated.

17.3 Relations within Families

Beyond family composition, legal family recognition, and the socioeconomic context of family units, relations *within* families are crucial for individual and family wellbeing. In this section, we focus on relationships between partners, between parents and children, with aging family members, and among other kin. We assess the empirical evidence on how these different relations contribute to family and individual wellbeing, keeping in mind the goal of the chapter to identify the conditions which allow families to flourish while ensuring individual autonomy and dignity. We do so with an emphasis on how the productive and reproductive role of families and family members can be made compatible with the individual search for dignity, opportunity, and protection.

17.3.1 Relationships between Partners

In much contemporary discourse, partner relationships are assumed to be based on altruism and solidarity, in the context of deep emotional attachment. While many unions may be underpinned by these sentiments and behavior, the overwhelming evidence also indicates that the distribution of power in a relationship matters not only for equality in the relationship but also for a broad range of factors related to individual and family wellbeing, from self-fulfillment, to freedom from violence, to child nutrition. Below we examine four dimensions of relations between partners – legal equality of partners, access to income and wealth, the gender division in paid and unpaid labor, and bodily integrity (reproductive choice and freedom from violence) – and what social science tells us about how they contribute to individual and family wellbeing.

Given that legalized same-sex unions are a very recent phenomenon, we focus here on heterosexual couples (whether married or in consensual unions), although much of the empirical evidence is likely relevant to same-sex couples as well, except that dynamics around gender roles are less established.

17.3.1.1 The Legal Framework on Gender Equality

The past century has witnessed a tremendous leap toward legal gender equality, albeit at different paces in different regions. A study of 100 countries using 17 indicators of potential gender inequality found that between 1960 and 2010, 28 countries removed all sources of gender inequality in family law, while an additional 29 reduced at least one

constraint; 18 countries stayed stagnant; hence, by 2010 53 of the 100 countries had achieved legal gender equality (Hallward-Driemeier, Hasan, and Rusu 2013).[13]

OECD countries and those of Eastern Europe and Central Asia had few explicitly discriminatory laws by 1960 and those remaining had been eliminated by 2010.[14] In Latin America, a region with relatively few indicators of gender inequality in 1960, considerable progress was achieved in this 50-year period. Countries of Sub-Saharan Africa had the greatest number of constraints in 1960; by 2010 the number of these had been halved, as in East Asia. There has been less progress and even some regression in the Middle East and North Africa as well as in South Asia. Many countries in these regions exempt religious and customary law from existing gender equality or anti-gender-discrimination provisions in their constitutions (Hallward-Driemeier, Hasan, and Rusu 2013). Another study, focusing on the 1975–2005 period, found that countries with the lowest gender equality in family law all apply Islamic family law but that there is considerable variation among them.[15]

The greatest progress toward gender equality in the family has been made with respect to married women's legal capacity. In all but a few countries of Sub-Saharan Africa, married women can now sign contracts, initiate legal proceedings, and open their own bank accounts. The most persistent constraints across world regions are those dealing with women's property rights and access to immovable assets: inequality in the inheritance rights of sons and daughters and in the property rights of surviving spouses. In addition, in some countries an adult married woman cannot be designated a household head on the same terms as her husband or seek a job or engage in trade or a profession without her husband's permission (Hallward-Driemeier, Hasan, and Rusu 2013: fig. 4).

The United Nations Convention on the Elimination of all Forms of Discrimination against Women (CEDAW) has played an important role in enshrining gender equality in the family globally since it came into effect in 1981.[16] As of 2017, CEDAW had been ratified by 189 countries, although many with reservations (UN Treaty Collection n.d.).[17] These reservations pertained mainly to Article 15, which stipulates that women's legal capacity should be "identical to that of men," and Article 16, which states that in marriage both spouses should have the same rights "in respect of the ownership, acquisition, management, administration, enjoyment and disposition of property" (UN 1980: part IV, 7–8).[18] The largest positive impact of CEDAW has been associated with the attainment of equal property rights between unmarried men and women, equal inheritance rights for daughters and widows, and

---

[13] The study investigated property rights, legal capacity, and constitutional protection. The indicators do not include regulations regarding divorce.

[14] Until 1978 in Spain and 1984 in Switzerland, wives needed their husbands' permission to be employed; in France, until 1985 only the husband could administer the marital property (Hallward-Driemeier, Hasan, and Rusu 2013).

[15] Bangladesh and Pakistan have made more progress in attaining gender equality than Egypt, Jordan, or Saudi Arabia. Also, not much progress has been attained in countries as diverse as India, Kenya, and Nigeria. Iran and Indonesia backtracked, scoring lower in 2005 than in earlier periods (Htun and Weldon 2011). Since 2005, Egypt, Morocco, and Tunisia have taken measures related to women's capacity to pass citizenship on to their spouses and children.

[16] CEDAW was an outcome of global organizing efforts associated with second-wave feminism. Its passage in 1979 built on momentum created by the first UN Conference on Women in Mexico City in 1975.

[17] Among the countries that have not ratified CEDAW is the United States, although it signed the convention.

[18] Byrnes and Freeman (2011) attribute much of this progress to subsequent UN Conferences on Women and other human rights conferences, as well as periodic review processes to which signature countries are subject.

17

several dimensions of legal capacity. This was felt most greatly in countries at lower levels of income and, in terms of inheritance rights, where the rule of law was weak. It should be stressed, however, that there is virtually always a gap between legal rights in principle and actual rights in practice, where the size of the gap is influenced by state capacity, among other factors. Thus, it is helpful to think of laws enshrining gender equality as a necessary first, but not only, step toward gender equality in practice.

Laws that regulate inheritance and property ownership in relation to marriage have a significant impact on how wealth is distributed between husbands and wives. Two broad marital regimes have emerged across different cultures. In separation-of-property regimes (a shared legacy of British common law, classical Islamic law, and the customary law of many sub-Saharan and Asian societies) each spouse retains ownership of the property acquired both before and during marriage, as well as any inheritance. In community-of-property regimes (a legacy of Roman law) all property acquired during a marriage belongs jointly to husband and wife; if the marriage is dissolved this property is split equally between them. Importantly, such regimes recognize the non-monetary contribution of wives (domestic and care labor) to the marriage.[19] In some countries of the West, in the case of divorce, reforms to separation-of-property regimes have required sharing on an equal or equitable basis those assets accumulated during the marriage, and in at least one, the community property regime has been reformed to allow equitable rather than equal sharing, thus blurring the distinction between these two regimes.

Inheritance and the degree of gender bias differ cross-culturally. Countries with legal systems derived from British common law often enjoy greater testamentary freedom, whereas in the Roman legal tradition children become forced heirs to most of their parents' estate. A relatively unique feature of the latter tradition is that sons and daughters are entitled to equal shares. In contrast, daughters are entitled to only half the share of sons under some schools of Islamic law. Dominant patterns of wealth ownership reflect the influence of different marital and inheritance regimes, as shown below.

Legal reform can have positive effects on both individual and family wellbeing. An analysis of the impact of inheritance reforms in two Indian states that equalized the land rights of sons and daughters in the mid-1990s found that it increased the probability of women inheriting land, getting married later, and having more education (Deininger, Goyal, and Nagarajan 2013).

Laws that regulate the age of majority and the age of consent for marriage, and social norms that influence actual marital age, are also important for individual wellbeing and gender equality in partnerships. Early age at marriage can deter schooling completion for both men

and women, with lifelong implications for their earnings capacity, while early motherhood can have detrimental effects on the health and employability of women. Also, large age differences between husbands and wives can aggravate power imbalances within couples.

Since the 1970s, the mean age at first marriage or union has been increasing for both men and women worldwide, and the gender age gap at marriage narrowing (UNDESA 2011). This trend is more marked in developed than in developing countries. In the US, for example, the mean age of legal marriage increased from 21 for women and 23 for men in 1970 to 27 and 29, respectively, by the late 1980s (Mintz 2015: 102). While the prevalence of adolescent marriage has fallen in developing countries, in a good number of countries in Sub-Saharan Africa and South Asia, 30 percent or more of women are married by the age of 18 (UNDESA 2011: 1). Having more years of schooling is associated with later age at marriage for women. This has led to a narrowing of the gender age gap and, potentially, greater female agency in marriage (Carmichael 2011).

Finally, how marital or common-law break-ups are regulated has a significant impact on the wellbeing of the individuals involved. Divorce potentially gives unhappy partners an exit option from insufferable marriages, and in the context of extant gender inequalities its regulation is especially consequential for the wellbeing of women and children. Its viability is conditioned by marital and inheritance regimes, access to income for the more vulnerable partner post-divorce, and social norms.

In the West, divorce based on mutual consent and/or unilateral, no fault divorce is now the norm. During the twentieth century, legal reforms in Muslim-majority countries found various ways to constrain the husband's power of unilateral divorce (including awarding compensation payments to divorcées and expanding the divorcée's temporary rights to the marital home) and widened the grounds on which a woman could apply for divorce; but generally a structural imbalance remained. Since 1984 at least ten Muslim countries have reformed their divorce regulations so that women as well as men can initiate a divorce or so that women can divorce their husband without his consent, parallel to the previous right of husbands (Hassani-Nezhad and Sjögren 2014: table 1).[20]

How property is distributed upon a divorce imposes significant conditions on the ability of individuals to exit unhappy or abusive relationships. As noted above, community property marital regimes (where both partners are automatically entitled to half the community property), or regimes where equal inheritance rights for sons and daughters prevail, make it easier for individuals to exit. In countries of the common-law tradition, such as the US and Canada, where separation-of-property regimes prevail, the trend over the past

17

---

[19] In full community property regimes, the principle of shared ownership applies regardless of when the property is acquired. In partial community property regimes, such as in most of Latin America, individual inheritances and property acquired before marriage continue to be recognized as the individual's during marriage, although earnings resulting from such property are generally still pooled. See Deere and Doss (2006).

[20] A remaining source of gender inequality in family law concerns custody and guardianship over children. In the ten Muslim-majority countries that reformed their divorce legislation between 1984 and 2006, the mother always gets custody of young children, but in seven countries, mothers lose custody of sons at a younger age (most frequently age ten) than they do daughters. The only two countries to treat children equally irrespective of sex are Jordan (where they remain with the mother until puberty) and Morocco (where they do so until age 15) (Hassani-Nezhad and Sjörgen 2014: table 1).

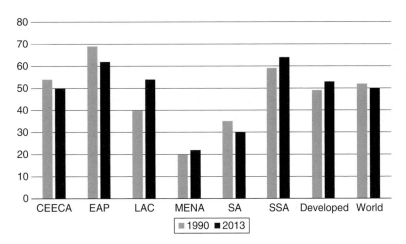

Figure 17.1 | Female labor force participation rates by region, 1990 and 2013.
Notes: Regions are as follows: CEECA (Central and Eastern Europe and Central Asia); EAP (East Asia and the Pacific); LAC (Latin America and the Caribbean); MENA (Middle East and North Africa); SA (South Asia); SSA (Sub-Saharan Africa); Developed (developed countries).
Source: Compiled from UN Women (2015: fig. 2.1), based on ILO data.

several decades has been toward the equal or equitable division of marital property upon divorce in recognition of wives' non-monetary contributions toward the marriage and childrearing. This enables the more vulnerable member to exit with some level of financial security. It also has implications for offspring. A study of Brazil's extension of alimony rights to couples in consensual unions found an increase in women's leisure time and the school enrollment of the eldest girl among households headed by couples in consensual unions, compared with those headed by married couples (Rangel 2006); there was no significant effect on men's time allocation.

Ensuring viable exit options for unhappy partners can mean a difference between life and death. Honor killings, which are widely documented in the Middle East, parts of South Asia, and North Africa, are sometimes targeted against women who seek to initiate divorce or separation, as well as reactions to female sexuality that transgresses social mores (Kabeer 2014). One study in the United States found that as a result of allowing for unilateral divorce, which increased women's exit options from oppressive relationships, suicide rates for women fell dramatically while those for men did not change. This legal change was also associated with a decrease in intimate partner violence as well as femicide (Stevenson and Wolfers 2006). A study in Canada found that following a reform which improved women's financial position upon divorce, suicide rates among older married women were reduced, while there was no change in the rate among men or younger unmarried women (Adam, Hoddinott, and Ligon 2011).

17.3.1.2   Access to Income and Wealth: Continuing Gender Gaps

Over the past half century there has been a tremendous increase in women's labor force participation worldwide, with half of adult women in 2014 being economically active (ILO 2012).[21] The increase in the share of households with more than one income earner in concert with rapid urbanization, rising educational levels, declining fertility

rates, and transformations in family composition have had profound implications for all facets of family life. Nonetheless, the increase in women's labor force participation has been uneven both across and within different regions. In addition, the conditions of women's employment continue to disadvantage them compared with men; for example, in 2014 the average global gender earnings gap remained at 24 percent (UN Women 2015). Moreover, while the increase in women's labor force participation is often associated with gains in women's access to and control over income and wealth, as well as more egalitarian relations among couples, this relationship is not linear or straightforward, although there is evidence of positive synergies in some dimensions. Figure 17.1 outlines female labor force participation rates by region between 1990 and 2013.

Figure 17.1 illustrates the heterogeneity in women's labor force participation rates across world regions and how, globally, these have fallen slightly since 1990. This decline is driven by trends in East and South Asia and Central and Eastern Europe. In India, for example, women's labor force participation fell from 33 percent in 1994 to 28 percent in 2012 (Neetha 2014). The largest gains have been in Latin America and the Caribbean, where the rate is now comparable to that of developed economies. While there have been gains in the Middle East and North Africa over the 1990–2013 period, this region continues to show the lowest rates of female labor force participation. The highest rate is exhibited by Sub-Saharan Africa, where agricultural employment still predominates.

Men's labor force participation rates also fell globally between 1990 and 2013, from 81 percent to 77 percent, decreasing in every world region (UN Women 2015: fig. 2.1). The lowest male rates are currently found in developed economies (68 percent) and Central and Eastern Europe (69 percent). Overall, these trends mean that the gender gap among the economically active population has narrowed over this period, being smallest in developed countries and in Sub-Saharan Africa.

---

[21]   For a detailed analysis of the factors contributing to this increase and long-term trends see Goldin (2006) and Blau and Kahn (2016).

Despite increases in the manufacturing and service sectors, women's employment in developing economies remains largely concentrated in family-based agriculture or informal work (ILO 2012). A substantial share are unpaid family workers (or "contributing family members") and do not necessarily have access to their own income. Gender inequality is central to this phenomenon. For example, in India men on family farms are more likely to be landowners or leaseholders and to be considered the primary farmer (self-employed), with women as their helpers (Neetha 2014). In Latin America, women are overrepresented in the informal sector. Moreover, the quality of women's informal-sector employment is generally more precarious than men's, with women concentrated either in domestic service or as unpaid family workers (Benería, Berik, and Floro 2016: fig. 4.2).

Women's earnings are also limited by a persistent gender wage gap. In developed countries, this gap has shrunk over the past half century, as women and men have developed similar levels of human capital, in both education and labor market experience. In the United States, by 2014, full-time female workers earned 79 percent of what men did annually, up from about 60 percent in the 1950s (Blau and Kahn 2016). The gender pay gap is even lower in Scandinavia and Southern Europe (Olivetti and Petrongolo 2016). The remaining gap is caused by discrimination, unequal bargaining conditions, different probabilities of career interruption (Goldin 2014), and occupational segregation, where women are often concentrated in occupations that suffer from what economists such as Nancy Folbre (2012) refer to as the "care penalty."

In developing countries, the gender wage gap has largely been maintained through the gendering of occupations and tasks. Female-dominated occupations generally have lower wages than those that are male-dominated, for example in the context of the garment industry in India and Bangladesh (Ghosh 2009; Custers 2012). This is rooted in the devaluation of domestic labor and the status of women as secondary earners, limiting the positive impact that gains in education could have on gender wage gaps (Kabeer and Natali 2013). In export industries, highly informal subcontracting arrangements employ women as part of a flexible workforce that hires and fires with fluctuations in export demand (Custers 2012). Women are sometimes home-based workers, where employers exploit systems of familial control, values, and cultural practices to create a docile, severely underpaid labor force (Cook and Dong 2011). In the service sector, increased female employment comes with a high degree of gender segmentation and wage gaps (Mazumdar and Neetha 2006).

Overall, the increase in women's wage work and self-employment has brought income into the hands of women and improved the economic wellbeing of their families. In developed countries, families where both parents work are less likely to be in poverty (Esping-Andersen 2009). For developing countries, a range of studies indicate broad gender differences in the practice of pooling earned income, with men often retaining some discretionary income and women pooling most of theirs, particularly when there are children at home (Bruce and Dwyer 1988).

Whether earning income improves women's position in marriage, largely depends on whether women are able to control the income that they earn. A study found that in 13 of 44 developing countries surveyed, 10 percent or more of the women sampled reported that they were not involved in decisions regarding the use of the income that they themselves earned (World Bank 2012: fig. 2.9).[22] Women in the poorest households are more likely to be uninvolved in such decisions than those in wealthier households. Malawi presents the most extreme case, with 45 percent of women in the lowest quintile not participating in these decisions, compared with 13 percent in the top income quintile.

Gender differences in income earnings and assets, combined with inequality in marital property regimes and inheritance, result in husbands having more wealth than wives. The most rigorous study of the gender wealth gap in a developed country to date, based on 2002 data for Germany, found that the mean net wealth of women was 69 percent of that of men; this gender wealth gap was greater for married women, who on average owned 64 percent of the wealth of men (Sierminska, Frick, and Grabka 2010).

In developing countries, the first large-scale surveys of individual wealth ownership that measured the intra-household distribution of wealth found tremendous differences across world regions. Nationally representative surveys in Ecuador and Ghana in 2010 reveal that in the former, partnered women own 44 percent of the wealth of the couple, compared with only 19 percent in the latter. A similar survey in the state of Karnataka, India, found that partnered women owned only 9 percent of couple wealth (Deere et al. 2013). This study argues that the governing marital and inheritance regimes largely explain these cross-country differences. In Ecuador, the default marital regime is partial community property, and inheritance laws treat children of both sexes equally. Assets such as land, housing, and other real estate tend to be owned jointly by spouses. In Ghana and India, where separation of property is the default marital regime, these assets are predominantly owned by men. Moreover, in both countries, sons are privileged in inheritance, resulting in a much lower share of wealth owned by partnered women.[23]

In South Asia, Latin America, and Sub-Saharan Africa, most land owners are male, and men own more land than women on average (Agarwal 1994; Deere and León 2001; Doss et al. 2015). The primary means through which agricultural land is acquired is inheritance. Thus, gender biases favoring men in inheritance – whether in law or in cultural practices – end up reproducing gender inequality within households and families. In more urbanized developing countries, housing rather than land is the most important component of household wealth. Data for Latin America suggest that ownership of the main residence is more equitably distributed than ownership of land;

---

[22] Based on the Demographic and Health Surveys sponsored by the United States Agency for International Development. Countries surveyed were in Sub-Saharan Africa, in addition to Bangladesh, Nepal, and India.

[23] Historical data for the US suggest that women typically fared better in community property states than in common-law states. A study of estate tax records in the 1950s found that women owned 49 percent of the reported wealth in community property states, but only 38 percent in common-law states (Lapman 1962 in Deere and Doss 2006).

nonetheless, in most countries, a larger share of homeowners are still men (Deere, Alvarado, and Twyman 2012).[24] All these factors reduce women's wealth compared with that of men, with implications for gender equality in families.

Gender wealth inequalities among couples often originate in what each partner is able to bring to marriage. Through local surveys conducted in six developing countries, a study found that husbands considerably exceed wives in either the number or the value of assets that they bring to marriage (Hallman et al. 2005).

Globally, dowry systems differ on whether assets are transferred from the bride's family directly to the wife (giving her an endowment at the time of marriage), as in China and historically in Latin America, or to the husband and/or his family, as in India. The latter system can result in substantial wealth inequality between husband and wife at the time of marriage, although it also depends on the composition of the dowry. If part is paid as gold jewelry, this tends to be considered the wife's property (Srinivasan and Bedi 2007). Differences in initial spousal wealth are then reproduced during the marriage due to gender differences in labor market opportunities and/or inheritance practices.

Research has shown that more equal access to income and wealth between husband and wife has positive effects on shared decision-making, more equal work burdens, and improved family wellbeing. A study of women in rural Bangladesh found that women who earned income had more say in purchasing decisions (Anderson and Eswaran 2009). Women's land ownership in Nepal was found to be associated with their having more autonomy not only in purchasing but also over their own health care and visits to family and friends, important for broader family wellbeing (Allendorf 2007). In the case of Ecuador, a study of how couples make decisions on whether or not to work and how to spend income found that women's share of couple wealth is a significant predictor of egalitarian decision-making (Deere and Twyman 2012).[25]

In countries where a woman's dowry is legally her property, its size has been found to be positively associated with the probability of husbands doing domestic labor, for example in Taiwan (Zhang and Chan 1999) and rural China (Brown 2009). This latter study also found that the size of a woman's dowry was positively related to the relative amount of time she dedicated to leisure activities, to household expenditures on "women's goods," and to her satisfaction with life. A small-scale study in Uganda focused on perceived differences in wealth and income between husbands and wives and found that husbands were more likely to participate in child care when wealth was considered to be equally distributed or shared than when there were differences between the spouses (Nkwake 2015).

Studies have also focused on the relationship between women's income and assets and other indicators of women's wellbeing, such as health and the incidence of intimate partner violence (the latter discussed in

Section 17.3.1.4b). In Indonesia, women's share of assets is associated with their obtaining prenatal and delivery care (Beegle, Frankenberg, and Thomas 2001). A higher female share of owned assets and income in marriage is also associated with improved outcomes for children – whether health outcomes in South Africa (Duflo 2003), Ethiopia (Fafchamps, Kebede, and Quisumbing 2009), or Nepal (Allendorf 2007); schooling attainment in Africa (Kumar and Quisumbing 2012; Doss et al. 2014); or both in urban Brazil (Thomas 1990) and Vietnam (Menon, van der Meulen Rodgers, and Huong 2014).[26] Studies of household budget shares have shown that women's ownership or share of assets is related to greater expenditures on education in Bangladesh, India, and South Africa (Quisumbing and Maluccio 2003) and on education and food in Ghana (Doss 2006).

In sum, there is substantial evidence, although not always consistent, that women's access to income and wealth is positively associated with an increase in their bargaining position within the household, more egalitarian gender relations, and enhanced family wellbeing, particularly of children.

17.3.1.3 The Gendered Division of Unpaid Labor in the Family

One of the main factors limiting women's labor force participation as well as the returns to their labor is the gendered division of unpaid labor in the family. Across the world, women bear more responsibility for unpaid housework and care labor than men. As noted in the introduction, in industrialized Western societies, the gap in the distribution of non-paid labor and care work between men and women has decreased considerably, although significantly more so in some countries than others (O'Brien and Shemilt 2003; Gauthier and DeGusti 2012; Nordenmark 2016). In no country, though, has this gender gap been eliminated. In most of the developing world, care and domestic labor still remain heavily the responsibility of women, limiting their ability to enter the labor force or make full use of their resources in the labor market. Overall, women's total labor time (paid and unpaid) tends to exceed men's, reducing their access to leisure and rest.

As Figure 17.2 shows, the gender gap in the time spent on unpaid labor in Latin America is large, particularly for women in their childbearing years, being around five hours per day. Moreover, when analyzed by household income quintiles, the gender gap is largest among the poorest households, since it is particularly poor women who dedicate the most time to unpaid labor, with little difference in the time spent by men across quintiles (ECLAC 2009).

Traditional gender roles tend to be reinforced when couples have children. Across cultures, being married and the presence of small children are found to lower the employment rates of women; the opposite is true for men (Esping-Andersen 2009; UN Women 2015). Indeed, men may typically receive what is referred to as a "fatherhood premium" (Budig and England 2001; Gangl and Ziefle 2009; Killewald and Gough

---

[24] Ranging from 73 percent in Guatemala to gender parity in Nicaragua and Panama.

[25] Egalitarian decision-making was defined as where both men and women report making these decisions jointly, and agree that the other spouse does in fact participate in them.

[26] See Doss (2013) for a summary of the intra-household bargaining literature and the methodological challenges involved, particularly the problem of endogeneity. The positive association between women's bargaining power and the various outcomes does seem to be sensitive to the choice of proxy and specific cultural contexts.

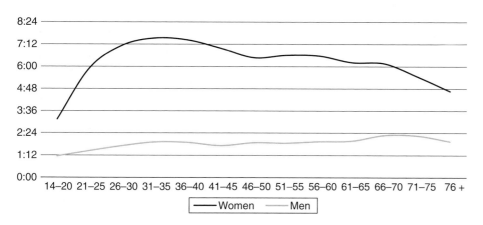

Figure 17.2 | Average time allocated to unpaid labor by sex and age, Latin America (daily hours).
Source: Compiled from ECLAC (2009, 2012: fig IV.26); unweighted average for five countries, for time-use surveys from mid-2000s.

2013). Many mothers exit the labor force or reduce their work hours upon having children, especially if they have a steady partner who works (Evertsson 2012; Baxter et al. 2015). In some cases, employers discriminate a priori on the basis of sex and gender role expectations and avoid hiring mothers of young children in both developed (Correll and Benard 2007; Budig 2014) and developing countries (Heymann 2006; Blofield and Madalozzo 2017).

Research shows that while some mothers prefer to stay at home with their children, especially in the first years, the availability and acceptability of alternative care arrangements increases mothers' labor force participation rates. Thus, when given the option, many women prefer to remain in the labor force after having children (De Laat and Sevilla-Sanz 2011; Boeckmann, Misra, and Budig 2014). Many analyses have demonstrated that expanding access to paid leave, child care, tax incentives for second earners, and flexible scheduling has increased women's labor force participation across OECD economies (Thévenon 2013). The literature on Latin America shows similar results; studies have found that access to affordable early childhood education and care (ECEC) or full-day school has a positive effect on mothers' labor force participation rates (Medrano 2009; Contreras, Paulina Sepúlveda, and Cabrera 2010). Other studies show that access to formal ECEC enables mothers to go from part time to full time and/or to switch from informal to formal work (Hallman et al. 2005; Chioda 2011).

Without changes in gender norms, well-intentioned policies can backfire. Long paid leaves and abundant part-time options risk "mommy-tracking" career-oriented women into part-time or lower-level positions (Blau and Kahn 2013). Thus, the challenge lies equally in fostering more paternal co-responsibility and changing the division of labor at home.

Studies show that when fathers participate more in care and housework, mothers are also more likely to work. So-called "father's quotas," which are individual non-transferable entitlements to paid parental leave, have been a way to provide strong incentives for men to become more involved at home (Moss 2015). The literature on

developed countries shows that such policies enable fathers' increased participation in care, including after the leave is over (Nepomnyaschy and Waldfogel 2007; Tanaka and Waldfogel 2007; Arnalds, Eydal, and Gíslason 2013), with better health and life satisfaction for fathers and increased gender equality both at home and in the labor market (O'Brien 2009; Huerta et al. 2013; Moss 2015).

Even when the gender gap in employment is due to preferences – mothers genuinely prefer to stay home with the children, and fathers prefer to work outside the home – it can aggravate gender inequalities within the family due to the reduction in women's income vis-à-vis men, with the effects outlined earlier. It can also endanger the material security of the family as a whole. These work interruptions reduce the wages and social protections of low-income households, increasing the financial hardship of these families. They also make old-age poverty among women, specifically, more likely (ILO/UNDP 2009; Gerecke 2013). Overall, evidence from advanced industrialized countries and Latin America indicates that dual-income families are less likely to be in poverty (ECLAC 2009, 2012; Esping-Andersen 2009).[27] The differential impact of these gender roles on women and men can, to an extent, be "equalized" by outsourcing. Women can ameliorate the "second shift" at home often by using their earnings on market substitutes for domestic work (Hochschild and Machung 1989; Killewald 2011). In many developing countries, and increasingly in many developed countries, this substitution has involved the hiring of paid domestic workers, who, given high rates of poverty and inequality either domestically or globally, are relatively inexpensive for the well-to-do (Hondagneau-Sotelo 2001; Palriwala and Neetha 2010; Parreñas 2015). States have historically "subsidized" this form of labor by maintaining discriminatory labor laws toward paid domestic workers, mandating longer legal work hours and lower benefits and protections (Blofield 2012). In Latin America, the region with the highest economic inequalities in the world, paid domestic workers made up a sizable 17.4 percent of female employment in 2010 (ILO 2013).

This dynamic of paid domestic labor shows that inequalities between families affect and are affected by inequalities within families in two

---

[27]   In low- and middle-income developing countries both partners' work may be insufficient to lift them above the poverty line, particularly if they are both employed in agriculture or in the urban informal sector.

ways. First, highly educated professionals tend to increasingly marry each other, thus earning higher incomes (Mintz 2015). Second, unequal gender roles tend to be less entrenched among more educated couples. These couples are better able to outsource, and at the same time more likely to share in domestic tasks, thus reducing the double burden on the woman (Esping-Andersen 2009).

The double burden tends to be most deeply felt among lower-income women, especially mothers, and especially in developing countries. Lower-income women are less able to outsource a share of their domestic burden given their lower purchasing power; at the same time, they are less likely to have participatory partners at home. Partly due to these factors, mothers in lower-income quintiles are less likely to be employed than mothers in higher-income quintiles, across countries. The employment gap is starkest in Latin America, where the employment rates of women aged 25 to 34 in 2013 were 80 percent in the highest income quintile, compared with 39 percent in the lowest (Filgueira and Martínez Franzoni 2017). In Sub-Saharan Africa and other areas of the world where rural subsistence economies predominate, gaps are lower due to the fact that both men and women work in agriculture, though they do not always have equal access to the fruits of their production, as discussed earlier.

Lower-income women, when employed, are more likely to work in the informal sector (often as nannies or maids for the well-to-do). They are likely to experience higher levels of stress than fathers as they juggle the competing demands of work and family with few resources (Heymann 2006; Blofield and Madalozzo 2017). While the vast majority of mothers continue to reside with their families, an increasing number migrate domestically from rural to urban communities or internationally from poor (particularly Indonesia and the Philippines) to rich countries. The migration of women results in an international division of reproductive labor (Parreñas 2000), or what Hochschild (2001) has referred to as a care chain. In it, women rely on migrant domestic workers, most often female, who in turn rely on other family members, virtually always female, to care for the family they have left behind in the process of migration.

17.3.1.4 Bodily Integrity

17.3.1.4a Reproductive Autonomy

Bodily integrity – in the form of sexual and reproductive autonomy, on the one hand, and freedom from violence on the other – are fundamental aspects of individual and family wellbeing. States provide the framework in which couples bear – or do not bear – children, and the conditions under which this occurs, including whether it takes place without undue physical, financial, or psychological hardship. The state also plays an important role in ensuring (or not) the bodily integrity of individuals in terms of both reproductive autonomy and freedom from violence, within – and beyond – families.

While male partners may be involved and affected, the consequences of the inability to avoid or terminate pregnancies, and to choose

when to have children, weigh much more heavily on women and girls. Terminating a pregnancy in unsafe conditions can result in bodily harm and even death of the woman, while carrying a child to term also holds significant health risks, especially in less-developed countries. Unwanted pregnancies affect the short-, medium-, and long-term schooling and careers of women to a much larger extent than those of men, reinforcing gender inequalities in relationships. Finally, in terms of the family as a whole, unintended or unwanted pregnancies are more likely to result in children living in poverty.

Control over reproduction and family planning has historically been in male hands, whether male heads of households, male religious authorities, or male state leaders. Individual autonomy in reproductive decisions has gradually become more broadly accepted as a dominant principle, although not without contestation. Concerns about public health, in particular, have driven practical concerns in the context of high rates of clandestine abortions and unwanted pregnancies, particularly among poor families. Progress has been slow and uneven. For example, in the United States, it was only in 1972 that the right of unmarried women to birth control was affirmed in a Supreme Court decision, following a century of very restrictive regulation of family planning.

In developed economies, liberalized access to contraception and abortion has provided women with more freedom to plan reproduction around their education and career instead of being forced to prioritize their domestic obligations (Goldin and Katz 2002). Along with these changes, medical advances have given women and couples more control over reproduction, both in prevention, termination, and assisted reproductive technologies such as in vitro fertilization.

Advances in technology have also given rise to commodified exchanges in reproduction via surrogacy, which is today a billion-dollar business. Due to legal restrictions and economic dynamics, surrogacy is concentrated in certain countries, including India, Thailand, the United States, Ukraine, and, more recently, Mexico (Pande 2014; Rudrappa 2015). More broadly, while reproductive technology has helped the reproduction of the privileged, it has a history of being used against the less privileged, for example with the forced sterilization of certain minorities in the United States (Roberts 1998; Briggs 2002; Gutierrez 2008).

In terms of actual behavior, there has been a dramatic decline in fertility rates across the world over the past half century; the global fertility rate has been halved from 5 children per woman in 1960 to 2.5 in 2012.[28] In 2014, all countries with fertility rates higher than 4.5 children per woman, with the exception of Afghanistan and East Timor, were in Sub-Saharan Africa, and all had low levels of development and low status of women.

Despite the decline in fertility, 40 percent of pregnancies worldwide are unintended. This is not simply a problem of developing countries; in the United States, half of pregnancies are unintended (AGI 2014; Sedgh et al. 2016). While unintended pregnancies are problematic

---

[28] See the World Bank Data Blog at https://blogs.worldbank.org/opendata/between960-and012-world-average-fertility-rate-halved5-births-woman.

across all age and income groups, they are particularly so for girls, with lasting socio-economic effects, including compromised educational and labor market opportunities (Micklewright and Stewart 2000; AGI 2015). Studies have repeatedly found that pregnancies among teenagers tend to be the result of lack of information about and access to contraception.

Closely linked to unintended pregnancies, an estimated 225 million women worldwide have an unmet need for modern contraceptives (Singh, Darroch, and Ashford 2014). Globally, 25 percent of pregnancies end in induced abortion, mostly as a result of unintended pregnancy, with a higher rate among married women. The rate in developed countries for the overall number of abortions per 1,000 women of childbearing age (15–44 years old) is lower, at 27 per 1000, down from 46 in the early 1990s, while in developing countries it has remained roughly the same at 37 per 1,000 women (Sedgh et al. 2016).

When performed by trained professionals, induced abortion is very safe for the woman. Restrictive laws, on the other hand, are not only ineffective in reducing the incidence of abortion but also force the procedure underground. The abortion rate in countries where abortion is prohibited altogether, or permitted only to save the woman's life, is 37 per 1,000 woman, while the abortion rate in countries that allow it on demand is 34 per 1,000 women (AGI 2016a; Sedgh et al. 2016). The main difference is that in countries that restrict access, almost seven million women are annually treated for post-abortion complications, and many who should be are not; it is estimated that 40 percent of those needing treatment do not receive it (AGI 2016a). Low-income women are most vulnerable to post-abortion complications (Blofield 2008).

The countries that best provide women and girls with the ability to exercise reproductive freedom are those with comprehensive family planning services, including sex education from an age when girls and boys begin sexual relations (rather than when authorities think they should start), access to contraception through public or subsidized health services, and access to abortion services on demand. These include most Western European countries, aside from Ireland. In these nations, abortion is used as a relatively rare last resort, with virtually all abortions performed safely.

In heavily patriarchal countries, abortions may also be used to engage in sex selection and female feticide, a widespread phenomenon in Asian countries, giving rise to an increasingly smaller share of girls born each year (Sen 2003).

States everywhere have grappled with the role and rights of the sexual partners of women, and the parents of girls, on issues of reproductive choice. The global trend has been to eliminate husbands' rights to veto wives' decisions in access to contraception and abortion. In the United

States, where abortion regulations remain a highly controversial issue, 38 states require parental involvement in the case of abortion for minors (AGI 2016b) despite evidence that such restrictions have led to clandestine abortions and even deaths from complications.

The other side of reproductive autonomy is the ability to choose to *have* children regardless of material and family circumstances, and to bear and raise a child without undue physical, financial, or social hardship. The most basic and brutal measure of the cost of bearing a child is maternal mortality. Efforts to reduce maternal mortality, bolstered by the Millennium Development Goals, have resulted in a 44 percent drop in rates between 1990 and 2015. Still, 830 women die from maternal mortality every day, and 99 percent of these women live in developing countries (WHO 2016a). These deaths are largely preventable.

The financial and social aspects of this dimension – bearing and raising a child without hardship – will be addressed in more detail below in the adult–child relationships section. Data from OECD countries suggests that the ideal family size of couples in the West tends to be around two children (Esping-Andersen 2009). Some countries face problems of "fertility crises," where fertility rates have dropped to way below replacement level. A very low fertility rate is problematic not only because it contradicts the expressed desires of couples, but also because it means that fewer future workers will bear the cost of supporting the elderly (Esping-Andersen 2009).

17.3.1.4b Intimate Partner Violence

There is no manifestation of individual harm in a relationship more severe than intimate partner violence (IPV) – physical, sexual, emotional, and economic violence suffered by a person, in the vast majority of cases a woman, at the hands of a current or former partner.[29,30] A recent World Health Organization (WHO) report considers IPV prevalence to be at "epidemic" proportions; 30 percent of women worldwide who have been married or have been in a consensual union have experienced physical or sexual violence (WHO 2013).[31] IPV rates vary by region, with the highest incidence of lifetime violence being reported in Southeast Asia, the Middle East, and Sub-Saharan Africa, and the lowest in high-income countries as well as East Asia.[32] The high IPV prevalence has tremendous economic, social, and health consequences for women, their families, communities, and societies.

Almost half of the women who experience physical or sexual IPV report sustaining physical injuries requiring medical assistance. Compared with women who have not experienced IPV, these women are more than twice as likely to have experienced an unintended pregnancy that ended in induced abortion, almost twice as likely to experience depression, and more likely to have a premature or low-weight birth (WHO

---

[29]   Violence against women also includes violence carried out by those other than spouses or partners, as well as all forms of sexual violence, trafficking of women, female genital mutilation, and honor killings (WHO 2013).

[30]   Men are also the victims of IPV at the hands of women. However, these rates are much lower in both developed and developing countries. For example, in the United States the prevalence is much lower than female victimization and tends to have fewer severe physical or emotional consequences; also, it often takes place in the context of bi-directional violence (Williams, Ghandar, and Kub 2008; WHO and London School of Hygiene and Tropical Medicine 2010).

[31]   The WHO study provides the most reliable regional and global estimates to date and is a mega-review of current studies. It did not include emotional violence, as this is measured less consistently across different studies. In most country-level surveys, the incidence of emotional abuse far exceeds that of physical or sexual IPV.

[32]   There can be considerable variation for countries within a region, as well as between rural and urban areas in a given country. See Abramsky et al. (2011).

2013: table 6). The economic consequences are large, ranging from direct health costs to the indirect costs of lost work days and earnings and lower productivity.[33] The starkest example of the high cost of IPV is when it leads to femicide. The WHO (2013) estimates that 38 percent of all female murders globally (compared with only 6 percent of male murders) are perpetuated by a current or former spouse or partner.[34]

Decades of research across disciplines in both developed and developing countries suggests a series of individual, relational, community, and societal risk factors associated with *both* women becoming victims of IPV, and men becoming perpetrators (Morrison et al. 2007; WHO and London School of Hygiene and Tropical Medicine 2010; Abramsky et al. 2011). Individual risk factors include witnessing their mother being the victim of abuse, experiencing physical or sexual abuse themselves as a child, the harmful use of alcohol as a trigger factor, and the acceptance of violence as justifiable behavior. Relational risk factors include controlling behavior by the husband, marital discord, and large age and educational gaps between spouses. Community-level risk factors include high neighborhood unemployment, poverty, and/or crime rates, a high proportion of illiteracy, and the presence of individuals who justify wife-beating.

Gender inequality is strongly associated with high rates of IPV. WHO studies emphasize that IPV is most prevalent where traditional gender norms based on male authority and control over women prevail:

> Gender inequality and male dominance reduces the opportunities for women to be involved in decision-making at every level; decreases the resources available to women; and increases acceptance of the use of violence against women. Furthermore, it contributes to gender-based inequalities in health and access to health care; in opportunities for employment and promotion; in levels of income; in political participation and representation; and in education. (WHO and London School of Hygiene and Tropical Medicine 2010: 26)

Considerable scholarly attention has been given to the relationship between a woman's status in family and society and the incidence of IPV. Most studies focus on whether women's education, employment, and/or earnings act as deterrents to IPV. Systematic reviews of the evidence from developing countries find that the most consistent result is that women's education is associated with a lower risk of physical violence, particularly, their having completed secondary schooling (Vyas and Watts 2009; Abramsky et al. 2011). Whether women are economically active is not associated with any consistent pattern in developing or developed countries for various reasons. While a number of studies have found a negative relation between women's employment and/or income and the odds of IPV, supporting the bargaining

power hypothesis (Farmer and Tiefenthaler 1997), others have found no relation, or even a backlash effect.[35] One of the main empirical problems in analyzing the precise relation between women's employment and IPV is that both the likelihood of employment and a lower risk of violence may be due to the same, unmeasured characteristics of the woman (a problem known as endogeneity).[36] Studies that control for endogeneity, either econometrically or by using experimental methods, tend to find support for the bargaining power hypothesis, such as among poor women in the US (Gibson-Davis et al. 2005), and in Mexico (Villareal 2007) and Uttar Pradesh in India (Bhattacharyya, Bedi, and Chhachhi 2011).

In the context of developing countries it has also been argued that women's access to employment or income might not strengthen women's fallback position in as powerful a way as might their ownership of assets (Panda and Agarwal 2005). Much depends on the type and quality of employment and whether women directly control the income they earn. Moreover, assets may provide more security than income, since ownership of a dwelling or land may provide women with a concrete exit option, a place to move to. The potential protective role of women themselves owning a dwelling has been confirmed in recent studies in India (Panda and Agarwal 2005; ICRW 2006; Bhattacharyya, Bedi, and Chhachhi 2011) as well as the United States (Resko 2010). Evidence of such a relationship in the case of land, however, is mixed, with some studies finding that it is associated with reduced risk of IPV (Panda and Agarwal 2005), others finding no effect (ICRW 2006), and still others that women's land ownership increases the likelihood of lifetime physical violence, such as in Uganda, where women owning land goes strongly against traditional norms (Ezeh and Gage 2000). Another study, drawing on the extensive literature on the role of status differences in couples, suggests that rather than examining the ownership of particular assets (whose importance may vary depending on the context), women's ownership of assets should be examined relative to their partners. In Ecuador, women's share of couple wealth was found to be a protective factor against physical IPV, and in Ghana, against emotional abuse (Oduro, Deere, and Catanzarite 2015).

The state plays a crucial role in ameliorating – or aggravating – gender inequalities. The expansion of legal assistance programs across the US after the Violence against Women Act of 1994 was passed has been associated with a dramatic decline in IPV: 21 percent between 1993 and 1998 (Farmer and Tienfenthaler 2003). Ease of access to protective orders and assistance with custody issues and child support all strengthen women's fallback position by making exit from a relationship more feasible.[37]

---

[33]   See Kabeer (2014: table 2) for a summary of the studies estimating the economic costs of IPV, for some countries reaching up to 2 percent of GDP.

[34]   In South Asia, another form of violence against women resulting in death is dowry-related violence or "bride burning," when the bride's family fails to meet the dowry demands of the husband and his family. Although dowry has been illegal in India since 1961, according to government data the number of reported dowry deaths increased from 6,995 in 2000 to 8,391 in 2010 (reported in Kabeer 2014).

[35]   This might be expected given the different methodologies employed, including the reference period (lifetime or past-year IPV), the group analyzed (current- or ever-partnered women), and how women's economic status is measured (absolutely or in terms of couple status differences).

[36]   Both variables might be determined by the same factor, for example, by the controlling behavior of the husband (Kishor and Johnson 2004). See Moe and Bell (2004) for a study on how IPV in the US negatively affects women's employment and employability.

[37]   This same analysis found that the increased provision of other services to victims at the county level, such as shelters and hotlines, did not impact the reporting of abuse. Other factors associated with the decline of IPV in the US include women's rising economic status and the aging of the population. According to the US Bureau of Justice Statistics, IPV has continued to decline in the US, falling 64 percent between 1993 and 2010 (BJS 2012).

Recognition in the global arena of the gravity of IPV for families and society and of women's right to live a life free of violence dates from the 1993 UN Declaration on the Elimination of Violence against Women, which recognized violence against women as a violation of women's human rights. The 1995 Beijing Declaration of the Fourth UN World Conference on Women provided even stronger condemnation and an agenda for action, and the issue was subsequently incorporated into the CEDAW reporting process by states. Regional conventions, such as the 1994 Belém do Pará Inter-American Convention on Violence against Women and subsequent treaties and resolutions in Africa, Europe, and the Middle East have played important roles in galvanizing states to develop more comprehensive legislation against IPV, including its criminalization, and to begin to address the causes and consequences of violence against women.[38]

Most studies conclude that a comprehensive effort is required at all levels (individual, relational, community, and societal) to reduce the prevalence of IPV and provide victims of abuse with access to justice and appropriate services (Morrison et al. 2007; WHO and London School of Hygiene and Tropical Medicine 2010). There is consensus that much depends on changing social norms among both men and women, and that strong legislation sanctioning IPV and promoting gender equality is a critical first step. For the overall wellbeing of current and former partners and their families, policies that give the more vulnerable member viable exit options without suffering devastating financial, physical, or emotional consequences are crucial. Having such viable exit options also allows couples to foster meaningful, positive relations.

In addition, partner relations exist within a broader community. Aside from the state, factors outside of the household such as the extended family and the community also play an important role, both directly and indirectly, in providing the conditions for fulfilling, meaningful, and egalitarian relationships. The extended family can enhance women's access to resources and ensure that they are able to exercise control over these resources. Their support may also reduce marital conflict, particularly where sons and daughters both inherit land and post-marital residence may just as likely be uxorilocal (near the wife's family) as patrilocal, such as in portions of the Andes of South America (Deere and León 2001). Social norms are often most keenly felt at the community level, particularly sanctions in support of traditional gender roles and behavior. And social practices can also be difficult to change. A good example is the practice of dowry in India, which, while illegal, continues and is associated with both IPV and other family violence against women, because either no dowry was paid to the husband's family or the amount was deemed insufficient, at the extreme leading to "bride burning" with relative impunity.

But communities are also an important driver of progressive change, such as when women organize to form their own organizations. The literature on women's empowerment shows how women's organizations can enhance women's self-esteem and how organized women may influence social norms, leading to positive changes in intra-household

relations and bargaining power (Agarwal 1997; Rowlands 1997; Pearse and Connell 2016).

In sum, there is good evidence that the overall tendency toward more gender-equitable family law and greater gender equality in education, labor force participation, and asset ownership is associated with improvements in women's bodily integrity, and in the wellbeing of the family as a whole. At the same time, these links are not automatic, and require concerted efforts by the state to both provide and enforce a legal framework in support of gender equality.

17.3.2 Adults and Children

One of the most important functions that families perform is the rearing of children. This section considers how societies can support families in providing the caretaking and human development that children need to become flourishing adults, while at the same time ensuring children's individual dignity and protecting them from harm. To do so, we consider three key dimensions of children's wellbeing: ensuring material provision; supporting caregiving for emotional, social, and human development; and protecting them from abuse and neglect.[39]

17.3.2.1   Material Provision for Children

Except in extraordinary circumstances, families are the unit in which children are raised into adults. They are also a key source of material provision for children. Children have little or no capacity to generate independent sources of labor income to meet their basic needs. They therefore need considerable material provision in their early years, and the only way these needs can be satisfied is through transfers – in the form of goods and services – from those whose production exceeds their consumption (Mason and Lee 2011). When families are primarily responsible for the transfers, the quantity and quality of the goods and services each child receives has a ceiling: that of their family's resources. In these conditions, income inequalities between families translate into inequality of opportunity for children. When such inequalities leave a large share of families with children below basic levels of wellbeing, they tend to cause long-lasting harm in child development, as documented in a large-scale study of families across developing countries (Heymann 2006). Indeed, all evidence shows that children's first years of life are *critical* in terms of further development and capacities.

State policies can ameliorate these inequalities. For example, taxes and spending can redistribute life chances and opportunities via public or subsidized education, health care, family allowances, in-kind transfers (food, clothes, transport), and other income transfers.

Table 17.1 shows the percentage of children and young people's monetary consumption, and specifically health and education consumption, that is financed by their own families or by the state in a select group

---

[38] As of 2015, 119 countries had some sort of legislation proscribing domestic violence and/or violence against women (UN Women 2015).

[39] The fourth dimension of participation has been emphasized in the Convention of Children's Rights, but as this has already been addressed in the section on family recognition we do not discuss it here.

Table 17.1 | Percentage of monetary consumption by children and young adults (ages 0–24) financed by the state or by families themselves, selected countries ~*2010

	Consumption		Health and education	
	Public share	**Private share**	**Public share**	**Private share**
All economies (23 countries)	33.9	66.1	69.4	30.6
Africa (2)	18.4	81.6	36.4	63.6
East Asia and China (3)	18.4	81.6	36.4	63.6
South and Southeast Asia (4)	22.9	77.1	61.1	38.9
Latin America (5)	27.9	72.1	62.4	37.6
Europe and US (8)	46.9	53.1	88.7	11.3

Note: * Synthetic cohort values.
Source: Mason and Lee (2011: 16).

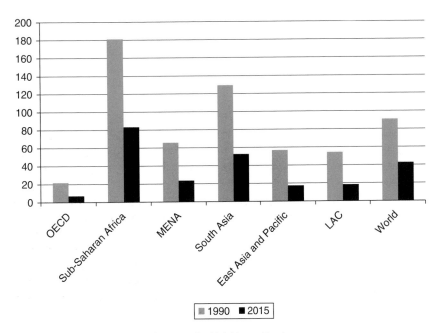

Figure 17.3 | Under-five mortality (per 1,000 live births) by world region.
Note: See Figure 17.1 for acronyms.
Source: Compiled from World Bank (2016).

of countries. While this data does not take into account non-market production (specifically, women's care labor in support of children), it demonstrates the stark differences across regions in state support for children.

As Table 17.1 shows, in the African and East Asian countries (including China), less than 20 percent of a child's or young person's consumption is financed on average by the state, while in Europe and the United States almost 50 percent is. In public health and education spending, the difference ranges from less than 40 percent in the African and East Asian countries, again, to almost 90 percent in Europe and the United States.

Of particular concern are the children whose family resources put them below basic levels of child physical wellbeing. Taking one proxy

for this – the under-five child mortality rate – Figure 17.3 shows that considerable progress has been made over the past quarter century; the rate globally has been cut in half. Significant regional inequalities, nonetheless, remain. Seven out of 1,000 children born in OECD countries will not survive to school age, while 83 out of 1,000 children in Sub-Saharan Africa – almost one in ten – will not.

Figure 17.4 shows regional rates of child poverty, as measured by the World Bank thresholds of income poverty based on living on less than $2/day (poverty) and less than $1.25/day (extreme poverty).[40] This measure gives us a glimpse of the extent of material deprivation among children around the world.

The unmet material needs of children vary by region: 80 percent of children in Sub-Saharan Africa and in South Asia; 60 percent of children in

---

[40] Material poverty is difficult to measure across countries and regions, due to a variety of challenges, including differences in the cost of living and access to non-monetary goods (e.g. subsistence agriculture). Nonetheless, the World Bank figures give us a general idea.

17

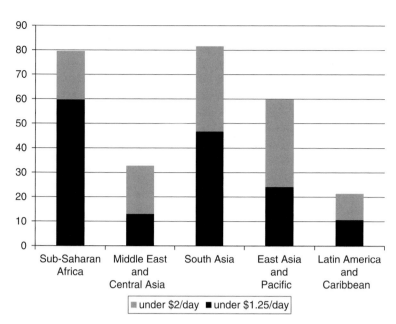

Figure 17.4 | Percentage of children living in income poverty.
Source: UNICEF (2014: 7).

East Asia and the Pacific; just over 30 percent of children in the Middle East and Central Asia; and 20 percent of children in Latin America and the Caribbean live on less than $2/day. In Sub-Saharan Africa, the majority of children live on less than $1.25/day. In all regions, rates of child poverty exceed poverty rates for the general population by 3 to 7 percent (UNICEF 2014:7).

Material poverty is of course less extreme in developed countries, and the share of the population living in poverty according to the above measures in these countries is negligible. Yet the OECD measure of relative poverty – the proportion of children living in households with average incomes below 50 percent of the median income – reveals a range of child poverty rates of just over 20 percent in the United States to less than 10 percent in the five Nordic countries, with Denmark and Finland at less than 3 percent (OECD 2017).

Certainly the causes of child poverty are varied. The role of the state, however, is central, as shown in Table 17.1. Countries that have relied more heavily on market provision generally have higher child poverty rates, the United States being a case in point. Despite its wealth, the United States has the highest child poverty rate of advanced industrialized countries. In the absence of a more assertive state role in providing material security and basic services, low-income families have not been able to ensure the material wellbeing of their children.

States address poverty and social risks through different sets of measures and levels of policy effort. Notwithstanding the wide variety of policies, the evidence indicates that the most efficient way to ensure a basic level of material wellbeing for families with children is to ensure them an income floor, whether through paid employment of adults accompanied by affordable care services, or through cash transfers. Most OECD countries (with the exception of the United States) and Eastern European and Central Asian countries, as well as China, already provide some kind of guaranteed minimum-income scheme (Lindert 2013: 8), and cash transfers to impoverished families

have become a widespread policy tool in developing countries in the past two decades. With the latter, it has become common to target mothers, given the evidence (as discussed earlier) that mothers more reliably spend the transfers on children and family wellbeing. Such transfers are most likely to reduce poverty when they are substantial in size, and provided on the basis of need, with non-restrictive criteria. Often they are conditional on ensuring school attendance and health checkups of children, as in most of Latin America, where by 2012 such programs reached 25 percent of the population (Stampini and Tornarolli 2012). By 2010, such conditional cash transfer programs had been adopted by 40 countries in Asia, Africa, the Middle East, and Latin America (Lindert 2013: 13).

Policies that ensure a financial floor for children seek to counter some of the policy legacies that heavily focus transfers on the elderly, a much more politically organized constituency across countries. A study on Spain and Italy in the 1990s found that the percentage of children in poverty increased after government taxes and transfers (Bradshaw 1999:402), and a study on Brazil in 2008 found that children were 20 times more likely to live in extreme poverty than the elderly (IPEA 2008).

Cash transfer policies are especially crucial for the increasing number of female-headed households around the world, which are often (though not always) more likely to be low-income and poor. A significant proportion of fathers who do not live with their offspring do not financially support them, and even fewer contribute to their caretaking, leaving mothers, and sometimes extended families, on their own with the burden of providing both sustenance and care (Bartfield and Meyer 2003; Smyth et al. 2014). Indeed, the social conditions of lone-mother families have been identified as a litmus test of social citizenship in the literature on advanced industrialized countries (see Orloff 1993; Lewis 1997). In the United States, where support for single mothers is meager, half of single-mother families live in poverty (Legal Momentum 2011). In many developing countries, single mothers struggle with both

17

higher material scarcity and lower state capacity to enforce policies such as child support. One study of 400 low-income families in São Paulo found that half of non-resident fathers never contributed any child support, and less than 5 percent cared for their child once a week or more (Blofield and Madalozzo 2017). Such struggles are even more prevalent in countries such as South Africa where 65 percent of families have only one parent present. The higher concentration of female-headed households among the lower-income quintiles also aggravates inequalities between families.

17.3.2.2   Caring for Children

In addition to material provision, children need significant caretaking during their early years to become flourishing adults. They also need stable attachments to at least a few adults. An increase in women's employment, more distance from extended family, and higher conjugal instability have transformed caring for children. Each of these challenges will be discussed in this section.

17.3.2.2a   Policies that Reconcile Work and Family

With the massive increase of women in the labor force, states have grappled with updating the maternalist assumptions that have implicitly or explicitly guided public policies, namely, that mothers will privately accomplish optimal levels of child care with some help from female relatives and fathers. States have two direct ways of helping parents reconcile paid and unpaid work responsibilities. The first, employment-based leave, allows mothers and increasingly fathers to take breaks from employment to care for children at home. The second way is to support the defamilialization of care by providing public or subsidized early education and care services that both promote children's development and enable parents to remain in paid employment.

17.3.2.2b   Parental Leave and Work–Life Balance

Market forces put considerable pressure on the time that parents have available for caregiving. Employment-based paid leave that allows workers time off to care for dependents plays an important part in both ensuring the financial security of families and meeting the need of young children for parental care. The overwhelmingly positive effects of paid maternity leave have been extensively documented, for the health of newborns (and thus an investment in child wellbeing and human capital down the road), for the health of the mother (recovery from childbirth, initiation of breast-feeding), for the ability of especially the mother to remain in the labor force, and for the income security of the family at a particularly vulnerable time (Gauthier 1996; Berger, Hill, and Waldfogel 2005; Aitken et al. 2015), as well as in the future, since mothers' employment is linked with child wellbeing (Esping-Andersen 2009). Thus, paid maternity leave has become globally accepted as almost a universal right in principle, with the exception of the United States, Papua New Guinea, and Suriname. Increasingly, such leave has been extended to fathers, although significant parental leave, and especially paternity leave beyond a few days, has mainly been restricted to advanced industrialized countries. Parental leave has also been extended to adoptive couples in many countries (Moss 2015).

How paid leave is financed, and the levels at which wages are replaced, dramatically affects access to leave for families at different income levels (Gornick and Meyers 2003; Ray, Gornick, and Smith 2009). Paid leave is generally provided through social insurance schemes funded by some combination of employee and employer contributions or through tax revenues (Moss 2015). Socializing the costs also helps reduce employer discrimination against those who are eligible for such leave, mostly mothers but sometimes fathers (Gornick and Myers 2003).

Given that more than half of the world's population works informally, many of them self-employed, laws on the books may mean little in practice. While the cash transfer schemes mentioned earlier have reached some of these families, they tend to be meager and in any case do not reach all informally working parents. Equally important are policies that encourage the extension of social security systems and the strengthening of state capacity more broadly, so that laws can benefit – and obligate – all citizens. For example, increases in formalization in Brazil led to maternity leave coverage going from 26 to 41 percent of new mothers between 2000 and 2011 (Blofield and Martínez Franzoni 2015).

Beyond legislated leave, encouraging reasonable, flexible work hours for both employees and the self-employed enables parents to spend time with their children in meaningful ways on a daily basis. Of course, providing more opportunities to spend time together does not guarantee families will do so, nor does it guarantee family wellbeing, but it makes both more likely. For example, sitting down together for a family meal is often seen as meaningful time together. One study found that eating meals together as a family was the most important predictor of adolescent flourishing, controlling for background characteristics (Zarrett and Lerner 2008, cited in World Family Map 2015: 39).

17.3.2.2c   Institutionalized Early Childhood Education and Care

Children's access to caretaking outside the home, especially after their first year, is also important for their development. The beneficial educational effects of good-quality early childhood care, in terms of promoting both equal opportunity and human capital overall, have been extensively documented (OECD 2012). Indeed, children's equal access to early childhood education and care services is crucial for child wellbeing, equal opportunities, and human capital later in life, since children who have been to ECEC do better in elementary and high school, and even much later in life, compared with other children (Esping-Andersen 2009; Nielsen and Cristoffersen 2009; Heckman 2012). Studies have also shown the cost-effectiveness of early education; in Canada, Akbari and McCuaig (2014) showed that for every dollar invested, $1.75 was recouped through taxes paid by parents and the reduced spending on social programs.

Early education and care services have been shown to be most effective in supporting family wellbeing when they focus not just on children's educational and social needs, but also on ensuring that both parents can work (Gornick and Meyers 2003). Most European countries have developed publicly supported day care institutions for children, and

17

coverage has increased. Denmark had the highest share of children aged 0–2 years in day care at 68 percent in 2013, closely followed by many others. The participation rates for children aged between three and five have also been increasing and are now over 80 percent in the majority of OECD countries (OECD n.d.). By contrast, in Asia and Latin America governments are slowly investing more in ECEC, but are still not keeping up with demand (Blofield and Martínez Franzoni 2015; Peng 2016).

Other countries, notably the United States, have invested far less in ensuring that children have access to high-quality ECEC (Gornick and Meyers 2003; Child Care Aware of America, 2013). The United States does not provide public day care or early education for young children, nor does it generally subsidize private day care for children, even for families who could not otherwise afford it. In addition, the United States has no compulsory federal standards for safety, staffing, or teaching curricula for early childhood care or education. The result is that most day care in the United States has been judged by experts to be poor to mediocre (Child Care Aware of America 2013). Moreover, these day care options are generally far more expensive than middle- and low-income parents can afford. In 2011, the average annual cost of center-based infant care was more than the annual in-state tuition at public four-year colleges in 35 states; for a four-year-old, average costs exceeded tuition costs in 19 states (Child Care Aware of America 2012). As a result, only 28 percent of children aged 0–2 in the US were enrolled in formal child care in 2010, and only 66.5 percent of children aged between three and five years.

17.3.2.2d   Paternal Care, Custody Arrangements, Role of Grandparents and Extended Family

In an era in which conjugal relationships dissolve frequently, special attention must be paid to ensuring children's continued ties to both parents. Considerable research establishes that children who maintain significant relationships with both parents do notably better than those who simply maintain ties to one parent, provided that the relationship between the parents is relatively low-conflict (Verschuere and Marcoen 1999; Sarkadi et al. 2008). Children's relationships with non-resident parents can play an important role in supporting child development, promoting academic success, and increasing self-esteem in children (Amato 2005; Amato and Gilbreth 1999). Studies also demonstrate a correlation between absent fathers and negative outcomes for children – including early sexual activity, risky behavior, and delinquency (Ellis et al. 2003; McLanahan, Tach, and Schneider 2013). Given this, all countries in the European Union, for example, recognize that children have the right to a personal relationship with both parents.

Shared physical custody is one means to support children's relationship with both parents. Shared parenting (in other words, frequent, continuing, and meaningful contact with both parents) is today permitted and often encouraged in most developed countries, although the specifics of the arrangements can differ markedly. Social science research strongly supports shared parenting as contributing to children's wellbeing when conflict is low and both parents agree to it (Buchanan, Maccoby, and Dornbusch 1996; McIntosh and Chisholm, 2008; Smyth et al. 2014). The empirical evidence is far less certain about the positive effects of shared parenting in circumstances beyond that in which both parents agree (Pruett and DiFonzo 2014; Smyth et al. 2016). Given that high-conflict custody arrangements can undermine the child's wellbeing, and especially when the threat of domestic violence is present (Pruett and DiFonzo 2014; Smyth 2014), imposing such arrangements in the absence of the consent of both parents is considerably more controversial.

Child support payments from the non-custodial parent are a critical source of income maintenance for children, particularly for lone parents in countries that do not have robust welfare states, which is most of the world. Although this means that single parents in countries that rely more on market provision, such as the UK, the US, and Canada, are especially dependent on child support, a much smaller percentage of such parents actually receive support than in countries with stronger welfare states. For example, in 2004, for those non-widowed lone parents in the US who received child support, this support made up 96 percent of the families' total social income transfers, compared with 24 percent in Sweden. Yet only 30 percent of non-widowed lone parents in the US received child support compared with 100 percent in Sweden, where the state guarantees the transfers (Hakovirta 2011: 254). We know less about developing countries, but research on Colombia suggests that, for custodial mothers in these countries, child support is less common but, when received, has an even greater impact on reducing poverty and extreme poverty for children than in developed countries (Cuesta and Meyer 2014: 70).

In the Nordic countries and Germany, the government directly provides child support whether or not the non-custodial parent pays it, ensuring that income to children (Skinner and Davidson 2009; Hakovirta 2011). In other countries, onerous child support awards can also have negative effects on the relationship between the non-resident parent, most often the father, and the children. Recent research in the United States suggests that in some circumstances children's relationships with the non-custodial parent can be thwarted by unrealistic child support requirements. The result is that these parents engage with their children less, hindering the potentially valuable contribution they could make to their children's lives (Harris 2011; Edin and Nelson 2013). In some countries, including Brazil, non-payment of formal child support obligations can land the father in prison, which will certainly guarantee non-payment for the duration of the sentence, as well as making parent–child contact more difficult. All this suggests an important intervening role for the state in providing support to children and collecting the financing from non-custodial parents.

Grandparents often play important roles in the lives of their grandchildren (Hagestad and Herlofson 2007; Silverstein and Giarrusso 2010). Increased life expectancy has reinforced this: Uhlenberg (1996) notes that a US child born in 2000 will be more likely to have a grandmother alive at the time he or she is 20 years old (91 percent chance) than a child born in 1900 would have been to have a mother still living at the same age (83 percent). As mothers have increasingly moved into the workplace, grandparents – usually grandmothers – have stepped in to fill gaps in care. The amount and regularity of this intergenerational caretaking varies considerably among countries based on a number of factors, including whether intergenerational co-residence is common, geographic proximity, cultural norms, work demands on the mother

17

or grandparents, and the availability of public support for caretaking (Guzman 2004; Hank and Buber 2009; Chen, Liu, and Mair 2011). As an example, in China, because intergenerational co-residence is common, 45 percent of children six and under have a grandparent living with them (Chen, Liu, and Mair 2011: 579). In developed countries, caretaking by grandparents is less likely to be as extensive, but is still important (Hank and Buber 2009). In transnational families, grandmothers, more so than fathers, often care for the children of migrant mothers (Parreñas 2005; Dreby 2010).

Grandparents in skipped-generation households are particularly crucial (Chen, Liu, and Mair 2011: 582). In China, for example, 10 percent of children live in skipped-generation households (Chen, Liu, and Mair 2011: 583), often because the parent has migrated for employment reasons. In Russia, 20 percent of children live in a household headed by their grandparents; in South Africa, 36 percent do, exacerbated by the AIDS crisis, which has left many children orphans across Sub-Saharan Africa (World Family Map 2015: 32). In the United States, circumstances including parental drug abuse, child abuse, teenage pregnancy, and incarceration result in grandparents assuming the custodial role (Fuller-Thomson and Minkler 2001).

17.3.2.3   Protection from Abuse

The last century has been referred to as the "age of the child" because of the increased emphasis on protections for children. All Western countries, and many non-Western ones, now have laws providing for child protection and child welfare. These laws authorize intervention by the state in the family in the case of child abuse. Internationally the construction of the Convention of the Rights of the Child (CRC) shows the global attention to protection of children. The CRC was adopted by the UN General Assembly in 1989, and in 2015 all countries except South Sudan and the US had ratified it, making the CRC the most widely ratified human rights treaty (UNICEF n.d.(a)). According to UNICEF the CRC has "changed the way children are viewed and treated – i.e. as human beings with a distinct set of rights instead of as passive objects of care and charity" (UNICEF n.d.(a)).

Physical and psychological violence in families has been demonstrated to pose great threats to the wellbeing and welfare of children, not only when the child is a victim but also when the child witnesses abuse (Hester, Westmarland, and Gangoli 2006). The CRC states that children should be protected against all forms of physical and psychological violence and physical and sexual abuse while remaining in the care of their parents. Indeed, in much of the world, substantial measures have been taken to prevent such violence, including extensive policies, laws, campaigns, and other public measures. Yet these efforts have been spotty geographically: in some countries family violence is not addressed as a serious problem (see Section 17.3.1.4b on intimate partner violence). Even in countries that have made significant efforts to prevent domestic abuse, the phenomenon may be so deeply rooted that it takes generations to eliminate. For example, as Björnberg and Ottosen (2013) point out, despite the Nordic countries' thoroughgoing efforts against domestic violence, significant numbers of women and children still fall prey to violence in their homes (Berglund 2010). In addition to physical violence, sexual abuse

within families poses a great threat to children's wellbeing worldwide (UNICEF n.d.(b)).

The use of violence to discipline children is a particular problem. Research demonstrates corporal punishment's ineffectiveness, its causal link to the development of violent behavior, and its association with other problems in childhood and later life (Strauss and Paschall 2009; Lansford et al. 2012; Gershoff 2013). Despite this, according to the World Health Organization corporal punishment kills thousands of children each year, as well as injuring and handicapping many more (UN Tribune n.d.).

Some countries have unequivocally prohibited such corporal punishment, for example, Norway and Sweden in the 1970s (Satka and Eydal 2004). Slowly other countries have followed in their footsteps. By 2014, 42 countries had enacted such laws (UN Tribune n.d.). Yet other countries, including many states in the United States, continue to treat such violence as a prerogative of parenting.

Mental illness and drug abuse has repeatedly been demonstrated to be an important causal factor in child maltreatment (Park, Solomon, and Mandel 2006; Department of Health and Human Services 2014). Therefore, policies that ensure parents' access to mental health services and drug treatment programs are critical to children's wellbeing (Haskins, Currie, and Berger 2015). In the United States, for example, under-resourced child welfare systems often lack resources to pay for parents' mental health treatment and are forced to apply available resources on only the most serious cases, hence the children that are removed from their families have in many cases already been harmed (Eichner 2010).

Poverty can also increase conditions associated with neglect and abuse (Paxson and Waldfogel 1999). In the United States, several studies show that a substantial percentage of children taken into foster care – in some studies as high as 30 percent – could remain safely in their own homes if their parents had access to decent housing (Lewin 1995; Harburger and White 2004). Ensuring material wellbeing for families is tightly linked to also providing a setting for higher psychological wellbeing and protection from abuse and neglect.

In sum, state efforts to improve children's welfare are most successful when they routinely support families in ways that forestall abuse and neglect rather than when they coercively remove children from their homes after child maltreatment occurs. Certainly there will still be situations in which the state will have to intervene coercively to protect a child from maltreatment, but many of these situations can be avoided by states' efforts to remedy the conditions that give rise to abuse. It is in their homes, given the right support to the family, rather than removed from the families, that children have the best chance of growing into flourishing adults (Doyle 2007, 2013; Eichner 2010; Björnberg and Ottosen 2013).

This section and the one below both deal with relations of actual and potential dependence and caregiving. For a breadth of reasons, a group of individuals need temporary or permanent care beyond their early years. The World Health Organization estimates that over one billion people around the world live with disabilities, of whom between 110 and 190 million have significant difficulties in functioning (WHO 2011). With the adoption of the United Nations Convention on the Rights of Persons with Disabilities in 2006, global attention to the health, social, and infrastructural needs of the disabled has been increasing. Despite this, the majority of individuals with disabilities in developing countries do not have their needs met, and even in high-income countries it is estimated that between 20 percent and 40 percent of people with disabilities generally do not have their needs met for "assistance with everyday activities" (WHO 2011: 9–10). As we discuss in the next section, population aging is contributing to higher prevalence of individuals with disabilities.

17.3.3   Aging Family Members

Life expectancy has increased at an impressive rate in both the developed and the developing world. This is due to both a dramatic decrease in infant mortality rates and an increase in longevity. This section outlines the role of families in providing care for older people around the world, and considers how public care protection, markets, and communities interact to confront the challenge of aging societies and longevity.

Globally, the proportion of the world's population aged 60 years or over is expected to double from about 11 to 22 percent between 2000 and 2050. By 2050, about 34 percent of Europe will be aged 60 years or over, Latin America and the Caribbean and Asia will have about 25 percent, while Africa, with the youngest population structure, is expected to see an increase from 5 to 10 percent in the 60-plus population (UN 2002; WHO 2016b). In terms of sheer numbers, the worldwide population aged 60 years or over is projected to increase from 900 million in 2015 to 1,400 million by 2030 and 2,100 million by 2050 (WHO 2016b). In mainland China alone, the number of 60-plus people will increase from the present 192 million to 450 million by 2050, or from 14 to 33 percent of the population (UN 2013).

As societies age, two challenges relating to families must be confronted. Many aging adults require, first, caregiving, including long-term care for routine activities; and second, financial support once they leave the labor market.

17.3.3.1   Caregiving for Aging Adults

As people age, many require care, much of which is currently provided "informally," meaning by non-professionals. For example, in 2006, around 20 percent of those 65 and older in the European Union received informal care, rising to between 30 and 60 percent for those 75 or older, depending on how informal care is defined (Eurostat 2006). One study estimated that 19 million persons provided a minimum of 20 hours a week of care to elders in 11 countries of the European Union (Grammenos 2005). Of these informal caregivers, about half provided more than 35 hours a week.

Care for the elderly across the world has most often been organized within the family and familial networks (Glendinning et al. 2009). Some countries, for example Cambodia and Vietnam, assign this responsibility to family members by law. Regardless of law, cultural norms have traditionally assigned this responsibility to family members. Some cultures specify a hierarchy of caretaking, for example assigning the oldest daughter or son as the preferred caretaker.

Partners and adult children (and their spouses) are the most frequent caregivers for family members, followed by broader family (Chapel 1985; Arber and Gilbert 1989). The increase in male life expectancy in particular has increased the availability of spouses as caregivers. It is women, however, often adult daughters or daughters-in-law, who disproportionately provide caregiving for family (Armstrong and Kits 2004; Parreñas 2005; Glendinning et al. 2009). This is the case regardless of differences in state policies, female labor market participation, and cultural values across countries.

Even when parents and adult children do not reside in the same household, they generally stay emotionally connected, with a strong sense of obligation, especially in conditions of crisis and need (Attias-Donfut, Ogg, and Wolff 2005; Hank 2007). In the United States, for example, at least 80 percent of parents speak to an adult child once a week; 69 percent of adults speak to their mother at least once a week; and 40 percent of adult children see a parent at least once per week (Lye et al. 1995; Swartz 2009). These ties are sufficiently meaningful to individuals that the presence of family members is an important factor when individuals decide to stay or move (Michielin, Mulder, and Zorlu 2008; Mulder and Malmberg 2014).

Urbanization, the increase in female employment, and changing family structures are transforming the available provision of informal care for the elderly (Heymann 2006). For example, more than 100 million rural Chinese are estimated to have moved to cities in search of work; combined with extremely low fertility (due in large part to the one-child rule), this reduces the availability of children to care for aging parents (Xiong 2009). Intergenerational living remains common in Asia, the Middle East, Latin America, and Sub-Saharan Africa, where at least 40 percent of children live in households that include adults besides their parents, in many cases grandparents (World Family Map 2015: 11). That said, the majority of families in most countries today live in a nuclear-family structure, apart from aging parents (World Family Map 2015). Further, an increasing number of older people live alone, sometimes as a result of divorce. Such family cleavages can weaken relationships between parents and children, and alter the extent to which adult children take on caregiving (Börsch-Supan, McFadden, and Schnabel 1996; Engers and Stern 2002).

Norms of filial obligation are also changing rapidly in many places. In South Korea, for example, the percentage of people who thought the family should be responsible for the support and care of their elderly parents declined dramatically from 90 percent in 1998 to 33 percent in 2012 (Peng 2013: 10). At the same time, the proportion of older people nominating their spouse as the preferred caregiver has increased (Knodel 2012). Of course, caring is an individual decision made in the context of a specific relationship, and as such, unpredictable.

Against this backdrop, most developed states in recent years have established or expanded government policies aimed at ensuring adequate caregiving for aging adults. Several European countries, plus

Japan and South Korea, have established universal long-term care (Leon, Ranzi, and Rostgaard 2014). Still, most advanced industrialized countries continue to limit publicly funded long-term care only to the poorest elderly (Scheil-Adlung 2015).

Many countries with the most universal and generous long-term care systems have moved in the last 15 years toward care in the home rather than in institutions. This policy of "ageing in place" is aimed at meeting with dignity the general desire among older people to remain in their own homes, but has also been a means to lower public expenditures on care provision (Rostgaard and Timonen, forthcoming). In China, the long-term care model is now seen to be one of family care as the main part, supported by community-based services and complemented by institutional care (Shang and Wu 2011). While such de-institutionalization can be both preferable to users and cost-effective, it may also transfer the burden of care to individuals and families who may not be able to ensure their own wellbeing or the wellbeing of care recipients (Rostgaard, Timonen, and Glendinning 2012).

Most developing countries are in the early stages of formulating long-term care systems. As the World Health Organization concluded, long-term care (LTC) needs "are increasing in the developing world at a rate that far exceeds that experienced by industrialized countries … [and] at levels of income that are far lower than those which existed in the industrialized world when these needs emerged. Therefore, the search for effective LTC policies is one of the most pressing challenges facing modern society" (WHO 2002: iii). In some countries, no formal programs exist to support long-term care. In others, at least some training of volunteers and some forms of community care are beginning to emerge. Integrating emerging long-term care programs into the health system, rather than fragmenting health care and social services programs, is one way to reduce costs and increase coordination of care (WHO 2002).

17.3.3.2   Financial Support for Aging Adults

Traditionally, aging adults co-resided with children who supported them financially. This still occurs, of course, as discussed earlier. In India, for example, more than three quarters of seniors live in three-generation households (Desai et al. 2010). Yet this is less and less common, while life expectancy has increased. Relying solely on the adult's savings, or on the financial resources of their families, results in harsh stratification, as well as undignified circumstances for a large swathe of these seniors.

Because of this, the vast majority of countries have mandated pension systems. These systems generally have two purposes: to help equalize seniors' incomes over the course of their life, rather than have this stream drop dramatically following retirement; and to reduce the incidence of poverty (MacKellar 2009). Most such public systems rely on pooled payroll taxes from current workers and employers; a few, including those of Bangladesh, Georgia, Botswana, and South Africa, are funded through the government's general funds. A minority of countries have systems requiring contributions to personal retirement accounts rather than to pooled pension funds.

Public pension systems have dramatically reduced poverty in many countries. Such schemes generally have high coverage rates for populations in high-income countries. For example, 90 percent of the labor force is covered in Japan, the United Kingdom, the United States, Australia, and Italy. In contrast, public pensions cover only one out of three people in China, and one out of ten in India. This difference is linked to the proportion who work outside the formal labor market sector and thus remain uncovered (MacKellar 2009). In India, for example, the main pension scheme excludes the self-employed, agricultural workers, and members of cooperatives with fewer than 50 workers (Social Security Administration 2013). To address this, India introduced an alternative defined contribution pension scheme in 2015.

Also, pension schemes tied to employment disadvantage the many women who have reduced paid work to assume unpaid caretaking, and thus have a shorter work history and lower earnings. To deal with this, some states have added supplements to women's pensions for such activities (Tinios, Bettio, and Betti 2015). Other states, for example Bolivia and Brazil, have established non-contributory pensions for low-income seniors.

Some states have moved away from public pension systems toward private individual retirement accounts. However, coverage in these countries remains limited, with payouts often insufficient to support citizens, and pension fund management companies have been criticized for high fees and weak competition. Further, these systems appear to work far better for higher- and middle-income workers, and less well for those below the median (James, Cox Edwards, and Wong 2003). Because of such issues, two countries – Argentina (2009) and Hungary (2011) – have closed their individual accounts systems and moved back to pooled pension funds for all workers. Chile, in 2008, reformed its pension system to add basic pensions for those not adequately supported by the individual account system (He et al. 2015).

17.3.4   Other Adult Relationships

Families include more than partners and direct descendants. Households may include extended kin, grandparents, siblings, uncles and aunts, cousins, and so on. Furthermore, whether extended family members live within the same household or in different households, they provide important emotional support, economic contributions, caretaking, and sometimes patriarchal control.

17.3.4.1   Extended Families

Norms and practices of extended family solidarity continue to play an important role in individuals' and families' lives (Yi and Farrell 2006; Uhlenberg 2009). They increasingly serve the purpose of supporting family members through the periods of marital and economic instability that often accompany contemporary life, as well as helping to buffer families' caretaking and human development activities from labor market pressures (Parreñas 2005; Swartz 2009).

While the nuclear family now dominates residential patterns in most developed countries, in many regions of the world, intergenerational

17

living continues to be widespread. Extended families are most widespread in Sub-Saharan Africa, followed by Asia and Latin America. As also mentioned earlier, in almost all of the countries for which data is available in Asia, the Middle East, Latin America, and Sub-Saharan Africa, at least 40 percent of children live in households that include adults besides their parents, in many cases extended family members. In India alone this figure is 50 percent; in Turkey, 58 percent. In Colombia and Nicaragua, the figure is 55 percent, in Mexico, 45 percent, and in Romania, 43 percent. The highest share is 70 percent, in South Africa (World Family Map 2015).

Relatedly, while in Asia and the Middle East the vast majority of children live in two-parent families, in Latin America and Sub-Saharan Africa a significant share of children live with only one or no parents. The latter types of households are more likely to include extended family members, who "may compensate for the absence of one or both parents" (World Family Map 2015: 3). In developed countries, the figures for extended family co-residence are lower but not insignificant, ranging from 15 percent in Canada to 29 percent in the United States and 34 percent in Spain (for the countries reported in the World Family Map). Living with adults other than parents can generate benefits for children, as the World Family Map (2015: 11) stresses, but, "depending on the circumstances, it can also produce difficulties such as overcrowding, violence, and abuse." In cases where poverty, orphanhood, or parental incarceration drive these arrangements, children may be in especially fragile situations. Another group of vulnerable children are those left behind by migrant parents in the country of origin (Parreñas 2005). Across the globe, migrant workers are denied the right to family reunification. This is particularly the case for low-wage migrant workers, including domestic workers.

Even where families live as nuclear families, extended family members still generally have a strong sense of attachment and obligation to one another, as discussed in the section on aging. Once this "latent kin network of support" has been activated (Riley and Riley 1993), family members often provide material support (financial and other resources), practical support (child care, household help, transportation, caregiving, or other services), and other types of aid (Eggebeen and Hogan 1990; Bengtson and Oyama 2007). Because this support is intermittent, it risks being a hidden means through which privilege is transferred between generations. These ties are sufficiently strong that even those who have strained relationships with aging parents still increase their support as parents grow older (Silverstein, Cong, and Li 2002). Further, while Americans live further from extended family than do people in many other countries, both there and elsewhere family geography often allows informal care to supplement institutional care (Swartz 2009).

17.3.4.2 Kinship Networks

Kinship networks that include grandparents, uncles and aunts, cousins, and adult brothers and sisters still have considerable power in individuals' lives in many developing and developed countries (Joseph 2000b; Luke and Munshi 2006). In a cross-national study of 27 countries, Murphy (2008) concluded that there was "a steady gradation" among

countries with respect to kinship contacts. At the high end of the scale are the Mediterranean countries (including Cyprus and Israel), and those with an Iberian colonial heritage, such as Brazil and, to a lesser extent, Chile. At the other end of the scale, low-contact countries include the Nordic and Anglo-Saxon countries. One factor associated with strong kinship networks is weak state governance, given that strong family ties may be a response to government corruption but may also promote it.

In countries with strong kinship systems, the kinship matrix may lie at the "the core of social identity, economic stability, political security, and religious affiliation" (Joseph 2000b: 171). It provides some stability in cultures in which conjugal relationships are relatively weak, and helps shore up the vulnerable position in which wives are placed by Muslim marriage law. Particularly in the absence of strong welfare support, these networks serve a variety of functions. As Singerman describes in lower-income communities in Cairo, for example:

> families are intimately and extensively involved in almost all realms of social, political, moral, and economic life, such as educating children, childrearing, securing employment, negotiating the bureaucracy and the political elite, establishing and maintaining businesses, saving money, promoting morality and status, distributing resources and information, securing credit, organizing migration, policing sexuality, etc. (Singerman 2006: 2)

Strong kinship systems provide caretaking for aging adults, particularly where the aging adult has no children (Schröder-Butterfill 2005). They also serve to buffer the harsher effects of market forces, particularly in the absence of robust state action. For example, in Russia, kinship networks that used to be central to "getting by" under the Soviet shortage economy have now become an important resource in coping with the widespread social and economic dislocations brought by the transition to capitalism (Walker 2010). Further, in some countries, such networks are a major factor in securing workers' job mobility (Bian and Ang 1997; Luke and Munshi 2006).

While kinship networks help provide members with stability and support, as Joseph (1994, 2000a, 2005) notes, some cultures fuse these goods with submission to patriarchal control. In Lebanon, for example, junior family members and women defer to family elders and to male kin generally with the expectation that they will in turn attend to their needs, security, and wellbeing, as well as safeguarding family honor. Sibling relationships frequently become the focus of these networks, and both brothers and sisters defer to the oldest brother in their natal family even after marriage (Meeker 1976; Joseph 2000a). These relationships therefore become vehicles for maintaining culturally appropriate gender roles that reproduce patriarchy (Joseph 1994).

Kinship ties take on a special role when relatives migrate either nationally or transnationally. Relatives often help one another in creating migratory routes, safe housing, transitional financial support, networking for jobs and creating relationships in new cities or countries (Menjívar 1997; Bashi 2007). Gender informs patterns and practices of assistance. For example, Mexican migrant women created female-centered networks to counter their exclusion from those of their male

17

counterparts (Hondagneu-Sotelo 1994). In the case of transnational families, migrant mothers likewise rely on the creation of a network of women for assistance with child care. When a mother migrates, care for children left behind is largely left to extended kin, primarily women, particularly grandmothers (both paternal and maternal), aunts, and older daughters (Parreñas 2005; Silverstein, Cong, and Li 2006). In contrast, the transnational families of migrant men rarely rely on other relatives for the care of their children but instead almost always solely depend on the care work of the left-behind wife (Parreñas 2005). This suggests a different structural formation for the transnational families of migrant men and women, as the households of migrant men are more likely to mirror traditional nuclear households, with a breadwinner father and stay-at-home mother, while those of migrant women reflecting female-centered extended households. These diverging household configurations challenge the assumption that women's migration results in increasing the care work carried out by other men.

17.4 Conclusion and Policy Recommendations

The vast majority of the world's population live most of their lives within family units, of all shapes and sizes. Regardless of their tremendous diversity, all families have certain commonalities. They all must confront the need to balance production and reproduction, or, in other words, ensure both income and care. Most families, at some point, raise children, and we all age if we are lucky enough not to die young. At best, families also provide us with a sense of meaning and belonging. At worst, families may grapple with severe material deprivation or be settings for neglect, abuse, and inequality in power relations, stunting the ability of their members to flourish as human beings. Here, we return to our key question: how can societies support conditions that allow families to flourish and at the same time promote individual dignity, equality, and choice? Below, we summarize our empirical evidence and provide policy recommendations based on the evidence.

The empirical evidence shows a broad trend toward legal acceptance of consensual adult partnerships, although with regional variation. On partner relations within families, the evidence shows that there is an overall tendency toward more gender-equitable family law and greater gender equality in education, labor force participation, and asset ownership, and that these are associated with improvements in women's bodily integrity and more shared decision-making, as well as enhanced wellbeing of the family as a whole. At the same time, these links are not automatic, and require concerted efforts by the state to both provide and enforce a legal framework in support of gender equality. On adult–child relations, the evidence shows that a state role in ensuring income floors for families with children is essential for children's physical and material wellbeing. Beyond this, ensuring a healthy balance of family (including paternal) care, and good-quality institutional care allows children and their families to flourish. Finally, state efforts to protect children are most successful when they routinely support families in preventive ways. Overall, care for older people around the world remains centered in the family as well. The looming challenge for aging societies is to ensure access to care services to relieve the burden on families, especially already overburdened women, and to ensure the dignity of older people.

We offer a set of policy recommendations based on the empirical findings. Three broad criteria guide our list of recommendations: (1) legal and cultural patterns should embrace the plurality of family types rather than punish them; that said, (2) embracing plurality should not foster family forms that are inegalitarian or authoritarian (for example, defending polygamy, the rights of parents to use physical punishment to discipline their children, or child wives) – on the contrary, states should actively promote more egalitarian relations and limit or outlaw harmful practices that are still present in many family arrangements; and (3) the burden that families carry regarding care, material support, and nurturing should not be constrained by private capacities but should become the target of collective, public support. First, we discuss legal rights and regulations; second, state policy more broadly, including transfers and services; and third, how to finance such policies.

17.4.1 Legal Rights and Regulations

17.4.1.1 Legal Recognition of Families

The goal of state policy should be to support the broader range of relationships in which people are organizing their family lives, consistent with promoting human dignity and fairness within and outside of these relationships. The following principles would further these goals:

- Same-sex couples should be treated the same as opposite-sex couples
- States may want to make available other formal partnership statuses besides marriage to support long-term caregiving that does not fit the traditional conjugal model and to ensure fairness for the partners if the relationship ends. Such formal statuses increase the likelihood that people will stay together to provide one another the care that each needs, and establish a stable relationship in the event of children.
- Even those couples who do not formalize their relationships should be accorded some rights and responsibilities when a relationship is long-term, especially when children are involved.
- We support the African Protocol of Women's Rights, which endorses monogamy but in the case of polygamy calls for measures that support the property rights of all wives, as well as their consent to future marriages of the husband.
- When determining which adults have parental rights and responsibilities, both biological and social factors should be given weight, and established relationships should trump biology alone. However, biological parenthood is a sufficient basis upon which to impose child support obligations.
- Children born to unmarried parents should receive the same rights and protections as children born within wedlock. By the same token, unmarried parents should have the same legal rights to parentage as married parents.
- Parents who live outside the child's household should be expected to pay a fair share of the child's support.
- Transnational families – a common form of household maintenance for migrant workers across the globe – forces the geographic separation of family members at the expense of their intimate

ties. National laws and international conventions should support the right to family reunification.

17.4.1.2 Regulating within Families

We recommend, broadly, laws that foster equality and dignity between partners and other adults, and respect and protection for children. More specifically, women and girls, married and single, must be considered equal to men and boys in every aspect of the law. For example, women should be able to sign contracts, initiate legal proceedings, open their own bank accounts and businesses, and have full property rights equal to men's, including full inheritance rights. Women and men must also have equal labor rights and full civic rights – such as passing citizenship on to their spouses and children, voting rights, rights to run for and hold public office, and the like – and women must have full reproductive autonomy. Further, women and men, girls and boys, should all have the right to live a life free from violence. In particular, we strongly support efforts to strengthen laws sanctioning intimate partner violence.

Research shows that more equal access to income and wealth between husband and wife has positive effects on shared decision-making, more equal work burdens, and improved family wellbeing. Egalitarian relationships within the family are preferable not only in and of themselves for reasons of self-fulfillment, dignity, and equity, but also for family wellbeing – especially for the children. Thus, laws that provide for more equitable relations between family members, based on respect, dignity, and protection (for children specifically), should be encouraged.

One issue that calls for particular attention involves constructing policies that encourage men to assume their share of domestic responsibilities. While women now work long hours in the workplace, men have been slower to adapt in the domestic realm. We recommend public policies that will encourage men to adapt, including public education campaigns and making use-it-or-lose-it paid paternity leave, sometimes known as "father's quotas," available. Promoting more involvement of men in care is not only beneficial to women in reducing their "double burden," and to children as care recipients, but to men themselves; indeed, a study in Sweden showed a reduced suicide rate among men who took more paternity leave.

In adult–child relations, we recommend a recognition of the best interests of the child in legal arrangements for parental care, and custody. This includes legal rights for same-sex couples, cohabiting couples, single parents, and parents not living with their children; and allowing for the legal recognition of the rights of grandparents to access to their grandchildren. We recommend building mechanisms into child support systems that ensure that the obligor parent has the capacity to pay support and flexible adjustments as needed (also addressed below).

17.4.2 State Transfers and Services

Beyond legal rights and regulations, we recommend a set of state policies in the form of transfers and services. Given the massive transformations that families have undergone over the past half century, we recommend a strong, two-fold role for the state to ensure flourishing families, well-equipped to deal with twenty-first-century challenges:

1. Transfers that guarantee a minimum income floor for all families with dependents (children, disabled, elderly) as well as for aging adults;
2. Publicly funded health, education, and care services with universal principles to allow families to maintain a healthy balance between the twin responsibilities of production and reproduction.

We address both in turn.

17.4.2.1 Transfers

First, as discussed, states that provide income transfers to families on a broad basis are best able to ensure low levels of material deprivation among families. With children, such transfers have important long-term effects in allowing nourished, educated children to become healthy adults. Thus, they are not only an investment in the present material wellbeing of families, but also an investment in future human capital. With older people and the disabled, transfers provide the ability to live in dignity, regardless of socio-economic status and/or family support. With dependent partners fleeing abuse, they provide the ability to support themselves. Such transfers should of course take into account local standards of living, but overall should guarantee the ability of a family to live in basic dignity. To the extent that pensions for seniors vary based on prior work history, they should be adjusted to take into account unpaid caregiving.

Beyond such guaranteed floors, we recommend an active state role in ensuring the payment of legal obligations between family members. This includes child support for children, spousal support between partners, and any legal support for aging parents owed by adult children. In all these cases, we recommend the state guarantee such transfers to the recipients while taking on the responsibility of collecting the revenue from the obligor. In this way, the recipient's material wellbeing is guaranteed, stresses associated with payment are less likely to be communicated to children, and the state has an incentive to ensure enforcement. That said, we recommend constructive rather than punitive ways to collect on financial obligations, taking into account the financial ability of the obligor (as mentioned above).

Policies to guarantee income floors to families also contribute to family wellbeing and children's welfare, since they ameliorate the conditions that foster abuse or neglect. It is far more conducive to children's welfare – and cost-effective in the long term – to ensure decent housing with their own parent(s) than to remove them on child maltreatment grounds to live with a stranger.

We also recommend a strong state role in regulating and ensuring income support for employment-based leave for care responsibilities and allowing for a reasonable balance between work and family responsibilities. Beyond maternity leave, which allows women to physically recover from childbirth and bond with and begin breast-feeding the newborn, such leave should also encourage paternal co-responsibility regarding children, and male engagement with other dependents. It should be available for same-sex and opposite-sex couples, for cohabiting partners, adoptive parents, and for other arrangements in which adults are called upon to care for children, older people, or the disabled and other dependents. Such leave should be funded either through social security or government tax revenue, to avoid labor market discrimination against potential recipients. Given that most people around the world work informally, efforts should focus as much on broadening coverage as on the legal reforms themselves. Without coverage extensions, reforms risk aggravating socio-economic inequalities between those who have formal jobs and those who do not.

17.4.2.2   Publicly Funded Health, Education, and Care Services

We call for publicly funded services to be broadly available in order to allow families to maintain a healthy balance between the twin responsibilities of production and reproduction. It is critical to provide such services to the poor. Yet providing them to individuals on a broader, even universal basis not only ensures access for everyone, but also fosters a political commitment to these services among the middle and upper classes. This is particularly important for services involving children, such as early education and care services, public education, public health facilities, and public spaces for leisure and sports. Ensuring that children from all socio-economic backgrounds access these services not only helps equalize opportunity in the short term, but also helps safeguard equal opportunities moving forward, through limiting exit options for those better off, whose parents will then use their political clout to ensure quality services.

The extension of publicly funded care services yields a multitude of other benefits. These services have the potential to improve the lives of family caregivers, the recipients of care, and care workers themselves. Given how feminized care remains, care services that "defamilialize" parts of family care, including early education and care services for children, and care services for the disabled and older people, can reduce the "double burden" especially on women. Such services – so long as they correspond to typical workdays – free women up, when they so choose, to participate in the labor market and earn an income, and thus materially support their families. This can at the same time enhance their bargaining power, providing for more egalitarian relationships. Overall, such services help families balance the twin roles of production and reproduction.

These services are also important for the wellbeing of the recipients. Research has overwhelmingly established that high-quality early childhood education and care has positive effects on children's wellbeing, equal opportunities, and human capital. High-quality care services for older people and the disabled are also vital in ensuring them dignity and autonomy, especially in societies with small or weak family units that are not able to care for their elderly and/or disabled family members. While informal family caregiving may work in specific areas, families need the relief provided by publicly funded services as well. If the services are outsourced to private,

for-profit companies, they need systematic government regulation and monitoring to ensure quality.

Policies to promote publicly funded care services also provide governments with an excellent opportunity to extend decent jobs with a living wage and benefit protections to care workers. These workers are overwhelmingly women who, because of the "care penalty" discussed earlier, tend to be paid less and to receive fewer protections, and often work in highly exploitative conditions. We recommend strong public regulation and guarantees of equal labor rights for all care occupations, both inside and outside households.

More specifically, we strongly recommend governments use the opportunity when investing in care services to create jobs in the formal sector with living wages and social security protections. This is not only a challenge for developing countries. A 2016 study found that 46 percent of child care workers in the United States had to meet their basic needs through at least one public safety-net program such as food stamps, contributing to high stress and high turnover among workers (Whitebook, McLean, and Austin 2016). This has negative effects on the workers as well as the children they care for. Decent jobs in the formal sector not only promote the wellbeing of these women and their families, as well as that of the children for whom they care, but can also foster the reduction of socio-economic inequalities between families.

We also recommend universal access to health care services. Universal coverage is important, of course, for recipients and thus for individual and family wellbeing, but it is also important for family caregivers. A recent study in *The Lancet* found that women provided billions of dollars' worth of unpaid work around the world caring for family members in the face of deficits in access to affordable health services (Langer et al. 2015).

While all aspects of health care coverage are important for individuals and their families, we would like to highlight two. First, coverage should include mental health. Ensuring parents' access to mental health care services reduces the potential for abuse and violence visited upon children, and helps keep families together. Second, of particular weight from the perspective of our normative goal are services that ensure individual agency and dignity regardless of family circumstances. Here, services that enable women and girls to have full control over their own reproduction have been shown to have the best results for individual and family wellbeing. The empirical data is unequivocal when it comes to abortion policies: restricting access to legal abortion does nothing to bring abortion rates down, but simply pushes the procedure underground, with very negative health effects. At the same time, while the evidence clearly demonstrates that legal and accessible abortion is a necessary element of ensuring women's and girls' health and wellbeing, the best way to promote a society with low abortion rates – something that many on both the reformist and the conservative sides of the issue can agree is a desirable goal – is to ensure comprehensive access to sexual education and contraceptive services, including long-term reversible contraception. We therefore call for a broad investment in the prevention of unintended and unwanted pregnancies, and in enabling wanted pregnancies, including ensuring access to pre- and post-natal care.

17

17.4.2.3   How to Pay for State Support for Flourishing Families?

State expenditures for all the above policies require state revenues, of course. While income-transfer policies require money and a way to deliver it, care services require more complex investments. Start-up costs for extending care services are likely to be especially high, as they require infrastructural investments. However, the investments we advocate will pay for themselves over the medium to long term in three ways. First, early childhood education and care services, as mentioned earlier, more than pay for themselves because every dollar invested produces more returns in the form of enhanced human capital and more stable, productive human beings later in life. Second, providing care services enables parents, especially women, to participate in paid work. In countries that make such services broadly available, taxes on mothers' increased earnings have been shown to pay for these services (Esping-Andersen 2009). Third, and finally, the newly formalized employees of care services also pay taxes on their income.

This said, we also make a strong call for tax reform. Many countries still have ample space to increase progressive taxation aimed at personal income and capital gains. Globally, taxes on capital mobility can contribute to financing global initiatives regarding the aforementioned policies. Also, we believe it is worth revisiting and recreating a strong inheritance and estate tax system. Inheritance laws that allow wealthy families to pass on substantial parts of their wealth intergenerationally cement inequalities between families, and worsen inequalities of opportunity for children. Without increasing inheritance taxes, global inequalities – between countries and within countries – will grow much worse. National or even global taxes on inherited wealth, or an internationally agreed-upon national tax on wealth, might go a long way in turning structural trends toward increasing inequality into trends toward equality. The revenue from such a tax could also be used to make the investments for which we call.

To conclude, families based on egalitarian principles, with supportive state policies that allow families to flourish, provide the most conducive setting to do what families can do at their best: provide a space where persons are loved and nurtured, love and nurture back, and are able to flourish to their fullest potential.

References

Abramsky, Tanya, Charlotte H. Watts, Claudia Garcia-Moreno, et al. 2011. "What Factors Are Associated with Recent Intimate Partner Violence? Findings from the WHO Multi-country Study on Women's Health and Domestic Violence." *BMC Public Health* 11/109: 1–17. http://biomedcentral.com/1471–2458/11/109.

Adam, Christoper S., John Hoddinott, and Ethan Ligon. 2011. "Dynamic Intrahousehold Bargaining. Matrimonial Property Law and Suicide in Canada." CUDARE Working Paper 1113. Berkeley: Department of Agricultural and Resource Economics, University of California.

Adebanjo, Adetoun Teslimat. 2015. "Culture, Morality and the Law: Nigeria's Anti-Gay Law in Perspective." *International Journal of Discrimination and the Law* 15/4: 256–270.

Agarwal, Bina. 1994. *A Field of One's Own. Gender and Land Rights in South Asia*. Cambridge: Cambridge University Press.

Agarwal, Bina. 1997. "'Bargaining' and Gender Relations: Within and beyond the Household." *Feminist Economics* 3/1: 1–51.

AGI (Alan Guttmacher Institute). 2014. "Facts on Induced Abortion in the US." Factsheet, July. New York: Alan Guttmacher Institute.

AGI. 2015. "Adolescent Pregnancy and Its Outcomes Across Countries." Factsheet, August. New York: Alan Guttmacher Institute.

AGI. 2016a. "Induced Abortion Worldwide." Factsheet, May. New York: Alan Guttmacher Institute.

AGI. 2016b. "Parental Involvement in Minors" Abortions." Factsheet, July. New York: Alan Guttmacher Institute.

Agrillo, C., and C. Nelini. 2008. "Childfree by Choice: a Review." *Journal of Cultural Geography* 25/3: 347–363.

Aitken, Z., C. Cameryn, B.H. Garrett, L. Keogh, J.S. Hocking, and A.M. Kavanagh. 2015. "The Maternal Health Outcomes of Paid Maternity Leave: A Systematic Review." *Social Science & Medicine* 130: 32–41.

Akbari, E., and K. McCuaig. 2014. *Early Childhood Education Report 2014*. Toronto: Ontario Institute for Studies in Education.

Akin, Bill. 2003. "The Challenge of Unmarried Cohabitation – The New Zealand Response." *Family Law Quarterly* 37: 303–27.

Allendorf, Keera. 2007. "Do Women's Land Rights Promote Empowerment and Child Health in Nepal?" *World Development* 35/11: 1975–1988.

Amato, Paul. 2005. "The Impact of Family Formation Change on the Cognitive, Social, and Emotional Well-Being of the Next Generation." *Child Development* 74/3: 801–821.

Amato, Paul R., and Joan Gilbreth. 1999. "Nonresident Fathers and Children's Well-Being: A Meta-analysis." *Journal of Marriage and the Family* 61: 557–573.

Anderson, Siwan, and Mukesh Eswaran. 2009. "What Determines Female Autonomy? Evidence from Bangladesh." *Journal of Development Economics* 90: 179–191.

Arber, S., and N. Gilbert. 1989. "Men: The Forgotten Carers." *Sociology* 23/1: 111–118.

Armstrong, P., and O. Kits. 2004. "One Hundred Years of Caregiving," in K. Willson (ed.), *Caring for/Caring about: Women, Home Care and Unpaid Caregiving*. Aurora, Ontario: Garamond Press Ltd.

Arnalds, Á., G.B. Eydal, and I.V. Gíslason. 2013. "Equal Rights to Paid Parental Leave and Caring Fathers – the Case of Iceland." *Stjórnmál og stjórnsýsla* 9: 323–344.

Attias-Donfut, C., J. Ogg, and F.C. Wolff. 2005. "Family support," in A. Börsch-Supan, H. Jürges Brugiavini, J. Mackenbach, J. Siegrist and G. Weber (eds.), *Health, Ageing and Retirement in Europe – First Results from SHARE*. Mannheim: MEA.

Badgett, M.V. Lee. 2011. "Social Inclusion and the Value of Marriage Equality in Massachusetts and the Netherlands." *Journal of Social Issues* 67/2: 316–334.

Bala, V., and Goyal, S. 2000. "A Noncooperative Model of Network Formation." *Econometrica* 68/5): 1181–1229.

Banda, Fareda. 2014. "Gender Discrimination and the Right to Family Life," in J. Eekelaar and R. George (eds.), *Routledge Handbook of Family Law and Policy*. Abingdon: Routledge.

Bartfeld, J., and D. Meyer. 2003. "Child Support Compliance among Discretionary and Nondiscretionary Obligors." *Social Service Review* 77/3: 347–372.

Bashi, V. 2007. *Survival of the Knitted: Immigrant Social Networks in a Stratified World*. Palo Alto, CA: Stanford University Press.

Baxter, J., S. Buchler, F. Perales, and M. Western. 2015. "A Life-Changing Event: First Births and Men's and Women's Attitudes to Mothering and Gender Divisions of Labor." *Social Forces* 93/3: 989–1014.

BBC World News. 2014. "Where Is It Illegal To Be Gay?" www.bbc.com/news/world-25927595.

Beegle, K., E. Frankenberg, and D. Thomas. 2001. "Bargaining Power within Couples and Use of Prenatal and Delivery Care in Indonesia." *Studies in Family Planning* 32/2: 130–146.

Benería, Lourdes, Günseli Berik, and Maria Floro. 2016. *Gender, Development, and Globalization: Economics as if People Mattered*. London: Routledge.

Bengtson, Verne, and Petrice S. Oyama. 2007. *Intergenerational Solidarity: Strengthening Economic and Social Ties*. New York: UN.

Berger, L.M., J. Hill, and J. Waldfogel 2005. "Maternity Leave, Early Maternal Employment and Child Health and Development in the US." *The Economic Journal* 115: 29–47.

Berglund, A. 2010. "Förekomst av våld mot kvinnor i Sverige och internationellt." *Utdrag ur NCK-rapport Att fråga om våldsutsatthet som en del av anamnesen* 2010: 04.

Bhattacharyya, Manasi, Arjun S. Bedi, and Amrita Chhachhi. 2011. "Marital Violence and Women's Employment and Property Status: Evidence from North Indian Villages." *World Development* 39/9: 1676–1689.

Bian, Yanjie, and Soon Ang. 1997. "Guanxi Networks and Job Mobility in China and Singapore." *Social Forces* 75/3: 981–1005.

Björnberg, U., and M.H. Ottosen. (eds.) 2013. *Challenges for Future Family Policies in the Nordic Countries.* Copenhagen: SFI.

BJS (Bureau of Justice Statistics, United States). 2012. "Intimate Partner Violence Dropped 64 Percent from 1993 to 2010." www.bjs.gov/content/pub/press/ipv9310pr.cfm.

Blau, F.D., and Kahn, L.M. 2013. "Female Labor Supply: Why Is the United States Falling Behind?" *The American Economic Review* 103/3: 251–256.

Blau, Francine, and Kahn, Lawrence. 2016. "The Gender Wage Gap: Extent, Trends, and Explanations." IZA discussion paper 9656. *Journal of Economic Literature* 55/3: 789–865.

Blofield, Merike. 2008. "Women's Choices in Comparative Perspective: Abortion Policies in Late-Developing Catholic Countries." *Comparative Politics* 41/4: 399–419.

Blofield, Merike. 2012. *Care Work and Class: Domestic Workers' Struggle for Equal Rights in Latin America.* College Park: Pennsylvania State University Press.

Blofield, Merike, and Regina Madalozzo. 2017. "Conciliando trabalho e família: Uma pesquisa para mensurar o hiato de gênero nas famílias de baixa renda em São Paulo." *Estudos Feministas* 25/1: 215–240.

Blofield, Merike, and Juliana Martínez Franzoni. 2015. "Are Governments Catching Up? Work–Family Policies and Inequality in Latin America." UN Women Discussion Paper 7. New York: UN.

Blumberg, Grace Ganz. 2001. "The Regularization of Nonmarital Cohabitation: Rights and Responsibilities in the American Welfare State." *Notre Dame Law Review* 76: 1265–1308.

Boeckmann, I., J. Misra, and M.J. Budig. 2014. "Cultural and Institutional Factors Shaping Mothers' Employment and Working Hours in Postindustrial Countries." *Social Forces* 93/4: 1301–1333.

Börsch-Supan, A., D. McFadden, and R. Schnabel. 1996. "Living Arrangements: Health and Wealth Effects," in D. Wise (ed.), *Advances in the Economics of Aging*, Chicago: University of Chicago Press.

Briggs, L. 2002. *Reproducing Empire: Race, Sex, Science and U.S. Imperialism in Puerto Rico.* Berkeley: University of California Press.

Brown, Philip H. 2009. "Dowry and Intrahousehold Bargaining: Evidence from China." *Journal of Human Resources* 44/1: 25–46.

Brown, Susan, and Alan Booth. 1996. "Cohabitation versus Marriage: A Comparison of Relationship Quality." *Journal of Marriage and Family* 58/3: 668–678.

Bruce, Judith, and Daisy Dwyer. (eds.) 1988. *A Home Divided. Women and Income in the Third World.* Palo Alto, CA: Stanford University Press.

Buchanan, Christy M., Eleanor E. Maccoby, and Sanford M. Dornbusch. 1996. *Adolescents After Divorce.* Cambridge, MA: Harvard University Press.

Budig, Michelle J. 2014. "The Fatherhood Bonus and the Motherhood Penalty: Parenthood and the Gender Gap in Pay". The Third Way. www.thirdway.org/report/the-fatherhood-bonus-and-the-motherhood-penalty-parenthood-and-the-gender-gap-in-pay.

Budig, M., and England, P. 2001. "The Wage Penalty for Motherhood." *American Sociological Review* 66/2: 204–225.

Byrnes, Andres, and Marsha Freeman. 2011. "The Impact of the CEDAW Convention: Paths to Equality," Background Paper. *World Development Report 2012. Gender Equality and Development.* Washington, DC: World Bank.

Carmichael, Sarah. 2011. "Marriage and Power: Age at First Marriage and Spousal Age Gap in Lesser Developed Countries." *The History of the Family* 16: 416–436.

Chapel, N.L. 1985. "Social Support and the Receipt of Home Care Services." *The Gerontologist* 25/1: 47–54.

Chen, Feinian, Guangya Liu, and Christine Mair. 2011. "Intergenerational Ties in Context: Grandparents Caring for Grandchildren in China." *Social Forces* 90/2: 571–594.

Cherlin, Andrew J. 2010. *The Marriage-Go-Round: The State of Marriage and the Family in America Today.* New York: Vintage Books.

Child Care Aware of America. 2013. "Ranking of States." http://web.archive.org/web/20130609004156/www.naccrra.org/sites/default/files/default_site_pages/2013/wcdb20rankings2020041013.pdf.

Child Care Aware of America. 2012. "Parents and the High Cost of Child Care: 2012 Report." National Association of Child Care Resource and Referral Agencies.

Chioda, Laura. 2011. *Work and Family: Latin American and Caribbean Women in Search of a New Balance.* Washington, DC: World Bank.

Cienfuegos, Javiera. 2014. "Tendencias familiares en América Latina: diferencias y entrelazamientos." *Notas de Población* 99: 11–36.

Cole, Alan. 2015. "Estate and Inheritance Taxes around the World." *Fiscal Fact 458.* Washington, DC: Tax Foundation.

Contreras, Dante, C. Paulina Sepúlveda, and Soledad Cabrera. 2010. "The Effects of Lengthening the School Day on Female Labor Supply: Evidence from a Quasi-Experiment in Chile." Santiago: University of Chile. http://ideas.repec.org/p/udc/wpaper/wp323.html.

Cook, S., and X.Y. Dong. 2011. "Harsh Choices: Chinese Women's Paid Work and Unpaid Care Responsibilities under Economic Reform." *Development and Change* 42/4: 947–965.

Correll, Shelley J., and Stephen Benard. 2007. "Getting a Job: Is There a Motherhood Penalty?" *American Journal of Sociology* 112/5: 1297–1339.

Cuesta, Laura, and Daniel R. Meyer. 2014. "The Role of Child Support in the Economic Wellbeing of Custodial Mother Families in Less Developed Countries: The Case of Colombia." *International Journal of Law, Policy and The Family* 28: 60–76.

Custers, Peter. 2012. *Capital Accumulation and Women's Labour in Asian Economies.* New York: Monthly Review Press.

De Laat, J., and A. Sevilla-Sanz. 2011. "The Fertility and Women's Labor Force Participation Puzzle in OECD Countries: The Role of Men's Home Production." *Feminist Economics* 17/2: 87–119.

Deere, Carmen Diana, and Cheryl Doss. 2006. "The Gender Asset Gap. What Do We Know and Why Does It Matter?" *Feminist Economics* 12/1 & 2: 1–50.

Deere, Carmen Diana, and Magdalena León. 2001. *Empowering Women. Land and Property Rights in Latin America.* Pittsburgh: University of Pittsburgh Press.

Deere, Carmen Diana, and Jennifer Twyman. 2012. "Asset Ownership and Egalitarian Decision-Making in Dual-Headed Households in Ecuador." *Review of Radical Political Economy* 44 /3: 313–320.

Deere, Carmen Diana, Gina Alvarado, and Jennifer Twyman. 2012. "Gender Inequality in Asset Ownership in Latin America: Female Owners versus Household Heads." *Development and Change* 43/2: 505–530.

Deere, Carmen Diana, Abena D. Oduro, Hema Swaminathan, and Cheryl Doss. 2013. "Property Rights and the Gender Distribution of Wealth in Ecuador, Ghana and India." *Journal of Economic Inequality* 11/2: 249–265.

Deininger, Klaus, Aparajita Goyal, and Hari Nagarajan. 2013. "Women's Inheritance Rights and Intergenerational Transmission of Resources in India." *Journal of Human Resources* 48/1: 114–141.

Department of Health and Human Services, Children's Bureau. 2014. "Parental Substance Use and the Child Welfare System." www.childwelfare.gov/pubPDFs/parentalsubabuse.pdf.

Desai, Sonalde, Amaresh Dubey, Brijlal Joshi, Mitali Sen, Abusaleh Shariff, and Reeve D. Vanneman. 2010. *Human Development in India: Challenges for a Society in Transition.* New Delhi: Oxford University Press.

Doss, Cheryl. 2006. "The Effects of Intrahousehold Property Ownership on Expenditure Patterns in Ghana." *Journal of African Economies* 15/1: 149–180.

Doss, Cheryl. 2013. "Intrahousehold Bargaining and Resource Allocation in Developing Countries." *World Bank Research Observer* 28: 52–78.

Doss, Cheryl, Sung Mi Kim, Jemimah Njuki, Emily Hillenbrand, and Maureen Miruka. 2014. "Women's Individual and Joint Property Ownership: Effects on Household Decision Making." IFPRI Discussion Paper 1347. Washington, DC: International Food Policy Research Institute.

Doss, Cheryl, Chiara Kovarik, Amber Peterman, Agnes Quisumbing, and Mara van den Bold. 2015. "Gender Inequality in Ownership and Control of Land in Africa: Myth and Reality." *Agricultural Economics* 46: 403–434.

Doyle, Joseph J. 2007. "Child Protection and Child Outcomes: Measuring the Effects of Foster Care." *American Economic Review* 97: 1583–1610.

Doyle, Joseph J. 2013. "Causal Effects of Foster Care: An Instrumental-Variables Approach." *Children and Youth Services Review* 35/7: 1143–1151.

Dreby, J. 2010. *Divided by Borders: Mexican Migrants and their Children.* Berkeley: University of California Press.

Duflo, Ester. 2003. "Grandmothers and Grandaughters: Old-Age Pensions and Intrahousehold Allocation in South Africa." *World Bank Economic Review*, 17/1: 1–25.

Dush, Claire Kamp, and Paul Amato. 2005. "Consequences of Relationship Status and Quality for Subjective Well-Being." *Journal of Social and Personal Relationships,* 22/5: 607–627.

ECLAC. 2009, 2012. *Social Panorama of Latin America*. Santiago de Chile: Economic Commission for Latin America and the Caribbean, United Nations.

Edin, Kathryn, and Timothy Nelson. 2013. *Doing the Best I Can: Fathering in the Inner City*. Berkeley: University of California Press.

Eggebeen, D., and D. Hogan. 1990. "Giving between Generations in American Families." *Human Nature* 1: 211–232.

Eichner, Maxine. 2010. *The Supportive State: Families, Government, and America's Political Ideals*. New York: Oxford University Press.

Ellis, Bruce J., John E. Bates, Kenneth A. Dodge, et al. 2003. "Does Father Absence Place Daughters at Special Risk for Early Sexual Activity and Teenage Pregnancy?" *Child Development* 74/3: 801–821.

Engers, M., and S. Stern. 2002. "Long-Term Care and Family Bargaining." *International Economic Review* 43: 1–44.

Esping-Andersen, Gøsta. 2009. *The Incomplete Revolution: Adapting to Women's New Roles*. Cambridge: Polity Press.

Euromonitor International. 2014. "The Rising Importance of Single Person Households Globally." https://blog.euromonitor.com/2014/06/the-rising-importance-of-single-person-households-globally.html.

Eurostat. 2006. *The Social Situation in the European Union 2005–2006*. Brussels: Eurostat.

Evertsson, M. (2012) "The Importance of Work: Changing Work Commitment following the Transition to Motherhood." *Acta Sociologica* 56/2: 139–153.

Ezeh, Alex C., and Anastasia J. Gage. 2000. "Domestic Violence in Uganda: Evidence from Qualitative and Quantitative Data." Working Paper 18. Nairobi: African Population and Health Research Center.

Fafchamps, Marcel, Bereket Kebede, and Agnes R. Quisumbing. 2009. "Intrahousehold Welfare in Rural Ethiopia." *Oxford Bulletin of Economics and Statistics* 71/4: 567–599.

Farmer, Amy, and Jill Tiefenthaler. 1997. "An Economic Analysis of Domestic Violence." *Review of Social Economics* 55/3: 337–358.

Farmer, Amy, and Jill Tiefenthaler. 2003. "Explaining the Recent Decline in Domestic Violence." *Contemporary Economic Policy* 21/2: 158–172.

Filgueira, Fernando. 2007. *Cohesión, Riesgo y Arquitectura de Protección Social en América Latina*. Serie Política Sociales 135. Santiago de Chile: ECLAC.

Filgueira, Fernando, and Juliana Martínez Franzoni. 2017. "The Difficult Road Ahead: Transforming the Latin American Care Regime from Stratified Home-Based to State Services." Contribution to the Panel on Recognising and Redistributing Care Work at "A Better Future For Women at Work: Legal and Policy Strategies," Oxford Human Rights Hub and ILO, May 18–19, Pembroke College, Oxford.

Folbre, Nancy. (ed.) 2012. *For Love and Money: Care Provision in the U.S.* New York: Russell Sage Foundation.

Fuller-Thomson, E., and M. Minkler. 2001. "American Grandparents Providing Extensive Childcare to their Children: Prevalence and Profile." *Gerontologist* 41: 201–209.

Gangl, M., and Ziefle, A. 2009. "Motherhood, Labor Force Behavior, and Women's Careers: An Empirical Assessment of the Wage Penalty for Motherhood in Britain, Germany, and the United States." *Demography* 46/2: 341–369.

García, Brígida, and Orlandina de Oliveira. 2011. "Family Change and Public Policy in Latin America." *Annual Review of Sociology* 37: 593–561.

Garrison, Marsha. 2008. "Nonmarital Cohabitation: Social Revolution and Legal Regulation." *Family Law Quarterly* 42/3: 309–331.

Gauthier, A., and DeGusti, B. 2012. "Time Allocation to Children by Parents." *Europe International Sociology* 27: 827–845.

Gauthier, H.A. 1996. *The State and the Family: A Comparative Analysis of Family Policies in Industrialized Countries*. Oxford: Clarendon Press.

Gerecke, Megan. 2013. *A Policy Mix for Gender Equality? Lessons from High-Income Countries*. Geneva: ILO.

Gershoff, Elizabeth T. 2013. "Spanking and Child Development: We Know Enough Now to Stop Hitting Our Children." *Children Development Perspective* 7/3: 133–137.

Ghosh, Jayati. 2009. *Never Done and Poorly Paid: Women's Work in Globalising India*. New Delhi: Women Unlimited.

Gibson-Davis, Cristina, Katherine Magnuson, Lisa Gennetian, and Greg T. Duncan. 2005. "Employment and the Risk of Domestic Abuse among Low Income Women." *Journal of Marriage and the Family* 67/5: 149–165.

Glendinning, C., Frits Tjadens, Hilary Arksey, et al. 2009. "Care Provision within Families and Its Socio-economic Impact on Care Providers." Report for the European Commission DG/EMPL Working Paper. York: University of York.

Goldin, Claudia. 2006. "The Quiet Revolution that Transformed Women's Employment, Education, and Family." *American Economic Review Papers and Proceedings* 96: 1–21.

Goldin, Claudia. 2014. "A Grand Gender Convergence: Its Last Chapter." *American Economic Review* 104: 1091–1119.

Goldin, Claudia, and Lawrence F. Katz. 2002. "The Power of the Pill: Oral Contraceptives and Women's Career and Marriage Decisions." *Journal of Political Economy* 110/4: 730–770.

Gornick, Janet C., and Marcia K. Meyers. 2003. *Families that Work: Policies for Reconciling Parenthood and Employment*. New York: Russell Sage Foundation.

Grammenos, S. 2005. "Implications of Demographic Ageing in the Enlarged EU in the Domains of Quality of Life, Health Promotion and Health Care." Studies on the Policy Implications of Demographic Changes in National and Community Policies, Lot 5. Brussels: Centre for European and Economic Policy.

Gutierrez, E.R. 2008. *Fertile Matters: The Politics of Mexican-Origin Women's Reproduction*. Austin: University of Texas Press.

Guzman, L. 2004. *Grandma and Grandpa Taking Care of the Kids: Patterns of Involvement*. Research Brief 2004-17. Washington, DC: Child Trends.

Hagestad, G.O., and Herlofson, K. 2007 "Micro and Macro Perspective on Intergenerational Relations and Transfer and in Europe," In *United States Expert Group Meeting on Social and Economical Implications of Changing Population Age Structure. Mexico City 31 August–2 September*. New York: UN.

Hakovirta, Mia. 2011. "Child Maintenance and Child Poverty: A Comparative Analysis." *Journal of Poverty and Social Justice* 19/3: 249–262.

Hallman, Kelly, Agnes R. Quisumbing, Marie Ruel, and Benedicte de la Briere. 2005. "Mothers' Work and Childcare: Findings from the Urban Slums of Guatemala City." *Economic Development and Cultural Change* 53/4: 855–885.

Hallward-Driemeier, Mary, Tazeen Hasan, and Anca Bogdana Rusu. 2013. "Women's Legal Rights over 50 Years. Progress, Stagnation or Regression?" Policy Research Working Paper 6616. Washington, DC: World Bank.

Hank, K. 2007. "Proximity and Contacts Between Older Parents and Their Children: A European Comparison." *Journal of Marriage and Family* 69: 157–173.

Hank, Karsten, and Isabella Buber. 2009. "Grandparents Caring for their Grandchildren: Findings from the 1004 Survey of Health, Ageing, and Retirement in Europe." *Journal of Family Issues* 30/1: 53–73.

Harburger, Deborah S., and Ruth A. White. 2004. "Reunifying Families, Cutting Costs: Housing-Child Welfare Partnerships for Permanent Supportive Housing." *Child Welfare* 8/5: 493–508.

Harris, Leslie J. 2011. "Questioning Child Support Enforcement Policy for Poor Families." *Family Law Quarterly* 4/2: 157–172.

Haskins, Ron, Janet Currie, and Lawrence M. Berger. 2015. "Can States Improve Children's Health by Preventing Abuse and Neglect?" Future of Children Policy Brief, spring. Princeton, NJ, and Washington, DC: Princeton University and Brookings Institution.

Hassani-Nezhad, Lena, and Anna Sjögren. 2014. "Unilateral Divorce for Women and Labor Supply in the Middle East and North Africa: The Effect of Khul Reform." *Feminist Economics* 20/4: 113–137.

Hasso, Frances. 2011. *Consuming Desires. Family Crisis and the State in the Middle East*. Palo Alto, CA: Stanford University Press.

Heckman, James. 2012. "Invest in Early Childhood Development: Reduce Deficits, Strengthen the Economy." https://heckmanequation.org/resource/invest-in-early-childhood-development-reduce-deficits-strengthen-the-economy/.

Hester, M., N. Westmarland, G. Gangoli. et al. 2006. *Domestic Violence Perpetrators: Identifying Needs to Inform Early Intervention*. Bristol: University of Bristol.

Hewitt, Belinda, Gavin Turrell, and Katrina Giskes. 2010. "Marital Loss, Mental Health and the Role of Perceived Social Support: Findings from Six Waves of an Australian Population Panel Study." *Journal of Epidemiology and Community Health* 66/4: 308–314.

Heymann, Jody. 2006. *Forgotten Families: Ending the Growing Crisis Confronting Children and Working Parents in the Global Economy*. New York: Oxford University Press.

Hochschild, Arlie. 2001. "The Nanny Chain." *The American Prospect*, December 19.

Hochschild, Arlie R., and Machung, Anne. 1989. *The Second Shift: Working Parents and the Revolution at Home*. New York: Viking.

Hondagneu-Sotelo, P. 1994. *Gendered Transitions: Mexican Experiences of Migration*. Berkeley: University of California Press.

Hondagneu-Sotelo, P. 2001. *Doméstica: Immigrant Workers Cleaning and Caring in the Shadows of Affluence*. Berkeley: University of California Press.

17

Htun, Mala, and Laurel Weldon. 2011. "Sex Equality in Family Law: Historical Legacies, Feminist Activism, and Religious Power in 70 Countries," Background Paper. *World Development Report 2012. Gender Equality and Development*. Washington, DC: World Bank.

Huerta, M.C., W., Adema, J., Baxter, et al. 2013. "Fathers' Leave, Fathers' Involvement and Child Development: Are They Related? Evidence from Four OECD Countries." OECD Social, Employment and Migration Working Papers 140. Paris: OECD.

ICRW (International Center for Research on Women). 2006. *Property Ownership and Inheritance Rights of Women for Social Protection-the South Asia Experience. Synthesis Report of Three Studies*. Washington, DC, and New Delhi: ICRW.

ILO. 2012. *Global Employment Trends for Women 2012*. Geneva: International Labour Office.

ILO. 2013. *Domestic Workers across the World: Global and Regional Statistics and the Extent of Legal Protection*. Geneva: International Labour Office.

ILO/UNDP. 2009. *Work and Family: Towards New Forms of Reconciliation with Social Co-responsibility*. Santiago: UNDP/ILO.

IPEA (Instituto de Pesquisa Econômica Aplicada). 2008. "Childhood and Poverty in Brazil." Powerpoint presentation delivered June 10 and July 1, Panama. www.unicef.org/socialpolicy/files/Childhood_and_Poverty_in_Brazil.ppt.

Jakovac-Lozic, Dijana. 2000. "Croatia's New Family Act and Its Implications on Marriage and Other Forms of Family Life." *California Western International Law Journal* 31/1: Article 20.

James, Estelle, Alejandra Cox Edwards, and Rebeca Wong. 2003. *The Gender Impact of Pension Reform: A Cross-Country Analysis*. Policy Research Working Paper 3074. Geneva: World Bank.

Joseph, Suad. 1994. "Brother/Sister Relationships: Connectivity, Love and Power in the Reproduction of Arab Patriarchy." *American Ethnologist* 21/1: 50–73.

Joseph, Suad. 2000a. "Civic Myths, Citizenship, and Gender in Lebanon," in S. Joseph (ed.), *Gender and Citizenship in the Middle East*. Syracuse, NY: Syracuse University Press.

Joseph, S. (ed.) 2000b. *Gender and Citizenship in the Middle East*. Syracuse, NY: Syracuse University Press.

Joseph, Suad. 2005. "The Kin Contract and Citizenship in the Middle East," in M. Friedman (ed.), *Women and Citizenship*. Oxford: Oxford University Press.

Kabeer, Naila. 2014. "Violence against Women as 'Relational' Vulnerability: Engendering the Sustainable Human Development Agenda." Occasional Paper. New York: UNDP Human Development Report Office.

Kabeer, Naila, and Natali, Luisa. 2013. "Gender Equality and Economic Growth: Is there a Win-Win?" IDS Working Paper 417. Brighton: IDS.

Killewald, Alexandra. 2011. "Opting Out and Buying Out: Wives' Earnings and Housework Time." *Journal of Marriage and Family* 73/2: 459–471.

Killewald, Alexandra, and Margaret Gough. 2013. "Does Specialization Explain Marriage Penalties and Premiums?" *American Sociological Review* 78/3: 477–502.

Kishor, Sunita, and Kiersten Johnson. 2004. *Profiling Domestic Violence: A Multi-country Study*. Calverton, MD: ORD Macro.

Knodel, J. 2012. "Inter-generational Family Care for and by Older People in Thailand." *International Journal of Sociology and Social Policy* 32/11 & 12: 682–694.

Koushal v. *NAZ Foundation*. 2013. Supreme Court of India. http://judis.nic.in/supremecourt/imgs1.aspx?filename=41070

Kumar, Neha, and Agnes R. Quisumbing. 2012. "Beyond 'Death Do Us Part': The Long-Term Implications of Divorce Perceptions on Women's Well-Being and Child Schooling in Rural Ethiopia." *World Development* 40/12: 2478–2489.

Langer, Ana, Afaf Meleis, Felicia M Knaul, et al. 2015. "Women and Health: The Key for Sustainable Development." *The Lancet* 386/9999, 1165–1210.

Lansford, Jennifer E., Laura B. Wager, John E. Bates, Gregory S. Pettit, and Kenneth A. Dodge. 2012. "Forms of Spanking and Children's Externalizing Behaviors." *Family Relations* 6/2: 224–223.

Lee, Kristen Schultz, and Hiroshi Ono. 2012. "Marriage, Cohabitation and Happiness: A Cross-National Analysis of 27 Countries." *Journal of Marriage and Family* 7/(5: 953–972.

Legal Momentum. 2011. "Single Mother Poverty in the US in 2010." The Women's Legal Defense and Education Fund. www.legalmomentum.org/sites/default/files/reports/single-mother-poverty-2010.pdf.

Leon, M., C. Ranzi, and T. Rostgaard. 2014. "Pressures towards and within Universalism: Conceptualising Change in Care Policy and Discourse," in M. Leon (ed.), *Care Regimes in Transitional European Societies*. Houndmills, Hampshire: Palgrave Macmillan.

Levy v. *Louisiana*, 391 U.S. 68 (1968).

Lewin, Tamar. 1995. "Child Welfare Is Slow to Improve Despite Court Order." *The New York Times*, December 30.

Lewis, Jane. 1997. "Gender and Welfare Regimes: Further Thoughts." *Social Politics* 4/2: 160–177.

Lindert, Kathy. 2013. "Social Safety Nets Core Course." Powerpoint. World Bank. www.worldbank.org/content/dam/Worldbank/Event/safetynets/1. 20Lindert_UCTs%20and%20CCTs%20for%20SSNCC.pdf.

Luke, Nancy, and Kaivan Munshi. 2006. "New Roles for Marriage in Urban Africa: Kinship Networks and the Labor Market in Kenya." *Review of Economics and Statistics* 88/2: 264–282.

Lye, D., D. Klepinger, P. Hyle, and A. Nelson. 1995. "Childhood Living Arrangements and Adult Children's Relations with their Parents." *Demography* 32: 261–280.

MacKellar, Landis. 2009. *Pension Systems for the Informal Sector in Asia (English)*. Social Protection Discussion Paper SP 0903. Washington, DC: World Bank.

Mason, A., and R. Lee. 2011. "Population Aging and the Generational Economy: Key Findings," in Lee Ronald and Andrew Mason, *Population Aging and the Generational Economy: A Global Perspective*. Cheltenham, Gloucestershire: Edward Elgar and IDRC.

Mazumdar, Indrani, and Neetha N. 2006. *Gender Dimensions: Employment Trends in India, 1993–94 to 2009–10*. New Delhi: Center for Women's Development Studies. http://archive.nyu.edu/bitstream/2451/34239/2/OcasionalPaper_56.pdf.

McIntosh, Jennifer E., and Richard Chisholm. 2008. "Cautionary Notes on the Shared Care of Children in Conflicted Parental Separations." *Journal of Family Studies* 14/1: 37–52.

McLanahan, Sara, and Pettit, Becky. 2003. "Residential Mobility and Children's Social Capital: Evidence from an Experiment." *Social Science Quarterly* 84/3: 6326–49.

McLanahan, Sara, Laura Tach, and Daniel Schneider. 2013. "The Causal Effects of Father Absence." *Annual Review of Sociology* 39: 399–427.

Medrano, Patricia. 2009. "Public Day Care and Female Labor Force Participation: Evidence from Chile." Series Documento de Trabajo 306. Santiago: University of Chile.

Meeker, M. 1976. "Meaning and Society in the Near East: Examples from the Black Sea Turks and the Levatine Arabs (II)." *International Journal of Middle East Studies* 7/3: 383–422.

Menjívar, Cecilia. 1997. "Immigrant Kinship Networks: Vietnamese, Salvadoreans and Mexicans." *Comparative Perspective Journal of Comparative Family Studies* 28/1: 1–24.

Menon, Nidhiya, Yana van der Meulen Rodgers, and Huong, Nguyen. 2014. "Women's Land Rights and Children's Human Capital in Vietnam." *World Development* 54/1: 18–31.

Mernitz, Sarah E., and Claire Kamp Dush. 2016. "Emotional Health across the Transition to First and Second Unions among Emerging Adults." *Journal of Family Psychology* 30/2: 233–244.

Michael H. v. *Gerald D.*, 491 US 110 (1989).

Michielin, Francesca, Clara H. Mulder, and Aslan Zorlu. 2008. "Distance to Parents and Geographical Mobility." *Population, Space and Place* 14: 327–345.

Micklewright, John, and Kitty Stewart. 2000. *The Welfare of Europe's Children: Are EU Member States Converging?* Florence: Policy Press and UNICEF.

Mintz, Steven. 2015. *The Prime of Life. A History of Modern Adulthood*. Cambridge, MA: Harvard University Press.

Moe, Angela M., and Myrtle P. Bell. 2004. "Abject Economics: The Effects of Battering and Violence on Women's Work and Employability." *Violence Against Women* 10/1: 29–55.

Morrison, A., M. Ellsberg, and S. Bott. 2007. "Addressing Gender-Based Violence." *World Bank Observer* 22: 25–51.

Moss, Jeremy. 2015. "How to Value Equality." *Philosophy Compass* 10/3: 187–196.

Mulder, Clara H., and Gunnar Malmberg. 2014. "Local Ties and Family Migration." *Environmental Planning* 46: 2195–2211.

Murphy, Michael. 2008. "Variations in Kinship Networks across Geographic and Social Space." *Population and Development Review* 34/1: 19–49.

Neetha, N. 2014. "Crisis in Female Employment: Analysis across Social Groups." *Economic and Political Weekly* 49/47: 50–59.

Nepomnyaschy, L, and J. Waldfogel. 2007. "Paternity Leave and Fathers' Involvement with Their Young Children. Evidence from the American ECLS-B." *Community, Work and Family* 10: 427–453.

Nielsen, A.A., and Christoffersen, M.N. 2009. *Börnehavens betydning for börns udvikling. En forksningsoversigt*. Köbenhavn: SFI –Det Nationale Forskningscenter for velfærd.

17

Nkwake, Apollo M. 2015. "Spousal Wealth and Fathers' Involvement in Childcare in Uganda." *Feminist Economics* 21/3: 114–141.

Nordenmark, M. 2016. "Gender Regime, Attitudes towards Childcare and Actual Involvement in Childcare among Fathers," in G.B. Eydal and T. Rostgaard (eds.), *Fatherhood in the Nordic Welfare States – Comparing care policies and practice*. Bristol: Policy Press.

O'Brien, M. 2009. "Fathers, Parental Leave Policies, and Infant Quality of Life: International Perspectives and Policy Impact." *The ANNALS of the American Academy of Political and Social Science* 624/1: 190–213.

O'Brien, M., and Shemilt, I. 2003. *Working Fathers: Earning and Caring.* Manchester: Equal Opportunities Commission.

Oduro, Abena D., Carmen Diana Deere, and Zachary Catanzarite. 2015. "Women's Wealth and Intimate Partner Violence: Insights from Ecuador and Ghana." *Feminist Economics* 21/2: 1–29.

OECD. 2012. *Starting Strong III – A Quality Toolbox for Early Childhood Education and Care.* Paris: OECD.

OECD. 2017. "Online Family Data Base." www.oecd.org/els/family/database.htm. Data corresponds to 2015 or latest available year.

OECD. n.d. "PF3.2: Enrolment in Childcare and Pre-school, OECD Family Database." Paris: Social Policy Division, Directorate of Employment, Labour and Social Affairs, OECD. www.oecd.org/els/family/database.htm.

Olivetti, Claudia, and Barbara Petrongolo. 2016. "The Evolution of Gender Gaps in Industrialized Countries," NBER Working Paper 21887. Cambridge, MA: National Bureau of Economic Research.

Orloff, Ann Shola. 1993. "Gender and the Social Rights of Citizenship: The Comparative Analysis of State Policies and Gender Relations." *American Sociological Review* 58: 303–328.

Palriwala, R., and N. Neetha. 2010. "Care Arrangements and Bargains: *Anganwadi* and Paid Domestic Workers in India." *International Labor Review* 149/4: 511–527.

Panda, Pradeep, and Bina Agarwal. 2005. "Marital Violence, Human Development and Women's Property Status in India." *World Development* 33/5: 823–850.

Pande, A. 2014. *Wombs in Labor: Transnational Surrogacy in India.* New York: Columbia University Press.

Park, J.M., P. Solomon, and D.S. Mandell. 2006. "Involvement in the Child Welfare System among Mothers with Serious Mental Illness." *Psychiatric Services* 57: 493–497.

Parreñas, R.S. 2000. "Migrant Filipina Domestic Workers and the International Division of Reproductive Labor." *Gender & Society* 14/4: 560–580.

Parreñas, R.S. 2005. *Children of Global Migration: Transnational Families and Gendered Woes.* Stanford, CA: Stanford University Press.

Parreñas, R.S. 2015. *Servants of Globalization: Migration and Domestic Work*, second edition. Stanford, CA: Stanford University Press.

Paxson, Christina, and Jane Waldfogel. 1999. "Parental Resources and Child Abuse and Neglect." *American Economic Review* 89/2: 239–244.

Pearse, Rebecca, and Raewyn Connell. "Gender Norms and the Economy: Insights from Social Research." *Feminist Economics* 22/1: 30–53.

Peng, Ito. 2013. "Reshaping and Reframing Gender, Care and Migration." Paper presented at the APSA Conference, August 29–September 3, Chicago.

Peng, Ito. 2016. "Shaping and Reshaping Care and Migration in East and Southeast Asia." Draft paper prepared for the International Sociological Association-RC19 Conference, August 23, University of Costa Rica, San José.

Perrin, E.C., and B.S. Siegel. 2013. *Promoting the Well-Being of Children whose Parents are Gay or Lesbian.* Elk Grove, IL: The American Academy of Pediatrics.

Pew Research Center. 2013. "The Global Divide on Homosexuality: Greater Acceptance in More Secular and Affluent Countries." www.pewglobal.org/2013/06/04/the-global-divide-on-homosexuality/.

Piketty, Thomas. 2014. *Capital in the Twenty-First Century.* Cambridge, MA: Harvard University Press.

Pruett, Marsha Kline, and J. Herbie DiFonzo. 2014. "Closing the Gap: Research, Policy, Practice and Shared Parenting: AFCC Think Tank Final Report." *Family Court Review* 52: 152–174.

Przeworski, Adam 2003. *States and Markets: A Primer in Political Economy.* Cambridge: Cambridge University Press.

Quisumbing, Agnes R., and John A. Maluccio. 2003. "Resources at Marriage and Intrahousehold Allocation: Evidence from Bangladesh, Ethiopia, Indonesia and South Africa." *Oxford Bulletin of Economics and Statistics* 65: 283–327.

Rangel, Marcos A. 2006. "Alimony Rights and Intrahousehold Allocation of Resources: Evidence from Brazil." *Economic Journal* 116/513: 627–658.

Ray, Rebecca, Janet C. Gornick, and John Schmitt. 2009. *Parental Leave Policies in 21 Countries Assessing Generosity and Gender Equality.* Washington, DC: Center for Economic and Policy Research.

Resko, Stella M. 2010. *Intimate Partner Violence and Women's Economic Insecurity.* El Paso: LFB Scholarly Publishing LLC.

Riley, M.W., and J.W. Riley, Jr. 1993. "Connections: Kin and Cohort," in F.L. Bengtson and W.A. Ahenbaum (eds.), *The Changing Contract across Generations.* New York: Aldine de Gruyter.

Roberts, D. 1998. *Killing the Black Body: Race, Reproduction and the Meaning of Liberty.* New York: Vintage.

Rostgaard, T. and V. Timonen. Forthcoming. "Turning the Problem into the Solution: Hopes, Trends and Contradictions in Home Care for Ageing Populations in Europe," in Thomas Boll, Dieter Ferring, and Jaan Valsiner (eds.), *Cultures of Care: Handbook of Cultural Geropsychology.* Charlotte, NC: Information Age Publishing.

Rostgaard, T., V. Timonen, and C. Glendinning. 2012. "Comparing Home Care Policies across Europe." *Health and Social Care in the Community* 20/3: 225–227.

Rowlands, Jo. 1997. *Questioning Empowerment. Working with Women in Honduras.* Oxford: Oxfam UK.

Rudrappa, Sharmila. 2015. *Discounted Life: The Price of Global Surrogacy in India.* New York: New York University Press.

Satka, M., and G.B. Eydal. 2004. "The History of Nordic Welfare Policies for Children," in H. Brembeck, B. Johansson, and J. Kampmann (eds.), *Beyond the Competent Child: Exploring Contemporary Childhoods in the Nordic Welfare Societies.* Roskilde: Roskilde University Press.

Sayare, Scott, and Maïa de la Baume. 2010. "In France, Civil Unions Gain Favor over Marriage." *The New York Times*, December 15.

Scheil-Adlung, X. 2015. "Extension of Social Security. Long-Term Care Protection for Older Persons: A Review of Coverage Deficits in 46 countries." ESS Working Paper 50. Geneva: ILO.

Schröder-Butterfill, Elisabeth. 2005. "The Impact of Kinship Networks on Old-Age Vulnerability In Indonesia." *Annales de Démographie Historique* 110: 139–163.

Sedgh, Gilda, Jonathan Bearak, Susheela Singh, et al. 2016. "Abortion Incidence between 1990 and 2014: Global, Regional, and Subregional Levels and Trends." *The Lancet*, May.

Sen, A. (2003). "Missing Women – Revisited: Reduction in Female Mortality Has Been Counterbalanced by Sex Selective Abortions." *British Medical Journal* 327/7427: 1297–1298.

Shang, X., and X. Wu. 2011. "The Care Regime in China: Elder and Child Care." *Journal of Comparative Social Welfare* 27/2: 123–131.

Sierminska, Eva M., Joachim R. Frick, and Markus M. Grabka. 2010. "Examining the Gender Wealth Gap." *Oxford Economic Papers* 61/4: 669–690.

Silverstein, M., and Giarrusso, R. 2010. "Aging and Family Life. A Decade Review." *Journal of Marriage and Family* 72: 1039–1058.

Silverstein, Merril, Zhen Cong, and Shuzhuo Li. 2002. "Intergenerational Transfers and Living Arrangements of Older People in Rural China: A Multi-Method Analysis." *Population and Development Review* 28/1: 31–57.

Silverstein, Merril, Zhen Cong, and Shuzhuo Li. 2006. "Intergenerational Transfers and Living Arrangements of Older People in Rural China: Consequences for Psychological Well-Being." *Journal of Gerontology* 61/5: S256–S266.

Singerman, Diane. 2006. "Restoring the Family to Civil Society: Lessons from Egypt." *Journal of Middle East Women's Studies* 2/1: 1–32.

Singh, S., J.E. Darroch, and L.S. Ashford. 2014. *Adding It Up: The Costs and Benefits of Investing in Sexual and Reproductive Health 2014.* New York: Alan Guttmacher Institute.

Skinner, Christine, and Jacqueline Davidson. 2009. "Recent Trends in Child Maintenance Schemes in 14 Countries." *International Journal of Law, Policy and the Family* 23/1: 25–52.

Skirbekk, Vegard. 2008. "Fertility Trends by Social Status." *Demographic Research* 18/5: 145–180.

Smyth, Bruce M., Jennifer E. McIntosh, Robert E. Emery, and Shelby L. Howarth. 2016. "Shared-Time Parenting: Boundaries of Risks and Benefits for Children," in L. Drozd, M. Saini, and N. Olesen (eds.) *Parenting Plan Evaluations.* New York: Oxford University Press.

Smyth, Bruce, Richard Chisholm, Bryan Rodgers, and Vu Son. 2014. "Legislating for Shared-Time Parenting After Parental Separation: Insights from Australia?" *Law and Contemporary Problems* 77: 109–149.

17

Social Security Administration. 2013. *Social Security Programs throughout the World: Asia and the Pacific, 2012*. Washington, DC: SSA Office of Retirement and Disability Policy Office of Research, Evaluation, and Statistics.

The Social Trends Institute. 2016. *The Sustainable Demographic Dividend*. Barcelona: The Social Trends Institute. http://sustaindemographicdividend.org/wp-content/uploads/2012/07/SDD-2011-Final.pdf.

Soons, Judith, and Matthijs Kalmijn. 2009. "Is Marriage More Than Cohabitation? Well-Being Differences in 30 European Countries." *Journal of Marriage and Family* 71/5: 1141–1157.

Srinivasan, Sharada, and Argun S. Bedi. 2007. "Domestic Violence and Dowry: Evidence from a South Indian Village." *World Development* 35/5: 857–880.

Stampini, Marco, and Leopoldo Tornarolli. 2012. "The Growth of Conditional Cash Transfers in Latin America and the Caribbean: Did They Go Too Far?" IZA Policy Paper 49. Bonn: Institute of Labor Economics.

Stevenson, Betsey, and Justin Wolfers. 2006. "Bargaining in the Shadow of the Law: Divorce Laws and Family Distress." *Quarterly Journal of Economics* 121/1: 267–288.

Strauss, M.A., and M.J. Paschall. 2009. "Corporal Punishment by Mothers and Development of Children's Cognitive Ability: A Longitudinal Study of Two Nationally Representative Age Cohorts." *Journal of Aggression, Maltreatment & Trauma* 18: 459–483.

Sutherland, Elaine. 2012. *The Future of Child and Family Law: International Predictions*. Cambridge: Cambridge University Press.

Swartz, Teresa Toguchi. 2009. "Intergenerational Family Relations in Adulthood: Patterns, Variations, and Implications in the Contemporary United States." *Annual Review of Sociology* 35: 191–212.

Tanaka, S., and Waldfogel, J. 2007. "Effects of Parental Leave and Work Hours on Fathers' Involvement with Their Babies: Evidence from the Millennium Cohort Study." *Community, Work and Family* 10: 409–426.

Thévenon, O. 2013. "Drivers of Female Labour Force Participation in the OECD." OECD Social, Employment and Migration Working Paper 145. Paris: OECD.

Thomas, Duncan. 1990. "Intra-Household Resource Allocation: An Inferential Approach." *Journal of Human Resources* 25/4: 635–664.

Tinios, Platon, Francesca Bettio, and Gianni Betti. 2015. *Men, Women and Pensions*. Luxembourg: Publication Office of the European Union/European Commission.

Tjaden, Patricia, and Thoennes, Nancy. 2000. *Extent, Nature, and Consequences of Intimate Partner Violence: Findings from the National Violence Against Women Survey*. Washington, DC: US Department of Justice.

Uhlenberg, Peter. 1996. "Mutual Attraction: Demography and Life Course Analysis." *Gerontologist* 36: 226–229.

Uhlenberg, Peter. 2009. "Children in an Acting Society." *The Journals of Gerontology: Social Sciences* 64(B)/4: S489–S496.

UN. 1980. *Convention on the Elimination of All Forms of Discrimination against Women*. New York: United Nations.

UN. 2002. *World Population Ageing 1950–2050*. New York: Population Division, DESA, United Nations. www.un.org/esa/population/publications/worldageing19502050/pdf/80chapterii.pdf.

UN. 2013. "World Population Prospects: The 2012 Revision, Key Findings and Advance Tables." http://esa.un.org/wpp/Documentation/pdf/WPP2012_20KEY%20FINDINGS.pdf.

UN Population Division. 2013. "World Population Prospects: The 2012 Revision." http://data.un.org/Data.aspx?d=PopDiv&f=variableID%3A54.

UN Treaty Collection. n.d. "Chapter IV: Human Rights. 8. Convention on the Elimination of All Forms of Discrimination against Women." https://treaties.un.org/Pages/ViewDetails.aspx?src=TREATY&mtdsg_no=IV-8&chapter=4&lang=en.

UN Tribune. n.d. "The 42 Countries that Have Banned Corporal Punishment." http://untribune.com/42-countries-banned-corporal-punishment/.

UN Women. 2015. *Progress of the World's Women 2015–2016. Transforming Economies, Realizing Rights*. New York: UN.

UNDESA (United Nations Department of Economic and Social Affairs). 2011. "World Marriage Patterns." *Population Facts* 2011/1.

UNICEF. 2014. "Issue Brief: Child Poverty in the Post-2015 Agenda." www.unicef.org/socialpolicy/files/Issue_Brief_Child_Poverty_in_the_post-2015_Agenda_June_2014_Final.pdf.

UNICEF. n.d.(a). "Convention on the Rights of the Child." www.unicef.org/crc/.

UNICEF. n.d.(b). "World Congress III against Sexual Exploitation of Children and Adolescents." www.unicef.org/protection/World_Congress_III_against_Sexual_Exploitation_of_Children_and_Adolescents(1).pdf.

Verschuere, Karine, and Alfons Marcoen. 1999. "Representation of Self and Socioemotional Competence in Kindergartners: Differential and Combined Effects of Attachment to Mother and to Father." *Child Development* 70/1: 183–201.

Vespa, Jonathan, Jamie M. Lewis, and Rose M. Kreider. 2013. "America's Families and Living Arrangements: 2012." *Current Population Reports* 20: 570.

Villareal, Andrés. 2007. "Women's Employment Status, Coercive Control, and Intimate Partner Violence in Mexico." *Journal of Marriage and the Family* 69/2: 418–434.

Vyas, Seema, and Charlotte Watts. 2009. "How Does Economic Empowerment Affect Women's Risk of Intimate Partner Violence in Low and Middle Income Countries? A Systematic Review of Published Evidence." *Journal of International Development* 21: 577–602.

Walker, Charles. 2010. "Space, Kinship Networks, and Youth Transition in Provincial Russia: Negotiating Urban–Rural and Inter-Regional Migration." *Europe Asia Studies* 62: 647–669.

Whitebook, M., C. McLean, and L.J.E. Austin. 2016. *Early Childhood Workforce Index – 2016. Executive Summary*. Berkeley: Center for the Study of Child Care Employment, University of California.

WHO (World Health Organization). 2002. *Long-Term Care in Developing Countries: Ten Case Studies*. Geneva: WHO/JDC-Brookdale Institute.

WHO. 2011. *World Report on Disability*. Geneva: World Bank/WHO.

WHO. 2013. *Global and Regional Estimates of Violence against Women: Prevalence and Health Effects of Intimate Partner Violence and Non-Partner Sexual Violence*. Geneva: WHO.

WHO. 2015a. Fact Sheet 348. November. www.who.int/mediacentre/factsheets/fs348/en/.

WHO. 2015b. *Imagine Tomorrow. Report on the 2nd WHO Global Forum on Innovation for Ageing Populations*. Geneva: WHO.

WHO. 2016a. "Maternal Mortality Fact Sheet." www.who.int/mediacentre/factsheets/fs348/en/.

WHO. 2016b. *Multisectoral Action for a Life Course Approach to Healthy Ageing: Draft Global Strategy and Plan of Action on Ageing and Health*. Report by the Secretariat. Provisional agenda item 13:4 A69/17. Geneva: WHO.

WHO and London School of Hygiene and Tropical Medicine. 2010. *Preventing Intimate Partner and Sexual Violence against Women: Taking Action and Generating Evidence*. Geneva: WHO.

Wight, Richard G., Allen J. LeBlanc, and M.V. Lee Badgett. 2013. "Same-Sex Legal Marriage and Psychological Well-Being: Findings from the California Health Interview Survey." *American Journal of Public Health* 103/2: 339–346.

Williams, Jessica R., Reem Ghandar, and Joan E. Kub. 2008. "Female Perpetration of Violence in Heterosexual Intimate Relationships: Adolescence through Adulthood." *Trauma, Violence and Abuse* 9/4: 227–249.

WLUML (Women Living Under Muslim Laws). 2003. *Knowing Our Rights: Women, Family, Laws and Customs in the Muslim World*. Lahore: WLUML.

World Bank. 2012. *World Development Report 2012. Gender Equity and Development*. Washington, DC: World Bank.

World Bank. 2016. "World Bank Database." https://data.worldbank.org/indicator/SH.DYN.MORT.

World Family Map. 2015. *Mapping Family Change and Child Well-Being Outcomes. Social Trends Institute*. New York and Barcelona: Institute for Family Studies.

Wyke, Sally, and Graeme Ford. 1992. "Competing Explanations for Associations between Marital Status and Health," *Social Science and Medicine* 34/5: 523–532.

Xiong, Y. 2009. "Social Change and Social Policy in China: National Adaptation to Global Challenge." *International Journal of Japanese Sociology* 18/1: 33–44.

Yi, C., and M. Farrell. 2006. "Globalization and the Intergernerational Relation: Cross-Cultural Perspectives on Support and Interaction Patterns." *Journal of Family Issues* 27: 1035–1041.

Zarrett, N., and R. Lerner. 2008. *Ways to Promote the Positive Development of Children and Youth*. Research-to-Results Brief. Washington, DC: Child Trends.

Zhang, Junsen, and William Chan. 1999. "Dowry and Wife's Welfare: A Theoretical and Empirical Analysis." *Journal of Political Economy* 107/4: 786–808.

18

Global Health and the Changing Contours of Human Life

Coordinating Lead Authors:[1]
Ama de-Graft Aikins, Dan Wikler

Lead Authors:[2]
Pascale Allotey, Gustaf Arrhenius, Uli Beisel, Melinda Cooper, Nir Eyal, Dan Hausman, Wolfgang Lutz, Ole F. Norheim, Elizabeth Roberts, Denny Vågerö

Contributing Author:[3]
Karim Jebari

[1]   Affiliations: AdGA: University of Ghana, Ghana; DW: Harvard University, USA.
[2]   Affiliations: PA: Monash University and United Nations University-International Institute for Global Health (UNU-IIGH), Malaysia; GA: Institute for Futures Studies, Sweden; UB: University of Bayreuth, Germany; MC: University of Sydney, Australia; NE: Harvard University, USA; DH: University of Wisconsin-Madison, USA; WL: IIASA, Austria; ON: University of Bergen, Norway; ER: University of Michigan, USA; DV: Stockholm University, Sweden.
[3]   Affiliations: KJ: Institute for Futures Studies, Sweden.

Summary

The "contours of human life" include childhood and adolescence, reproduction, the experiences of health, illness, disability, and death. These stages and aspects of life are universal and will remain so. However, social, environmental, and scientific changes are transforming their timing, texture, and patterns – and these transformations are not universally shared. Serious inequalities persist, among and within countries and regions, in longevity, morbidity, and disability, control over reproduction and sexuality, and care at the end of life. This chapter addresses these changing contours of human life in six sections: coming into being; longevity; diminished health; reproduction; enhancement; and death and dying.

We come into being as infants, children, and adolescents. In most parts of the world, life expectancy of infants and children has improved. Yet an infant's chances of surviving to adulthood are strongly linked to country of birth. The persistence of unmet need for disease intervention and avoidable suffering among millions of children is concentrated in poor regions and countries. There, adolescents also, whose numbers are at an all-time global high, are vulnerable to infectious diseases affecting other children, as well as harm from injury, violence, and alcohol and drug abuse.

Globally, on average, we live longer and better lives. Success in reducing infant and child mortality contributes greatly to increasing life expectancy and the convergence in age at death globally. Yet some countries and groups lag behind or even experience rising mortality. In rich countries, those with more education tend to live longer than those with less education; shorter lives are more common in many poor countries, among those burdened by the HIV/AIDS pandemic, and in post-communist Eastern Europe. While overall gains in life expectancy and longevity are substantial and promising, national and global data indicate divergence as well as convergence.

Diminished health compromises the value of longevity. Diminished health is also of concern for occasioning pain and discomfort, limitations or impediments to important activities, and social isolation and stigma; and often for the need to seek and pay for care, which may be both urgent and financially catastrophic. The most vulnerable adult populations are people from the poorest wealth quintile, women, older people, and people who are unemployed with low educational qualifications. In low- and middle-income countries, these groups bear a significant proportion of the cost of diminished health and disabilities because weak health and social care systems undermine lived experiences and health/social outcomes.

The extent to which people can make choices about their sexual and reproductive health is invariably intertwined with issues of disadvantage, inequity, and rights violations. This stratification of reproduction is evident in forms of access to maternal health services, global fertility control strategies, abortion and contraception management, and access to assisted reproductive technologies. Across these domains, poor women in poor countries are the most disadvantaged.

The important changes to the human condition that enhancement is likely to bring about will be social and cultural, rather than biological. This is likely to be mediated through the social effects of the widespread adoption of practices such as off-label use of stimulants like Ritalin. Still, these changes raise issues of inequality and will require regulation and rethinking of long-established principles in health policy.

Death and dying constitute an intimate and complex admixture of biomedical, social, cultural, and personal elements that are in a dynamic process of change and transformation. Wealth and poverty – at personal, social, and national levels – determine not only when and from what cause death will occur but also the experience of dying. In poor countries there is a notable deficit in palliation. In rich countries there is an abundance of resources, which also has drawbacks in the form of overreliance on institutional care and life-extending efforts that go past the point of diminishing returns.

The chapter sections illustrate that the value of longevity is compromised by an increasing number of people living with diminished health under inequitable systems of health and social care. Vigilant monitoring of these inequalities, combined with forceful engagement with their economic and social determinants, are needed to ensure that the favorable trends in the contours of human life become each person's birthright.

18.1   Introduction

For all of the great variations in history and culture among the world's peoples, and despite momentous changes in society, technology, and the environment over the past several hundred years, most human lives have had similar contours. We are conceived and born; if we avoid premature mortality, we go on to live as children, then as adolescents, then as adults; we form relationships based on kinship, love, and friendship; most of us have children of our own; we age; and we die. Each of us can respond with recognition and emotion to the stories and literatures of peoples remote from us in geography and time, for these universal contours of life constitute the human condition.

In the decades to come, these common patterns will continue to structure human lives, but their rhythms and textures will change greatly for many, reflecting personal and social consequences of economic growth and scientific and technological advances, and the continuing evolution of political and moral aspirations and norms. In the main, these are welcome developments. Two centuries ago, even in the richest nations, parents could expect to see many of their children die. Not infrequently, mothers died in childbirth. Though these tragedies still occur regularly in less affluent parts of the world, infant mortality rates are now below 1/100 in the vast majority of countries, and maternal death rates are in most countries well below 1/1,000. Death rates have fallen across the lifespan, and people everywhere can expect to live longer and healthier lives. Raising children, which used to occupy a large part of people's adult lives, now occupies a third or a half. We can anticipate further improvement in the duration and quality of life, including the avoidance of illness and disability; and the prospect of both biological and technological enhancements of our capacities is now coming into view.

As impressive as these gains have been, however, their distribution across and within human societies has been staggeringly uneven. Identifying these inequalities serves both to identify important trends in these key concerns of each human's life and to contribute to a moral agenda dedicated to bringing these benefits to all (see Box 18.1 for a note on concepts and measures of inequality). In this chapter, we chart both these advances and their unequal achievement, and make projections into the near future.

18.2   Coming into Being

For most of the history of our species, childhood was a grim fight for survival. At the dawn of the industrial age, one of five children would die before age five even in good times; in a bad year, the early death was the rule rather than the exception. With the rise in living standards in much of the West and in Japan, mortality rates for children dropped steadily; but most children lived in low- and middle-income countries, where death in childhood remained stubbornly high. Indeed, the presence or absence of mortal threats to health during childhood represented one of the most tangible differences in the experience of growing up in poor and rich countries, respectively.

These long-standing patterns changed markedly over the past three decades. Child mortality in low- and middle-income countries has plummeted. Moreover, because relatively few children in wealthy countries were dying, the huge improvement in child mortality in lower-income countries effectively narrowed global health disparities. Having transitioned from universal high child mortality to sharply unequal child mortality, humankind is currently progressing rapidly in the direction of universal low child mortality. Happier stories than this are hard to come by.

Despite these very welcome advances, child mortality remains stubbornly high in some countries, particularly in Sub-Saharan Africa; and significant disparities persist also within countries, both rich and poor. Moreover, there are grounds for concern that the resources and strategies that have secured the recent gains in child survival may be reaching their limit, requiring a more direct attack on sources of social inequality than may be possible with the means currently in use.

18.2.1   Infancy and Child Mortality

Two thirds of the great reduction of global child mortality during the past half century took place between 1970 and 2013 (Wang et al. 2016). The under-five mortality rate has almost halved since 1990, dropping from 90 to 46 deaths per 1,000 live births between 1990 and 2014 (UNICEF 2014a). With the notable exception of Sub-Saharan Africa, the greatest absolute declines have generally been reported among the poorest households.

Yet despite these promising trends, there remains significant cause for concern. The absolute burden of under-five deaths is still very high: worldwide, 223 million died before the age of five between 1990 and 2013 (UNICEF 2014a). These premature deaths are overwhelmingly concentrated in Sub-Saharan Africa and South Asia, which together account for four out of five under-five deaths worldwide. In Sub-Saharan Africa, 1 in 11 children dies before age five, compared with 1 in 159 in high-income countries (UNICEF 2014a). The vast majority of these deaths are preventable. Proven interventions exist to avert the most common causes of unnecessary death among children and adolescents – from pneumonia, diarrhea, malaria, and HIV/AIDS to road injuries and drowning – pointing to continued failures of political will and global coordination.

Moreover, the global reduction in child deaths continues to elude the youngest of children. Neonatal deaths – that is, deaths occurring in the first 28 days of life – make up almost half of all under-five deaths and are declining more slowly than other childhood deaths (UNICEF 2014a). Preterm and labor-related complications account for almost 60 percent of neonatal deaths. These complications are correlated with the education level of the mother and are more common among low-income, rural households.

Large disparities in child survival exist also between countries. With 157 deaths out of 1,000 births, Angola is the country with the highest under-five child mortality, while Finland, Iceland, and Luxemburg, with 2 deaths per 1,000 births, have the lowest mortality (UNICEF 2015).

Box 18.1 | A Note on Concepts and Measures of Inequality

Following the approach adopted in Chapter 3 on "Inequality and Social Progress," the conception of inequality used in this chapter is evidence-based (not merely perceived), static (not dynamic), and relative (not absolute). Note, however, that at different points, the present chapter uses different notions of equality and of distributive justice in health. Using either Chapter 3 or philosophical parlance (Cohen 1989; Lippert-Rasmussen and Eyal 2012), the differences pertain to how things are distributed (the distributive "pattern"), what is being distributed (the distributive "currency"), and the area in which that assessment is made (the distributive "locus").

- *The distributive pattern*: Sometimes we focus on the gap or inequality in health as a morally significant fact in itself. At other times, we emphasize the avoidable health gaps exposed or caused by social and structural inequality, especially in the case of individuals or populations who are worse off. The concern with health gaps can reflect a straightforward utilitarian approach or a prioritarian approach. Prioritarianism puts greater weight on the health or wellbeing of those who are worse off rather than focusing specifically on the gap between them and those who are better off. At other points in this chapter, we emphasize the avoidable or even intentional wrongful human and structural barriers to better health which inequality merely exposes. For example, inequalities in numbers of injuries may reflect officially sanctioned violence against minorities. When we indicate inequalities in terms of various indices, this usually reflects pragmatic measurement needs rather than deeper thoughts on what fundamentally constitutes a health inequality, or the health inequality that matters.

- *The distributive currency*: The chapter focuses on inequalities in the availability of health services, but we also explore inequalities in other distributive "currencies," such as longevity or freedom from disability. Additionally, we discuss inequalities in probabilistic spaces like life expectancy and risk of disability. Our chapter lays emphasis on equality of true access to services. Cases in point would include ramps that equalize access to health facilities for wheelchair-reliant patients and language translators who equalize access across linguistic lines. An alternative emphasis is on equality in the resources being offered to all, for example in whether all are allowed to use the staircase to the clinic. Related to the question of which currency is being used is the question of whether it is important to use multiple currencies. We sometimes focus on equality in a single component of health (e.g. in diabetes status, in ambulatory functioning), potentially suggesting that these may matter independently of one another. At other times, what we assess is equality in a summary measure of health (e.g. in overall disability status), or even in a related summary measure of utility or capability to which health is only one contributor (e.g. in welfare or in health-related quality of life). In current philosophical debates concerning equality, one also finds a very different notion of equality that focuses on equality of fundamental social status. Although distinct from a concern about distribution of fungible goods and services, fundamental equality in the relations among members of a population is rarely obtainable when inequalities in money, power, and, to some degree, health and health care, are large.

- *The distributive locus*: The present chapter is concerned both with inequalities within districts, countries, and regions of the world and with inequalities between them. Sometimes we discuss inequalities among individuals, as is common in economics (inter-individual inequality or, as per chapter 3, "vertical inequality"), but usually we focus on inequalities among social groups (inter-group inequality or "horizontal equality"). The groups whose health or access to health care we compare include different income quintiles, levels of education, racial and ethnic groups, age groups, and genders. These groups are marked out either by their tendency to attract advantages and disadvantages across many – potentially reinforcing (Crenshaw 1993; Kabeer 2010) – distributive spheres, or by their social salience and relevance to personal identity. That said, often these two group definitions overlap (e.g. when a racial minority group both is socially salient and faces multiple disadvantages). Sometimes we focus on inequalities in contemporaneous health states but we do so largely for pragmatic or measurement reasons: what ultimately matters with respect to health (as opposed to access to health care) is inequality in lifetime health or inequalities within life stages. Sometimes we examine inequalities in the prevalence of certain health states (such as living with HIV). At other times we assess inequalities in the incidence of health states (such as when HIV infection took place).

Box 18.2 | Infant/Child Deaths and the Cultural Construction of Personhood

The continued high incidence of infant and child death in some countries plays a significant role in determining how personhood is bestowed over time, sometimes at a child's first or even fifth birthday instead of at birth (Scheper-Hughes 1993; Conklin and Morgan 1996). In her study of early child deaths in Brazil, Scheper-Hughes (1993) shows how mothers learn to allow themselves to only bond with children who are likely to survive. At other times, naming ceremonies are postponed from the moment of birth to later in life. These practices of gradual personhood contrast sharply with the trend toward marking child, infant, and even "prenatal" death much earlier in wealthier countries, through funerals and other forms of memorialization, as infant and child death becomes comparatively rare (Scheper-Hughes 1993).

"A child born in the highest under-five mortality country faces about 80 times the risk of dying before age 5 as her or his counterpart in the lowest mortality country" (UNICEF 2015: 27). Additional inequalities exist within regions and within countries. Within the European Union, for instance, infant mortality is highest in Romania with 9.8 deaths per 1,000 live births and lowest in Finland with 2.3 (European Union 2013). In 2010, Romanian children also experienced the poorest survival chances in the EU, with 37 deaths per 100,000 boys and 30 for girls. Child death rates have dropped to as low as 10 among 100,000 Slovenian boys and 7 among Danish girls (European Union 2013: 21). Box 18.2 considers the impact of infant and child deaths on the cultural construction of personhood.

The fourth of the Millennium Development Goals (MDGs) was to reduce child mortality (under-five mortality) by two-thirds between 1990 and 2015. Many countries, including Bangladesh and China, managed to reach this goal, while others, such as India, did not, and the world taken as a whole also failed (UN 2015). So, while we can observe that on a global level overall child mortality has been decreasing significantly since the 1970s, a closer look at this trajectory reveals a more complicated spatial picture of ongoing progress in some countries and regions and pockets of remaining challenge in others. Nor has progress been temporally continuous. The reduction in child mortality began to slow down in 1985 and reversed direction in 1994 (−1/2 percent) before resuming its former downward trend in 1997 (UN 2015). Uneven progress must be expected in an effort to mobilize the entire globe toward the goal of sharply reducing child mortality; nevertheless, the patterns that emerged during this period may be explained by attending to the socio-economic context in which the planning and execution of these programs took place.

18.2.2   Child Mortality and the Changing Contours of Global Public Health

The 1980s and 1990s were the period in which global financial institutions such as the World Bank and IMF used debt restructuring (known as Structural Adjustment Programs or SAPs) to force through draconian "reforms" of the public health sector in the global South. These reforms included mass privatizations, cutbacks in public spending, public-sector employee redundancies, user-fee systems of health care access, and a preferred model of public-private partnership in health care provision leading to the "NGOization" of the health care sector (Pfeiffer and Chapman 2010). The generalization of this regime had dramatic negative effects on public health, leading to a visible deterioration of public health indicators across Africa, the former Soviet Union, and other countries in the throes of economic liberalization (Kim et al. 2002).

This evisceration of the public health sector across the global South – combined with mass unemployment, growing inequalities, and the imposition of a new intellectual property rights regime at the hands of the World Trade Organization – could not have occurred at a less auspicious time. Many countries affected by World Bank and IMF debt restructuring in the late 1980s and 1990s were also facing a significant HIV/AIDS epidemic and found themselves without the means (such as affordable medications) to implement any effective response. As a result, countries, especially in Sub-Saharan Africa, saw horrific increases in child and adolescent mortality during this period (Farmer 2001; Poku 2006).

By the turn of the millennium, as the devastating impact of World Bank, IMF, and WTO policies became difficult to ignore, this model came under increasing scrutiny. The adoption of the MDGs by the United Nations in 2000 signaled a new resolve to develop a more progressive global health strategy at odds with the brutal fiscal conservatism of the global financial institutions. Under the strain of overwhelming criticism, the World Bank itself adopted a new focus on the social aspects of growth, initiating what some refer to as the post-Washington Consensus era in global development policies (Bedford 2009). This turning point coincided with the arrival of a new set of institutional actors, including new private foundations such as the Gates Foundation, new national and global programs to combat specific infectious diseases (PEPFAR, the Global Fund), and new global alliances such as the Global Alliance for Vaccines and Immunization (GAVI), which have together profoundly transformed the landscape of global health interventions (McGoey, Reiss, and Wahlberg 2011; Williams and Rushton 2011; Gonzàlez-Block et al. 2012). This new global health complex has reinvested in health care at a time when states have retreated, and has generated a renewed focus on infectious disease research among pharmaceutical companies, who had neglected the area for many years. As a consequence of their interventions, we have seen remarkable progress in the treatment of HIV/AIDS, neglected tropical diseases, and other infectious diseases, and faster-than-expected decreases in child and adolescent mortality. Mortality from infectious disease among children and adolescents remains high, but appears to be steadily declining (Kyu et al. 2016). Child deaths from HIV/AIDS peaked in 2005 and have declined thereafter, no doubt as a consequence of greater access to anti-retroviral treatments (Kyu et al. 2016).

However, there are significant limitations in this new model of global public health. New institutional actors such as the Gates Foundation have no doubt made important contributions to the prevention and treatment of infectious disease and have had a marked positive impact on slowing the progression of HIV/AIDS in particular. At the same time, these actors have adapted to, rather than restructured, the public-private infrastructure of health care imposed by the first-generation Washington Consensus, and they continue to rely on a mix of non-profit, philanthropic, and private (pharmaceutical) entities to address public health challenges. The new global health actors work in close collaboration with big pharma and are to a large extent driven by the desire to generate a new drug innovation model and a new stream of revenue flows for the pharmaceutical industry, which has been faced with an innovation deficit and expiring patents for more than a decade now (Cooper 2013). In this way, "public health" is being resurrected as a profitable area of investment in ways that shape the kinds of health care interventions that are prioritized and foreclose the revival of a truly *public* health care infrastructure (Clark 2014). The result has been a pattern dominated by vertical funding schemes that focus on single diseases and a prioritization of distinct, commercializable medical interventions over environmental or infrastructural improvements in public health. While these schemes have contributed significantly to the decrease in child mortality overall, their vertical orientation has equally created a fragmented health care landscape, a new dominance of public-private initiatives and other para-state actors over national actors (Geissler 2013; Rees 2014), and a move toward "projects" as units of action (Whyte et al. 2013; Krause 2014), resulting in an uneven geography of "the global health complex" (McGoey, Reiss, and Wahlberg 2011). To illustrate these shortcomings, we will now look at child and adolescent health and development in more detail.

18.2.3   Infancy Health and Development

Even as child mortality remains a priority at a global level, most children survive even in the poorest of countries, and there is an imperative to ensure that they thrive and remain healthy. In this respect, the new Sustainable Development Goals (SDGs) (UN 2015) offer a much more rounded perspective than the MDGs did, addressing issues relating to development over and above the reduction in mortality.[4]

This emphasis on the interrelationship between development and child health followed on several decades' research on a hypothesis by the epidemiologist David Barker (1938–2013) that health over the life course was strongly influenced by fetal and infant development; indeed, that by the time children are born, events that have already

occurred predict much of their future health, and even the health trajectories of their progeny. Barker hypothesized that environmental influences, such as nutrition, interact in utero with genetic factors to program development, a process then referred to as "biological programming." The theory was originally attacked by both geneticists and social epidemiologists, the latter arguing that Barker failed to account for social influences on development (Ben-Shlomo and Smith 1991; Susser and Levin 1999). In fact, Barker was fully aware that biological programming was a process that was socially stratified and tied to family social circumstances. However, he overstated the reach of his hypothesis (Barker 1990) and claimed that health inequalities were already programmed in utero (Barker 1991), a claim which has been heavily criticized since (Vågerö and Illsley 1995).

The vast amount of work that was triggered by the formulation of the fetal origin hypothesis has led to its reformulation in the form of a "developmental origins of adult disease hypothesis." According to the so-called DOHAD hypothesis, adult disease is heavily influenced by what happens during the first part of your life. This insight was first formulated in 1934 in an influential paper in *The Lancet* (Kermack, McKendrick, and McKinlay 1934) which suggested that the first 15 years of life shape survival chances in later life. The modern DOHAD hypothesis simply recognizes the fact that social and environmental factors influence child development in a broad way, and through this process also influence adult health, in particular circulatory disease and diabetes (Barker 2013). The biology of the process is better understood today with the rise of epigenetics, which explores the ways in which the environment "talks to" the genome and influences gene expression (Carey 2011). Nutritional shock, trauma, and infections are examples of external factors that may trigger epigenetic change in children and affect their long-term development. Whether or not such epigenetic change can trigger a response in later generations remains controversial (Davey Smith 2012; Pembrey, Saffery, and Bygren 2014).

If epigenetic processes can indeed exert such broad influence, programs targeting children and overall economic development may have long-term consequences for adult health and survival. A focus on school is certainly necessary, but at the age when children normally start school the earliest environmental influences on them have already been at work. Attachment between child and parents (Roisman and Fraley 2012), children's language skills (Laplante et al. 2004), and non-cognitive social skills (Heckman, Stixrud, and Urzua 2006) are all influenced by parents' experience, and affect children's development and long-term health.

War, famines, and trauma represent large-scale social influences with the potential to influence public health broadly. Children who survived the famine during the siege of Leningrad, 1941–44, suffered "Leningrad siege hypertension" decades later. As adults, their mortality from circulatory disease was elevated (Vågerö et al. 2013). Children who survived the Ukrainian famine of 1932–33 were more likely to suffer diabetes as adults than children who were not exposed to the famine (Lumey, Khalangot, and Vaiserman 2015). The "great leap forward" in China led to mass starvation in 1959–61; children born during

---

[4]   See SDG 3 and SDG 4.

those years were more likely than other children to develop schizophrenia as adults (Xu et al. 2009). Though the world is less convulsed by war and famine than in previous times (Pinker 2012), these have by no means been eliminated, and their consequences are likely to stretch long into the future. For example, the average duration in the instability of refugee camps is 17 years. Children who survive such calamities may nevertheless be scarred by their experience, suffering from impairments to health and wellbeing decades later.

18.2.4   Child Health

Much of the recent success in reducing child mortality can be attributed to overall improvements in socio-economic status worldwide, to the improvement and wider availability of basic health care measures, and to the rapid scale up of the WHO's Expanded Program on Immunization (EPI) since the 1970s. Furthermore, there has been significant success in the elimination of mother-to-child transmission of HIV (Chi, Stringer, and Moodley 2013; Mofenson and Cotton 2013; Wang et al. 2016). Early childhood education in this age group is critical to laying the foundations for cognitive development, but this is also closely associated with other factors that affect general health and wellbeing such as good nutrition, safe drinking water to protect again diarrhoeal diseases, sanitation, and safety. A significant body of work identifies particular risks to the girl child through the workings of gender-based norms that may limit access to resources and education and provide preferential treatment to one gender over another. As girls grow older, other structural factors impede access to education, such as poor sanitation in schools which impacts on menstrual hygiene (Kansai, Singh, and Kumar 2016; Phillips-Howard et al. 2016).

Global health inequalities in child health remain pertinent: children from Sub-Saharan Africa, South Asia, lower-income countries, and fragile contexts still have the highest under-five mortality rates (UNICEF 2015), as well as being disproportionately affected by disease, illhealth, and unhealthy living environments. However, health inequalities within countries are widespread too, with the consequence that national and regional comparisons based on country league tables must be nuanced by attention to intraregional disparities.

Ghana is an instructive example. While economic growth has averaged 7 percent over the last decade, with the result that Ghana is now labeled as a lower-middle-income country, economic disparities are not only persistent but in some areas widening (UNICEF 2014b; Aryeetey and Kanbur 2017). Poverty reduction has mainly succeeded in the country's more urbanized south, while in the agricultural north little progress has been reported. Yet the majority of the population continues to live in rural areas and depends on agriculture. In fact, poverty has increased substantially in the Upper West region, the poorest in Ghana, provoking the World Bank to declare that Ghana's success story in reducing poverty is confined to its southern and urban areas only (World Bank 2011, quoted in UNICEF 2014b: 2).

In addition, Ghana's 2010 Population Census found that "over 86% of Ghana's workforce are employed in the informal sector, making both job security and revenue generation a substantial challenge"

(UNICEF 2014b: 3). The economic gaps between urban and rural and between formal and informal sector are starkly visible in health trends and outcomes in the country. A recent comprehensive survey of living conditions and health in Accra, the capital, calculated that under-five mortality "ranges from 21 per 1,000 in some parts of the city to 78 per 1,000 in other areas within the city" (Weeks, Hill, and Stoler 2013: 6).

Such large disparities in health services and outcomes are not confined to economically poor countries. In the United States of America, for instance, access to health services for children is highly unequal; minority children are much less likely to be insured. These racial inequalities are closely correlated with socio-economic disparities: "Given these differences in income distributions, the shorter average life expectancy at age 25 for poor adults applies to more than 1 in 5 Black and Hispanic adults and fewer than 1 in 10 White adults" (Braveman et al. 2010: S192; see also NCHS(US) 2016).

In the European Union, where universal health insurance is the norm, stark inequalities in health outcomes mirror social and economic disparities both between and within countries. Male life expectancy at birth, for example, varies by 11.8 years across the EU. These "intersecting inequalities" (Kabeer 2010) in child mortality and health within regions and countries draw our attention to the fine-grained geographies of health care access and quality, as well as to how health prospects intersect with race, gender, and economic status. They also point to the importance of going beyond country-wide and regionwide league tables in evaluating progress in child mortality and health.

18.2.5   Adolescent Mortality and Health

Mortality rates among adolescents are much lower than those of children and have shown a slight decline since the turn of the millennium. Recent data on the global burden of disease, collected for 2013, show that more than 80 percent of overall deaths among those under 19 occurred in younger children, while adolescents represented more than 60 percent of years lived with disability (Kyu et al. 2016). The leading causes of death in this age group are road injury, HIV, suicide, lower respiratory infections, and interpersonal violence ((Kyu et al. 2016: 276). Lower respiratory infections rank among the top five causes of adolescent deaths in all regions except for high-income countries and the Western Pacific Region, with more deaths occurring among younger adolescents (under 14). Diarrheal diseases are also a significant cause of mortality, particularly in 10–14-year-olds. Diarrheal diseases, lower respiratory infections, and meningitis together account for about 20 percent of deaths in this age group in the Africa and Southeast Asia regions (WHO 2014a; Kyu et al. 2016).

In other respects, however, mortality rates among adolescents evidence distinct singularities. One area of particular concern is the rise in HIV/AIDS mortality among adolescents, which has increased since 2000, bucking the overall trend toward improvement visible among all other age groups (Kyu et al. 2016). Most of these premature deaths are concentrated in the African region. It is possible that the increase reflects improvements in the treatment of pediatric HIV, as infected children survive into the second decade of life (WHO 2014a). Adolescents who were infected in childhood face particular challenges in adapting to the realities of chronic disease and in accessing successive anti-retroviral drug regimens, particularly given the existence of extensive drug resistance in multi-drug-treated children. Adolescent HIV care must focus on morbidity related to long-term HIV care and treatment adherence (Mofenson and Cotton 2013).

We also see an increased vulnerability to *new* HIV infections between the ages of 10 and 19 and the emergence of a marked gender differentiation. Before adolescence, little difference is discernible between males and females, while after adolescence, girls begin to contract new infections at a much greater rate. This trend is the same across countries but is starkest in Sub-Saharan Africa, where we find 85 percent of cases of adolescents living with HIV (Idele et al. 2014). In countries with generalized epidemics, more than 80 percent of new infections among adolescents are in girls (Idele et al. 2014). The overwhelming majority of these new infections are transmitted through sex; research indicates that adolescent girls in particular have very poor knowledge about HIV and very limited access to proven means of prevention such as condoms (Idele et al. 2014).

During adolescence, we see a distinct set of vulnerabilities emerge. The leading causes of disability-adjusted life years (DALYs) lost among this age group are depression (specifically unipolar depressive disorders); iron-deficiency anemia; asthma; alcohol and substance misuse; accidental and non-accidental injuries including road traffic accidents, violence, and suicides; back and neck pain; and HIV (WHO 2014b). Alcohol misuse was the highest risk factor for DALYs for young people aged 20–24 years, while unsafe sex as a risk factor increased from the thirteenth rank to the second for both sexes aged 15–19 years from 1990 to 2013 (Mokdad et al. 2016). Smoking, which remains the number one risk factor for premature death worldwide, is a habit that typically begins during adolescence. Though its principal health effects are experienced later in the life course, its initiation reflects and is partly explained by the distinctive vulnerabilities of the adolescent phase.

During these years, gender, sexuality, sexual practice, and sex/gender identity begin to play an important role in shaping experiences of health and exposure to health risk. Many young people have their first sexual experiences in adolescence, while many young girls get married or give birth during these years, in many instances through coercion. Provision of comprehensive sexual health and sexuality education, as well as access to youth-friendly health services, is critical to mitigating these risks. It is also important to acknowledge the influence of family, technology, social media, and peers in the development of risky and health-seeking practices in youth.

Other significant gender influences are evident in rates of injury and death from violence, with adolescent girls experiencing much higher rates of emotional and physical violence from intimate partners, while adolescent boys encounter increased risk from physical violence by other boys or men (see Chapter 10 for a more extensive discussion). The continued practice of female genital mutilation (FGM) is one example of gender-based violence that is still present in an estimated 28 countries, in Africa, the Middle East, and Southeast Asia (Muthumbi et al. 2015). While the African Charter on Human and

People's Rights on the Rights of Women in Africa recognizes FGM as a violation of women's rights and a form of gender-based discrimination (Muthumbi et al. 2015: 33), an estimated 125 million women and girls have undergone the procedure and many more are at risk (UNICEF 2013).

It is clear from the preceding discussion that adolescent health presents unique challenges that would best be met by targeted, gender-sensitive interventions. However, the available data on adolescent health are extremely patchy when compared with data on children and adults, making it difficult to assess past successes or to plan future interventions (Idele et al. 2014). Thus, despite the relatively low level of mortality rates in this age group, adolescents are confronted with a unique set of vulnerabilities which until recently have been somewhat neglected by the leading global health actors. For example, adolescence is the time when many people experience significant mental health problems for the first time. Globally, depression, anxiety disorders, and schizophrenia are among the top ten causes of disability among adolescents and young adults, and suicide was the second leading cause of death among 15–29 year olds in 2015 (GBD 2015 Disease and Injury Incidence and Prevalence Collaborators, 2016). A recent *Lancet* investigation into adolescent health and wellbeing concluded that increased attention to adolescent health is crucial for the world's future, as adolescence is "characterised by dynamic brain development in which the interaction with the social environment shapes the capabilities an individual takes forward into adult life," and is thus critical for achieving human potential (Patton et al. 2016). Initiatives to lobby for and promote adolescent health are important and welcome.

18.2.6   Conclusion

In most parts of the world, death rates among infants and young children have sharply decreased over the past four decades. These successes, which seem to be little noticed by the general public, constitute a remarkable achievement. Nevertheless, they represent only partial fulfillment of the goal of ensuring a healthy childhood for each person. An infant's chances of surviving to adulthood are strongly linked to country of birth. Death rates in Sub-Saharan Africa remain very high. The charted progress in reducing child mortality substantially achieves the objectives of a coordinated effort, targeted by the UN's MDGs and mobilized by both public agencies and philanthropists, relying in large part on successful deployment of immunization and other technologies within single-disease interventions. However, the persistence of unmet need and avoidable suffering among millions of children, concentrated particularly in Sub-Saharan Africa, illustrates some of the limitations of this approach. For instance, adolescents, whose numbers are at an all-time high, are vulnerable to infectious diseases affecting other children (and more vulnerable to HIV/AIDS) as well as harm from injury, violence, and alcohol and drug abuse. The distinctive health needs of this age group, including those specific to gender, remain relatively less studied and less frequently targeted compared with those of other children. The SDGs on health (SDG 3), education (SD4), and gender equity (SDG 5) provide benchmarks for reducing child mortality and enhancing the wellbeing and development of children, adolescents, and youth over the coming decades.

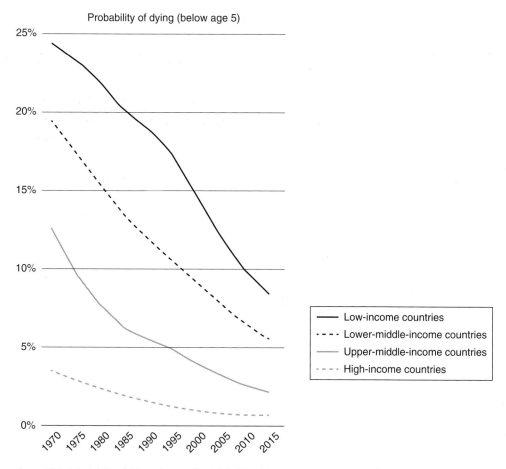

Figure 18.1 | Probability of dying before age five, by World Bank income region, both sexes, 1970–2015.
Source: UNPD (2015).

But achieving a world in which each newborn, regardless of place and circumstances of birth, can be expected to proceed to a healthy and thriving childhood and adolescence will require that we go beyond the SDGs. Initiatives of the past three decades that have improved health for so many millions of children worldwide were the result of an alignment of public and private resources and initiatives whose impact may have reached its maximum. To continue to improve health systems in low-income countries will require sustained and well-funded engagement with the underlying economic, structural, and social determinants of child and adolescent health throughout the world.

18.3 Longevity, Life Expectancy, and Inequalities in the Risk of Dying

18.3.1 Introduction: Social Progress in Health and Longevity

Compared with half a century ago, people all over the world now have a reasonable expectation not only of surviving childhood but of living longer and healthier lives (Peto, Lopes, and Norheim 2014). Avoiding premature mortality is possible for a majority of the world population, even for the bottom billion, given the right circumstances and the right

policies (CSDH 2008; UNPD 2012; Norheim et al. 2015). This section looks at the vast improvements in global health, measured as rising life expectancy; but also at inequalities in life expectancy and longevity, conceived as differences either between individuals or between groups, within countries as well as globally.

As mentioned above, the general public may be unaware of the very welcome story that a review of global health trends tells. Globally, on average, we live longer and better lives, and even if many countries and groups lag behind and some may even reverse their previous progress, overall inequalities in average age at death between individuals are decreasing. This reflects a two-centuries-old process of reduction of infant, child, and early mortality, discussed in Section 18.2, which probably represents the single most important achievement of modern humanity (Smits and Monden 2009). This is a reason to celebrate.

Yet, in contrast to converging child mortality trends (Figure 18.1), adult mortality trends 1950–2015 appear *not* to be converging globally. The global picture is complex and mixed, showing both convergence and divergence. Despite the progress evident in much of the world, whole regions have faced long-term stagnation or deterioration, such as in the former Soviet Union in 1970–2005, or in Sub-Saharan Africa in the 1990s.

Box 18.3 | Data and Methods on Estimating Inequality

To estimate inequality in life expectancy and longevity (age at death), we used UN Population Division (UNPD) historical life tables in their latest revision (Preston, Heuveline, and Guillot 2001; UNPD 2012). These cover each five-year time period from 1950 to 2015, where the last five-year period is partly estimated. There are separate life tables for each country, World Bank income regions, and the world as a whole. Since age distributions differ between countries, and within countries over time, all life tables are age-adjusted. For every fifth year from 1970 to 2010, we estimated the death rates by averaging the age-specific risks in the five-year periods before and after it (so our 1970 rates describe 1965–1975); this smooths out any sudden mortality changes. It should be noted that many countries lack vital registration, so UNPD mortality trend estimates are only approximate.

Inequality within each population is estimated by Le Grand's method: Gini applied to age at death (Le Grand 1987; Smits and Monden 2009; Norheim 2010). We shall hereafter use the term "longevity" for age at death, and we are interested in whether inequality in longevity is increasing or decreasing. This terminology is important. Longevity is the actual age at death for each individual in a life table (and inequality in longevity can therefore be seen as an ex-post measure), while life expectancy is an ex-ante measure of average health for the whole population.

$Gini_h$ can be calculated in different ways and takes the values 0 for perfect equality and 1 for complete inequality (Asada 2007). We use the formula:

$$Gini_h = \frac{1}{2} \sum_{i=1}^{n} \sum_{j=1}^{n} \frac{|y_i - y_j|}{n^2 \mu},$$

where y_i is the age at death for the ith person, n is the number of people in the population (100,000 in our life table model), and μ is average health (life expectancy at birth) in the population. We extracted the expected final distribution of people dying in different age groups from the $_nd_x$ column in the life table.

We only present results for both sexes combined. Gender inequality in mortality is an interesting field of inquiry in itself, but for ease of presentation, we do not present separate figures for females and males. Life tables by sex are available from UNPD.

Inequalities in mortality rates also persist within countries, mirroring differences in income, wealth, class, and level of education. In many countries, these widening gaps are due to the success among the better-off in forestalling death, leaving their less fortunate compatriots behind. Indeed, before the great rise in material wealth and in biomedical science brought on by industrialization, the lifespans of lord and commoner may have been fairly similar; when the means for living longer became available, the best-off were the first to benefit (Deaton 2013). These inequalities proved to be transient, at least in part, where similar benefits eventually accrued to the less well-off. But this easing of inequality is not inevitable. Worse still, substantial inequalities persist and expand also when segments of the adult population in a country experience rising mortality trends, as has been the case in both the USA and Russia recently. Much more can be done to accelerate social progress in health.

In this section we track the trends and patterns in longevity, life expectancy, and inequalities in the risk of dying: our data and methods and terminology are briefly explained in Boxes 18.3 and 18.4.

18.3.2 Trends in Life Expectancy at Birth

18.3.2.1 Life Expectancy at Birth in the 25 Largest Countries (1955–2015)

Figure 18.2 shows trends in life expectancy from 1955 to 2015 for the world (thick line) and for the 25 most populous countries in the world. The average improvements for the world are immense: from 48 years in 1955 to above 71 years in 2015. This is an increase of 23 years over a time span of 60 years, or (put differently) more than an additional four months per year.

Box 18.4 | Terminology on Mortality and Associated Concepts

Mortality refers generally to the process of dying and its intensity.

(Crude) death rate is the number of deaths that occur in a given year in a given population in relation to the population at risk, mostly expressed as deaths/1,000 population.

Age-adjusted mortality rates (or *age-standardized death rates*) are used to compare population groups with different age distributions. They are calculated by applying age-specific mortality rates to a standard age distribution and hence allow a fair comparison between populations with different age structures.

Age-specific mortality rates refers to the number of deaths of a certain age divided by the population at risk of that age over a year, such as infant mortality (mortality before age one); child mortality (usually mortality before age five) or adult mortality, usually measured by five-year age groups.

Life expectancy is calculated by using a life table in which empirically measured age-specific mortality rates in a given year are converted into survival probabilities at each age and subsequently multiplicatively combined to calculate life expectancy at birth or at any other age (such as life expectancy at age 60). They give expected length of life after that age, assuming that present age-specific mortality rates would apply during the further life course of the person.

Longevity is a general term (usually) measured as the average age at death in a given population in a given year. This average depends crucially on the age distribution in that population. Assuming that two populations have identical age-specific mortality rates, the younger population will have more deaths at younger ages and consequently a lower average age at death. The age-at-death measure used here to compare populations or to study time trends adjusts for this.

18.3.2.2 Inequality in Life Expectancy between the 25 Largest Countries

Life expectancy differs between countries, and on first impression Figure 18.2 seems to indicate that the dispersion is about the same in 1955 as in 2015 (about 35 years between the two countries with highest and lowest life expectancy). However, if we make pairwise comparisons in life expectancy between all 25 countries and sum up the average relative difference, as the Gini measure does, we find that there has been substantial decrease in inequality between countries (Figure 18.3).

Figure 18.3 shows that in 1955, Gini$_h$ for inequality in life expectancy between these countries was about 0.13, falling to about 0.06 in 2015 (a lower Gini$_h$ coefficient represents more equality than a higher coefficient). The lower line in Figure 18.3 shows inequality between countries when they are weighted by population size. This indicates even more inequality reduction by 2015 since large countries like China and India have had substantial mortality reductions at early ages and contribute more than small countries.[5]

18.3.2.3 Contrasting Trends in Life Expectancy at Birth in 36 Developed Countries

In a recent paper, Timonin et al. (2016) found that in 36 developed countries mortality trends are strongly patterned by global region, showing a widening east–west gap in mortality and life expectancy during the period 1970–2005. After 2005 it appears to narrow. This gap coincided with the East–West geopolitical division (see Figure 18.4).

18.3.2.4 Trends in Global Life Expectancy Inequalities

Moser, Shkolnikov, and Leon (2005) published a comparison of life expectancy trends for 1950–2000 in the 152 countries with more than one million inhabitants. The authors used population-weighted pairwise comparison of every country with every other country to calculated a global "dispersion measure of mortality" (DMM) for both adults and infants, and found that while differences in infant mortality steadily narrowed, adult mortality trends after 1990 caused life expectancy to diverge (see Figure 18.5). Goesling and Firebaugh (2004), comparing

---

[5]   The standard Gini$_h$ is population size invariant, and we have not adjusted for population size in the other results given below.

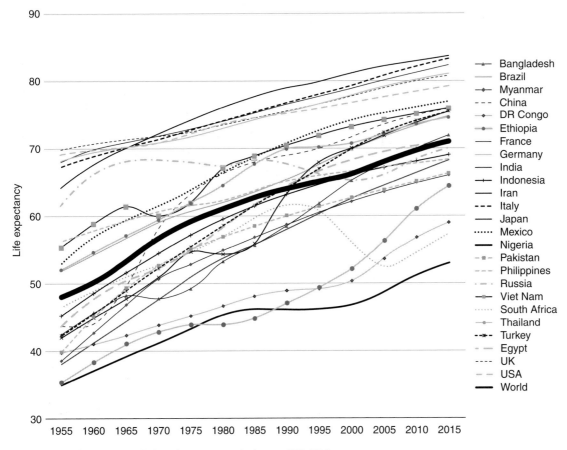

Figure 18.2 | Life expectancy at birth, 25 largest countries, both sexes, 1955–2015.
Source: UNPD (2015 revision).

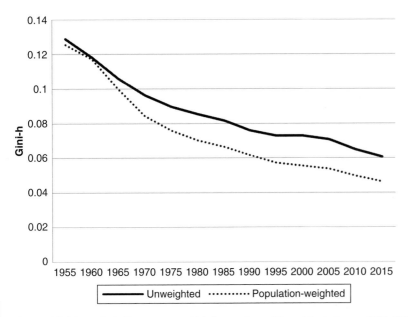

Figure 18.3 | Inequality in life expectancy at birth, between largest 25 countries, both sexes, 1955–2015.

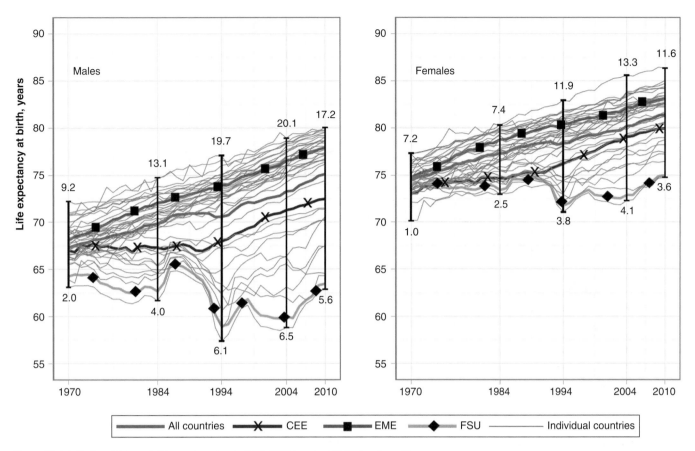

Figure 18.4 | The East–West gap in life expectancy trends, 1970–2010, based on 36 developed countries.
Note: CEE – Central and Eastern European countries; EME – Emerging Market Economy countries; FSU – Former Soviet Union countries.
Source: Timonin et al. (2016).

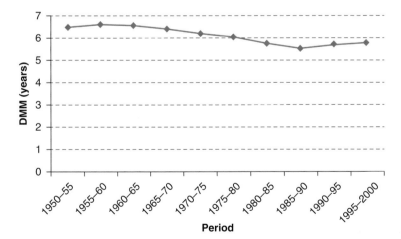

Figure 18.5 | Worldwide Convergence and Divergence of Life Expectancy, 1950–2000, Based on Pairwise Comparisons of 152.
Source: Moser, Shkolnikov, and Leon (2005).

18

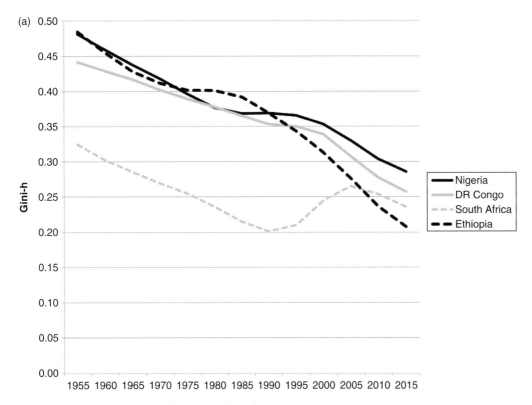

Figure 18.6a | Inequality in longevity for four Sub-Saharan African countries.

169 countries through 2000, also found that mortality convergence was replaced by mortality divergence in 1990.

18.3.3   Inequality in Longevity

18.3.3.1   Inequality in Longevity within World Bank Income Groups and the World

In the literature on measures and indices of inequality, there is an important distinction between inequality within populations and between populations (Murtin et al. 2017). It arises also in understanding inequalities in health. When we compare life expectancy or longevity between countries we are comparing average values, by country. This ignores within-country inequality, and may lead to underestimation of total inequality.

Inequality remains high in each of the four World Bank income regions (low-income, lower-middle income, upper-middle income, and high-income), but the trend in age at death is toward more equality. Here, we treat each group of countries (or the whole world) as one population and compare longevity for each individual within that population. Within-group inequality for the world was much higher in 1955 ($Gini_h = 0.36$) than between-country inequality ($Gini_h = 0.14$), although both within-group and between-group inequalities fell in the period (to 0.16 and 0.07 respectively in 2015). In our view, within-group and between-group inequalities are both relevant for monitoring trends.

18.3.3.2   Inequality in Longevity within Selected Countries

Figures 18.6a–c show inequality in age at death within some of the 25 most populous countries in the world. Although the trend is toward more equality, some countries are still at high levels, and there are interesting inter-country variations in patterns.

Figure 18.6a shows inequality trends in four Sub-Saharan African countries. Ethiopia's reduction of inequality has been more rapid in the last 25–30 years compared with that of Nigeria and the Democratic Republic of the Congo. South Africa stands out, with a period from early 1990 to early 2000 during which inequality *increased* because of very high age-specific mortality in children and young adults due to HIV/AIDS.

Figure 18.6b shows time trends in India, Russia, Iran, and China. Inequality in India is highest, but is steadily falling. Iran's reduction in inequality was interrupted by high adult male mortality between 1975 and 1985. China made a big improvement after around 1965, while Russia showed no narrowing of inequality during this period, and in some intervals inequalities worsened.

Figure 18.6c shows trends for five high-income countries: USA, UK, France, Japan, and Italy. Inequality in each of these countries is relatively low. Japan enjoyed high rates of decline in inequality early in the period while the US lagged somewhat behind after 1970, a trend that continues today.

Summing up, we find that inter-individual inequality in longevity (age at death) within countries is decreasing. Reduction of infant and child

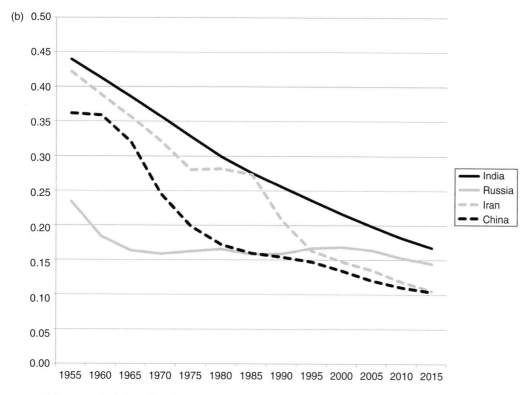

Figure 18.6b | Inequality in longevity for four large countries.

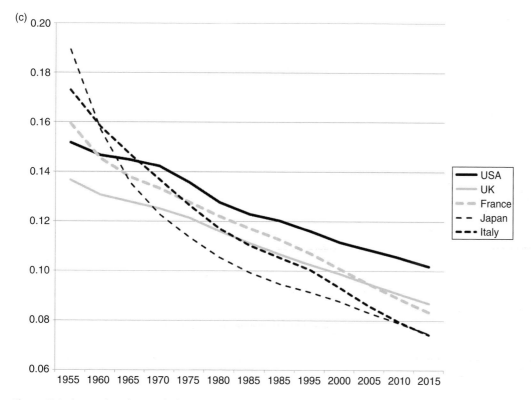

Figure 18.6c | Inequality in longevity for five high-income countries.

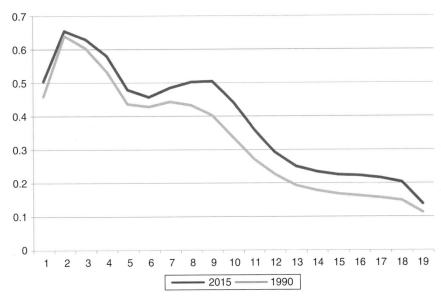

Figure 18.7 | Relative difference in age-specific mortality rates, world, both sexes, 1990 and 2015.
Source: calculated from UNPD data, 2015 revision.

mortality is most important for this development. Some countries still experience high inequality and some countries have even had periods of rising inequality in age at death (South Africa and Russia).

Overall, we find that there is, at the same time, convergence in age at death within and between countries, driven by falling early-life mortality, and increasing differences in life expectancy between some countries. The latter is driven by adult mortality trends, especially in Eastern Europe. The survival curve for the world is mostly moving in the direction of rectangularization, but this is not found everywhere and not in every segment of the population.

18.3.4   Global Inequalities in Age-Specific Mortality

When we look at age-specific mortality rates, the picture becomes both more complete and complex.

Figure 18.7 shows that the *relative* difference (measured as Gini) in all *age-specific mortality rates* between all countries in the world *increased* in the period 1990 to 2015. This happens when the relative decrease in age-specific mortality for countries with lower mortality is faster than for countries with higher mortality, or when there is a rise in age-specific mortality in countries with high mortality (such as in Russia 1970–2005) and a fall among most other countries. This finding is the basis for the general observation that health inequalities within countries are increasing (see also the next section below).[6]

Increases in relative inequality are important for two reasons. First, even if inequality in age at death is decreasing (because of convergence in

under-five mortality), the increase in relative difference in age-specific mortality rates shows that the speed of mortality improvement for high-mortality countries is slower than for lower-mortality countries (and especially so in adults). Thus, the picture is not all positive. In particular, as can be seen from the graph, adult (ages 30-plus) mortality rates are more unequal in 2015 than they were in 1990. Second, we must keep in mind that data on child and maternal mortality alone – the only mortality trends taken into account by the MDGs – do not tell us all that must be taken into account in assessing how people fare over their lifetimes.[7]

18.3.5   Social Inequalities in Mortality and Life Expectancy within Countries

18.3.5.1   Mortality Differentials by Level of Education

Education is one of the most important sources of observable social heterogeneity in all countries, and it is a very common social stratification variable in health studies as well. Its differential impact on health and mortality is strong. There is ample evidence (Lutz and Skirbekk 2014) that education empowers people in various dimensions, and thus has a direct and causal effect on health-related behavior, health, mortality, and longevity. In all countries of the world, child mortality is significantly lower for children of more educated women even after adjusting for the effect of income and wealth (Pamuk, Fuchs, and Lutz 2011). Life expectancy of university-educated men and women exceeds that of those with basic education by as much as 12 years. In most developed countries the differentials have actually increased in recent years.

---

[6]   See for example Michael Marmot: "Health is improving globally … Within many countries … inequalities in health are increasing – the health of the best off is increasing more rapidly than that of the worst off. The best and worst of times coexist" (Marmot 2015).

[7]   It is important to note that the choice of health measure may affect our results. Measures of child mortality and measures of maternal mortality are both important, and analysts should always make clear what kind of health inequalities are reported.

This phenomenon and the role played by the modern welfare state, have figured prominently in recent discussions of what is called the "welfare state paradox." Recent comparative studies of the size of health inequalities in a number of European countries tested the hypothesis that comprehensive welfare states of the Nordic model should present the smallest inequalities. This might have been true in the 1980s, or earlier (Vågerö and Erikson 1997), but later data suggest that it is no longer the case (Mackenbach et al. 2008). Most Western European states now offer a minimum of welfare provisions and social protection, but a divide has nevertheless become apparent between Eastern and Western Europe. Social inequalities in mortality are much more pronounced in the former communist countries of Eastern Europe – both a legacy from the past and a response to the system collapse in the 1990s (Vågerö 2010).

18.3.5.2   Social Inequalities in Life Expectancy and Mortality within Countries: The Long View

Social class differences in mortality have been tracked for over a century by the decennial supplements of occupational mortality published by the Office of Population Statistics (OPCS) in Britain. The reports, which compare the all-cause mortality of five occupationally defined social classes, show the same gradient in mortality in every decade. Mortality in social class V (unskilled workers) is typically about twice as high as in class I (professionals) with classes II, III (consisting of non-manual (IIINM) and manual (IIIM)), and IV falling in between. The continuity in this pattern, decade after decade, in spite of a gradually changing disease panorama, impressive economic growth, modern medicine, and welfare state provisions, is quite remarkable (OPCS 1995). It suggests that health differentiation is a fundamental social process, closely tied to the general stratification in society.

The "Black Report," presented by Sir Douglas Black to the British government in 1979, and immediately dismissed by the Conservative government of that time, sought to understand these regularities and to suggest means of changing the situation. The Report's account of why social class differences in health reappear again and again in every new generation, which triggered academic and political controversy, focused on the contribution to health of poverty and material circumstances in adult life. One critique of the Report argued that issues of selection were not dealt with properly. Health and vitality in early life may to some extent determine social career and contribute to the social differentiation of health in adult life.

Such arguments about "selection" versus "causation" were once quite bitter. The introduction of a life course perspective has changed this. Today, this conflict has been resolved, at the theoretical level, by the insight (as discussed in Section 18.2.3) that health in early life is heavily influenced by the social circumstances of the previous generation (Vågerö and Illsley 1995; Kuh and Ben-Shlomo 2004). Public health scientists today generally agree that lifelong social circumstances have a dominant influence on people's health and survival and that health conditions may influence economic activity and social mobility, reinforcing the pattern of social inequalities in health (Greenhalgh 2008).

The publication of and controversy over the Black Report inspired a new generation of researchers who have produced a vast literature

on health inequalities, now shown to exist in every country that has data to make a study possible. It is a general phenomenon, observable in rich and poor countries alike, on every continent and in every social system (CSDH 2008).

Social inequalities have typically been conceived as differences by occupational class, by education, sometimes by income or by residence in deprived areas versus affluent areas. In very general terms patterns of inequality are similar across these social boundaries, but anomalies exist, often reflecting and looking at specific causes of death, or specific health conditions. Breast cancer among women, for instance, is generally higher among highly educated women than among those with low education.

Even if occupation, education, and income are closely correlated in most societies, they cannot be interchanged for each other – though this is a common practice in social epidemiology. Education, occupation, and income tap into different etiologies and predict mortality and longevity independently of each other (Geyer et al. 2006). Theoretical understanding of social inequalities in health, mortality, and longevity in the adult population has to allow for several determinants and risk factors, distributed across the lifespan and within the previous generation. There is a complex and dynamic set of relations between those factors.

Access to health data is poorest in low- and middle-income countries. However, the Program for Demographic and Health Surveys (DHS), running since 1984, has been quite successful in providing data on child mortality by household economic level. Tanja Houweling, using World Bank country reports and DHS data for 43 low- and middle-income countries to compare the richest fifth of households with the poorest fifth in each country (Houweling 2007), found that child mortality in poor households was around double that of rich households in the same country. Wagstaff et al., using Living Standard Measurement Study data for nine countries, found very similar results (Wagstaff 2000). Hosseinpoor et al. (2005), using regionally representative DHS data for Iran in the year 2000, found a gradient in infant mortality from income quintile 1 to income quintile 5; infant mortality was more than twice as high among the poor than among the rich. This is the typical pattern in any country, although the estimated size of mortality differentials is sensitive to the method of defining household income (income, assets, expenditure) (Houweling, Kunst, and Mackenbach 2003) and varies between countries.

A scarcity of data prevents us from assessing how social inequalities in child mortality change over time within many countries (Victora et al. 2003). A study by Moser, Shkolnikov, and Leon (2005) that uses country data to estimate global trends in infant mortality suggests that there may be a convergence in infant mortality worldwide. This is in contrast to global trends in adult mortality, which they suggest to be diverging after 1985 to 1990.

18.3.6   Four Distinct Patterns of Health Change within Countries

Trends in social inequalities in mortality and longevity within developed countries and among adults are better studied and known. It appears that the dominant trend is one of increasing adult mortality differences.

We can distinguish four main patterns of how mortality in general and also social inequalities in mortality have changed during the last few decades. The first three patterns describe growing mortality inequalities. We list them by the degree of moral concern they raise, with the most problematic pattern first.

- Pattern 1: Sharply fluctuating (falling, rising, falling) life expectancy trends nationally. Growing social inequalities in mortality and/or life expectancy, combined with falling life expectancy in large segments of the population.
- Pattern 2: Increasing life expectancy trends nationally. Growing social inequalities in mortality and/or life expectancy, combined with falling life expectancy in large segments of the population.
- Pattern 3: Increasing life expectancy trends nationally. Growing social inequalities in mortality and/or life expectancy, combined with increasing life expectancy in all segments of the population.
- Pattern 4: Increasing life expectancy trends nationally, combined with narrowing of the social gradient in mortality.

The first pattern can be illustrated by Russian mortality trends 1970–2005, where a long-term trend of falling or sharply fluctuating life expectancy dominated from 1965 to 2005. It is combined with increasing mortality differentials by education, at least for the period 1980–2001, during which period low-educated men and women experienced falling life expectancy (Murphy et al. 2006). Similarly, Estonia demonstrated dramatically growing mortality inequalities both by education and by ethnicity during the 1990–2000 period, driven by rising mortality and falling life expectancy among the low-educated and in the Russian minority (Leinsalu, Vågerö, and Kunst 2003, 2004). South Africa probably fits this pattern too.

The second pattern can be illustrated by United States. Case and Deaton (2015) have recently noted that middle-aged white Americans experienced increasing mortality during the 1999–2013 period. However, this trend only applied to low-educated whites, not to those of middle or high education. Behind the phenomenon is a longer trend of generally widening mortality differences between educational groups, and not only in middle-aged men and women, since at least 1990. The mortality of white men and women with less than 12 years' schooling has been growing gradually worse over time (Olshansky et al. 2012).

The third pattern is much more common than the first two. Countries that are doing quite well in general life expectancy trends often demonstrate increasing social inequality in mortality and life expectancy, including many countries in Western Europe. Steingrímsdóttir and colleagues (2012) published annual life expectancy data for men and women in three educational groups in Norway from 1960 to 2009. This series, perhaps the longest series of mortality differentials by education that we have, shows a continuously growing gap between all three educational groups over the 50-year period. The lowest-educated group is making progress, but at a slower pace than the other two groups. Shkolnikov, Andreev, and Jdanov (2012) demonstrated the same pattern in a comparison of Finland, Norway, and Sweden for the 1970–2000 period. In all three countries, mortality is falling in all educational groups, but the rate of decrease has been greater with higher educational attainment, resulting in a growing life expectancy gap.

Leinsalu et al. (2009) demonstrated the same pattern for Poland and Hungary, for 1990–2000.

The choice of inequality measures makes a difference. The study of six Western European countries by Mackenbach et al. (2003) showed a widening mortality gap by education in all of them, when using a relative inequality measure. Differences in mortality were more stable when an absolute measure was used, except for in Finland. Reducing absolute mortality differences should be easier than reducing relative ones when mortality rates are falling.

The long-term increase in absolute mortality differences and in life expectancy between men and women of different educational backgrounds in Finland, Norway, and Sweden is therefore quite remarkable. Much attention has been devoted by social epidemiologists to understanding this "welfare state paradox." The influence of global market forces and corporate actors over national income distributions, labor markets, consumption patterns, taxes, and welfare policies in general may now be too powerful for national governments to balance.

The fourth pattern of mortality differentials and trends, outlined above, corresponds to what most governments aim for. The policy documents of the WHO and of national governments, such as the Rio Political Declaration on Social Determinants of Health, October 2011, call for improved health in combination with smaller health inequalities. But this remains only an aspiration; in reality, most governments will have to cope with the first three scenarios. The fourth pattern, of growing life expectancy and smaller health inequalities is not consistent with "business as usual," according to the influential report of the Commission on Social Determinants of Health (2008). Though this field remains an area of intense interest in policy-making, the way forward is not very clear.

18.3.7   Conclusions

People are living longer. There has been a tremendous increase in life expectancy and longevity throughout much of the world. Success in reducing infant and child mortality contributes greatly to increasing life expectancy and the convergence in age at death globally. Adult mortality trends and life expectancy demonstrate a long-term convergence globally that was sustained until about 1990. The divergence after that point primarily reflects developments in two regions of the world, Sub-Saharan Africa (where life expectancy has again been improving since 2000) and the former Soviet Union. Adult mortality is strongly socially differentiated in all countries, as is child mortality in low- and middle-income countries. Lower death rates have been achieved in many populations at each stage of life, with a small but growing number achieving active lives through eight and nine decades.

Nevertheless, others lag behind or even experience rising mortality. Within the richer countries, those with more education tend to live longer than those with less education; shorter lives are more common in many of the less-developed countries – often caused by high adult mortality rates and those the HIV/AIDS pandemic – and many in post-communist Eastern Europe. While overall gains in life expectancy and longevity are substantial and promising, national and global data indicate divergence as well as convergence. Achievement of better health and more equal lifespans remains a priority in the global health and development agenda.

18.4 Diminished Health: Morbidity, Disability, and Chronic Conditions

Diminished health compromises the value of longevity: the prospect of longer lifespans has less appeal – or, in extreme cases, none at all – if those years are accompanied by poor health. Diminished health is also of concern independently for occasioning pain and discomfort, limitations or impediments to important activities, social isolation and stigma; and often for the need for seek and pay for care, which may be both urgent and financially catastrophic.

These are not merely biomedical considerations. Social acceptance can reduce or eliminate the stigma that many experience as a result of chronic or infectious diseases such as HIV/AIDS or cancer. Disabilities resulting in limitations on mobility, hearing and vision, and even cognitive function are much less burdensome in welcoming, tolerant social and physical environments. Serious illness does not lead to bankruptcy where there is social insurance.

A purely biomedical understanding of diminished health and disability would miss subtle but important dimensions of these issues (Scully 2004; Jones, Podolsky, and Greene 2012; Hausman 2015). Dyslexia (a learning disorder consisting in a difficulty reading) is problematic in some social and natural contexts and of no importance in others, while other health conditions, such as migraine headaches, cause hardships in every context. Some health problems, such as disfigurement, limit people's activities only because of social customs and the actions of others, while others would limit or harm people even given optimal social accommodations. Some health issues, such as the loss of an arm, provide no compensating benefits. Other problems, such as blindness, while limiting a crucial capacity, may sharpen the other senses and heighten the satisfactions individuals receive from them. There are many different ways in which humans may flourish, and health conditions that interfere with some of these ways need not prevent individuals from living well. When some activists in the Deaf community maintain that deafness is not a disability, they obviously do not mean that it does not limit a significant human capacity. They envision an environment with access to facilities that enable an excellent quality of life. In lower-income countries and communities where a significant proportion of people with hearing loss do not have access to hearing aids, their deafness limits the attainment of wellbeing (The Lancet 2016).

This chapter section is in four parts. In part one, we examine the different concepts of diminished health and make a case for choosing disability as our overarching conceptual framework. In part two, we present the current epidemiological and public health evidence on disability across the life course and in global context. In part three, we present the perspectives of affected communities, through four case studies of chronic illness and disability experiences. In part four we discuss potential responses to the challenges of disability, particularly in poor countries with limited resources for health and social care.

18.4.1 Examining Concepts of Diminished Health

The concept of "diminished health" is often used interchangeably with associated terms such as "morbidity," "disability," "impairment," "handicap," "injury," "disease," "pathology," and "illness." Obviously, these are not the same, and picking any term as a catch-all risks serious confusion. If, for example, one regards any diminution of health as a loss in "health-related quality of life," as the most common generic health measurement schemes maintain, then one provokes the justified response of the Deaf community that although the lives of the deaf are *different* than those of people who can hear, they are not clearly of lesser quality. This is a significant debate that was raised in the conceptualization of disability weights – a quantitative and comparative scoring of disabilities that is used in descriptive epidemiology and in priority-setting (Salomon et al. 2012). Similarly the physiological state of infertility is voluntarily induced by millions of women, while the same physiological state is cause for medical intervention in others, highlighting again the contextual nature of the interpretation of *illness* or *sickness*.

Instead of conceptualizing health decrements as involving lesser health-related quality of life, one prominent approach maintains that health limitations can all be conceived as limitations on activities and hence as "disabilities" of one sort of other. This language may be misleading as well inasmuch as it describes health problems as diminishing quality of life or overall ability. It is at the very least awkward to describe burns, rashes, and pains as disabilities. It would probably be least misleading to speak of "health decrements, limitations, or problems" but since "disability" is so widely used by demographers, epidemiologists, and health economists, we shall often speak of all shortfalls of health as disabilities. Still, it is important to recognize that "disability" is herein a technical term for any sort of health issue, many of which would not in everyday language be called "disabilities." The remarkable improvements in longevity and life expectancy documented in Section 18.3 do not automatically imply any diminution in disability. To the contrary, if the extension of life leaves individuals with more mental and physical limitations, then people may end up gaining longer life at the expense of more years with disability. But it is important not to be misled here. Along with the health problems that come with the additional years are all the good things that those years provide. Apart from the rare cases in which the additional lifespan consists in extreme suffering or humiliation, longer life is usually desirable.

One may question the conclusion that longer life is usually a benefit in two ways. First, an extended period of disability at the end of one's life changes its overall "narrative" (Velleman 1991). Some would argue that a long period of substantially diminished physical, cognitive, or emotional capacities decreases how well that life as a whole has gone, compared with the life of a vigorous, competent, and authoritative person that ends with no long period of dependency on others, mental confusion, or inability to contribute to the maintenance of a household. We do not take a stance on this controversial question. Second, even if a longer life is almost always a benefit to the individual, it may be costly to others. If individuals live into their nineties and retire in their sixties, then even if they do not require expensive care, they still require support from the working-age population. They may provide

Box 18.5 | Leading Causes of Disability across the Life Course

Age group	Leading causes of disability
Younger children (<5 years)	Iron-deficiency anemia, skin diseases, protein-energy malnutrition, diarrhea
Older children (5–14 years)	Iron-deficiency anemia, skin diseases, asthma, mental health disorders including conduct disorders, autistic spectrum disorders, anxiety disorders
Adolescents and young adults (15–39 years)	Iron-deficiency anemia, skin diseases, depression, lower back and neck pain, migraine, anxiety disorders, schizophrenia
Middle-aged adults (40–64 years)	Musculoskeletal disorders, mental health disorders – in particular depression, diabetes, sense organ disorders
Older adults (>65 years)	Sense organ disorders, musculoskeletal disorders, chronic obstructive pulmonary disease
Oldest adults (>80 years)	Ischemic heart disease, Alzheimer's and other dementias

Source: GBD 2015 Disease and Injury Incidence and Prevalence Collaborators (2016)

some compensation in the form of the wisdom and cultural continuity that they pass along, but providing for them can be a struggle especially in societies in which there have been recent decreases in fertility and hence there are relatively few working-age adults to support them (Reidpath et al. 2015). The severity of this burden on younger individuals is greatest in societies that lack social support systems for aging dependents (WHO 2002a, 2002b).

18.4.2   Global Trends in Disability

The World Report on Disability (WHO 2011) and the systematic analysis of disability data by the GBD 2015 Disease and Injury Incidence and Prevalence Collaborators (2016) provide the most recent and comprehensive insights into global trends in disability. Both publications outline different types of disability, including those affecting movement, vision, hearing, thinking and learning, and mental health. They highlight levels of severity encompassing very mild, mild, moderate, severe, and profound.

Between 785 million (15.6 percent of the world population) and 975 million (19.4 percent) of people aged 15 years and older are estimated to live with some form of a disability. Among them, 110 million (between 11 percent and 14 percent) have significant difficulties in functioning: this refers to severe/profound disability for conditions such as quadriplegia, severe depression, and blindness. It is estimated that 95 million children aged 0–14 years (5.1 percent) live with disability. Of these, 13 million (0.7 percent) have "severe disability." The GBD analysis shows that over the last 25 years, the proportion of people of all ages living with disabilities (mild or greater) has increased (although as mentioned above this partly reflects increased longevity). Their data suggest that as we move across the life course the causes of disability shift from common infectious diseases (diarrhea, skin diseases) among children, to adult-onset chronic non-communicable diseases (diabetes, cancers) and mental health disorders (e.g. depression, anxiety) (see Box 18.5). Furthermore, as the number of people living with co-morbid and multi-morbid conditions rises, the prevalence rates of associated physical disabilities and mental health disorders also rise (Barnett et al. 2012; Leone et al. 2012).

The most vulnerable adult populations globally are: (1) people from the poorest wealth quintile; (2) women; (3) older people; and (4) people who are unemployed with low educational qualifications. In child and adolescent populations, groups from poorer households and from ethnic minority groups have a significantly higher risk of disability (see Sections 18.2 and 18.3 on the effects of child poverty on physical health and mortality). The intersections of these vulnerabilities complicate subjective experiences and the development of appropriate interventions.

Not all people with disabilities are equally disadvantaged. Women with disabilities arising from neglected tropical diseases (such as lymphatic filariasis or onchocerciasis) experience more pronounced gendered discrimination and stigma compared with men living with the same conditions (Allotey and Gyapong 2005). Children with physical impairments fare better than children with intellectual or sensory impairments at school. Among the adult population, people with mental health and intellectual impairments are more likely to be excluded from the labor market. Low- and middle-income countries (LMICs) are disproportionately affected by chronic non-communicable diseases (NCDs), and the double burden of NCDs and infectious diseases. Within these LMICs the poorest citizens and increasingly those in productive years under age 40 experience the greatest burdens (Bukhman, Mocumbi, and Horton 2015). These groups are more likely to bear a significant proportion of rising levels and cost of disabilities because weak health and social care systems undermine lived experiences and health/social outcomes.

18.4.3   Living with Disabilities: Case Studies of Two Debilitating Chronic Conditions

There is a general lack of standardized culturally sensitive data on disability. The WHO (2011: 20) observes that "methodologies for collecting data on people with disabilities need to be developed, tested cross-culturally and applied consistently." The data that exist suggests that people with disabilities have poorer secondary health outcomes (e.g. greater vulnerability to preventable secondary conditions, co-morbid chronic conditions and age-related conditions; higher risk of being exposed to violence), less economic participation, higher rates of poverty (frequently a vicious cycle), increased dependency, and restricted participation in social life. Children with disabilities have lower educational achievements.

We present and discuss two case studies on the lived experiences of diabetes and dementia.[8] These case studies trace the complex trajectories of subjective and family experiences of serious chronic conditions, and highlight the ways these experiences are mediated by the physical and medical impact of the condition, as well as the social, cultural, economic, and structural contexts of individual and family lives.

Some aspects of chronic illness experiences are shared across social and geographical categories. Most individuals (and their caregivers) make cognitive and psychological adjustments to a diagnosis of chronic illness or disability over time. They struggle to come to terms with their relationship with self and illness, and with self and society (see the case studies below). As illness progresses, the subjective quest to regain one's lost self and former social roles cuts across illness experiences, regardless of condition or location (Bury 1982; Reeve et al. 2010).

The differences in illness outcomes and life trajectories arise when social, cultural, economic, and structural factors are considered. Negative attitudes and stigma associated with impairments can be greater barriers to normal functioning than the impairments themselves. For example, in socio-cultural contexts where conditions like diabetes or dementia are poorly understood and are perceived through the traditional lens of spiritual causes, there is a higher likelihood of stigma, with associated impediments to normal functioning by individuals living with such conditions.

Severe chronic conditions have an economic impact for most sufferers: in addition to threatening one's livelihood, diet and other expensive lifestyle changes must be made, and medicines must be purchased. When one lives with a chronic condition like diabetes in a rural or urban poor community in Africa, Asia, or Latin America, structural and individual poverty permeates all aspects of the illness experience (see Case Study 18-1). As Capewell and Graham (2010) observe, poor communities experience health disadvantage at multiple stages: from "the person's beliefs about health and disease, and actual behaviour, to presentation, screening, risk assessment, negotiation, participation, programme persistence and treatment adherence."

Culture shapes the illness experience in specific ways. Case Study 18-2 tells the story of a family's experience of dementia in the UK, a country with one of the most advanced systems of dementia care in the world. In the UK, dementia threatens "valued elements of life" (Lawrence et al. 2011) for all sufferers, regardless of ethnic group, and people with dementia can live meaningful lives if their unique core values of self and social roles are understood, legitimized, and supported. Yet in the UK cultural and structural factors can create barriers to comprehensive dementia care for black and ethnic minority groups. It is estimated that Black African and Caribbean

elders have a higher prevalence and earlier onset of dementia than the White UK population (Berwald et al. 2016). Yet they present later to dementia specialist services, receive diagnoses when the disease is at a more advanced stage, and experience poorer health outcomes. Studies focusing on how communities, caregivers, and dementia sufferers from minority ethnic groups make sense of dementia highlight important ethnic and cultural differences in perceptions and responses (Lawrence et al. 2011; Berwald et al. 2016). African and Caribbean groups tend to perceive dementia as "old white people's disease" or as "memory problems" and are less likely to recognize the severity of it; they are more likely to see psychiatric services as institutionally racist and care homes as undesirable, and therefore present their problems late and rely exclusively on family support. Their experiences of poorer dementia health outcomes are partly attributed to these cultural factors.

Two further cross-cutting themes emerge in the case studies. First, it is clear that living with a debilitating or disabling condition affects the mental health of sufferers and their caregivers. Anxiety and frustrations arising from challenges in or disagreements over everyday management are salient in the diabetes and dementia case studies. Individuals living with diabetes under conditions of poverty express despair (and suicidal ideation) about their difficult life circumstances. Stigma restricts the lives of sufferers and their significant others and deepens emotional conflicts and tensions within families. This shared experience underscores the importance of understanding the co-morbid relationships between common chronic physical conditions (diabetes, hypertension), and between chronic physical conditions and mental health disorders (diabetes and depression). Poor mental health has been strongly associated with poor self-care, poor self-efficacy, and poor chronic illness management (Prince et al. 2007). Caregiver stress has been associated with poor physical and mental health outcomes (Schulz and Sherwood 2008).

Finally, the case studies underscore the practice of health-seeking and healer-shopping across pluralistic medical systems. Individuals search for meaning and respite when they fall seriously sick and they experiment with available (recommended) health services as they seek solutions to their problems. In African and Asian contexts, healer-shopping for a cure to chronic conditions is common (de-Graft Aikins et al. 2010; Yasin et al. 2012). As Case Study 18-1 shows, healer-shopping for herbal cures occurs for a range of reasons including the high cost of biomedical care, the perceived ineffectiveness of pharmaceutical medications, and trust in the recommendations of significant others. Similar dynamics are reported in the context of dementia care among UK black and ethnic minority groups, where individuals may seek diagnosis for early-onset dementia symptoms in the "black church" and try alternative therapies to stall the advancement of dementia (Berwald et al. 2016). These practices highlight the importance of traditional cultural beliefs about the etiology of various health conditions, evolving explanatory models about the body and mind, and how medical pluralism is perceived, legitimated, and used across contexts. Ethnographic and phenomenological studies on lived experiences of chronic conditions are rare, but they present important

---

[8]   The longer online version of this chapter (available at www.ipsp.org) presents four case studies, on diabetes, blindness, dementia, and a rare condition, Harlequin Ichthyosis.

Case Study 18-1: Diabetes Experiences In Rural Ghana

Ruth* (a middle-aged widow) lived with severe uncontrolled diabetes and chronic physical impairments: loss of appetite, severe weight loss, joint pains, and body sores. This had a pervasive impact on her life. She was unable to carry out the simplest everyday chores and had had to abandon her previous job as a food hawker. In the early years, she had financial support from her extended (paternal) family – but she was on insulin, which was expensive, and gradually financial support had been withdrawn. Three caregivers were identified: an older daughter, Adjoa* (29), widowed, with three children, all of whom lived with Ruth; a son who lived locally, visited rarely, but made her yearly insurance contributions; and a niece, Cynthia* (40), a teacher, who helped financially when she could. Other forms of financial and social support came from sympathetic hospital staff and self-help group members. Ruth and her family attributed her diabetes to a mix of diet, lifestyle, and spiritual causes.

Ruth's inability to treat her diabetes had led to acute weight loss. For a middle-aged woman who, prior to getting diabetes and prior to abandoning regular treatment, had had a healthy body image, the sudden change to her physical identity had caused some shock to her family and community. Shock turned to community speculation and gossip that Ruth may have contracted AIDS. Ruth experienced disruption to her social relationships: she was shunned by her friends and taunted in the streets by school children, and lost customers.

> When I sent food to the school to sell, the children wouldn't buy, because the teacher told them I have HIV/AIDS. (Ruth)

Her family became "tainted" with this identity: they lived with "courtesy stigma" (stigma by association). Adjoa's attempt to take over her mother's food-hawking business failed, because people were unwilling to buy food from an individual living in close proximity with an alleged AIDS sufferer.

> You see, at first, my mother was selling rice water [rice pudding]. Due to her illness I had to take over and sell it but people didn't buy it anymore. Some people thought she had got AIDS. This perception … made people stop buying her rice water. (Adjoa)

Ruth's relationship with her significant others was fraught with emotionally charged misunderstandings. Ruth was convinced that her family had abandoned her because they perceived her as either an AIDS sufferer or a witch. Adjoa did not refer to her mother either as an AIDS sufferer or a witch. However Adjoa's narratives suggested that she did experience and project onto her mother's condition conflicting emotional responses, and that these were underpinned by a dual struggle to cope with her own life circumstances (low-income, self-employed single parent with three children) and attend to the extra daily burden brought on by her mother's physical disability and dependency. Even as Adjoa recognized the extent of her mother's impairments, she glossed over her disabilities. She stressed her intention to provide support, and she also hoped for an end to her mother's suffering, either through a miracle cure or death, to ease the emotional burden she lived with.

> When the impact of the disease increases, I feel a lot of pressure. She worries me a lot and so I make up my mind to travel and leave her, if we leave and later we hear that she is dead, then we can come back and bury her. But I have second thoughts and then decide to stay and take care of her. (Adjoa)

Ruth adopted three regular strategies to address (her) diabetes. She took herbal tonics (which were often unsafe) to regain physical strength; she prayed and attended church regularly for spiritual support; and she attended self-help group meetings for advice and support. Self-help group members noted that while they all faced varying forms of physical disruption, Ruth experienced a particularly heavy social-psychological burden. Her life circumstances were presented by group members as an acute illustration of the fate of rural poor living with diabetes. Ruth's interview narratives were dominated by despair and suicidal ideation.

Recently, I even thought of committing suicide by poisoning myself. And I say it each day. But I remind myself later on that, it is the Lord who brought me into this world. And if I make my mind up about poisoning myself there would be a punishment for me one day. But I think of it very much. (Ruth)

*not their real names. Abridged case study. Source: de-Graft Aikins (2006)

Case Study 18-2: Living with Dementia in the UK

In 2016 the British Broadcasting Corporation (BBC) produced a rare multi-textured documentary filmed over two years on one family's experience with dementia: Chris Roberts, from north Wales, his wife Jayne, and their youngest daughter Kate.

From making the decision to choose his own care home to writing a living will, getting lost in his own house and not recognising his family, Chris chronicle[d] his changing life as his independence slip[pped] away. Once a businessman and a keen biker, he now struggle[d] to walk and talk – his life [wa]s beset by frustration, yet his remarkable insight allow[ed] us into his world. (www.bbc.co.uk/programmes/b07dxmyh)

This is an edited version of a review of the documentary.

At 55 years old, Chris Roberts often gets lost in his own home. At times he has to ask his wife, Jayne, how to get to the bathroom and regular household appliances, such as a kettle, can confuse him. Five years ago, the former property manager was diagnosed with both vascular dementia and early onset Alzheimer's disease after he started displaying behavior that was out of character, such as unwarranted anger.

"The best thing you can do after your diagnosis is read up about it, find out all you can. It's the unknown that scares us," Chris says in the program. "Some people try and hide from their dementia, hiding is easier than facing up to it sometimes. But you can only run for so long – dementia will catch you up. You will have to face it, you will have to live with it."

The documentary follows their highs and lows, from bittersweet moments like Christmas day to a heartbreaking scene where Jayne struggles to comfort Chris as he screams in distress for no apparent reason.

"The person I miss most, is me," Chris says.

In one clip, Chris explains what it's like to wake up in the morning, confused about where he is and what's happening. He wanders around, shouts and searches for his wife, then says: "Trouble is, I don't know whether I'm dreaming or not. Can't find any notes … It's really strange when you don't know what's real and what isn't."

The program also reveals what it's like to be a family member of someone with dementia. Jayne opens up about her feelings of guilt as she drops her husband off to a daytime respite center and Kate says having a dad with dementia "isn't all doom and gloom" as in many ways the illness has made them all closer.

"I need respite and I didn't think I'd ever say that," Jayne says. "He wants to go in and have respite overnight for himself. I'm not ready to let him do that. One of my biggest worries is that I won't want him to come home. I might like him being there."

The family decided to take part in the one-off program as they wanted to dispel myths about dementia and raise awareness of what living with Alzheimer's disease is really like.

"I really hope that the programme helps people and doesn't scare them. I haven't done this to scare anybody," Chris says. "You've seen that I still live, I still have a life. Just a different quality."

"Panorama – Living With Dementia: Chris's Story" on BBC One. Review Source: Ross (2016)

Box 18.6 | Politics of Disability and Mental Health Care in Ghana

In Ghana, the prevalence of physical disability is estimated at 7–10 percent and the prevalence of common mental health disorders is estimated at 10 percent (de-Graft Aikins and Koram 2017). Adults and children living with disabilities lack access to appropriate health and social care and experience stigma and associated socio-cultural responses that are life-restricting. Epilepsy, a neurological condition, is typically treated as a mental health disorder with underlying supernatural causation. Adults and children from poor and rural communities are likely to be hospitalized in psychiatric institutions or treated at traditional shrines and prayer camps, rather than receive neurological treatment (Read, Adiibokah, and Nyame 2009). The confluence of wrong medical and social diagnoses creates excluded communities of epilepsy sufferers and caregivers, who are served by under-resourced mental health NGOs (Cohen et al. 2012).

Ghana has a disability policy and a mental health policy. Both policies took over a decade to formulate; both are informed by contemporary global discourses and benchmarks on disability and mental health and focus on rights-based prevention and intervention. However, neither policy has been fully implemented as no funds have been allocated to support governing authorities and service delivery. Inequalities in care persist especially for children, rural communities, and older adults (de-Graft Aikins and Koram 2017). Similar gaps between policy rhetoric and action relating to disability and mental health are reported in other African countries (Faydi et al. 2011; Akyeampong, Hill, and Kleinman 2015) and in other regions (Prince et al. 2007; Saxena et al. 2011).

multifaceted insights. These insights underscore the importance of integrating medical and social models of disease and disability in research, practice, and policy.

18.4.4 Addressing Diminished Health and Disabilities

Resources required to support or enhance the quality of life differ significantly within and between countries. In low-income countries, it is estimated that less than 5 percent of those living with disabilities gain access to rehabilitative and associated services (WHO 2011). The barriers to providing ideal disability care in these countries include inadequate policies and standards; negative social and professional attitudes; lack of provision of services; problems with service delivery; inadequate funding for disability services; lack of accessibility (environmental, social, institutional); lack of consultation, involvement, participation in the formulation and implementation of policies; and lack of evidence and data (WHO 2011; see also Box 18.6 on the politics of heath care in Ghana).

Paraplegia in a low-income-country setting, for instance, could still result in a reasonable quality of life with access to a wheelchair or crutches to be used in an urban environment built to support it. Similarly, with resources to ensure activities of daily living and access to physiotherapy, function and ability to engage within the community can be enhanced. Poorer families within the same lower-income country may not have access to wheelchairs and even if they did, may not live in a built environment that would enable the adequate functioning of a wheelchair. Indeed, there is evidence to suggest that life expectancy in such settings is significantly reduced by complications of the disability that would not arise in an environment

where there was access to basic rehabilitation, nursing, and social care (Allotey et al. 2003). In contrast, a similar injury that results in comparable reduction in physiological function in a high-income country would lead to a different experience in which social support and social protection, access to technology, high-quality physiotherapy and rehabilitation, and a disability-friendly environment would result in better health outcomes (Allotey et al. 2003). Participation in the Paralympics provides a stark indication of the inequalities in disability support across countries (Le Clair 2012).

Continuing progress in addressing disability, however, should not be understood in purely biomedical terms. In addition to efforts to prevent disabling injury and morbidity, and to find and implement the means for restoring function, there remains a strong and complex social component. People living with disability should be able to expect extensive accommodations in their physical and cultural environment and access to technological aids that reduce or even eliminate the associated personal burden. These range from motorized wheelchairs and alternative means of communication to building designs, education of the non-disabled public to overcome prejudice and misunderstanding, and efforts to minimize social isolation. The goal of supporting and enhancing the autonomy of those living with disabilities includes assistance in self-care, and support for affected communities and associations (The Lancet 2016).

With increasing life expectancy, there is a growing need to identify and provide support for aging- and chronic-disease-related poor health. In lower-income countries, extended families are socially expected to provide that support. However with the dynamism of globalization and urbanization there are growing numbers of the elderly living alone (Wan Ibrahim, Zainab, and Redzuan 2012).

Box 18.7 | State Power and Reproduction: Birth Registration in Malaysia

The demonstration of a state's power over reproduction is manifest in various ways.

Registration of births in Malaysia is mandatory in order for the child to gain access to services as a citizen. However this registration process is also used as a means to penalize individuals through a range of religion/society-imposed sanctions. The National Registration Department in Malaysia requires the presentation of the *surat nikah* (marriage certificate) in order to register the birth of a child. Children of unmarried couples are not allowed to have their fathers registered on their birth certificates. If the birth occurs less than nine months after the date of the marriage, the child is considered conceived out of wedlock and is not allowed to have the name of the father recorded on the birth certificate, denying the child any corresponding future patrilineal rights.

Source: www.crin.org/en/library/news-archive/malaysia-birth-registration-authority-denies-baby-right-identity.

18.4.5   Conclusion

The prospect of longer lifespans will be attractive only if the added years are not seriously compromised by diminished health, disability, and chronic illness. The "squaring of the morbidity curve" (see Section 18.3) remains a theoretical ideal whose prospects remain uncertain.

Disability has both biomedical and social components. What makes a condition disabling for an individual may depend on the physical environment and on social attitudes as much as, or even more than, compromised function. Support and respect for those living with disabilities requires affirmative efforts of accommodation, assistance, toleration, and respect for the perspectives and priorities of "differently abled" communities.

18.5   Reproduction

Reproduction includes the biological processes and management of sexual practice, pregnancy, menstruation, abortion, birth, the treatment of infertility, reproductive technologies, birth control, adoption, conception, miscarriage, sterilization, and menopause. The study of reproduction also includes the collection of vital statistics, the analysis of demographic trends, population management, the codification of the categories of maternal and infant mortality, the management of family formation, parenthood (both same-sex and heterosexual), and childrearing (see Box 18.7). More than any other area of global health, reproduction engenders strong views that are based on demography, politics, social values, ideology, religion, and morality. The extent to which people can enjoy their sexual and reproductive health is invariably intertwined with issues of disadvantage, inequity, and rights violations: encompassing gender-based violence; stigmatization on the basis of sexuality; and structural and system-wide barriers to accessing quality care. Who has sex, how and when they have it, whether, when, and how often they reproduce, or have access to information and care for their sexual and reproductive health, is in large part determined by gender roles and power, societies, laws, politicians, and increasingly, global funders (Allotey et al. 2011).

Given this chapter's focus on how inequality shapes the changing contours of human life, we deploy "stratified reproduction," a concept coined by the anthropologist Shellee Colen to describe "the power relations by whom some categories of people are empowered to nurture and reproduce while others are disempowered" (Colen 1995, cited in Ginsburg and Rapp 1995: 3). The lens of reproductive stratification demonstrates how resources and class position shape reproductive phenomena. The concept can be used in analyzing the difference in reproductive horizons of West Indian nannies and the affluent families in New York City who they work for, how IMF- mandated austerity measures and structural adjustment in the developing world have exacerbated differences in global rates of maternal mortality, and how reproductive processes align with a distinction between communities that need "productive children" who contribute to household economies and communities that cultivate "priceless" children whose joyful company is consumed by their parents (Zelizer 1985).

We also see stratification in forms of access to maternal health services and the quality of care received. Julio Frenk, former Minister of Health in Mexico, remarked in opening statements at the 2007 Women Deliver conference in London that maternal and child health are the best entry points to improving health care systems, and crucial to maternal and child health is the quality of birth attendance. Birth attendance is a frequently contested issue. With the exception of Sub-Saharan Africa, rates of births assisted by a medically trained attendant have shown impressive increases over the past 15–20 years and today data indicate that 59 percent of LMIC births are assisted by a medically trained professional. The large majority of these births occur in a health facility.

18.5.1   Measuring Reproduction

Understanding the measurement of reproduction is critical to the domains across which inequities can be assessed. Demography plays a key role where reproduction is discussed primarily in the context of its importance to "reproduction" of the population and to the control of the size of the population. From a gender and rights perspective, disaggregation of the data is critical to understanding who is reproducing,

18

Box 18.8 | Notes on Measuring Reproduction

Birth statistics usually start from the absolute counts of births that are registered in a given territory over a certain period, typically a calendar year. In countries that do not have complete vital registration systems this information is often estimated with surveys. To calculate the crude birth rate (often called only the birth rate), this absolute birth count is related to the mid-year resident population in the territory under consideration. The crude birth rate can be used to compare birth intensities of different populations across time and space, but does not consider the influence of age structure.

More sophisticated measures of reproduction differentiate birth by the age of mothers at the time of birth. The use of age-standardized fertility rates has become the norm for comparative analyses in reproduction. There are three dominant indicators : (1) total fertility rate (TFR) is the sum of age-specific fertility rates (all children born to women of a certain age group divided by the number of women in this age group); (2) gross reproduction rate (GRR) only considers female babies and thus gives the average number of daughters born to women over their lives; (3) net reproduction rate (NRR) considers the survival of the child from birth to the mean age of childbearing and thus gives the extent to which one generation of mothers is replaced by another one. A NRR of 1.0 means that the following generation of women reaching reproductive age will be exactly the same as the previous one; a NRR of 2.0 means that the population doubles each generation.

Another important distinction in the measurement of reproduction is that between a period and a cohort perspective. While period rates summarize the reproductive experience of different age groups of women in one period (typically a calendar year), cohort rates describe the experience of birth cohorts of women. During times of changes in reproductive behavior, such as postponement of childbearing (measured through an increase in the mean age of childbearing), the two kinds of rates can show very different pictures. Period TFRs can be artificially depressed (tempo effect).

Recently, methods have been developed to estimate tempo-adjusted period TFRs that can be interpreted as the "period quantum" of fertility or the mean number of children per woman as implied by reproductive behavior in recent periods. A naïve interpretation of the period TFRs as the mean number of children can result in misleading conclusions.

---

at what age, and how often. This also provides some measure of fertility control and choice, as a proxy indicator of inequities. In Box 18.8 we present notes on measuring reproduction. Demographers measure reproduction by a set of indicators which vary considerably in their meaning; the interpretation of time trends or differentials in reproduction requires careful attention to these precise meanings (Lutz 2013).

18.5.2   Determinants of Reproduction

The literature on the determinants of fertility distinguishes between proximate determinants and underlying determinants. The proximate determinants are the factors that are immediately causing pregnancy and birth in a biological sense. These determinants include the age of beginning of sexual activity and the frequency of intercourse, the prevalence and effectiveness of contraception, the prevalence of induced abortion (plus spontaneous intra-uterine mortality), and the duration of post-partum infecundity. Any change in observed fertility levels occurs through changes in one or more of these proximate determinants, which explain the mechanisms but not why women and couples are changing their behaviors.

When discussing the underlying social, economic, and political determinants of fertility it is useful to distinguish between the secular decline in fertility levels which is part of the demographic transition from pre-modern high to modern low levels, and the variations within low-fertility societies. The global fertility transition began in France in the nineteenth century and by the beginning of the twentieth century had started in most industrialized societies. It then spread globally during the second half of the last century. Except for a few pockets of still very high traditional fertility levels in Africa, this secular fertility transition has been completed or is under way in virtually all parts of the world. The global TFR has declined from 5.0 in 1960–1965 to 2.4 in 2010–2015 (UNPD 2015). But even before the onset of the demographic transition, fertility levels varied among populations due to different marriage patterns and different lengths of post-partum infecundity, which are associated with different breast-feeding patterns. In Western Europe, fertility levels in the eighteenth century were lower than in Eastern Europe and most of the rest of the world due to a distinct "European marriage pattern" (Hajnal 1965) which was characterized by a rather late age at marriage and high proportions of men and women remaining unmarried. On the other hand, some traditional hunter and gatherer populations showed remarkably low fertility levels due to unusually long birth intervals that are associated with extended breast-feeding (Howell 1979). But despite these different levels of overall fertility, one finds no significant evidence of parity-specific fertility control in any of these traditional societies.

According to demographic transition theory, conscious family limitation has been a social innovation that was brought about by social and economic factors as well as cultural diffusion processes. While in traditional cultures there is evidence for some methods of avoiding pregnancies as a consequence of non-marital sex, this seems to have been largely unthinkable within marriage. Based on an analysis of historical fertility transitions in Europe, Ansley Coale (1973) specified a set of three preconditions for a lasting fertility decline: (1) Fertility must be regarded as being within the realm of conscious choice. This factor seems to be closely associated with female basic education, but cultural diffusion and mass media can also play a role. (2) There must be objective advantages to lower fertility. These can range from economic factors to urbanization to health reasons. (3) Acceptable means of fertility control must be available. What is considered acceptable is dependent on the specific cultural context, particularly with respect to abortion. In the context of the current fertility decline in low-income countries, this factor also relates directly to the availability of modern reproductive health services.

How low fertility rates will fall in the later phases of demographic transition and what differentials within and between societies will prevail are topics of intense scientific discussions. Basten, Sobotka, and Zeman (2014) provide the most comprehensive recent summary of fertility trends and differentials in low-fertility countries, as well as the different theories, approaches, and arguments that can help to explain and forecast these differentials. Fuchs and Goujon (2014) provide a comparable assessment for countries whose fertility levels are still higher (with TFRs above 2.5). These assessments are based on the input of hundreds of internal population experts and cover all world regions. They discuss the drivers of fertility in four broad domains: (1) reproductive health: including availability of family planning, side-effects of contraceptives, traditional methods, abortion, and religious attitudes to contraception; (2) economic costs and benefits: child labor, cost of urban upbringing, old-age security, and value of education; (3) status of women: arranged marriage, age at marriage, female educational status, autonomous contraceptive choice, male support of contraception, and female labor force participation; (4) cultural change: ideal family size, son preference, politically promoted norms, attitude to childlessness, and educational differentials. In the case of low-fertility countries there are much more detailed analyses regarding the nature of the partner relationship as well as different forms of combining employment and family care. Given this very broad range of relevant factors determining reproduction in different societies, we can in the following sections discuss only selected aspects.

18.5.3 Population Growth, Fertility Control, and Reproduction Governance

The development of the nation-state produced a new focus on internal populations and vital statistics and the measurement of fertility. This focus codified sexuality and reproduction as processes that should be governed as a matter of great interest to the nation (Greenhalgh 2008; Morgan and Roberts 2012). The development of the legal and medical management of reproduction sought to control reproductive behavior in both colonizing and colonized nations. Examples of these new regulatory forms included the late nineteenth-century initiation of laws and morality campaigns directed toward making prostitution, abortion, and homosexuality illegal activities. Additionally, birth attendance (banning midwifery), fertility rates, infant feeding, and contraception were all newly regulated through legal, moral, and medical means in the efforts to create strong working and fighting populations within nation-states. Throughout the twentieth century and into the twenty-first, concerns about over- and underpopulation have been paramount in defining nations, often through coercive means, such as eugenic programs or the inducement to reproduce.

With the exponential rise of world population, new regulatory measures to curb population growth were instituted by nation-states and international agencies, especially in LMICs. Fertility rates are highest in lower-income countries in Africa and Asia. China and India now have the largest populations, with the United States in third place. In LMICs, the management of reproduction during the Cold War and beyond took the form of internationally driven programs to limit and control specific populations. Deriving from early twentieth century nationalistic, eugenic policies, these programs sought to limit the population growth of developing nations to enrich their populations and make the world safe from communism. Conversely, wealthier nations in Western Europe and Japan have seen population decline often described as a harbinger of national decline.

To combat this top-down approach to population control, the Cairo International Conference on Population and Development in 1994 and the Fourth World Conference on Women in Beijing in 1995 developed programs of action through a human-rights-based approach to reproductive health. The approach advocated for individual rights, particularly women's rights over fertility choices, with the underlying assumption that given these forms of control, fertility would be curtailed. These efforts met with significant resistance, on religious and political grounds (Berer 2011). Countries such as the United States placed limits on aid funding based on reproductive policies. The Catholic Church also had significant influence over how reproductive rights played out in several countries. Despite these obstacles, international discussions of reproduction since Cairo have tended to be framed in terms of individual rights. Other countries developed controversial population-level strategies to limit fertility, such as the one-child policy in China and forced sterilizations in parts of the Americas.

Thirty years later, birth rates have dropped dramatically. However, the rights-based approach to reproduction also remains controversial. In emphasizing rights, this approach has made it natural to conceptualize some of the issues as a competition between the "right to life" of the unborn and the "reproductive rights" of women. Control of women's fertility has been exercised in other coercive forms in conflict situations through the use of "breeding programs" (Hoile et al. 2002; Allotey and Reidpath 2015) and pressure, including through incentives, toward redistribution of resources across ethnic groups (Asiaweek, 1993).[9]

---

[9] Similar strategies are deployed in Singapore, Japan, and Italy – although most tend to give some one-off small incentives rather than make affordable child care more widely available so women can work.

We can see the stratification at work in terms of the selective focus on population as over- or underpopulation. For instance, much of the global anxiety about overpopulation is directed toward Sub-Saharan Africa, which is also the site of the world's largest infertility belt due to the iatrogenic effects of poor health care infrastructure. Little attention is paid to this form of subfertility in aid programs.

18.5.4　Abortion and Contraception

The control of fertility and birth through contraception and abortion has been one of the most controversial aspects of reproductive policy. One explanation is that these issues place women in control of the shape of their lives and sexuality, challenging traditional female roles. Sterilization is also controversial, in part for the same reason, but also because of the history of forced sterilization among devalued groups within many nation-states. Modern contraceptive methods became widely available in the early part of twentieth century and have been partially responsible for lowering fertility rates worldwide. The use of contraception and abortion are highly stratified. Even where certain means of fertility control such as abortion are illegal, women with more resources have greater access. Women have access to contraception in most high-income countries and in many LMICs that were considered overpopulated.

More coercive population control can be found in China, in its one-child policy, in India, which lowers fertility rates though giving ration cards in return for sterilization, and in Tibet, Haiti, and Peru – often with certain groups considered unworthy of reproducing (Adams and Pigg 2005). Accepting the eugenic logic of the earlier twentieth century, governments have sought to limit the reproduction of minority groups, low castes, and indigenous communities. While development experts have understood lowered fertility rates to be key to economic development, many subaltern groups have framed population reduction policies and programs as forms of genocide (Ginsburg and Rapp 1995).

Abortion only became illegal from the late nineteenth century on, when states came to see robust and large populations as key to building strong nations. Illegality was framed around morality and the perceived risk of the procedure. The anthropological literature on personhood reveals North American debates about when life begins as local and specific. In different non-Western contexts, personhood can commence at various times, often post-birth; and the concept of individual life is not relevant to how children are made at all (Conklin and Morgan 1996; Kaufman and Morgan 2005). Even within the Catholic Church, currently one of the staunchest opponents of abortion, the definition of beginnings of life have changed over time (Noonan 1986).

The most recent estimates suggest that 56 million abortions are performed each year, of which 88 percent occur in LMICs (Sedgh et al. 2016). Abortion conducted by trained practitioners and under sterile medical conditions can be safer than carrying a child to term. But in LMICs unsafe abortions are common, and almost 70,000 women die each year from complications due to unsafe abortion, a figure that constitutes 13 percent of maternal mortality rates. Illegality and censure do not prevent the practice of abortion. Despite the continued illegality of on-demand abortion in Latin America, except in Cuba and now Mexico City, the subcontinent now has some of the highest abortion rates in the world (Sedgh et al. 2016). In Latin America women with means can access safe abortion, while women without means cannot.

Gender-based mobilization for the right to abortion has been variable. In Latin America for instance, it has been hampered because – unlike the right to vote – abortion's illegality affects women differentially by class. Because clandestine abortion is easily available and relatively safe for women with means, there has been little impetus to work toward legalization (Htun 2003; see also Mooney 2009: 51). The current model for abortion decriminalization in developing countries makes the case for the right to public health, rather than the North American "right to choose" (Morgan and Roberts 2009, 2012).

Medical abortion (pharmaceutically induced) is changing the abortion landscape by providing women a safe and discrete means to abort outside of clinical settings. Reproductive stratification is also evident in access to medical abortion, given that a combination of mifepristone and misoprostol achieves the highest efficacy with the fewest side-effects. In many regions of the world, only mifepristone is available (Winikoff and Sheldon 2012).

18.5.5　Assisted Reproductive Technologies and Selective Reproductive Technologies

The late twentieth century saw the rapid development of assisted reproductive technologies that facilitate fertility and selective reproductive technologies that facilitate and prevent the births of children. As several social scientists and scholars of the social studies of science have argued, reproduction has always been assisted and children have always been selected through various kinds of social arrangements and practices, as well as familiar technologies of infant formula, paperwork, and forceps. The availability and reach of assistance and selection has, however, never been greater. This availability falls along stratified lines.

We can see stratification at work in the development and use of assisted reproductive technologies and selective reproductive technologies around the world. In the developed world, assisted reproductive technologies, such as in vitro fertilization, intracytoplasmic sperm injection (ICSI), egg donation, and surrogate motherhood have produced anxieties about interference with nature. In LMICs, assisted reproduction is now geared toward combating iatrogenic infertility – which perhaps involves ignoring larger structural causes for the high rates in these areas.

Rather than aiming to overcome infertility, selective reproductive technologies are used to determine which children are born. Two of the most common purposes are sex selection and preventing the birth of children with certain developmental conditions. In societies with extensive public prenatal programs fewer and fewer children are born with conditions such as Down's syndrome. Disability rights advocates criticize this as an injustice, while defenders point to the difference between choosing not to bring someone with disabilities into existence and violating the rights of or showing disrespect to those who have disabilities (Gammeltoft and Wahlberg 2014).

In many LMICs the private use of selective technologies like amnio-centeses and pre-implantation genetic diagnoses has resulted in a skewed sex ratio in favor of boys. This form of sex selection is partially explained by the fact that in the past, extended families have prospered through the propagation of boys. In fact in some places in Sub-Saharan Africa, women who only have daughters are considered infertile because they have not produced what is necessary for family continuity (Inhorn and Balen 2002).

18.5.6 Developmental and Environmental Approaches to Reproduction

A developmental/environmental approach has started to shift the focus of reproductive policy, from an approach framed by genetic determinism toward more general environmental factors. This environmental approach also allows social and biological scientists to shift the focus away from the individual reproductive body to larger global environmental conditions that shape reproduction in disparate and stratified ways. For example, declines in human male sperm production and the falling age of female menstruation worldwide have been linked to factors ranging from increased nutrition to synthetic chemical compounds like endocrine disruptors, BPA phthalates and antibiotics, and growth hormones (Steingraber 2007).

One site where environment seems to be of particular importance is gestation. Epigenetic researchers examine environmentally triggered mechanisms (e.g. DNA methylation, histone modifications, and DNA-binding proteins) that affect and regulate gene expression. Epigenetic researchers broadly define environment in terms of climate, stress, and nutrition, emphasizing particular environmentally plastic reproductive moments such as embryogenesis, early gestation, and the neonate period. Thus, the bulk of epigenetic research focuses on the effects of the maternal body and maternal behavior on the "fetal programming" of offspring. Thus, as discussed in Section 18.2, researchers have shown that children born to women stressed or starved during wartime have much higher levels of adulthood disease and lower educational attainment – characteristics that might be passed on to their children.

Epigenetics and studies of the social determinants of health have the potential to reshape social welfare policy toward more collective and distributed action, enlisting broader support for environmental regulation, public education, and health care (CSDH 2008). But within current neoliberal economic regimes in the United States and Western Europe, epigenetics researchers have focused on the implications of their findings for the behavior of pregnant women.

Similarly, governments and NGOs in LMICs find it more feasible to fund programs targeting pregnant women and infants than to restructure decayed public institutions such as schools and health care facilities. Pharmaceutical companies are attempting to produce drugs that will activate epigenetic mechanisms, including a drug that calms children who experienced "bad mothering" in the neonate period. Such a drug obviously does nothing to address the larger (and, from the perspective of a pharmaceutical company, profitless) political and economic factors that produced "bad mothers" to begin with. The targets of these discussions and interventions are women of reproductive age who are made, yet again, to bear the bulk of responsibility for how their offspring fare. Epigenetics might reshape our understanding of socio-biological existences, or they might instead reinforce the policing of the behavior of pregnant women.

18.5.7 Conclusions

The historian of science Michelle Murphy argues that if we ask, "Where does biological reproduction reside?" the answer "The body" is simply not up to the task (Murphy 2011). Murphy advances a framework of "distributed reproduction" that allows us to examine "what counts as biological reproduction by tracking the dispersion of sexed living beings into their infrastructural and political economic milieu" (Murphy 2011, 22). The notion of the individual body is not up to the task, for instance, of understanding how only 35 boys are born for every 100 girls among the First Nations Aamjiwnaang peoples in Eastern Canada, where, in the local waterways, the gonads and sex ratios of fish, fowl, and reptiles have also been dramatically altered (Murphy 2013). To grasp the determinants of reproduction, Murphy argues that we need to move beyond individual bodies and sort through the specific tangles of diverse causal factors.

Murphy's insights are similar to those of a host of other scholars of reproduction, reviewed in this section, who caution against locating reproduction within individual women's bodies, and encourage a more expansive view of reproduction that examines reproductive phenomena as produced through larger structural factors such as inequality, gender roles, environmental health, and family organization.

18.6 Enhancement: Better than Well?

This section will explore the possible implications of human enhancement interventions, present and future, on the limits of health care and the fair distribution of medical resources. We shall suggest that many expectations and concerns regarding the biological transformation of humans by enhancement may be exaggerated. The important changes to the human condition that enhancement is likely to bring about will be social and cultural and mediated through the social effects, sometimes subtle, of the widespread adoption of such practices. Still, these changes will require regulation and rethinking of long-established principles in health policy.

18.6.1 What Is Enhancement?

Several practices that can be considered human enhancements are prevalent today. Examples are performance-enhancing drugs in sports and off-label use of stimulants such as Ritalin (methylphenidate), but also common products such as coffee. According to a standard definition among bioethicists, an intervention is an enhancement if and only if it improves a biological functioning beyond what restores or sustains health.[10] Such improvements can be physical (e.g. muscle strength), cognitive (e.g. attention span), and conative (e.g. mood). Enhancement is often contrasted with *treatment*, which is a biomedical intervention that restores or sustains health (Daniels 2000). The same medical procedure can sometimes be used both for treatment and for enhancement. For example, the drug Modafinil is used as a treatment for disorders such as narcolepsy and as such not considered an enhancement. However, it is also used by, e.g. the United States Air Force to enhance cognitive functioning in sleep-deprived pilots during extended missions.[11]

We shall also distinguish between radical and non-radical enhancement. An intervention is a radical enhancement if and only if it improves a biological function such that it surpasses the current human range.[12] For example, a medical intervention that would extend a person's lifespan to 150 years would be a radical enhancement. By contrast, nonradical enhancement includes interventions that leave the improved abilities well within the human range. As most current and emerging human technologies belong to the latter group, our focus will be on non-radical enhancement (henceforth "enhancement").

What to count as an enhancement is not as straightforward as it might first seem, however. First, according to the standard definition, human enhancement is distinct from interventions that impair or don't improve human biological functioning, such as tattoos, piercing, genital cutting, cosmetic surgery, and other body modifications. We face here an interesting complication with the standard definition since some body modifications impair body functioning but confer a social advantage in some contexts. For example, skin bleaching harms the biological function of the skin (Olumide et al. 2008; WHO 2011). However, this practice would hardly be so popular if it didn't improve the social prospects of its practitioners. In several countries in Africa and Asia, lighter skin improves job prospects, wages, and other social goods (Hunter 2007). Thus, how *improvement* should be characterized with regard to human enhancement is not straightforward and the distinction between health-related and social improvements is sometimes difficult to maintain. This threatens to make the standard definition (where functioning does not include social functioning) too narrow.

Second, the standard definition depends crucially on what one means by "health." The meaning of this term varies across cultural and historical contexts, often depending on whether a condition is normal in the statistical sense.[13] For example, the diagnosis "idiopathic short stature" is defined as being of a height two standard deviations below the mean of a specific population (Rosenbloom 2009). This means that children of the same height can be diagnosed differently between countries with different average height. This in turn will determine, according to the standard definition, whether growth hormone therapy will be considered a treatment or an enhancement: For one child, it

might just be treatment, but for another child of the same height but in another country it will be classified as an enhancement.

Moreover, claims about whether an intervention is an instance of enhancement or restores health may also be partly normative, since health is commonly seen as a desirable good that ought to be promoted. If health is defined as the absence of disease, and associated with a "normal" state, then interventions that restore human functioning to this normal state can be partly justified by virtue of promoting health. By contrast, if an intervention is defined as an enhancement it will lack this justification. On this view, growth hormone therapy is, other things being equal, more justified if it is a treatment rather than an enhancement. Thus, to state that an intervention is an instance of enhancement rather than a treatment may be not merely a descriptive claim but also a normative one.

Third, whether an intervention is an enhancement also depends on what is perceived to be part of a person's abilities rather than something the person can do with the help of technologies external to the person. Enhancement technologies are often seen as artifacts that are to a certain degree integrated with the body, for instance performance-enhancing stimulants or implants. While rarely stated explicitly, this view is consistent with our folk-psychological notion of the boundaries of a human body. The account of enhancement technologies as necessarily attached to or integrated with the body is complicated by the view of cognition as essentially embodied and extended (Menary 2010). On this view, cognitive processes are deeply embedded in artifacts and other objects in our environment. If a person's cognitive processes are regulated and (partially) executed by their environment, why should things such as calculators, maps, whiteboards, etc., not be considered enhancements? Arguably, some tools affect the human condition much more than some instances of bodily integrated enhancement. The view that a certain technology is an instance of enhancement only if it is inside the skin seems to be poorly justified.

These considerations show that what should be classified as an enhancement is not a straightforward matter, and is contested. This complicates the picture for those who ascribe special moral significance to the distinction between treatment and enhancement (e.g. Wasson 2011).

18.6.2   Enhancement and Priority in Health Care

While most accept that human enhancement is in at least some instances permissible, there remains considerable controversy with regard to how such interventions should be prioritized when distributing limited health care resources. Modern medical practice and health care policy-making face an increasing number of conditions

---

[10]   Cf., e.g. Juengst and Moseley (2015). Our definition differs slightly from theirs. See also Tännsjö (2009) for a different definition (more on this below).

[11]   Air Force Special Operations Command Instruction 48–101 (sects. 1.7.4), US Air Force Special Operations Command, November 30, 2012.

[12]   Cf. Tännsjö (2009), who distinguishes among "negative medical interventions (intended to cure disease), positive interventions (intended to improve, within the normal range, functioning) and enhancement (where a person is pushed beyond species normal functioning)." What Tännsjö calls "positive intervention" and "enhancement," we call "non-radical enhancement" and "radical enhancement" respectively.

[13]   Note that what is statistically normal is distinct from what is normal in the physiological sense, even though these states are often coextensive. For example, statistical deviations from the norm in heart shape are often associated with abnormal heart function.

that could be addressed through medical interventions. A general principle that is often, implicitly or explicitly, used to guide deliberations in the face of this challenge is the principle that conditions which qualify as diseases (i.e. that impair health) yield a special normative claim to medical resources. Let us call this principle "Disease Priority." A strong version of this principle states that medical interventions that do not restore or sustain health are morally wrong.[14] A weaker version of Disease Priority states that all interventions that treat or prevent disease are to be prioritized before any other interventions. This weaker notion is part of standard approaches to prioritization in the health care system. For example, the National Board of Health and Welfare in Sweden explicitly states that medical services not associated with disease or harm have the lowest priority with respect to the distribution of medical resources (Larsson 2007).

According to Disease Priority, enhancement interventions, as we have characterized them above, would either be morally impermissible or in the lowest priority group. However, although Disease Priority may sound initially plausible, it conflicts with some instances of standard medical practice. Unwanted pregnancies, for instance, are generally considered to be a medical problem that ought to be addressed by the health care system, even though being pregnant or fertile is not a disease.

An alternative and more pragmatic approach to the distribution of health care resources would avoid a strict reliance on the enhancement/treatment distinction but would instead base decisions about extending medical interventions to new areas on considerations such as cost-effectiveness and fairness. For example, it may now (or in the near future) be possible to partly address some social problems with modern medicine. According to a new study in the *New England Journal of Medicine*, the medication of prison inmates diagnosed with ADHD with the stimulant methylphenidate seems to lead to a reduction in reoffending (Lichtenstein et al. 2012). The same medication seems to improve math and reading skills among students with ADHD, according to a study in the *Journal of Pediatrics* (Scheffler et al. 2009). Though debate continues over whether ADHD is a genuine disease (Greenberg 2010), the pragmatic approach suggested here would not base a decision on the use of this drug for these students on the outcome of this debate. It would instead shift the focus to whether the symptoms typically associated with ADHD can be effectively addressed with medical interventions at a reasonable cost, and whether it would be desirable to do so. This approach could guide decisions on using medical interventions to ameliorate social problems in a wide variety of contexts, whether or not the results should properly be regarded as treatments of a disease or enhancements. What matters is the safety, fairness, cost, and direct and indirect effects of the intervention.

18.6.3   The Limits of Human Enhancement

In general, existing enhancement interventions have limited medical benefits compared with many medical treatments. As we discussed

above, sometimes enhancements are biologically harmful or neutral but may provide a social benefit. The pragmatic outlook proposed here suggests that it is not only medical benefits that are worth taking into consideration when assessing the relative importance of a specific intervention but also other benefits. For example, contraceptives have in most cases little or no medical net benefit but have quite substantial social benefits, such as reproductive autonomy and increased female workplace participation. Some of the effects of such interventions may not be very noticeable at the individual level at the same time as the group effect is significant, and this should also be taken into account. For example, we may hypothesize that if a large fraction of children would receive medication for certain behavioral traits, and this intervention was effective, then we should expect this to have significant consequences for youth culture and social norms. Bostrom and Roache have suggested that macroeconomic gains from increased cognitive function due to the removal of lead in gasoline have been considerable (Bostrom and Roache 2008). Similar gains could be the result of the proliferation of cognition-enhancing drugs, even when the effects of such drugs would be practically imperceptible at the individual level.

With respect to existing enhancement options, however, restoring human functions that have been impaired by disease is typically more effective than improving the functions of a healthy body. For example, fortifying food with essential micronutrients such as iodine to address iodine deficiency (not an enhancement, as defined here) is a much more effective way to improve intelligence (in those with said deficiency) than any existing cognitive enhancer. This does not imply, of course, that existing human enhancements have little or no effect, as is illustrated by the effects of anabolic steroids (and in elite sports, even small improvements can be decisive in determining who wins).

The apparent difficulty of enhancement interventions to radically enhance (in contrast to just enhancing; see the definitions above) biological functions is in many cases explained by the fact that human bodies are complex systems where different subsystems coexist in an equilibrium such that improving one function over a certain baseline often reduces some other functions. For example, while caffeine improves some cognitive functions, such as alertness and wakefulness, it has a detrimental effect on other functions, such as emotional stability (Vilarim, Rocha Araujo, and Nardi 2011). Hence, unless an individual is prepared to accept considerable medical risks, radical enhancement is rarely possible, as illustrated by the many side-effects that athletes using performance-enhancing drugs have suffered. This may suggest that Disease Priority could still be used as a rule of thumb to assess the medical effectiveness of an intervention where enhancement and treatment compete for the same resources, although it is not an appropriate general principle for prioritizing between interventions.

In the discussion of how to allocate medical resources, it is useful to make a distinction between enhancements that confer a positional advantage and those that confer a non-positional advantage. For instance, the enhancement of executive functions (self-control, planning, concentration) is better for the enhanced individual because

---

[14]   Along these lines, Sandel (2004) observes: "It is more plausible to view genetic engineering as the ultimate expression of our resolve to see ourselves astride the world, the masters of our nature. But that promise of mastery is flawed. It threatens to banish our appreciation of life as a gift, and to leave us with nothing to affirm or behold outside our own will."

such functions are very helpful in avoiding costly mistakes. The same enhancement may also confer a positional advantage in that the person may benefit from being better off relative to others with respect to these abilities, but it would still be good for the individual even without such a positional advantage. Other enhancements, such as doping in elite sports and cosmetic surgery, typically confer only or mainly a positional advantage. Such enhancements are beneficial to the individual only if they improve a specific function in comparison with other people. Were everyone to use the same performance-enhancing drug in a contest, then it is possible that no one would be positionally better off as a result of taking the drug, and, considering the side-effects, all would probably be worse off with respect to their wellbeing.

While individuals most often cannot be expected to adapt their behavior in such problematic collective-action situations, policy-makers should consider these problems when making decisions with regard to the allocation of medical resources. This is a typical collective-action problem, where each individual stands to be better off by performing a certain act no matter what the others do, yet when everyone performs this act each individual is worse off than she would have been had everyone not performed the act. Collective-action problems of this kind are most often best solved by the intervention of an external actor (a regulatory body such as WADA, the World Anti-Doping Agency, for example) which can impose costs, such as fines or banning athletes from future competitions, for such actions and thereby align the individual and the collective interest.

18.6.4   Enhancement and Global Inequality

The world's resources are dramatically unequally distributed, and this inequality has significant effects on human health, wellbeing, and life prospects. Lack of access to clean water, vaccines, and other crucial resources not only kills, but also stunts physical and cognitive development. For people that live under these conditions, non-enhancement interventions are likely to play a much larger role in improving their lives. Granting equal access to nutritious food, clean water, education, and other basic goods is both cheaper and more likely to have a greater positive impact than any enhancement technology.

Yet when it comes to biological functioning, humans are to a large extent born roughly equal when their most basic needs have been met. Some opponents of human enhancement fear that enhancement might change this. The worrying prospect is that human enhancement would create a cognitive elite who not only had superior material resources to perpetuate inequality but also were genetically or otherwise biologically superior to the poor (Fukuyama 2002; Habermas 2003). While this scenario is indeed worrisome, it may be less plausible than is typically assumed.

First, just as non-enhancement interventions that improve cognitive ability usually have declining marginal impact, so do known enhancements (Ilieva, Hook, and Farah 2015). In other words, enhancement interventions typically improve function most in individuals whose functions are on the lower end of what can be expected from healthy individuals. For example, methylphenidate, discussed

above, seems to have a limited effect on "normal" people and the effect seems to be roughly proportional to the deficiency in attention and other related functions (Agay et al. 2014).

Genetic selection for increased cognitive ability is also likely to have a similar declining marginal impact. The number of genes associated with intelligence is large, and since each gene that can improve an average person's intelligence has only a very small effect, selecting for very intelligent offspring is rarely feasible (Bostrom and Shulman 2014). Yet, a few mutations are known to cause mental impairment; these have a comparatively large effect and could feasibly be selected against. Selecting against such mutations could be used not only to avoid cognitive impairment, but also to enhance intelligence among individuals with normal but below-average intelligence. As such mutations are likely to be relatively rare among more intelligent individuals, this suggests that, to the extent that social inequality is a result of a cognitive difference, enhancement could be a useful tool to reduce social inequality.

Second, detractors of enhancement typically assume that such interventions will be expensive. This largely depends on what kind of intervention one considers, however. A drug that improves cognition in the general population would have a very large pool of potential consumers, and could therefore be quite cheap (setting aside market failures such as monopolies). If such drugs are effective and positive externalities are considerable, as suggested by Bostrom and Roache (2008), it would be an appealing option for policy-makers to subsidize them. Some other potential interventions are likely to be more expensive. On the other hand, transcranial direct current stimulation, a technique which might enhance learning, would be more expensive to administer on a large scale (Cohen Kadosh et al. 2012).

The prospect of enhancement reinforcing prevailing inequalities, while speculative, still raises concerns regarding unequal access to enhancement. For enhancement interventions that yield a considerable advantage, it is desirable that policy-makers ensure that access to such interventions is universal, or at least that the use is regulated. The current situation in some countries in which off-label use of cognitive stimulants is widespread in academia might very well favor elites with easy access to medical technology and give them even further positional advantage (Arria et al. 2008). Yet, reforms to address these trends might be difficult to implement in an era when social and economic elites exert disproportionate political influence on government priorities (see, e.g., Gilens 2014). Moreover, as discussed above, it is important to consider the possible beneficial social effects on groups and populations from enhancement, not least from a global perspective. If some countries gain access to such enhancements before others, we might see increased inequalities between countries.

18.6.5   Conclusions

This section has discussed some important considerations for policy-makers regarding human enhancement, with a focus on issues that we are likely to face in the close future rather than science-fiction-inspired speculations about future radical enhancements. We have suggested that many expectations and concerns regarding enhancement may be exaggerated. The important changes that enhancement

Box 18.9 | Cultural Representations of Death and Dying

During the 2014/2015 Ebola outbreak, mainstream press accounts focused on how African religious beliefs and customs like touching the dead in order to become ancestors, or the female sharing of veils in Christian congregations, served to spread Ebola in Liberia and Sierra Leone (Grundy 2014). This narrative about cultural attitudes toward death obscured the fact that years of structural adjustment policies had stripped the region of the health infrastructural supports needed to establish and follow quarantine protocols and emergency public health services (Nyarko et al. 2015; Robinson and Pfeiffer 2015). According to politicians, doctors, and clergy in Egypt in the early 2000s, low rates of organ donation were due to Egyptian's culturally backward religious beliefs about death and the afterlife. Rates of organ donation picked up, though, through and after the Arab Spring, stemming from a realigned relationship of trust between subjects and the state, after years of corruption and poor medical care. Low organ donation rates had little to do with cultural beliefs about death (Hamdy 2016). Death and dying as well as biomedicine can be analyzed, then, as phenomena shaped through history and political economic realities that often produce inequality (Lock and Gordon 1988; Singer and Baer 1995).

is likely to bring about will be social and cultural and mediated through the social effects of the widespread adoption of such practices. Still, these changes raise some worrisome issues regarding inequality and collective-action problems which will require regulation and rethinking of long-established principles in health policy. We pointed out a number of problems with the distinction between enhancement and treatment for policies regarding the distribution of health care resources. Instead, we suggested a pragmatic approach, to the effect that decisions about extending medical interventions to new areas should be based on considerations of cost-effectiveness and fairness.

18.7 Death and Dying

Death is the one certainty awaiting every human being. None of us can expect to avoid this calamity, but if we are fortunate death will come late in life and will be preceded by a minimum of suffering and indignity. The gains in longevity enjoyed in much of the world in recent decades, surveyed in Sections 18.2 and 18.3 of this chapter, fulfill the first of these hopes for many; and palliative care at the end of life helps an increasing number to achieve the second. Extending these gains to all is a goal that heads the health agenda for the present century.

What constitutes a "good" death is understood differently by different peoples. In the Netherlands, what matters may be the manner of dying: "at home, without violence or pain, with the dying person being at peace with his [sic] environment and having at least some control over events" (Seale and van der Geest 2004: 885). In Ghana, a good death is marked by extravagant public funerals (van der Geest 2000) – resources are expended in order to celebrate the life, maintain ongoing relationships, and facilitate the passage to what lies beyond this life. Some of these seemingly culture-bound variations may reflect underlying socio-economic deprivation (see Box 18.9).

We focus on four key themes relating to the complexity of death and dying in the global context: (1) dying unequally; (2) palliative care; (3) assisted dying; and (4) changing conceptions of death.

18.7.1 Dying Unequally

The last century saw huge transformations in what people die of and how they die. In developed nations, people are living longer lives, with few mortalities resulting from communicable or infectious diseases (see Section 18.3). With longevity come chronic conditions and complex diseases of aging that are costly to manage, e.g. more people living with heart disease, rather than dying of a heart attack. These transformations in cause of death will radically reshape how people die, where, with whom, and under what emotional and physical circumstances. Key to this transformation is the fact that in poor nations, non-communicable causes of death are usually multi-factorial, stemming from multilevel, multifaceted, largely structural causes including poverty, lack of access to health care, and weak health systems and policy (Bukhman, Mocumbi, and Horton 2015; de-Graft Aikins and Agyemang 2016).

The result of inequality is that, too often, death and dying in poor nations does not approach the global health ideal of a "good death," with its connotations of a peaceful end at home in bed, perhaps surrounded by loved ones – an ending unobtainable when life ends as a result of violence, suicide, death from natural disaster, or what we call "death by modernity."

18.7.1.1 Violent Death

While violent death does not make it onto the top ten list of causes of death worldwide, it tends to be considered one of worst ways to die, and the most traumatizing for the bereaved. Violent death occurs disproportionately within poor and marginalized groups around the world and in countries experiencing complex humanitarian emergencies. Nations in Central America and South America – including El Salvador, Brazil, Venezuela, Honduras, and Guatemala – have the highest country-wide rates of violent death in the world (Gagne 2017). In the United States homicide is the highest cause of death among black men aged 15–44, and African-Americans are almost eight times as likely as white Americans to be homicide victims; firearm injuries constitute the third leading cause of death and the second leading cause of injury-related death among US children aged 1–17 (Fowler et al. 2017). Boys, minorities, and older children are disproportionately affected. In complex humanitarian emergencies in countries like Syria, violent deaths occur among internally displaced people and refugees (Heudtlass, Speybroeck, and Guha-Sapir 2016).

18.7.1.2   Suicide

Suicide rates have increased worldwide by 60 percent over the last 45 years, making it now the 15th leading cause of death. Among 15–29-year-olds suicide is now the highest cause of death (WHO 2014a). Guyana has the highest rates of suicide, with 44.4 deaths per 1,000, with South Korea at second place with 28.9 per 1,000. Eight Eastern European nations are represented in the top 25. If we look at groups within nations, however, the highest suicide rates in the world exist among first nations peoples in the Americas, where loss of life ways and intergenerational continuity, poverty and violence, and dispersed settlement patterns contribute to these high rates. In Nunavut, the mostly Inuit province of Canada, suicide is the cause of 27 percent of all deaths.

State and NGO interventions have been implemented at population, sub-population and individual levels to prevent suicide and suicide attempts among these groups. Much of this attention is medicalizing, geared toward improving mental health within individuals instead of focusing on larger structural issues that shape the often bleak collective life conditions for communities most affected by suicide (Stevenson 2014). The complex cultural representations of suicide are also ignored. While suicide can seem puzzling and pointless or even immoral from a modern global health perspective, it has been used and still is used to communicate sacrifice, honor, or political resistance within collective life, which can then be celebrated and admired, especially when death is not experienced as completely disconnecting the dead from the living (Asad 2007; Staples and Widger 2012). A critical question for global health, then, is what suicide prevention is meant to do: save individual lives or create more equitable conditions that make life worth living?

18.7.1.3   Disaster

The term "disaster" connotes randomness, but social science research on tsunamis, earthquakes, floods, hurricanes, heatwaves, droughts, and famines has amply demonstrated that human action, social organization, and stratification determine whether a random natural event will produce a human disaster; likewise, they determine who is most likely to be harmed or killed. Fifty-six percent of disasters happen in high-income countries, while these same countries only experience 32 percent of the lives lost related to disaster, while low-income nations experience 44 percent of the disasters but 68 percent of the deaths from disaster (CRED 2015). The psychic toll can be long-term for disaster survivors when whole communities and life ways are obliterated in short order.

Heatwaves are a representative example. With the increase in elderly people living alone, the degradation of shared urban space, and increased temperatures from global warming in the late twentieth and early twenty-first centuries, there has been a massive upswing in the rate of heat-related death among the elderly. In 2003 over 11,000 people died in France during a heatwave, most of them elderly and low-income, and in Chicago in 1995 over 800 people died, mostly elderly poor residents living alone in dangerous urban neighborhoods, who could not afford air conditioning. They had no place to go for heat relief (Klinenberg 2002).

18.7.2   Quality of Death: Palliative and Hospice Care

"Quality of life" indices have paved the way for discussions around "quality of death," which is measured in terms of access to palliative and hospice care. Palliative care is now considered part of the right to health, defined by the WHO as "an approach that improves the quality of life of patients and their families facing the problems associated with life-threatening illness, through the prevention and relief of suffering" (WHO 2017). Essential medicines for palliative care were included in the 18th WHO Essential Medicines List in 2013, and in May 2014 the World Health Assembly (WHA) passed a landmark resolution urging member states to support access to essential medicines, and to strengthen palliative care as an integrated component of universal health coverage throughout the life course, stating that palliative care is an ethical responsibility of health systems (WHA, 2014).

Access to palliative care, however, is unequally distributed. It has been largely absent from the global health dialogue and consequently a low priority for donor investment (Powell et al. 2015). Hospice and palliative care is either non-existent or in its infancy in many parts of the world, and an estimated 5 billion people have insufficient or no access to medications to control severe or moderate pain (WHO 2017). Meanwhile, in high-income countries, medical services have all too often focused on preventing death rather than helping people meet death without suffering pain, discomfort, and stress (EIU 2010).

A key assumption underlying "quality of death" is that cause of death will be a single non-communicable disease, like cancer or heart disease, hopefully at the end of life, that can be palliated through the care of symptoms. Death from a single non-communicable disease occurs more frequently in high-income nations, where resources exist for both early disease diagnosis and the end-of-life palliation of pain. The situation is different for LMICs, where deaths arise from a burden of intertwined infectious and chronic non-communicable disease and a higher prevalence of co-morbidities and multi-morbidities. HIV/AIDS, diabetes, and neurodegenerative diseases present an enormous need for palliative care in low-income countries and populations, and cancer is a growing cause of death in low-income countries (de-Graft Aikins and Agyemang 2016). In low-income countries, late diagnosis and lack of resources for palliative care make death by non-communicable disease a traumatic experience for the dying and their families (Livingston 2012). Furthermore, pain control is essential but largely unavailable in low-income countries even in cases of severe injury, acute infections, and epidemics (e.g. Ebola), and the fall-out of natural disasters. Despite this widespread need, only 20 nations in total (8.5 percent) have integrated palliative care adequately into their health care system (EIU 2010).

Most studies associate palliative care with less health spending. Palliative care is perceived to reduce costs associated with hospital stays and emergency admissions, because the proportion of community and home care is increased.

The costs associated with non-cancer palliative care are higher than for cancer-related care. And as the population ages, more end-of-life care will be needed overall. While the utilization of both hospital-based and in-home hospice and palliative care services significantly reduced the cost of care, while providing equal- if not better-quality care, studies to date are primarily from high-income countries. Additionally, any measurement of the true cost of palliative care would need to take into account that most of the innovative palliative care programs in low-income nations are resourced through a patchwork of NGOs and volunteering groups, obscuring much of the labor costs involved in providing this kind of care, and making expenditures hard to measure.

The hospice movement, which advocates for end-of-life care at home or a home-like setting, was developed in the UK. The UK now ranks first among nations in providing quality of end-of-life care, based on indicators such as public awareness, training availability, access to painkillers, and doctor–patient transparency. The failure of many wealthy nations to achieve similar results has been attributed to poor resource allocation and policy coordination, and a focus on hospital medical care programs and reliance on oncologists and other medical specialists rather than hospices (EIU 2010). In the US, for example, hospice care is available, but it is only covered by health insurance if the patient is declared terminal. This narrows the scope of who it can serve and discourages its use. In the context of the US health system's focus on intensive care and heroic measures (Kaufman 2005), moving to hospice care can seem like "giving up."

Though this fear of "giving up" might appear to be a cultural belief that could be alleviated through the right education, it is better explained by the pattern of rewards and incentives. Medical providers are paid for procedures rather than outcomes, while hospices are paid on a daily basis, usually regardless of length of care. As more and more people spend longer living with chronic illness, the challenge will be to come up with payment models that allow for hospice care at an earlier stage, which could reduce the inevitability of heroic measures, and the unwarranted assumption that hospice represents not a choice among alternatives but rather resignation when no alternatives remain. One barrier to palliative care around the world is unequal access to opioids for pain relief, because of either lack of resources or strict narcotics control, which contributes to acute suffering in the dying (Stonington 2015). In India, one of the largest producers of opium and morphine, access by the poor to end-of-life pain relief is minimal because of complicated regulations put in place by the British in the nineteenth century to control their opiate supply for export (Jacob and Mathew 2017). Kerala, a state with a long history of community organizing and high literacy rates, has bucked this trend through the development of comprehensive palliative care centers where pain relief is available, and a network of volunteer health aids who provide home health care. Recently this program has inspired some change in opioid regulation at the national level (EIU 2010).

Another pharmaceutical trend in palliative care in many high-income nations is that increasingly the dying are medicated for anxiety as well as pain, in order to make the experience less stressful for the family who are not accustomed to seeing the agitation that imminent death can cause among the dying.

Palliative care is also shaped by disclosure practices, which vary widely. In much of the world it is common practice for family to keep information about negative prognosis from the dying because this knowledge would dampen their health and spirit (Gordon and Paci 1997). Non-disclosure can seem problematically paternalistic and highly antithetical to notions of autonomy and consent so valued in many high-income nations. However, if we understand non-disclosure as part of the ecology of family care necessary in many low-income nations we can see how this ethic serves to maintain the emotional wellbeing of families. In some cases palliative care has in fact been structured around non-disclosure. For instance, in Thailand hospice care is provided without the explicit disclosure of imminent death to the patient (Stonington 2013).

18.7.3   Assisted Dying

While death is governed less than reproduction, euthanasia (pharmaceutical death administered by physicians) and assisted suicide (pharmaceutical death carried out by and within the family of the dying) provoke reaction, controversy, and legal regulation, even though they affect only a tiny proportion of the terminally ill, and account for only a tiny fraction of all suicides. Nonetheless, pressure brought to bear on policy-makers over these issues can be a catalyst for the improvement of palliative care services – as in Australia, where the federal overturning of a Northern Territory euthanasia law in 1996 may have had the effect of increasing national funding for end of life (EIU 2010).

There is some momentum globally to legalize and regulate both euthanasia and assisted suicide under the umbrella term "assisted dying," although in some locales where assisted dying has been legal, such as Switzerland, stricter controls are under consideration (EIU 2010). At this time, however, there are only eight nations where forms of assisted dying are permitted: Colombia, Switzerland, Canada, Albania, the Netherlands, Belgium, Luxembourg, and the US, where in some cases state laws, rather than federal laws, permit these practices.

The premise of these laws is that for some individuals, a *chosen* death – i.e., a death that occurs at a time and in a manner under the control of the individual – is closer to a "good death" than that which would otherwise occur. For example, the individual might prefer to avoid prolonged decline in an unfamiliar hospital setting. Where patients fear becoming dependent on machines whose use is determined largely through the impersonal imperatives of hospital organization within a nexus of ventilators, insurance reimbursement codes, state legislation, and pain relief (Kaufman 2005) – as is the case too often in the United States – "patients' rights" are asserted in the sense not of entitlement to treatment, but rather of liberty to decline it (Roberts 2009). In less-resourced contexts, there tend to be fewer concerns about the artificiality of these technologies, with more focus on how they can strengthen family relationships through intensive care for the dying (Stonington 2013).[15]

18.7.4 Changing Conceptions of Death

Beginning in the 1960s, legislation in some Western countries broadened the legal definition of death so that it applied to certain comatose patients who, thanks to mechanical ventilators and other intensive care, continued to breathe, circulate blood, and even continue gestation. Whether this constituted a historic change in our conception of death remains a matter of debate. For some, the acceptance of the new definition by some countries is evidence that death has become less a sharp boundary of the end of life than an ill-defined nether region presided over by those who control machines according to their own purposes (such as maintaining organs slated for eventual transplantation). In an alternative perspective, the change in the legal definition of death signaled no new understanding of what death is, but was rather a stratagem to ensure that those who removed vital organs for transplantation (with the permission of the patient or next-of-kin) would not be held legally responsible for the patient's death (Wikler 1993).

The most radical reconception of human death would be its abolition; indeed, the hope for immortality is both eternal and doomed. The closest approximation that might be achieved would be an open-ended lifespan. Though the percentage of the "oldest old" (age 85-plus) in the wealthiest countries has been increasing rapidly, hardly any human beings live past age 110. Scientific opinion is divided over whether there is an immutable upper limit, although funding for research seeking a route to indefinite life extension has been abundant, in part from donations by aging billionaires.

18.7.5 Conclusions

As with many of the "contours of human life" examined in this chapter, death and dying constitute an intimate and complex admixture of biomedical, social, cultural, and personal elements that are in a dynamic process of change and transformation. As in other domains, wealth and poverty – at personal, social, and national levels – are factors determining not only when and from what cause death will occur but also the experience of dying. For the under-resourced there is a notable deficit in palliation. Abundance of resources, however, also has its drawbacks, in the form of overreliance on institutional care and life-extending efforts that go past the point of diminishing returns. The advent of technologies that sustain life processes after permanent loss of consciousness, and are used to facilitate successful organ transplantation, creates new existential categories whose contours remain contested across cultural contexts.

18.8 Chapter Conclusion

The "contours of human life" include childhood and adolescence, reproduction, the experience of disability and chronic conditions, and death. These stages and aspects of life are universal. They will remain so, but scientific, social, and environmental changes are transforming their timing, texture, and patterns.

There is much to celebrate in the trends we have examined. Most populations are living longer. Child mortality has decreased enormously in recent decades, even in many of the poorest countries. Where overpopulation was only recently among humankind's greatest concerns, birth rates have fallen. Science offers the prospect of welcome enhancements in coming decades. For many, more extensive use of palliation has eased the agony of dying.

These advances, however, are not universally shared. Serious inequalities persist in longevity, morbidity, and disability; control over reproduction and sexuality; and in care at the end of life. Some of these disparities are widening, and the availability of enhancements could exacerbate these injustices. Vigilant monitoring of these inequalities, combined with forceful engagement with their economic and social determinants, are needed to ensure that the favorable trends in the contours of human life become each person's birthright.

References

Adams, V., and S.L. Pigg. 2005. *Sex in Development: Science, Sexuality, and Morality in Global Perspective*. Durham, NC: Duke University Press.

Agay, N., E. Yechiam, Z. Carmel, and Y. Levkovitz. 2014. "Methylphenidate Enhances Cognitive Performance in Adults with Poor Baseline Capacities Regardless of Attention-Deficit/Hyperactivity Disorder Diagnosis." *Journal of Clinical Psychopharmacology* 34/2: 261–265.

Akyeampong, E., A. Hill, and A. Kleinman. (eds.) 2015. *Culture, Mental Illness and Psychiatric Practice in Africa*. Bloomington: Indiana University Press.

Allotey, P., and M. Gyapong. 2005. *The Gender Agenda in the Control of Tropical Diseases: A Review of Current Evidence*. Geneva: WHO/TDR.

Allotey, P., and D.D. Reidpath. 2015. "Sexual and Reproductive Health and Rights Post 2015–Challenges and Opportunities." *BJOG: An International Journal of Obstetrics and Gynaecology* 122/2: 152–155.

Allotey, P., S. Diniz, J. DeJong, T. Delvaux, S. Gruskin, and S. Fonn. 2011. "Sexual and Reproductive Health and Rights in Public Health Education." *Reproductive Health Matters* 19/38: 56–68.

Allotey, P., D. Reidpath, A. Kouamé, and R. Cummins. 2003. "The DALY, Context and the Determinants of the Severity of Disease: An Exploratory Comparison of Paraplegia in Australia and Cameroon." *Social Science and Medicine* 57/5: 949–958.

Arria, A.M., K.M. Caldeira K.E. O'Grady, et al. 2008. "Nonmedical Use of Prescription Stimulants among College Students: Associations with Attention-Deficit-Hyperactivity Disorder and Polydrug Use." *Pharmacotherapy* 28: 156–169.

Aryeetey, E., and R. Kanbur. 2017. *The Economy of Ghana: Sixty Years after Independence*. Oxford: Oxford University Press.

Asad, T., 2007. *On Suicide Bombing*. New York: Columbia University Press.

Asada, Y. 2007. *Health Inequality: Morality and Measurement*. Toronto: University of Toronto Press.

Asiaweek. 1993. "Malaysia: Where Big Is Still Better. For Malays, Large Families Are Part of the Plan." November 3: 30.

Barnett, K., S.W. Mercer, M. Norbury, et al. (2012). "Epidemiology of Multimorbidity and Implications for Health Care, Research, and Medical Education: A Cross-sectional Study." *The Lancet*, 380/9836 : 37–43.

Barker, D. 1990. "The Fetal and Infant Origins of Adult Disease: The Womb May Be More Important Than the Home." *BMJ* 301/6761: 1111.

---

[15] This is not the case, however, in Northern Thailand, where relatives keep their dying relatives hooked up to machines to pay off their "debt of life," and at the last possible second bring them home, where they can die surrounded by loved ones and their possessions. In these cases, machines like mechanical ventilators are not experienced as new problematic impositions but as a means to expend resources to pay off family debts (Stonington 2013).

Barker, D. 1991. "The Foetal and Infant Origins of Inequalities in Health in Britain." *Journal of Public Health Medicine* 13: 64–68.

Barker, D. 2013. "The Developmental Origins of Adult Disease." *Journal of the American College of Nutrition* 23/sup. 6: 588S–595S.

Basten, S., T. Sobotka, and K. Zeman. 2014. "Future Fertility in Low Fertility Countries," in W. Lutz, W. Butz, and K.C. Samir (eds.), *World Population and Human Capital in the 21st Century*. Oxford: Oxford University Press.

Bedford, K. 2009. *Developing Partnerships: Gender, Sexuality and the Reformed World Bank*. Minneapolis: University of Minnesota Press.

Ben-Shlomo, Y., and G. Davey Smith. 1991. "Deprivation in Infancy or in Adult Life: Which is More Important for Mortality Risk?" *The Lancet* 337: 530–534.

Berer, M. 2011. "Repoliticising Sexual and Reproductive Health and Rights." *Reproductive Health Matters* 19/38: 4–10.

Berwald, S., M. Roche S. Adelman N. Mukadam, and G. Livingston 2016. "Black African and Caribbean British Communities' Perceptions of Memory Problems: 'We Don't Do Dementia.'" *PLoS ONE* 11/4: e0151878.

Bostrom, N., and R. Roache. 2008. "Human Enhancement: Ethical Issues in Human Enhancement," in J. Rydberg, T.S. Petersen, and C. Wolf (eds.), *New Waves in Applied Ethics*. Houndmills, Hampshire: Palgrave Macmillan.

Bostrom, N., and C. Shulman. 2014. "Embryo Selection for Cognitive Enhancement: Curiosity or Game-changer?" *Global Policy* 5/1: 85–92.

Braveman, P.A., C. Cubbin, S. Egerter, D.R. Williams, and E. Pamuk. 2010. "Socioeconomic Disparities in Health in the United States: What the Patterns Tell Us." *American Journal of Public Health* 100/S1: S186–S196.

Bukhman, G., A.O. Mocumbi, and R. Horton. 2015. "Reframing NCDs and Injuries for the Poorest Billion: A Lancet Commission." *The Lancet* 386: 1221–1222.

Bury, M. 1982. "Chronic Illness as Biographical Disruption." *Sociology of Health and Illness* 4:167–182.

Capewell S., and H. Graham. 2010. "Will Cardiovascular Disease Prevention Widen Health Inequalities?" *PLoS Medicine* 7/8: e1000320.

Carey, N. 2011. *The Epigenetics Revolution: How Modern Biology Is Rewriting Our Understanding of Genetics, Disease and Inheritance*. London: Icon.

Case, A., and A. Deaton. 2015. "Rising Morbidity and Mortality in Midlife among White Non-Hispanic Americans in the 21st Century." *PNAS* 112: 15078–15083.

Chi, B.H., J.S.S. Stringer, and D. Moodley. 2013. "Antiretroviral Drug Regimens to Prevent Mother-to-Child Transmission of HIV: A Review of Scientific, Program, and Policy Advances for Sub-Saharan Africa." *Current HIV/AIDS Reports* 10/2: 124–133.

Clark, J. 2014. "Medicalization of Global Health 3: The Medicalization of the Non-Communicable Diseases Agenda." *Global Health Action* 7: online. http://dx.doi.org/10.3402/gha.v7.24002.

Coale, A.J. 1973. "The Demographic Transition," in *International Union for the Scientific Study of Population: International Population Conference*, vol. 1. Liege: IUSSP.

Cohen, G.A. 1989. "On the Currency of Egalitarian Justice." *Ethics* 99/4: 906–944.

Cohen, A., S. Raja, C. Underhill, et al. 2012. "Sitting with Others: Mental Health Self-Help Groups in Northern Ghana." *International Journal of Mental Health Systems* 6/1.

Cohen Kadosh, R., N. Levy, J. O'Shea, N. O'Shea, and J. Savalescu. 2012. "The neuroethics of non-invasive brain stimulation." *Current Biology* 22/4: R108–R111.

Conklin, B.A., and L.M. Morgan. 1996. "Babies, Bodies, and the Production of Personhood in North America and a Native Amazonian Society." *Ethos* 24/4: 657–694.

Cooper, M. 2013. "Double Exposure: Sex Workers, Biomedical Prevention Trials, and the Dual Logic of Global Public Health." *S & F Online* 11/3: 1–11.

CRED (Centre for Research on the Epidemiology of Disasters). 2015. *The Human Cost of Natural Disasters. A Global Perspective*. Brussels: CRED.

Crenshaw, K. 1993. "Mapping the Margins: Intersectionality, Identity Politics and Violence against Women of Color." *Stanford Law Review* 43: 1241–1299.

CSDH (Commission on the Social Determinants of Health. 2008. *Closing the Gap in a Generation. Health Equity through Action on the Social Determinants of Health*. Geneva: WHO.

Daniels, N. 2000. "Normal Functioning and the Treatment-Enhancement Distinction." *Cambridge Quarterly of Healthcare Ethics* 9/3: 309–322.

Davey Smith, G. 2012. "Epigenetics for Epidemiologists: Does Evo-Devo Have Implications for Population Health Research and Practice?" *International Journal of Epidemiology* 41: 236–247.

Deaton, A. 2013. *The Great Escape: Health, Wealth, and the Origins of Inequality*. Princeton, NJ: Princeton University Press.

de-Graft Aikins, A. 2006. "Reframing Applied Disease Stigma research: A Multilevel Analysis of Diabetes Stigma in Ghana." *Journal of Community and Applied Social Psychology* 16/6: 426–441.

de-Graft Aikins, A., and K. Koram. 2017. "Health and Healthcare in Ghana, 1957–2017," in E. Aryeetey and R. Kanbur (eds), *The Economy of Ghana: Sixty Years after Independence*. Oxford: Oxford University Press.

de-Graft Aikins, A. and C. Agyemang. (eds.) 2016. *Chronic Non-communicable Diseases in Low and Middle-Income Countries*. Wallingford, Oxfordshire: CABI Publishing.

de-Graft Aikins, A., N. Unwin, C. Agyemang, et al. 2010. "Tackling Africa's Chronic Disease Burden: From the Local to the Global." *Globalization and Health* 6:5.

EIU (The Economist Intelligence Unit). 2010. *The Quality of Death. Ranking End-of-Life Care Across the World. A report by The Economist Intelligence Unit commissioned by the Lien Foundation*. London: Economist Intelligence Unit.

European Union. 2013. *Health Inequalities in the EU*. Final report of a consortium. Consortium lead: Sir Michael Marmot. European Commission Directorate-General for Health and Consumers.

Farmer, P. 2001. *Infections and Inequalities: The Modern Plague*. Berkeley: University of California Press.

Faydi, E., M. Funk, S. Kleintjes, et al. 2011. "An Assessment of Mental Health Policy in Ghana, South Africa, Uganda and Zambia." *Health Research Policy and Systems* 9/17: 2–11.

Fowler, K.A., L.L. Dahlberg, T. Haileyesus, C. Gutierrez, and S. Bacon. 2017. "Childhood Firearms Injuries in the US." *Pediatrics* 140/1: 1–11.

Fuchs, R., and A. Goujon. 2014. *Future Fertility in High Fertility Countries*. Oxford: Oxford University Press.

Fukuyama, F. 2002. *Our Posthuman Future: Consequences of the Biotechnological Revolution*. New York: Picador.

Gagne, D. 2017. "InSight Crime's 2016 Homicide Round-up." www.insightcrime.org/news-analysis/insight-crime-2016-homicide-round-up.

Gammeltoft, T.M., and A. Wahlberg. 2014. "Selective Reproductive Technologies." *Annual Review of Anthropology* 43: 201–216.

GBD 2015 Disease and Injury Incidence and Prevalence Collaborators. 2016. "Global, Regional, and National Incidence, Prevalence, and Years Lived with Disability for 310 Diseases and Injuries, 1990–2015: A Systematic Analysis for the Global Burden of Disease Study 2015." *Lancet* 388/10053: 1545–1602.

Geissler, P.W. 2013. "The Archipelago of Public Health. Comments on the Landscape of Medical Research in 21st Century Africa," in R.J. Prince and R. Marsland (eds.), *Making and Unmaking Public Health in Africa: Ethnographic and Historical Perspectives*. Athens: Ohio University Press.

Geyer, S., O. Hemström, R. Peter, and D. Vågerö. 2006. "Education, Income, and Occupational Class Cannot Be Used Interchangeably in Social Epidemiology. Empirical Evidence against a Common Practice." *Journal of Epidemiology and Community Health* 60: 804–810.

Gilens, M. 2014. *Affluence and Influence: Economic Inequality and Political Power in America*. Princeton, NJ: Princeton University Press.

Ginsburg, F.D., and R. Rapp. 1995. *Conceiving the New World Order: The Global Politics of Reproduction*. Berkeley: University of California Press.

Goesling, B., and G. Firebaugh. 2004. "The Trends in Inequality in Health." *Population and Development Review* 30: 131–146.

Gonzàlez Block, M.A., A.B. Akosa, M. Chowdhury, and A. de-Graft Aikins. 2012. "Health Systems Research and Infectious Diseases of Poverty: From the Margins to the Mainstream," in WHO/TDR, *Global Report for Research on Infectious Diseases of Poverty*. Geneva: WHO/WHO TDR.

Gordon, D.R., and E. Paci. 1997. "Disclosure Practices and Cultural Narratives: Understanding Concealment and Silence around Cancer in Tuscany, Italy." *Social Science and Medicine* 44/10: 1443–1452.

Greenberg, G. 2010. *Manufacturing Depression: The Secret History of an American Disease*. New York: Simon & Schuster.

Greenhalgh, S. 2008. *Just One Child: Science and Policy in Deng's China*. Berkeley: University of California Press.

Grundy, T. 2014. "Kissing Corpses is Helping Spread Ebola, Expert Says." *Washington Post*, September 26. www.washingtonpost.com/national/religion/kissing-corpses-is-helping-spread-ebola-expert-says/2014/09/26/bdb3fe5e-4597-11e4-8042-aaff1640082e_story.html?utm_term=.86bfa561de2e.

Habermas, J. 2003. *The Future of Human Nature*. Cambridge: Polity Press.

Hajnal, J. 1965. "European Marriage Patterns in Perspective," in D.V. Glass and D.E. Eversley (eds.), *Population in History: Essays in Historical Demography*. Chicago: Aldine Publishing Company.

Hamdy, S. 2016. "All Eyes on Egypt: Islam and the Medical Use of Dead Bodies Amidst Cairo's Political Unrest." *Medical Anthropology* 35/3: 220–235.

Hausman, D. 2015. *Valuing Health: Well-Being, Freedom, and Suffering*. New York: Oxford University Press.

Heckman, J., J. Stixrud, and S. Urzua. 2006. "The Effects of Cognitive and Noncognitive Abilities on Labor Market Outcomes and Social Behavior." *Journal of Labor Economics* 24/3: 411–482.

Heudtlass, P., N. Speybroeck, D. Guha-Sapir. 2016. "Excess Mortality in Refugees, Internally Displaced Persons and Resident Populations in Complex Humanitarian Emergencies (1998–2012): Insights from Operational Data." *Conflict and Health* 10/1: 15.

Hoile, O.V., G. Green, S. Jathanna, and T. Stewart. 2002. "Violence against Women." *The Lancet* 360/9329: 343.

Hosseinpoor, A.R., K. Mohammad, R. Majdzadeh, et al. 2005. "Socioeconomic Inequality in Infant Mortality in Iran and across Its Provinces." *Bulletin of the World Health Organization* 83: 837–844.

Houweling, T.A.J. 2007. "Socio-economic Inequalities in Childhood Mortality in Low and Middle-Income Countries." Doctoral thesis, Erasmus University Medical Center, Rotterdam, the Netherlands.

Houweling, T.A.J., A.E. Kunst, and J.P. Mackenbach. 2003. "Measuring Health Inequality among Children in Developing Countries: Does the Choice of the Indicator of Economic Status Matter?" *International Journal for Equity in Health* 2/1: 8.

Howell, N. 1979. *Demography of the Dobe !Kung*. New York: Academic Press.

Htun, M. 2003. *Sex and the State: Abortion, Divorce, and the Family under Latin American Dictatorships and Democracies*. Cambridge, UK, and New York: Cambridge University Press.

Hunter, M. 2007. "The Persistent Problem of Colorism: Skin Tone, Status, and Inequality." *Sociology Compass* 1/1: 237–254.

Idele, P., A. Gillespie, T. Porth, et al. 2014. "Epidemiology of HIV and AIDS among Adolescents: Current Status, Inequities, and Data Gaps." *Journal of Acquired Immune Deficiency Syndromes* 1: S144–53.

Ilieva, I.P., C.J. Hook, and M.J. Farah. 2015. "Prescription Stimulants' Effects on Healthy Inhibitory Control, Working Memory, and Episodic Memory: A Meta-analysis." *Journal of Cognitive Neuroscience* 27/6: 1069–1089.

Inhorn, M.C., and F. van Balen. 2002. *Infertility around the Globe: New Thinking on Childlessness, Gender, and Reproductive Technologies*. Berkeley: University of California Press.

Jacob, A., and A. Mathew. 2017. "End-of-Life Care and Opioid Use in India: Challenges and Opportunities." *Journal of Global Oncology* 3/6: 683–686.

Jones, D.S., S.H. Podolsky, and J.A. Greene. 2012. "The Burden of Disease and the Changing Task of Medicine." *New England Journal of Medicine* 366/25: 2333–2338.

Juengst, E., and D. Moseley. 2015. "Human Enhancement." *The Stanford Encyclopedia of Philosophy*.

Kabeer, N. 2010. *Can the MDGs Provide a Pathway to Social Justice? The Challenge of Intersecting Inequalities*. New York: United Nation Development Program.

Kansai, S., S. Singh, and A. Kumar. 2016. "Menstrual Hygiene Practices in Context of Schooling: A Community Study among Rural Adolescent Girls in Varanasi." *Indian Journal of Community Medicine* 41:39–44.

Kaufman, S., 2005. *And a Time to Die: How American Hospitals Shape the End of Life*. New York: Scribner.

Kaufman, S., and L. Morgan. 2005. "The Anthropology of the Beginnings and Ends of Life." *Annual Review of Anthropology* 34: 317–341.

Kermack, W.O., A.G. McKendrick, and P.L. McKinlay. 1934." Death-Rates in Great Britain and Sweden. Some General Regularities and Their Significance." *The Lancet* 31: 698–703; reprinted in *International Journal of Epidemiology* (2001) 30: 678–683.

Kim, J.-Y., J.V. Millen, A. Irwen, and J. Gershman. 2002. *Dying for Growth: Global Inequality and the Health of the Poor*. Monroe, ME: Common Courage Press.

Klinenberg, E. 2002. *Heat Wave: A Social Autopsy of Disaster in Chicago*. Chicago: University of Chicago Press.

Krause, M. 2014. *The Good Project. Humanitarian NGOs and the Fragmentation of Reason*. Chicago: Chicago University Press.

Kuh, D., and Y. Ben-Shlomo. 2004. *A Life Course Approach to Chronic Disease Epidemiology*, second edition. Oxford: Oxford University Press.

Kyu, H.H., C. Pinho, J.A. Wagner, et al. 2016. "Global and National Burden of Diseases and Injuries among Children and Adolescents between 1990 and 2013: Findings from the Global Burden of Disease 2013 Study." *JAMA Pediatrics* 170: 267–287.

The Lancet. 2016. "Hearing Loss: An Important Global Health Concern." *The Lancet* 387/10036: 2351.

Landecker, H., and Aaron Panofsky, A. 2013. "From Social Structure to Gene Regulation, and Back: A Critical Introduction to Environmental Epigenetics for Sociology." *Annual Review of Sociology* 39: 333–57.

Laplante D., R.G. Barr, A. Brunet, et al. 2004. "Stress During Pregnancy Affects General Intellectual and Language Functioning in Human Toddlers." *Pediatric Research* 56: 400–410.

Larsson, J. 2007. *Prioriteringar i hälso- och sjukvården. Socialstyrelsen analys och slutsatser utifrån rapporten "Vårdens alltför svåra val?"* Copenhagen: Socialstyrelsen (2017, 103–104).

Lawrence, V., K. Samsi, S. Banerjee, C. Morgan, and J. Price. 2011. "Threat to Valued Elements of Life: The Experience of Dementia across Three Ethnic Groups." *Gerontologist* 51/1: 39–50.

Layne, L.L. 2003. *Motherhood Lost: A Feminist Account of Pregnancy Loss in America*. New York: Routledge.

Le Clair, J., 2012. "Introducing Global Organizational Change in Sport and the Shifting Meaning of Disability," in J. Le Clair (ed.), *Disability in the Global Sport Arena. A Sporting Chance*. Oxford: Routledge.

Le Grand, J. 1987. "Inequalities in Health." *European Economic Review* 31: 182–191.

Leinsalu, M., I. Stirbu, D. Vågerö et al. 2009. "Educational Inequalities in Mortality in Four Eastern European Countries: Divergence in Trends during the Post-Communist Transition from 1990 to 2000." *International Journal of Epidemiology* 38: 512–525.

Leinsalu, M., D. Vågerö, and A. Kunst. 2003. "Estonia 1989–2000: Enormous Increase in Mortality Differences by Education." *International Journal of Epidemiology* 32: 1081–1087.

Leinsalu, M., D. Vågerö, and A. Kunst 2004. "Increasing Ethnic Differences in Mortality in Estonia after the Collapse of the Soviet Union." *Journal of Epidemiology and Community Health* 58: 583–589.

Leone, T., E. Coast, S. Narayanan, and A. de-Graft Aikins. 2012. "Diabetes and Depression Comorbidity within Poor Settings in Low and Middle Income Countries (LMICs): A Mapping of the Evidence." *Globalization and Health* 8: 39.

Lichtenstein, P., L. Halldner, J. Zetterqvist, et al. 2012. "Medication for Attention Deficit–Hyperactivity Disorder and Criminality." *New England Journal of Medicine* 367/21: 2006–2014.

Lippert-Rasmussen, K., and N. Eyal. 2012. "Equality and Egalitarianism," in R. Chadwick (ed.), *Encyclopedia of Applied Ethics*, second edition. San Diego: Elsevier Academic Press.

Livingston, J. 2012. *Improvising Medicine: An African Oncology Ward in an Emerging Cancer Epidemic*. Durham, NC: Duke University Press.

Lock, M.M., and D. Gordon. 1988. *Biomedicine Examined*. Dordrecht and Boston: Kluwer Academic Publishers.

Lumey L.H., M. Khalangot, and A. Vaiserman. 2015. "Association between Type 2 Diabetes and Prenatal Exposure to the Ukraine Famine of 1932–33: A Retrospective Cohort Study." *The Lancet Diabetes and Endocrinology* 3/10: 787–794.

Lutz, W. 2013. "Demographic Metabolism: A Predictive Theory of Socioeconomic Change." *Population and Development Review* 38/s1: 283–301.

Lutz, W., and V. Skirbekk. 2014. "How Education Drives Demography and Knowledge Informs Projections," in W. Lutz, W.P. Butz, and Samir KC (eds.), *World Population and Human Capital in the 21st Century*. Oxford: Oxford University Press.

Mackenbach, J.P., V. Bos, O. Andersen, et al. 2003. "Widening Socioeconomic Inequalities in Mortality in Six Western European Countries." *International Journal of Epidemiology* 32/5: 830–837.

Mackenbach, J., I. Stirbu, A.R. Roskam, et al. 2008. "Socioeconomic Inequalities in Health in 22 European Countries." *New England Journal of Medicine* 358: 2468–2481.

Marmot, M. 2015. *The Health Gap*. London: Bloomsbury.

McGoey, L., J. Reiss, and A. Wahlberg. 2011. "The Global Health Complex." *BioSocieties* 6/1: 1–9.

Menary, R. 2010. *The Extended Mind*. Cambridge, MA: MIT Press.

Mofenson, L.M., and M.F. Cotton. 2013. "The Challenges of Success: Adolescents with Perinatal HIV Infection." *Journal of the International AIDS Society* 16: 1–3.

Mokdad, A.H., M.H. Forouzanfar, F. Daoud, et al. 2016. "Global Burden of Diseases, Injuries, and Risk Factors for Young People's Health during 1990–2013: A Systematic Analysis for the Global Burden of Disease Study 2013." *The Lancet* 387/10036: 2383–2401.

Mooney, J.E.P. 2009. *The Politics of Motherhood: Maternity and Women's Rights in Twentieth-Century Chile*. Pittsburgh: University of Pittsburgh Press.

Morgan, L., and E.F.S. Roberts. 2009. "Rights and Reproduction in Latin America." *Anthropology News* 50/3: 12–16.

Morgan, L., and E.F.S. Roberts. 2012. "Reproductive Governance in Latin America." *Anthropology and Medicine* 19/2: 241–254.

Moser, K., V. Shkolnikov, and D. Leon. 2005. "World Mortality 1950–2000: Divergence Replaces Convergence from the Late 1980s." *Bulletin of the World Health Organization* 83/3: 202–209.

Murphy, M. 2011. "Distributed Reproduction," in M.J. Casper and P. Currah (eds.), *Corpus: An Interdisciplinary Reader on Bodies and Knowledge*. New York: Palgrave Macmillan.

Murphy, M. 2013. "Distributed Reproduction, Chemical Violence, and Latency." *The Scholar and Feminist* 11.3/1: online.

Murphy, M., M. Bobak, A. Nicholson, R. Rose, and M. Marmot. 2006. "The Widening Gap in Mortality by Educational Level in the Russian Federation, 1980–2001." *American Journal of Public Health* 96: 1293–1299.

Murtin, F., J.P. Mackenbach, D. Jasilionis, and M.M. d'Ercole. 2017. *Inequalities in Longevity by Education in OECD Countries: Insights from New OECD Estimates*. OECD Statistics Working Papers 2017/2. Paris: OECD.

Muthumbi, J., J. Svanemyr, E. Scolaro, M. Temmerman, and L. Say. 2015. "Female Genital Mutilation: A Literature Review of the Current Status of Legislation and Policies in 27 African Countries and Yemen." *African Journal of Reproductive Health* 19/3: 32–40.

NCHS (National Center for Health Statistics) US. 2016. *Health, United States, 2015. With Special Feature on Racial and Ethnic Health Disparities*. Report 2016–1232. Hyattsville, MD: National Center for Health Statistics (US).

Noonan, J.T. 1986. *Contraception: A History of Its Treatment by the Catholic Theologians and Canonists*. Cambridge, MA: Belknap Press of Harvard University Press.

Norheim, O.F., 2010. "Gini Impact Analysis: Measuring Pure Health Inequity before and after Interventions." *Public Health Ethics* 3/3: 282–292.

Norheim, O.F., P. Jha, K. Admasu, et al. 2015. "Avoiding 40% of the Premature Deaths in Each Country, 2010–30: Review of National Mortality Trends to Help Quantify the UN Sustainable Development Goal for Health." *The Lancet* 385: 239–252.

Nyarko, Y., L. Goldfrank, G. Ogedegbe, S. Soghoian, A. de-Graft Aikins, and NYU-UG-KBTH Ghana Ebola Working Group. 2015. "Preparing for Ebola Virus Disease in West African Countries Not Yet Affected: Perspectives from Ghanaian Health Professionals." *Globalization and Health* 11: 7.

Olshansky S.J., T. Antonucci L. Berkman, et al. 2012. "Differences in Life Expectancy due to Race and Education Are Widening, and Many May Not Catch Up." *Health Affairs* 31/8: 1803–1813.

Olumide, Y.M., A.O. Akinkugbe, D. Altraide, et al. 2008. "Complications of Chronic Use of Skin Lightening Cosmetics." *International Journal of Dermatology* 47/4: 344–353.

OPCS (Office of Population Censuses and Surveys). 1995. *Occupational Health. The Registrar General's Decennial Supplement for England and Wales*. Edited by Frances Drever. London: HMSO.

Pamuk, E.R., R. Fuchs, and W. Lutz. 2011. "Comparing Relative Effects of Education and Economic Resources on Infant Mortality in Developing Countries." *Population and Development Review* 37: 637–664.

Patton, G.C., S.M. Sawyer, J.S. Santelli, et al. 2016. "Our Future: A Lancet Commission on Adolescent Health and Wellbeing." *The Lancet* 387/10036: 2423–2478.

Pembrey, M., R. Saffery, and L.O. Bygren. 2014. "Network in Epigenetic Epidemiology. Human Transgenerational Response to Early-Life Experience: Potential Impact on Development, Health and Biomedical Research." *Journal of Medical Genetics* 51: 563–572.

Peto, R., A.D. Lopes, and O.F. Norheim. 2014. "Halving Premature Death." *Science* 345/6202: 1272.

Pfeiffer, J., and R. Chapmann. 2010. "Anthropological Perspectives on Structural Adjustment and Public Health." *Annual Review of Anthropology* 39: 149–165.

Phillips-Howard, P., B. Caruso, B. Torondel, et al. 2016."Menstrual Hygiene Management among Adolescent Schoolgirls in Low- and Middle-Income Countries: Research Priorities." *Global Health Action* 9/1: online.

Pinker, S. 2012. *The Better Angels of Our Nature: Why Violence Has Declined*. London: Penguin.

Poku, N. 2006. *AIDS in Africa: How the Poor Are Dying*. Cambridge: Polity Press.

Powell, R.A., F.N. Mwangi-Powell, L. Radbruch, et al. 2015. "Putting Palliative Care on the Global Health Agenda." *Lancet Oncology* 16/2: 131–133.

Preston, S., P. Heuveline, and M. Guillot. 2001. *Demography: Measuring and Modeling Population Processes*. Oxford: Blackwell Publishers.

Prince, M., V. Patel, S. Saxena, et al. 2007. "No Health without Mental Health." *The Lancet* 370: 859–877.

Read, U.M., E. Adiibokah, and S. Nyame. 2009. "Local Suffering and the Global Discourse of Mental Health and Human Rights: An Ethnographic Study of Responses to Mental Illness in Rural Ghana." *Globalization and Health* 5: 13.

Rees, T. 2014. "Humanity/Plan; or, On the 'Stateless' Today (Also Being an Anthropology of Global Health)." *Cultural Anthropology* 29/3: 457–478.

Reeve, J., M. Lloyd-Williams, S. Payne, and C. Dowrick. 2010. "Revisiting Biographical Disruption: Exploring Individual Embodied Illness Experience in People with Terminal Cancer." *Health* 14/2: 178–195.

Reidpath, D.D., S. Gruskin, P. Allotey. 2015. "Is the Right to Health Compatible with Sustainability?" *Journal of Global Health* 5/1: 010301.

Roberts, F.S.E. 2009. "American Death." *Focal – European Journal of Anthropology* 54:114–119.

Robinson, J., and J. Pfeiffer. 2015. "The IMF's Role in the Ebola Outbreak: The Long-Term Consequences of Structural Adjustment." *Global Research*, February 7. www.globalresearch.ca/the-imfs-role-in-the-ebola-outbreak-the-long-term-consequences-of-structural-adjustment/5429970.

Roisman, G.I., and R.C. Fraley. 2012. "The Legacy of Early Interpersonal Experience." *Advances in Child Development and Behaviour* 42: 79–112.

Rosenbloom, A.L. 2009. "Idiopathic Short Stature: Conundrums of Definition and Treatment." *International Journal of Pediatric Endocrinology* 1: 47038.

Ross, R. 2016. "BBC's 'Panorama: Living with Dementia' Captures the Reality of Life after Diagnosis." The Huffington Post, June 2. www.huffingtonpost.co.uk/entry/bbc-panorama-dementia-chris-story_uk_575051f8e4b04a0827f146e3.

Salomon, J., T. Vos, D.R. Hogan, et al. 2012. "Common Values in Assessing Health Outcomes from Disease and Injury: Disability Weights Measurement Study for the Global Burden of Disease Study 2010." *The Lancet* 380: 2129–2143.

Sandel, M. 2004. "The Case Against Perfection." *The Atlantic*, April.

Saxena, S., A. Lora, J. Morris, et al. 2011. "Mental Health Services in 42 Low- and Middle-Income Countries: A WHO-AIMS Cross-national Analysis." *Psychiatric Services* 62/2: 123–125.

Scheffler, R.M., T.B. Timothy, B.D. Fulton, et al. 2009. "Positive Association between Attention-Deficit/ Hyperactivity Disorder Medication Use and Academic Achievement during Elementary School." *Pediatrics* 123/5: 1273–1279.

Scheper-Hughes, N. 1993. *Death without Weeping: The Violence of Everyday Life in Brazil*. Berkeley: University of California Press.

Schulz, R., and P.R. Sherwood. 2008. "Physical and Mental Health Effects of Family Caregiving." *American Journal of Nursing* 108/9 (Suppl): 23–27.

Scully, J.L. 2004. "What Is a Disease?" *EMBO Reports* 5/7: 650–653.

Seale, C. and S. van der Geest. 2004. "Good and Bad Death: Introduction." *Social Science & Medicine* 58/5: 883–885.

Sedgh, G., J. Bearak, S. Singh, et al. 2016. "Abortion Incidence between 1990 and 2014: Global, Regional, and Subregional Levels and Trends." *The Lancet* 388/10041: 258–267.

Shkolnikov, V., E.T. Andreev, D. Jdanov, et al. 2012. "Increasing Absolute Mortality Disparities by Education in Finland, Norway and Sweden, 1971–2000." *Journal of Epidemiology and Community Health* 66/4: 372–378.

Singer, M., and H. Baer. 1995. *Critical Medical Anthropology*. Amityville, NY: Baywood Pub. Co.

Smits, J. and C. Monden. 2009. "Length of Life Inequality around the Globe." *Social Science & Medicine* 68: 1114–1123.

Staples, J., and T. Widger. 2012. "Situating Suicide as an Anthropological Problem: Ethnographic Approaches to Understanding Self-Harm and Self-Inflicted Death." *Culture Medicine and Psychiatry* 36/2: 183–203.

Steingraber, S. 2007. *The Falling Age of Puberty in US Girls: What We Know, What We Need to Know*. San Francisco: Breast Cancer Fund.

Steingrímsdóttir, Ó.A., Ø. Næss, J.O. Moe, et al. 2012. "Trends in Life Expectancy by Education in Norway 1961–2009." *European Journal of Epidemiology* 27/3: 163–171.

Stevenson, L., 2014. *Life beside Itself: Imagining Care in the Canadian Arctic*. Oakland: University of California Press.

Stonington, S., 2013. "The Debt of Life: Thai Lessons on a Process-Oriented Ethical Logic." *New England Journal of Medicine* 369/17: 1583–1585.

Susser, M., and B. Levin. 1999. "Ordeals for the Fetal Programming Hypothesis: The Hypothesis Largely Survives One Ordeal but Not Another. Editorial." *British Medical Journal* 318/7188: 885–886.

Tännsjö, T. 2009. "Medical Enhancement and the Ethos of Elite Sport," in J. Savulescu and N. Bostrom (eds.), *Human Enhancement*. Oxford: Oxford University Press.

Timonin, S., V. Shkolnikov, D. Jasiolinis, et al. 2016. "Disparities in Length of Life across Developed Countries: Measuring and Decomposing Changes Over Time within and between Country Groups." *Population Health Metrics* 14/29: 1–19.

UN. 2015. *Sustainable Development Goals*. https://sustainabledevelopment.un.org/sdgs.

UNICEF. 2013. *Female Genital Mutilation*. New York: UNICEF.

UNICEF. 2014a. *Committing to Child Survival: A Promise Renewed*. New York: UNICEF.

UNICEF. 2014b. "Inequality in Ghana: A Fundamental National Challenge." Briefing Paper, April 2014.

UNICEF. 2015. *Committing to Child Survival: A Promise Renewed. Progress Report 2015*. New York: UNICEF.

UNPD (United Nations Population Division). 2012. *World Population Prospects: The 2012 Revision*. Washington, DC: UN.

UNPD. 2015. *World Population Prospects: The 2015 Revision*. Washington, DC: UN.

Vågerö, D. 2010. "The East West Health Divide in Europe: Growing and Shifting Eastwards." *European Review* 18/1: 23–34.

Vågerö, D., and R. Erikson. 1997. "Socioeconomic Differences in Morbidity and Mortality in Western Europe." *The Lancet* 350/9076: 516.

Vågerö, D., and R. Illsley. 1995. "Explaining Health Inequalities: Beyond Black and Barker." *European Sociological Review* 11: 219–241.

Vågerö, D., I., Koupil, N., Parfenova, and P. Sparén. 2013. "Long-Term Health Consequences Following the Siege of Leningrad," in L. H. Lumey and Alexander Vaiserman (eds,), *Early Life Nutrition and Adult Health and Development: Lessons from Changing Dietary Patterns, Famines and Experimental Studies*. New York, Nova Science Publishers.

van der Geest, S. 2000. "Funerals for the Living: Conversations with Elderly People in Kwahu, Ghana." *African Studies Review* 43/3: 103–129.

Velleman, J.D. 1991. "Well-being and Time." *Pacific Philosophical Quarterly* 72/1: 48–77.

Victora, C.G., A. Wagstaff, J.A. Schellenberg, et al. 2003. "Applying an Equity Lens to Child Health and Mortality: More of the Same Is Not Enough." *The Lancet* 362: 233–241.

Vilarim, M.M., D.M. Rocha Araujo, and A.E. Nardi 2011. "Caffeine Challenge Test and Panic Disorder: A Systematic Literature Review." *Expert Review of Neurotherapeutics* 11/8: 1185–1195.

Wagstaff, A. 2000. "Socio-economic Inequalities in Child Mortality: Comparison across Nine Developing Countries." *Bulletin of the World Health Organization* 78: 19–29.

Wan Ibrahim W.A., I. Zainab, and M. Redzuan. 2012. "Living Arrangement of Older Population in Rural Malaysia." *Advances in Natural and Applied Sciences* 6/3, special issue 2): 383–387.

Wang, H., C.A. Liddell, M.M. Coates, et al. 2016. "Global, Regional, and National Levels of Neonatal, Infant, and Under-5 Mortality during 1990 and 2013: A Systematic Analysis for the Global Burden of Disease Study 2013." *The Lancet* 384: 957–979.

Wasson, K. 2011. "Medical and Genetic Enhancements: Ethical Issues that Will Not Go Away." *American Journal of Bioethics* 11/1: 21–22.

Weeks, J.R., A.G. Hill, and J. Stoler. (eds.) 2013. *Spatial Inequalities: Health, Poverty, and Place in Accra, Ghana*. Dordrecht: Springer.

WHO. 2002a. *Current and Future Long-Term Care Needs: An Analysis Based on the 1990 WHO Study The Global Burden of Diseases*. Geneva: WHO.

WHO. 2002b. *Ethical Issues in Long-Term Care: What Does Justice Require?* Geneva: WHO.

WHO. 2011. *World Report on Disability*. Geneva: WHO.

WHO. 2014a. *Health for the World's Adolescents: A Second Chance in the Second Decade (Full Report)*. Geneva: WHO. http://apps.who.int/adolescent/second-decade/

WHO. 2014b. *Injuries and Violence – the Facts*. Geneva: WHO.

WHO. 2017. "WHO Definition of Palliative Care." www.who.int/cancer/palliative/definition/en/.

Whyte, S.R., M.A. Whyte, L. Meinert, and J. Twebaze. 2013. "Therapeutic Clientship: Belonging in Uganda's Mosaic of AIDS Projects," in J. Biehl and A. Petryna (eds.), *When People Come First: Critical Studies in Global Health*. Princeton, NJ: Princeton University Press.

Wikler, D. 1993. "Brain Death: A Durable Consensus?" *Bioethics* 7: 239–246.

Williams, O.D., and S. Rushton. 2011. "Private Actors in Global Health Governance," in O.D. Williams and S. Rushton (eds.), *Partnerships and Foundations in Global Health Governance*. London: Palgrave.

Winikoff, B., and W. Sheldon. 2012. "Use of Medicines Changing the Face of Abortion." *International Perspectives on Sexual and Reproductive Health* 38/3: 164–166.

Xu, M.Q., W.S. Sun, B.X. Liu et al. 2009. "Prenatal Malnutrition and Adult Schizophrenia: Further Evidence From the 1959–1961 Chinese Famine." *Schizophrenia Bulletin* 35/3: 568–576.

Yasin, S., C.K. Chan, D.D. Reidpath, and P. Allotey. 2012. "Contextualizing Chronicity: A Perspective from Malaysia." *Global Health* 8/1: 4.

Zelizer, V.A.R.. 1985. *Pricing the Priceless Child: The Changing Social Value of Children*. Princeton, NJ: Princeton University Press.

19

The Contribution of Education to Social Progress[*]

Coordinating Lead Authors:[1]
Christiane Spiel, Simon Schwartzman

Lead Authors:[2]
Marius Busemeyer, Nico Cloete, Gili Drori, Lorenz Lassnigg, Barbara Schober, Michele Schweisfurth, Suman Verma

Contributing Authors:[3]
Bilal Bakarat, Peter Maassen, Rob Reich

[*] Acknowledgments: The panel acknowledges the helpful comments and suggestions from Maria Balarin, Emilio Blanco, Ricardo Cantoral, Martin Carnoy, Juan Espínola, Leonardo Garnier, Cornelia Gräsel, Blanca Heredia, V.V. Krishna, Johan Muller, Juan Carlos Navarro, Silvia Ortega, Lila Pinto, Kerstin Schneider, Isabel F. Schwartzman, Ian Whitman.

[1] Affiliations: CS: University of Vienna, Austria; SS: Institute for Studies on Labor and Society, Brazil.

[2] Affiliations: MB: University of Konstanz, Germany; NC: CHET, South Africa; GD: Hebrew University of Jerusalem, Israel; LL: Institute for Advanced Studies, IHS Vienna, Austria; BS: University of Vienna, Austria; MS: University of Glasgow, UK; SV: Panjab University, India.

[3] Affiliations: BB: IIASA, Austria; PM: University of Oslo, Norway; RR: Stanford University, USA.

19

Summary

Education is the process of learning and expanding culture, and, as it contributes to the improvement of the human condition through better knowledge, health, living conditions, social equity, and productivity, is a central tool for social progress. Education is expected to foster social progress through four different but interrelated purposes: humanistic, through the development of individual and collective human virtues to their full extent; civic, by the enhancement of public life and active participation in a democratic society; economic, by providing individuals with intellectual and practical skills that make them productive and enhance their and society's living conditions; and through fostering social equity and justice.

The expansion of formal education, which was part of the emergence of the nation-states and modern economies, is one of the most visible indicators of social progress. In its expansion, education created a complex web of institutions distributed according to different paths along the life course, from early education through the school cycles to the final stages of higher education, continuing with the provision of lifelong education. This web of institutions is subject to breaks and cleavages that reflect their diverse and multiple historical origins and purposes and the asynchronous developments in different regions. From primary schooling, education institutions grew horizontally (by learning fields, subjects, or occupations) and vertically (by levels and credentials). The allocation of children and young people to different tracks and institutions, by a mixture of choice and assignment, is a core process in formal education that often reflects and reproduces pre-existing inequalities.

The chapter presents the main dilemmas and actions needed to allow education to fulfill its promises. Education policies, informed by the knowledge created by social research, should lead to more equity and productivity, while giving more emphasis to its civic and humanistic purposes, with special attention to teacher education. Governance structures should be flexible, participatory, accountable, and aware of their social and cultural context.

The new agenda of *Sustainable Development Goals for 2030* established in 2015 calls for a new cooperative paradigm based on the concept of "full global partnership" and the principle that "no one will be left behind." Sustainable Development Goal 4 for Education aims "to ensure inclusive and quality education for all and promote lifelong learning." This provides a broad framework for education's contribution to social progress. To achieve this, it is necessary: (1) to expand access and improve the quality of early childhood education, as a precondition for lifelong educational success in all its goals; (2) to improve the quality of schools, in aspects such as the learners' direct interactions with their peer groups, educators, and the surroundings; institutional characteristics such as group size, student–teacher ratio, teacher qualifications, and spatial and material conditions; and the provision of a meaningful and relevant curriculum; (3) to enhance the role of educators, considering that teachers are not just carriers of knowledge and information, but role models that have a significant impact on children's dispositions toward learning and life more generally; (4) to make higher and vocational education more inclusive and socially relevant, thereby enhancing the opportunities for students of all sectors of society to further their education in meaningful and practical ways, eliminating social and cultural restrictions to access and reducing the dividing lines between high and low prestige and esteem between institutions and careers. Additionally, appropriate use of the opportunities created by the new digital technologies is recommended. These are not a magic bullet that will replace existing educational institutions and create a new learning world. But they can be powerful instruments to improve the quality and relevance of education and its contribution to social progress.

19.1 Introduction: Education and Social Progress

Culture, classically described as "that complex whole which includes knowledge, belief, art, morals, law, custom and any other capabilities and habits" (Tylor 1870), is the most distinctive feature of human societies. Education is the process of learning and expanding culture, and, as it contributes to the improvement of the human condition through better knowledge, health, living conditions, social equity, and productivity, is a central tool for social progress. Education takes place informally, starting with the interaction of children with their parents and significant others and by learning by doing in life, but becomes to a large extent formal in complex societies, as it is codified (in primers, manuals, catechisms, handbooks) and provided by specialized institutions (religious organizations, schools, universities, professional guilds, academies, apprenticeships) according to different methods (collaboration, demonstration, experimentation, interpretation, lecturing, memorization, practice). This chapter deals with the complex field of formal education, which has always been closely related to the power of political institutions and is shaped and influenced by competing political parties, movements, and processes that try to enact their purposes and programs.

Education is expected to foster social progress through four different but interrelated purposes. Historically, the first is the humanistic goal, the development of individual and collective human virtues to their full extent. Traditionally, the issues related to the humanistic and enlightenment roles of education have been considered in terms of the knowledge and values imbued in the European classical school curricula. More recently, the attention has shifted to the students' school and learning experience, and how these develop capabilities which learners and societies value as intrinsically worthy. In higher education, key issues are the use of science and technology for understanding and the improvement of the human condition, the appreciation of the study of the humanities, emphasis on human responsibility, and, increasingly, the collective responsibility to save the environment and other species against the overuse of planetary resources.

The second contribution of education to social progress is the enhancement of civic life and active participation in a democratic society, not only by teaching the contents of civic education, but also through the practical experience of living and working with others in the school environment and community service. Well-educated persons are expected to be informed, responsible, and engaged citizens, better able to understand and participate in the broad tasks of creating, maintaining, and improving the complex institutions of contemporary societies.

The third contribution is economic productivity. Education should provide individuals with intellectual and practical skills that make them productive and enhance their living conditions; societies with a better-educated citizenry tend to be richer and more productive. The links between education and productivity can be direct, as when students learn the specific skills and competencies for a craft or a profession, or more general, when they acquire the broad humanistic, social, and intellectual competencies required by contemporary work organizations.

The fourth contribution is the furthering of social equity and justice. Education is sought by individuals and their families and supported by governments and social organizations as a mechanism of social mobility and inclusion, expected to break the barriers of social, ethnic, and cultural exclusion and fragmentation; but it may also contribute to reproducing divisions in society and to maintaining inequalities. Furthering social equity requires policies to counter the discriminatory effects of education, including the use of resources to assure universal equitable access to quality education.

The analysis of the contribution of education to social progress is thus both a normative and an empirical endeavor. We need to spell out what education can be expected to provide, how these expectations are met in different contexts and historical times, whether these expectations are still worth pursuing, and what can be done to achieve them, based on empirical evidence. The general assumption of this chapter is that all four purposes are important and interrelated, and that social progress is hindered when any of them is neglected to the benefit of others.

The chapter is structured as follows. Section one provides the broad historical and contemporary context in a global perspective, focusing on the two dominating trends of education expansion and differentiation at all levels. Section two deals with how education policies can contribute to the fulfillment of education's main four purposes. Section three elaborates on the contribution of pedagogy and the curriculum, and section four on governance. The final fifth section presents the main actions needed to allow education to fulfill its promises to promote social progress.

19.1.1 The Context: Expansion and Differentiation

The expansion of formal education, which was part of the emergence of nation-states and modern economies, is one of the most visible indicators of social progress.

The notion that all persons should be able to read the sacred books was part of the Jewish, Protestant, and Muslim traditions, but was never fully practiced and was mostly limited to men (Gawthrop and Strauss 1984; Vincent 2000; Hanna 2007; Botticini and Eckstein 2012). This notion was adapted and spread out by the modern, industrialized Western nation-states, and exported to their colonies and areas of influence. In other cultures, education institutions shaped societal divisions or selected elites, e.g. the Brahman educational monopoly or the Confucian examination system. By the end of the nineteenth century, the United States, Australia, Canada, and New Zealand had already reached universal schooling, followed closely by Northern Europe. In Asia, expansion of primary education started in Japan, followed later by Taiwan, Thailand, Sri Lanka, and the Philippines. In Latin America and Africa, it expanded first in areas with strong European immigration, such as Argentina, Chile, Uruguay, and southern Brazil, as well as in South Africa and Zimbabwe (Benavot and Riddle 1988). Socialist countries have historically put much emphasis on the set-up of mass education, strongly linked to the planned economy, and imbued by their political ideology. In 1950, about 47 percent of children aged 5–14 in the world were enrolled in school. In 2010, 89.1 percent were.

Table 19.1 | Gross enrollment rates in education by region (2014)*

	Preschool	Primary	Secondary	Tertiary
Arab states	27.0	99.8	73.0	28.3
Latin American and the Caribbean	73.0	108.4	94.1	39.0
Africa	23.3	99.6	48.3	13.1
Asia	41.3	106.8	75.5	31.1
Europe	92.4	103.0	109.1	63.6
Oceania	97.7	108.5	101.4	51.9

* Total number of children enrolled, regardless of age, expressed as a percentage of the population in the relevant official age group. Can be more than 100%.

Source: UNESCO Institute of Statistics, http://data_uis_uneseo.org.

Table 19.1 compares contemporary enrollment rates across different global regions.

Secondary education, which used to be mostly a preparatory stage for universities, became part of the regular school system, starting with the "high school movement" in the United States in the early twentieth century, and spreading later to Europe and other countries. Worldwide, the number of secondary school students went from 187 to 545 million between 1970 and 2010, a threefold growth, capturing 63 percent of the relevant age group.

Until the early nineteenth century, advanced learning was limited to a small elite of religious leaders, bureaucrats, and specialists, educated in universities and other prestigious learning centers, usually associated with religious institutions. In the second half of the twentieth century, higher education became a mass phenomenon, reaching 32 million students worldwide in 1970 and 182 million in 2010 (Goldin and Katz 1997; Trow 2000; Schofer and Meyer 2005; Schwartzman, Pinheiro, and Pillay 2015; World Bank 2015).

This extraordinary expansion of formal education – in volume, reach, and scope – resulted from a combination of factors. For the modern nation-states, public education was considered a tool for social cohesion and citizenship, and a means to develop the human resources necessary for running the state and enhancing the economy. Religious organizations and churches continued to participate strongly in education, sometimes in partnership and sometimes in dispute with nation-states. Business sectors also got involved, either creating their own systems of vocational education or participating in the shaping of education policies.

This growth was also a response to expanding aspirations. For a growing number of persons, access to education was perceived as a channel for social mobility. More than a tool for access to public and private jobs, education came to seen as a personal right, expected to pave the way for other forms of participation, including the benefits of individual choice, good employment and income, and social prestige. After World War II, the right to education was enshrined in the Universal Declaration of Human Rights and embodied in the work of international organizations such as UNESCO, that not only spread the gospel of expanding education but also helped countries to organize their school systems. In 1990, the Jomtien World Conference on Education for All set the target to provide free and compulsory primary education for all children in the world, with the financial and technical support of public and private donors. This was expanded with UN Millennium Development Goal 2, which aimed to achieve universal completion of a full cycle of primary education, and in 2015 with the new Sustainable Development Goal 4, which emphasizes the quality and learning dimensions. Beginning in the 1990s, different institutions started to implement worldwide assessments of student achievement in language, mathematics, and science, with the assumption that, beyond local languages and cultural traditions, all persons in the world were supposed to acquire the same set of basic cognitive and non-cognitive competencies required for full citizenship in contemporary societies (Mullis et al. 2003; Spring 2008; Kautz et al. 2014).

In the following, we describe the differentiation of educational paths and institutions in more detail. Higher education and universities are presented in a distinct sub-section as they differ in many directions from other institutions of formal education.

19.1.2 Differentiation: Main Issues and Dilemmas

As education expanded, it created a complex web of institutions distributed according to different paths along the life course, from early education through the school cycles to the final stages of higher education, continuing with the provision of forms of lifelong education. This web of institutions is subject to breaks and cleavages that reflect their diverse and multiple historical origins and purposes and the asynchronous developments in different regions. From primary schooling, education institutions grew horizontally (by learning fields, subjects, or occupations) and vertically (by levels and credentials). The allocation of children and young people to different tracks and institutions, by a mixture of choice and assignment, is a core process in formal education that often reflects and reproduces pre-existing inequalities.

19.1.2.1 Early Education and Care

Early education and care concerns the age span between birth and the beginning of primary education, in which the family is an important agent and has a high degree of responsibility, and the processes of socialization and informal learning are very prominent (Kamerman 2006). Early formal education starts at different points (between ages three and seven), and the participation rates vary widely among regions and countries. Here, formal education often still competes with the informal education processes in families, and with mere caring functions, and the drive for the expansion of early education is strongly related to the expansion of feminine work. There is growing evidence that good-quality earlier education has multiplicative effects for further learning, but young children most in need are often deprived not only of access to early education but also of several necessary background conditions and care, and one issue is how to balance the functions of education and care at the early age (Heckman 2006; Lubotsky and Kaestner 2016).

19.1.2.2 Primary Education

Primary education is the first core part of compulsory education. Progress toward the goal of reaching universal access to primary education worldwide has improved, but it has not been fully reached by 2017. Attention has over time shifted from access to equity, quality, and persistence of learning, since high proportions of school children do not acquire basic competencies and often also drop out early, particularly among those in low-income communities. This shift of emphasis required the development of methodologies for measuring and assessing learning results, which depends on the mapping and definition of needed basic competences, with increasing attention given to those beyond basic literacy and numeracy (the so-called non-cognitive skills). More recently, the measurement of character and civics education are also gaining ground (Learning Metrics Task Force 2013).

19.1.2.3 Secondary Education

Secondary education, which builds on primary education, is much more differentiated, often first by stages of lower and upper cycles (which provide credentials of different paths inside or outside formal education), and then within these cycles. Participation at lower secondary level is close to that in primary education (85 percent globally; however, only at 50 percent in the least-developed countries and in Sub-Saharan Africa). At the upper secondary level, various configurations of sub-sectors arise according to the career patterns in education and the world of work. Differentiation between academic and vocational strands or sub-sectors, and between groupings or tracks of different aspirations, perceived ability, and levels, may start already at the lower secondary level. Main issues are the common school agenda vs. the degree of differentiation at the lower secondary level, and how this relates to the further academic–vocational divide; how the increase of access and expansion at the upper secondary level can be guided and managed; and the purpose, orientation, and distribution of programs.

19.1.2.4 Vocational Education

Vocational education might be situated in or outside the mainstream secondary education system, related to employment (as in the European systems of dual apprenticeship, which combine public and private actors in complex ways), to labor market institutions (as in the Mediterranean and Latin regions), or to postsecondary or tertiary levels (as with further education or community colleges in the Anglophone world). Indeed, a main trend is that vocational education and higher education increasingly overlap. About one third of young people have already terminated their formal education career at the stage of upper

secondary education globally, and the controversy about whether the expansion of secondary education should be directed toward the academic or vocational strands is still alive (Heikkinen and Lassnigg 2015).

19.1.2.5 The Apprenticeship Model

The apprenticeship model developed in Europe from a long tradition of professional guilds, expanded with industrialization, and, at least in some countries, has been adapted successfully to the challenges of the service economy. While there are certainly significant differences across countries in the importance of vocational education and training (VET) compared with general academic education, the former remains an important pathway to the labor market for a substantial proportion of youth. In 2014, 48 percent of secondary students in OECD countries were enrolled in VET programs at the upper secondary level (OECD 2016: 294). This is, on average, the same level as in the late 1990s (OECD 2000: 146). The United States never developed a distinctive vocational education sector, but, in practice, provided it within high schools and community colleges as an option for students unwilling to follow, or not properly prepared for, the path to full college education.

As the relative size of employment in the industrial sector diminished and access to higher education expanded, maintaining the attractiveness of VET as an alternative to academic education became more challenging. Much emphasis is currently put on the further development of vocational education and training to adapt it to the new circumstances (Lassnigg 2016), eliminating or postponing tracking to the end of compulsory education, creating paths from vocational to higher education, creating comprehensive schools expected to combine general and vocational education, and putting more emphasis on general skills, such as language and mathematics, in vocational schools. Hence, even in the age of the service-oriented knowledge economy, vocational education remains a popular alternative to general academic education at the secondary level.

Less-developed countries often lack the established industrial and business sectors that facilitate good-quality vocational education in richer countries. For them, formalized vocational education remains at best very limited in size, and at worse a second-class education for the poor. However, as the manufacturing and service sectors become important sources of employment growth in many developing and transition economies, there is potential for further developing VET as an instrument to promote both economic growth and social inclusion.

19.1.2.6 Teacher Education

Teacher education can be conceived as a distinct sector of formal education. There is strong evidence that the main driver of education quality is the professional qualification of teachers (Barber and Mourshed 2007). Well-prepared teachers are key not only in terms of good teaching, supporting the learning process, but also in supporting and enhancing cultural and intellectual values.

There is no standard approach to where and how teachers should be prepared, and a lack of studies on that topic. The IEA Teacher

19

Education and Development Study in Mathematics (TEDS-M) showed considerable variation in national policies related to quality assurance, entry requirements, program length, and the opportunities to learn, as well as differences in the organization and types of teacher education programs within and across the participating countries. Countries with programs providing the most comprehensive opportunities to learn university- and school-level mathematics tended to have higher scores on the TEDS-M tests. The data further indicated a positive relationship between the strength of quality-assurance arrangements and future teachers' mathematics and pedagogy knowledge (Ingvarson et al. 2013). But the debates on teacher education are not just a matter of identifying the best practices, since they are intermingled with the interests of powerful players in the education sectors, such as governments, public and private teaching networks, publishing corporations, governmental and non-governmental organizations, religious movements, and teacher unions (Grubb and Lazerson 2004).

The overlap of secondary and higher education in vocational and professional education is reflected in the institutional development of teacher education. Institutions of teacher education are interlinked to the professional profile of teachers, which in turn reflects the divisions within education systems, the power divisions among various stakeholders, and the political emphasis given to education. Big debates include to what extent teacher education should be included in universities, and how it should be related to research, on the one hand, and how the relationship to education policies should be organized, on the other. Teacher education also is important for the spread of lifelong and lifewide learning behaviors, reflected in the access of teachers themselves to further and continuing education, as well as in the focus on skills required for continuous learning.

19.1.2.7   Lifelong Education

Since the 2000s, the expanding notions of lifelong and lifewide learning emphasize the demand and necessity for broad and diversified learning throughout life. Learning does not necessarily have to be provided by formal education. The previous visions of the late twentieth century of building an additional formal adult education sector are being replaced by much more fluid and market-oriented visions, including self-oriented learning and digital provision, making extensive use of the new information and communication technologies. Despite the strong rhetoric about the benefits of adult learning, even its economic benefits are disputed, as in the seminal "Heckman curve" that postulates that the life-cycle returns for adult education are mostly negative (Singh, Schuller, and Watson 2009).

19.1.3   Higher Education and Universities

The higher education sector is undergoing a very expansive development, starting from few homogeneous elite universities and emerging into a wide, diverse, and differentiated tertiary sector comprised of several types of organizations and institutions (Trow 2006). The university is still the core institution, combining, at its best, high-quality teaching and research, and, more recently, expanding toward the "third missions" of technological innovation and community outreach.

Universities, as cultural, professional, and political institutions, reach far beyond the education system, and are thus – beyond their economic role – more closely involved in the processes of wider societal and political development and change than other educational organizations. Consequently, these institutions are often at the center of critical political movements, as well as being the target of authoritarian policies.

The medieval religious teaching universities were already internationally oriented; today, science, research, and higher education are, to a large extent, global endeavors, and the leading universities are global institutions in their impact, personnel, and student bodies. However, the sector is tremendously diverse, and overlaps with vocational education. The Bologna Process, supported by the European Union, is seeking to develop a common framework for the combination and integration of different types and levels of higher education, and has spread to 48 countries far beyond Europe.

19.1.3.1   The Impact of Modern Universities

Universities played a central role in the rapid socio-economic development of the 1950s and 1960s in North America, Western Europe, and Australasia. University research produced much of the knowledge that led to the biotechnology, nanotechnology, and information and communication technology revolutions, and university graduates became the core knowledge workers in the industries that emerged and blossomed in the wake of these revolutions (Mazzucato 2013). In addition, new types of higher education institutions and sectors emerged, focusing on welfare professions in the public and private sectors, spreading professional models of work life, enrolling first-generation students in higher education, and bringing them and their families into the middle classes.

Somewhere along the line the trust-based relationship between social progress and higher education was altered. The first reason was the dramatic increase in the size of higher education: massification of student numbers was followed by rapidly increasing staff numbers and new higher education institutions, leading to a dramatic costs explosion. Second, since the 1960s, the belief in the linear relationship between the publicly funded products of higher education (knowledge, early-stage new technologies, and qualified graduates) and social progress became increasingly challenged. Third, in several regions, including the USA, South America, and various East Asian countries, a large private, for-profit higher education sector emerged. While private, not-for-profit higher education has a long history and is, like public higher education, anchored in enlightenment values, for-profit higher education is a new phenomenon, and differs in its basic values fundamentally from the traditional not-for-profit institutions and systems, which are also being infiltrated by this new ethos (Altbach and Levy 2005; Levy 2006; Marginson 2016).

19.1.3.2   International Competitiveness and World-Class Universities

The growing focus on the economic role of higher education led many governments to reform the governance of their higher education systems to increase their universities' links to the economy and contribution to the global competitiveness of their countries. While there are variations among these national reform agendas, there are also clear similarities related to the ideas of strengthening the "third mission" of higher education: universities should become "integrated strategic actors," led by professional leaders and managers, expected to guide their institution into a fitting "niche" and make sure that their institution's engagement with society intensifies. All institutions are expected to be socio-economically relevant, to contribute to the innovative capacity of private-sector companies and public-sector organizations, to the creation of jobs, and to the solving of the grand challenges that are confronting our societies.

Part of this trend is the efforts of some leading universities, such as Harvard, MIT, and Columbia, to become global institutions, establishing branches and offices in different countries, and of governments to concentrate resources into a selected group of institutions to reach "world-class" excellence in teaching and research, as in the National Universities Research Program in Russia, the "excellence initiative" in Germany, and the "double first class" plan in China. This drive was spurred by the enormous attention gathered by the first global university ranking in 2003 (the so-called Shanghai Ranking) that inspired the introduction of various global and regional rankings, some of which have a commercial character.

On the positive side, this movement has stimulated many institutions to improve their standards of teaching and research and to introduce new governance practices. The actual ability of these initiatives to make universities truly global and to increase their countries' international economic competitiveness, however, is still to be seen. At the same time, there are cautious views pointing to indications of overeducation, mismatch, and potentially inflationary effects of global competition (Brown 2000; Altbach and Balán 2007; Altbach and Salmi 2011) and the risks associated with the development of a globalized, technocratic "scientist" elite around the culture of science and technology in higher education (Drori and Meyer 2006). Other contested topics are the issues related to "academic capitalism," "entrepreneurial universities," and the enforcement of privatization and the market, supposedly required to foster the "knowledge triangle" of education, research, and innovation (Brunner and Uribe 2007; Maassen and Stensaker 2011; Lassnigg et al. 2017); and the apparent decline of the cultural mission of the university in democratic societies, including strong humanities and social sciences to support critical intellectual discourses.

19.2   The Purposes of Education

The four different but interrelated purposes through which education is expected to foster social progress were briefly described in the introduction. This section aims at a more concrete presentation of how they have been attained so far, and might be further achieved. A common understanding today is that policies should be assessed by their achievements, in terms of access to schooling, academic proficiency, professional credentials, and integration with the labor market. Broader impacts, such as economic benefits at various levels, social positioning and mobility, and wider cultural outcomes such as civic

participation or value patterns, cannot be achieved by education alone. The understanding of these wider economic, social, and cultural outcomes is, moreover, affected by difficulties and controversies in measurement, and policies in education have been driven by untested beliefs in its wider results for a long time.

Since the mid-twentieth century, sociological research has started to analyze the wider impact of education on social structures and mobility, and, in parallel, economics has applied the models of growth accounting and the production function to education, and has developed the understanding of human capital, both with strong and controversial effects on policy-related discourses. The main indicators for these analyses were the data on access, participation, and finance, to which was added, more recently, large-scale data on student achievement. This has changed the political focus toward the results of learning, still limited, however, by a bias toward cognitive outcomes, and a narrow understanding of the "production function" (how education "produces" the learning results) and of the impact of the results on social progress more widely. These latter include economic growth, innovation, social stratification and further aspects of wellbeing, political participation, and deeper cultural dimensions.

Besides the cognitive outcomes, educational settings develop tacit personal "soft skills" such as self-regulation, behavioral management, and social and communication skills. Research shows that those with such traits are more likely to take better care of their own health (not to smoke, for instance), and less likely to be depressed or to commit crimes. Educated individuals are also more likely to interact more positively in social networks and local governments (Vorhaus et al. 2008: 13). Additionally, a review of the economics research evidence on the social externalities of education in cities found that "increases in the aggregate stock of human capital can benefit society in ways that are not fully reflected in the private return of education. Human capital spillovers can in theory increase aggregate productivity over and above the direct effect of human capital on individual productivity. Furthermore, increases in education can reduce criminal participation and improve voters' political behavior" (Moretti 2003). An extensive review of the evidence on the links between education and social cohesion finds a very significant association between equity in education and the presence of trust, civic cooperation, and low crime, which are core components of a well-functioning civic society. Effective education on pluralism, global citizenship, patriotism, and elections seems to lead to higher levels of tolerance, but there was no relationship to levels of trust, which depend very much on the country-level context (Green, Preston, and Janmaat 2006).

19.2.1   The Humanistic and Enlightenment Roles of Education

In the current humanistic understanding of education's purpose, the emphasis is not on human beings' usefulness to the state or the economy or to a religious order, but on their own personal development and the sustaining and growth of cultural traditions as goods in themselves and necessities for social progress. The origins of this goal,

19

in the Western tradition, can be traced back to the Greek concept of *Paidea* and the European classical curriculum of grammar, poetry, rhetoric, history, and moral philosophy, which were deemed necessary to infuse students with values, knowledge, and the abilities required to flourish as human beings and participate fully in their society. With the Enlightenment, education in the West became imbued with the values of rationality, science, and human progress, including pragmatism and more practical orientations.

In higher education, the main issues are research and innovation, reflection, and the humanities. The modern research university, which emerged after centuries of scholastic stagnation, gradually started to be a carrier of enlightenment values, such as rationality, scientific attitudes, and the intellectual traditions of scholarship. Its classical model was the Humboldtian university of the early nineteenth century, glorifying *Wissenschaft* and creativity, in the sense of education through the creation of new knowledge, as preconditions for meaningful thinking and sound judgments and drivers of social progress. The German research university, together with the French model of high-quality professional *Grandes Écoles*, became the main templates for modern universities worldwide, carrying enlightenment values into the twentieth century (Ben-David 1977). The US invention of the graduate school is seen as a next institutional step that has further improved the research function and contributed to differentiation of levels and functions in universities (Geiger 1993, 2004). Most higher education institutions throughout the world in the twenty-first century are adaptations, not always very successful, of the German, French, and American models.

There are also a few cases of new universities which seek to develop an alternative, "postcolonial" culture, through the recovery, creation, and recreation of the knowledge and language of original nations and peoples, supported by social movements and intellectuals in different parts of the world. Examples include a Zapatista-supported school in Chiapas, México, Universidad de la Tierra; the Universidad Indígena Boliviana Aymar Tupak Katari; and the Universidad Indígena Tawantineyu, in Bolivia. The Gawad Kalinga Village Farm University in the Philippines, while not a formal degree-awarding institution, shares some of the same goals in celebrating traditional ways of life and in distancing itself from Eurocentrism (de Oliveira Andreotti et al. 2015; Burman 2016; Takayama, Sriprakash, and Connell, 2017).

19.2.1.1   The Place of the Humanities in the Academic Culture

The academic cultures of science and technology, on one hand, and the humanities and literature, on the other, and more recently that of the social sciences, are very often in tension and do not communicate well, but are all key components of the enlightenment tradition (Snow 1959; Lepenies 1988). Humanities and the social sciences overlap to some extent, but, while the social sciences rely on empirical approaches similar to those of the natural sciences, as in economics, sociology, and political science, the humanities tend have a different approach, which includes, among other things, the study and interpretation of language, linguistics, literature, history, jurisprudence, philosophy, ethics, and esthetics and their use for reflection on the human environment, with particular attention to our diverse heritage, traditions, and

history (US Congress and House Committee on Education and Labor 1965). The humanities are important not only for their own sake, but for their potential to place the overwhelming priority given to economic and technological rationality in a broader context that includes the preservation of the environment, a responsible way of dealing with innovation, and the securing of just and equitable access to cultural goods. By upholding the principles of non-discrimination and multiculturalism, the humanities contribute to the purposes of identity building and the support of esteem and recognition, helping young people to deliberate about their plans and potentials, a key dimension of a just and progressive society.

19.2.1.2   The Students' Experience and Identity

If we extend the humanistic purpose to include psychological perspectives on personal identity, a more recent consideration is the role of education and the school experience in building this.

Who am I? What shall I do with my life? Questions of identity can and do arise at many points in life, and are particularly intense during adolescence. Individuals have multiple identities – one can be Indian, female, and planning to be a teacher – which, together, define one's personality, or "self" (Schwartz, Zamboanga, and Jarvis 2007; Spiel 2017). In addition to being shaped by dispositions, motivations, and individual experiences, the process of identity development can be influenced by the social and cultural environment. Schools, as the place where students spend much of their waking time, can play a crucial role in helping them to sort out who they are and their places in society (Zimmermann et al. 2015).

As the transition from adolescence to adulthood becomes far more extended, individualized, and complex than in the past, schools need to provide opportunities for students' exploration of life and support identity formation in domains such as occupation, culture, religion, politics, and gender roles.

Cultural background and gender are central aspects of identity, in which schooling plays a significant role. In contexts of diversity, shared learning places provide opportunities for prolonged first-hand contact with people from different cultures and ethnic backgrounds, and have the potential to afford positive opportunities like friendships, learning about other cultures, and understanding other ethnic groups; as well as negative experiences such as prejudice and racism, rejection and social exclusion, bullying and victimization (Schofield 1995).

19.2.2   Education and Citizenship

The civic purpose of education is clearly stated in the internationally agreed Sustainable Development Goals, with the expectation that, by 2030, "all learners acquire the knowledge and skills needed to promote sustainable development, including, among others, thorough education for sustainable development and sustainable lifestyles, human rights, gender equality, promotion of a culture of peace and non-violence, global citizenship and appreciation of cultural diversity and of culture's contribution to sustainable development" (UN 2017).

The initial drive for the expansion of public education in the modern era was a concern for the need to imbue the population with the knowledge, values, and habits of citizenship. Thomas Jefferson believed that "if a nation expects to be ignorant and free, it expects what never was and never will be." In Latin America, Andrés Bello and Domingo Sarmiento established the first public school systems in Chile and Argentina in the 1840s, arguing for the importance of public education for nation-building and economic wellbeing (Jaksic 2006). Since the 1918 Reform Movement in the city of Córdoba, Argentina, demanding university autonomy and governance with strong participation of students, academics, and alumni, universities in Latin America have played a crucial role in replacing the traditional oligarchic regimes with democratic governments, expanding enfranchisement, and paving the way for a new generation of leaders groomed in the university benches and student organizations (Walter 1968, 1969; Altbach 1981; Levy 1981; Bernasconi 2007). In 1968, in Paris, Berkeley, and Prague, students took to the streets to demand more participation, less war, and more democracy, changing forever the post-war political consensus that may have existed in their countries (Judt 2006: chapter 13).

The role of schools, as expressed by Émile Durkheim in France in the early twentieth century, was to make students understand their country and their times, to make them feel their responsibilities, to initiate them into life, and thus to prepare them to take their part in collective tasks, providing a link between private life in the family and public life in society; fully educated citizens should be disciplined, attached to their social group, and endowed with autonomy and self-determination, provided by rationality (Durkheim 1922; Nisbet 1965; Wesselingh 2002). Sociologists developed the concepts of civic culture, social cohesion, social trust, and social capital as key ingredients for the proper functioning of modern democracies and complex economies (Almond and Verba 1963; Harrison and Huntington 2000; Putnam 2001, 2002). Reactions to the conservative tone of the Durkheimian tradition, in the context of a changing world, led to alternative pedagogical approaches putting more emphasis on critical thinking, communitarian values, and individual liberation and self-determination (Freire 1970; Apple 1996; Benson, Harkavy, and Puckett 2007; Peterson 2011; Biesta, De Bie, and Wildemeersch 2014; Dalton and Welzel 2014).

Thus, the main thrust of promoting citizenship via education is toward social engagement, democratization, and enlightenment, but it should also be kept in mind that non-democratic regimes might purposely use education as a propaganda instrument to bolster support for authoritarian forms of government. Hence, the contents of civic education in school curricula depend very much on the prevailing cultures and ideologies in different countries and times: they can be strongly nationalistic, cultivating national glory and heroes; driven by notions of obedience to family and nation; or shaped by the current worldviews of the teaching profession.

An analysis of the official school curricula in seven Latin American countries in the 1990s found a clear decline of strong symbolic contents related to the national community, replaced by a new emphasis on general values and local identities; and found that history had lost its role of forging national identities and horizontal solidarity, since the past was replaced by expectations about the future (Cox, Lira, and Gazmuri 2009). In the 1990s, the International Association for the Evaluation of Education Achievement carried out a comparative survey of civic education in 38 countries, assessing to what extent 14-year-old students gained the knowledge, engagement, and attitudes expected from citizenship in a modern society. One of their findings was that "in most countries, young people's views of political parties are relatively negative. In place of giving allegiance to parties and to what many perceive as hierarchical political organizations ruled by an older generation, they are instead gravitating to social movements as the arenas in which good citizenship can be manifested" (Torney-Purta et al. 2001: 189).

This disaffection with the political establishment is likely to be a consequence of the malaise affecting political institutions in general, rather than a negative effect of education. While good education can improve the student's intellectual and personality tools to enable them to take part more fully in social life, the content of this participation depends more on the broad social and political context than on the school curricula as such.

In general, it has to be considered that formal public education, provided or guided by the state, is always embedded in the wider processes of informal learning and socialization, which de facto provide the main thrust of civic education through everyday life. The processes of school life and governance, and the role model activities of adults, also provide civic education through the hidden curriculum. Schools should provide space for reflecting these experiences, and learn participatory and solidarity practices, including them in the curriculum as well as in setting up appropriate procedures of school life.

19.2.3   Education and Economic Development

Economists coined the expression "human capital" to refer to their interpretation of education as a factor of production. Since the pioneering work of Schultz, Becker, and Mincer (Schultz 1970; Becker 1973; Mincer 1974), empirical research has shown again and again that investment in education leads to higher income, and that countries that expand and improve the quality of education are more likely to develop their economy (Harmon, Oosterbeek, and Walker 2003; Sianesi and Reenen 2003).

If education is an economic investment, it should be possible to measure its rates of return, both for individuals and for societies, and actors are expected to decide their investments accordingly. If this is so, data on rates of return can be used to establish priorities in education policy by finding out where the return is higher, in primary, secondary, or higher education – as practiced by the World Bank in the 1990s and still widely used (Leslie 1990; Psacharopoulos 1994).

A recent study found that, across 140 countries, there has been a significant shift in the rate of private (individual) returns to education. They found that returns to schooling declined from the early 1980s to post-2011 (from 13 percent to around 10 percent) and they ascribe this to the unprecedented increase in schooling (three more years globally). The study also found that, except in high-income economies, primary education has higher returns than secondary education, and that higher education has the highest private returns, despite the large increase in the number of students and graduates, with Sub-Saharan Africa having the highest rates in the world (21 vs. 14.6 percent on average) (Montenegro and Patrinos 2014).

Despite this study's intriguing findings, the use of rates of return for setting up priorities and assessing the quality of investments in education is controversial, because of its underlying assumptions and policy implications. The rates of return are calculated from the wages individuals receive in their lifetime, compared with their investment in completing their education. In most countries, education is subsidized with public resources, and the social benefits are calculated as private returns net of public costs. However, Heckman and associates show that "people do not only (or even mainly) make their schooling decisions by looking at their monetary returns in terms of earnings" (Heckman, Lochner, and Todd 2006),

Also, how policies should deal with differentials in returns is not a trivial question. A strict market-based approach would leave the investment–return logic on its own. An interventionist approach must deal with the question of why the public should support areas where the returns are high anyway, or where they are low and there is a risk of efficiency losses. Thus, policy choices are necessary in any case. A fundamental question is: which factors contribute to the levels and differences of returns, and how are these differences influenced by the degree of income inequality and social reproduction of educational credentials in a region? As the British sociologist Alison Wolf argues, "wages reflect a great deal more than productivity. The amount paid to different groups and different individuals also depends heavily on the way in which a society is organized overall: how it runs services such as health and education; how much its public and civic culture values equality; how professionals' fees are regulated" (Wolf 2002).

19.2.3.1   Education and the Regulation of the Marketplace

There are important differences in the ways the labor market is organized and relates to the education sector, depending in part on whether countries have a tradition of market coordination or liberalization, and how they react to the technological changes related to deindustrialization and the expansion of the services sector (Thelen 2007, 2012).

In some countries, the regulation and protection of the job and professional markets and of education may be part of a broader political consensus on the values of social equity, implemented by the prevailing political parties; in others, the segmentation of the job market may derive from the political power of specific professional end economic groups.

In the former Soviet Union, education was tightly linked to the productive sector and unemployment, by definition, did not exist, but this arrangement proved to be inefficient and did not survive the opening of the economy (Soltys 1997; Froumin and Kouzminov 2015). A usual pattern is for countries to protect the better-organized sectors of the market with legal provisions of job stability and unemployment benefits, while leaving other parts of the labor market unprotected, with low salaries, in the "informal" economy, or excluded from the labor market altogether,

establishing segmented job markets enforced by legal and sometimes ethnic or social barriers (Carnoy 1978; Wilkinson 2013).

When the labor market is regulated, it also extends this regulation to education. A classic example is the link between the industrial sector and the apprenticeship system in Germany, Austria, and Switzerland, and the role played by medical and legal associations in defining the numbers, duration, resources, and content of education in their respective fields, while others may be left unattended-to and unfunded (Rosenbaum 2001; Lassnigg 2016).

19.2.3.2   Higher Education and the Economy

Higher education contributes to economic development both in general, by enabling the population to participate more fully and evenly as producers and consumers in the complex industrial and services society, and, more specifically, by providing the skilled staff required by different sectors of the modern, knowledge-intensive economy. In higher education, a key issue is innovation and the role of science for economic competition in different parts of the world. Prominent approaches that focus on the "race between education and technology" put very high emphasis on university education (Acemoglu and Autor 2011). The expansion of application- and development-oriented higher education institutions has several important consequences. First, new study programs are introduced in areas such as agriculture, engineering, business, forestry, architecture, education, and mining. Second, it brings new forms of professional training to higher education through the introduction of discussion classes, experiments, field trips, and laboratories, as well as through the emphasis on national languages as the language of instruction (instead of, in the distant past, Latin and Greek). Third, it stimulates a more direct coupling of higher education with economic and political actors and agendas (Gibbons et al. 1994; Etzkowitz 2008; Mazzucato 2013). Finally, it opens higher education to non-traditional students.

A comprehensive analysis of the relationships between higher education and economic development has shown that expanding higher education may promote faster technological catch-up and improve a country's ability to boost its economic output (Bloom, Canning, and Chan 2006). The detailed study of Sub-Saharan Africa suggests that a one-year increase in higher education stock could boost incomes by 3 percent after five years and by 12 percent eventually. Considering that incomes have been falling in some African countries, such growth would be significant, and strongly suggests that higher education can play a recognizable role in promoting economic growth. However, it must be said that higher education can only be built on the earlier stages of education, and presupposes the necessary contextual conditions for the development of quality education; thus, there is no real policy choice between these different sectors, and the whole system must be considered.

19.2.3.3   Policy Choices

In sum, the broad links between education and productivity are clear in principle, and must be considered in the contribution of education to social progress. However, there are many policy choices left that do not directly follow from the economic evidence as such. Policies must embed the expected economic impacts into the broader potential impacts of education, and consider the controversial economic approaches. Traditional growth theory and market-led reasoning give much less weight to education for economic growth and competitiveness than do new growth theory and more institutional and innovation-oriented approaches. The former sees much more danger in overeducation, as when education keeps expanding and the economy changes or stagnates, leaving educated people without jobs, uncertain of their place in society, and having to migrate or find work in activities below their qualifications (Hersch 1991). The more innovation-led approaches see higher education lagging in the race with technology, even in the US of today, with its large system and its already high level of participation, and see rising inequality as an effect of this lag.

Striving for social progress requires the placing of the imperatives of economic growth and innovation into a broader framework of well-being beyond GDP, and dealing with the dark sides of innovation and the limits of growth.

19.2.4   Education and Equity

As education expands, it also plays a role in sorting people according to their attainment, the social prestige of the places they study and their careers of choice. Beyond its value in terms of skills and competencies, formal education is also a "positional good," meaning that individual benefits depend on one's place within the distribution of access and attainment. This results in intense pressure and competition for more education and credentials, which may conflict with the actual requirements or possibilities of the job market (Hollis 1982; Brown 2003; Brighouse and Swift 2006). Education systems are stratified in terms of the prestige and opportunities provided by different types of schools and universities, and access and achievement are strongly correlated with the social conditions of students and their families, leading some authors to argue that the main effect of education is to maintain and even reinforce existing social inequalities and the monopolies of social status through the administration of credentials. Education credentials can be a useful mechanism to signal one's competencies to potential employers in a competitive job market, but can also be associated with market segmentation and professional monopolies (Bourdieu and Passeron 1970; Spence 1973; Collins 1979; Wolf 2002).

19.2.4.1   The Global Efforts to Reduce Inequality

To deal with the problems of access and quality of education globally, with emphasis on low-income countries, the United Nations has been promoting important collective actions, starting with the 1990 Jomtien World Conference on Education for All, continuing with the 2000 Millennium Development Goals and culminating in the 2030 Agenda, in the form of 17 Sustainable Development Goals (SDGs), aimed at a shift in the economic and political relationships between high-, middle-, and low-income countries.

Between 1999 and 2012, the number of out-of-school children dropped from approximately 115 to 57 million. Among all regions, South Asia experienced the most accelerated progress. However, the rate of progress has significantly stagnated since 2007. Almost 30 percent of low- and middle-income countries are off-track to meet the goal of universal primary education and more than 20 percent are off-track to meet the goal of gender parity (World Bank 2012). Those remaining out of school are among the most disadvantaged: children in conflict-affected countries, children with disabilities, and children from the poorest families. In West and Central Africa, children of primary school age from the poorest quintile are on average six times more likely to be out of school than those from the richest.

19.2.4.2   Gender Parity

Progress has also been made toward gender parity in terms of primary school enrollment, with approximately 70 percent of countries reaching this quantitative goal, but local cultural perspectives on the value of education to girls in some contexts have also led to exclusion. Providing girls with an education helps break the cycle of poverty: educated women are less likely to marry early; less likely to die in childbirth; more likely to have healthy babies; and more likely to send their children to school. Poverty and other forms of social disadvantage magnify gender disparities. In most Sub-Saharan African countries, girls from the poorest households remain most disadvantaged in terms of school participation. The *World Development Report* on gender equality and development (World Bank 2012) shows that there are still 31 million girls out of school, and nearly four million "missing" women annually (meaning the number of women in low- and middle-income countries who die relative to their counterparts in high-income countries). The systematic exclusion of girls and women from school and the labor force translates into a less educated workforce, inefficient allocation of labor, lost productivity, and diminished progress in economic development. This is particularly worrisome in some Gulf States countries, where gender inequality in access to education is very high (UNDP 2017).

However, even in egalitarian societies, gender differences still exist in students' performance and motivation, in vocational aspirations, in salaries, and in participation in different fields. Men are expected to develop traits related to agency (such as aggression, forcefulness, independence, and decisiveness), whereas women are expected to develop traits related to communal virtues (such as kindness, helpfulness, beauty, and concern for others) (Kite, Deaux, and Haines 2008); and these expectations lead to self-fulfilling prophecies that perpetuate biases (Jussim, Eccles, and Madon 1996). In the context of education, gender-stereotyped expectations occur in the interests, abilities, and vocational aptitudes attributed to girls and boys (Kollmayer, Schober, and Spiel 2016).

19.2.4.3   The Role of Schools in Reducing Inequality

The role of education in reducing inequality depends on schools' ability to compensate for the effects of students' pre-existing social and individual disadvantages, providing them with equal opportunities for learning, social participation and work. The *Coleman Report*, published in 1968 in the US, influenced research and policies for decades by showing that public schools had little or no effect in reducing the inequalities associated with race (Coleman 1968). However, school characteristics were specified only narrowly, e.g. by resources, and the results were always contested. Since then, the assessment of the "school effects" on student achievement, compared with pre-existing conditions, and the expansion of opportunities through social inclusion and better schools and teaching, has become a major subject of education research (Coleman 1966, 1968; Hanushek 1986). These studies are being in turn criticized for neglecting the processes in place within schools. A similar controversial study (Rutter 1982) has set a counterpoint by trying to point out that "school would matter" and has stimulated more emphasis on processes and inner school factors. These gaps between different methodologies result in different kinds of policy recommendations (Hedges et al. 2016). Alternative types of modeling have also been developed in the economics of education that take a wider perspective on the whole structure of education and on different kinds of longer-term impacts, with quite different results on peer effects, tracking, and vocational education (Brunello and Checchi 2007).

There are many strategies to make education more attractive, meaningful, and accessible, but the fact remains that millions of students, some in rich countries but mostly in low-income countries, go through school without learning to read and understand a simple text or solve a simple arithmetic problem, or gaining a grasp of very simple scientific facts. Inequality of outcomes is impacted by lack of equity in access to distinct forms/types of schooling (public fee-paying, public non-fee-paying, self-funded private, or grant-funded private schools); by inequity in provision in respect to dosage (class size, student–teacher ratios, teaching and learning time, ability to learn at home, language choice, technology, infrastructure); and by inequity in quality (teaching standards, pedagogical methodology, materials, curriculum and curriculum coverage). Educational governance, institutions (schools) and educators, curriculum, and pedagogy all matter a great deal. Where students from poor or marginalized communities are exposed to less rigorous content and lower expectations or to a less engaging pedagogical method, the risk of inequality in the opportunity to learn is high. Grade attainment (completing more grades) will not improve educational outcomes or downstream income earnings if little learning happens per grade. More schooling is therefore not necessarily equal to a better education (Hanushek and Wössmann 2012; Hanushek et al. 2015).

Inequality in Preschool and Primary Education

Inequality in education achievement starts in the early years, and can be cumulative: "reading acquisition is a process that begins early in the preschool period, such that children arrive at school having acquired vastly differing degrees of knowledge and skill pertaining to literacy. Attention has thus turned to whether preschool differences in language and literacy development are reliable prognostic indicators, and perhaps direct causes, of later reading (dis)abilities" (Scarborough 2009: 23). Good-quality preschool education is crucial to reducing these differences, combined with literacy methods emphasizing phonological awareness, letter recognition, print concepts, retention of verbal material, and oral language skills (Goswami and Bryant 1990; Brady and Shankweiler 2013). In primary education, inequality can increase if students arriving with different conditions are not supported with differentiated action to ensure that they acquire the required competencies in reading, writing, and arithmetic in the first one or two years. In highly unequal societies with decentralized school systems, poor students may end up enrolled in local schools with less resources and lower teacher quality, which can increase the gap between them and those coming from richer and better-educated families that go to better-equipped and pedagogically stronger schools (Lee and Burkam 2002; Park and Kyei 2011).

Inequality in Secondary and Vocational Education

At the secondary school, a central issue is the existence of separate academic and vocational study streams. The fact that students reach secondary education with widely different interests, motivations, and competencies means that they cannot be required to follow the same curricula and be assessed by the same standards. To deal with this issue, several countries have developed highly differentiated systems, with general and vocation education tracks going up to the tertiary level. One common criticism of this differentiation is that tracking often takes place too early in the students' life, and is related more to the students' social origins than to their intellectual potential, worsening class biases in access to education (Hanushek and Wössmann 2006; Pfeffer 2008; Van de Werfhorst and Mijs 2010). However, the separation between academic and vocational tracks might have beneficial effects, since it allows for the inclusion of a large variety of students in schools, increases the supply of vocational skills in the economy, and facilitates the transition from school to work (Shavit and Muller 2000; Hall and Soskice 2001; Schwartzman 2011). Furthermore, there is empirical evidence that levels of socio-economic, not educational, inequality are lower in countries with extensive vocational training systems (Estevez-Abe, Iverson, and Soskice 1999; Solga et al. 2014; Busemeyer and Thelen 2015) because vocational training opens access routes to well-paid and secure employment for those with few academic skills.

Inequality In Higher Education

Higher education can contribute to inequality by providing additional benefits to those that are successful in completing secondary education and going through the selective processes of university admissions. In general, the wage differential between those with higher education and those without it is affected by the relative scarcity of persons with high education in a country and the demands for highly skilled persons in the economy, but also by the ability of persons with less education to protect their income through strong union organization and minimum wage legislation. Historical data for the US shows that the earning gap in favor of higher education has been increasing since 1979, which is explained by the limited growth of higher education participation, the expanding demands for highly skilled personnel, and the deterioration of the earnings of less-skilled workers (Autor 2014).

19.3 The Contribution of Pedagogy and the Curriculum

The role of education in promoting social progress is enhanced by pedagogy and the curriculum. Pedagogy is a complex and highly culture-bound process, and this is part of the explanation for the limited attention it receives by researchers and funders. The traditional Western curriculum, and the way it is presented to students, used to be taken for granted as the only appropriate direction. Sociologists of education, however, have shown that school curricula are related to the values, culture, and social standing of specific social groups, and, as education expanded, new groups and sectors started to criticize the standard practices and demand alternative curricula, more meaningful for them (Bowles and Gintis 1973; Whitty 1985; Beyer and Liston 1996). There is a permanent and lively debate among educators about the contents and ways in which the teaching of virtues such as criticism, feminism, personal identity, pluralism, empathy, and tolerance should occur (Noddings 1995; White 2003). Postcolonial perspectives also signal the need for alternative views of "the good life" and the very foundations of knowledge, which move beyond dominant Western definitions and ways of seeing the world.

19.3.1 Pedagogy

Pedagogy consists of the observable methods and interactions that take place in educational settings. It also includes the beliefs, philosophies, and theories that underpin these in the minds of educators. All lessons have shared and familiar ingredients: tasks, activities, teacher judgments, and interactions, structured through the use of time, space, and student institutions, and, in the school context, over the cycles of the school year, routines, rules, and rituals (Alexander 2001a,b).

Despite cultural variations and recurring controversies among different pedagogic traditions, learner-centered education has gained prominence as a policy and promoted practice. The broad term "learner-centered education" (LCE) is an umbrella for a wide range of practices which emphasizes inquiry-based learning, activity-based learning, and critical pedagogy. Its best-known expression was the "progressive education movement," started in the late nineteenth century in Europe and related to well-known names in the education literature such as Johann Heinrich Pestalozzi as a forerunner, Maria Montessori, Jean Piaget, Lev Vygotsky, and John Dewey (Reese 2001; Hayes 2006). What they all have in common is their reaction against teacher-centric approaches such as lecturing and drilling, and their emphasis on learner participation in what is studied and how.

LCE has been associated with social progress in many ways (Schweisfurth 2013). By encouraging active participation by all individual learners, and by giving them greater control over the curriculum, it upholds children's rights conventions and is assumed to facilitate the development of democratic skills. Critical versions of LCE encourage questioning of received knowledge and authority, deemed essential for democracy and social progress. By acknowledging and accommodating individual differences in terms of interests, talents, and preferred approaches to learning, LCE has, in theory, the potential to stimulate engagement with schooling, by generating and channeling motivation, thereby raising achievement across all groups of learners. LCE is also expected to prepare all learners for the knowledge economy by creating flexible, lifelong learning practices that can respond to rapid change and the information revolution.

Whatever the potential of LCE, it cannot be implemented within mainstream schooling where teachers and educational organizations are not well prepared or where it does not embed into local systems. And in many lower-income countries where it has been an import, there have been unintended consequences of the introduction of LCE through policy reform.

Research in the UK has suggested that not all learners are equally equipped to participate in learner-centered lessons, with already advantaged learners being more accustomed to stimulating learning activities and more practiced at expressing themselves (Bernstein 1971). It has also been argued that if it draws primarily on learners' pre-existing understandings, LCE can reduce access to knowledge and skills that disadvantaged learners need to flourish (Young 2013). This condition applies to most students in public schools in low- and middle-income countries, where the adoption of extreme constructivist approaches that deny the importance of phonological awareness in literacy and the more structured and content-laden teaching of mathematics, literature, and science is considered one of the causes of the extremely high levels of functional illiteracy among school children (Goswami and Bryant 1990; Boghossian 2007; Hyslop-Margison and Strobel 2007; Mascolo 2009; Brady and Shankweiler 2013). In this regard, the successful experience of public schools in Ceará, Brazil, in their adoption of a combination of high expectations, strong involvement of students, teachers, and principals, and structured curriculum in one of the poorest regions of the country, is an important example (Gall 2016).

Despite the challenges, it is striking how successful LCE has been in alternative schools outside of the mainstream, such as those that follow the Montessori model, and in some public experiences such as the Escuela Nueva initiative in Colombia (Psacharopoulos, Rojas, and Velez 1992; Schiefelbein 1992). What is needed is a broader understanding of the learning process and how to approach it. Contents and processes are often depicted as opposite and conflicting education ideologies, but can best be considered two indispensable faces of any successful education system.

A synthesis of hundreds of meta-analyses of research related to student achievement confirms that education works best when teachers have explicit goals and high expectations about what the students should and can learn, including the necessary fluency in reading, writing, and mathematical reasoning, which can only be obtained through practice; when the students are actively engaged in the education process; and when teaching is aimed at three equally important "worlds of achievement." These "three worlds" are: "surface knowledge of the physical world, the thinking strategies and deeper understanding of the subjective world, and the ways in which students construct knowledge and reality for themselves as a consequence of this surface and deep knowing and understanding" (Hattie 2008: 26).

Policy-makers and teachers can embrace the potential of student-centered and critical education to uphold rights, encourage critical thinking and democratic exercise, and support the development of love for learning. However, it is essential that educational reform does not impose individualistic approaches where more collectivist ways of working are more culturally valued and have been educationally successful. Cultural awareness, in turn, should not be used to condone pedagogical practices that violate rights, such as the use of corporal punishment, or perpetuate or create inequalities, such as excluding girls and students with less cultural capital.

19.3.2　The Curriculum

A significant part of the current debates on the curriculum relates to decisions by governments to establish national mandatory curricula, mostly for primary and secondary education, but in some cases including also vocational and higher education. Such curricula describe the subjects and themes that are considered the basis for the individual and social competencies required for twenty-first-century life and progress (Trilling and Fadel 2009; Rotherham and Willingham 2010).

National curricula set out the knowledge that learners are expected to command, and define the skills they should acquire and sometimes the values that are intended to be inculcated. The level of detail varies among countries, ranging from minute listing of "facts" to be covered and learned and competencies to be attained, to very loose guidelines within which schools and teachers make some of the most important decisions, allowing for differentiation for and by individual learners based on their needs and interests. When the national curriculum is tightly framed, it is also common to have state-prescribed textbooks that buttress this control over content.

19.3.2.1　The Global Core Curriculum

Despite the large national differences, it is possible to talk about an emergent global curriculum, which is being implemented worldwide by imitation or the influence of international organizations and technical assistance. In 2006, the European Community proposed a framework of eight "key competences for lifelong learning" that included (1) communication in the mother tongue; (2) communication in foreign languages; (3) mathematical competence and basic competences in science and technology; (4) digital competence; (5) learning to learn; (6) social and civic competences; (7) sense of initiative and entrepreneurship; and (8) cultural awareness and expression (Halász and Michel 2011). In 2012, it created the European Qualifications Framework, to establish equivalences among the qualification frameworks of the different countries, according to eight levels, from basic general knowledge to the advanced frontiers of scholarship and research (Bohlinger 2008; Grollmann, Spottl, and Young 2008).

Whereas post-World War II international education policies concentrated mostly on basic literacy, currently the global core curriculum includes a much-expanded list of subjects and themes. Chief among them is STEM (science, technology, engineering, and mathematics), adjusted per education level to build the required general science and math knowledge and skills. In its expanded form, STEM also includes environmental education, chemistry, physics, and computer sciences (Trilling and Fadel 2009). The global core curriculum may also include citizenship education, such as civic and political skills, studies of international relations and human rights, and multiculturalism and tolerance (Cogan and Derricott 2014); and contents related to lifelong learning and non-formal education, acknowledging the ever-changing conditions of global society and the need for continuous education and skilling of the labor force (Tuijnman and Boström 2002; Jakobi 2009). These three general curricular areas – STEM, citizenship, and lifelong learning – differ in their worldwide appeal. STEM is the most internationally standardized curricular area, whereas citizenship and lifelong subjects are treated with greater sensitivity to local traditions. Still, overall, all three curricular areas are included in international policy recommendations regarding education and progress.

Much discourse around curriculum reform is couched in terms of preparing students for economic productivity, whether that means learning "the basics" of literacy and numeracy, studying vocational subjects as preparation for specific jobs, or focusing on the so-called twenty-first-century skills. The nature of civics as a subject area or cross-curricular theme – for example whether it is limited to knowledge about governmental structures and prescriptions about obedient citizens, or is taught through critical approaches that question inequalities and power – shapes understandings of the possibilities and limits of democratic political and civic participation. The curriculum has the potential to contribute to the redistribution of opportunity by debunking myths of in-group superiority; equally, it can reinforce social stratification when different curricula are offered to different groups of students and those groups align with pre-existing privilege. Textbooks and other curricular resources can communicate messages to students that build or undermine their confidence in terms of what they can achieve. While the curriculum can potentially support equity by equalizing entitlement, the use of imposed state curricula to oppress citizens in totalitarian or racist regimes is also well documented.

Whatever the explicit learning outcomes might be, the contents of teaching and learning also have an implicit dimension, known as the hidden curriculum, which conveys strong but tacit messages. For example, the ways that women are portrayed in textbooks – the jobs they do, the ways they communicate, the clothes they wear, who is loved and who is not – set out a normative framework that has deep effects on the students' own identities and understandings of what to expect from others, even if the official line advocates equality for women as a learning goal; likewise, school textbooks carry implicit cultural norms regarding tolerance, rights, and equity (Meyer, Bromley, and Ramirez 2010).

19.3.3　The Assessment of Learning

The implementation of national or core standards in the curriculum requires external assessments that are used to establish benchmarks, often linked to international assessments such as OECD's PISA and TIMMS, to identify underperforming sectors or schools and the factors that may explain the differences, and to guide policies aimed at improving the quality of education. This trend has been criticized as being too intrusive and threatening to the autonomy of schools and the teaching profession. Other controversies concern the role of formative and summative assessment, high- or low-stakes testing, the relationship of assessment to motivation, and the distinction between intrinsic and extrinsic motivation. The notion that the focus on outcomes and assessment would, through sanctions and material rewards, change practices in education is opposed by more professionally oriented approaches that focus on the improvement of the processes. The focus of these assessments on core competencies such as language and STEM is criticized as leading to the neglect of other dimensions of education such as the humanities, the social sciences, and civic education, and replacing education in a broad sense with "teaching to the tests," which in fact may occur (Schwartzman 2013; Ravitch 2016).

To avoid these risks, the Finnish National Core Curriculum, implemented since 2016, combines strong standards with local autonomy and flexibility. A key factor is the presence of a highly qualified teaching profession, which is often missing in lower-income countries and regions, where the adoption of a combination of explicit standards, the provision of structured teaching materials, and accountability of schools and teachers seems to work best (Bruns, Filmer, and Patrinos 2011).

19.4   Governance and Public Policy

Public policies seek to steer the educational processes happening in the classroom by, for example, regulating the training and employment conditions of teachers, establishing standards and external evaluation procedures, and providing moneys to finance buildings and salaries, as well as many other things. Policy-makers shape the governance and institutional set-up of education by defining the variety of educational pathways, the conditions of access and the involvement in governance of stakeholders such as teacher unions and parents. Educational policy-making does not play out in a political vacuum: decisions about governance are often contested between different actors. Therefore, the mobilization of public support for education policies is a critical factor.

19.4.1   Public Support in Education: Differences and Benefits

In most societies, there is strong consensus about the promises of education to contribute to social progress. Studies of election programs in Western Europe and public opinion polls in Asia, Africa, and Latin America show that no political parties openly oppose the expansion of education opportunities, and education tends to be the most popular policy program, along with health care (Jakobi 2011; Kosack 2014; World Values Survey Association 2014; Busemeyer, Lergetporer, and Wössman 2017).

The apparent widespread support for public education contrasts with the fact that, in many countries, persistent educational inequalities are still unresolved. Furthermore, levels of public investment in education and efforts to expand enrollment and educational opportunities are often below expectations. For instance, in the OECD countries, public spending on education has been more negatively affected by fiscal pressures related to austerity than spending on other social policy programs (Streeck and Mertens 2011; Breunig and Busemeyer 2012).

There are two potential explanations for why the gap between aspirations and actual policy-making might be larger in education than in other sectors. First, public support for education might be less robust than assumed. Expanding educational opportunities creates benefits in the long rather than the short term, both for individuals and for society. The long-term maturation of educational investments stands in contrast to the short-term benefits of many other social policies such as health care, social transfer programs, and old-age pensions (Busemeyer et al. 2017). Second, political parties might agree on the need to expand education in general, but, when it comes to the details, education is a highly contested policy area. Conservative and liberal parties tend to support education policies that limit the role of the state in financing the provision of education, while encouraging the involvement of non-state actors. Left-wing parties, in contrast, are more in favor of a strong role for the central state.

The institutional design and capacity of education systems vary dramatically among countries, levels of government, and sectors. Political conflicts about the institutional design or the governance of education systems are related to underlying material interests of those affected (Iversen and Stephens 2008; Ansell 2010; Dobbins and Busemeyer 2015). Historical conflicts about the shape of education systems have strong implications for present governance, since, once established, institutions create powerful path-dependency effects, constraining the leeway for large-scale changes (Pierson 1993; Thelen 1999). The feedback effects of established institutions affect strategies, preferences, and power resources of individual and collective actors. Once policy choices for the design of education systems have been made at critical junctures, large-scale change is unlikely thereafter (Dobbins and Busemeyer 2015).

Ideally, democracy, education, and economic development can positively reinforce each other, with education promoting both citizenship and economic skills, which promote the further development of democratic structures. These in turn can ensure a continued opening of access to higher levels of education (Ansell 2008, 2010). But there is no deterministic association between the institutional structure of education and economic development. Western countries with similar levels of economic development can have hugely different institutional arrangements for their education: more or less centralized, with differentiation among academic and vocational tracks in secondary and higher education and unified or diversified higher education systems, which are often more related to historical paths than to recent policy options.

Countries differ regarding how much they invest in education and how they distribute funding across the different sectors. However, there is no apparent association between the total level of investment in education and educational performance (Castles 2013). In addition, there is significant cross-national variation in the division between public and private sources of funding (Wolf 2009, Wolf and Zohlnhöfer 2009), which mostly include tuition and school fees. There are indications that very high tuition fees effectively block students from low-income backgrounds from participating in higher education (Mettler 2014). Furthermore, high levels of private spending can also have feedback effects on citizens' expectations vis-à-vis the welfare state: when individuals have invested a considerable amount of money in acquiring their education, they are less likely to support high levels of taxation and redistribution, since this would lower the returns on their educational investments (Busemeyer 2013).

19.4.2   Decentralization in the Provision of Education

Another important dimension in the governance of education is how different stakeholders are included in decision-making. In some countries, decision-making is centralized in the hands of governmental bureaucrats, while in others, different stakeholders are involved, e.g. parents and students, in the running of local schools, as well as representatives of trade unions and employers' associations in the administration of vocational training schemes.

Since the 1980s, many education systems have undergone a process of decentralization of provision. Decentralization of education governance means that decisions over management, financing, curriculum design, and personnel are delegated to regional and local governments as well as to schools and school districts. The rationale is that decentralization allows for greater involvement of local stakeholders, parents, teachers, and students in designing the pedagogical content of the curriculum and stimulating good performance, and promoting their local embeddedness.

Even though decentralization is a powerful international trend, national contexts influence how it plays out in different countries. In the US and the United Kingdom, the governance of education was already decentralized before the 2000s, with many powers transferred to local education authorities or school districts. In this context, further decentralization amounts to the delegation of responsibilities to individual schools that are independent from the local educational authorities (e.g. charter schools in the US or academies in England). In other cases, for instance Germany, decentralization implied the delegation of autonomy to individual schools within existing governance structures, i.e. from the *Land* to the school level. In Sweden, far-reaching reforms in the 1990s paved the way for the emergence of "independent schools," which are run by private providers, though financed with public moneys (Klitgaard 2008). In some cases, decentralization is accompanied and conditioned by a parallel trend toward privatization (Gingrich 2011). Examples are African countries, Brazil, India, and the Russian Republic (Schwartzman 2015). In these places, private households are increasingly willing and able to pay for higher education, while state institutions often lack the fiscal and administrative capacities to meet the increasing demand both from households and employers. Hence, private institutions increasingly play an important role in filling this gap.

19.4.3   The Regulation of Private Education

The traditional structures of formal public education are being challenged by new trends that blur the distinctions between public and private education and create new divisions and structuring within education. Private formal education has always coexisted with the public sector in most countries, managed by religious, philanthropic, or communitarian associations, and supported in whole or in part with public funds, as with the Catholic schools in Canada and Ireland, the Catholic University in Chile, and the Madrassa schools in many Muslim-majority countries (Levy 1986, 2006). The new trends include the growth of a large for-profit private education industry, the move to replace public schools with charter schools, the introduction of student vouchers and loans instead of direct subsidies to public schools, the charging of tuition in public schools and universities, and the adoption of business-like practices in management. In low-income countries, when public schools are failing because of governance problems related to mismanagement, corruption, and lack of accountability, private schools may be considered as an attractive alternative, delivering better teaching and achieving better learning outcomes at lower costs (Ashley et al. 2014). In higher education, private education fills the niches created by failures of the public sector, either by improving access to low-cost, bare-bones professional qualifications for students who cannot access the best elite universities, or, on the contrary, providing elite education when the public sector is bloated, inefficient, and politicized.

These issues are often debated in strong ideological terms, as if they were all part of the same package, but need to be assessed in terms of their different impact on the equity, quality, and relevance of education provision for the broad purposes of education. Not surprisingly, the evidence is contradictory, depending very much on the context and the way these policies are implemented (McEwan and Carnoy 2000; Angrist et al. 2002; Somers, McEwan, and Willms 2004; Howell and Peterson 2006; Ashley et al. 2014; Elacqua 2015). Education is not an exclusive task of public institutions and cannot be considered a service business like any other: it is the role of public governance to seek a proper balance for each context, looking for the best mix that enhances the goals of relevant content, equity, the enhancement of civic values, and economic productivity.

In the Western world, there are good reasons to believe that privatization and marketization will and does already have negative consequences regarding social and educational inequality, as well as social progress in general. In the developing countries, marketization may promote educational expansion in the short run, compensating for the lack of responsiveness on the part of the public education system. In the long run, however, the entrenchment of a private sector may contribute to segregation, as it has done in some rich-world democracies. A crucial factor in this respect is the extent to which competition between schools and higher education institutions is constrained by public regulations. When institutional autonomy in resource management and pedagogical matters is accompanied by a decentralized system of education finance, decentralization can result in a growing heterogeneity between institutions. Wealthy schools would then increasingly be concentrated in wealthy districts, being able to attract better students and better teachers. Once an institutional regime is established, entangled with housing and residential patterns and career choices, it can be very difficult to change.

19.4.4 Research-Informed Policy-Making

Public policies in education, health care, and welfare are being increasingly informed by research-based evidence, which is promoted as providing a solid and more rational – namely, professional and value-neutral – basis for decision-making on matters of supervision, control, capacity, efficiency, operations, and structure (Drori and Meyer 2006; Espeland and Sauder 2007). The assumption is that partisan and ideological conflicts are best addressed by delegating decisions to well-informed experts. The problem of distinguishing scientific evidence from other kinds of knowledge and information has been currently seemingly resolved with the adoption of a "gold standard" of randomly controlled trials or highly sophisticated quasi-experimental econometric methodology. However, the model of evidence-based or evidence-informed policy is still very sparsely understood and controversial (Lassnigg 2012). Applied to education, it is heavily biased toward certain aspects and understandings of the education field; i.e. it has primarily looked at and introduced practices of assessment (such as measurement of education outcomes, in terms of comparative performance) and of education provision and administrative capacity (such as management of financial and human resources). Facts and certain kinds of evidence are often reified toward value-neutral "truths" at the expense of a proper understanding of the need for theory and concepts to give the "facts" sense and meaning.

The idea of using research knowledge for policy-making is an old one and has undergone several waves in Western history, being inspired by the enlightenment and, in the US, by the empirical turn to evaluation and operations research in the 1960s driven by the US Great Society programs (Wells and Roda 2016). The more recent turn toward "evidence-based-policy" in the 2000s is more specifically inspired by ideas of the knowledge society and a better use of research-based knowledge, as in medicine. Globally, most evident is the policy fascination with internationally comparative testing, such as PISA and TIMSS, under the assumption that curricula and student achievements are indeed universal and comparable (Kamens and McNeely 2009; Meyer and Benavot 2013; Crossley 2014; Lingard et al. 2015). The rise of this international assessment and accountability regime has encouraged the diffusion of practices for the assessment of education also at the national and subnational levels, bringing the mode of "governing by numbers" to all world regions (Grek 2009) and many countries (Feniger, Livneh, and Yogev 2012; Sung and Kang 2012). A softer version is to give priority to "evidence-informed" rather than "evidence-based" policies (Burns and Schuller 2007).

The shift toward research-based or research-informed policy can lead to changes in the main actors responsible for policy implementation, since government agencies usually lack the extensive research capability required to substantiate policy-making and may need to outsource it to outside experts and think-tanks (Sellar and Lingard 2013). However, major policy cannot and should not be delegated to technocratic committees, as it has distributive and normative implications that

can only be decided in democratically elected decision-making bodies. While few would doubt that policy decisions should be informed by research and evidence as far as possible, it is also important to be aware of its conceptual and political limitations, which are often neglected by the rhetoric of technocratic discourse. Education is a field that is heavily driven by diverse ideological and political influences which cannot be bridged by "facts" but only by careful and serious discourses that secure deliberate judgment, and a balancing between the basic actors of the state, the private sector, parents/students, and professionals (Gutmann and Ben-Porath 2015).

Finally, there is no guarantee that policy solutions proposed by experts and researchers will automatically be supported by the public. In fact, there are many cases where this is not the case. For example, even though empirical educational research has produced robust evidence that early tracking of students onto separate academic and vocational tracks in secondary education enhances educational inequality, reforming school structures on the secondary level has been very contentious politically in many countries (Dobbins and Busemeyer 2015). Thus, to advance educational reforms promoting social progress, it is not sufficient to identify good policy solutions – it is also important to ensure that these policies will be supported by the public and influential stakeholders.

19.4.5 Global Governance

Education is formally enshrined in numerous international treaties as a human right guaranteed to all, and policies are set – nationally, internationally, and transnationally – in accordance with this spirit. In Europe, the Bologna process, which started out as an effort of international coordination in higher education governance, has contributed to the establishment of a transnational governance framework based on voluntary cooperation between governments. This framework achieves some sort of coordination in higher education policy, such as the introduction of Bachelor and Master degrees throughout Europe and the establishment of common quality management procedures, while also respecting national peculiarities. Hence, it is a good example of how complex governance arrangements are both necessary and possible in the global era (Voegtle, Knill, and Dobbins 2011).

Education worldwide is promoted by a transnational advocacy network, composed of both intergovernmental and transnational nongovernmental organizations. This diverse set of organizations, which have proliferated in the last decades, has been instrumental in formulating transnational objectives, most notably the Global Campaign for Education and the Education for All agenda, as well as placing education as a pinnacle of the Millennium Development and Sustainable Development Goals. While intergovernmental organizations affect national education agendas through the activation of inter-state treaties, most other transnational organizations influence education agendas through "soft law" mechanisms, for example by setting standards in the form of comparative assessments (Kamens and McNeely 2009; Meyer and Benavot 2013). This international and transnational education governance intersects with national and subnational education policy-making in numerous ways and influences its trajectory. It establishes what is taken to be "best practice," defining universal standards for curriculum, pedagogy, evaluation, and the like. Global organizations have imprinted curricula worldwide by introducing discourses of social sciences (Wong 1991), environmentalism (Bromley, Meyer, and Ramirez 2011), and human rights (Suárez 2007) to textbooks in schools worldwide and by promoting programs for girls' education (Vaughan 2013) and lifelong learning (Jakobi 2009). They have also driven the rapid institutionalization of universal mass schooling (Boli, Ramirez, and Meyer 1985; Meyer, Ramirez, and Soysal 1992) and of higher education (Schofer and Meyer 2005), particularly in poorer countries with weaker national polities (McNeely 1995; Steiner-Khamsi and Stolpe 2006; Vaughan 2013). And still, the worldwide isomorphism that resulted from the decades of policy borrowing and lending has nevertheless preserved cross-national differences in education capacities and outcomes (Baker and LeTendre 2005).

Whereas global and cross-national education policies focused, until the 1980s, on mass schooling and, with the advent of the global knowledge economy, also on higher education and innovation, the focus today is on lifelong learning. The orientation toward education as a continuous, and often also self-motivated, learning and skilling is spurred by the rapid changes of the global economy and the labor force. Such changes include the longevity of individuals, which extends the employability of working adults; they also introduce great uncertainty as to the competencies that are required for future gainful and productive employment. These uncertainties, and the "over the horizon" planning that they impose, call not only for promotion of continuous learning but also for changes in the contents of education. Indeed, contemporary education policies globally and cross-nationally advocate a paradigm shift in pedagogy – toward flexible and non-formal education, toward digital literacy, and toward agentic learners. This global governance regime regarding lifelong and lifewide learning is formalized in such intergovernmental initiatives as the 2010 Belém Framework for Action, coordinated by such intergovernmental programs as the UNESCO Institute for Lifelong Learning, and advocated by the European coalition of nongovernmental organizations known as The Lifelong Learning Platform (formerly EUCIS-LLL).

19.5 Moving Forward: Bolstering the Contribution of Education to Social Progress

This final section presents the main actions needed to allow education to fulfill its promise to promote social progress, considering the four purposes of education. On a global level for moving policy forward, we recommend a balanced approach to educational reform, including teacher education, while putting more emphasis on the civic and humanistic purposes. More research-informed policy is required, taking into account different methodological approaches focusing on all four purposes of education – beyond PISA and university rankings – that combine global and local research perspectives. Concerning governance structures, we recommend that they are flexible, participatory, and accountable, considering the political and social contexts.

In the following we present six specific recommendations bolstering the contribution of education to social progress and coping with twenty-first-century challenges.

19.5.1   Implementing the Sustainable Development Goals

One key area of international debate revolves around the implementation of initiatives and agendas such as Education for All and the Millennium Development Goals. It has been frequently argued that international efforts have focused far too narrowly on increasing access to formal education, without attending to the quality and contents of learning. Another criticism is that international initiatives to expand and improve education may tend to rely on a "Western" view of what constitutes "development." Authors such as Amartya Sen, Martha Nussbaum, Arturo Escobar, Robert Chambers, and James Ferguson have argued for a range of alternative conceptualizations of the term, capable of providing space for indigenous and local knowledges; diverse understandings of what constitutes a "good life;" and acknowledgment of the effects of unequal global relationships (Sen 1999; Alkire 2005; Hulme 2007). This shift in academic discourse has run parallel to a shift in international development policy, which is increasingly moving away from an idea of "development" being organized *for* the global South *by* actors in the global North (Skinner, Blum, and Bourn 2013).

Notwithstanding the validity of many criticisms, the nature of globalization demands that educational programs in all countries prepare young people to understand global relationships and concerns, cope with complex problems, and live with rapid change and uncertainty. Insufficient recognition of the importance of these issues undermines international efforts to engage all citizens around the world with developmental processes and debates on providing quality education to all.

The new agenda of Sustainable Development Goals for 2030 calls for a new cooperative paradigm based on the concept of "full global partnership" and the principle that "no one will be left behind." The scale and scope of the ambition requires particularly strong partnerships at every level with young people, who are already engaged in making the goals a reality (UN 2016).

The stated Sustainable Goal for education is to "ensure inclusive and equitable quality education and promote lifelong learning opportunities for all." This goal greatly expands the ambitions of the previous agendas in scope, geographical coverage, and policy focus: from access to primary education to quality learning opportunities at all levels of education in a lifelong perspective; from low-income and conflict-affected areas to a universal agenda applicable to all countries; from formal education to a concern for equitable access to post-basic education and training for youth and adults through appropriate learning opportunities; and a strong focus on the relevance of learning outcomes for work and citizenship in a global and interconnected world. The knowledge, skills, values, and attitudes required by citizens should be acquired through education for sustainable development and global citizenship education, which includes peace and human rights education, as well as intercultural education and education for international understanding (UNESCO 2016).

Implementing these goals at country level implies an effort to align national policies and plans to the targets and focus areas reflected in the 2030 agenda for sustainable development. UNESCO has started a series of regional meetings to build a common understanding of the Sustainable Development Goals for education and to set the foundation for supporting its implementation. However, agreements reached at international conferences do not translate easily into actual policies by individual countries or the international community, since these depends more on the internal conditions of the countries than on their commitment to the goals.

19.5.2 Expanding Access and Improving the Quality of Early Childhood Education

Numerous studies demonstrate that early childhood education brings a wide range of benefits, both social and economic: better child wellbeing and learning outcomes; more equitable outcomes and a reduction in poverty; increased intergenerational social mobility; greater female labor market participation and gender equality; decreased fertility rates; and better social and economic development for society at large (Campbell et al. 2002; OECD 2006). The health, wellbeing, and economic benefits are particularly strong in lower-income countries (UNICEF 2007).

However, it is not only the length of attendance that matters, but also – and even more so – the quality (Espinosa 2002; Sheridan 2007; Tietze 2010; Britto, Yoshikawa, and Boller 2011). In the short term, a good, supportive environment contributes to the child's linguistic-cognitive development. In the long run, it leads to better final school degrees, higher income, and lower rates of criminality. High-quality preschool education leads to better cognitive, language, and math performance, broader scholastic abilities, and the ability to cope with everyday situations. Children from disadvantaged families and migrant backgrounds who attend high-quality early education have reduced rates of grade retention in their study life. However, if the subsequent school has low quality, the positive effects of high-quality preschool education is reduced (Campbell et al. 2002).

As money invested in early childhood development and education can yield significant public returns, governments are increasingly working to assist families and support children (Gertler et al. 2013). Between 1998 and 2011, public expenditure on young children in the form of child care and preschool increased 55 percent on average across OECD countries. However, there are large differences in the percentage of GDP that countries spent on child care and preschool. Even in the OECD countries, preschool places for very young children are lacking (OECD 2015). Furthermore, the quality of child care and preschool education is very mixed. To move forward the contribution of education to social progress, expanded access to early childhood education is needed, as well as improvement in its quality.

19.5.3 Improving the Quality of Schools

Despite the large differences among countries and cultural settings, there is a strong consensus on what makes education institutions

perform well and meet their expected goals, in three broad quality areas: *quality of processes*, the learners' direct interactions with their group, with the educators, and with surroundings; *quality of structures*, institutional characteristics such as group size, student–teacher ratio, teacher qualifications, and spatial and material conditions; and *quality of orientation*, curriculum, institutional-specific concepts, educational approach, and staff goals and values. Sustainably successful schools need to combine these factors, as they are highly related. This classification scheme of quality is primarily used in research on early childhood education (Tietze, Roßbach, and Grenner 2005) but also applies to general education (Scheerens 2000).

Research on the quality of schools tends to deal mostly with the effectiveness and quality of school management, and the findings of a vast literature can be summarized in six dimensions: (Bonsen and Bos 2010; Scheerens, Glas, and Thomas 2003): (1) Achievement orientation: high but appropriate expectations for both teachers and students provide a positive stimulus for the school's pedagogical work. (2) Well-structured learning atmosphere: students learn better and take responsibility for themselves in an environment where everybody feels valued and secured. This includes a positive school climate, among students as well as between students and the teaching staff. (3) Professional cooperation among teachers: there should be broad consensus among the teaching staff in terms of pedagogical goals; teachers should work together in formulating goals and in planning and developing their classroom instruction. (4) Pedagogical leadership: the school's leadership should go beyond purely administrative matters. The responsibilities of school leaders include supporting, evaluating, and developing teaching quality; goal-setting, assessment, and accountability; strategic financial and human resource management; and collaborating with other schools. (5) Quality of the enacted curriculum: schools need to ensure alignment between the intended, enacted, and received curriculum. This requires school-level reflection regarding its pedagogical work. (6) Evaluation focus: evaluation is important, and systematic monitoring of student performance, feedback on instruction, and internal as well as external evaluations need to take place at the institutional level.

Effective schools are *results-oriented*, *output-oriented*, and *competency-oriented*, and educators and school leaders are required to define learning goals, take targeted measures to achieve these goals, measure and assess whether and to what extent goals have been achieved, derive new measures as a consequence of this, initiate and conduct internal evaluations (i.e. effectiveness analyses), and handle and make use of the results of external evaluations (Schober et al. 2012). Consequently, investment should be made in high-quality training for teachers and leaders with differentiated quality-assurance arrangements providing a multitude of comprehensive learning opportunities (Ingvarson et al., 2013).

19.5.4 Enhancing the Professional Role of Educators

There is a high degree of consensus worldwide about the crucial role of teachers in reaching the four purposes of education. Teachers are not just carriers of knowledge and information, but also play an important role in the cultural and political discourse. They have a significant impact on children's quality of life – including their relationships with peers and adults, and their dispositions toward learning and life more generally. They are role models and conveyors of implicit values and modes of behavior, which cannot be simply codified in books or transmitted through new technologies (Sachs 2003).

Not all teachers are effective, not all teachers are experts, and not all teachers have powerful effects on students (Rivkin, Hanushek, and Kain 2005; Hanushek and Rivkin 2006; Hattie 2008). In the most successful education systems, teaching is a prestigious and well-paid profession, and teachers are recruited from among the best-educated students. In others, particularly in low- and middle-income countries, teaching does not attract the most talented. In these contexts, teaching education institutions tend to be also of low prestige and less endowed than other higher education institutions, and teachers are often not properly prepared to deal with the high expectations and often difficult tasks of providing good-quality education for children coming from poor socio-economic environments.

A common reaction, well documented in Latin America and elsewhere, is that teachers, particularly in the public sector, get organized in trade unions and political movements which allow them to assure some benefits in terms of salary, job stability, and working conditions, but oppose the establishment of external standards and assessments, placing the responsibility for poor outcomes on the general conditions of the population or the lack of support from their governments (Bastick 2000; Liang 2000; Murillo et al. 2002; Sachs 2003; Vaillant 2004). In this situation, in countries like Mexico and Brazil, which have some of the worst results in international assessments such as PISA, efforts to reform and improve public education alternate between entering into confrontation with the teachers' unions, as in Mexico, or attending their demands without the corresponding responsibilities, as in Brazil. In these situations, many families that can pay prefer to put their children in private schools, which often can recruit the best teachers, further depressing the quality of the public sector. In other countries such as Finland and Canada, teacher unions and/or professional organizations have become important supporters and drivers of progressive educational reform. Hence, it is important to design governance arrangements in such a way as to ensure that stakeholders engage in collective problem-solving rather than zero-sum bargaining for particularistic benefits (Sahlberg 2014; Fullan and Rincon-Gallardo 2016).

19.5.5 Making Higher and Vocational Education More Inclusive and Socially Relevant

Access and quality issues in general education in low- and middle-income countries have led governments and international organizations to give priority to investments in primary education. This view was supported by studies, since the 1970s, showing that the rates of return were higher at this level than for higher education, which should not be supported because it would be a diversion of public money to the benefit of small elites (Psacharopoulos and Hinchliffe 1973).

This understanding has changed since the year 2000 with the publication, by an international task force convened by UNESCO and the World Bank, of a report which stressed the importance of higher education. The report questioned the use of rates of return to justify existing education priorities, arguing that they were inadequate to capture the broad social and cultural impact of higher education, and also its role in innovation (The Task Force on Higher Education and Society 2000). The task force argued that higher education was essential to provide increasing numbers of students, especially those from disadvantaged backgrounds, with specialized skills; to produce a body of students with a general education that encouraged flexibility and innovation; to teach students not just what is currently known, but also how to keep their knowledge up to date; and to increase the amount and quality of in-country research.

To fulfill these purposes, higher education would need to develop a set of core qualities, including: sufficient autonomy, with governments providing clear supervision, while avoiding day-to-day micro-management; explicit differentiation, allowing institutions to play to their strengths and serve different needs, while competing for funding, faculty, and students; cooperation as well as competition; and increased openness, encouraging higher education institutions to develop knowledge- and revenue-sharing links with business and to deepen dialogue with society, which would lead to stronger democracy and more resilient nation-states.

This broad view of the importance of higher education is shared by scholars and significant sectors of the higher education communities in the United States and Europe, who are concerned about the trend of giving extreme priority to the role of higher education institutions as agencies for workforce training and technological innovation, to the detriment of the classical values of academic quality, collegiality, autonomy, and intellectual freedom, which were the basis for the development of the best university traditions in many countries. Studying the new entrepreneurial universities, Burton C. Clark finds that, at their best, they provide "new foundations for the rebuilding of internal collegiality and external autonomy … [and] ways to integrate … many disparate parts around the assertion of a distinctive character" (Clark 2001: 23). The same need to rebuild the university's core foundations occurs in Europe, where "the University has had to re-think its rationale, identity and foundations, its ethos, codes of behavior and primary allegiances and loyalties. There has been a need to explain and justify foundational institutional principles and rules and, for example, to give policy-makers and citizens good reasons for accepting university autonomy and individual academic freedom" (Gornitzka et al. 2007: 184).

Besides higher education, scholars and policy-makers should pay more attention to the potential of vocational as an alternative to academic higher education. Both in the OECD world and in lower-income countries and transition economies, VET can promote social inclusion and labor market participation for young people who do not make it to college or university. However, maximizing the potential of VET hinges on several conditions: VET needs a significant degree of commitment both from the public sector and from employers to become an attractive choice for youth. It also needs to be well connected to pathways toward higher and further education.

19.5.6 Fulfilling the Promises of Digital Technologies

The diffusion of microcomputers and the internet in the 1990s was perceived by many as heralding a profound revolution in education. The opportunity to communicate via technology was supposed to mark a massive shift in the experience of teaching and learning, breaking the schools' walls and freeing students and teachers from the rituals of sequential education and rote learning, to be replaced with individualized education and the ability to have all the world's information at one's fingertips. In 2005, the Media Lab of the Massachusetts Institute of Technology announced the "One Laptop Per Child" program, which was expected to start with the production of one million computers by 2007, initially priced at one hundred dollars each, and was soon adopted by many governments in low- and middle-income countries. In the 2000s, many universities, non-profit organizations, and private companies started to roll out "Massive Open Online Courses" (MOOCs) that were supposed to provide access to high-quality learning opportunities, often for free anywhere in the world and at any time.

Assessments of these first experiences replaced the original enthusiasm with cautious optimism. It was clear, from the onset, that a major obstacle for the dissemination of these technologies in low- and middle-income countries was the lack of appropriate communications and support infrastructure, raising concerns about an emerging "digital divide" (Norris 2001; Sorj 2003; Warschauer 2004). A careful analysis of the One Laptop Per Child program in Peru in 2002 did not find any evidence of impact in school participation or improvement in achievement in language and mathematics, although it did find some improvement in general cognitive abilities (Cristia et al. 2013). An analysis of the links between access to computers and student achievement using data from PISA in 2004 found that, once family background and school characteristics were controlled for, the relationship between student achievement and the availability of computers was negative for home computers and insignificant for school computers (Wössmann and Fuchs 2004). The initial enthusiasm for MOOCs was dampened by the large number of enrolled students who never completed their courses, which is also the case for the more traditional distance education programs.

The recent spread of low-cost mobile phones, even in poorer regions, has softened concerns about the digital divide, though high-quality internet in schools is still a challenge. But the current consensus is that sheer availability of communications hardware does not replace the need for good teaching, proper school environment, effective learning tools, and standards.

The earlier priority of providing access is being replaced by efforts to develop science-based software to deliver the required contents to the students in the best possible way and teaching methodologies to turn technological devices into instruments that engage students with learning. Instead of individualized, distance learning or unsupervised networking, the current emphasis is on blended learning, which combines digital media with new teaching methodologies in the classroom, attempting to reach a diversity of student needs through a combination of group and individualized work. Personal interaction of students with teachers remains indispensable, but the new technologies can provide even less-qualified teachers with tools and support to improve their performance (Arnett 2016), while students can be guided in their learning process by software that adjusts the lessons to their specific needs.

Two recent reports by the New Media Consortium, an international network of experts in education technology, present an updated outline of what to expect from the contribution of technology to education. For primary and secondary education, the main trends are in redesigning learning spaces, rethinking how schools work, the development of collaborative learning, coding as literacy, and making the students creators; and the main challenges are the development of authentic learning experiences and the need to rethink the role of teachers. For higher education, the main trends are the development of blended learning designs and collaborative learning, leading to advanced cultures of innovation and deeper learning approaches; and the main challenges include improving digital literacy, integrating formal and informal learning, managing knowledge obsolescence and rethinking the roles of education (Adams Becker et al. 2016; Adams Becker et al. 2017).

In the same vein, the Office of Educational Technology of the US Department of Education lists as central trends the engagement and empowerment of learning through technology, the combination of teaching with technology, the importance of leadership in the new digital context, and assessment of results (US Department of Education 2017). For UNESCO, the main issues related to ICT in education are developments in teacher education, mobile learning, open educational resources, lifelong learning, and the development of management information systems to guide education policies (UNESCO 2017).

The new information and communication technologies are not a magic bullet that will replace existing educational institutions and create a new learning world. But they can be powerful instruments to improve the quality and relevance of education and its contribution to social progress, once they grow from the current early stages of experimentation and trial and error into more established and proven practices.

References

Acemoglu, Daron, and David Autor. 2011. "Skills, Tasks and Technologies: Implications for Employment and Earnings." *Handbook of Labor Economics* 4: 1043–1171.

Adams Becker, S., A. Freeman, C. Giesinger Hall, M. Cummins, and B. Yuhnke. 2016. *NMC/CoSN Horizon Report: 2016 K-12 Edition*. Austin, Texas: The New Media Consortium.

Adams Becker, S., M. Cummins, A. Davis, A. Freeman, C. Hall Giesinger, and V. Ananthanarayanan. 2017. *MC Horizon Report: 2017 Higher Education Edition*. Texas: The New Media Consortium.

Alexander, Robin J. 2001a. "Border Crossings: Towards a Comparative Pedagogy." *Comparative Education* 37/4: 507–523.

Alexander, Robin J. 2001b. *Culture and Pedagogy: International Comparisons in Primary Education*. Oxford: Blackwell.

Alkire, Sabina. 2005. *Valuing Freedoms: Sen's Capability Approach and Poverty Reduction*. Oxford University Press on Demand.

Almond, Gabriel Abraham, and Sidney Verba. 1963. *The Civic Culture: Political Attitudes and Democracy in Five Nations*. Princeton, NJ: Princeton University Press.

Altbach, Philip G. 1981. *Student Politics, Perspectives for the Eighties*. Metuchen, NJ: Scarecrow Press.

Altbach, Philip G., and Jorge Balán. 2007. *World Class Worldwide: Transforming Research Universities in Asia and Latin America*. Baltimore, MD: The Johns Hopkins University Press.

Altbach, Philip G, and J. Salmi. 2011. *The Road to Academic Excellence: The Making of World-Class Research Universities*. Washington, DC: World Bank Publications.

Altbach, Philip G., and Daniel C. Levy. (eds.) 2005. *Private Higher Education: A Global Revolution*. Rotterdam: Sense Publishers.

Angrist, Joshua, Eric Bettinger, Erik Bloom, Elizabeth King, and Michael Kremer. 2002. "Vouchers for Private Schooling in Colombia: Evidence from a Randomized Natural Experiment." *American Economic Review* 92/5: 1535–1558.

Ansell, Ben W. 2008. "University Challenges: Explaining Institutional Change in Higher Education." *World politics* 60/2: 189–230.

Ansell, Ben W. 2010. *From the Ballot to the Blackboard: The Redistributive Political Economy of Education*. Cambridge: Cambridge University Press.

Apple, Michael W. 1996. *Cultural Politics and Education. The John Dewey Lecture*. New York: Teachers College Press.

Arnett, Thomas. 2016. *Teaching in the Machine Age: How Innovation Can Make Bad Teachers Good and Good Teachers Better*. Redwood City, CA: Christensen Institute.

Ashley, Laura Day, Claire McLoughlin, Monazza Aslam, et al. 2014. "The role and Impact of Private Schools in Developing Countries." Education Rigorous Literature Review. Birmingham: University of Birmingham.

Autor, David H. 2014. "Skills, Education, and the Rise of Earnings Inequality among the 'Other 99 Percent'" *Science* 344/6186: 843–851.

Baker, David, and Gerald K. LeTendre. 2005. *National Differences, Global Similarities: World Culture and the Future of Schooling*. Stanford, CA: Stanford University Press.

Barber, Michael, and Mona Mourshed. 2007. *How the World's Best-Performing School Systems Come Out on the Top*. London: McKinsey & Company.

Bastick, Tony. 2000. "Why Teacher Trainees Choose the Teaching Profession: Comparing Trainees in Metropolitan and Developing Countries." *International Review of Education* 46/3: 343–349.

Becker, Gary Stanley. 1973. *Human Capital: A Theoretical and Empirical Analysis, with Special Reference to Education*, third edition. Chicago and London: The University of Chicago Press.

Benavot, Aaron, and Phyllis Riddle. 1988. "The Expansion of Primary Education, 1870–1940: Trends and Issues." *Sociology of Education* 61: 191–210.

Ben-David, Joseph. 1977. *Centers of Learning: Britain, France, Germany, United States: An Essay*. New York: McGraw-Hill.

Benson, Lee, Ira Richard Harkavy, and John L. Puckett. 2007. *Dewey's Dream. Universities and Democracies in an Age of Education Reform: Civil Society, Public Schools, and Democratic Citizenship*. Philadelphia: Temple University Press.

Bernasconi, Andrés. 2007. "Is There a Latin American Model of the University?" *Comparative Education Review* 52/1: 27–52.

Bernstein, Basil. 1971. *Class, Codes and Control. Volume 1: Theoretical Studies Towards A Sociology of Language*. London: Routledge & Kegan.

Beyer, Landon E., and Daniel P. Liston. 1996. *Curriculum in Conflict: Social Visions, Educational Agendas, and Progressive School Reform*. New York: Teachers College Press.

Biesta, Gert, Maria De Bie, and Danny Wildemeersch. 2014. *Civic Learning, Democratic Citizenship and the Public Sphere*. Dordrecht: Springer.

Bloom, D.E., D. Canning, and K. Chan. 2006. *Higher Education and Economic Development in Africa*. Washington, DC: World Bank.

Boghossian, Paul. 2007. *Fear of Knowledge: Against Relativism and Constructivism*. Oxford: Clarendon Press.

Bohlinger, Sandra. 2008. "Competences as the Core Element of the European Qualifications Framework." *European Journal of Vocational Training* 42/1: 96–112.

Boli, John, Francisco O Ramirez, and John W Meyer. 1985. "Explaining the Origins and Expansion of Mass Education." *Comparative Education Review* 29/2: 145–170.

Bonsen, M., and W. Bos. 2010. "Bildungspsychologie auf der Mesoebene: Die Betrachtung von Bildungsinstitutionen [Educational Psychology on the Meso-Level: Considering Educational Institutions]," in C. Spiel, P. Schober, P. Wagner, and R. Reimann (eds.), *Bildungspsychologie*. Göttingen: Hogrefe.

Botticini, Maristella, and Zvi Eckstein. 2012. *The Chosen Few*. Princeton, NJ: Princeton University Press.

Bourdieu, Pierre, and Jean Claude Passeron. 1970. *La reproduction; éléments pour une théorie du système d'enseignement*. Paris: éditions de Minuit.

Bowles, Samuel, and Herbert Gintis. 1973. *Schooling in Capitalist America*. New York: Basic Books.

Brady, Susan A, and Donald P Shankweiler. 2013. *Phonological Processes in Literacy: A Tribute to Isabelle Y. Liberman*. New York: Routledge.

Breunig, Christian, and Marius R. Busemeyer. 2012. "Fiscal Austerity and the Trade-Off between Public Investment and Social Spending." *Journal of European Public Policy* 19/6: 921–938.

Brighouse, Harry, and Adam Swift. 2006. "Equality, Priority, and Positional Goods." *Ethics* 116/3: 471–497.

Britto, Pia Rebello, Hirokazu Yoshikawa, and Kimberly Boller. 2011. "Quality of Early Childhood Development Programs in Global Contexts: Rationale for Investment, Conceptual Framework and Implications for Equity." *Social Policy Report* 25/2.

Bromley, Patricia, John W. Meyer, and Francisco O. Ramirez. 2011. "The Worldwide Spread of Environmental Discourse in Social Studies, History, and Civics Textbooks, 1970–2008." *Comparative Education Review* 55/4: 517–545.

Brown, Phillip. 2000. "The Globalisation of Positional Competition?" *Sociology* 34/4: 633–653.

Brown, Phillip. 2003. "The Opportunity Trap: Education and Employment in a Global Economy." Cardiff: School of Social Sciences, Cardiff University.

Brunello, Giorgio, and Daniele Checchi. 2007. "Does School Tracking Affect Equality of Opportunity? New International Evidence." *Economic Policy* 22/52: 782–861.

Brunner, José Joaquin, and Daniel Uribe. 2007. *Mercados universitarios: el nuevo escenario de la educación superior [University markets: The New Scenario of Higher Education]*. Santiago: Ediciones Universidad Diego Portales.

Bruns, Barbara, Deon Filmer, and Harry Anthony Patrinos. 2011. *Making Schools Work: New Evidence on Accountability Reforms*. Washington, DC: World Bank Publications.

Burman, Anders. 2016. "Damnés Realities and Ontological Disobedience: Notes on the Coloniality of Reality in Higher Education in the Bolivian Andes and Beyond," in Ramón Grosfoguel, Roberto Hernández, and Ernesto Rosen Velásquez (eds.), *Decolonizing the Westernized University*. Lanham, MD: Lexington Books.

Burns, Tracey, and Tom Schuller. 2007. "The Evidence Agenda," in OECD (ed.), *Evidence in Education: Linking Research and Policy*. Paris: OECD.

Busemeyer, Marius R. 2013. "Education Funding and Individual Preferences for Redistribution." *European Sociological Review* 29/6: 1122–1133.

Busemeyer, Marius R., and Kathleen Thelen. 2015. "Non-standard Employment and Systems of Skill Formation in European Countries," in W. Eichhorst and P. Marx (eds.), *Non-Standard Employment in Post-Industrial Labour Markets: An Occupational Perspective*. London: Edward Elgar.

Busemeyer, Marius, Philipp Lergetporer, and Ludger Wössmann. 2017. "Public Opinion and the Acceptance and Feasibility of Educational Reforms," in *European Expert Network on Economics Education*. Luxembourg: Publications Office of the European Union.

Busemeyer, M. R., J. L. Garritzmann, E. Neimanns, and R. Nezi. 2017. "Investing in Education in Europe: Evidence from a Survey of Public Opinion in Eight European Countries." *Journal of European Social Policy* 28/1: 34–54.

Campbell, Frances A., Craig T. Ramey, Elizabeth Pungello, Joseph Sparling, and Shari Miller-Johnson. 2002. "Early Childhood Education: Young Adult Outcomes from the Abecedarian Project." *Applied Developmental Science* 6/1: 42–57.

Carnoy, Martin. 1978. *Segmented Labor Markets: A Review of the Theoretical and Empirical Literature and Its Implications for Educational Planning*. IIEP Working Paper. Paris: UNESCO; International Institute for Educational Planning.

Castles, Francis G. 2013. "The Real Issue for Future Comparative Policy Research: Does Government Matter?" in Klaus Armingeon (ed.), *Staatstätigkeiten, Parteien und Demokratie: Festschrift für Manfred G. Schmidt*. Dordrecht: Springer.

Clark, Burton R. 2001. "The Entrepreneurial University: New Foundations for Collegiality, Autonomy, and Achievement." *Higher Education Management* 13/2: 9–24.

Cogan, John, and Ray Derricott. 2014. *Citizenship for the 21st Century: An International Perspective on Education*. New York: Routledge.

Coleman, James S. 1966. *Equality of Educational Opportunity*. Washington, DC: US Department of Health, Education, and Welfare.

Coleman, James S. 1968. *Equal Educational Opportunity*. Cambridge, MA: Harvard Educational Review.

Collins, Randall. 1979. *The Credential Society*. New York: Academic Press.

Cox, Cristián, Robinson Lira, and Renato Gazmuri. 2009. "Currículos escolares e suas orientações sobre história, sociedade e política: significados para a coesão social na América Latina" [School Curricula and Their Orientation Regarding History, Society and Politics: Implications for Social Cohesion in Latin America] in Simon Schwartzman and Cristián Cox (eds.), *Políticas Educacionais e Coesão Social – uma agenda latinoamericana* [Social Cohesion: A Latin American Agenda]. Rio de Janeiro and São Paulo: Elsevier; Instituto Fernando Henrique Cardoso.

Cristia, Julián P., Pablo Ibarrarán, Santiago Cueto, Ana Santiago, and Eugenio Severín. 2013. "Tecnología y desarroll en la niñez: Evidencia del programa Una Laptop por Niño" [Technology and Child Development: Evidence from the One Laptop per Child Program]. IDB Working Papers. Washington, DC: International Development Program.

Crossley, Michael. 2014. "Global League Tables, Big Data and the International Transfer of Educational Research Modalities." *Comparative Education* 50/1: 15–26.

Dalton, Russell J, and Christian Welzel. 2014. *The Civic Culture Transformed: From Allegiant to Assertive Citizens*. New York: Cambridge University Press.

de Oliveira Andreotti, Vanessa, Sharon Stein, Cash Ahenakew, and Dallas Hunt. 2015 "Mapping Interpretations of Decolonization in the Context of Higher Education." *Decolonization: Indigeneity, Education & Society* 4/1: 21–40.

Dobbins, Michael, and Marius R Busemeyer. 2015. "Socio-economic Institutions, Organized Interests and Partisan Politics: the Development of Vocational Education in Denmark and Sweden." *Socio-economic Review* 13/2: 259–284.

Drori, Gili S., and John W. Meyer. 2006. "Global Scientization: An Environment for Expanded Organization" in G.S. Drori, J.G. Meyer, and H. Hwang (eds.), *Globalization and Organization*. Oxford: Oxford University Press.

Durkheim, Émile. 1922. *Éducation et Sociologie* [Education and Sociology]. Edited by Jean-Marie Tremblay. Les Classiques des Sciences Sociales. Chicoutimi: Université du Québec à Chicoutimi.

Elacqua, Gregory. 2015. "Chile: The Quality of For-Profit Schooling," in S. Schwartzman (ed.), *Education in South America*. London: Bloomsbury Academic.

Espeland, Wendy Nelson, and Michael Sauder. 2007. "Rankings and Reactivity: How Public Measures Recreate Social Worlds 1." *American Journal of Sociology* 113/1: 1–40.

Espinosa, Linda Marie. 2002. *High-Quality Preschool: Why We Need It and What It Looks Like*. New Brunswick, NJ: National Institute for Early Education Research.

Estevez-Abe, Margarita, Torben Iversen, and David Soskice. 1999. "Social Protection and the Formation of Skills: A Reinterpretation of the Welfare State." 95th American Political Association Meeting, Atlanta.

Etzkowitz, Henry. 2008. *The Triple Helix: University-Industry-Government Innovation in Action*. New York and London: Routledge.

Feniger, Yariv, Idit Livneh, and Abraham Yogev. 2012. "Globalisation and the Politics of International Tests: The Case of Israel." *Comparative Education* 48/3: 323–335.

Freire, Paulo. 1970. *Pedagogy of the Oppressed*. New York: Herder and Herder.

Froumin, Isak, and Yaroslav Kouzminov. 2015. "Supply and Demand Patterns In Russian Higher Education," in Pundy Pillay, Romulo Pinheiro, and Simon Schwartzman (eds.), *Higher Education in the BRICS Countries: Investigating the Pact between Higher Education and Society*. Dordrecht: Springer.

Fullan, Michael, and Santiago Rincon-Gallardo. 2016. "Developing High-Quality Public Education in Canada: The Case of Ontario," in Frank Adamson, Björn Åstrand, and Linda Darling-Hammond (eds.), *Global Education Reform. How Privatization and Public Investment Influence Education Outcomes*. New York: Routledge.

Gall, Norman. 2016. "Shakespeare in Quixeramobim: Ceará Goes to School." *Braudel Papers* 49: 1–20.

Gawthrop, Richard, and Gerald Strauss. 1984. "Protestantism and Literacy in Early Modern Germany." *Past and Present* 104: 31–55.

Geiger, Roger L. 1993. *Research and Relevant Knowledge: American Research Universities since World War II*. New York: Oxford University Press.

Geiger, Roger L. 2004. *To Advance Knowledge: The Growth of American Research Universities, 1900–1940*. New Brunswick: Transaction Publishers. Original edition Oxford University Press, 1986.

Gertler, Paul, James Heckman, Rodrigo Pinto, et al. 2013. "Labor Market Returns to Early Childhood Stimulation: A 20-year Followup to an Experimental Intervention in Jamaica." Washington, DC. World Bank.

Gibbons, Michael, Camille Limoges, Helga Nowotny, et al. 1994. *The New Production of Knowledge: The Dynamics of Science and Research in Contemporary Societies*. London: SAGE.

Gingrich, Jane R. 2011. *Making Markets in the Welfare State: The Politics of Varying Market Reforms*. New York: Cambridge University Press.

Goldin, Claudia, and Lawrence F. Katz. 1997. "Why the United States Led in Education: Lessons from Secondary School Expansion, 1910 to 1940." *National Bureau of Economic Research* w6144: 683–723.

Gornitzka, Åse, Peter Maassen, Johan P. Olsen, and Bjørn Stensake. 2007. "'Europe of Knowledge': Search for a New Pact," in P. Maassen and J.P. Olsen (eds.), *University Dynamics and European Integration*. Dordrecht: Springer.

Goswami, Usha, and Peter Bryant. 1990. *Phonological Skills and Learning to Read*. Hove, East Sussex: Psychology Press.

Green, Andy, John Preston, and Jan Janmaat. 2006. *Education, Equality and Social Cohesion: A Comparative Analysis*. Houndmills, Hampshire: Palgrave MacMillan.

Grek, Sotiria. 2009. "Governing by Numbers: The PISA 'effect' in Europe." *Journal of Education Policy* 24/1: 23–37.

Grollmann, Philipp, Georg Spottl, and Michael Young. 2008. "Towards a European Qualifications Framework: Some Cautionary Observations." *Journal of European Industrial Training* 32/2: 128–137.

Grubb, W. Norton, and Marvin Lazerson. 2004. *The Education Gospel: The Economic Power of Schooling*. Cambridge, MA: Harvard University Press.

Gutmann, Amy, and Sigal Ben-Porath. 2015. "Democratic Education," in *The Encyclopedia of Political Thought*. Wiley Online Library.

Halász, Gábor, and Alain Michel. 2011. "Key Competences in Europe: Interpretation, Policy Formulation and Implementation." *European Journal of Education* 46/3: 289–306.

Hall, Peter A., and David Soskice. 2001. *Varieties of Capitalism: The Institutional Foundations of Comparative Advantage*. Oxford: Oxford University Press.

Hanna, Nelly. 2007. "Literacy and the Great Divide' in the Islamic World, 1300–1800." *Journal of Global History* 2/02: 175–193.

Hanushek, Eric A. 1986. "The Economics of Schooling: Production and Efficiency in Public Schools." *Journal of Economic Literature* 24/3: 1141–1177.

Hanushek, Eric A., and Steven G. Rivkin. 2006. "Teacher Quality"," in E.A. Hanushek and F. Welch (eds.), *Handbook of the Economics of Education, vol. 2*. Amsterdam: Elsevier.

Hanushek, Eric A, and Ludger Wössmann. 2006. "Does Educational Tracking Affect Performance and Inequality? Differences-in-Differences Evidence across Countries." *The Economic Journal* 116/510: C63–C76.

Hanushek, Eric A., and Ludger Wössmann. 2012. "Schooling, Educational Achievement, and the Latin American Growth Puzzle." *Journal of Development Economics* 99/2: 497–512.

Hanushek, Eric A, Guido Schwerdt, Simon Wiederhold, and Ludger Wössmann. 2015. "Returns to Skills around the World: Evidence from PIAAC." *European Economic Review* 73: 103–130.

Harmon, Colm, Hessel Oosterbeek, and Ian Walker. 2003. "The Returns to Education: Microeconomics." *Journal of Economic Surveys* 17: 115–156.

Harrison, Lawrence E., and Samuel P. Huntington. 2000. *Culture Matters: How Values Shape Human Progress*, first edition. New York: Basic Books.

Hattie, John. 2008. *Visible Learning: A Synthesis of Over 800 Meta-analyses Relating to Achievement*. Abingdon, Oxfordshire: Routledge.

Hayes, William. 2006. *The Progressive Education Movement: Is It Still a Factor in Today's Schools?* Lanham, MD: Rowman & Littlefield Education.

Heckman, James J. 2006. "Skill Formation and the Economics of Investing in Disadvantaged Children." *Science* 312: 1900–1902.

Heckman, James J., Lance J. Lochner, and Petra E. Todd. 2006. "Earnings Functions, Rates of Return and Treatment Effects: The Mincer Equation and Beyond," in E. Hanushek and F. Welch (eds.), *The Handbook of the Economics of Education, vol. 1*. Amsterdam: Elsevier.

Hedges, Larry V., Terri D. Pigott, Joshua R. Polanin, et al. 2016. "The Question of School Resources and Student Achievement: A History and Reconsideration." *Review of Research in Education* 40:143–168.

Heikkinen, Anja, and Lorenz Lassnigg. (eds.) 2015 *Myths and Brands in Vocational Education*. Newcastle upon Tyne: Cambridge Scholars Publishing.

Hersch, Joni. 1991. "Education Match and Job Match." *The Review of Economics and Statistics* 73: 140–144.

Hollis, M. 1982. "Education as a Positional Good." *Journal of Philosophy of Education* 16/2: 235–244.

Howell, William G., and Paul E. Peterson. 2006. *The Education Gap: Vouchers and Urban Schools*. Washington, DC: Brookings Institution Press.

Hulme, David. 2007. *The Making of the Millennium Development Goals: Human Development meets Results-Based Management in an Imperfect World*. Manchester: Brooks World Poverty Institute, University of Manchester.

Hyslop-Margison, Emery J., and Johannes Strobel. 2007. "Constructivism and Education: Misunderstandings and Pedagogical Implications." *The Teacher Educator* 43: 72–86.

Ingvarson, Lawrence, John Schwille, Maria Teresa Tatto, et al. 2013. *An Analysis of Teacher Education Context, Structure, and Quality-Assurance Arrangements in Teds-M Countries: Findings from the IEA Teacher Education and Development Study in Mathematics (Teds-M)*. Amsterdam: IEA.

Iversen, T., and J. D. Stephens. 2008. "Partisan Politics, the Welfare State, and Three Worlds of Human Capital Formation." *Comparative Political Studies* 41/4–5: 600–637.

Jakobi, Anja P. 2009. "Global Education Policy in the Making: International Organisations and Lifelong Learning." *Globalisation, Societies and Education* 7/4: 473–487.

Jakobi, Anja P. 2011. "Political Parties and the Institutionalization of Education: A Comparative Analysis of Party Manifestos." *Comparative Education Review* 55/2: 189–209.

Jaksic, Ivan. 2006. *Andrés Bello: Scholarship and Nation-Building in Nineteenth-Century Latin America*. New York: Cambridge University Press.

Judt, Tony. 2006. *Postwar: A History of Europe Since 1945*. London: Penguin.

Jussim, Lee, Jacquelynne Eccles, and Stephanie Madon. 1996. "Social Perception, Social Stereotypes, and Teacher Expectations: Accuracy and the Quest for the Powerful Self-Fulfilling Prophecy." *Advances in Experimental Social Psychology* 28: 281–388.

Kamens, David H., and Connie L. McNeely. 2009. "Globalization and the Growth of International Educational Testing and National Assessment." *Comparative Education Review* 54/1: 5–25.

Kamerman, Sheila B. 2006. "A Global History of Early Childhood Education and Care." In *Paper Commissioned for the Education for All (EFA) Global Monitoring Report 2007*. Paris: UNESCO.

Kautz, Tim, James J. Heckman, Ron Diris, Bas ter Weel, and Lex Borghans. 2014. *Fostering and Measuring Skills: Improving Cognitive and Non-Cognitive Skills to Promote Lifetime Success*. Paris: OECD.

Kite, Mary E., Kay Deaux, and Elizabeth L. Haines. 2008. "Gender Stereotypes." *Psychology of Women: A Handbook of Issues and Theories* 2: 205–236.

Klitgaard, Michael Baggesen. 2008. "School Vouchers and the New Politics of the Welfare State." *Governance* 21/4: 479–498.

Kollmayer, Marlene, Barbara Schober, and Christiane Spiel. 2016. "Gender Stereotypes in Education: Development, Consequences, and Interventions." *European Journal of Developmental Psychology* online (June 6): 1–17.

Kosack, Stephen. 2014. "The Logic of Pro-poor Policymaking: Political Entrepreneurship and Mass Education." *British Journal of Political Science* 44/02: 409–444.

Lassnigg, Lorenz 2012. "'Use of Current Best Evidence' – Promises and Illusions, Limitations and Contradictions in the Triangle of Research, Policy and Practice." *International Journal of Training Research* 10/2: 179–203.

Lassnigg, Lorenz. 2016. "Apprenticeship Policies in Comparative Perspective. ET-Structures, Employment Relationship, Export." Sociological Series Working Papers. Vienna: Institute for Advanced Studies.

Lassnigg, Lorenz, Jakob Hartl, Martin Unger, and Iris Schwarzenbacher. 2017. "Higher Education Institutions and Knowledge Triangle: Improving the Interaction between Education, Research and Innovation." IHS Sociological Series Working Paper 118. Vienna: Institute for Advanced Studies.

Learning Metrics Task Force. 2013. *Toward Universal Learning: What Every Child Should Learn*. Montreal and Washington, DC: UNESCO Institute for Statistics and Centre for Universal Education at Brookings.

Lee, Valerie E., and David T. Burkam. 2002. *Inequality at the Starting Gate: Social Background Differences in Achievement as Children Begin School*. Washington, DC: Economic Policy Institute.

Lepenies, Wolf. 1988. *Between Literature and Science: The Rise of Sociology*, vol. 10. Cambridge: Cambridge University Press.

Leslie, Larry L. 1990. "*Rates of Return as Informer of Public Policy with Special Reference to World Bank and Third World Countries*." *Higher Education* 20/3: 271–286.

Levy, Daniel C. 1981. "Student Politics in Contemporary Latin America." *Canadian Journal of Political Science* 14/2: 353–376.

Levy, Daniel C. 1986. *Higher Education and the State in Latin America: Private Challenges to Public Dominance*. Chicago: University of Chicago Press.

Levy, Daniel C. 2006. "The Unanticipated Explosion: Private Higher Education's Global Surge." *Comparative Education Review* 50/2: 217–240.

Liang, Xiaoyan. 2000. *Teacher Pay in 12 Latin American Countries: How Does Teacher Pay Compare to Other Professions? What Determines Teacher Pay? Who Are the Teachers*? Washington, DC: World Bank, Latin America and the Caribbean Regional Office.

Lingard, Bob, Wayne Martino, Goli Rezai-Rashti, and Sam Sellar. 2015. *Globalizing Educational Accountabilities*. New York: Routledge.

Lubotsky, Darren, and Robert Kaestner. 2016. "Do Skills Beget Skills? Evidence on the Effect of Kindergarten Entrance Age on the Evolution of Cognitive and Non-cognitive Skill Gaps in Childhood." *Economics of Education Review* 53: 194–206.

Maassen, P., and Stensaker, B. 2011. "The Knowledge Triangle, European Higher Education Policy Logics and Policy Implications." *Higher Education* 61/6: 757–769.

Marginson, Simon. 2016. *Higher Education and the Common Good*. Melbourne: University Publishing Limited.

Mascolo, Michael F. 2009. "Beyond Student-Centered and Teacher-Centered Pedagogy: Teaching and Learning as Guided Participation." *Pedagogy and the Human Sciences* 1/1: 3–27.

Mazzucato, Mariana. 2013. *The Entrepreneurial State: Debunking Public vs. Private Sector Myths*. London: Anthem.

McEwan, Patrick J, and Martin Carnoy. 2000. "The Effectiveness and Efficiency of Private Schools in Chile's Voucher System." *Educational Evaluation and Policy Analysis* 22/3: 213–239.

McNeely, Connie L. 1995. "Prescribing National Education Policies: The Role of International Organizations." *Comparative Education Review* 39/4: 483–507.

Mettler, Suzanne. 2014. *Degrees of Inequality: How the Politics of Higher Education Sabotaged the American Dream*. New York: Basic Books.

Meyer, Heinz-Dieter, and Aaron Benavot. 2013. *PISA, Power, and Policy: The Emergence of Global Educational Governance*. Oxford: Symposium Books.

Meyer, John W., Patricia Bromley, and Francisco O. Ramirez. 2010. "Human rights in social science textbooks: Cross-national analyses, 1970–2008." *Sociology of Education* 83 (2): 111–134.

Meyer, John W., Francisco O. Ramirez, and Yasemin Nuhoğlu Soysal. 1992. "World Expansion of Mass Education, 1870–1980." *Sociology of Education* 1992: 128–149.

Mincer, Jacob. 1974. *Schooling, Experience, and Earnings. Human Behavior and Social institutions, 2*. New York: National Bureau of Economic Research; distributed by Columbia University Press.

Montenegro, Claudio E., and Harry A. Patrinos. 2014. "Comparable Estimates of Returns to Schooling around the World." World Bank Policy Research Working Paper 7020. Washington, DC: World Bank.

Moretti, Enrico. 2003. "Human Capital Externalities in Cities." Working Paper. Cambridge, MA: National Bureau of Economic Research.

Mullis, Ina V.S., Michael O. Martin, Teresa A. Smith, and International Association for the Evaluation of Educational Achievement. 2003. *Timss Assessment Frameworks and Specifications 2003*. Chestnut Hill, MA: International Study Center, Lynch School of Education, Boston College.

Murillo, Victoria, Mariano Tommasi, Lucas Ronconi, and Juan Sanguinetti. 2002. "The Economic Effects of Unions in Latin America: Teachers' Unions and Education in Argentina." IDB Working Paper 171. Washington, DC: Inter-American Development Bank.

Nisbet, Robert A. 1965. *Émile Durkheim: Makers of Modern Social Science*. Englewood Cliffs, NJ: Prentice-Hall.

Noddings, Nel. 1995. *Philosophy of Education*. Boulder, CO: Westview Press.

Norris, Pippa. 2001. *Digital Divide: Civic Engagement, Information Poverty, and the Internet Worldwide*. Cambridge: Cambridge University Press.

OECD. 2000. *Education at a Glance: OECD Indicators*. Paris: OECD.

OECD. 2006. *Starting Strong II. Early Childhood Education and Care*. Paris: OECD.

OECD. 2015. *Education at a Glance. OECD Indicators*. Paris: OECD.

OECD. 2016. *Education at a Glance: OECD Indicators.* Paris: OECD.

Park, Hyunjoon, and Pearl Kyei. 2011. "Literacy Gaps by Educational Attainment: A Cross-national Analysis." *Social Forces* 89/3: 879–904.

Peterson, Andrew. 2011. *Civic Republicanism and Civic Education: The Education of Citizens.* Houndmills, Hampshire: Palgrave Macmillan.

Pfeffer, Fabian T. 2008. "Persistent Inequality in Educational Attainment and Its Institutional Context." *European Sociological Review* 24/5: 543–565.

Pierson, Paul. 1993. "When Effect becomes Cause: Policy Feedback and Political Change." *World politics* 45/4: 595–628.

Psacharopoulos, George. 1994. "Returns to Investment in Education: A Global Update." *World Development* 22/9: 1325–1343.

Psacharopoulos, George, and Keith Hinchliffe. 1973. *Returns to Education: An International Comparison.* Amsterdam and New York: Elsevier.

Psacharopoulos, George, Carlos Rojas, and Eduardo Velez. 1992. "Achievement Evaluation of Colombia's Escuela Nueva: Is Multigrade the Answer?" Policy Research Working Papers. Washington, DC: Technical Dept. Latin America and the Caribbean Region, World Bank.

Putnam, Robert D. 2001. *Bowling Alone: The Collapse and Revival of American Community.* New York: Touchstone.

Putnam, Robert D. 2002. *Democracies in Flux: The Evolution of Social Capital in Contemporary Society.* Oxford and New York: Oxford University Press.

Ravitch, Diane. 2016. *The Death and Life of the Great American School System: How Testing and Choice Are Undermining Education.* New York: Basic Books.

Reese, William J. 2001. "The Origins of Progressive Education." *History of Education Quarterly* 41/1: 1–24.

Rivkin, Steven G., Eric A. Hanushek, and John F. Kain. 2005. "Teachers, Schools, and Academic Achievement." *Econometrica* 73/2: 417–458.

Rosenbaum, James E. 2001. *Beyond College for All: Career Paths for the Forgotten Half.* American Sociological Association's Rose Series in Sociology. New York: Russell Sage Foundation.

Rotherham, Andrew J., and Daniel T. Willingham. 2010. "'21st-Century' Skills." *American Educator* 34: 17–20.

Rutter, Michael. 1982. *Fifteen Thousand Hours: Secondary Schools and Their Effects on Children.* Cambridge, MA: Harvard University Press.

Sachs, Judyth. 2003. *The Activist Teaching Profession.* Buckingham, Buckinghamshire: Open University Press.

Sahlberg, Pasi. 2014. *Finnish Lessons 2.0: What Can the World Learn from Educational Change in Finland?* New York: Teachers College Press.

Scarborough, Hollis S. 2009. "Connecting Early Language and Literacy to Later Reading (Dis)abilities: Evidence, Theory, and Practice., in F. Fletcher-Campbell J. Soler, and G. Reid (eds.), *Approaching Difficulties in Literacy Development: Assessment, Pedagogy, and Programmes.* London: SAGE.

Scheerens, Jaap. 2000. *Improving School Effectiveness.* Paris: UNESCO International Institute for Educational Planning.

Scheerens, J., C. Glas, and S.M. Thomas. 2003. *Educational Evaluation, Assessment, and Monitoring – A Systematic Approach.* Lisse: Swets & Zeitlinger.

Schiefelbein, Ernesto. 1992. *Redefining Basic Education for Latin America: Lessons To Be Learned from the Colombian Escuela Nueva.* Paris: UNESCO; International Institute for Educational Planning.

Schober, B., J. Klug, M. Finsterwald, P. Wagner, and C. Spiel. 2012. "Ergebnisorientierte Qualitätsentwicklung von Schule: Spezifische Kompetenzen von Lehrkräften, Schulleiterinnen und Schulleitern [Outcome-Oriented Quality Development in Schools: Specific Competencies of Teachers, Students and Principals]," in B. Herzog-Punzenberger (ed.), *Nationaler Bildungsbericht Österreich 2012, Band 2: Fokussierte Analysen bildungspolitischer.* Graz, Austria: Leykam.

Schofer, Evan, and John W. Meyer. 2005. "The Worldwide Expansion of Higher Education in the Twentieth Century." *American Sociological Review* 70/6: 898–920.

Schofield, Janet Ward. 1995. "Improving Intergroup Relations among Students." www.researchgate.net/publication/234671774_Improving_Intergroup_Relations_among_Students.

Schultz, Theodore William. 1970. *Investment in Human Capital: The Role of Education and of Research.* New York: Free Press.

Schwartz, Seth J, Byron L Zamboanga, and Lorna Hernandez Jarvis. 2007. "Ethnic Identity and Acculturation in Hispanic Early Adolescents: Mediated Relationships to Academic Grades, Prosocial Behaviors, and Externalizing Symptoms." *Cultural Diversity and Ethnic Minority Psychology* 13/4: 364–373.

Schwartzman, S. 2011. "Academic Drift in Brazilian Education." *Pensamiento Educativo. Revista de Investigación Educacional Latinoamericana* 48/1: 14–26.

Schwartzman, S. 2013. "Uses and Abuses of Education Assessment in Brazil." *Prospects* 43/4: 269–288.

Schwartzman, S. 2015. "Demand and Policies for Higher Education," in S. Schwartzman, R. Pinheiro, and P. Pillay (eds.), *Higher Education in the BRICS Countries – Investigating the Pact between Higher Education and Society.* Dordrecht: Springer.

Schwartzman, S., R. Pinheiro, and P. Pillay. (eds.) 2015. *Higher Education in the BRICS Countries – Investigating the Pact between Higher Education and Society.* Dordrecht: Springer.

Schweisfurth, Michele. 2013. *Learner-Centred Education in International Perspective: Whose Pedagogy for Whose Development?* Abingdon, Oxfordshire: Routledge.

Sellar, Sam, and Bob Lingard. 2013. "The OECD and Global Governance in Education." *Journal of Education Policy* 28/5: 710–725.

Sen, Amartya. 1999. *Commodities and Capabilities.* New Delhi: Oxford University Press.

Shavit, Yossi, and Walter Muller. 2000. "Vocational Secondary Education – Where Diversion and Where Safety Net?" *European Societies* 2/1: 29–50.

Sheridan, Sonja. 2007. "Dimensions of Pedagogical Quality in Preschool." *International Journal of Early Years Education* 15/2: 197–217.

Sianesi, Barbara, and John Van Reenen. 2003. "The Returns to Education: Macroeconomics." *Journal of Economic Surveys* 17/2: 157–200.

Singh, M., T. Schuller, and D. Watson. 2009. *Learning Through Life. Inquiry into the Future for Lifelong Learning.* Leicester: NIACE.

Skinner, A., N. Blum, and D. Bourn. 2013. "Development Education and Education in International Development Policy: Raising Quality through Critical Pedagogy and Global Skills." *International Development Policy/ Revue internationale de politique de développement* 4/3.

Snow, C.P. 1959. *The Two Cultures and the Scientific Revolution.* Cambridge: Cambridge University Press.

Solga, Heike, Paula Protsch, Christian Ebner, and Christian Brzinsky-Fay. 2014. "The German Vocational Education and Training System: Its Institutional Configuration, Strengths, and Challenges." WZB Discussion Paper. Berlin: WZB Berlin Social Science Center.

Soltys, Dennis. 1997. *Education for Decline: Soviet Vocational and Technical Schooling from Khrushchev to Gorbachev.* Toronto: University of Toronto Press.

Somers, Marie-Andree, Patrick J. McEwan, and J. Douglas Willms. 2004. "How Effective are Private Schools in Latin America?" *Comparative Education Review* 48/1: 48–69.

Sorj, Bernardo. 2003. *Brazil@digitaldivide.com: Confronting Inequality in the Information Society.* Brasília: UNESCO Brasil.

Spence, Michael. 1973. "Job Market Signaling." *The Quarterly Journal of Economics* 87/3: 355–374.

Spiel, C. 2017. "Education and the Shaping of Identitites," in P. Webinger and A. Shahbasi (eds.), *Who Are You? States and the Quest for Identity.* Bitterfeld: Echoverlag.

Spring, Joel. 2008. "Research on Globalization and Education." *Review of Educational Research* 78/2: 330–363.

Steiner-Khamsi, Gita, and Ines Stolpe. 2006. *Educational Import: Local Encounters with Global Forces in Mongolia.* New York: Palgrave Macmillan.

Streeck, Wolfgang, and Daniel Mertens. 2011. "Fiscal Austerity and Public Investment: Is the Possible the Enemy of the Necessary?" MPIfG Discussion Paper 11/12. Cologne: Max Planck Institute for the Study of Societies.

Suárez, David F. 2007. "Human Rights and Curricular Policy in Latin America and the Caribbean." *Comparative Education Review* 51/3: 329–352.

Sung, Youl-Kwan, and Mi Ok Kang. 2012. "The Cultural Politics of National Testing and Test Result Release Policy in South Korea: A Critical Discourse Analysis." *Asia Pacific Journal of Education* 32/1: 53–73.

Takayama, Keita, Arathi Sriprakash, Raewyn Connell. 2017. "Toward a Postcolonial Comparative and International Education." *Comparative Education Review* 61/S1: 1–24.

The Task Force on Higher Education and Society. 2000. *Peril and Promise: Higher Education in Developing Countries.* Washington, DC: World Bank.

Thelen, Kathleen. 1999. "Historical Institutionalism in Comparative Politics." *Annual Review of Political Science* 2/1: 369–404.

Thelen, Kathleen. 2007. *How Institutions Evolve: The Political Economy of Skills in Germany, Britain, the United States, and Japan*. Cambridge: Cambridge University Press.

Thelen, Kathleen. 2012. "Varieties of Capitalism: Trajectories of Liberalization and the New Politics of Solidarity." *Annual Review of Political Science* 15: 137–159.

Tietze, Wolfgang. 2010. "Bildungspsychologie des Vorschulbereichs [Educational Psychology in Early Childhood Education]," in C. Spiel, P. Schober, P. Wagner, and R. Reimann (eds.), *Bildungspsychologie*. Göttingen: Hogrefe.

Tietze, W., H.G. Roßbach, and K. Grenner. 2005. *Kinder von 4 bis 8 Jahren. Zur Qualität der Erziehung und Bildung in Kindergarten, Grundschule und Familie [Children from 4 to 8. Towards Higher-Quality Education in Preschool, Elementary School and in the Family]*. Weinheim: Beltz.

Torney-Purta, Judith, Rainer Lehmann, Hans Oswald, and Wolfram Schulz. 2001. *Citizenship and Education in Twenty-Eight Countries: Civic Knowledge and Engagement at Age Fourteen*. Amsterdam: International Assocation for the Evaluation of Educational Achievement.

Trilling, Bernie, and Charles Fadel. 2009. *21st Century Skills: Learning for Life in Our Times*. San Francisco: John Wiley & Sons.

Trow, Martin. 2000. "From Mass Higher Education to Universal Access: The American Advantage." *Minerva* 37/4: 303–328.

Trow, Martin. 2006. "Reflections on the Transition from Elite to Mass to Universal Access: Forms and Phases of Higher Education in Modern Societies since WWII," in J.F. Forest and P. Altbach (eds.), *International Handbook of Higher Education*. Dordrecht: Springer.

Tuijnman, Albert, and Ann-Kristin Boström. 2002. "Changing Notions of Lifelong Education and Lifelong Learning." *International Review of Education* 48/1: 93–110.

Tylor, Edward Burnett. 1870. *Researches into the Early History of Mankind and the Development of Civilization*. London: John Murray.

UN. 2016. "Global Sustainable Development Report 2016." https://sustainabledevelopment.un.org/content/documents/2328GSDR 2016.pdf.

UN. 2017. "Sustainable Development Goals – Goal 4 – Ensure inclusive and quality education for all and promote lifelong learning." UNESCO. www.un.org/sustainabledevelopment/education/.

UNDP (United Nations Development Programme). 2017. *Arab Human Development Report 2016. Youth and the Prospects for Human Development in a Changing Reality*. New York: UNDP.

UNESCO. 2016. *Unpacking Sustainable Development Goal 4 Education 2030*. Paris: UNESCO.

UNESCO. 2017. "ICT in Education." UNESCO. www.unesco.org/new/en/unesco/themes/icts/policy/.

UNICEF. 2007. *A Human Rights-Based Approach to Education for All: A Framework for the Realization of Children's Right to Education and Rights within Education*. New York: UNICEF.

US Congress and House Committee on Education and Labor. 1965. *National Foundation on the Arts and the Humanities act of 1965*. Washington, DC: US Government Printing Office.

US Department of Education. 2017. *Reimagining the Role of Technology in Education: 2017 National Education Technology Plan Update*. Washington, DC: Department of Education.

Vaillant, Denise. 2004. *Construcción de la profesión docente en América Latina: tendencias, temas y debates [The Construction of the Teaching Profession in Latin America: Tendencies, Themes and Debates]*. Washington, DC: Preal.

Van de Werfhorst, Herman G., and Jonathan J.B. Mijs. 2010. "Achievement Inequality and the Institutional Structure of Educational Systems: A Comparative Perspective." *Annual Review of Sociology* 36: 407–428.

Vaughan, Rosie Peppin. 2013. "Complex Collaborations: India and International Agendas on Girls' and Women's Education, 1947–1990." *International Journal of Educational Development* 33/2: 118–129.

Vincent, David. 2000. *The Rise of Mass Literacy: Reading and Writing in Modern Europe, Themes in History*. Cambridge: Polity Press.

Voegtle, Eva M, Christoph Knill, and Michael Dobbins. 2011. "To What Extent Does Transnational Communication Drive Cross-national Policy Convergence? The Impact of the Bologna-Process on Domestic Higher Education Policies." *Higher Education* 61/1: 77–94.

Vorhaus, John, Kathryn Duckworth, David Budge, and Leon Feinstein. 2008. *The Social and Personal Benefits of Learning: A Summary of Key Research Findings*. London: Centre for Research on the Wider Benefits of Learning, Institute of Education, University of London.

Walter, Richard J. 1968. *Student Politics in Argentina: The University Reform and Its Effects, 1918–1964*, vol. 2: New York: Basic Books.

Walter, Richard J. 1969. "The Intellectual Background of the 1918 University Reform in Argentina." *The Hispanic American Historical Review* 49/2: 233–253.

Warschauer, M. 2004. *Technology And Social Inclusion: Rethinking the Digital Divide*. Cambridge, MA: The MIT Press.

Wells, Amy Stuart, and Allison Roda. 2016. "The Impact of Political Context on the Questions Asked and Answered: The Evolution of Education Research on Racial Inequality." *Review of Research in Education* 40/1: 62–93.

Wesselingh, Anton A. 2002. "Durkheim, Citizenship and Modern Education," in William S.F. Pickering and Geoffrey Walford (eds.), *Durkheim and Modern Education*. New York: Routledge.

White, John. 2003. *Rethinking the School Curriculum: Values, Aims and Purposes*. Abingdon, Oxfordshire: Routledge.

Whitty, Geoff. 1985. *Sociology and School Knowledge: Curriculum Theory, Research and Politics*. London: Methuen & Co. Ltd.

Wilkinson, Frank. 2013. *The Dynamics of Labour Market Segmentation*. Amsterdam: Elsevier.

Wolf, Alison. 2002. *Does Education Matter? Myths about Education and Economic Growth*. London: Penguin.

Wolf, Frieder. 2009. "The Division of Labour in Education Funding: A Cross-national Comparison of Public and Private Education Expenditure in 28 OECD Countries." *Acta Politica* 44/1: 50–73.

Wolf, Frieder, and Reimut Zohlnhöfer. 2009. "Investing in Human Capital? The Determinants of Private Education Expenditure in 26 OECD Countries." *Journal of European Social Policy* 19/3: 230–244.

Wong, Suk-Ying. 1991. "The Evolution of Social Science Instruction, 1900–86: A Cross-National Study." *Sociology of Education* 64: 33–47.

World Bank. 2012. *World Development Report 2012: Gender Equality and Development*. Washington, DC: World Bank.

World Bank. 2015. "World Databank - Education Statistics - All Indicators." http://databank.worldbank.org/data/reports.aspx?source=education-statistics-~-all-indicators.

World Values Survey Association. 2014. *World Values Survey Wave 6 2010–2014 Official Aggregate* v. 20141107. Madrid: Asep/JDS.

Wössmann, Ludger, and Thomas Fuchs. 2004. "Computers and Student Learning: Bivariate and Multivariate Evidence on the Availability and Use of Computers at Home and at School." CESIfo Working Paper 1321. Munich: CESIfo.

Young, Michael. 2013. "Overcoming the Crisis in Curriculum Theory: A Knowledge-Based Approach." *Journal of Curriculum Studies* 45/2: 101–118.

Zimmermann, Grégoire, Lyda Lannegrand-Willems, Claire Safont-Mottay, and Christine Cannard. 2015. "Testing New Identity Models and Processes in French-Speaking Adolescents and Emerging Adults Students." *Journal of Youth and Adolescence* 44/1: 127–141.

20

Belonging

Coordinating Lead Authors:[1]
Akeel Bilgrami, Prabhat Patnaik

Lead Authors:[2]
Faisal Devji, Michele Lamont, Ernesto Ottone, James Tully, Nira Wickramasinghe, Sue Wright

[1]   Affiliations: AB: Columbia University, USA; PP: Jawaharlal Nehru University, India.
[2]   Affiliations: FD: University of Oxford, UK; ML: Harvard University, USA; EO: University Diego Portales, Chile; JT: University
       of Victoria, Canada; NW: University of Leiden, Netherlands; SW: Portsmouth University, UK.

Summary

This chapter consists, first, of an extended *theoretical analysis* of the concept of belonging in three dimensions: belonging as "identity," belonging as "solidarity," and belonging as "the unalienated life." And second, there is an extended *empirical survey of different regions of the world* where belonging in one or other of its analytical dimensions has surfaced in certain socially, politically, and economically situated contexts.

Belonging as identity, it is argued, can be both subjective and objective, and it is the former that is most obviously present in identity politics since people tend to politically mobilize themselves on the basis of identities when they subjectively *identify* with some important aspect of their social lives – their class, their caste, their race, their gender, their nationality, etc. A detailed effort is made to consider the relation between the subjective and objective sides of identity, to define each of these, to locate the historical conditions in which each is prompted, and to address the question whether some of these identities (class identity, for instance) are more fundamental than others.

Belonging as solidarity, it is argued, may occur both in mobilizations toward some immediate and shared political goal but also in the broader social and cultural context when different groups with vastly different cultural and social and moral values may nevertheless seek to engage with one another via an empathetic form of reasoning. In the latter case they exhibit a form of solidarity in a more conceptual sense than in mere political activism.

Finally, belonging in the form of an unalienated life is considered as a very specific form of social relation that overcomes the individualistic atomization that is so prevalent in modernity, in particular a form of social relation that repudiates the pervasive individualist mentality that constantly threatens the possibilities of social cooperation toward the common good (whether it be the common good of a just political economy or sustainable environment).

Each of these three dimensions of identity raise very complex theoretical and practical issues and the chapter makes some detailed effort to address the most important of these.

On the question of social progress, both the theoretical analysis and the empirical survey of different regions of the world yield an overarching normative conclusion about the relations between these three dimensions of identity: There is social progress when belonging as identity – through deliberate social and political efforts at wider solidarities and socially grounded overcoming of individual-centered alienation – *becomes* more rather than less inclusive (the "becomes" here suggesting an essentially dynamic nature of the constitution of belonging).

How such progress is made may emerge from a variety of conditions and may be variably pursued, but our regional surveys suggest that central to these various possibilities is the need to stress and to integrate two different agencies in any large-scale effort toward these ends: on the one hand the role of the state and the policies and reforms it can enact, and on the other the element of democratic mobilization. The latter has two functions. Movements first of all put pressure on the state to enact policies that promote the conditions of cohesion that generate solidarities, civic rather than divided participation, and eventually unalienated social relations. But movements are also locations of public education through democratic collective deliberation, which, if sustained over time, helps to create solidarities that transcend particular sites of language, ethnicity, religion, etc. to a common register of common concepts and ideals. What forms these movements might take and what policies exactly they seek from the state will, of course, differ in different regional contexts.

Our different regional surveys throw up a range of further, more specific, conclusions. We very briefly and abbreviatedly list below two or three of these, just to give a vastly summarizing sense of the detail that may be found in these surveys.

The reports from Canada and Sri Lanka propose startlingly different policies, the former weighing in favor of recognition of communitarian identities that should be dialogically brought together, while the Sri Lankan report stresses a more top-down state intervention that discourages such communitarian differences in favour of a more civic form of popular participation. One report on Europe traverses the vexed forms of exclusion that owe to language, in particular how deliberative democracy may be blocked by language constraints – first by lack of knowledge of the language of debate and then further by lack of access to the conceptual register of debate. The report on Islamic nations is a historical account of how identities formed and ideologies developed into an ethical register, despite seemingly politically articulated goals.

Throughout the chapter, there is a sustained and sturdy conviction in a methodological stance that the ideal of belonging (in these aspects of the unalienated life and solidarity and inclusive identity) is what most deeply *underlies* the other great ideals of modern political thought, those of liberty and equality, and that if we lost sight of this more fundamental underlying ideal, then the pursuit of liberty and equality would be in danger of being reduced to an exercise in social engineering.

20.1   Introduction

Belonging is a relation that an individual bears to society or to some more specific group defined in terms of family, ethnicity, caste, tribe, nation, race, indigeneity, class, language, citizenry … This chapter will begin with an analytical elaboration of the theoretical issues at stake in the concept of belonging and then proceed with an extensive empirical report on how these questions of belonging have surfaced in different parts of the world. Though there is no effort to be globally comprehensive in this empirical reach, it will nevertheless briefly cover areas as far-flung as Europe, North America, Latin America, the Middle East, and South Asia.

20.2   Theoretical Issues: Belonging as Identity, Solidarity, and the Unalienated Life

The concept of belonging has been discussed along at least three different conceptual lines. One has to do with how and in what sense belonging bestows "identity." The concept of identity has over some decades become central, ever since the rise of identity politics, a form of politics that people are poised to mobilize themselves toward when they identify with a religion, a nationality, a caste, or a race – as a Muslim, as it might be, or a Québécois, or a Dalit, or African-American…

Another line of discussion has to do with interpreting belonging in terms of feelings of solidarity or fraternity with others in the wider group. A third has to do with the condition when belonging goes missing or is thwarted and difficult; often such a condition is discussed under the label "alienation," and belonging, therefore, is equated with the unalienated life.

The first of these – belonging as identity – is a more or less descriptive issue, whereas the second and third – belonging as entailing supportive emotions of compassion and solidarity, and belonging as the unalienated life – tend to be seen in normative terms, as ideals or values that we should aspire to. There is a vast amount of literature on each of these ways of thinking about belonging but there will be no effort to summarize it here.

20.2.1   Belonging as Identity

Though the concept of belonging as identity has been the focus of interest since the rise of identity politics in the last several decades, its significance is more general than its manifestation in such a form of politics. For one thing, a great deal of what has come to be called "identity politics" consists in movements with short-term instrumental goals to gain one or other benefit for certain groups in society. As such, however necessary and important it may be, its links with the concept of identity can be temporary and relatively shallow. For another, identities need not by any means always give rise to identity politics. The most that can be said of the link between the concept of identity and

identity politics is, as was said earlier: identities make one poised to be mobilized in identity politics.

It is useful at the outset to observe that belonging and identity have an objective and a subjective side. One may, for instance, belong to a family or nation by criteria that are relatively objective: birth to certain parents, for example, or possession of a certain passport. But frequently one may not subjectively care for this objective fact about oneself. One may feel no subjective identification with one's family or country. If so, one has only an objective familial or national identity.

It is only when one endorses the objective fact about oneself that an objective identity is accompanied by subjective identity. Sometimes, though much less frequently, one may even imagine or declare oneself by choice to have a certain identity which has no substantial objective co-relative, as when some who had never even been to New York said in the aftermath of September 11, 2001, "We are all New Yorkers now." But for the most part subjective identity consists in identifying with some feature that is also objectively present. That is why it is misleading to say that subjective identity is a matter of choice. It is usually a matter of endorsement of what is given to one, only rarely a matter of choosing one's identity de novo, as it were.

Biological criteria for identity are frequently considered objective or given to one, which does not mean that they do not leave one with a subjective choice about the matter, since (increasingly) one's biology may be altered by one's own voluntary decision. And even when there is no radical intervention in the biology, some may, without denying the objective fact, be indifferent to and refuse to positively endorse the gender or the race that is biologically given to them.

Moreover, though gender or racial identity were long considered to be objective and based purely on biological considerations, in the past few decades the very idea of a purely objective criterion of identity of this kind has been put into question, and gender, race, and a variety of other such forms of identity are thought to be "socially constructed." This does not necessarily mean at all that they are not objective. They may still be more on the objective than the subjective side of identity, especially if the process of social construction occurs independently of subjective endorsement and choices on the part of the individual agents. The entire question of social construction is a complex and interesting topic that cannot be pursued here in any detail, except to say that it complicates the notion of objective identity and to that extent qualifies the distinction between objective and subjective identity or belonging.[3]

Objective identities are much more interesting when they are social rather than biological, and in a way even more problematic; and this bears some detailed discussion. Perhaps the most classic and frequently discussed example of this is class identity. One familiar way of understanding class identity is owed to Marx, but how exactly to understand what Marx said about it is a matter of interpretation and dispute. An objectivist reading of Marx goes roughly like this: one's class belonging or identity is not a matter of subjective identification

---

[3]   For an illuminating discussion of the issues around "social construction," see Hacking (2000).

but an objective given that derives from history, and history is to be understood by an objective account of it found in what has come to be called "historical materialism" – though that is not an expression in Marx's own writing.[4] On this account, which class one belongs to has nothing to do with one's identifying with any given class. Whether or not one identifies with a given class, one belongs to it simply because of the objective unfolding of successive economic formations in history. Thus, for instance, proletarian identity is entirely a matter of specific forms of class employment ("working" class) in a certain economic formation (capitalism) in a certain period of history (modernity). One may have no commitment to that class, have no class consciousness or solidarity with other working people, pursuing only what Marx called "bourgeois" aspirations – still, one's true identity or "self" or consciousness is proletarian, even if, in such cases, it is hidden from oneself by layers of ideology or false consciousness. It is the task of revolutionary social transformation to mobilize the proletariat to overcome this false consciousness and to realize their true "selves," their proper or objective revolutionary class role in history.

Such a view has given rise to much anxiety, especially in liberal thinkers like Isaiah Berlin who saw in such an ideal of emancipation or self-realization a form of liberty – what he called "positive" liberty – which he thought to be tyrannical, because one can be "forced to be free" (to be someone other than what one subjectively views oneself to be) by a vanguard, armed with an objective theory of history (Berlin 1990). Though in Berlin's case this was a cold warrior's anxiety, there is a deeper, more theoretically motivated, underlying worry about such objectivity, which is that someone is being attributed a self or identity and belonging that he or she may explicitly disavow or – as is perhaps more often the case – may have no self-knowledge of. That is to say, it may be that nothing whatever in one's behavior reflects the identity being attributed, not even in one's unconsciously motivated behavior (in this respect Marx – on this objectivist reading – is distinguishable from Freud, who at least insisted on unconscious behavioral manifestations of identity). The intuition against objectivism of this sort in the matter of identity is that to attribute a self or identity or belonging to someone when there is no behavioral sign of it nor any self-awareness of it (perhaps even disavowal of it) is to disregard the agency of the subjects, seeing them merely as reflections of an objectively conceived theory of history. The intuition in favor of the objectivist side arises most pressingly when subjects of a group are deeply oppressed and yet acquiescent in their oppression. The intuition is that such subjects are oppressed, despite their acquiescence in the oppression, by standards that have nothing to do with the behavior, the awareness, the avowals of the subjects. This theme surfaces implicitly at various points in the empirical survey and most vividly in the section on caste in India.

One possible solution to the difficulty is this: Frequently, in history, populations that have been acquiescent in their oppression have transformed abruptly and in very large numbers and joined movements of social and political transformation and even revolution. This could, of course, be a change of mind on their part, a change from acquiescence to dissatisfaction and revolutionary consciousness. That is

how the opponent of objectivism would insist on presenting it – one subjectivity being replaced by another. But both the abruptness and the large numbers to whom this sometimes happens suggests that a "change of mind" is not a plausible explanation, since changes of mind tend to emerge through deliberation or acculturation toward something new, processes that are both slow and proceed from small numbers of people to larger numbers via a variety of accumulated efforts at public education. A better explanation of the volatility and numerical strength of such transformations is to attribute retrospectively, a latent dissatisfaction in the population even when they were explicitly acquiescent in their behavior and avowals. This solution does not give up the link between agency and behavior. It simply does not require that the link be simultaneous. It may be thought that if there is this link to behaviour, something of the "objectivity" in the objectivist position is compromised. But it should not be seen as a wholesale cancellation of objectivity, since objectivist positions that do not require even this minimal theoretical link with behavior and agency are, in any case, marred by an ulterior form of transcendence in the understanding of identity that seems irrelevant to the study of society and history. Again, these issues are exemplified in the discussion of caste in India in the regional survey below.

Turning from objective to subjective belonging and identity, it is worth noting that much of subjective belonging, when it is long-standing and deeply rooted, is un-self-conscious and unarticulated. It is only people who undergo some sort of dislocation from their deep and long-standing roots who ask questions such as "Who am I?" or "To which group, do I belong?" Of course, the dislocation that makes them raise these questions about identity or belonging, though it is often so, need not always be physical or geographical (as in migration) but can also occur when one is sedentary – as a result of unsettling (material and psychological and cultural) conditions owing to a variety of either external influences or internal transformations.

Often, subjective identifications are formed under conditions of defeat and feelings of powerlessness and helplessness. Thus, much of Muslim identity in the Middle East today has been formed under (explicitly articulated) anti-Western feelings of being subjugated by what is perceived as a long history of colonization that continues in revised forms to this day, despite decolonization. Islam, under such conditions, came to be seen by a demoralized population as a source of autonomy and dignity. But sometimes identities are formed through triumphalist feelings as well. Linda Colley (1992) describes how Scots came to endorse a British identity only when Britain became a great empire; and much identification of American Jews with Israel occurred in the aftermath of Israel's smashing victory in 1967. So, also, some Jihadi identifications with Islam formed through triumphalist feelings in the light of what were felt to be "Mujahideen" victories after the Soviet withdrawal from Afghanistan.

Nationalism has played its role in the formation of identities. In Europe, many religious and other forms of identity were formed as a result of nation-building exercises after the Westphalian peace. Nationalism of this kind was based on a self-consciously majoritarian identity

---

[4]   A clear statement of what has come to be called "historical materialism" may be found in Marx (1955: 362–364).

formation – finding an external enemy within, despising and subjugating it, and claiming that the nation is "ours" not "theirs" (the Jews, the Irish, Protestants in Catholic-majority countries, Catholics in Protestant-majority countries …). Often this created self-conscious backlash minoritarian identities among these populations. (In fact, secularism, as a doctrine, was formulated to repair the damage of religious and civil strife done by conflicts among religious identities formed by these nation-building majoritarianisms and the minoritarian backlashes against them.) A familiar form of identity formation of majorities and minorities also grew out of colonial policies of "divide and rule" in countries of the south, an importing of European nation-building ideas into the colonies. Many of these sources of identity and belonging and the mobilizations that they give rise to in the public and political sphere are further traversed in the regional surveys of this chapter below.

But quite apart from the sources that give rise to it, there is the prior theoretical question about what *is* subjective identity. How shall we characterize or define it?

There is a tendency in some social theorists who shun identity politics to confuse normative and descriptive questions and take a skeptical stance on the very idea of subjective identity, claiming that any given individual subject cannot be said to have any firm or clear singular identity because she identifies with far too many wider groups – her gender, her family, her profession, her religion, her nation, her class, her caste, her company of people with shared mutual interests… and so indefinitely on and on. But this skepticism, though it may have a normative point in commending those who have an ecumenical and supple social outlook, cannot be grounds to dismiss the importance of notions of subjective identity, since for many subjects, descriptively speaking, one or other of these identifications will be far more important and loom much larger in certain contexts and, when that is so, they will be much more likely to mobilize themselves in public life and politics on the basis of that identity. Thus, a Muslim may also be an Iranian, a father, a doctor… but in certain contexts (such as those mentioned above) it is his Islamic values that he elevates above his nationalist, family, professional… values, and he mobilizes himself on that basis and not others in public and political life. Such strongly felt singular identity, and the politics that is sometimes based on it, has been an undeniable descriptive fact in our social and political lives, however multiple our identities may be – and ought to be.

But to say that subjective identity is not thus dismissible is not yet to define it. And defining it is no easy matter. We have said that subjective identity usually consists in *endorsing* certain facts about oneself – one's nationality, race, gender, caste, class… – and in doing so allowing oneself to be poised to be mobilized in public and political life on their basis. So the question is: what sort of state of mind or commitment is this endorsement? At first sight the answer might be that these endorsements are simply one's valuing one's nationality, religion, etc., more strongly or intensely than other things one values. However, "intensity" (with which one holds a value) is not exactly a theoretically tractable idea and even if it were, it is not sufficient to define subjective identity, since one may have these intensely held values and find that they are not quite rational in oneself, even often wishing one didn't have them. If so, it would be perverse to define

subjective identity in terms of them. Some further constraint must be added to the presence of these values to reveal identity in the subjective sense. It is tempting to think that the further constraint is simply a second-order attitude of valuing one's first-order values. That would rule out the cases in which the first-order values seem unwanted and alien to oneself. But this is insufficient too since our second-order states of approval and disapproval of one's first-order states may also seem irrational or neurotic to one – as, for instance, when one thinks that one's second-order disapproval of some first-order value or disposition is too prim, too much of a superego phenomenon. And suggesting a step up to the third order threatens to merely render an infinite regress. What other constraint might there be, then, that helps to characterize subjective identity?

One possible answer is to see these values as accompanied by a very specific sort of property, the property of viewing them as something one ought not to revise – as in the case of Ulysses and the sirens, whereby one ties oneself to the mast of these values so that even if one were tempted by circumstances to cease to have those values or commitments, one would still be living by them. This elaborates analytically the intuition that subjective identity consists in one's self-conception, how one conceives oneself to be. Such self-conceptions are often intuitively expressed in such remarks as, "I wouldn't recognize myself if I betrayed my country" (or my family, or class, etc.), or even as in British schoolboy identity expressed by E.M. Forster: "I wouldn't recognize myself if I betrayed my friends." In other words, one views departures from these values as moral or political weakenings and, therefore, departures from one's identity. Values, held in this way, may properly be thought of as identity-imparting values. So, for instance, the Iranian clergy in Iran might – in this Ulysses fashion – think of Islamic values in such a way that they are willing to entrench Islam in their society so that if they were to weaken in the face of what they conceive to be the pernicious siren-songs of modernity, they would still be living by Islamic values. This idea of subjective identity cannot be dismissed as a form of fanatical irrationality, since even those with a liberal identity share this constraint on how they hold their values. This is evident in the fact that liberals elevate some of their values (such as freedom of speech) to fundamental rights, the point of which is precisely to prevent themselves from acting when they weaken in their resolve and wish to censor some odious viewpoint (neo-Nazism, say) that has surfaced in society. This echoes exactly the same structural constraint on how values are held as in the case of the Islamic clergy mentioned above. Such a constraint (of holding values in the Ulysses-and-the-sirens form) captures how deeply one identifies with some point of view (Islam, liberalism, etc.) at any given time and may properly be thought to be a reflection of subjective identity (at that time). Much more can be said to elaborate on this, but it will not be pursued here.

As said earlier, the notion of identity came to prominence with the rise of the identity politics of race, gender, caste, language, etc., since the 1960s and 1970s and has been with us since in many parts of the world. (All of these are briefly surveyed in the summary regional studies that follow below.) A good deal of this was necessitated by the fact that standard universalist formulations of liberal ideals refused to acknowledge these particular identities, dismissing them as parochializing public life in one form or another. More interesting was their refusal by traditional Left politics which claimed that class identity was the more fundamental identity, not race or gender or linguistic identities, and that a lofty focus on class struggles would usher out the other deprivations that each identity politics was seeking to usher out with more specific struggles of its own. There was undoubtedly something blinkered about this refusal too, since it refused to recognize the extent to which disrespect can come from other sources than class distinctions. Even so, there is a sense in which it seems as if the category of class is more basic, and one needs to find a way of putting it without failing to recognize the point about the multiple sources of disrespect. A way to approach how it is more basic is to point out the following: Though substantial gains have certainly been made on the racial, gender, caste… fronts in the last many years as a result of identitarian struggles, these gains would never have been allowed if they deeply undermined the basic structure of the capitalist society and in particular if they jeopardized the key interests of corporations, which have such a sway on policy-makers nowadays. This is, of course, a speculation. But given the conspicuous power of vested interests, we can make the speculation with confidence. If so, there is no gainsaying the fundamental importance of class identity over others, and this speculative formulation is the right way to present it rather than a formulation that does not recognize the importance of other forms of identity. (Of course, one should also explore parallel speculations, for instance by speculating that if any gains have been made on the class front, they would not be allowed if it deeply undermined patriarchy. But, though it is certainly worth exploring, it is not perhaps as immediately obvious that one has as full a grip on what such a speculation would be based on.)

20.2.2 Belonging and Solidarity

Another aspect of belonging has been elaborated in terms of the notions of fraternity or feelings of brotherhood and sisterhood – in short, feelings of solidarity within the members of a society. Solidarities often presuppose a common point of view and that is why it is an ideal that is very often found in struggles and movements toward an ideal. Thus, for instance, there is talk of "working-class solidarity" where there is a common goal, a common perspective on what is to be done by all those within a group. But of course such a common purpose and point of view may be present in a society at large, not just in groups struggling for some idea or cause. When this is so, solidarity shades into what is called "fraternity."

If this point about a common point of view as making possible belonging as solidarity and fraternity is correct, then it is safe to say that when societies were relatively homogeneous (if they ever were

so), solidarity perhaps came more easily and without too much effort. But the hard question is what belonging as solidarity amounts to when there is widespread cultural heterogeneity. In the modern period, when societies – due to migration or conquest or due to internal fragmentation – are inevitably comprised of multiple groups and points of view, solidarity is more of an achievement (and also more of an urgent necessity), since solidarity cannot be taken for granted across groups as it can be perhaps within a group. When there is plurality of religion, ethnicity, etc., there is bound to be at the very least difference and often even conflict in values and beliefs. When this happens a whole range of issues arise about how cohesion, solidarity, fraternity, etc., are even so much as possible, and what they amount to if they are possible. What could solidarity mean across groups (rather than within them) when groups conflict deeply over beliefs and values?

There are three prominent doctrines that address the question of difference and disagreement over values and beliefs among groups.

The first and the most long-standing doctrine of modernity has been liberal universalism, whose lofty stance has been that when there is conflict of this kind between two sets of values, only one can be right (two contradictory positions cannot both be right) and so difference and disagreement are not occasions to shed one's universalist aspirations. Points of view that one disagrees with may be "tolerated" (and liberalism elevates toleration into a primary virtue) but that is not a concession to their truth or rightness. Thus, despite its commitment to toleration of other points of view, its eventual ideal is group solidarity that comes from within a single point of view, the universally right one which transcends difference.[5]

A second doctrine, cultural relativism, recoils from this universalism and allows that different cultures and groups may claim truth relative to their cultural points of view, denying that there is any way of assessing truth from an Archimedean position outside of these points of view. Solidarity across points of view is not a coherent ideal; it is only to be had within cultures and groups.[6]

A third position, pluralism, defines itself in partial opposition to both of these doctrines. Against the first it argues that toleration is the wrong ideal with which to address the question of difference. The very term "toleration" suggests that one is putting up with something for which one might not have any respect. If toleration entails respect it is only of a very abstract kind – respect for a citizen's autonomy to hold whatever views she wishes, even if one does not specifically respect her for her views. Pluralism, by contrast, respects difference, not merely the autonomy of citizens to be different. And respect is a first step toward building solidarity across cultures.[7]

---

[5] Universalist forms of liberalism go back to John Locke, through John Stuart Mill, down to John Rawls in our own time, to name three of the most well-known figures. For canonical texts, see Locke (2017 [1689]); Mill (2017 [1859]); Rawls (1971). John Rawls struggled throughout his intellectual career following that major work to make liberal universalism more responsive to the problems posed for it by cultural heterogeneity, especially as they came to be posed by religious points of view.

[6] Cultural relativism for the most part has been a doctrine to be found in anthropology, though some of its more rigorous formulations have emerged in philosophy, focusing more generally on conceptual relativism and frequently also on moral relativism. Among anthropologists, Franz Boas was a leading early figure (see particularly Boaz 1963 [1911]; see also Ruth Benedict (1934). Among philosophers, conceptual relativism emerged first with full force due to the influence of Thomas Kuhn (1962) and found its full and explicit flowering in Paul Feyerabend's writings (see particularly Feyerabend 2010). For a good discussion of moral relativism within the larger claims of conceptual relativism, see Williams (1981); see also Harman (1975) for an argument and elaboration of relativism about values in particular.

[7] What is being labelled here as "pluralism" shades into what is frequently theoretically elaborated under the label of "multiculturalism," and much of the literature on the subject tends to use the latter label. For good discussions of the subject, see Taylor (1994); Kymlicka (1995); Tully (1995).

20

But it is pluralism's contrast with the other doctrine, cultural relativism, that pushes the ideal of solidarity deeper than merely showing respect for other cultures. This is where all the interest and complexities of the subject of solidarity lie. Relativism holds that there are values and beliefs that are true (or false) only relative to particular cultures, and so such truth (or falsity) as they have does not speak at all to other cultures. It is incommensurate with the values and beliefs of other cultures. One culture may recognize that another culture holds certain beliefs, adheres to certain values, but that recognition is purely detached and disengaged: it is merely an academic or ethnographic comprehension of another. There is no engagement of one culture by another. If so, how can there be any inter- (rather than intra-) group solidarity? At best, one can go to another culture and be converted by "going native," a form of defection rather than transformation via influence or dialogue or persuasion. Thus, solidarity conceived as the building of bridges across difference is ruled out. By contrast, pluralism, despite acknowledging genuine difference between the values of different cultures, does not consider values across cultures to be incommensurate in this way. That is to say, difference does not engender detachment and indifference; rather it leaves it completely open that one may learn from other cultures and seek to influence other cultures, in turn, through mutual engagement.

This distinctness from cultural relativism makes it clear that nothing in pluralism requires one to stamp every commitment of every culture as true or right simply because of the fact that it is avowed by a culture. Respect for cultures does not concede to them that automatic form of self-validation. One may certainly find some values of another culture (as indeed of one's own culture) to be wrong and indeed that is precisely why one, unlike with relativism, often seeks to engage with that culture – seeking to change its mind and thereby overcome the disagreement over values and practices. So long as such engagement is done with the respect that defines the pluralist ideal, as expounded in its contrast with liberal toleration, pluralism may insist that differing cultures are commensurate and can find each other to be wrong without giving up on the pluralism. So, a question then arises: what is it to show solidarity and engage with respect with a culture with which one disagrees and moreover, crucially, to do so with a more specific form of respect than merely the general and abstract form of respect that liberalism grants, the respect for all persons' autonomy and right to an opinion, however false? How is that more specific form of respect toward another to be shown while one is disagreeing with her and seeking to change her values and beliefs? This is the hard question, because without a good answer to it, solidarity in the face of deep cultural disagreement and difference has not been clarified.

The specific form of respect that is the hallmark of pluralism bestows a very specific quality on such engagement with another culture with which one disagrees. The engagement must take the form of attempting to persuade another culture by appealing to some grounds or reasons that are *internal to the commitments of the other culture*. That displays a respect for the other culture that goes beyond, that is more specific than, respect owing to the abstract recognition of the right of all to have their opinions, however wrong. It respects their substantive moral and psychological economies rather than merely their autonomy, and seeks to reason with them *within the detail of their worldview*, taking its particular substantive values seriously and engaging with them so

as to persuade it to change its mind or practice on the matter on which there is disagreement. Thus, solidarity in the face of deep difference and disagreement – unlike solidarities that exist within a group with a common point of view – may necessarily take a rather abstract form. Within a shared point of view, solidarity may consist of routine forms of support and mutual understanding. But when there is no common point of view, when there are different and conflicting points of view, the ideal of engaging with others from within their point of view is what solidarity amounts to. This is not easily recognizable as the traditional ways of thinking about fraternity and brotherhood with others that hold within homogenously characterized societies.

Is it even right to call this solidarity and belonging? There is no reason to deny that it is. People may find or form themselves to be a fraternity at all sorts of levels – and empathy of this rarified kind (engagement with conflicting others from within their point of view) is one source of solidarity – a uniquely modern source, given the tensions, conflicts, and fragmentations of modern society. One way to see that it is still a form of fraternity might be elaborated in terms of the ideal of brotherhood that fraternity implies. As was said above, attitudes of both liberal toleration and (especially) cultural relativism yield no substantive engagement with other points of view. The first tolerates them without requiring substantive engagement; the latter thinks substantive engagement is not possible since moral and political truth is to be understood from within cultural points of view because it does not straddle different points of view. By contrast, the engagement that pluralism requires suggests a quite different outlook, and one stark way to express the contrast between these outlooks that brings brotherhood to center stage might be this: pluralism would have each group among plural groups saying to others, "You must be my brother" and seeking to engage with others from within their points of view to overcome conflicts in moral and political values and beliefs. By contrast, the outlook of (especially) cultural relativism and (even) liberal toleration is better summed up as "You need never be my brother." Toleration recoils from the slogan, "You must be my brother." And that may give the impression that the slogan suggests intolerance. But that is not the point of the slogan. The point of the slogan is not to express coerciveness but to express the commitment to engaging with other points of view that conflict with one's own, with the goal of learning from them or convincing them to transcend difference, and this form of engagement is an expression of a form of fraternity with all others, however different they may be. It is fraternity because it reflects the fact that one cares about others and that is why one seeks to share the moral and political truth, as one sees it, with them; and one does so by entering their point of view and seeking to convince them from within it rather than simply by claiming a universality to one's own point of view. (The regional survey section on Canada speaks to and conveys the importance of some of the possibilities of such engagement.)

It may be that in some societies, conflicts and tensions between conflicting groups can never be overcome while there are economic and political conditions that encourage conflict and division. Historically, in some colonized countries in which conflicting groups had emerged as a result of colonial policies of "divide and rule," as mentioned above, nationalist struggles for independence from colonial rule sought to mobilize groups pluralistically, transcending these conflicts in an inclusive anti-imperialist struggle; but some decades after independence was gained, it has become increasingly clear that the neoliberal political economies that many countries of the south have acquiesced in (acquiesced, that is, in a new and revised form of imperialism, despite decolonization) revive, perpetuate, and intensify traditional religious, ethnic, and tribal conflicts among groups, because of various mechanisms that make development policy ineffective or that even directly corrupt local politics in the interests of transnational corporations and international finance. To the extent that this is so, group conflict will only be marginally ameliorated by the solidarities of empathetic engagement outlined above. It will only be transcended if there are also effective struggles of a more fundamental kind against the prevailing institutions linked to the international economic system.

These interconnections between, on the one hand, the politics of pluralism and, on the other, the struggles of a more fundamental nature are very important to fully understand and explore, not merely theoretically but in political practice that aspires to a deeper eventual fraternity and solidarity among groups. They are essentially two different forms or modes of political activism – the first is dialogical and negotiative engagement; the second is resistance. The reason for this is obvious. Pluralist engagement of the sort outlined above is only possible among relative equal conflicting groups, whereas the struggle against neoliberal economic forces is a struggle against a range of dominating tendencies and structures with which it makes no sense to speak of dialogue or negotiation. How two such diverse political efforts must be combined and pursued has no easy answer, though what is obvious is that the latter, the resistance form of political activism, unlike the former, is essentially a matter of mobilizing people in movements.

20.2.3   Belonging as the Unalienated Life

Though, as discussed above, belonging may have important relations to identity and to ideals of solidarity, it is, at its core, a notion that is most deeply of a piece with and inseparable from the ideal of an unalienated life. It is hard to conceive what a life of belonging would be, if it were also alienated. But what is it to be alienated and unalienated? Many different answers may be found in the vast theoretical treatment of the subject from Hegel, Marx, and before, to Sartre, Arendt, and after.

One revealing (even if insufficient) clue about what is meant by alienation may be found in the fact that most social theorists who have written on the subject have claimed that alienation is a malaise of the modern period. However defective pre-modern societies (societies that we summarize with such omnibus labels as "feudal") might have been, alienation does not seem to have been a defect that characterized them. For all the extraordinary oppression that serfs and slaves, and indeed women, suffered in an earlier period, they did not want for a sense of belonging in their social lives. That suggests that alienation has as its source the fragmentation of individual lives that was generated by the capitalist political economies that emerged in the modern period. More recently it has emerged that the modern period has also generated a deep alienation of human subjects not only from each other but also from nature. The unalienated life of belonging, therefore, is an ideal not just regarding social belonging but of our belonging in nature as its inhabitants.

Though this linking of alienation with the rise of capital and the social (and other) relations it generates makes it clear that there are material sources to alienation, it must be remembered that alienation itself is an experiential phenomenon, something felt and experienced by individuals, a malaise whose symptoms, therefore, are to be found in the mentality of individuals. What are the features of such a mentality?

If pre-modern societies allowed for a sense of belonging as unalienatedness, whatever else they did not allow for, the question arises as to whether it is that sense of belonging that needs to be recovered in the modern period. This question cannot possibly receive an affirmative answer, at least not without betraying a nostalgia for feudal societies. The reason for this is simple. The pre-modern sense of belonging or unalienatedness was crippled by the absence of two ideals that emerged only in the modern period – the ideals of liberty and equality. Belonging with a pervasive absence of liberty and equality is not an ideal worth recovering. And if belonging were to be recovered without deep unfreedoms and inequalities, the very meaning of the term "belonging" would be transformed from its pre-modern meaning.

But now, if this is so, there is an interesting set of complexities that follow because of similar issues arising with the concepts expressing the ideals of liberty and equality that were introduced in Enlightenment modernity to correct these defects of the earlier period. It is a familiar curiosity, indeed a perversity, that as soon as the great ideals of liberty and equality were articulated it became increasingly clear that they could not be jointly implemented. This was for many reasons, two of the more familiar being that liberty became attached to two things that put it in irresolvable tension with equality. First, the possession of property bestowed upon its possessor a form of liberty that became enshrined in the law of the land as a right, and the inequalities that this gives rise to have been widely studied, most powerfully, of course, by Marx. And second, though this is less widely studied, liberty became associated with the notion of desert, the right of each individual to reap the rewards of her or his talent, thereby incentivizing talent in a competitive form and giving rise to inequalities in ways that are everywhere visible in our societies. So, liberty and equality, though they were formulated in the modern period to correct for the defects of pre-modern societies, were equally hobbled as ideals by this deep internal tension with each other. It would follow, then, that if the notions of liberty and equality are to be made compatible, they cannot be the ideals as they have been elaborated by the accounts they were given in the political Enlightenment. Indeed if they were to be made compatible, they cannot mean what they are taken to mean by these standard accounts. This is just the situation with the ideal of the unalienated life, whose very meaning must change, as was said earlier, if it is to avoid the highly defective social surroundings within which it was embedded in pre-modernity. It is apparent from all this that all three ideals are inadequate: the ideal of the unalienated life of pre-modernity, and the ideals of liberty and equality in the modern period brought in to correct the inadequacies of the feudal past. They, all three, need to be holistically transformed all at once in their meaning. How might this be done?

One way to do this might be to first remove liberty and equality from the center-stage position they have been given in our time and replace them with the idea of belonging qua unalienated life as the most fundamental concept of the three, and then re-introduce liberty and inequality, by the back door as it were, with less centrality than they have had, merely now as necessary conditions for the more fundamental goal of achieving the unalienated life. So reconfigured, the tension between liberty and equality may subside, but so also, if it now had liberty and equality as its necessary conditions, the life of belonging would no longer be the unalienated life of pre-modernity. This approximates Marx's early understanding of what is needed, since he stressed the unalienated life in his early work, and throughout his life's work thought of liberty and equality as articulated by political liberalism to be "bourgeois" notions, which, in the form of tension we have observed above, they certainly are. The triangular and concerted reconfiguration of all three ideals just proposed would take the notions of liberty and equality some distance from the notions they were articulated as in the context of the capitalist society that Marx was criticizing, and moreover liberty and equality would be in the service of creating something of more fundamental importance: an unalienated society of belonging for all – more fundamental, that is, than the social engineering goals that ameliorations toward equality and liberty amount to in the present political framework of collective bargaining.

What, in particular, is meant by reconfiguring liberty and equality as merely necessary conditions for the more fundamental goal of belonging, so that they are not likely to be in tension with one another as they have hitherto been? As noted above, liberty gives rise to tensions with equality because it attaches to the possession of property and to talent. One would need to see how and why it is defined to do so, in order to understand how the reconfiguration might be pursued. For the sake of simplicity, let us focus on the grounds in liberal theory for the possession of property.

The justifications of the privatization of property from the commons in liberal doctrine are well captured in a famous argument known as "the tragedy of commons," an argument that summarizes a centuries-long way of thinking about the rationality of privatized economic arrangements that are at the heart of the tensions between liberty and equality we have noted (Hardin 1968). The argument goes as follows: If there was to be no privatization of land there would instead have to be a collective cultivation of the commons. Such an arrangement is only possible if each individual commoner cooperates in its collective cultivation. But such cooperation is irrational. Why? Because cooperation requires each commoner to pay a certain cost (often restraint is a cost that must be paid, since often overcultivation is the problem). If each individual commoner pays the cost, of course everyone gains. But each individual commoner will have to consider that if he does not cooperate (i.e. does not pay the cost), the gains are immediate, whereas the gains from cooperation are long-term. Moreover, the gains from non-cooperation are all for himself whereas the gains from paying the cost are spread over the whole group. And above all he is never sure that if he pays the cost others will do so too, so there is always the qualm that each has that he will pay the cost and others won't, which will be the worst possible outcome for him. So it is rational for each individual commoner to not cooperate. But if that happens the commons are doomed to destruction. Thus, the tragedy. So: privatization is a better bet.

A standard response to this argument is to say that it does not prove the rationality of privatization but rather proves that we need to detect, police, and punish non-cooperation. Nobody can be opposed to such an effort to solve the problem – obviously we should try and police and punish non-cooperation when it happens. But the trouble is that, quite apart from the difficulty of detecting subtle forms of non-cooperation, the very same tragedy-style argument arises as to why it is rational to cooperate in a system of policing and punishment if we can get away with bribing or threatening those who administer the system or those – witnesses, for example – who cooperate with the running of it. This is in fact widespread in many societies, and in societies that congratulate themselves in having gotten rid of the culture of bribes and threats, the non-cooperation is frequently carried out more formally by exploiting loopholes in the law.

The ideal of an unalienated life points the way to a more non-standard and simpler but deeper repudiation of the tragedy-of-the-commons argument. It rejects the entire way of thinking that gives rise to the tragedy by pointing out that to even have the qualm and ask the question that leads to the tragedy of the commons – "What if I paid the cost and others did not?" – is to be thoroughly alienated. In an unalienated society, such a question does not arise in the mentality of the commoner. It is important to note here that to say this is not to say that it is morally wrong to have the qualm and raise that question. Rather, if one is unalienated, it is incoherent, a form of non-sense, to raise it. That is one central logical consequence of the unalienated life: it simply preempts the mentality that leads to the tragedy of the commons.

If we see unalienatedness this way, how does seeing liberty as a necessary condition for such an ideal of unalienatedness reconfigure the notion of liberty and make it more compatible with equality, thus transforming equality as well from the liberal notion of equality? To see individual liberty along lines that are of a piece with such a notion of belonging and unalienatedness, we have to first note that individual liberty is a matter of individual self-governance, and then point out that individual self-governance need not be conceived individualistically. Just to be clear, that does not make it a notion of collective liberty. Collective liberty may be an interesting notion on its own, but it is not of relevance here. The liberty involved here is felt and exercised by individuals just as alienation and its overcoming is felt and experienced in the mentality of individuals. The idea rather is to conceive of individual liberty in non-individualistic terms. This sounds paradoxical only because we have for too long conceived of liberty as determined by a mentality that underlies the privatization of property and the incentivization of talent, a mentality that lends itself to arguments for the tragedy of the commons. To see individual liberty instead as involving a mentality that is of a piece with the ideal of an unalienated life, each individual, when she governs herself (and thereby exercises her liberty) by making decisions about how to live and act, must see the world not just from her point of view but from a larger point of view; she must see the world from everyone's point of view. Consider the following analogy: When one drives a car on a road (as opposed to, say, when one walks on the road), one does not see the world from one's own bodily point of view, but from the point of view of something larger, the point of view of the whole car. The world (the road) makes certain demands on us when we drive and if we did not orient ourselves to the world from a larger perspective, the car's perspective, we would crash the car. The tragedy of the commons, thus, is like the tragedy of the car crash, the result of meeting the normative demands made on us by the world from the wrong perspective on the world. To exercise liberty from the reconfigured and right perspective (i.e., each one of us making the decisions that shape our lives and actions in our self-governance from a larger point of view than our own) silences the possibility of even expressing the qualm and question that generates the tragedy of the commons. And if liberty is understood in this way, as a form of making the decisions that go into self-governance by looking at the world's normative demands from everyone's point of view, then equality would not be some further or external ideal with which liberty stands in trade-off relations; rather, it would tend to be an internal outcome of the deliverances of liberty itself. And liberty can only be understood this way if we see it as a necessary condition for the unalienated life, a society in which the qualm and question that is raised by the tragedy-of-the-commons argument *is not so much as intelligible.*

The very last point that has been italicized is of real significance. This ideal of an unalienated life does not at all amount to saying that one should be supportive and compassionate toward and concerned for others in the group. Those are all good things to be, but not all good things are the same good thing, and the good thing that unalienatedness is, is quite different from these attitudes of sympathy and support. It is a more abstract ideal, one which disallows as unintelligible the entire mentality that renders liberty and equality as in tension with one another. That is why the ideal of an unalienated life constitutes an entirely distinct notion of belonging from the ideal of solidarity or fraternity, which has to do with such feelings of brotherhood and support and compassion toward others.

The foregoing remarks elaborate how the notions of liberty, equality, and the unalienated life must be transformed in concert, all three at once. They do not tell us how these triangulatedly transformed ideals are to be implemented. Marx, as we know, did not think that the unalienated ideal could be achieved except by transcending capitalism. Others will no doubt have different ideas about what makes for their implementation. What is clear, even in our present non-ideal condition, is that each one of us goes in and out of alienation. Alienation is by no means ubiquitous. In many contexts, it does not occur to us to ask "What if I cooperated and others did not?" Most often this is so when the contexts are decentralized – families, perhaps small communities. But in many other contexts, especially in contexts when our minds are distorted by orthodox ways of thinking about society, politics, political economy, we tend to think in deeply alienated ways. The large question, therefore, is how we may use the conceptual resources we possess and wield in the former contexts to criticize how we think in the latter contexts. Or to put it differently, the question is: how do we scale up the mentality we exhibit in the decentralized contexts to the larger contexts of modern social, political, and economic life and governance?

The argument has presented one central aspect of the mentality of alienation – as it surfaces in certain ways of understanding liberty, when it is individualistically conceived. The malaise of alienation is,

however, a wider notion and can surface in many other forms than the way it does in the question and qualm that leads to the tragedy of the commons. The underlying claim has been that, whichever form of alienation we focus on, the overcoming of alienation in the ideal of an unalienated life *is a more fundamental goal than the ideals of liberty and equality.* One way to bring this out is to point out that alienation affects everyone, both the well-off and the badly off in an unequal society. A slogan that expresses this might be: "No one is well-off if someone is badly off." The slogan is not a normative claim about the need for equality so much as a descriptive claim about the effects of inequality: in a deeply unequal society, even those who are "well-off" are only seemingly so. Of course the symptoms of the malaise and mentality of alienation may be very different among the well-off and the badly off. Thus, just to give one example, in unequal societies fear and anxiety pervade the lives of "the well-off," leading them to recluse themselves from the world around them in the thoroughly artificial lives of gated communities; the alienation of "the badly off" has been painstakingly elaborated by many theorists, with Marx, focusing mostly on the nature of the work of laboring people, but pointing out that even their lives away from work are deeply alienated, reduced to a form of leisure that is mostly rest and idle recreation, with no possibility of developing their creative urges.

This point about the greater centrality of the ideal of the unalienated life brings out some of the insufficiencies of notions of equality and liberty, if thought of wholly independently of a further ideal of an unalienated life. Vis-à-vis equality, the point, as elaborated above, is that simply resting with equality without situating equality in the larger goal of an unalienated life would render the achievement of equality a mere form of social engineering. Vis-à-vis liberty, the point, as elaborated above, is that an ideal of liberty conceived along non-individualistic lines that are tied to the ideal of an unalienated life coheres far more with the ideal of equality than some of the standard ways of understanding liberty in the last few centuries of liberal thought and its practice in most of the societies we live in.

None of this is to deny that there are other notions of liberty and equality that have been developed in recent years, which also repudiate the standard ways of thinking about them, even if they do not do so by stressing, as above, the centrality of the unalienated life. Perhaps one way to bring out appeal of the latter's centrality is to say a little bit more by way of comparison about one or two of these alternative ideas of liberty and equality that do not make it central.

Let us look at two alternative approaches to explore this, the capability approach to liberty or freedom and the luck egalitarian approach to equality, neither of which shares the features of the notion of liberty discussed above – its tie to the incentivization of *talent*, in particular. (The stand these two accounts, especially the capability approach, take in relation to the liberty that is tied to the possession of *property* is a complicated matter, which can't be discussed here.)

The capability approach is often said to yield a conception of liberty or freedom that has to do with each person's capacity to live a life and carry out functions and activities that they each have reason to value. This has no particular place for the notion of liberty that attaches to the incentivization of talent, since it makes no appeal to notions of desert and the right of each to reap the rewards of their talents. Rather, what "development" or what the state and political economy must seek to provide is the flowering of the capacity of each person, understood in terms of what each person has a reason to value. How does such a view of liberty relate to the one on offer in the analysis given above that is of a piece with the ideal of an unalienated life? There are two points of comparison worth making. First, suppose it is the case that freedom as capability, so understood, is by and large established in a given society. It may still be possible that what happens once it is established is that the world values the output of some persons' capabilities far more than that of others', and that this becomes harnessed in "the market" to create deep inequalities. Presumably the answer will be that these inequalities, however deep, do not matter, so long as each person's capacities that they have reason to value are flowering. And that is why it is *only* when we bring to view how fundamental the ideal of an unalienated life is, and thereby bring to view the point that deep inequalities lead to a malaise that is shared by everyone (those who are well-off and those who are badly off), that we might see some of the limitations of the capability view of freedom, even if we grant its superiority to views of liberty that are tied to the incentivization of talent. A second point is this: The capability approach asks states and the arrangements of a political economy to pursue a notion of development that increases the freedom *qua capability* of each person. But why should someone who is unmoved by such an ideal of freedom, and seeks no other ideal of liberty or freedom than the one that attaches to talent and desert, despite its tension with inequality, have any reason to sign up to such arrangements of the political economy? It is only when we point out that everyone is worse off in a society where these deep inequalities exist that they might be moved by it. And only bringing in the centrality of the unalienated ideal allows one to point that out.

What, then, of the approach of luck egalitarianism? How does that relate to the dialectic set up earlier via the tension between notions of liberty (which attaches to the possession of property and to the idea of desert and the incentivization of talent) and equality? The luck egalitarian approach can certainly point out that it has no place for the incentivization of talent, and even if it has a place for private property it has no place for *heritable* private property, since the point of luck egalitarianism is to give each person the same opportunities at the start, cancelling the luck of both talent and inheritance. Unlike as in the argument of this chapter, where a certain non-individualistic notion of individual *liberty* (that is of a piece with the idea of an unalienated life so as to make liberty cohere better with equality) is constructed to replace the individualistic notion of individual liberty (that attaches to property and the rewards of talent, thereby giving rise to tensions with the notion of equality), the luck egalitarianism approach seeks to construct a notion of *equality* that rules out the notion of liberty attaching to (heritable) property and to talent and its rewards. But there are striking difficulties with this latter approach. First, it takes for granted that if the inequalities of talent are somehow leveled, then all reward will go to effort alone rather than to the luck of one's talent. But it is not so clear, in general, that there can be any clean and radical separation of talent and effort, since no talent is even so much as identifiable without a considerable amount of effort being exercised. And second, it is also not clear how the ideal of luck egalitarianism

works intergenerationally, since the *effort* of some parents may lead to accumulation of privilege and income which *in their lifetime* can be used to give great advantages to their children's development, missing in the lives of children of other parents who make less effort and are less successful. Without actually having the state take children away from parents and bring them up with leveled opportunities, a grotesquely inhuman proposal (something only a philosopher would think of proposing, as Plato did), this does not seem like equality even of opportunity. For these reasons, among others, many political and economic theorists seek – just as the argument presented in this section on belonging as the unalienated life does – equality of outcome rather than the equality of opportunity that luck egalitarianism posits.

So far the focus has been only on belonging in the *social* sense. What, then, about the possibilities for unalienated relations that we might have with the *natural world* we inhabit?

We have said that alienation is a matter of experience and mentality, even if this has its source in material and economic foundations. A basic aspect of this mentality, noticed by thinkers as diverse as Rousseau, Marx, Gandhi, Sartre, and Arendt, is an increasing detachment of attitude – where detachment is opposed not to attachment so much as to engagement. In all their work, the general idea is that the social relations induced by the nature of capital puts people in detached or disengaged relations with one another, each fragmented in their individual lives. And we have tried in the extended discussion above to see in a general way how the ideal of an unalienated life might overcome this mentality of individualist fragmentation of our individual self-governance. As is well known, Marx made more detailed specifications of such a notion of detachment in the economic sphere, thus speaking of how the relations of production in capitalism made each laborer detached from his own work and the products of his work, and commodity production under capitalism even succeeded in making detached the commercial relations between human agents. What, then, is the specific form of detachment of our alienated relations with nature, as these are set in in the modern period?

We get a glimpse of such detachment when we ask the question: how is it that the concept of nature got transformed, in modernity, into the concept of natural resources? The process of detachment that the question asks of seems to have had two conceptual steps. The first is to see nature exhaustively as what the natural sciences study, that is to say, to deny that nature contains any properties that are not countenanced by the natural sciences. Natural sciences take a purely detached attitude toward nature, seeing it only as an object of explanation and prediction. They do not see in nature any properties that engage our practical (as opposed to theoretical) agency by making normative demands on us, properties such as values, for instance. This is a relatively recent transformation, perhaps no earlier than the seventeenth century. Much of this transformation came from the desacralization of nature in that period with the rise of modern science, and that is why Weber called it "the disenchantment of the world." With the loss of sacralized conceptions of nature, there remained no metaphysical or theological obstacle to taking from nature's bounty with impunity, and that constitutes the second stage of the transformation of the idea of nature – into the idea of natural resources.

The chronic (and acute) environmental crisis we are now landed with has led to a lot of rethinking on these matters, and increasingly there seems to be a recognition of the wisdom in traditional indigenous cultures still active today in different parts of the world (Bolivia, for example), which claims that nature has rights that cannot be violated any more than the rights of human beings. This need not be a sacralized view of nature – it may simply be a secular form of enchantment – but if it is right, we cannot just view nature in a detached way as the object of explanation and prediction, nor just as a resource; we have to see it also as possessing value properties, and this means that it possesses properties that natural science cannot study, that it is not the business of natural science to study. If the thought that forests and trees and rivers have rights and make normative demands of practical engagement and respect on us as value, in general, does, is startling today, that is only to be expected. It took us long centuries to come to believe, and to create institutions for, the idea that human beings possessed rights. What is clear is that we cannot wait for centuries to rebuild such unalienated relations with nature.

20.3 Empirical Regional Survey

20.3.1 Canada: Belonging in Deeply Diverse Federations

There is an enormous amount of scholarship on belonging in the Canadian federation. The main lessons learned are summarized below.[8]

First, it is not possible to study individual examples of belonging in isolation from others or from the form of federalism that coordinates them, or fails to do so. The reason is that deeply diverse societies are composed of interdependent, crisscrossing, and overlapping social relationships that constitute multiple forms of association, identification, and belonging. There is not only a plurality of forms of association and belonging of various kinds. They also overlap and interact in complex ways. These associations include not only formal linguistic, legal, political, and economic associations such as over 600 indigenous peoples or nations, the Quebec nation and majoritarian and minoritarian nationalisms, provinces, territories, municipalities, regions, linguistic and cultural minorities of various kinds and sizes, both official and unofficial, corporations, cooperatives, unions, and political parties. They also include informal forms of belonging, such as eco-regions (place-based belonging), economic classes, persons with disabilities, persons of color, racialized minorities, gender, sexual orientation, pan-indigenous decolonization networks, social movements, local-global networked associations, and so on. Studying this multiplicity of forms of belonging has brought into being a learning curve from the initial focus on big and powerful forms of belonging to the growing awareness of the depth and diversity of other, crisscrossing forms of belonging.

Second, to study the lived experience of belonging in this complex lifeworld is to study the interdependent and interactive relationships of power, knowledge, authority, and identity formation of members, both within overlapping associations and among them. Through participation in these multiple relationships that govern their conduct, members come to have corresponding forms of self-formation and self-awareness (belonging or identity) of subject positions in their associations. These relational identities usually come along with stereotypical contrastive identities of members of other associations. These relationships govern members' conduct, individually and collectively, but, reciprocally, as agents, members contest and reform them. They are normalizing and normative. They are also "federal." That is, members of associations of belonging relate to other associations in diverse ways, relative to their diverse ways of belonging, just as in the cases of the larger and more formal federal relationships among diverse provinces, territories, and indigenous nations.

Third, a central concern has been to study the "dynamics of interaction" within and over these relationships of cooperation and contestation both within and among overlapping communities of belonging. The dynamics of interaction include the many types and cycles of cooperation, contestation, reconciliation, cooperation, and recontestation: for example, working together, grievance, dissent, protest, struggle, negotiation, conflict resolution or irresolution, implementation or non-implementation, review, and beginning again. These are the agonistic and democratic activities of individual and collective subjects of these always imperfect relationships of governance through which they become free, active, and responsible co-agents of the specific associations to which they belong and of the more general federal, coordinating associations to which they also belong: seeking to test them and, if necessary, negotiate their modification or transformation over generations as circumstances change and new injustices and social suffering come to light. They are carried out through the courts, parliaments, constitutional change, referenda, truth and reconciliation commissions, reasonable accommodation commissions, civil disobedience, boycotts, non-cooperation, revolution, enacting alternative ways of living socially and ecologically, and, at the ground of it all, the everyday negotiation of the relationships in which human live and interact, and on which they interdepend. All these discursive and non-discursive (embodied) dynamics of interaction are referred to as "dialogical." The historical interactions between the two official language groups, French and English, have been of central importance in struggles over belonging. These struggles highlighted the inseparability of language from culture, nationality, and other forms of belonging, and thus brought to awareness struggles of minority and indigenous language communities as deeper struggles for forms of cultural recognition and belonging.

Fourth, although research began with the powerful actors and high-profile contests over perceived injustices to their senses of belonging, such as language and indigenous and non-indigenous nationalism, it soon expanded to the expression or repression of voices of the powerless who were either outside and unrecognized by these contests or silenced and subordinated within by actors who claimed to represent them. It became obvious that appropriate forms of dialogical mutual recognition and participation of "all affected" by the perceived injustice

---

[8]   For an introduction to the points summarised in this brief survey, see the many publications of Groupe de recherché sure les sociétiés plurinationale (GRSP), and Centre de recerche interdisciplinaire sur la diversité et la democratie (CRIDAQ). Both are under the direction of Professor Alain-G. Gagnon at the Université de Québec à Montreal. For three representative studies, see Tully (2008); Webber (2015); Borrows (2016).

at issue, not just the most vocal and well organized, are essential for reasons of justice, stability, and trust. Running roughshod over the less powerful, presuming agreement, or feigning consultation in each stage of the contest creates further injustices: non-recognition and mis-recognition. These generate distrust, resentment, enmity, and further conflict. Thus, the study of deep diversity includes "intersectionality" (Dhamoon 1990).

Fifth, among the "all affected" by these human systems of social relationships of belonging are the ecosystems in which they are deeply embedded and to which they belong, yet which they are systematically destroying at an unprecedented rate. Therefore, it is no longer possible to study systems of social belonging without studying their positive and negative interrelations with the biotic communities to which they belong. This insight joins together social and ecological justice. Moreover, the deep diversity of ecosystems that has sustained life on earth for the last three billion years is similar in some respects to the diversity of human social systems. Thus, it may be possible to learn some lessons on how to design sustainable social systems of sustainable belonging by learning from how ecosystems sustain life on earth (Hardin 1968).

Sixth, the conclusion researchers and the Supreme Court of Canada draw is that contests over the relationships between and among multiple, interacting, and interdependent communities of belonging are a permanent feature of diverse societies. Accordingly, non-violent dialogical practices of civic engagement of all affected need to be built into the social relationships of free and democratic associations: that is, into the cycles of dissent, negotiation, implementation, and openness to renewed dissent and negotiation. Since these practices are themselves systems of social relationships, they too should be open to contestation. Such practices of listening (*audi alteram partem*), engagement, and negotiation have come into increasing use in the last decades and they are another focus of research: for example, practices of citizen participation and consultation, mediation practices, deliberative democracy, treaty negotiations between indigenous peoples and settlers, the representation of damaged and threatened ecosystems in negotiations over resource development, the duty to consult across the private and public spheres of contemporary societies, practices of transitional and transformative justice in pre- and post-conflict situations, and new practices of engagement beyond consultation. These are the demanding conditions under which any form of association and belonging can present itself as a "we" and exercise its constituent powers acceptably and fairly in circumstances of interdependent diversity.

The oldest examples of the conditions of diverse belonging in Canada are treaty negotiations and treaty relationships among indigenous peoples and non-indigenous people (the Crown) since the early seventeenth century. These indigenous–settler relationships of negotiation of self-rule and shared rule, and shared land use – called treaty federalism – coordinate diverse peoples and their diverse ways of belonging over centuries.[9]

These treaty relationships of belonging differently among indigenous and non-indigenous peoples grow out of the much older indigenous

peoples' understanding and practice of the way they belong to Mother Earth. They often say that the "earth does not belong them [as private property]; they belong to the living earth." That is, all humans belong in and to cyclical gift–reciprocity relationships of interdependency with all living beings, human and non-human, and thus have reciprocal responsibilities to take care of the plants, animals, and biotic communities that sustain them. This kin-centric way of being in the world with "all our relatives" is strengthened by the clan system of belonging, in which each clan is related to an animal family (bear, raven, etc.). This contrasts with species-centrism of most non-indigenous forms of belonging. Moreover, clan belonging establishes relationships of kinship across tribal belonging because there are similar clans in every tribe. Sharing of overlapping uses of the same bioregions by several tribes with each other and the plants and animals also deepens the primacy of interdependent belonging and negotiation. These institutions contrast with the primacy of exclusive independence and friend/enemy binary of many modern forms of belonging to nations, states, movements, and civilizations (Dhamoon 2009).

Ever since non-indigenous peoples invaded North America, dispossessed indigenous peoples of their traditional territories, exterminated 80 percent of the population, and asserted that the earth belonged exclusively to them, indigenous peoples have resisted this genocide, struggled to sustain and regenerate their ways of belonging, and explained that the only legitimate way indigenous people could belong with non-indigenous people in North America is through consensual treaty-making and sharing use and care of the land. They, and indigenous peoples throughout the world, have won recognition of this in the United Nations Declaration of the Rights of Indigenous Peoples and, to a lesser degree, in the Canadian courts (Rees 2010; Capra 2015).

In summary, the relationships of power in these multiple associations of belonging are, when successful, exercised cooperatively and agonistically within associations and, federally, in cooperation and contestation with other interdependent associations of belonging. This follows from the premise of interdependency that runs through all six conditions of the complex lifeworld. Indeed, the unilateral exercise of power by presumptively independent groups of belonging is the major cause or exacerbation of the injustice and distrust that give rise to struggles over non-recognition and mis-recognition in conditions of multiple belonging.

The long-term remedy these lessons suggest is the cultivation of a culture of democratic cooperation and contestation of the conditions of belonging in any association, and of the relationships of interdependency that coordinate diverse forms of belonging among all affected partners. Insofar as this complex form of democratic federalism enables the agency of members within communities of belonging and within federal associations that coordinate them, the members generate senses of belonging to both. Through participation in both associations members learn from each other that their ways of belonging must be always adjusted so that they are compatible with the ways of belonging of their interdependent relatives if they are to live in peace. They also learn that when this kind of mutual accommodation fails, as

---

[9]   For the research on which this analysis is based, see the many publications of GRSP and CRIDAQ.

it often does, they have recourse to institutions of contestation and reform (Hardin 1968).

20.3.2 The Middle East and Islam: Belonging and Global Islam

Despite our use of idiomatic phrases like "global citizen," is it really possible to possess a sense of belonging to the globe? Perhaps one way of imagining such an experience is to place the globe in its referential context. The world, for instance, continues in many ways to remain a metaphysical category referring to another or other worlds of a quite different sort, as in the originally religious but now also profane use of words like "worldly" and "otherworldly," to say nothing of "this world" and "the next." And for its part "the earth" is a term that takes its meaning from the solar system of which it is a planet, though it may also partake of the world's metaphysical character in phrases like "earthly existence" or "earthly remains." Both words are also routinely used as synonyms of "globe," though they don't cover all its meanings even in a colloquial register.

Interesting about "the globe" is the fact that it appears to have no context, and is instead entirely self-referential in its popular as well as scholarly usage. Global issues such as overpopulation or climate change cannot be spoken about in galactic or otherworldly terms. Indeed the globe has the paradoxical role of naming vast spaces and populations at the same time as stressing their finitude. Surely this contradictory pairing of large and small is precisely what the archaeology of global issues so well illustrates, from worries about a nuclear holocaust during the Cold War to global warming in our own times, by way of overpopulation in the era of decolonization. On the one hand we call "global" any phenomenon too large to master in a conventional way, and on the other use the word to describe a shrinking habitat that makes escaping such phenomena impossible.

In keeping with its self-referential character or lack of context, "the globe" possesses a single true subject that is also its object. Whether it is mutually assured destruction or climate change, humanity represents the simultaneous agent and victim of all such global phenomena. An asteroid hitting the earth belongs in another context altogether, constituting a planetary rather than a global possibility, one that makes of humanity one species among others at risk. Perhaps the breakdown of national, ethnic, and other forms of identity in certain parts of the Muslim world, as a result of political and economic circumstances, has made of Islam a privileged site for experiments in global belonging. While other communities and traditions might possess equally global visions, then, it is in Islam that these have been fully activated or translated into experience.

At first glance, of course, it seems odd to pair a self-referential and finite view of the globe with a religion for which transcendence of various kinds, including a deity, paradise, and angels, is so crucial. But we shall see that Islam's globalization, whether in its liberal, conservative, or even militant form, is premised upon the attenuation of such transcendence, and the consequent effort of believers to take responsibility for Muslims as a global community, one that is in addition seen to represent the human race. This narrative, however, doesn't completely dominate even that modern entity called the Muslim world, and is interrupted by other forms of belonging, of which the Arab Spring and Kurdish nationalism provide two important examples.

20.3.2.1   Islam Made Global

The origins of Islam as a global entity can be traced to nineteenth-century European imperialism, which was characterized by a novel focus on territory and demography, one defined by cartographic and statistical practices that were evaluated from an international and comparative perspective. Older categories, like the ummah or Muslim community, and the dar al-Islam or domain of Islam, had been metaphysical and juridical rather than empirical in nature. They didn't refer to a global Muslim population on the one hand, or a globally defined Muslim territory on the other. Instead the ummah described Muslims as a theological and trans-historical rather than enumerable entity, one that might include those already dead and yet to be born. Similarly the dar al-Islam (and its contrary, the dar al-harb or domain of war) named a legal not a cartographic or even political jurisdiction. So clerics in British India, as elsewhere in European empires, were able in the first half of the nineteenth century to declare them part of the dar al-Islam, since Muslims were free to fulfill their obligations there.

By the end of the nineteenth century, however, such notions had taken on the empirical and so enumerable and measurable character of modern categories, with the word "Islam" itself losing its once common adverbial form as a kind of action to become a proper name for a set of beliefs and practices that also included novel and non-theological attributes such as population and territory. The emergence of the notion as much as reality of pan-Islamism during this period provides a good example of this process. For the Ottoman claim to represent Muslims outside their own domains, initially as a regional and eventually as a global community, was first made late in the eighteenth century following the Russo-Turkish treaty of Kuchuk-Kainardji, in response to the right given the Romanovs to protect Christians in the Sultan's territories.

Unlike their Muslim predecessors, European empires were scattered across the globe, and came to provide Muslims with new models of identity and belonging. In their effort to compete with the Ottomans, for example, the British made much of the fact that they ruled more Muslims than the Sultan did, and were so entitled to call themselves the "greatest Mohammedan power," as viceroys, proconsuls, and prime ministers routinely did. Important about this identification was that it defined Islam in demographic and territorial as much as theological terms (which the British included under religious freedom). As the the rise of Islam gave Christendom a territorial designation, as Peter Wilson argues in his recent book on the Holy Roman Empire (2017), so did that of European empires allow Muslims to reconceive themselves as a globally dispersed people inhabiting a territory that came to be known as the Muslim world.

Like other colonized intellectuals, Muslim thinkers during this period sought to engage with and even contest European ideas of their own

20

universality, manifested as it was by their unprecedented power over large parts of the world. And they frequently did so by claiming to represent these ideals better than the British or French themselves, whom they either urged to fulfill their self-proclaimed missions of civilization and freedom in the colonies, or dismissed by arguing that Muslims were more capable of such universality. The resonance of these apologetics continues to be heard in contemporary Muslim polemics, and indeed Asian and African polemics more generally, which still take as their theme the alleged hypocrisy of European and now American claims to embody universal values.

The two great categories that such men struggled with were race and civilization, each of which had significant legal implications within European empires and even outside them, as illustrated by the "standard of civilization" that was required for non-European powers to be treated as equals and included within the bounds of international law. While race was routinely if often rather disingenuously rejected by Muslim thinkers, who sought to argue that Islam was not discriminatory along these lines, civilization was a category they tended to engage with more intimately, by saying that Islamic history represented it more perfectly than Christian Europe. In either case, however, Islam was held up as being a truly universal religion because it supposedly repudiated the hierarchies of race and civilization (to which was added class in the twentieth century) and staked its claim on humanity as a whole.

Beginning late in the nineteenth century, this argument continues to be made today, and characterizes both liberal and conservative, indeed even militant, Muslims, for all of whom Islam is the universal religion for mankind not simply because they think God says so in the Koran, but by reason of its being the one closest to nature. Whatever the pre-modern view of Islam as a natural religion, in other words, its conformity with the "laws of nature" and so with rationality rather than superstition was what modern Muslims focused on. Itself an offshoot of European debates originating in the seventeenth century, such a focus on nature allowed Muslim reformers of various political and ideological hues to purge Islam of customs and practices they considered unnatural, artificial, and decadent. They were also critical of regional cultures, which were seen as being too particularistic, and tried to bring a truly universal Islam into being – one fit for humanity in the same way as the universal declarations of rights announced by states and international bodies would be.

20.3.2.2   Mobilization and Militancy

While in the nineteenth and for much of the twentieth century Muslim concerns with representing humanity remained theoretical, the Cold War suddenly gave this otherwise abstract category a novel materiality. If the human race had achieved an empirical reality by being enumerated and made subject to various forms of planning and development, it was the possibility of a nuclear apocalypse that lent it a new kind of retrospective and even posthumous truth. Bringing as it did the religious language of apocalypse back to secular life, the Cold War threat of mutually assured destruction allowed Muslim thinkers to imagine the ummah's extinction alongside that of the human race.

In fact the early-twentieth-century theme of Islam's destruction by Western imperialism, common among colonized peoples from all religious persuasions, was updated to imagine the physical as much as political and psychological liquidation of the global Muslim community, which represented in this way the fate of the human race as a whole. After the Cold War, the atomic danger was supplemented if not replaced by that of climate change, and so it is no accident that Al-Qaeda's leaders, Osama bin Laden and Ayman al-Zawahiri in particular, routinely mentioned both threats to humanity when condemning their enemies in both East and West. In this narrative the Muslim community represents both the global force of resistance to such dangers, and the first global victims of the states and companies that make them possible.

Al-Qaeda, of course, emerged at the end of the Cold War to occupy a new global arena that came into view after the collapse of its superpower conflict. With the globe no longer defined by the hemispheric division of East and West in ideological, political, or economic terms, an opportunity arose to remake it in religious and other ways. Just as old-fashioned state sovereignty was being questioned in the 1990s, then, Al-Qaeda burst onto the scene with its networked form of militancy which neither required the state (indeed it was only capable of being organized and operating in so-called failed states) nor aspired to create one – despite its visions of a global caliphate. Crucial rather were global figures like the ummah or the West, neither of which possessed any institutional reality.

It was not only by way of jihad, however, that Islam became globalized after the Cold War. Indeed militancy was preceded by another form of mobilization whose first occurrence was in 1989, the very year in which the bipolar global order came to an end. Starting with the Rushdie affair, then, we have already seen three global mobilizations protesting some alleged insult to the Prophet. Each incident has taken place in Europe, allowing the demonstrations that ensued to invoke a narrative of conflict between East and West, Islam and Christendom, that predates the Cold War. So while there might well be controversies and violence over blasphemy against Muhammad in other parts of the world, most of all in Pakistan but increasingly also Afghanistan, these never take on a global character and remain local or national events.

Interesting about the global protests over insults to the Prophet is the fact that they not only originate in the West, but perversely also make use of a liberal vocabulary in stating their demands. Thus, what is called for are apologies, recognition, and respect, which is to say invitations, however coercive, to build a new kind of relationship of civility between East and West. The language of jihad is absent from such mobilizations, which have in the past even interrupted and overshadowed Al-Qaeda's domination of Islam as a media spectacle without once referring to it. Even blasphemy, a category often deployed by Muhammad's passionate defenders, is taken from a Christian rather than a Muslim theological tradition, and during the Rushdie affair there were many who said that they only wanted Islam to enjoy the same legal protection that the (since abrogated) blasphemy laws provided the Church of England.

One reason why Muhammad, rather than, say, God, has come to play the role of victim in these great mobilizations has to do with his being gradually stripped of all transcendent or metaphysical character, as a super-human or miracle-working figure, beginning late in the nineteenth century. Having been made fully human, and thus the chief representative of Islam's faithfulness to nature, the Prophet, unlike God, has now become vulnerable enough to merit the protection of his followers, and at the same time to stand as a representative of a virtuous and victimized humanity. The great dramas of outrage over insults to Muhammad, of course, are also made possible by 24-hour satellite television coverage, with Muslim audiences around the world now able to see protests in different places occurring in real time and to mirror them without the need of any organization, political project, or even common goals.

If television as a medium of collective viewing allowed the ummah to realize itself in a new if still only transient way, by waves of mobilization that arose only to decline into nothingness, the internet made for an equally dispersed but highly individualized form of militant recruitment through the spectacle of martyrdom. The decisive shift here was from the older and perversely liberal language of accommodation and equality, to the apocalyptic one of elimination that entailed a war for Islam's very survival. By describing the same fantasy and experience of global connectedness as the internet, therefore, Al-Qaeda addressed the simultaneous reality and unreality of entities like the Muslim community and humanity, both of which had indubitably come to exist in some sense, if only because their extinction could be contemplated, but which were not yet able to represent themselves.

Al-Qaeda dealt with the paradoxical existence and non-existence of such entities by claiming to represent the Muslim community and therefore humanity itself, each connected to the other by its alleged status as a global victim. By elevating individual acts of sacrifice, such as suicide bombing, into its media brand, Al-Qaeda sought not simply to mobilize otherwise abstract entities like the ummah, as protests over insults to the Prophet did, but also to represent humanity itself through the universality of death. Bin Laden and Zawahiri had always contrasted this negative and indeed nihilistic universality with what they saw as the West's unjust restriction of the right to life and security for its own citizens. Like Muslim reformers of the nineteenth century, then, militants were demanding the universalization of Western ideals; but unlike them they went on to substitute the equality of death for the still unavailable one of life.

20.3.2.3   From State to Caliphate

While the global phenomena we have been looking at are anti-statist in nature, there exists, of course, an equally important and older narrative of Muslim state-building as well. For our purposes the relationship between the two can be compared to that between anarchism and communism as distinct ways of representing the proletariat, itself the first truly global subject of politics and thus the savior or rather creator of humanity in Marx's view. Like Al-Qaeda's militants, anarchists in the past relied upon individualized acts of sacrifice and freedom to build transnational networks, while the Islamists who succeeded them chose to follow the communist example and proceed in a collective way by fortifying what promised to be a global revolution in one state after another.

The thinkers and founders of Islamic states have always drawn upon Marxist, and sometimes fascist, ideas of the ideological state, while dispensing with their focus on class or race. The first two Islamic republics, Pakistan and Iran, were both established during the Cold War, as part of a more general political fashion in what was then known as the Third World to establish ideological states, whose rather tenuous links with socialism were more often than not manifested in their controlled economies. Revolutionary Iran, for instance, invoked a famous Third-World trope in claiming, like the Non-Aligned Movement, to represent a middle way between Western capitalism and Eastern communism. And yet Islamist politics has also retained a certain anarchistic element in its deep distrust of the state form, inherited as this was from the colonial past and seen as the chief instrument of Western power. In this the Islamists joined figures like Gandhi who sought to foreground society and its self-governance rather than the modern state in their politics.

If Lenin, then, thought to conquer the state only to have it wither away once the dictatorship of the proletariat had performed its function, Islamists were similarly concerned with taking over the state only to roll it back from interfering in a supposedly autonomous society defined by the religious norms seen as being natural to it, and by extension to humanity. By following European Orientalists in criticizing the Muslim princes of the past for their allegedly decadent and un-Islamic ways, the Islamists deprived themselves of an inherited political language that they might have developed, as Europeans had done by translating monarchical into republican forms of sovereignty. Their focus on society, therefore, has had the curious consequence that Islamists, ostensibly dedicated to politicizing Islam, are led in fact to criticize the conventional and institutional forms that politics takes.

This suspicion of the state is characteristic of Sunni versions of Islamism more than of Shia, with Khomeini, for instance, subordinating Islamic law to the expediency of the nation-state. For the Sunnis this can only signal Iran's hypocrisy as an Islamic republic, since by recognizing state sovereignty it allows dictatorial or populist power to breach defenses that the sacred law is meant to have placed between Muslim society and the possibility of tyranny. In this view only God can lay claim to sovereignty, and so the law is meant to operate in a preventive and managerial rather than an agentive way to protect society. It should be clear that such a vision can describe more than one political form, and if the Cold War's Islamists were its earliest interpreters, today the idea of a self-regulating Muslim society can also be found among neoliberal capitalists in countries like Turkey and Malaysia.

Perhaps the most violent heir to this form of thinking about the place of law in society is the Islamic State in Iraq and Syria. ISIS takes such juridical logic to breaking point by trying to destroy every person and practice that cannot be defined or made visible in the vocabulary of divine law. Marked by a deep fear that heretics, atheists, and unbelievers are either openly or surreptitiously laying claim to the transcendence and therefore sovereignty that properly belongs to God, the Islamic State is dedicated to rooting out and eliminating all such illicit acts and beliefs, if only by making inner life itself impossible in demanding the absolute transparency of all social relations. Breaking with the traditional Sunni emphasis on protecting the privacy of domestic life, ISIS reworks totalitarian forms of surveillance to substitute a supposedly real society for the false one it has inherited. And in doing so it brutally seeks to create a second nature that can then be said govern itself through a sacred law that is based in the social rather than the political realm, upheld as it is by clerics whose link to the state is tenuous and intermittent at best.

We can trace the genealogies of global Islam in militant cartographies. Al-Qaeda's and more especially the Islamic State's maps, for example, are arranged in accordance with two criteria that bear no necessary relationship to each other. One of these is territory defined by its past Muslim ownership, thus including places like Spain or Sicily that do not have a significant Muslim population. And the other is demography, which allows for the inclusion of areas like the Rakhine state of Myanmar, which is home to the Rohingya minority, or Mindanao in the Philippines, inhabited by the Moro people, both considered victims of Buddhism, Catholicism, or even the West seen to be supporting them. Despite the ideal of humanity's final conversion to Islam, these visions still presume a division of the globe into two or more political parts, and in this way place themselves in a context that includes both imperial and Cold War politics.

Interesting about this use by militants of the initially colonial categories of territory and demography is the fact that they are kept distinct from one another. And while the rights of conquest might possess a theological justification, those of numbers only do so in potentially democratic terms. It also remains unclear whether these global cartographies are to be considered part of a single empire like the caliphate, or taken to constitute an alternative international order, thus demonstrating the variety of sometimes contending influences that go into making Islam global. Even ISIS, for instance, uses the name "state" or "dawla" for itself, as well as "caliphate" or "khilafah," though the two are by no means equivalent. The state, after all, belongs in the common register of political entities, while the caliphate is part of another genealogy that allows ISIS to take the Ottoman Empire as its immediate predecessor.

Unlike these global geographies, however, the regional ones that define Pakistani terrorist groups like the Lashkar-e Tayyaba or Jamaat al-Dawa invoke other kinds of genealogies. Taking India rather than the West as its great enemy, the Lashkar's map of a victorious future draws upon the cartography of British India as much as the history of Pakistani nationalism. So it imagines a subcontinent fragmented into Hindu, Muslim, Sikh, Dravidian, and even Dalit or Untouchable states. In addition to demanding the territory of Muslim princely states as they existed in colonial times, and whatever their present demographic composition, the Lashkar also stakes claim to areas like Kashmir with a majority Muslim population. And in this way, of course, it deploys the same pair of divided criteria as ISIS.

Instead of claiming the much larger part of India that had once been ruled by the Muslim dynasty of the Mughals, however, the Lashkar takes as its model the cartography of the British raj, with its princely states and populations divided into religiously defined electorates. The immediate inspiration for this map seems to be those produced during the 1930s by Choudhry Rehmat Ali, who had coined the name "Pakistan" and sought to disperse the subcontinent into a mosaic of religious and ethnically defined nationalities, each with its own state,

thus eliminating the prospect of Hindu majority rule. As with the Islamic State, therefore, the Lashkar appears to desire another kind of international order, and that, too, a curiously pluralistic one in which no one group can dominate the subcontinent.

20.3.2.4   A Global Inheritance

Drawing from rather different regional histories, militant narratives nevertheless share some of the criteria that define their global geographies. But they are not the only players in the field, and just as militant imaginaries rework colonial and other categories from the past, so too do their enemies and rivals in different ways. Indeed the emergence of a global arena deprived of political definition after the Cold War, has resulted in the reimagining or transformation of older and apparently defunct political forms. The so-called Arab Spring, for example, spread across the Middle East in much the same way as demonstrations against insults to Muhammad had done globally. Starting with a sacrificial act of protest in Tunisia, mobilizations were provoked that mirrored each other by way of media reports, but without serious organizational links.

And yet these self-proclaimed revolutions also drew from another tradition, one defined by the capture of a state. Rather than referring to the Islamist model of revolution, however, whose only successful instance has been Iran, to say nothing of the communist or nationalist examples predating it, the Arab Spring's closest precedents in time as much as experience were the color revolutions of Eastern Europe. In both cases, after all, we saw mobilizations without a political party to lead or even appropriate them – for even in Egypt the Muslim Brotherhood came to power hesitantly and without having led the revolution. Partly as a consequence, in both cases the overthrow of the government, when it was achieved, did not result in the making of a new kind of state – except perhaps in Tunisia. It is almost as if the protests were in some sense negative and even anti-political in nature, able to overturn the state but not to replace it with one of another kind.

Can we see the many interesting rituals of mobilization in the Arab Spring, including the ceremonies of solidarity in Cairo's Tahrir Square or setting up of citizens' committees to clean its streets, as a recrudescence of the older Islamist ideal of social self-governance which looked askance at the evil of statecraft and its politics? Or did the movement sweeping the region represent the first time in decades that the previously statist ideology of Arab nationalism achieved a popular reality – albeit without ever becoming a subject of debate in its own right? It is even possible to speculate, as one historian of the Fatimid Empire did, that these mobilizations invoked the heretical counter-caliphate set up by the Ismaili movement. For remarkable about the Arab Spring was the fact that it took hold in the very areas that defined and supported the Fatimid Empire, which is to say Tunisia, Libya, Egypt, Syria, Yemen, and Bahrain.

Fantastic as this interpretation might appear, it signals the sheer variety of older narratives and geographies that have reappeared in new guises during and since the Middle Eastern revolutions. The Kurdish national struggle in Rojava, for example, which was made possible and also elevated to celebrity status by the civil wars in Iraq and Syria,

20

has declared its faith in a novel form of self-critical nationalism that dedicates itself to humanity. Drawing once again upon anti-statist and even anarchist themes, the movement's imprisoned leader, Abdullah Ocalan, condemns the state form itself as oppressive and imperialist. He calls for the freedom and equality of women, seen as representing history's first colony, and derides the xenophobic and homogenizing tendencies of nationalism, together with the environmentally destructive capitalism that underlie them.

While these ideas, now being put into practice in the war against ISIS, may well come out of Ocalan's reading of Western theorists of the left, it should be clear that they draw upon themes of long provenance in the region and, indeed, in the Muslim or former Third World as well. But what does it mean to revive nationalism, or for that matter revolution and Arab unity, as empty or at least non-sovereign forms? Clearly they are far more than mere symbols, but to deploy the nation as a category, for instance, while condemning it on principle, is an extraordinary if not quite unprecedented act. Does it illustrate the difficulty of imagining a suitable politics for the new global arena, or simply the poverty of imagination on the left? To suggest that the old and the new exist in uneasy combinations at a time of transition may be true, but it has also become an analytical stereotype.

In one sense, of course, Kurdish nationalism bears some resemblance to its more settled and secure peers elsewhere. For economic forms of globalization have deprived nation-states in general of one of the foundations of old-fashioned sovereignty, leading to the increasing importance of cultural and indeed religious forms of identity, of which the European Union alone provides us with several instances on both the right and the left. In addition to that continent's xenophobic parties, after all, there also exist Scottish or Catalan movements for independence, which no longer imply the claim to traditional forms of sovereignty but instead rely upon the existence of the EU for their financial and security needs. While the Kurdish movement certainly does not incline toward a vast, European-style bureaucracy, its effort to hold together local and global modes of belonging are familiar to new national movements more generally.

What is crucial about the many rival groups and ideas that battle for space in the global arena is how much even the most violently opposed among them share. Whether it is Islamists, militants, or new nationalists, all appear to have a deep suspicion of the state, a focus on the social, and a questioning attitude toward sovereignty. The battle for this arena, in other words, isn't ideological so much as one about where to lay emphasis in a shared narrative. Despite the enormous and sometimes violent differences between such groups, then, their mutual struggles may well end up being about nuance rather than principle. From the ideological opposition of the Cold War, we seem to have moved into a situation where shared global narratives entail entirely divergent consequences.

20.3.3   Caste, Community, and Belonging: The Indian Case

The caste system is rooted in, and constitutes a further proliferation of, the four varna system of ancient India comprising the Brahmins (priestly class), the kshatriyas (warrior class), and the two classes of workers recruited largely from conquered tribes: the vaishyas (artisans and other producers) and the shudras (menial laborers) (Kosambi 1965). It is an arrangement of hierarchically organized endogamous groups, each consisting of persons belonging to a particular occupation that is carried on in a hereditary manner. It is also associated with abhorrent practices like "untouchability" and "unseeability," which presume that a person from the "upper castes" gets "polluted" just by touching or even setting eyes on someone from the "menial" castes. People from these "menial" castes were traditionally debarred from owning any land and even leaving the village. This was to ensure that an adequate supply of labor for the "upper-caste" landowners was always available, in a situation where cultivable land existed outside the village premises and would have otherwise pulled laborers away to cultivate on their own (Habib 1995).

Colonial rule introduced the formal idea of equality (equality before law) into this society of institutionalized social and economic inequality. But it also generated new forms of inequality in the material sense, via the destruction of domestic handicraft industry by the import of metropolitan goods ("deindustrialization") and the appropriation gratis of local commodities by the metropolis (using locally raised tax revenue to pay for them, a process called the "drain of surplus"), which worsened the material conditions of the "lower" castes.

It was the anti-colonial struggle (which paralleled a struggle for social emancipation in the late nineteenth and the early twentieth centuries and was affected by it) that led to the adoption of a constitution, after independence, which supplemented formal equality before law with democratic governance through elections based on universal adult suffrage, and affirmative action in the form of "reservations" for certain "scheduled castes" and "scheduled tribes" (dalits) in the legislatures and government institutions. "Reservations" were later extended to some other "backward" castes as well.

The experience of post-independence India, however, shows that constitutional measures meant to end caste oppression cannot do so, as long as the caste system, i.e. the division of people into different caste groups within a hierarchical order, remains. It is this hierarchical order itself that is oppressive. Even if through such measures, for argument's sake, the caste distribution of persons employed within each occupation becomes the same as that of the population as a whole, which is a necessary condition for ending caste oppression, given the enormously long history of the system and the ideology sustaining it, to which both its perpetrators and its victims have subscribed in the past, such oppression will still continue in society. The ending of caste oppression in the economy, in short, will not put an end to it in society. What is required is an obliteration of caste identity itself, the very "annihilation of caste," as Ambedkar (2014) puts it, in contrast with Gandhi's belief that the caste system could continue without hierarchy or caste oppression through a breaking down of the occupational division of labor and everyone participating in all activities, i.e., through a satisfaction of the above-mentioned necessary condition. (Toward this end, in his ashrams Gandhi used to insist on everyone sharing menial tasks like cleaning toilets.)

This is relevant to our question of belonging. Everyone in society can have a sense of belonging to, or of being at home with, a particular group, a caste group, and yet there can be oppression, rooted in the continuing disrespect of one group toward another, even if social progress (our theme) has been made on the front of material equality among the groups. Such social progress remains poignantly incomplete.

Moreover, this oppression would exist even if the oppressed are (ideologically) conditioned into accepting it as a "normal" state of affairs. Such acquiescence on their part might be accompanied by a sense of belonging within their caste; but this "belonging," experienced by members of a particular caste, within an overall oppressive order in which this caste is located and in which they acquiesce, is not necessarily a laudable thing.

Some may argue that it is denying the agency of those who are supposedly being oppressed if such oppression is posited despite their own denial of it. But underlying their denial is often the nurturing of a latent grievance that at some point bursts into explicit articulation and thus retrospectively reveals itself. Taking the apparent acquiescence of the oppressed in an oppressive order at face value thus not only raises normative questions, but also amounts to giving credibility to a false impression. It follows that only that "belonging" counts as social progress which is objectively free of the wrong of caste oppression; such "belonging" alone has the potential to endure.

To recapitulate, what is required is a transcendence of this oppressive order, both of these particular separate belongings, and of any overall sense of belonging to the order based on an ideology of inequality. What is required is the annihilation of caste. Not until then can "belonging" of a sort that would count as genuine social progress be possible.

Post-independence India has addressed the question of caste in various ways. There has been affirmative action in the form of "reservations" in government employment and government educational institutions. There has also emerged an "identity politics" of the oppressed castes in the electoral field, seeking, via the "one-person-one-vote" system, to use their numbers to put in power political parties that represent their material, social, and cultural interests. Yet other strategies have been in the air, such as efforts to have a larger number of dalit capitalists, so that caste categories are dissociated from class categories, unlike at present. But these moves still belong to a universe of separate belongings. They must of course be supported, as part of the traverse toward a society without caste oppression, but they do not constitute the end of that traverse. They do not take us toward the annihilation of caste.

Even the elimination of the dissociation between the caste distribution of the population and the caste distribution in particular occupations will not end caste oppression. But such elimination, assumed for argument's sake, will not even occur through the pursuit of pure identity politics or identity-based demands. This is because the existing distribution of social and political power in society, which is in favor of the "upper castes," will never allow such pure identity-based demands to be fulfilled. Even if they are conceded in a given conjuncture, efforts will be made to negate them in practice, or even to roll them back.

At present in India, for instance, "reservations" in favor of dalits and other "backward" castes are being sought to be undermined by two strategies: first, through a shrinking of the domain of the state sector where reservations exist, to conform ostensibly to the neoliberal economic policies that the state itself has adopted; and second, through a demand for further extension of such "reservations" even to obviously non-"backward" caste groups, such as Jats and Patels, with these groups resorting to their own brands of identity politics, which would necessarily attenuate the existing "reservations" for the genuinely oppressed castes. (One form of attenuation will be the additional introduction of "income criteria" and other such qualifications.) This second strategy amounts to a pure caste-versus-caste struggle, or what we might call a pure clash of group "belongings." Identity politics, in short, will not achieve a lessening of caste oppression at the economic level, let alone the elimination of caste.

What is required for the elimination of caste is the creation of a new "belonging" that transcends caste as a category altogether, a new belonging where both the oppressed castes and even members of other castes can find common ground, a higher community of belonging beyond caste. Breaking existing caste belongings through cultural phenomena such as inter-caste marriages, dropping of caste names, and the like, used to be considered an effective means toward this end; and these approaches do have a role to play. But their effectiveness is limited. The higher belonging transcending caste can only be created through common struggles built on supra-caste solidarity.

The Marxist perception in India, influenced by the European experience, has traditionally been that the development of capitalism would bring in such supra-caste solidarity through class struggle. Capitalism in Europe had destroyed the "old community" that existed under feudalism (the involuntary "community" that derived from being born within a feudal society) and had absorbed those displaced through such destruction into its own workforce. These workers in turn had, starting with what Marx had called "combinations," gone on to create a "new community." This experience, Marxists have assumed, would be repeated in India.

This, however, is unlikely. Behind both the destruction of the old community and the formation of the new, under the aegis of capitalism in Europe, was a massive emigration of labor to the temperate regions of European settlement. It is this which produced the requisite tightness in the labor market (i.e. kept down the relative size of the "reserve army of labor") to create effective "combinations" among workers, and ensured that those displaced through the destruction of the old community were not forced, owing to the absence of employment opportunities outside, just to linger on in their old habitats as a pauperized mass. Such emigration is impossible today from countries like India. At the same time, labor absorption under capitalism is so meager that it even falls short of the sum of the natural increase of the workforce and those displaced from petty production through its unviability owing to capitalist penetration. The result is a growing unemployment that manifests itself not as open unemployment existing alongside workers who are "fully employed," but rather as a proliferation of casual employment, intermittent employment, disguised unemployment, and the like. There is, in short, a shortage of "proper," or what the ILO calls "decent," employment. Because of this, a pauperized mass lingers on in the countryside, even as the mass of workers outside, i.e. under capitalism, is fragmented, with weak "combinations" and little solidarity.

This provides the condition for a flourishing of "identity politics" including caste identity politics. Capitalist commodity production tends to fragment the workers, to force them into competing against one another, as individuals and even as groups. This is the opposite of "combinations" – fragmentation. "Combinations" serve precisely to overcome such fragmentation. But when "combinations" are difficult (due to chronic impermanence and informalization of employment), then fragmentation persists, and "identity politics" in the realm of the polity is the counterpart of such fragmentation. "Neoliberal" capitalism in countries like India, no matter how rapidly the gross domestic product grows under it, produces economic fragmentation among workers because of its incapacity to create adequate employment; it correspondingly also produces "identity politics" in the realm of the polity.

Such economic fragmentation, together with the fact that caste itself becomes a barrier to combinations among agricultural laborers in the countryside, as it used to be in the early years of the trade union movement in the cities too (prompting Ambedkar, who led a dalit workers' union, to stipulate as a condition for cooperating with a Communist-led union that the workers of both unions should drink from the same water tap on the factory floor), makes working-class solidarity as a means of transcending "caste group belonging" difficult. The fact that the working class itself (both urban and rural workers) remains relatively small within a vast mass of petty producers makes things more difficult. The supra-caste "community of belonging" therefore cannot simply be a working-class belonging.

Where, then, do we search for supra-caste" belonging that would count as genuine social progress? Perhaps the answer lies in the ideal of a "fraternity of equal citizens." This is what the Indian Constitution promises, but its realization has been thwarted by the inadequate employment opportunities created for the mass of the people by the "spontaneous" working of neoliberal capitalism. A mobilization of people in supra-caste struggles for the realization of a set of universal and justiciable economic rights, similar to the political rights that already exist within the Constitution, can provide a way of transcending caste belongings for a higher community, that of citizens. Such a struggle for universal economic rights transcends identity politics. It pushes caste into the background, though it does not entail, as argued below, any withdrawal of the "affirmative action" strategy that already exists.

Among these rights one can list for immediate practical implementation a right to food, a right to employment, a right to state-provided free and quality health care, a right to state-provided free and quality education to all up to a certain level, and a right to adequate old-age pension and disability allowance.

The demand for such universal rights can bring together people belonging to different caste groups and hence build up supra-caste solidarity. And since a universal right to employment will not per se overcome the concentration of "lower castes" in menial and lesser-paid occupations, the elimination of the disjunction between the caste distribution of the population and the caste distribution within particular occupations will still need to be addressed, for which affirmative action in the form of "reservations" will be still required. The demand for such universal rights therefore does not obviate the need

for "reservations;" at the same time the achievement of such universal rights serves to reduce "upper-caste" opposition to "reservations." It achieves supra-caste solidarity, a condition for the annihilation of caste, in lieu of the caste antagonism that identity politics, if exclusively pursued, generates.

There is an important related issue here. Caste divisions are not the only fault-lines in Indian society; what in India are labeled "communal" divisions, above all between Hindus and Muslims, have occupied center stage recently. The two issues are related: the vast bulk of the Muslims in the Indian subcontinent are converts from the "lower castes" and continue to remain wretched and excluded. Unlike the Hindu "lower castes," they do not enjoy the benefits of "reservations" (since caste does not formally exist among Muslims), because of which, on certain social indicators like educational attainment, they have fallen even below the dalits, who were traditionally the most oppressed. In recent years some states have included reservations for certain purposes for "backward" Muslims within the overall quota for the "backward" castes (the maximum quota for all categories taken together is legally stipulated through a Supreme Court ruling); but the persistent attempt of the Hindu Right to arouse anti-Muslim passions within the majority community has put a restraint even on such ameliorative measures. The strengthening of a notion of "citizenship" through enlarging the set of rights, by incorporating economic rights in addition to the political ones, provides a possible direction of advance.

The foregoing does not mean a substitution of class struggle by some form of a "citizens' struggle." What it suggests is that class struggle itself must be oriented toward ensuring for every citizen the right to a minimum standard of material and cultural life.

The question arises: are such rights feasible? The answer depends on what we take to be the constraints, i.e. what is assumed to be unchangeable in the given situation. If the entire ensemble of relationships that underlies the given situation is taken as a constraint and assumed to be unchangeable, then obviously the only feasible outcome is what exists. Any change, therefore, toward a supra-caste and supra-(religious) community "belonging," must take only some elements of the existing situation as constraints but not others. Whether the proposed rights are feasible depends on what elements we take as constraints.

An example will clarify the point. Implementing such rights will certainly require additional public expenditure. The enforcement of some rights will no doubt automatically facilitate the achievement of others (e.g. implementing the right to education will increase employment of teachers, maintenance staff, and construction workers, which will make the right to employment that much easier to realize); but even so, around 8 to 10 percent of the GDP will be needed for this purpose. Since India has one of the lowest tax–GDP ratios in the world, raising these resources should pose no objectively serious problem. But if it is argued that any such fiscal effort will affect "investors' confidence" and hence be unfeasible within the current neoliberal capitalist order, then the preservation of the existing order is being made a constraint.

This is illegitimate. The desired social system should be one that makes the institution of such rights possible (provided that the objective availability, i.e. the supra-system availability, of resources permits it), rather than the institution of such rights being made secondary to the preservation of the economic arrangement that underlies the existing social system. No movement toward a new belonging is possible if we adopt the latter position.

One can go further. Neoliberal capitalism which shuns state intervention, except for improving investors' confidence, imbues the system with a "spontaneity," where its own immanent tendencies get full scope to work themselves out. These include a basic inequalizing tendency, which arises for reasons already discussed – namely, the non-diminution of the relative size of the labor reserves, which keeps real wages at a subsistence level even as labor productivity increases, thus raising the share of the economic surplus, accruing to the propertied classes and their largely high-income service providers, in total output. This inequalizing tendency, when superimposed on a pre-existing unequal socio-economic order, entails a widening, both economically and socially, of caste and religious-communal inequalities. The move toward a wider belonging therefore must restrain this inequalizing tendency; it cannot take the neoliberal capitalist order as a constraint upon its efforts. Doing so will not only thwart any wider belonging; it will be a panacea for acute and increasing social conflicts.

20.3.4 The Unfinished Project of Citizenship in Sri Lanka

20.3.4.1 Introductory Remarks

The question of belonging and identity in Sri Lanka today is inevitably tied to the aftermath of a civil war. The dominant position on how to usher in reconciliation in Sri Lanka after the end of the civil war in 2009 is founded on a faulty epistemology. The notion that each group inhabits some kind of culture and that the boundaries between these groups and the contours of their cultures – namely majority Sinhalese Buddhists (70 percent of the population) and minority (Sri Lankan and Indian) Tamil Hindus (12 percent) – are specifiable and easy to depict is deeply flawed (Benhabib 2004). Importantly, how most well-meaning policy-makers think inequities among groups should be addressed – and diversity and pluralism furthered – is still influenced by this culturalist approach.

According to this flawed epistemology, people are seen as and expected to belong to a single primordial community and to behave accordingly. The solution to the sovereignty claim made by Tamil separatists and crushed by the state forces remains, for believers in the distinctness of cultures, to divide the country on ethno-cultural lines, instituting a more or less advanced federal constitutional arrangement. We would like to suggest instead that turning to the political subject may prove to be salutary. If we follow Fanon's dream of articulating a subject "who becomes a citizen by participating in the formation of a people to come, a people that has not yet been imagined or invented" (Isin 2012: 565) we may be able to complete the unfinished project of citizenship.

20.3.4.2 False Integration

Since reconciliation has been premised on a faulty reading of society as composed of clearly delimited authentic cultural communities, the importance of mélange in society has been devalued. One can argue that the colonial taxonomical graft has in many ways inflected how attempts at reconciliation between conflicting parties have been shaped over the past 30 years. In its institutions and bureaucracies, traces of the colonial mold are still present (Wickramasinghe 2010). The urge to classify groups according to distinct cultural traits is at the center of the liberal state that has grown from the shards of the colonial state. The official status of cultural groups is regulated by the national identity cards citizens carry with them, the forms they fill in for state and non-state institutions to enter their children into schools, the religious instruction they receive in state schools, applications for scholarships, employment, and bank loans. One of the conventions in today's state is the "impermissibility of fractions, or to put it the other way round, a mirage-like integrity of the body" (Anderson 1998: 36).

20.3.4.3 Communities in Formation

Before advocating a turn to a new form of citizenship and to fluid cultural forms of belonging one needs to highlight certain traits among the peoples of Sri Lanka that add credence to this approach. First of all, the social formations called Sinhalese and Tamil are historically produced communities that are still in flux. The Sinhalese encompasses all Sinhalese-speaking people, including Buddhists, Catholics, and Christians. From the fifteenth century onwards, migrants from Tamil- or Malayalee-speaking south India streamed into the coastal areas of the island, adopted the Sinhalese language, converted to Buddhism or later Christianity, and became part and parcel of the Sinhalese community, forming the three intermediary caste groups in the maritime provinces. In contrast to the common perception that shapes school curricula and the public arena that Sinhalese people are direct descendants of the Aryan prince Vijaya, his lion grandfather, and his rowdy companions, the reality of the mixedness of the Sinhalese community in an island society, colonized for 400 years, is rarely claimed or lauded. A single culture as it is commonly understood still remains what makes you, and who you are, in Sri Lanka. But reality is quite different; people are moving between cultures, as documented in Amarnath Amarasingham and Daniel Bass's (2016) fascinating account of the way more and more young up-country Tamils who live outside the plantations identify themselves not as Indian Tamils – a term that refers to the people who had worked on the plantations since the mid-nineteenth century – but as Sri Lanka Tamils, a category that for census officials refers to Tamils whose family roots can be traced far back to the northern or eastern province. In a paradox of history the census, once an agent of fixity, is playing a role in destabilizing categories and promoting mobility. These playful subversions invite us to display some incredulity toward the claim that some scholars make over the importance of cultural recognition as the key to historical reconciliation.

Another complicating factor is that the distribution of communities varies from one region to another. While there are areas with a majority of over 80 percent (Tamil in the far north, or Sinhalese in the far south) there are also areas with approximately 25 percent minority populations and areas with approximately equal representation between groups – for example the plantation district of Nuwara Eliya and the Trincomalee and Amparai districts in the east. The state ten years ago denied the option of straddling many identities. But in everyday life and not only in border areas, anthropologists have shown that communities, men and women, spoke and still speak two languages and continue to visit all places of worship – catholic churches, Buddhist temples, and Hindu devales. The formation of cultural enclaves as a solution to the demands for justice by the Tamils of Sri Lanka is troubling, inadequate, and insufficient. Since more than half of the Tamil-speaking people live outside what would be devolved regions, it is the Sri Lanka state in its entirety that needs drastic change. Autonomy for the other can only happen in a state that nurtures pride in cultural mélange and hybridity rather than in the fantasy of the purity and authenticity of cultures.

20.3.4.4 Citizenship and the Making of Majoritarianism

Citizenship is an unfinished and until now flawed project. Since 1948, the year Sri Lanka became independent, citizenship or "being a citizen" has been experienced by the people of Sri Lanka in different ways. "Majorities are made, not born," posited Dru Gladney (1998). Indeed, by consolidating the majority community in the twenty-first century – as a political group and as a people unified by a common love for the land – the government of Mahinda Rajapaksa (2005–15) was in fact finishing a project that had been initiated in the late 1920s. With the abolition of communal representation and the introduction of universal suffrage in 1931, the voice of the rural Sinhalese majority gained a new prominence. The next step in border-drawing was initiated through the Citizenship and Franchise Acts, which were hurriedly passed by the new nation-state in 1948–49. These laws altered the balance of power among the various communities and helped consolidate a majority within the polity. Two types of citizenship – citizenship by descent and citizenship by registration – were devised while the status of citizenship became mandatory for the right of franchise. In both cases, documentary proof was required for applicants, a procedure that disqualified the majority of Indian Tamil workers, who were illiterate. Through these laws, a person who could not prove that she belonged to the new nation-state was defined as an alien (Wickramasinghe 2015). The issue of statelessness for over 900,000 people was finally "resolved" when in 1964 India and Sri Lanka signed a pact giving them citizenship in one or the other state.

After 1956 the Sinhala language was made the official language (Sinhala Only Act 33 of 1956), and over the following decades a growing perception of the state as bestowing public goods selectively began to emerge, breeding mistrust between ethnic communities. The changes introduced in the criteria for university admission known as "standardization," giving weight to the Sinhalese youth from underprivileged areas, was read by its adversaries as an unfair form of affirmative action. This led to a permanent crisis in higher education. The failure of the state to guarantee social mobility through education and the unequal distribution of education entitlements were central issues in the southern insurrections and the Tamil insurrection in the north and east in the 1970s. While issues of unemployment led the Sinhala rural educated youth to rebel in 1971, the early Tamil militancy was energized by the issue of standardization. As Cheran suggests, this explains the middle-class character of the early Tamil militancy in Jaffna, which only in the late 1970s spread to less-privileged social groups (Cheran 2009). The 1970s university admission schemes

represent a crucial moment in the process of transformation of this core perspective on the state, which was no longer seen as a harbinger of social justice but as an impediment to some peoples' very "capacity to aspire," to borrow Arjun Appadurai's words (2004). For a generation of Tamil youth, the affirmative action schemes of the 1970s constituted irrevocable evidence of the partiality of the state vis-à-vis the majority Sinhalese. The 1970s crisis illuminates how the lack of public debate on issues of equality of opportunity can lead to distrust and misinterpretations that linger.

20.3.4.5 Civic Nationalism?

After the end of the civil war, the state formulated a new politics of patriotism, which coupled state and nation. Sri Lanka, it was proclaimed, would no longer have minorities. This statement in effect redefined the idea of multicultural society embodied and endorsed in the Thirteenth Amendment to the Constitution of 1987. In the new civic nation, citizens/patriots would be ethnically undifferentiated, although promise was made that all religions and ethnic identities would be respected.

The idea of a civic nation is commendable but utopian. Any attempt to construct "one people" involves marginalizing some. Furthermore, all examples of civic nations – the United States and France are cases in point – have anchored their liberal principles in a particularistic legacy. Most liberal democratic political cultures reflect the norms, history, habits, and prejudices of majority groups. They usually attempt to foster a political identity whose political content makes it compatible with a variety of practices and beliefs. Moreover the new patriotism enunciated has little in common with the post-national or constitutional patriotism that has been theorized as an alternative form of loyalty, compatible with universal values but distinct from and superior to nationalism. It has little in common even with a civic patriotism that recognizes the public sphere cannot be neutral (Canovan 2000). On the contrary, the vision of the victorious government merged the nation and state and promoted a love of country based on a particular reading of the history and foundation myth of the Sinhala people in which all other groups – those formally known as minorities – were present merely as shadows, not as constitutive elements of a common political culture.

20.3.4.6 Nurturing a Sense of Belonging

The new government voted in in 2015 inherited a state that, instead of ushering in ethnic reconciliation, political equality, and economic distribution, systematically and purposefully created conditions for a further sharpening of ethnic divides and a deeper marginalization of Sri Lankan Tamils, Muslims, and up-country Tamils.

Turning toward the citizen is a possible way out of the impasse, not as the disciplined citizen-patriot that Rajapaksa's ten years in power attempted to construct but as Tagore's citizen who has a responsibility to be disloyal to national and subnational prisons.

The challenge may be today to try to revitalize "disloyal citizenship" as an alternative to multiculturalism and federal arrangements in a way

20

that reaches further than legal rights and entitlements, within a state structure that recognizes multiple identities through multiple acts of identification. This would mean acknowledging the limits of pluralism and devising criteria to determine what is admissible and what is not. If non-Sinhalese are to identify with a superordinate identity that transcends their attachment to a group, to feel that they belong, the state needs to be sensitive to the ways in which certain expressions of "banal nationalism" can easily alienate cultural minorities. Continuing to flag Sinhala Buddhist nationhood, a practice that started in the mid-1950s, might not be the most judicious way for the state to win over members of other communities to the goal of civic patriotism. Inclusion alone is not enough, as all citizens enjoy rights according to the Constitution. Economic rights alone are not enough.

The ideal of pluralism that was espoused to describe and order what were read as distinct cultures within a society also led to the production of differences and hierarchies.

A new citizen needs to be created whose sense of belonging would question the notion that she inhabits a single discrete culture. She would speak multiple languages, Sinhala, Tamil, and English. In school, instead of following instruction about her religion of birth she would learn about world religions; instead of learning a skewed national history she would learn about the interconnectedness of histories; she would then create state institutions where multiple identifications and mélange are valued rather than tolerated. What is needed is to put into practice the ideal that people inhabit a complex world of meaning that does not correspond to a single, bounded, authentic, and unchanging notion of culture.

20.3.5   France and the United States

Contrasted definitions of belonging are at the center of major tensions between ethno-racial groups across advanced industrial societies.[10] Alternative logics of social segmentation are often at work, and they can be identified by focusing on categories through which members view one another as significant others who share fundamental moral worldviews and/or cultural traits. More specifically, it is possible to consider the symbolic boundaries that individuals trace when they are asked to describe the kinds of people they like and dislike, whom they feel inferior and superior to, and whom they are similar to and different from. In the process, differences that are at the center of individual maps of perception emerge, as well as the differences that are not salient in the way people discuss worth, status, and, indirectly, community membership. The result is a comparative analysis of models of inclusion/exclusion that operate on the basis of different status cues, such as color, class, and immigrant status.

A comparison of institutionalized national "models" of social segmentation reveals contrasted patterns in France and the United States in particular. One can argue that the French model combines strong external boundaries and weak internal boundaries.[11] For French workers in particular, "us" includes all the French, but with increasing frequency, "les français de souche" only, while a large portion view immigrants – and particularly Muslim immigrants – as unable to assimilate to a universalistic French culture. In the early 1990s, the poor and blacks were still included in the definition of the French "us," as understandings of the social bond structuring French society downplayed internal divisions to emphasize humanitarianism, collective responsibility toward indigent fellow citizens, as well as a certain universalism qua republicanism. By the late 2000s, under the influence of neoliberalism, the boundaries drawn toward the poor had become more rigid in France, as they had in large segments of Europe (Mijs, Bakhtiari, and Lamont 2016). Boundaries toward Muslims and blacks had also rigidified (Lamont and Duvoux 2014). In contrast, in the early 1990s, American workers already drew strong internal boundaries against the poor and African-Americans, largely on a moral basis, i.e. in the name of work ethic and responsibility. These external boundaries were more mixed: immigrants who partook in the American dream were more easily made part of "us" than African-Americans, but strong boundaries were also present toward illegal immigrants. By 2010, after 30 years of neoliberalism, boundaries toward the poor have also become more acute, as manifested, for instance, in the fact that data from the American National Election Survey shows that many more college-educated blacks opposed government spending for the poor in 2012 than in 1980 (Hochschild, Weaver, and Burch 2012: 1253) Although a culture of diversity has become more broadly diffused and institutionalized (Berrey 2015), discrimination toward African-Americans is persistent and a strong boundary separating non-blacks and blacks remains a dominant feature of American society (Gans 1999). According to the 2000 General Social Survey, whites prefer a neighborhood that is more than half white and less than a third African-American. For their part, on average, African-Americans prefer a neighborhood that is a third African-American and less than half white. Both groups prefer to live near in-group members, but African-Americans prefer to live in more racially mixed neighborhoods than do whites.

Understanding patterns of boundary work is particularly urgent in a context of mounting neoliberalism and xenophobia, which both entail a narrowing of bonds of solidarity. Both models involve exclusion, but boundaries are structured differently across cases. In particular, the relative decoupling of racism and blackness in the French case in the early 1990s sheds light on the American case by putting it in perspective.

The "imagined communities" are not necessarily primarily framed in political terms: in France as in the United States, individuals use moral and cultural arguments about differences and similarities to define "people like us." They refer to the struggles of their own daily lives, which are central to their own concept of self, and negatively judge others whom they perceive as not meeting basic moral standards (in terms of work ethic, sense of responsibility, perseverance, etc.) In the worldview of many of these workers, moral, racial, and class

---

[10]   This section draws from Lamont (2002), with permission of University of Minnesota Press.

[11]   Based on an interview-based study of French and American workers conducted in the early 1990s (Lamont 2000), updated through a detailed review of changing boundaries in France (Lamont and Duvoux 2014; see also Fassin and Fassin (2009).

boundaries work hand in hand to provide them a space for self-worth and dignity.

20.3.5.1   French Cultures of Solidarity

In a Durkheimian vein, Jeffrey Alexander (1992: 291) argues that:

> members of national communities often believe that "the world," and this notably includes their own nation, is filled with people who either do not deserve freedom and communal support or are not capable of sustaining them (in part because they are immoral egoists). Members of national community do not want to "save" such persons. They do not wish to include them, protect them, or offer them rights because they conceive them as being unworthy, amoral, and in some sense "uncivilized."

In contemporary France, these unworthy people are primarily the growing number of Muslim immigrants originating from North Africa, as "Islam marks the frontier of what is foreign" (Kastoryano 1996: 63).

Between 1960 and 1974, the majority of immigrants to France came from North Africa (Morocco, Algeria, Tunisia), and they arrived often under temporary permits directing them into the worst-paid, least-desirable jobs in manufacturing, mining, and public work. These immigrants were a visible minority who, after 1974, could establish their families on French soil. Their numbers grew rapidly. A sense of competition and the breakdown of traditional working-class culture eventually translated into xenophobia and calls for repatriation of non-Europeans. This movement amplified and resulted in a major breakthrough when, in the 1984 European parliamentary election, the Front National, whose main program was to oppose immigration, received more than 11 percent of the vote. This party continues to lament the disappearance of the old white and culturally homogeneous France, one where neighborhoods were safe and truly French, where popular culture and collective identity coexisted in an organic way, undisturbed by the mores, smells, and bizarre clothing of non-European immigrants.

Today, many native French workers draw strong boundaries toward North Africans, and in doing so they use three primary types of moral argument: First, they are viewed as lacking in work ethic and sense of responsibility, and as having access to a larger share of the collective wealth than they are entitled to. This is particularly unbearable to workers because it violates their sense of group positioning (Blumer 1958). Interestingly, whereas American workers condemn blacks for their lack of self-reliance, French workers are angry that immigrants are favored by a disloyal paternalist state, at a time when the quality of life and education in working-class neighborhoods is perceived as being in steady decline.

Second, French workers draw boundaries against North Africans on the basis of their lack of civility: they spit in front of people, never apologize, are rude, and lack respect for others. They also have barbarous mores (e.g. they kill goats on their balconies at Ramadan). They destroy French quality of life and should go back home.

The third and most fatal failing of North African immigrants is their inability or refusal to assimilate, which violates republican ideals and is perceived by workers as a major threat to their personal and national identity. Republican ideals include the Jacobean notions of equality, universalism, and national unity. These ideals negate particularism based on religion, locality, race, corporate membership, and birth. They also presume a voluntaristic or contractual approach to political participation: anyone can join in the polity as long as they assimilate and come to share the same political culture. That North Africans are perceived as refusing this contract (by resisting assimilation) invalidates their right to reside in France. In contrast, throughout French history, other immigrant groups have not been as intensely stigmatized because they were perceived as assimilating quickly (through the army, unions, schools, or left-wing political parties), or as being there only temporarily (Noiriel 1988). This refusal to assimilate is particularly resented because being French is one of the most high-status aspects of workers' identity, and because French political culture defines this republicanism as quintessentially French, and even as one of the most sacred contributions of the French nation to the world.

It is largely because they are Muslims that North African immigrants are construed by native French workers as either particularly resistant to assimilation or unable to assimilate. Indeed, as Muslims they are described as fundamentally other, and in some cases as culturally incompatible with the French ("they don't respect women," "they don't believe in human rights," "their education is different"). Undoubtedly, this rejection is linked to the defense of a "true French culture" that is threatened not only from the inside by foreigners but also from the outside by Americanization. Moreover, colonial notions of France's "mission civilisatrice" and of French superiority remains present in the minds of many workers, especially when it comes to "barbaric" former African colonies. Elements of these available cultural repertoires are appropriated by French workers to reinforce boundaries against Muslims: differences in the degree of their religious involvement are downplayed, and even "beurs" (i.e., second-generation children of immigrants) who have French citizenship are widely perceived to be immigrants.

The importance of immigrants in the boundaries that the French interviewees draw is particularly remarkable when compared with the place that these men give to alternative bases of community segmentation in their discourse on "the Other," and particularly the place they give to racial Others (mostly blacks) and to the poor. Their boundaries toward blacks have been historically weaker, although they have gained in importance in recent years. There is a decoupling between racism and blackness that is surprising from an American perspective. As French citizens, black Martiniquais and Guadeloupians are by right and de facto fully and equally included in the national collectivity, again on the basis of republican ideals. A survey in the early 1990s showed that when asked which category of immigrants posed the greatest difficulty for integration, 50 percent of the French respondents identified North Africans, far more than the 19 percent who pointed to black Africans or the 15 percent who named Asians (Horowitz 1992: 19). More recent survey data consistently provide evidence that negative feelings toward North African immigrants are much stronger than negative feelings toward blacks, toward European immigrants, or toward other racial minorities (Lamont and Duvoux 2014).

A number of factors combine with the culture of republicanism to create weak boundaries against blacks, as compared with North Africans: (1) Most North Africans are first- or second-generation immigrants. Blacks are more heterogeneous: while some are recent immigrants from Sub-Saharan African, those from the overseas territories and departments ("Dom-Toms") have been French for several generations. This works against defining "us" in opposition to "blacks," and partly trumps the low status of blacks as formerly colonized people. (2) Blacks living in France are more heterogeneous religiously than North Africans – for instance the Senegalese are predominantly Muslims while the Congolese are Catholic (Tribalat 1995) – which also works against institutionalizing a clear distinction between "us" and "blacks." While North Africans include a small Jewish population, they are often presumed to be homogeneously Muslims. (3) Muslims are more salient to French workers because they constitute a larger group than blacks (again, they make up almost 5 percent of the French population as compared with less than 2 percent for blacks). (4) The process of decolonization was much more peaceful in French Sub-Saharan Africa than in North Africa, which sustained less negative stereotypes of blacks than of North Africans. And (5), historically, a sizable proportion of black African immigrants came to France to be educated. This population was of a more elite background and was more assimilated than many low-skilled North African workers. Their presence worked against negative views of blacks, at a time when low-skilled black Africans had less easy access to French shores than their North African counterparts due to geographical distance.

The arrival of a rapidly increasing number of West African immigrants might be undoing this relative dissociation between blackness and racism. In particular, the policy of family reunification that was put in place after 1974 brought in large numbers of African families, which made Muslim African migration more visible in part by focusing public attention on polygamy and female genital mutilation (Barou 1996). Nevertheless, overall, the combined characteristics of blacks living in France work against a clear polarization between "Frenchness" and "blackness" in a manner unparalleled for North Africans. Racial "Others," such as Asians, have assimilated very successfully. They contribute to the playing down of racial differences as a basis for internal differentiation within French society.

French workers also downplay the internal segmentation of their society by integrating among "people like us" individuals located in the lower echelons of society. But boundaries toward this group have become more salient in recent years. Republicanism, Christianity, and socialism all provide elements of cultural repertoires that favor such weak internal boundaries toward the poor. French workers have historically put great emphasis on solidarity and this continues to shape how they understand their fate and the role of structural forces in explaining their plight.

20.3.5.2　Collectivity, American-Style

In the mind of many American workers, social and cultural membership remain largely equated with being white and being at least lower-middle or working class. They more often evaluate people on the basis of their "success" and more readily draw boundaries against individuals below themselves on the socio-economic ladder, as compared with the French. They often resort to arguments having to do with work ethic and ambition in doing so, distinguishing superior and inferior people: "some people out there I think that could do better and don't try. There's nothing wrong if you don't want to become something, but don't blame somebody else for it."

There appears to be a close association between moral and class boundaries in the United States. The literature has clearly documented the association between poverty and irresponsibility, laziness, and lack of self-sufficiency (e.g. Katz 1989). Thus, after declaring proudly that he is a diehard Republican, a worker explained that being Republican means "Don't give anything for nothing. Incentive … Go get a job … [We should not] make it so easy to stay on unemployment, on welfare." Such men are angry that they have to pay so much in taxes to support the poor who "don't work at all and get everything for free." They more often stressed traditional aspects of morality (e.g. the Ten Commandments and the defense of traditional work ethic) than the French. When asked to choose, from a list, traits that they dislike most, half chose "lazy," in contrast to a fifth of their French counterparts.

When asked to whom they feel superior and inferior, the majority of American interviewees constantly and subtly shifted from moral to racial boundaries, drawing both at once, and justified racist attitudes via moral arguments. The rhetoric they used to draw boundaries against blacks resembles that which they use to reject the poor: they stressed their alleged lack of work ethic and sense of responsibility. They also pointed to their inability to educate their children properly, particularly in moral matters, and their lack of self-sufficiency. An electronics technician summarized the way many perceive the situation when he said: "It's this whole unemployment and welfare gig. What you see mostly on there is blacks. I see it from working with some of them and the conversations I hear … That's bullshit. It may be white thinking, but, hey, I feel it is true to a point." This passage illustrates how for some American workers, class, racial, and moral boundaries work hand in hand in such a way that the community of "people like us" is defined very narrowly and certainly excludes blacks, who are largely constructed as living off working people.

That boundaries against the poor and blacks in the United States are so strong is undoubtedly related to the fact that these two groups are associated with one another. (In contrast, in the French context, the long-term unemployed are mostly white French workers who are victim of economic restructuring.) Hence, in the United States, blackness and poverty trace the limits of social membership, and this trend is likely to become more accentuated as we move toward an opposition between all non-blacks and blacks (Gans 1999), despite the centrality of egalitarianism in American political culture (de Tocqueville 1945; Lipset 1979).

In this context, immigrants, and particularly immigrants who attempt to achieve the American dream, are easily made part of "us" (Lieberson 1980). These immigrants still hold a privileged place in the country's self-image in part because it is first a country of immigrants. Tthe United States remains a nation of nations, where external boundaries remain relatively weak. When describing their mental maps, few workers pointed to immigrants, and when they did, it was rarely to single out their moral failures. Some pointed to failure to assimilate, and are slighted by what they perceived to be a lack of desire to learn English among immigrants. However, they tended to be more concerned with the dangers this represents for the decline of the relative status of the nation, than for immigrants' moral character. National surveys also show that in the early 1980s, the percentage of Americans who did not perceive immigrants as "basically good, honest people" was only around 20 percent, and the percentage who did not consider them as hardworking was only 18 percent (Lapniski et al. 1997, p. 367). Moreover, Espenshade and Belanger's (1998) survey analyses reveal that if Americans have negative feelings toward immigrants, these are ambivalent and not strongly held. These boundaries have become more rigid over the last 20 years, propelling Donald Trump to the presidency of the United States in 2017.

20.3.5.3   Conclusion

This brief sketch of the external and internal boundary patterns that prevail in France and the United States still begs qualification and raises a number of questions. However, in a nutshell, it does suggest the presence of somewhat contrasted models in which moral boundaries play a key role: in France, strong boundaries are erected toward Muslim immigrants, whose culture is viewed as fundamentally incompatible with a universalistic French culture. Simultaneously, boundaries against blacks and the poor have been downplayed in the name of French universalism and a view of morality that stresses solidarity, egalitarianism, and humanism and is influenced by Christianity, socialism, and republicanism. In contrast, in the United States we continue to find strong moral boundaries drawn against the poor and African-Americans on the basis of responsibility and work ethic, while legal immigrants who partake in the American dream are made part of the collective "us."

Analyzing how workers define worth and cultural membership is particularly pressing today, in our era of neoliberalism. We know that national welfare systems reveal implicit rules about conceptions of merit and social citizenship that vary across societies. Yet, conceptions of moral communities and cultural membership that underlie policy choices remain under-examined. We described conceptions of moral communities by focusing on the schemas of evaluation used by ordinary citizens. National social policies are more likely to be adopted if they resonate with conceptions of the boundaries of the community that citizens upheld. Moreover, boundary ideologies also have a powerful impact on the agenda of political parties and the electoral strategies they use. Hence we must study these conceptions if we are to make sense of some of the most important social and political changes that we are facing today, at a time when community boundaries appear to be narrowing and when principles of solidarity seem to apply to an increasingly small number of "people like us."

20.3.6   The Role of Language in Belonging and Identity: Some Thoughts from Europe

Being able to express ideas in language allows human beings to remember the past, organize the present, and plan the future. Language permits individuals to negotiate with each other, cooperate, and live in groups. This utility of language is thus its fundamental attribute. However, the fact that this human skill has developed as languages rather than language has added another very important function: the use of a language variety defines the parameters of a group; it includes as members all those who are speakers and excludes all those who cannot speak the language. Language thus plays a key role in the construction of political/social identity as communication takes place and social interaction cements relationships among all those who can understand each other. It seems to us that being able to communicate is a fundamental requirement in belonging, and we agree with George Steiner (1975) that at best incomprehension produces "zones of silence" and "cultural isolation" while at worst it fosters the construction of those with whom we cannot communicate as "Other" or "Enemy."

The question of language difference has not always been of concern to rulers. Feudal suzerains, absolutist monarchs, and emperors did not habitually require their subjects to speak one and the same language. As long as there were adequate bilinguals in the chains of command there was little pressure for linguistic unity. This changed radically as the world became a mosaic of nation-states and democracy began to spread. The ideal in nationalism is that people, language, and territory are congruent and the state the home of a homogeneous nation. This was, of course, rarely the case and a good deal of social engineering was required to harmonize populations. Language was a particular challenge, since belonging to a community of communication is different to many other forms of belonging. One cannot change language simply by an act of will; one cannot "convert" to a language; language shift for individuals and communities comes only after a long (and usually hard) apprenticeship.

Achieving national communities of communication has not been unproblematic. It was always the language of a power group that was enshrined as national language, and those with other cultural and linguistic heritages were constrained to converge or shift to this language variety. Since linguistic conformity was equated with loyalty, the system produced monolinguals as many accepted the national language as their sole medium for communication and identity needs. Those who maintained separate language communities (either through their own choice or through exclusion) became "minorities," often to their detriment. The nation-state system divided the world linguistically as well as politically, producing a mosaic of national languages. Contact across language frontiers was accomplished by learning foreign languages.

We cannot claim that this world is now part of history; the nation-state is clearly still a very potent force in the world and a key focus of belonging. However, the flows, exchanges, and networks of an increasingly globalizing world are challenging the strict division of populations into national groups whose main communication takes place within that group. There is greater contact as migration increases under the pressures of continuing global economic inequality and the extreme political insecurity in war zones and lawless states. There is greater contact as increasingly global structures of economic activity produce a highly mobile workforce on all continents. There is greater (virtual) contact as fact and opinion circulate on the internet, to which approximately a third of humanity has access. In all of these fast-evolving aspects of globalization there is also a linguistic dimension. Who is talking to whom and in what language? How are new virtual communities of communication being constructed? Who is excluded? Who has access to knowledge? Who does not? For all of us concerned with belonging and solidarity, language raises significant and complex issues. As it always has.

20.3.6.1 Europe, the Nation-State, and After

Europe was the continent on which the concept of the nation-state was first elaborated. As a mosaic of nation-states developed slowly in the modern era, an important component of national citizenship was competence in the national language. In some states, knowledge of the national language is an objective criterion of belonging. Some constitutions (e.g. the Spanish) demand it explicitly. In other states (e.g. the UK) the requirement is unwritten but universally accepted.

Many different processes and activities combined to help the spread of national languages in Europe. There was overt, top-down policy: a single language variety was chosen, codified, and standardized. It became the medium in national education and in state institutions. Citizens were pressed to shift to show loyalty (particularly in times of war). Other developments had unplanned effects on language convergence: industrialization and urbanization provided melting pots where the national language was the lingua franca; the establishment of national frontiers cut the dialect continuum; the printing industry with its reluctance to cater for diversity and its desire for large markets produced texts for a national readership in the national language. National language acted as social glue. Individual citizens would never meet all their co-citizens, but, as Anderson (1983) observed, they felt they belonged to an "imagined community" because in theory they could communicate with all members of the group.

The imagined community had, of course, good and bad effects. On the positive side, it was a factor in the development of the welfare state; tax and redistribution seemed more acceptable when the recipients came from the same community of communication. It was also integral to the democratic process; an imagined community helped build consensus and balance interest groups within the polity. On the negative side, a strong sense of national belonging was one element in the slide to total war; the world wars of the twentieth century had their root in European nationalisms.

It was recognition of this that led to an ambitious project to create structures that would rein in dangerous ways of belonging. The European project started with the creation of the European Steel and Coal Community in 1952, which pooled control of the industries that are the motor of modern warfare. In 1958 the creation of the European Economic Community dismantled some aspects of national sovereignty in the commercial domain. The merging of member states' economic and political responsibilities continued with the Single European Act (1986) and the Treaty on European Union (1991), which introduced the idea of the single market with free movement of capital, goods,

people, and services and gave citizens of member states citizenship of the Union.

The European Union experiment has been successful in that it appears to have aided political stability during economic recession. It has promoted democracy within states in transition. It has ensured the rule of law and press freedoms. It encouraged new economic thinking in failing command economies. If dangerous nationalisms have not been eradicated, they have been corralled. However, there has not been universal support for the ever closer union envisaged by the founding fathers. The clearest rejection of the vision has come recently from the UK electorate, which narrowly voted to leave the Union in June 2016, but there are pockets of resistance in most member states.

There are a multitude of reasons why populations or parts of populations have not transferred their allegiance wholesale from the national to the European level. First, nation-building was a very successful process and the elements that coalesced to make it so cannot be readily dismantled; national education, national media, national democracy, national welfare, etc. continue to produce profound feelings of national belonging. Second, there is a widespread feeling that the European Union is an elite project which bypasses the ordinary citizen and which in its leaning to neoliberalism benefits big business more than workers. Third, many perceive a democratic deficit at the heart of the EU, because there is no forum for the democratic practice of debate.

At the heart of much of this third cause for negativity is the linguistic fragmentation of the EU. Citizens lack channels for debate across language boundaries. Europe-wide media lack profile and influence compared with national media. There is no regular political interaction among the different populations. But, although the lack of a European forum and the absence of a European demos both have a linguistic dimension, problems of communication are rarely discussed. The political class of the EU tends to play down the language issue and maintains strict respect for the nation-state language tradition; the legal equality of all the national languages of member states is a fundamental of the treaties. Perhaps this could not have been otherwise given the weight of the nation-state legacy, in which language is linked with sovereignty and hierarchy. Respect for national languages, however, means that no general community of communication is developing among European populations.

This, however, is not the case among elites, who transcend linguistic enclosure to run the institutions of the EU and profit from the single market. They participate in the networks and activities of the multilingual polity either by having constant access to quality translation and interpretation, through their own personal multilingualism, or by using the current lingua franca. These channels are not easily available to ordinary citizens. Translation and interpretation are expensive services to purchase, knowledge of a number of prestige European national languages presupposes a high education level, and even functional knowledge of English, the current lingua franca, suggests more than basic-level qualifications and opportunities for travel and practice. In consequence the European community of communication, such as it exists, tends to be an elite phenomenon.

From a theoretical perspective it seems curious that the elites of the EU, who relinquished so much economic and political sovereignty to the European project, shied away from tackling the linguistic/communication issues inherent in polity-building. In practice, it is easy to see why elite-led development of any kind of European community of communication was and is impossible. Any top-down language planning on the model of nation-state-era planning is blocked by the very success of that earlier process.

20.3.6.2   Language as System; Language as Dialogic Creativity

One aspect of the linguistic problems of the EU as a community is the respect for language as system. Each national language is standardized, its norms have been relatively stable over a long period and its speakers are held to be homogeneous. A much used metaphor is that of "nation as container" (Gellner 1983), which evokes the idea of speakers securely corralled within their community of communication. Thus, in cross-border communication we have competing national standards.

The first national language to play the role of lingua franca in the EU was French. In the last decades it has become English and fluent mastery of standard English is the current passport to participation in European political, commercial, financial, scientific, and educational domains. UK or US national standards are taught in education, are the norm for publication, are a prerequisite for elite employment and seem to be prized in lingua franca exchange. With native-speaker standards as the model, most non-native speakers are constructed as having a linguistic deficit. But isn't it curious that citizens of the EU submit to nation-state norms, when they are using English as a lingua franca in what is in many ways a post-national situation? If Europeans need a medium of exchange, does it have to be the full-scale adoption of a national language? Why is there is an unthinking default to UK or US standard Englishes?

There is an alternative paradigm to the de Saussurean "language as system" model. Wittgenstein and Bakhtin (among others) proposed that language is co-construction, a work constantly in progress. Wittgenstein (2002) suggests that a language user is an agent, someone who contributes to agreement on rules. These must be reasonably consistent within a community if the propositions made using them are to have meaning for members of the community, but it is the community of speakers that continuously adjudicates and constructs the system of rules. Agreement on use comes from within the group. In Bakhtin's (1981) analysis, language is dialogic creativity where speakers (whose linguistic backgrounds are necessarily different even within the same community of communication) constantly accommodate in order to interact and co-create meaning. Such a perspective allows language users more fluidity and flexibility. It removes the straitjacket of the alien standard. Lexis can change as connotations develop and language users can feel free to simplify grammar and

syntax to suit their purposes. In this view, those who use the language own it and are not measured against national language standards.

The problem is complex. Europeans might hesitate to develop their own brand of English as a lingua franca because they are part of global networks as well. And the corporate executives of neoliberal capitalism, the high-ranking employees of international and supranational bodies and high-profile figures in the spheres of sport, art, and entertainment, together with a globally mobile group with lesser power and influence (technical experts, middle management, scientists, educationalists, engineers, etc.), constitute a "transnational ruling class" (Lauder 2015: 172) that lives, works, and socializes in standard English. Of course, this global elite is not comprised solely of native English speakers. Many from other linguistic groups have learned English as a necessary (if not sufficient) condition of becoming members. They acquire their standard English in international schools and in prestige universities. Qualifications in standard English (e.g. the British IELTS or the American TOEIC) are gatekeepers for access to education and employment.[12]

At the moment there is immense resistance to any linguistic leeway, as hostile reactions to the work of linguists[13] who document deviation from standard English in international settings demonstrate. Such hostility probably stems from the way that new practices undermine the inherited cultural capital of those whose first language has become the lingua franca of power and the acquired cultural capital of those who have learned that lingua franca with much effort and investment. There is thus no impetus from elites to reduce the high bars to entry to their community of communication. Native speakers enjoy their advantage gained without effort, and non-native speakers seem to prize the distinction they have achieved (Bourdieu 1979).

There is also disdain for linguistic creativity in interaction across language borders. "Globish" is dismissed as inferior, and the resourcefulness evident in the current superdiversity of European cities (Vertovec 2007) is rejected as "pidgin." However, instances of exchange in settings of diversity reveal intensely creative linguistic behavior. Linguists[14] have recorded individuals who communicate without extensive knowledge of each other's languages, cooperate to use the linguistic resources available, and adopt, adapt, blend, and negotiate. We could argue that in such exchanges, we have useful models for dealing with the complex heteroglossia of global flows. However, such language dexterity is neither valued nor rewarded. On the contrary, European states increasingly require proof of high levels of competence in their national languages for those who apply for residence permits and citizenship. Those who have ambitions to remain in the European destinations in which they find themselves must acquire the standard language of the state.

So at all societal levels there is gatekeeping that ensures that standard language is the criterion for belonging. There is little appreciation of the utility of linguistic flexibility in heteroglossic settings, little

---

12   This is classic hegemony – in Gramsci's (1971) sense.
13   E.g. J. Jenkins, B. Seidlhofer, and A. Mauranen.
14   E.g. K. Arnaut, J. Blommaert, B. Rampton, M. Spotti, T. Milani, S. Leppannen. For a recent study see the 2014–18 project on translanguaging in four UK cities, directed by A. Blackledge and A. Creese. www.birmingham.ac.uk/generic/tlang/working-papers/index.aspx.

understanding that those with skills derived from negotiating changing language environments are better adapted to a globalizing world than those who conceive language as rigid systems. Our present language ideologies allow little tolerance for the development of new language practices. Europeans in general are very ill at ease with linguistic fluidity and negotiation and exclude any new linguistic development as "error." We are not open to allowing the development of new languages to suit new human groupings and relationships.

20.3.6.3   Conclusion

So the question arises: does our modern love of linguistic normativity aid or hinder belonging? Certainly an agreed standard gives clarity to the linguistic aspect of entry into a group. It does, however, set the bar high.

We might be minimally hopeful that attitudes to national standards will change because of the new e-technologies. On past evidence we should expect alteration in language behavior. The technologies of communication (writing, printing, audio-visual) all played crucial roles in the way that communities of communication and languages developed. Now that e-technologies democratize authorship and permit multiple voices, there is likely to be change as digital literacies and multimodality permit and encourage new linguistic freedoms. Now that three billion human beings have access to the internet, we could surmise that a proportion are seeking to cross linguistic frontiers. And as they do so, will they continue to adhere to the strict system of national standards or will they increasingly negotiate meaning with the linguistic repertoires at their disposal? At an early stage of the process and with ever increasing numbers involved, it is perhaps too early to predict exactly how practice will develop.

It seems very idealistic to suggest that linguistic belonging could arise from negotiated meaning rather than from acquisition of stable national languages. However, challenging prevailing attitudes to language could reduce the linguistic gatekeeping associated with global elite networks, could give value to linguistic repertoires that are effective but unrewarded, could start to dismantle the reign of the rigid standard, where so many operate in deficit mode. In Europe, an approach to communication that permits some negotiation and accommodation would allow Europeans to use English in a way that gives them ownership. In general, a less rigid adherence to the language ideology and practices of the nation-state might open up communication practices that allow for wider networks of belonging and greater solidarity.

20.3.7   Social Cohesion and Belonging in Latin America

Latin America does not possess a systematic, coherent set of subjective indicators for social cohesion. However, what information is available, although fragmented, does help to illustrate the situation of certain variables associated with social cohesion in Latin America.

One source of information is Latinobarómetro, an opinion survey that covers a wide range of subjects. This survey also has certain limitations,

however, so the data it provides must be treated as purely illustrative in nature. On the plausible assumption that social cohesion is an essential condition for belonging, the purpose of this survey is to explore forms of belonging in Latin America by looking at the problems and prospects for social cohesion in its various societies.

20.3.7.1   Perceptions of Justice

Latinobarómetro indicates that a large percentage of the population regards the legal system as unfair, discriminatory, and, what is more, inefficient. Only a little over a third of those interviewed in 17 countries (36 percent in 2001 and 35 percent in 2003) say that they agree or strongly agree with the statement "There are sharp differences across countries," however. In Argentina and Paraguay, fewer than one person in five (18 percent on average) agrees with the statement, while in Nicaragua and Uruguay almost half (47 percent on average) do so. There are also differences between respondents of different ethnic origins.

In Bolivia, Guatemala, and Peru, the percentages agreeing with this statement are significantly lower among indigenous people than in the population at large (12, 7, and 17 percentage points, respectively).

This finding should be borne in mind, because differences by ethnic origin become more significant when we turn to personal attitudes and predispositions, which are subjective factors.

20.3.7.2   Job Insecurity

Many Latin Americans also express concern about the possibility of losing their current position in the near future, and this does not seem to have changed since the mid-1990s. In 2005, three out of every four working people said they were "very concerned" or "concerned" when asked "How concerned would you say you are that you will be left without work or unemployed during the next 12 months?" A review of the Latinobarómetro series for this question shows a rise in concern about the possible loss of employment peaking at 80 percent in the regions in 2002, partly owing to the increase in Argentina (from 72 percent in 2000 to 86 percent in 2002) and Uruguay (from 63 percent to 74 percent in the same years). There were also increases in Brazil, Chile, Honduras, and Panama in the early years of the decade.

20.3.7.3   Trust in Institutions

This type of trust can be defined as "the belief that a person or group will be able and willing to act appropriately in a given situation." It thus constitutes "a temporary suspension of the basic uncertainty surrounding the actions of others."

Levels of trust fall dramatically when people evaluate the institutions most directly linked to political power: the judiciary, the legislature, and political parties. As many as 13 percent of those surveyed expressed mistrust in all persons and institutions, a pattern that is most pronounced among people of indigenous origin (and women more than men) and the poorest.

20.3.7.4   Multiculturalism and Discrimination

The emergence in the region of the issue of multiculturalism means a manifestation of diversity and the coexistence in society of different groups, which can influence a country's degree of social cohesion.

The fact is that exclusion and discrimination in all their forms (against women, indigenous populations, older adults, the disabled, the poor, religious, or ethnic minorities, those evincing non-heterosexual preferences), based on what are almost always ascriptive characteristics in terms of symbolic and cultural representations of what constitutes "difference," fracture and undermine the sense of belonging to a society among those affected and, consequently, impair social cohesion. This is a complex phenomenon (and one with clear historical and cultural roots in the case of discrimination against indigenous peoples) that manifests itself subjectively in socio-cultural representations, stereotypes, traditions, and stigmas, and in symbolic expressions of inequity, which do not always have a direct link to people's material living conditions and which, in any event, transcend them (Véase Székely 2006).

As for discrimination, it would be a mistake to think that these attitudes and the practices associated with them were more powerful or occurred only or mainly in countries with a larger proportion of indigenous people, such as Peru, Mexico, Bolivia, and Guatemala. The racial mixing characteristic of Latin America complicates the picture sometimes subtly, sometimes not so subtly; discrimination also affects people of mixed race who, chiefly because of their physical appearance, are restricted in their opportunities for recognition, status, and access to wellbeing on equal terms with the Caucasian population. In a number of Latin American countries, furthermore, it is race rather than membership in indigenous groups that provides the basis for discrimination against those of African descent.

20.3.7.5   Social Solidarity

Within this context, the concept of solidarity, i.e., unity or agreement of feeling or action, refers especially to mutual support given in difficult circumstances, the degree of solidarity exhibited by fellow citizens, and the importance people assign to the need for greater solidarity. As may be seen, while on average more than half the population in these countries think their fellow citizens tend to show solidarity, a strikingly higher percentage of people have a negative perception in poorer societies with substantial proportions of indigenous people. Conversely, the countries where people perceive the greatest social solidarity among others are the ones with the most robust social policy institutions, the most active anti-poverty efforts, and, generally speaking, the highest levels of trust.

In the light of the information given about trust and solidarity, the question arises as to whether some "social fissure" is undermining

social solidarity and limiting it to collaboration within the immediate community, and whether this fracture is specifically linked to social exclusion and discrimination.

20.3.7.6   Social and Community Participation

Participation can be understood as any collective action aimed at attaining particular ends, implying the existence of a collective identity rooted in shared values, interest, and motivations. As for community participation, this can be understood as the rational, conscious, and voluntary organization of individuals inhabiting a particular geographical territory with a view to devising initiatives that meet their needs, identifying common interest and values, collaborating in the realization of public works and the provision of public services, and influencing the decision-making of groups exercising power in that territory.

Appreciation of Democracy

The information provided by Latinobarómetro, based on a set of indicators included in the 2002 census round and data for 1996, shows a decline from 61 percent to 57 percent in the share of respondents stating that they prefer democracy over any other regime.

According to the index of support for democracy (UNDP 2004: 132, 133), 43 percent of Latin Americans qualified as democratic, 26.5 percent as non-democratic, and 30.5 percent as ambivalent.

The evidence from Latinobarómetro and Eurobarometer is that, in both Latin America and the European countries, only a little over half of all citizens are satisfied with the workings of democracy in their country; in Latin American this percentage fell by ten percentage points between 1996–97 and 2004–05 (from 62 percent to 52 percent) while in the European Union (15 countries) it increased by eight percentage points (from 48 percent to 56 percent).

Indifference to Politics and the Rejection of Parties

It has already been noted that a willingness to participate in organized deliberations and collective planning is one of the types of behavior and attitudes that contribute to social cohesion.

Overwhelmingly, the evidence is that Latin Americans are uninterested in politics. Although negative replies to the question "How interested are you in politics?" could have different motivations, the fact is that since the mid-1990s, between two thirds and three quarters of those interviewed by Latinobarómetro have replied that they are only "a little" or "not at all" interested. The 2005 data show 74 percent of the populations sharing this low level of interest, and this attitude is consistent with the low frequency of political participation. Just 27 percent of the population said that they talk about politics frequently or very frequently; 17 percent said that they frequently or very frequently try to convince someone of their political ideas; and just 6 percent said that they work or have worked for a political party or candidate.

A lack of interest in politics is accompanied by a growing rejection of political parties. Between 1996 and 2005, the proportion of respondents who rejected political parties rose by five percentage points, on average (from 35 percent to 40 percent), in the 17 countries covered.

As might be expected, the failure to ascribe value to political parties, which are the principal mediators between the aspirations and interests of citizens and the possibility of their expression in the state, is closely associated with a feeling of detachment from them. In 2003, 58 percent of Latin Americans felt that they were not close to any political party, a rise of 12 percentage points from the low reached in 1997.

The attitude of rejection toward political parties and the tendency to abstain from voting are generally on the rise, indicating a lack of interest in political participation, which is an important aspect of social participation. Are these attitudes a consequence of social fragmentation resulting from exclusion and discrimination and expressed in a lack of appreciation for democracy and in a feeling of discontent, whose effects are heightened in poor and highly unequal societies? The social exclusion and lack of citizenship reflected in these attitudes of rejection and alienation from politics do nothing to strengthen the sense of belonging to society. Both impede democratic governance and the achievement of stable social agreements or covenants.

In summary, the limited and fragmented empirical data available paint a disturbing picture of the variables associated with the sense of belonging, the strength of people's ties of solidarity, insecure employment, and the very doubtful legitimacy of democratic institutions, all of which demonstrates that social cohesion needs to be placed quite high up on the region's agenda.

20.3.7.7   A New Social Contract

Latin America needs to take a qualitative leap if it is to capitalize on the opportunities opened up by globalization. Attaining this objective will require high and sustained growth rates; efficient public policies to reduce income inequalities, educational divides, and employment problems; large investments in education, science, and technology; a shift toward a meritocratic society that respects diversity; and an end to long-standing discriminatory practices.

This entails the creation of a new social contract. Long-term policies to strengthen cohesion need to be underpinned by a contract that is endorsed by a wide range of stakeholders willing to negotiate and accept far-reaching agreements. This implies that stakeholders must be ready to sacrifice some of their personal interests for the benefit of all. It also needs to be understood, however, that this relinquishment of private interests for the common good is not a purely altruistic action, inasmuch as it arises out of the belief that the common good is the best guarantee of individual interests.

To create the right political conditions for social cohesion, the Economic Commission for Latin America and the Caribbean (ECLAC) believes that one of the first priorities is to establish clear fiscal rules covering the levels and sources of contributory and non-contributory

solidarity financing. These rules must also be based on explicit, guaranteed, and enforceable thresholds for the exercise of social rights. Universally recognized rights cannot be applied at the discretion of certain individuals or left to the workings of the market.

In accordance with the principles of universality and solidarity, such a social cohesion covenant must ensure that resources are used transparently and effectively. It also needs to be oriented toward reaching a consensus on the following points.

- Guaranteeing a certain threshold of social protection to which all members of society are to have access simply by virtue of their citizenship. This threshold should be set at a realistic level in terms of the society's stage of development and viable levels of intersectoral redistribution and transfers, which means that political viability is a necessary consideration.
- Raising thresholds of social protection, welfare, and investment. Both the rate of increase and its sequencing and progressiveness should be calculated to optimize the relationship between growth and equity. Redistributive mechanisms must safeguard competitiveness and the sustainability of growth.
- Creating tangible manifestations of solidarity. The exact mechanisms may vary from country to country for reasons of age, gender, employment status, income, and specific vulnerabilities.
- Forging an institutional structure with sufficient authority and legitimacy.
- Using regulatory mechanisms, as well as other measures, to ensure that the principle of solidarity is effectively applied in fiscal and contributory financing.
- Strengthening solidarity in the case of contributory systems, through the social optimization of contributions.
- Care should also be taken to make sure that contributions are rewarded by established levels of benefits so as to prevent abuses in the name of solidarity. Thus, the contributory efforts of individuals should be linked to both the quantity and the quality of actual benefits as well as to the principle of solidarity.
- Increasing the progressiveness of social spending and the tax burden and ensuring that the benefits are openly channeled to the most vulnerable groups in the forms of social investment.
- Adopting certain standards in terms of the impact on social cohesion of any increase in available resources, which the state should assume as one of its obligations under the covenant.

The most significant proposals being made in this connection establish a link between public finances and social cohesion. They suggest that the social contract should be combined with a fiscal covenant by means of certain "general rules of the game" which fiscal authorities undertake to apply. Only if the constraints imposed by these rules are respected will it be possible to ensure the financial viability of the goals and provisions of a social contract under which citizens do not just demand rights, but also agree upon ways of guaranteeing them and rendering them enforceable.

A social contract embedded in a fiscal covenant that is consistent with contributory systems, cementing the link between public finances and social cohesion, confers legitimacy upon public financing policies designed to reconcile economic viability with social effects that expand access to social benefits and to opportunities for human capital formation for the most deprived sectors of society.

As we have seen, this contributes to social cohesion in a variety of ways. The interaction of public finances with social protection can be seen as both a point of departure and a point of destination for cohesion, as a locus of dialogue based on a shared language and on procedural rules accepted by all parties. Thus, this interaction can also serve as the foundation for a state policy whose aims are greater equity, less exclusion, and guaranteed social rights for all, a policy that will instill a greater sense of belonging and distributive justice, thereby engendering confidence in the future and trust in social institutions.

20.4   Some Conclusions, Prospects, and Possibilities

How might we conceive the ideal of belonging in terms of our overall theme of social progress? As we see it, progress in the realm of belonging occurs when it becomes less fixed and more inclusive. In terms of the three aspects of belonging (identity, solidarity, and the unalienated life) this would amount to overcoming identities in the narrow sense, and this emerges as a result of increasingly unalienated social relations and the cultivation of greater solidarities over different groups rather than within groups.

How such progress is made may emerge from a variety of conditions and may be variably pursued. But our regional surveys suggest that central to these various possibilities is the need to stress and to integrate two different agencies in any large-scale effort toward these ends: on the one hand the role of the state and the policies and reforms it can enact, and on the other the element of democratic mobilization. The latter has two functions. Movements first of all put pressure on the state to enact policies that promote the conditions of cohesion that generate solidarities, civic rather than divided participation, and eventually unalienated social relations. But movements are also locations of public education through democratic collective deliberation, which, if sustained over time, helps to create solidarities that transcend particular sites of language, ethnicity, religion, etc. to a register of common concepts and ideals. What forms these movements might take and what policies exactly they seek from the state will, of course, differ in different regional contexts.

Our different regional surveys threw up a range of further, more specific, conclusions. We very briefly and abbreviatedly list below two or three of these, just to give a vastly summarizing sense of the detail that may be found in these surveys.

The reports from Canada and Sri Lanka propose startlingly different policies, the former weighing in favor of recognition of communitarian identities that should be dialogically brought together, the Sri Lankan report stressing a more top-down state intervention that discourages such communitarian differences for a more civic form of popular participation. One report on Europe traverses the vexed forms of exclusion that owe to language, in particular how deliberative democracy may be blocked by language constraints – first by lack of knowledge of

the language of debate and then further by lack of access to the conceptual register of debate. The report on Islamic nations is a historical account of how identities formed and ideologies developed into an ethical register, despite seemingly politically articulated goals.

References

Alexander, J. 1992. "Citizen and Enemy as Symbolic Classification: On the Polarizing Discourse of Civil Society," in M. Lamont and M. Fournier (eds.), *Cultivating Differences: Symbolic Boundaries and the Making of Inequality*. Chicago: University of Chicago Press.

Amarasingham, A., and D. Bass. (eds.) 2016. *Sri Lanka. The Struggle for Peace in the Aftermath of War*. New York: Oxford University Press.

Ambedkar, B.R. 2014. *Annihilation of Caste*. New Delhi: Navayana.

Anderson, B. 1983. *Imagined Communities*. London: Verso.

Anderson, B. 1998. *The Spectre of Comparisons. Nationalism. Southeast Asia and the World*. London: Verso.

Appadurai, A. 2004. "The Capacity to Aspire: Culture and the Terms of Recognition," in V. Rao and M. Walton (eds.), *Culture and Public Action: A Cross-Disciplinary Dialogue on Development Policy*. Stanford, CA: Stanford University Press.

Bakhtin, M. 1981. *The Dialogic Imagination*, transl. M. Holquist and C. Emerson. Austin: University of Texas Press.

Barou, J. 1996. "Les immigrations africaines," in D. Assouline and M. Lallaoui (eds.), *Un Siècle d'immigration en France: 1945 à Nos Jours. Du Chantier a la Citoyenneté?* Paris: Diffusion Syros.

Benedict, Ruth. 1934. *Patterns of Culture*. Boston: Houghton Mifflin.

Benhabib, S. 2004. *The Claims of Culture: Equality and Diversity in the Global Era*. Princeton, NJ: Princeton University Press.

Berlin, Isiah. 1990. "Two Concepts of Liberty," in *Four Essays on Liberty*. Oxford: Oxford University Press.

Berrey, E. 2015. *The Dilemma of Diversity*. Chicago: University of Chicago Press.

Blumer, H. 1958. "Race Prejudice as a Sense of Group Position." *Pacific Sociological Review* 1: 3–7.

Boaz, Franz. 1963 [1911]. *The Mind of Primitive Man*. New York: Collier.

Borrows, J. 2016. *Freedom and Indigenous Constitutionalism*. Toronto: University of Toronto Press.

Bourdieu, P. 1979. *La Distinction. Critique sociale du jugement*. Paris: Éditions de Minuit.

Canovan, M. 2000. "Patriotism Is Not Enough." *British Journal of Political Science* 30/3: 413–432.

Capra, F. 2015. *The Systems View of Life*. Cambridge: Cambridge University Press.

Cheran, R. (ed.) 2009. *Pathways of Dissent. Tamil Nationalism in Sri Lanka*. New Delhi: SAGE.

Colley, Linda. 1992. *Britons: Forging the Nation 1707–1837*. New Haven, CT: Yale University Press.

de Tocqueville, A. 1945. *Democracy in America*. New York: Vintage.

Dhamoon, R. 2009. *Identity/Difference Politics: How Difference Is Produced and Why It Matters*. Toronto: UBC Press.

Espenshade, T.J., and M. Belanger. 1998. "Immigration and Public Opinion," in M. Suarez-Orozco (ed.), *Crossings: Mexican Immigration in Interdisciplinary Perspectives*. Cambridge, MA: Harvard University Press.

Fassin, E., and D. Fassin. (eds.) 2009. *De la question sociale à la question raciale?* Paris: La Découverte.

Feyerabend, Paul. 2010. *Against Method*. London: Verso.

Gans, H. 1999. "The Possibility of a New Racial Hierarchy in the 21st Century United States," in M. Lamont (ed.), *The Cultural Territories of Race: Black and White Boundaries*. Chicago and New York: University of Chicago Press and Russell Sage Foundation.

Gellner, E. 1983. *Nations and Nationalism*. Oxford: Blackwell.

Gladney, D. 1998. *Making Majorities: Constituting the Nation in Japan, Korea, China, Malaysia, Fiji, Turkey and the United States*. Stanford, CA: Stanford University Press.

Gramsci, A. 1971. *Selections from the Prison Notebooks*, transl. and ed. Q. Hoare and G. Nowell Smith. London: Lawrence & Wishart.

Habib I. 1995. "Caste in Indian History," in *Essays in Indian History*. New Delhi: Tulika.

20

Hacking, Ian. 2000. *The Social Construction of What?* Cambridge, MA: Harvard University Press.

Hardin, Garrett. 1968. "The Tragedy of the Commons." *Science* 162/3859: 1243–1248.

Harman, Gilbert. 1975. "Moral Relativism Defended." *Philosophical Review* 84/1: 3–22.

Hochschild, J.L., V. Weaver, and T. Burch. 2012. *Creating a New Racial Order: How Immigration, Multiracialism, Genomics, and the Young Can Remake Race in America.* Princeton, NJ: Princeton University Press.

Horowitz, Donald L. 1992. "Immigration and Group Relations in France and the United States," in D. Horowitz and G. Noirel (eds.), *Immigrants in Two Democracies: French and American Experience.* New York: New York University Press.

Isin, E.F. 2012. "Citizenship after Orientalism: An Unfinished Project." *Citizenship Studies* 16/5–6: 563–572.

Kastoryano, R. 1996. *La France, L'Allemagne et leurs immigrés: négocier l'identité.* Paris: Armand Colin.

Katz, M. 1989. *The Undeserving Poor: From the War on Poverty to the War on Welfare.* New York: Pantheon.

Kosambi D.D. 1965. *The Culture and Civilization of Ancient India.* London: RKP.

Kuhn, Thomas. 1962. *The Structure of Scientific Revolution.* Chicago: University of Chicago.

Kymlicka, Will. 1995. *Multicultural Citizenship.* Oxford: Oxford University Press.

Lamont, M. 2000. *The Dignity of Working Men: Morality and the Boundaries of Race, Class and Immigration.* Cambridge, MA: Harvard University Press.

Lamont, M. 2002. "Working Men's Imagined Communities," in U. Hedetoft and M. Hjort (eds.), *The Postnational Self: Belonging and Identity.* Minneapolis: University of Minnesota Press.

Lamont, M., and N. Duvoux. 2014. "How Neo-Liberalism Has Transformed France's Symbolic Boundaries." *French Politics, Culture and Society* 32/2: 57–75.

Lapniski, J. S., P. Peltola, G. Shaw, and A. Yang. 1997. "The Pools-Trends. Immigrants and Immigration." *Public Opinion Quarterly* 61: 356–383.

Lauder, D. 2015. "International Schools, Education and Globalization: towards a Research Agenda," in M. Hayden, J. Levy, and J. Thompson (eds.), *The Sage Handbook of Research in International Education.* Los Angeles: SAGE.

Lieberson, Stanley. 1980. *A Piece of the Pie: Black and White Immigrants since 1880.* Berkeley: University of California Press.

Lipset, Seymour Martin. 1979. *The First New Nation: The United States in Historical and Comparative Perspective.* New York: W.W. Norton.

Locke, John. 2017 [1689]. "Second Treatise on Government." www.earlymoderntexts.com/assets/pdfs/locke1689a.pdf.

Marx, Karl. 1955. "Preface to a Contribution to a Critique of Political Economy," in K. Marx and F. Engels, *Selected Works*, vol. 1. Moscow: Foreign Languages Publishing House.

Mijs, J., E. Bakhtiari, and M. Lamont. 2016. "Neoliberalism and Symbolic Boundaries in Europe: Global Diffusion, Local Context, Regional Variation." *Socius: Sociological Research for a Dynamic World* 2: 1–8.

Mill, John Stuart. 2017 [1859]. *On Liberty.* www.earlymoderntexts.com/assets/pdfs/mill1859_1.pdf.

Noiriel, G. 1988. *Le creuset français. Histoire de l'immigration, XIXe–XXe siècle.* Paris: Seuil.

Rawls, John. 1971. *A Theory of Justice.* Cambridge, MA: Harvard University Press.

Rees, W. 2010. "Thinking Resilience," in R. Heinberg (ed.), *The Post-Carbon Reader.* Corvallis, OR: Post-Carbon Institute.

Steiner, G. 1975. *After Babel: Aspects of Language and Translation.* Oxford: Oxford University Press.

Taylor, Charles. 1994. "The Politics of Recognition," in Amy Gutman (ed.), *Multiculturalism: Examining the Politics of Recognition.* Princeton, NJ: Princeton University Press.

Tribalat, Michèle. 1995. *Faire France. Une enquête sur les immigrés et leurs enfants.* Paris: La Découverte.

Tully, James. 1995. *Strange Multiplicity.* Cambridge: Cambridge University Press.

Tully, James. 2008. *Democracy and Civic Freedom.* Cambridge: Cambridge University Press.

UNDP. 2004. *Democracy in Latin America: Towards a Citizen's Democracy.* New York: UNDP.

Véase Székely, Miguel. 2006. *Un nuevo rostro en el espejo : Percepciones dobre la discriminación y la cohesión social en México.* Serie Políticas Sociales 128. Santiago: CEPAL.

Vertovec, S. 2007. "Superdiversity and Its Implications." *Ethnic and Racial Studies* 30/6: 1024–1054.

Webber, J. 2015. *The Canadian Constitution: A Contextual Approach.* London: Bloomsbury.

Wickramasinghe, N.K. 2010. "Sri Lanka's Independence: Shadows over a Colonial Graft," in B.R. Brass (ed.), *Routledge Handbook of South Asian Politics. India, Pakistan, Bangladesh, Sri Lanka, and Nepal.* Abingdon, Oxfordshire: Routledge.

Wickramasinghe, N.K. 2015. *Sri Lanka in the Modern Age. A History.* New York: Oxford University Press.

Williams, Bernard. 1981. "The Truth in Relativism," in *Moral Luck.* Cambridge: Cambridge University Press.

Wilson, Peter. 2017. *The Holy Roman Empire: A Thousand Years of Europe's History.* London: Penguin.

Wittgenstein, L. 2002. *Philosophical Investigations*, transl. G. Anscombe. Oxford: Blackwell.

Concluding Chapters

The Multiple Directions of Social Progress: Ways Forward

Forward

Coordinating Lead Authors:[1]
Nancy Folbre, Erik Olin Wright

Lead Authors:[2]
Jenny Andersson, Jeff Hearn, Susan Himmelweit, Andrew Stirling

[1] Affiliations: NF: University of Massachusetts, Amherst, USA; EOW: University of Wisconsin-Madison, USA.
[2] Affiliations: JA: Sciences Po, France; JH: University of Huddersfield, UK; SH: Open University, UK; AS: University of Sussex, UK.

Summary

This chapter engages with three important themes of the larger report: the meaning of progress, its uneven nature, and obstacles to future progress.[3] It also considers a number of political and economic alternatives aimed to overcome these obstacles, emphasizing the need for diverse strategies, open-minded experimentation, and scientific assessment.

While it may be impossible to ever reach agreement, the effort to calibrate different interpretations of progress remains an important exercise for political deliberation about how to make the world a better place. The very hope of moving forward implies some agreement on a destination. All of us must take responsibility for the future.

Our discussion emphasizes the complexity and multidimensionality of the interpretive debate, but also calls attention to its ideological character. Social actors – individuals, groups, and even academic disciplines – tend to define progress in ways that serve their own interests. In a way, distributional conflict undermines our very efforts to better understand and mediate such conflict.

The uneven character of progress is manifest in many different domains. Increases in the global reach of formally democratic institutions have been accompanied by growing concerns about their stability, efficacy, and consistency with democratic ideals. Successful economic development has created a new category of "middle-income" countries, even as it seems to have contributed to income polarization within many at the top.

The so-called "welfare state" was a major advance in the twentieth century. Government programs have expanded education, improved health, and created new forms of social insurance in many areas of the world. But slower economic growth and intensified social divisions in recent decades have created pressure for cutbacks. Many governments can no longer effectively tax or regulate corporations that have the power to relocate and minimize such inconveniences. In both Europe and the US, austerity-based policies are reducing public support and services for many vulnerable groups, including single mothers, students, the long-term unemployed, and pensioners.

In most, if not all, countries, women have gained greater access to education, political rights, and economic opportunities. However, increases in their formal labor force participation seem to have stalled in many countries, and women continue to shoulder a disproportionate share of the burden of caring for dependents. Public policies that support family work, such as subsidized child care and paid parental leave from work, vary considerably in coverage both within and across countries. In the US, highly educated women are able to bargain for family-friendly benefits; in large metropolitan areas they can easily hire low-wage women migrants to reduce their own family care burdens. Gender differences are now heavily inflected by differences based on citizenship, race, and class.

Economic inequality has also undermined progress toward environmental sustainability. Innovative new technologies offer ways of averting disastrous levels of climate change and ecological damage. But their implementation is often blocked by groups with powerful interests in the status quo who are protected from (or unconcerned by) the long-run consequences of their actions. Likewise, both political and economic power shape the direction of scientific and technological change, with little scope for democratic participation.

Why has progress been so uneven? Existing forms of capitalism both concentrate economic power and discourage the provision of public goods. But class differences alone cannot account for patterns of inequality based on citizenship, race/ethnicity, gender, and many other dimensions of group identity. Differences in collective bargaining power often lead to unfair and inefficient outcomes. While democratic institutions offer a means of negotiating better solutions, they currently seem inadequate to the task. Social science itself has yet to provide much assistance.

Yet social science theory and research suggest that a number of emerging institutional innovations could contribute to the development of a more collaborative, democratic, and egalitarian society. Rather than putting democracy at the service of the market, we could put the market at the service of democracy. The expansion of non-capitalist firms, including worker cooperatives, employee stock ownership, social enterprises, and other hybrids, could contribute to the development of a "cooperative market economy." Improved regulation of private enterprises – especially

3   Acknowledgments: We are grateful to Nick Couldry, Nico Cloete, Ronaldo Munck, and especially Shahrashoub Razavi for detailed engagement with earlier drafts. Leila Gautham provided invaluable assistance with copy-editing.

the financial sector – could protect the public interest. Progressive tax-and-transfer policies could reduce economic inequality. The public sector could improve, streamline, and expand the provision of health, education, and care services,

Some specific examples of these strategies include successful large-scale worker-owned businesses such as Mondragon, community-based credit unions, forms of co-management by owners and workers known as "economic bicameralism," and proposals for universal basic income and care services. Possible innovations in political decision-making include sortition legislatures (which, like juries, require the random participation of citizens) and participatory budgeting.

Social scientists don't have all the answers. But the only way we will ever find them is by moving beyond the critique of existing institutions toward a more focused and inventive process of exploring new ones.

21

21.1   Introduction

There are strong historical links between the social sciences and the idea of progress. The modern social sciences were part and parcel of the building of nation-states in Europe from the seventeenth century on. They came together around Comte's positivist notion of change, according to which modern societies evolved through predictable stage-driven trajectories. Social scientists, hoping to master messy processes of social change in capitalist societies, aspired to displace the authority of previous beliefs in human destiny. The idea of progress represented a shift from notions of religious sovereignty to the idea of human-made change based on scientific rationality, steady improvement in technology, and secular political will. Such Enlightenment conceptions marched the social sciences into the contemporary era. Notions of linear change were reproduced in twentieth-century conceptions of modernization as a process of universal development steps. Such notions remain deeply embedded in both Marxist and pro-capitalist world views. They were, however, never universally shared, and evoked considerable criticism. By the 1960s, the Western-centric worldviews of modernization theory were vehemently challenged, and so were attempts to use the social sciences to implement a Western worldview of modernization.

The 1960s, marked by a return of critical theory and Marxism, and the rise of feminism and postcolonialism, saw both a formidable outreach of social science and growing awareness of its problematic relationship with the exercise of political and economic power. As collateral damage, confidence in the possibility that social science could successfully shape reformist projects was undermined. The very notions of "progress" and "modernity" were problematized, often bracketed in an effort to inoculate against their ideological undertones. At the same time, a turn to narrative, discourse, and subaltern voices created a great plurality in conceptions of social change while emphasizing that notions of progress directly linked to capitalism, technology, and forms of growth constituted a historically contingent Western process of modernization (see discussion in Chapters 3 and 4). Many of these critiques have been led by intellectuals and activists from and in the global South, and the Third or postcolonial worlds, where faith in progress has long been questioned (see, for example, Said 1978; Spivak 1987; Mies 1999; Santos 2014, among many others).

Challenges to progress are rooted in profound inequalities in world development that endured during the long post-war period of Western-driven world integration and in unexpected defections from commitments to democracy itself. The International Panel on Social Progress stands at a crossroads. The social sciences urgently need to produce an account of progress that stresses its universal aspects while not losing sight of social differences, plural values, and multi-dimensional priorities. These profound issues demand a global perspective that takes account of both social conditions and scholarship in postcolonial, Third-World, global-South perspectives, as well as insights from feminist and critical race theory.

The chapters of this report build some consensus on how social scientists define progress, but they also stress the late hour. The global climate has been destabilized. The financial crisis has created new uncertainties regarding turbulent market forces. Intensified economic inequality and insecurity, surges in international migration and refugee flows, and a resurgence of nationalism and racism, among other threats, loom large. In 2017, the Bulletin of the Atomic Scientists set its famous doomsday clock to two minutes to midnight, where it had not been since the Cuban missile crisis of 1962.

The central values of progress include democracy, equality of opportunity, mutual aid and care for dependents, and ecologically and socially sustainable economic development. While such values will never have a universal and fixed meaning, they constitute, as the Panel in its totality proposes, a compass for arriving at a sense of whether world developments are moving in the right or wrong direction. Rejecting a teleological view of progress is not at odds with retaining a rational kernel in the very approach to progress. This rational kernel is the idea that there are important *potentials* in the present for large-scale social improvements, and that these can be realized through action on a set of different levels of world politics, citizen participation, and collective agency. These potentials may never be fully actualized, but they form the basis for human struggles to make a better world. We may no longer have good reason to predict progress, but must nonetheless work toward it.

In this chapter, we contribute to this effort by: first, reexamining the meaning of progress in a contemporary world; second, describing the uneven shape of progress as social improvement; third, identifying the main obstacles to progress in the world today; and fourth, outlining a set of ideas or practical utopias for the twenty-first century.

21.2   The Meaning of Progress

The concept of progress in the Western tradition is directly linked to the notion of the future. The invention of the future, as the German historian Reinhart Koselleck (2004) has remarked, came from the idea that coming horizons of time would embody improvements wrought by rationality, technology, and industry. The future, unlike destiny, would emerge as a secular space made by people. This secularization of destiny gave birth to the modern idea that progress would require changing the power structures of absolutist societies. The Enlightenment conception of modernity also gave rise to the notion that European societies occupied the lead on an axis of time, with other parts of the world lagging behind.

Many twentieth-century social theorists (including Dewey 1935; Luhmann 1995; Elias 1996) also emphasized the crucial link between the future, human rationality, and social imagination, arguing that the concept of utopia could help counter notions of social development predetermined by economy or technology. But while a future equated with progress has long shaped the social sciences, the relationship between the two has been called into question since at least the 1970s. The IPSP also challenges confidence in a technologically preordained better future based on the liberal, democratic values of Western capitalist societies.

Social scientists must confront the possibility of future crises that threaten the very idea of progress, raising issues of growing inequality within affluent countries, between countries of the North and the South, and also between living and unborn generations of humanity. We must take long-term perspectives into account, and encourage what sociologists Barbara Adam and Chris Groves term "caring for the future" (Adam and Groves 2007), especially in the face of the possible irreversibility of social and environmental changes.

21.2.1   Progress as Social Improvement

However difficult it may be to maintain confidence in any grand narrative of progress, many of the chapters in this report show that the world has witnessed significant improvements since the mid-twentieth century. Technological advances have helped bring the people of the world closer together, reduced hunger, and improved life for many people. Medical science has made extraordinary advances. Global literacy has expanded and the gender gap in literacy has been significantly reduced. Infant mortality has declined and longevity increased. Economic productivity has grown. But other, less positive trends are apparent. Economic development has been accompanied by environmental degradation and looming climate catastrophe. The social environment too has suffered, with intensified inequality, erosion of communities, and heightened vulnerability and precarity for many people in many parts of the world. Improvements in women's access to education and opportunity in many parts of the world have been accompanied by multiple revivals of patriarchal authority. The traumas of abrupt globalization have triggered a backlash of nationalist and, often, racist mobilization. This report as a whole paints a picture of humanity equipped with enormous unrealized potential.

To identify progress as social improvement rather than as a driving force of history immediately poses a number of difficult issues. Five are especially important: the multidimensionality of social progress; disagreements over the values that constitute progress; conflicting interests at stake in progress; beliefs about the causes of and solutions to impediments to progress; and political struggles over progress.

21.2.2   Multidimensionality

First, the ideas of "social improvement" that necessarily underlie any understanding of progress are irreducibly complex, multidimensional, and plural (Norgaard 1994). There are many values and goals relevant to making the world a better place and no way of meaningfully collapsing them into a single metric of improvement (Stirling 2011). The list is long and heterogeneous, and this inevitably means that there will be tensions, trade-offs, and even contradictions among them (Ophuls 1997). Some of these are familiar. For example, for many people, two important values in play in social improvement are individual freedom and democracy: a world with more freedom and more democracy is better than one with less freedom and less democracy (Freire 2001). However, individual freedom includes, among other things, freedom to spend money as one wishes, and in a society with large inequality of income and wealth, this undermines democracy. In this instance, a full realization of democracy would require restrictions on individual freedom by either limiting private donations to political campaigns or

significantly redistributing income and wealth. What this means is that even where there is a broad consensus on the list of values that constitute the stuff of progress, there can be considerable disagreement on the relative desirability of particular priorities and trade-offs.

21.2.3   Disagreement over Values

Beyond disagreements over priorities, there is, of course, no real consensus on the underlying values themselves (see discussion in Chapters 1 and 2). This is the second difficult problem in talking about progress: some values used to judge progress are nearly universal; others are deeply controversial; and in some instances, the very meaning of a value is contested. Consider, for example, the widely discussed United Nations Sustainable Development Goals (UN 2015a). Driven by decades of collective action by social movements (Redclift 1987; Doherty and Geus 1996; Bloom and Breines 2003; Perreaul, Bridge, and McCarthy 2015), the 17 internationally adopted Sustainable Development Goals, were generated by an arduous process of international deliberation that sought some kind of broad consensus for what the report calls a "new universal agenda." As one might expect, most of the goals are not especially controversial. For instance, the second goal is "end hunger, achieve food security and improved nutrition and promote sustainable agriculture." Virtually no one would deny that ending hunger is a social improvement – although the inclusion of multiple indicators and targets by which to account for progress toward this goal may nonetheless be challenging to certain interests. But other goals in the agenda are much more controversial, such as the fifth goal, "achieve gender equality and empower women and girls," or the tenth goal, "reduce inequality within and among countries." While the desirability of eliminating abject poverty might be a near universal, gender equality certainly is not, and many people think that there is nothing especially objectionable about economic inequality as such. Furthermore, goals that are not on the list – such as religious freedom and tolerance, democracy, freedom of association, and so on – would be even more controversial internationally.

Conflicts over the values that constitute social progress occur not just cross-culturally. Deep political and ideological divides over the values that are relevant for judging social progress occur within countries as well. Of particular salience are sharp disagreements over the values connected to equality and social justice. On the one hand, there are political orientations, typically identified with the "right" of the political spectrum, which are deeply skeptical of egalitarian understandings of social justice. For many traditional conservatives, this skepticism comes from a view of society as an organic whole with functionally necessary hierarchies and inequalities. For some strands of libertarian conservatism, the rejection of egalitarian values is anchored in a survival-of-the-fittest worldview in which inequalities are celebrated, democracy is viewed with suspicion as empowering the weak, and aggressive competition is seen as legitimately producing winners and losers. While few people defend the idea of "might makes right" as a moral ideal, political movements often embody this principle as a practical orientation. From this perspective, social progress might be understood as people taking responsibility for their own welfare without expecting others to bail them out when they fail.

On the other hand, political orientations generally associated with the "left" and often referred to as "progressive," are anchored in a more horizontal worldview committed to egalitarian ideals of social justice and democratic ideals concerning the distribution of power. From this perspective, social progress can be defined by the degree to which a society assumes collective responsibility for individual wellbeing and fosters equality in access to the social and material conditions required for people to flourish.

Even when people seem to agree on the importance of certain values, it can still be the case that the real meaning of those values may be contested. Consider the value "gender equality." For many people, gender constitutes of a simple binary rooted in nature. The value of gender equality is then simply a question of equality – especially equality of opportunity and power – between men and women. For others, gender is a much more complex idea, not simply because gender relations are socially constructed rather than given by nature, but because gender is not a simple binary. Attending to gender includes the gendered construction and differential gender power of diverse femininities and masculinities; inequalities connected to gender diversity and sexual diversity, including LGBTIQA+ (lesbian, gay, bisexual, transgender, intersex, queer, asexual, and further non-normative genders and sexualities); and *gendering* as a process over time. The meaning of "gender equality" as a value is very different if one sees gender as a complex, multidimensional, and fluid social form.

21.2.4   Interests and Power: Social Progress for Whom?

Social progress is not simply a matter of a plurality of social values. The social changes implicated in social progress also affect the interests of different categories of people and institutions in multiple ways. There are winners and losers endowed with contrasting kinds and degrees of power. Everyone might agree that a world with less poverty is better than a world with more poverty. But since eliminating poverty requires significant redistribution, there will be opponents to the policies needed to eliminate poverty. And the very fact of privileged access to resources means that these interests will often tend to enjoy greater power in the resulting struggles. These issues are especially acute when we think of social progress globally. Policies which advance certain values in the wealthy parts of the world may be at the expense of the less advantaged parts of the world. For example, nation-based anti-pollution regulations for a clean environment in wealthy countries may result in the displacement of polluting industries or polluting waste to the global South (Allen 1992; Grossman 2006). Likewise, a reduced burden of domestic labor for citizens of the North may rely on the caregiving services of immigrant women withdrawn from their own families and communities (see Chapters 1 and 17).

Interests and values derive partly from different social positions, such as age, class, gender, and race, and their intersections. In some situations such dimensions may be analytically separable, with different logics and dynamics (Verloo 2006). Interests and values may look very different from changing individual and collective positions; what may benefit, say, young people may not benefit those older – hence calls for intergenerational and other cross-dimension solidarities (Hearn 1999; Bengtson and Oyama 2007).

In addition, both capitalism and authoritarian regimes, whether political, religious, or technological in flavor, are important in shaping, indeed driving, media formats and the privileging of certain technologies and technological platforms with the social adaptations they require. Such politico-technological developments are increasingly relevant in the very construction of interests and values through the power and influence of media, education, and many other institutional forces.

21.2.5   Uncertain Means and Ends

Deeply connected to the complexity of the values and interests implicated in social progress is a fourth problem: conflicting beliefs about how to improve the realization of any given dimension of social progress. This is where social science probably has the most to contribute. In order to realize the potential for social improvement we need to properly diagnose what it is about existing social structures, institutions, and processes that fosters or impedes progress on different values; and, given the diagnosis, we need good social-scientific understanding of viable alternatives in order to formulate proposals for social change that would effectively foster those values. Neither ends nor means are self-evident to those concerned, and thus the spontaneous beliefs about what needs to be done to improve things are often deeply flawed. Given these diagnoses, the formulation of proposals for social change that would effectively foster desired values requires good social-scientific understandings not only of diverse viable alternatives, but also of the pluralities of relevant perspectives that are taken on these (Stirling 2011).

Of particular importance here is the problem of unintended consequences of efforts at social improvement (Veld 2010). It is one thing to argue that a particular policy of social change would benefit certain groups of people or directly advance some social value, and quite another to anticipate the full range of side-effects that might harm other values or even ultimately undermine the original direct purposes of the policy. A good example is the contrast between means-tested and universalistic programs for reducing poverty (Wilson 2012). On the face of it, means-tested programs might seem preferable since for any given level of state funding more money can be directed at poverty if only poor people receive the funds. But universal programs may actually provide more real benefits to the poor. Means-tested programs define a clear division between beneficiaries and non-beneficiaries of the policy; universal programs create a broader coalition of people who receive some benefit, and thus, in the long term, universal programs receive greater public support. More focused social-scientific research is needed to establish and analyze this dynamic of policy feedback.

Beliefs about the best means to achieve a given social goal are filled with controversy, both because social-scientific analyses frequently go against common-sense explanations of social problems and their solutions, and also because among social scientists there are often serious disagreements over the diagnosis of problems and the desirability of alternative solutions. To take just one example, nearly everyone agrees that reducing poverty would constitute social progress. The mainstream "common-sense" understanding of poverty by many people in wealthy countries (Allan, Adam, and Carter 1999; Curran 2002; Hess and Kalb 2003; Edwards and Cromwell 2006; Christophers 2009; Le 2010; Dator, Sweeney, and Yee 2015) is that poverty exists because poor people generally lack a work ethic and other personal attributes needed to get out of poverty. Such highly individualistic "blame the victim" explanations are also prominent in the mass media. If one accepts this diagnosis, then the solution is to increase pressure on poor people to take more responsibility for their own fate. Relatively few social scientists agree with this "common-sense" diagnosis, but they disagree over what are the most critical social causes of poverty and therefore what needs to be done. Some argue that the core problem is deficits in human capital caused by inadequate school provision, chaotic neighborhoods, and other social conditions. The solution, therefore, is intensive efforts at improving educational opportunities for the poor. Others argue that the most fundamental problem is the nature of job opportunities, labor markets, and class structures in capitalist economies. Real progress to eliminate poverty, therefore, requires a transformation of these basic socio-economic structures.

21.2.6   The Politics of Social Progress

Because of the issues we have been discussing – the multidimensionality of social progress, disagreements over values, conflicts of interest, and asymmetric power – the possibility of social progress is always deeply contested. Some discussions make it seem that a highly idealized conception of a "good social planner," well informed by relevant evidence and social theory, could simply nudge society in the right direction. For such an enlightened social planner, the main problem to be solved is finding the "optimal" policy, not overcoming the powerful interests and coalitions opposed to particular forms of progress. This is a fantasy. Social progress requires more than simply enlightening people; it requires political struggle.

The challenge of overcoming opposition to social progress is especially acute when progress involves matters of inequality and social justice. Those who benefit most from injustice are also powerful. Indeed, the very processes that generate unjust inequalities in income and wealth also generate associated inequalities in power sufficient to obstruct progress. What this means is that it is insufficient to have a clear understanding of what needs to be changed in order for there to be improvements in social justice; there also need to be sufficient solidarity and collective capacity to successfully challenge the powerful in political struggles over the needed social changes.

This gets to the heart of perhaps the most difficult problem in thinking about social progress. We know much about the causes of a wide range of social problems. We can track the trajectory over time in how some things have become better, and others worse, with respect to different values. There are many good, viable proposals for how to make things better, and we even know much about the obstacles to implementing these proposals. What we do not really know is how to create and assemble the necessary political forces to overcome these obstacles.

21.3   The Uneven Direction of Progress and Problems of Reversal

There is no simple "bottom line" in taking stock of social progress in the world today. The issue is not simply that the *pace* of progress varies both across the different dimensions of progress and across different regions of the world. A crucial additional challenge lies in questions of orientation (Stirling 2010). Complex interactions between the forces through which social progress occurs along its diverse dimensions and the contingency of political struggles mean that the direction of social progress is often uncertain (Collingridge 1983; Leach, Scoones, and Stirling 2010; Stirling 2012; Hess 2016). For instance, the social movements that social science has associated with progressive coalitions in the past might have a more ominous role in the present, as populist mobilization increases in strength. A turn to individualization as the major force for social change in recent decades may also erode capacities for collective action, and force the need to find new mechanisms of democratization and new vehicles of group politics. Many of the problems of the world, ranging from climate change to development issues and the rise of authoritarianism, are not manageable at the level of the individual but will require collective solutions on levels from supranational and world institutions, to interest groups, class action, social movements, and party politics.

The chapters of this report chart many of the uneven, precarious trends on different dimensions of social progress, and we will not attempt to summarize all of these here. Instead, we will focus on those dimensions of – and directions for – social progress that pose the most serious challenges for the world today: democracy; class, inequality, and economic precarity; the welfare state; gender; the environment; and science and technology.

21.3.1   Democracy

Assessing the extent and forms of progress (and sometimes regress) on the dimension of democracy is especially complex both because of disagreements over the meaning of democracy and because of the highly context-dependent nature of the specific institutional forms that advance the value of democracy in different historical conditions.

The value of democracy has been specified in many different ways. Sometimes it is restricted only to the formal procedures through which political officials in the state are chosen. Other times it taps a much broader idea of political equality and collective self-determination. In this broader notion, the fundamental value underlying the ideal of democracy is that *all people should have equal access to the necessary means for empowered participation in decisions that affect their lives* (Wright 2010: chapter 2). Understood in this way, democracy as a value does not apply simply to the state; it applies to all arenas of social life in which decisions significantly affect one's life. One can speak of a democratic workplace, a democratic family, a democratic church, as well as a democratic state.

If equal access to the necessary means for empowered participation in decisions is the central criterion for democracy, then a core indicator for democratic progress is the extent to which the least powerful segments of a society gain access to such participation. This is where the problem of context-dependence enters. In highly unequal societies with significant segments of the population being marginalized, the ability of the most disadvantaged to engage in vigorous public protest, including disruptive protest, could count as an indicator of increasing democracy. In a much more egalitarian society in which there are effective channels of meaningful political participation for all, disruptive protests could signal an erosion of democracy. In some contexts, forms of direct, participatory democracy can be highly empowering to the least powerful segments of society; but in other settings, participatory democracy can be manipulated by the rich and powerful, special interests, or sinister forces.

In considering the means to pursue democracy in this sense, one of the most important insights from the social sciences today is that social progress does not necessarily display a ratchet-like character in which gains along some dimension, once achieved, cannot be reversed. While sociologists have noted the "disorganization" of Western capitalism in the period from the 1970s onwards, with ensuing fractures of national communities and progressive coalitions, until recently most social scientists saw democracy as an unquestioned, broadly held value, at least in the Western world, and believed that processes of democratization, once achieved and stabilized, were irreversible. Chapter 1 of this report proposes that this is not the case and this deserves to be underlined in the light of ongoing developments. This raises the question of the conditions under which democracy might prove in fact to be fragile even in long-standing liberal regimes and to just what extent the current authoritarian turn might threaten democracy.

Two broad, contradictory trends have marked the progress of democratic values in recent decades. On the one hand, the proportion of the world's population that lives in states with nominally democratic institutions is greater today than at any time in the past. The dissolution of the former Soviet Union led to the emergence (or in some cases, re-emergence) of a number of democratic states. And while it is more difficult to establish the extent to which these formal institutions meet the minimum criteria for substantive democracies – the rule of law, "free and fair" elections that incumbents can lose, open political debate, and so on – progress seems evident on this front as well. Easy access to new information and communication technologies has improved the potential for political organization and participation, even if such technologies have also enabled parallel and sometimes false channels of information, and a new propaganda war.

On the other hand, in certain critical ways the "democraticness" of democratic institutions has declined in many traditional stable liberal democracies, and the future prospects for democracy in countries without a long tradition of liberal democracy are less promising than was once thought. There are many indicators of declining democratic health in what are generally thought of as secure democracies:[4]

- declining levels of traditional forms of political participation in most nations;
- a decline of traditional mechanisms in the media and political parties for robust public deliberation of political issues;
- the development of new media and communication technologies, such as social media, which has generated a proliferation of channels of false information, hate speech, and propaganda, in turn altering democratic debates significantly, albeit in ways that it is today difficult to fully evaluate;
- increasingly sophisticated forms of state surveillance through the use of information technologies;
- increasing levels of popular cynicism about politicians and declining trust in democratic institutions;
- the erosion of voting rights through national or state-level restrictions in the United States;
- an increasing institutional "democratic deficit" because of displacement of significant forms of decision-making from democratically accountable bodies to various kinds of unelected commissions.[5]

Taken together, these processes are reflected in the serious challenge to liberal democracy embodied in the rise of illiberal authoritarian politics, as demonstrated by the election of Donald Trump in the US and the rise in popularity of ultra-right-wing parties in Germany, Austria, the Netherlands, and France. In recent years, these parties have gone further than their earlier populist attacks on liberal values: they are mounting a strategic and systemic attack on liberal institutions, including fundamental rights of citizenship, the rule of law, free press, and cultural life. They are seriously threatening ethnic, political, and sexual minorities. The European Union, which had its origins not only in desires for market integration, but also and importantly, in response to fascism, in the hope for enduring peace on the European continent, has become a central arena of extreme right-wing parties, threatening not only the potential of the EU to respond to both financial crisis and the needs of migrants, but also its very capacity to defend democracy.

In countries without stable traditions of liberal democracy, the prospects for democracy in the future are also much more ambiguous than previously thought. While there were always debates on these issues, until recently social scientists generally argued that economic development would eventually lead to democratic reform more or less automatically. This expectation has been discredited. The example of China has shown not only that authoritarianism can be a successful development strategy, but that development can reinforce rather than undermine authoritarianism, although the long-term future of politics in China is quite open. Furthermore, quite apart from the ambiguities in the connection between economic development and democracy, the advance of democratic institutions in some parts of the world has been undermined by significant increases in various forms of political violence. Many political boundaries established through international negotiation have proven unstable, with ethnic conflict fanning the flames of civil war. Increased international economic competition has

---

[4]   Many of these trends are discussed in Chapters 9 and 14.

[5]   This has been especially salient in the European Union, where elected bodies at the European level are particularly weak, but many decisions of considerable importance are nevertheless made at that level of governance.

also been linked to the intensification of ethnic conflict in many countries (Chua 2004).

What is perhaps especially worrisome for the global prospects for democracy is that in some countries in which formal democratic institutions were instituted in recent decades and where democracy seemed to be consolidating, strong, illiberal, and authoritarian movements have emerged. This is especially striking in Russia, where democracy has become a shell, but similar trends are present in certain other Eastern European countries, as well as Turkey, the Philippines, and, in a more ambiguous way, India.

21.3.2   Inequality

Despite many disruptive fluctuations in economic growth, global labor productivity has grown significantly over the last four decades, with vast potential for improvement in living standards. The actual gains, however, have been unequally distributed, at both international and national levels (see discussion in Chapters 3 and 14).

New sources of historical and contemporary data offer important new insights into distributional trends, revealing somewhat contradictory outcomes. On the one hand, rapid economic growth in countries such as China, Korea, and Mexico has created a global category of middle-income countries that confound a long-standing tradition of sorting countries into the binary categories of developed and developing. On the other hand, the difference in living standards between countries at the top and the bottom of the global income distribution has widened considerably, creating enormous pressure for the migration of economic as well as political refugees. By one estimate, about 60 percent of a person's income is determined merely by where she or he was born (Milanovic 2012).

Most empirical attention to economic inequality focuses on the national level, where its multidimensional aspects can be more fully explored. Here too, progress seems ambiguous. On the one hand, material standards of living have improved for most people within developed economies since the middle of the twentieth century. Expanded public provision of health care and pensions in the second half of the twentieth century has had a particularly important effect on raising real living standards of people at the bottom of the income distribution (Weil 2015). And even in terms of the components of living standards purchased in the market, the material standards of living of people in the lower deciles of the income distribution have generally improved even in the face of growing inequality in labor market earnings. Virtually all low-income households in wealthy countries have refrigerators, modern heating and electricity, and televisions; over two-thirds of households in the bottom quartile own smartphones.

On the other hand, both income and wealth inequality have increased dramatically in many developed economies. In recent decades income from capital has far outpaced income from labor, and the rate of return on capital has exceeded the rate of economic growth. In the US, where public policies have done little to mitigate these trends, the top 1 percent of the population has dramatically increased its share of income and the average household income of the bottom 50 percent has stagnated since the 1970s (Piketty 2014). In France, by contrast, the incomes of the bottom 50 percent of income recipients grew at approximately the same rate as national income per adult over the same period.[6] Earnings inequality has also intensified sharply in the US. Some economists explain this trend as the result of technological changes that have increased the demand for skill, combined with a reduction in the supply of college graduates. However, median earnings of college graduates have changed little in recent years, and growth in earnings is concentrated at the very top, especially among employees in the financial sector (Lin and Tomaskovic-Devey 2013; Folbre 2016).

Meanwhile, at the bottom of the earnings distribution, the decline of unionized industrial employment has been accompanied by a rise in precarious employment, including temporary and involuntary part-time jobs. These changes have been driven largely by globalization and institutional restructuring, though technological change may also have played a role (Kalleberg 2011).

A global "precariat" has also emerged, a harbinger of what may be a major change in class structure (Standing 2011). Migrant workers who lack citizenship rights are particularly vulnerable to insecure employment. Their interests are often, in contemporary consumer capitalism, in conflict with those of white workers whose faltering wages in the last decades have led to a demand for ever cheaper consumer goods. This global conflict in the division of labor is increasingly played out not only as a division between increasingly skilled labor in the Western world and manual labor in the developing South, but also as conflicts and perceived conflicts of interests between white workers and immigrant labor in the West. Brexit showed the unpredictable nature of the political responses that might stem from this, and future elections in Europe and elsewhere may underscore that, even if migrant workers do not reduce jobs available to the white working class, feelings of threat provide a breeding ground for right-wing populist politics which make it ever more difficult to articulate notions of common class interests and progressive coalitions.

21.3.3   Progressive Coalitions and the Erosion of the Welfare State

In the decades following World War II, many social scientists believed that progress could be understood as the completion of Marshall's social citizenship revolution through an expanding welfare state that redirected a significant proportion of the resources produced by the economy to social purposes (Marshall 1950). Virtually all the democracies that climbed the ladder to affluence in the twentieth century devoted an increasing share of their GDP to social insurance and protection, vastly improving the health and income security of their populations and reducing inequality in living standards (Lindert 2004). Most research to date on social policy and the welfare state has focused on Western Europe, North America, Australia, and New Zealand. The focus is now shifting, and with good reason: most of the

---

[6]   For a summary of more recent but as yet unpublished research by Thomas Piketty, Emmanuel Saez, and Gabriel Zucman that makes this comparison, see Cohen (2016).

world's population lives in less affluent countries, and policy trajectories there differ substantially and offer new possibilities for innovation. Increases in public spending in Latin America, in particular, represent an important trend (UNRISD 2010, 2016).

However, the once powerful expectation that expansion of the welfare state would accompany economic growth has been shaken. In 16 of the most affluent democracies, government spending as a percentage of GDP declined between the late 1980s and 2008 (Brady and Lee 2014). OECD statistics show further declines in many countries since that year.[7] In the UK, a period of public investment between the mid-1990s and the mid-2000s came to a halt with dramatic cuts in expenditure and soaring levels of poverty, including a dramatic rise in the use of food banks and in the number of children growing up below the poverty threshold. Following the break-up of the Soviet bloc, centrally planned redistributive programs have been replaced by various national systems, and those with authoritarian political systems have largely eviscerated those social programs (Orenstein 2008). The financial crisis of 2008 had devastating effects on social spending in southern European countries in particular, where cuts in unemployment and pension benefits have imposed shocking hardships (Petmesidou and Guillén 2014). In Greece, hit by the twin challenges of the refugee crisis at Europe's borders and its own debt-ridden economy, life expectancy is decreasing and suicide rates are rising.

Nevertheless, the welfare state remains a fundamental element of social progress. As demonstrated in many chapters of this report, social scientists generally believe that a publicly funded and redistributionist welfare state is necessary to mitigate the shortcomings of capitalism. Public spending still represents considerably more than 30 percent of GDP in the US, Canada, Australia, Japan, most European countries, and a handful of other countries, and has been expanding in some areas of the world, especially Latin America. While some economists have blamed public sectors for faltering growth rates, empirical analysis of the relationship between government spending and economic growth in the US and Europe has led to the opposite conclusion: public spending buffers the business cycle, boosts consumer demand, improves the capabilities of the working-age population (Lindert 2004), and is a form of social investment (Morel, Palier, and Palme 2012).

Social spending helps spread the costs and risks of caring for young, the old, the sick, and the disabled. Unlike private insurance, which is subject to problems of adverse selection, public insurance can pool risk efficiently. Most redistribution through the state takes place over the life-cycle, with the working-age population helping pay for both the education of the young and pensions and health care of older people. Socialization of support for dependents has particularly important implications for women, who have traditionally devoted more resources and more effort than men to family care. Some empirical studies of the distributional impact of social spending in both the US and the UK show that members of most income groups receive benefits that are broadly similar to what they financially contribute (Folbre 2008; Hills 2014). Still, public transfers have an equalizing effect on opportunities for young children, in particular.

Social spending also has symbolic as well as economic valence, reflecting deeply held ideals of economic justice and concern for others. What, then, accounts for the faltering role and declining size of the public sector despite positive – albeit slower – rates of economic growth? Part of the explanation lies within the public sector itself. Voters find it difficult to accurately assess the value of its contributions. Public spending sometimes fuels distributional conflict, especially when transfers are specifically targeted to a low-income population through means-testing. Continuing increases in the relative share of the elderly population, combined with improvements in longevity and slower wage growth, have raised legitimate fears regarding the sustainability of public commitments to retirees.

The bigger factors, however, derive from institutional changes that have taken place outside the public sector. The devolution of the formerly centrally planned economies set the stage by removing the political pressure of competition from a more egalitarian – though clearly undemocratic – economic system (Petras 2012). Austerity policies have led to major budget cuts, often with disproportionate impact on women and low-income families (Bargawi, Cozzi, and Himmelweit 2017). Starved of necessary funds, some public programs have been forced to cut either the quantity or the quality of services provided, further undermining public support.

Increased globalization and capital mobility have made investors less dependent on any specific national labor force and less vulnerable to regulation. Transnational corporations can relocate at will in search of lower wages and lower taxes. In recent years a large share of private as well as corporate wealth has essentially gained immunity from public oversight and taxation (Zucman 2014). Concomitant effects of globalization, such as the decreased power of labor unions, have contributed to political realignments. Increased international migration and ethnic diversity, combined with intensified income inequality, may also have undermined support for public spending (Alesina, Baqir, and Easterly 1999).

The conviction that free trade is always and everywhere economically advantageous functions as a key tenet of radical pro-market advocacy. On the other hand, feelings of economic vulnerability may lead to rash responses and false promises that protectionism will recreate once flourishing national industries. Far-right populist parties on the European continent advocate a conservative form of welfare nationalism that channels funds in ways designed to maintain national and local authority. While social protection can in principle buffer vulnerable populations from the disruptions of globalization, it can also become a means of cementing clientelism and implementing old and new forms of gender and ethnic segregation.

The future nature of the state itself is in question. Research on the strong pro-market policies of recent decades emphasizes increased subordination of states to markets, and the increasingly tight connection between political and financial elites, as well as new possibilities for veto points and "winner-takes-all" politics. Public debt leaves governments profoundly dependent on financial markets, rendering large populations vulnerable to even small changes in

---

[7]   See the OECD database at https://data.oecd.org/gga/general-government-spending.htm.

interest rates. Regulatory failures have lead to financial bailouts and encouraged international tax evasion. Economic and political elites have more in common with their counterparts in other countries than their own fellow citizens, creating resentments that fuel populist backlash. Financialization and marketization have clearly reduced the egalitarian leverage of the welfare state.

21.3.4 The Uneven Progress of Gender Equality

There is broad agreement among social scientists that in the past half century there has been significant, if uneven, progress toward gender equality, gender equity, and gender justice in many parts of the world. Much of this progress is connected to improved access to education for girls and women in most – though certainly not all – countries around the world. Important gains have also been made in the area of legal, political citizenship, and property rights. But these gains are not universal, and may not be permanent, especially when intersecting inequalities based on race, ethnicity, gender, citizenship, and other dimensions of collective identity come into force. Some right-wing populist governments have taken aim at immigrants, including refugees, and this can have particularly serious effects on the status of immigrant women. In sum, "the elaboration of gender equality is closely aligned with the development of gendered citizenship, seen as inclusive of political and economic entitlements, access, and belonging and encompassing rights and obligations" (Hearn and Husu 2016; see also Oleksy, Hearn, and Golanska 2011).

Another important area concerns health and bodily autonomy. Improvements in medical technology have reduced child mortality, and increased access to safe and reliable means of contraception and early-stage abortion have given many women more control over their reproductive decisions than they enjoyed in the past. Violence against women and other forms of gender-based violence remain a major challenge for gender equality, even though they are now highlighted on many international governmental agendas. Interestingly, cross-national and cross-state statistical analysis of reduction in gender inequalities suggests that these may serve men's interests as well (Holter 2014).

Evidence of economic progress is more mixed. Trends in formal labor force participation, relative earnings, the division of labor in unpaid work, and financial responsibility for the care of dependents reveal persistent – and in some cases worsening – gender inequalities. Women's participation in formal employment remains variable, relatively low in the Middle East and North Africa, and relatively high in OECD countries. Women increased their share of formal employment in OECD countries rapidly during the last third of the twentieth century. This trend has now leveled off. The record for low-income countries is more complex, with significant increases in women's employment over the last 20 years in Latin America, and declines in South Asia (especially India) (Elborgh-Woytek et al. 2013).

The stagnation of global manufacturing employment, combined with the growth of precarious and part-time employment and expansion of informal employment, does not bode well for future trends in female employment. Indeed, some economists argue that male employment patterns are converging toward female patterns, rather than vice versa (Standing 1999).

In virtually all countries for which data is available, levels of occupational segregation by gender remain quite high (Charles and Grusky 2004), although there has been some erosion especially in professional occupations requiring high levels of education. With the exception of some export-oriented manufacturing platforms in low-income countries, women tend to be concentrated in service-sector jobs with relatively low wages. Even when they attain professional or managerial status, they are clustered in care industries (often in the public sector), where wages are more compressed.

Women continue to devote far more time to unpaid work and family care than men do, a factor that constrains their opportunities in paid employment. The impact of such constraints varies considerably by race and class as well as citizenship. Affluent families can outsource many domestic tasks to low-wage workers. In many developing countries, the absence of basic infrastructure like piped water at the domicile, easily accessible fuel, and adequate and accessible sanitation facilities is particularly critical for reducing the burden of unpaid domestic work that is placed disproportionately on women and girls.

In the US, many European countries, and some Asian and Middle Eastern countries, large pools of low-wage migrants provide a cheap source of purchased care for children and the elderly, enabling them to send money home but depriving them of opportunities for a family life of their own. The global inequalities that induce them to migrate on these terms reduce the pressure on affluent countries to provide more public support for care.

Many policies embedded in the welfare states of northwestern Europe (but now seriously threatened by budget cuts) make it easier for women to combine family work with paid employment, with positive consequences for female employment, family formation, and birth rates. Many Latin American countries have adopted progressive work–family policies in recent years. In general, however, public support for family care remains low and uneven. Austerity policies aimed at reducing public spending in many developing countries since the 1980s and, more recently, in Europe, have set back progress toward gender equality. Such policies have had a disproportionately negative effect on those taking on responsibilities for unpaid care (mainly women), households with children (notably lone parents), and single women pensioners (Bargawi, Cozzi, and Himmelweit 2017).

Changes in the organization of family life also reveal both positive and negative trends (see Chapter 17). On the one hand, time-use survey data from many countries indicate that differences between men's and women's total work day (including both market and non-market work) are generally lower in high-income than in low-income countries (Burda, Hamermesh, and Weil 2013). In many countries, modest increases in men's relative contributions to both housework and child care since the 1970s have been well documented. On the other hand, increasing rates of non-marriage and/or unstable partnerships in many high-income countries have made childrearing a more risky and uncertain proposition. Below-replacement fertility levels may offer some environmental benefits, but they also disrupt intergenerational transfers (whether through the family or the welfare state). Growth in the percentage of children maintained by women alone, especially in the US, Latin America, and southern Africa, has contributed to increasing child poverty. In some instances, mothers' improved access to earnings has been partially counter-balanced by a decline in fathers' contributions to the costs of supporting and raising children.

While gender equality, and gender relations more generally, are often seen as related primarily to either family relations (as in the above examples), or formally labeled gender policy issues (for example, the gender pay gap and violence against women), they are also relevant to what may appear to some as gender-neutral arenas, such as foreign policy, transport policy, or environmental policy. Embedded gendering processes persist in what may be represented as seemingly "gender-neutral" or "non-gendered" arenas, such as state functioning, budgetary allocations, economic development, international relations, mobility, and so on (Hearn 2015).

Also, values and aspirations other than (gender) equality, such as democracy, freedom, or simply care, are also constructed through gendered processes (Steans 2013). Economic crisis has highlighted gendered aspects and biases in policy development. Although some voices at both the World Bank and the International Monetary Fund emphasize that gender equality can promote economic growth, most members of the global financial community maintain a "strategic silence" on the gendered effects of macroeconomic policies. Deflationary policies and cuts in social spending tend to have a more negative effect on women than men (Young, Bakker, and Elson 2011). In some countries, economic crises have initially depressed men's employment more, with larger delayed effects on women. The allocation of government expenditures, investments, and spending on research and development often has more positive effects on men than women (Neumayer 2011). Male employment tends to be more concentrated in the private, corporate sector than female employment, encouraging men to identify more closely with that sector.

Gender equality policies offer important progressive tools, but are not unproblematic. The meanings of gender and sexuality are not fully captured by the male/female binary, and their multiplicity requires more serious attention in both theory and practice. If narrowly conceived, gender equality may feed an ideology of equality based on misleading and superficial appearances (Spade 2011). It may also reproduce heteronormativity and a form of Western neo-imperialism, as exemplified in the debate on homonationalism (Duggan 2003; Puar 2007). But however circumscribed some gender equality policies may be, they should not be dismissed or underestimated (Hearn and Husu 2016).

21.3.5 Uneven Progress on the Environment

One of the most striking features of world politics over the past half century has been the rising salience of concerns about the environment. Initially driven by grassroots environmental and other social movements and now forming the single most voluminous arena for international law, pressures for improved international environmental

governance have been major drivers of the institutional regimes constituting globalization.

Social processes have tremendous effects on the environment and environmental flows. Unlike the formal organization of international political orders, the earth itself knows no borders. Social, economic, and political processes intersect and influence environmental processes. Economic and political justice are closely linked to environmental justice. Social and economic inequalities, including those based on class, gender, ethnicity, and citizenship, are antithetical to sustainability (Wilkinson and Pickett 2009; Neumayer 2011).

By the mid-2000s, the US and Canada, with 5 percent of the global population, accounted for 27 percent of global oil consumption; Europe, with around 10 percent of the global population, accounted for 24 percent. Per capita emissions within regions are also extremely variable. North America produces 20 tons of carbon dioxide per person per year, Europe about 8 tons, Africa 1 ton (World Bank 2007). The rate of increase in fossil fuel consumption in Brazil, Russia, India, and China is especially rapid.

Although worldwide debates over the environment are now dominated by the imperative need to halt anthropogenic global climate change, human assaults on nature also take many other forms, threatening similarly uncertain but possibly catastrophic consequences (Harremoës et al. 2002; Gee et al. 2013). Climate change and sea level rise (IPCC 2015), chemical contamination (Cranor 2011), accumulating toxic wastes (Allen 1992), atmospheric pollution (OECD 2012), ecological destruction (MEA 2008), soil erosion (International Resource Panel 2014), population growth (UN 2015b), urban spread (UNDESA 2015b), resource depletion (Meadows, Randers, and Meadows 2005), food insecurity (IAASTD 2009), water deprivation (FAO and WWC 2015), ocean acidification (Burke et al. 2011), landscape degradation (CPRE 2013), novel pandemic risks (Jonas 2013), antimicrobial resistance (Neill 2016), foodborne diseases (WHO 2015), nuclear accidents (FAIC 2012), ionizing radiation (UNSCEAR 2016), genetic interference (UNCTAD and CGIAR 2013), weapons of mass destruction (OTA 1979), disruption of global material cycles (Rockström et al. 2009), and direct forms of oppression of other living beings (Singer 2002) all represent distinctive environmental challenges across various definitions of social progress. The grave intensity of each of these human impacts combines in a potentially exponential "perfect storm" of cumulative interactions (Beddington 2009; WEF, Waughray, and Workman 2014).

As with other aspects of social progress, however, general implications are easier to discern than specific imperatives for action. Despite many divergent views regarding the implications, magnitude, and urgency of environmental challenges, convergence toward technocratic solutions is evident (Stirling 2015). One form of technocratic environmentalism is the view of many economists that a suite of technically sophisticated tax and subsidy policies could incentivize sufficient environmentally respectful behavior to effectively deal with most environmental problems. A more radical technocratic view, associated with analyses of the advent of a new "Anthropocene" geological epoch (Hamilton, Bonneuil, and Gemenne 2015), calls for intensified human control over the earth, involving "management" of "planetary control variables" (Rockström et al. 2009). In such views, "progress" becomes exemplified by new global institutions and infrastructures such as those argued to be required for "climate geoengineering" in order to address global warming (Shepherd et al. 2009). Here, the emphasized gravity and urgency of environmental challenges are increasingly held to demand moves toward new forms of "environmental authoritarianism" (Beeson 2010) under which democracy is openly dismissed as a "luxury" that should be "put on hold" (Hickman 2010).

Under an alternative perspective, however, it is exactly these kinds of "fallacies of control" (Stirling 2015) and associated "cockpit-ism" (Hajer et al. 2015) that constitute the core of the problem. In this view, proliferating forms of environmental degradation are caused by the same kinds of oppressive social relations as those resisted by democratic struggle (Grove 1995; Castree and Braun 2001; Stirling 2014b). Alongside other more human forms of exploitation, environmental destruction can in this sense be seen as a symptom of powerful interests and privileged groups being insulated from the consequences of their exploitative practices (Goldman and Schurman 2000; Perreaul, Bridge, and McCarthy 2015). In this view, the task of reversing adverse impacts on vulnerable natural environments presents effectively the same political challenge as resistance to more exclusively human forms of oppression. And in this analysis, social progress is best realized not by concentration of power in vertical global structures for planetary control, but by the reinforcing of mutualistic horizontal relations of solidarity, under which people in more equal societies are incentivized to exercise greater care not only for each other, but also for the environments in which all live (Stirling 2016).

21.3.6   Uneven Progress of Science and Technology

Arguably, no other area of life is more implicated in debates about social progress than practices and discourses around science and technology, including related investments in education. More than any other aspect of society or politics, it is science and technology that tend to be afforded the main credit for the remarkable historical improvements around the world in which many people in different societies are experiencing unprecedented qualities of health and wealth, energy and communication services, mobility and leisure, shelter and material comfort (Huesemann 2003; Broers 2005). Yet it is equally important to acknowledge that not all consequences of research and innovation are positive, and that beneficial directions for science and technology do not unfold automatically (Sveiby, Gripenberg, and Segercrantz 2012).

Few would argue, for instance, that new kinds of tax avoidance, covert state or corporate surveillance (Zuboff 2015), or weapons of mass destruction constitute positive applications of science and technology. Yet many of these are highly active areas in contemporary innovation. Indeed, it is currently the case that the single largest area for public investment in science and technology around the world lies in military- and security-related applications (Government Office for Science 2014b). The balance between benefits and risks in other areas of education, science, research, and innovation depends on the effectiveness with which these are governed.

In other words, not all technological innovation is driven most strongly by science. Collective action by governments or social movements can often be as important as academic, commercial, or public research in steering progressive directions for technology. For instance, it is difficult to envisage the formative advent of nineteenth-century urban sewerage systems without the driving energy of Victorian philanthropism (Geels 2006). Nor are the enormous late-twentieth-century gains in health care credibly explained without reference to the enabling effects of welfare states.

Currently burgeoning forms of renewable energy, sustainable agriculture, and ecological production were likewise all pioneered by marginalized activist organizations – often strongly opposed by institutions associated with mainstream science and technology (Joergensen and Karnoe 1991). Appreciation of this breadth in the drivers of social progress is currently informing rising interest in the importance of social and grassroots innovation as means to achieve social progress (Smith et al. 2016).

A further irreducibly social and political factor shaping the roles of science and technology in the assisting or obstructing of social progress lies in crucial processes of resource allocation within research and innovation. Across areas as diverse as agriculture, pharmaceuticals, energy, and materials, a host of economic and institutional factors determine patterns of investment across alternative possible trajectories for innovation (Stirling 2014a). Many of these are entirely distinct from any direct measure of social progress. Indeed, the principal incentives bearing on existing research and innovation systems typically arise not in manifest public benefits, but in pressures to maximize private returns on investment. Even publicly funded research tends to be strongly disciplined by prospects for onward commercialization, and this applies equally to the marketization of education, especially higher education, in many parts of the world.

So rather than focusing directly on wider human wellbeing, innovation activity in most countries of the world tends to be concentrated disproportionately around commercial considerations: the potential for raising rents on intellectual property (Hilgartner 2009; Chou and Shy 2013); appropriating value in associated supply chains (Kaplinsky 2000); or increasing market share across mutually interdependent products (La Porte 1991). Innovations which do not seem as likely to offer prospects of these kinds of private benefits are typically much less enthusiastically developed. Open-source innovation, distributed social practices, or preventive health behavior may often be more effective at realizing social progress in any given area (Government Office for Science 2014a). But these will typically be disfavored by a preference for scientific and technological advances that better enable the securing of private benefits.

However social progress is construed, then, there are no guarantees that interests and incentive structures operating within scientific research or technological innovation systems will successfully focus attention on challenges and opportunities prioritized in the wider society. Nor is this just a reflection of market failure to meet social needs, since so much effort in research and innovation systems driven by public-sector institutions is preoccupied with military and security technologies (Alic 2007; OECD 2013). Of course, the regular occurrence of "spin-off" does to some extent mitigate the effects of this mismatch – where technologies pursued for one purpose yield benefits in some contrasting area (Chesbrough 2003). But this is a general phenomenon that applies irrespective of the main purpose in question. So, whatever the incidental benefits may be in particular areas, there can be no denying that efforts to realize social progress through science and technology can experience serious divergences between private incentives and the public good.

There are many reasons, then, to challenge the notion of any simple relationship between technological change and wider social progress. Without the right kinds of cultures, institutions, and political economies, it is not possible for the most socially progressive innovations to develop in the first place – nor for them to be prioritized or to diffuse or advance in the required ways. The potential of science and technology to help realize social progress remains enormous. But it is essential to ensure appropriate incentives and encourage clarity, transparency, and accountability.

Policy debates overwhelmingly view the formative relation between technology and society in a one-way fashion. Each new innovation is seen as ushering in a wave of apparently necessary forms of onward organizational, behavioral, cultural, and political adaptation, rather than the other way around. Various forms of "technology roadmap" currently proliferate through much research and innovation policy (Phaal, Farrukh, and Probert 2004). What is striking, however, is the extent to which political imaginations are constrained merely to the two possibilities of "forging ahead" or "falling behind." The main point of any roadmap, surely, is to enable steering in the right direction. Yet these policy documents typically feature just a single "way forward." The particular scientific and technological trajectories in any given sector that are highlighted in this way as the natural orientation for "advance" are not necessarily those that best realize social progress, but rather are those that are most favored under incumbent interests in that sector.

With futures increasingly conceived in these terms, wider debates also become preoccupied with competitive pressures merely to "accelerate" emerging and converging technologies, rather than steering their directions. As anxieties grow over the implications of ever more competitive modes of globalization, these visions of disproportionately science- and technology-driven forms of social progress are intensifying. Meanwhile, governments and businesses around the world increasingly emphasize similarly driving roles of science and technology, asserting the importance of developing "population innovation readiness" (Eurobarometer 2005) for "knowledge societies" (Felt and Wynne 2008) and "pro-innovation policies" (Sveiby, Gripenberg, and Segercrantz 2012). Again, what is striking about this language is how much it is advanced without any reference to exactly which kinds of science, technology, or innovation it is intended to favor and which to discourage.

In this way, adverse public reactions to some particular technology (like GM crops or nuclear power) are routinely branded "anti-science" – as if they represented indiscriminate opposition to science in general (Felt et al. 2013). This again entirely excludes the actuality that science and

technology (like other kinds of institutional change) are branching evolutionary processes rather than a one-track race (Nelson and Winter 1977; Dosi and Nelson 1994; Williams and Edge 1996; Fagerberg 2003). Just as market competition is held to favor the maximizing of economic performance, so political contestation in democratic societies ideally would help to steer the trajectories for science and technology in the most socially desirable directions. In this light, all the language and apparatus summarized here around supposedly generally "pro-innovation" policies or indiscriminately "anti-science" public reactions not only are deeply irrational and misleading, but actively serve to undermine this democratic process of steering (OECD 2010).

The implications of this picture of the politics of science and technology for the present report on social progress could hardly be more profound. Despite their uneven and contingent success, research and innovation are typically characterized as primary drivers of progress. Rather than being recognized as a choice among plural directions across multiple dimensions, they are reduced to a single one-track race. Scope for debate is thus restricted merely to queries over "how much," "how fast," or "what risk." Crucial questions are neglected over "which way," "who says," and "why" (Stirling 2008). This seriously suppresses scope for democratic struggle and mature political deliberation over both the speed and the direction of social progress.

21.4   Obstacles to Progress

Some aspects of social progress may sometimes happen "behind the backs" of actors as simply the cumulative, unintended side-effect of human action, but generally progress requires purposeful action – albeit often distributed and mutualistic rather than vertically controlled (Kennedy, Eberhart, and Shi 2001, Pellizzoni 2004; Gloor 2006; Fligstein and McAdam 2011; Stirling 2015; Muñoz-Erickson and Cutts 2016). Social progress doesn't just happen; it is made. The problem of generating progress on any dimension, therefore, depends in critical ways on the ability to identify the forces and processes that impede progress and the opportunities for reducing (or getting around) those obstacles.

In what follows we will review four obstacles to continued social progress: existing forms of capitalism; collective conflicts based on class, gender, race, and citizenship; the current limits of democracy; and social science.

21.4.1   Existing Forms of Capitalism as Obstacles to Progress

The term "capitalism" gets used in a wide variety of different ways by social scientists. Sometimes it is used as almost the equivalent of market economy. Other times, as a way of talking about a broad social system, not just an economic structure. When we use the term "capitalism" as a general, abstract concept, we are referring to a particular form of market economy: a market economy consisting of privately owned, profit-seeking firms employing labor hired from a labor market. Concrete capitalist economies come in a wide variety of forms. It is also the case that in all real economies, different varieties of capitalism are entangled, often hybridized, with other hierarchical systems or social

SICK workers = less production

contracts based on gender, race, and citizenship (Mills 1999; Folbre 2013), as well as a wide variety of non-capitalist forms of economic activity including welfare state provisions that contribute to the reproduction of its labor force, various forms of subsistence production, and a wide range of non-market, collaborative community-based economic activity (Gibson-Graham 1996).

Capitalism has always had a deeply contradictory relationship to social progress. On the one hand, capitalist modes of production and exchange emerged in the interstices of a patriarchal feudal system in Western Europe and gradually weakened traditional forms of authority based largely on inherited status. The expansion of competitive markets created incentives for innovation, and new forms of labor discipline contributed to the expansion of low-price commodity production. Capitalism, as its defenders emphasize, has been an engine of technological change, increased productivity, and the erosion of some forms of hereditary status inequalities.

On the other hand, capitalist forms of production created a new elite capable of pursuing its own interests at the expense of society as a whole. Capitalist economic growth, highly concentrated within the nation-states where it first emerged, enabled imperial nations to colonize weaker countries and extract resources, labor, and profits from them. By the same token, colonial expansion, accompanied by military domination, slavery, and debt peonage, as well as wage employment, fueled capitalist economic growth.

Because of the different historical conditions in which capitalism emerged and developed in different times and places, there have always been great variations in the concrete forms of capitalism across nations. Today, however, the many different kinds of capitalism are rapidly becoming "denationalized." The current era features concerted efforts to relax regulation of capitalist enterprises and expand their scope, and to roll back state interventions in the economy. Radical pro-market ideology emphasizes the virtues of competition unencumbered by concerns for human needs or social justice. Radical pro-market policy rejects progressive taxation and brandishes the putative merits of budgetary austerity to cut public spending. Economic strategy is defined on the national level by efforts to replace public provision with market-based services (including privatized pensions and school vouchers) and on the international level by increased resistance to paying taxes (such as utilization of offshore tax shelters), relocation of investment to low-wage venues, and greater reliance on global supply chains.

These dimensions of recent pro-market, anti-state tendencies complement one another. The globalization of investment makes employers less dependent on the health, education, and other capabilities of a national labor force, reducing the potential costs to them of cuts in social spending. Offshoring and outsourcing, as well as financial shells designed to minimize global tax liability, force countries into a bidding war to offer the most favorable business climate. These strategies increase the profitability and the power of large firms relative to both workers and their small-business competitors.

But while globalization is offering capitalism itself new stepping stones, it is also creating stumbling blocks to further expansion (see discussion in Chapter 12). If all governments underinvest in the health and education of their workforce, productivity growth is likely to decline. Capitalist employers, like everyone else, would benefit from a sustainable and healthy natural environment that minimizes the threat of disruptive climate change. Financialized capitalism, however, often devises ways to maximize profits by offloading risks. In the absence of international regulation, capitalist competition creates incentives for short-run profit-maximizing strategies that could prove catastrophic in the longer run.

Capitalist employers, like everyone else, would also benefit from a sustainable and healthy social environment that minimizes the threat of war, terrorism, and crime. In the absence of both national and international regulation, however, market-driven inequalities in opportunities and income fuel many forms of social conflict. International migration and refugee flows are one indicator of the resulting tensions. Political backlash against both immigration and free trade is another.

As with other hierarchical systems, capitalism reproduces itself over time though a number of different mechanisms: the concentration of wealth, investment in political influence, and promotion of a specific individualistic ideology and culture. However, it also derives legitimacy from two other sources: the promise of delivering economic growth, and competitive dynamics that encourage political conflicts among subordinates ("divide and conquer").

Recurrent financial crises, such as those that sparked the Great Recession of 2007, have been accompanied by relatively slow growth in earnings and employment in high-income countries. Confidence that a rising tide will lift all boats is undermined when it becomes clear that many boats remain stuck in the mud. On the other hand, the political realignments now taking place in the US and Western Europe seem to be contributing more to a revival of nationalism than a reform of capitalism, and they also draw to an important extent on state structures, drawing the state into the complex of financial capitalism. It remains unclear how these alignments will play out over the next decade.

21.4.2 Collective Conflicts Based on Class, Gender, Race, and Citizenship

Popular mobilization and other forms of collective action both express an ideal of democracy and offer a potential force for progressive change. But traditional theories of popular mobilization, always susceptible to wishful thinking, seem increasingly out of date. The expectation that wage-earners bound by common economic interests in the workplace would easily join hands to restrain or even abolish capitalist prerogatives has proved simplistic. The slogan of the Occupy Movement in the US, "We are the 99 percent," effectively called attention to power concentrated in the hands of the top 1 percent. However, it did not enable the 99 percent to overcome their internal divisions and effectively combat increased inequality.

Class is not the only dimension of collective interests that has proven mutable. Confidence that "people of color" would always unite around a common agenda or that women would always pursue common gender interests has also been shaken, replaced by a new appreciation of unpredictable cycles of contingent solidarity.

Collective interests are difficult to define, much less effectively pursue, in a multi-layered global economic system where information is abundant, but difficult to organize and interpret. Strategic complexity makes prediction difficult. Optimal strategies for individuals depend in large part on those adopted by others, leading to tipping points and other non-linear dynamics (Axelrod 1997; Arthur 2013). Political mobilization is susceptible to small exogenous shocks and feedback loops that further add to unpredictability.

Collective interests themselves cannot be defined in one-dimensional terms, because people typically belong to intersecting groups that offer different levels – and different forms – of privilege and disadvantage. On the one hand, a white working-class woman in the US enjoys substantial benefits from her citizenship and her race, but on the other hand she pays certain costs related to her gender and her class. She is embedded in a matrix of group memberships to which even more variables, such as religion, sexuality, marital status, and physical appearance, could be added.

An explicit theory of "intersectionality" grew out of the criticisms that black and Third-World feminists leveled at feminist theories which largely ignored significant differences among women based on race, ethnicity, and citizenship (Crenshaw 1989). But the concept of intersectionality has important antecedents. Karl Marx described the ordinary English worker of his day in these terms: "In relation to the Irish worker he feels himself a member of the ruling nation and so turns himself into a tool of the aristocrats and capitalist of his country against Ireland, thus strengthening their domination over himself … his attitude towards him is much the same as that of the 'poor whites' to the 'niggers' in the former slave states of the U.S.A."[8]

Similarly, theories of a "comprador bourgeoisie" pursuing its class interests at the expense of contributions to national economic development and splits between the center and the periphery of the global capitalist system explicitly invoke intersectional complexities (Frank 1967). Another interesting antecedent emerges from research on contradictory class locations in the US, an approach that emphasizes implications for political mobilization (Wright 1998).

Intersectional theory is sometimes equated with "identity politics," a term often used describe political movements that focus on a particular dimension of collective identity, such as race, gender, or sexuality. This term is accurate, insofar as it emphasizes the extent to which individuals may or may not identify with others who they perceive as similar. However, "identity politics" is often contrasted with politics based on "economic justice" as though identity politics rests entirely on a cultural and political, rather than an economic, footing, or as though economic interests are synonymous with class interests.

This contrast is misleading. Mobilization around economic interests requires identification with at least some fellow interest-holders (in some instances known as class consciousness). Collective action based on group identities such as race, gender, and citizenship is often motivated by economic interests and has specific economic consequences. Intersectional analysis can be taken to extremes, denying the existence of categories such as "women" or "class." On the other hand, it can also help progressive coalitions develop unified strategies to turn diversity into strength.

Such coalitions are particularly important given the rise of populist and in some cases proto-fascist movements around the world, which seem to reflect mobilization around privileged national and racial identities. Historical analysis of the rise of fascism in Europe in the 1920s offers important parallels between what happened then and what is happening now in the US, Europe, and some other countries, including India. The promise that aggressively nationalist policies will deliver significant benefits to a dominant ethnic group may be false, and it may never be realized. It offers, nonetheless, almost hypnotic appeal, in part because it typically evokes a nostalgic past of unquestioned dominance that assuages fears of the future (Paxton 2004).

The social psychology of intersectionality may also help explain this particular political alignment. Social scientists have traditionally focused on forms of political mobilization that represent collective efforts to challenge exploitation or oppression, which have certainly changed the course of history. But experimental research suggests that people are generally more eager to avoid losses than to risk gains ("loss aversion"), an asymmetry that reinforces resistance to change. Experimental research also suggests that people who belong to intersecting groups are more eager to identify with those that enjoy the higher status (Fiske 2012). In other words, a working-class white man may identify more with his race and gender than his class, because these dimensions offer him a stronger relative position and self-esteem. While the concept of intersectionality clearly requires further elaboration, it helps explain why conflicting interests and divided loyalties play such an important role in political debate, and it lends weight to the more narrative accounts of the effectiveness of "divide and conquer" strategies.

Taken together, these many complexities in the formation of coherent, collective interests and solidarities constitute one of the most difficult obstacles to social progress. Social progress depends to a significant extent on the capacity of people to engage in collective action in pursuit of the values that constitute progress. For this to occur requires overcoming the cross-cutting interests and identities in contemporary societies, formed and fractured at different scales of social organization.

21.4.3 The Current Limits of Democracy as an Obstacle to Progress

Democracy is a work in progress. But inherent to this is the recognition that some political activities ostensibly undertaken in the name of "democracy" may actually impede social progress. In order

---

[8] Karl Marx, Letter to Meyer and Vogt, cited in Elster (1985: 21).

to be progressive, "democracy" requires continual critical vigilance. And in any case, whatever their forms, ideals of democratic governance are seldom fully achieved in practice. So, the resulting inevitable disappointments can undermine confidence in both collective decision-making and the role of the public sector in the economy. As earlier chapters of this report (particularly Chapters 9 and 14) explain, much theory and practice concerning "democracy" now seem increasingly obsolete.

Political theory has traditionally focused on the design of constitutions aimed to provide checks and balances on majoritarian rule. But it has become increasingly clear that the analysis of political institutions cannot be separated from the analysis of economic institutions that influence the distribution of wealth and income. Not long ago, economists often described democracy as a kind of luxury good that countries could not afford until they achieved affluence (Barro 1994). Today it is widely recognized that democracy contributes to forms of empowerment that both reduce inequality and promote economic growth (Acemoglu and Robinson 2012). Democracy can enhance trust, encouraging cooperation, improving health and education, and helping foster robust demand for new goods and services. It can help overcome ethnic inequalities and foster effective provision of public goods and regulation of public "bads."

Unfortunately, the trajectory of social and economic change threatens to both intensify ethnic conflict and undermine democracy. Global competition undermines cooperation (Chua 2004). Political investments give the wealthy disproportionate influence. In the affluent nations, increased inequality among voters leads to a greater divergence of interests, intensifying distributional conflicts that are often destabilizing as well as unproductive. The immediate symptoms include declining voter turnout, disengagement from existing political parties, and lack of trust and cooperation in governance.

International inequalities are also relevant, contributing to horrific military conflicts, refugee crises, and persistent underdevelopment and poverty in some areas of the world. All these factors have fueled a conflagration of systematic terrorist activities, with profoundly frightening and demoralizing effects around the world. Efforts to respond to terrorist threats have provoked many states to seize new, intrusive police powers for monitoring and interrogating residents.

The largely unregulated accumulation and concentration of global wealth creates enormous potential for corruption of democratic processes through campaign finance contributions, manipulation of mass media, and revolving doors between government regulatory agencies and the private sector. As Arundhati Roy puts it, "free elections, a free press, and an independent judiciary mean little when the free market has reduced them to commodities available on sale to the highest bidder" (2004: 55).

Low-income countries and even low-income regions within rich countries are forced into bidding wars, where those that offer the most generous subsidy and least regulation of corporate investments are the winners (see, for instance, Barboza 2016). The diminished economic significance of national borders has significantly reduced the efficacy of national government, a point that is widely but rather helplessly acknowledged. The journalist William Grieder pointed to the increased disjuncture between global capitalism and national government in his 1997 book, *One World, Ready or Not*, and a question he asked 20 years ago has become even more relevant today: "If capitalism is now truly global, what are the global social obligations that accompany it?" (1997: 334).

From a libertarian perspective, the answer to that question is "none." The liberal tradition has typically pictured democracy as a set of rights, with hardly a mention of the word "obligation." Threats such as cataclysmic climate change and nuclear war dramatize the limitations of this approach. Future inhabitants of the planet do not have a vote; they are represented only through our concern for them. The feminist theorist Joan Tronto makes a case for centering democratic politics on responsibilities for care and ensuring that "democratic citizens are as capable as possible of participating in this assignment of responsibilities" (2013: xv).

Existing national democracies are unlikely to take on such a task, and the most powerful and affluent countries in the world exercise disproportionate international influence through completely undemocratic institutions such as the World Bank and the International Monetary Fund. More representative institutions such as the United Nations remain relatively powerless. The United Nations General Assembly set up a commission to propose important global economic and financial reforms, but its recommendations fell on deaf ears.[9] The outcome of UN deliberations in Addis Ababa in 2015 on "Financing for Development" was similar. Developing countries asked for a global tax regulatory body to be created under the auspices of the UN, but developed countries bulldozed the idea, insisting that global tax matters be left to the OECD (UNDESA 2015a).

Units of democratic decision-making must be enlarged. At the same time, they must also be extended downward. The narrow confinement of democracy to a political sphere of limited relevance to most people's lives has contributed to a cynical professionalization of government and increase in bureaucratic passivity. The public sector of the economy is indispensable to the provision of health, education, and social services, as well as other public goods. Its centralized and hierarchical administration, however, has often fostered hostility and resentment. The punitive, carceral side of the state is often the most visible one. Given a choice between "the market" and "the state," many citizens remain ambivalent and undecided, creating wide political openings for coordinated efforts to privatize public services.

Citizens who lack opportunities to develop the skills required for collective decision-making and management on a daily basis may not be able to effectively maintain political democracies. Efforts to develop more cooperative economic institutions, whether described as "shared capitalism" or as "democratic socialism," could both reduce inequality and improve capabilities for conflict resolution. The future

---

9   See www.un.org/ga/econcrisissummit/docs/FinalReport.

global north?

of democracy itself hangs on its extension beyond the political to the economic realm.

21.4.4   Social Science as an Obstacle to Progress

We are at a crossroads at which it is urgent to defend not only the social sciences in themselves, but also their insights into possibilities for building a better world. Many worrisome trends, including the recent persecution of over 250 academics in Turkey (the signatories of Academics for Peace), have shown that fascism and authoritarianism are not a thing of the past. Strong political forces today are ready to sideline the inconvenient contributions of both the social and the natural sciences. Faced with this threat, some scholars in some disciplines have begun the difficult exercise of reconsidering yet again their relationship to power, and some have also raised voices of collective protest. What will be the role of social science for the coming era? Will it be one of active contribution, hibernation, or resistance?

Social scientists are, in general terms, sharply divided along both inter- and intra-disciplinary lines, and our differences of opinion both reflect and shape deep political divisions. The IPSP is an effort in consensus-building, and represents what might be called a progressive consensus among social scientists. Nonetheless, it is worth noting that the social sciences themselves can also create significant obstacles to progress.

In our view, four specific problems stand out. First, there is the continuing dominance of social science originating in and reflecting the perspective of the global North. This derives from several sources, including resource inequalities, Anglophone hegemony in publishing and related activities, and also colonial, neo-colonial, imperialist, and neo-imperialist legacies and practices (Graham, Hale, and Stephens 2011), as part of the broader global division of labor of research infrastructure, libraries, data banks, and research centers (Hountondji 1997; Connell 2014).[10] This is important not only in terms of substantive research analyses and specific research topics and priorities, but also more broadly for epistemology, ontology, and knowledge constructions (Santos 2014). Postcolonial scholarship, now well developed in and across some disciplines, recognizes the limitations of analyses that are derived only from the global North.[11] In addressing the global political organization of research, the Beninese philosopher Paulin Hountondji (1997) has analyzed the historical practices of science whereby the global periphery has supplied data, and then later applied science from the metropole in practical ways. He also makes the stronger case for less external orientation that seeks legitimation of knowledge from the global North on the part of global Southern researchers. These issues are also very much part of debates on transforming the postcolonial condition in Africa and elsewhere (Mbembe 2001). What might be suggested by such work is that global Southern- and global Northern-based research and researchers should find better, less colonialist or imperialist ways of working, as in "mutual learning across boundaries."[12] Developing a truly global social science of knowledge and knowledge construction is an aspiration in process (Connell et al. 2017).

Second, and in some ways related to the first point, a tendency toward narrow professionalism and specialization has discouraged efforts to communicate with a larger public and contribute to the development of public policy. In current debates on development policies, observations that are not based on stylized – and often problematic – randomized control trials are often discounted. Increased competition for university jobs and emphasis on publication in academic journals has reduced the support and respect once offered to "public intellectuals." At the same time, the increasingly precarious character of the academic job market (along with that for journalism) means that scholars lack the institutional stability required for the process of knowledge creation. Such precarity undermines the capacity of the academy to defend itself against political intrusion. Further, social scientists are now operating in an information environment dominated by oligopolies such as Google, even as new social actors proliferate information that is either unverifiable or not exposed to scrutiny.

A third problem concerns a failure to reinforce the importance of scientific inquiry and standards of evidence in policy debate, leaving public discourse increasingly vulnerable to ideological bias and media manipulation. Some social scientists cling to positivist convictions that prevent them from expressing an opinion on political issues when irrefutable empirical evidence is not available. At the opposite extreme, some embrace a postmodernist skepticism that challenges any distinction between truth and falsehood. Social scientists need to carve a wider path between "everything true is measurable" and "nothing is true." As E.P. Thompson put it, the facts are there not to disclose their own meaning, but to "be interrogated by minds trained in the discipline of attentive disbelief" (1978: 29).

A fourth problem of social science needs particularly serious inquiry – its frequent deployment on behalf of the powers that be. One vivid example is provided by the American Psychological Association's support for psychologists' involvement in US military interrogations, which raises serious ethical questions (Pope 2015). Another example is provided by the neoclassical economic "proof" that unfettered market forces lead to efficient outcomes. While not all economists by any means endorse this view of the market (the otherwise correct mathematical result relies on many assumptions that are not realized in practice), this assertion undergirds the implementation of radical pro-market policies on a global level and encourages disregard for environmental sustainability. Although it is confined to efficiency analysis, it also bizarrely serves to validate the existing distribution of power and income. In defense of individuals in the top 1 percent, Harvard economist Gregory Mankiw explains the standard neoclassical economic framework as follows: "The rich earn higher incomes because they contribute more to society than others do" (2013: 29). Similarly, economist Tyler Cowen's (2013) recent book, *Average is Over*, celebrates the claim that market forces increasingly reward

---

10   See http://geography.oii.ox.ac.uk/?page=the-location-of-academic-knowledge.

11   These issues are very much on international agendas, for example, the initiative of the International Sociological Association on the *Global Dialogue* online journal series (http://isa-global-dialogue.net/). See also Bhambra and de Sousa Santos (2016).

12   We are grateful to Kopano Ratele for this clarification.

Something wrong w/ This?

excellence and innovation. These propositions are based on spurious assumptions that inherited advantages, power, and networks play no significant role within capital and labor markets.[13] The inordinate influence on policy-making, at both the national and international levels, of economists and ill-trained business executives who broadly accept this ideological interpretation of economic theory undermines the potential for social science to contribute to social progress.

21.5   Overcoming Obstacles

The obstacles to *sustainable* social progress – progress that is robust and continues into the future – are enormous in the world today, and the prospects for overcoming those obstacles seem daunting (see discussion in Chapter 8). What is more, there is real urgency in the need to overcome these obstacles. Just muddling through does not seem a viable option. Even if the apocalyptic visions of some environmentalists are overstated, unless there are significant changes in the direction we are collectively moving in, global warming and climate disruption will generate enormous suffering and destructive conflict. Disastrous effects, concentrated in the poorer parts of the world least able to cope, will cause demographic pressures from escalating flows of refugees, including future climate refugees, putting tremendous strains on host countries. Increasing economic marginalization and precariousness for significant parts of the population within both rich and poor countries, combined with increasing concentrations of wealth and power, will further undermine democratic institutions. Personal, family, and community life will be profoundly disrupted.

The long-term consequence of simply trying to muddle through is likely to be social regress on many dimensions, not progress. These tendencies are all complicated by trends in science and technology, including the advance of biotechnologies, automation, and artificial intelligence, which may intensify existing inequalities.

We need to mitigate, if not overcome, social divisions by developing a persuasive vision of a more collaborative, democratic, and egalitarian society.

The proposals and initiatives most relevant for promoting social progress would obviously vary enormously depending both on political context and a wide range of socio-economic factors. We will not attempt to map out these variations here. We will also not attempt to lay out a comprehensive institutional design for an alternative socio-economic system. What we can do is give some sense of the kinds of proposals that reflect this broad strategic vision.

Proposals for new institutions can be evaluated on three principal grounds: their *desirability*, their *viability*, and their *achievability*.

Desirability refers to the extent to which proposals embody desirable values. In our discussion here, we emphasize the values of democracy, equality, and solidarity, but certainly other values would be relevant as well. Viability refers to the extent to which a proposal, if instituted, would in fact generate in a sustainable way the anticipated desirable consequences. In particular, some proposals may look very good "on paper," but if instituted would have self-destructive, perverse side-effects. This was at least part of the problem with the idea of socialism as comprehensive, central planning of entire economies. Finally, achievability refers to the extent to which we can get from here to there. In particular, for many kinds of proposals, this means assembling the social forces and collective actions needed politically to implement a proposal. In some ways, this is the most problematic of the three criteria, for while it may be possible to make sensible claims about what sorts of political forces can be mobilized for social change in the immediate contexts of the present, it is extremely hard to say anything very precise about what might be possible even a few decades in the future; there simply are too many contingencies and unknowns about the nature of crises and particular concatenations of events that might suddenly make what seemed impossible, possible. In what follows, therefore, we will stress the desirability and viability of various proposals, rather than their achievability. In any case, among the things that may contribute to the achievability of social progress are arguments about the desirability and practical viability of different proposals.

21.5.1   Transcending the Economic Structure of Capitalism

At the heart of any plausible vision of constraining and eventually displacing capitalism[14] as the dominant form of economic organization in a modern economy are three broad kinds of initiatives.

First, displacing the dominance of capitalist organizations requires expanding non-capitalist forms of market activity. While markets may be an essential feature of any viable complex economy, markets need not be dominated by capitalist firms, capitalist investment, and capitalist rules. A "cooperative market economy" is one alternative way of organizing market-oriented production. A variety of non-capitalist types of firms could populate such an economy: worker cooperatives; employee stock-owned firms; community-owned firms; hybrids of various sorts; individual proprietorships. And these firms could interact under rules which dampen competition and foster cooperation among cooperatives, for instance on providing employment security to workers, without encouraging collusion against customers.

Second, instead of a "market-conforming democracy," we can imagine new institutional devices to create a "democracy-conforming market."[15] Vigorous, effective, democratically imposed regulations

---

[13]   Labor markets are imperfect and incomplete because workers do not choose their initial endowments of capital or skill and are vulnerable to many outside forces that they cannot possibly anticipate. Even in the absence of explicit interference with market outcomes, many forms of power shape wage determination.

[14]   We use the specific term "capitalism" here, rather than the more encompassing term "market economy" for several reasons: (1) Not all market economies are capitalist; capitalism is a particular form of organization within the market economy. (2) The term "capitalism" points to the role of political and economic power in the economy rather than simply the "site" of economic transactions. (3) In any case, it is a misnomer to describe contemporary economies as simply "market economies," since the public sector constitutes a substantial share of both employment and output, and unpaid work accounts for about half of all labor time.

[15]   The expression "market-conforming democracy" comes from Angela Merkel. The expression functions much like Margaret Thatcher's well-known "There is no alternative" to suggest that a capitalist market economy constitutes a hard constraint on society. From this perspective, democracy should not try to subordinate the market to collectively decided priorities; such efforts are doomed to fail.

21

on the market and on the strategies of capitalist firms are needed to ensure that they serve the broad interests of people. This should include redistributive tax-and-transfer policies that would significantly reduce the destructive economic inequalities generated by under-regulated competition, as well as new mechanisms through which democratically determined priorities could shape the allocation of investments for different social objectives. Such policies would necessarily require interference with the unfettered private exercise of power by owners of capital and managers of firms. Of particular importance in the current era would be new forms of effective democratic regulation of finance designed to reduce both the power of finance and the systemic risks posed by financialized capitalism. While such democratic regulation of capitalism may also help to stabilize capitalism, it nevertheless renders it less purely capitalistic.

Third, we need to expand decisively the direct role of the state or community in meeting human needs. One of the hallmarks of the recent era in policy-making is the idea that the market, particularly the market dominated by profit-motivated private firms, generally provides the optimal way of meeting virtually all human needs. This claim has underwritten the privatization of state services and the general decline in the support for the state's role in creating a broad array of public goods and services. The provision of an expansive set of non-commodified, publicly provided goods and services is critical for social progress. This includes the typical services closely tied to caregiving and social reproduction: early child care services; elder care and disability care services; health; and education. But it also concerns a range of public amenities that enable people to engage in non-capitalist economic activities: community centers; performance spaces for non-commercial arts; makerspaces and fablabs (facilities where people share various arrays of machines for individual and collective projects); meeting rooms for public events; spaces for social and solidarity economy activities.

What follows is a series of more specific proposals for each of these three ways of transforming capitalism.

21.5.1.1   Building a Vibrant Cooperative Market Sector

The idea of "cooperatives" includes a rather heterogeneous set of economic organizations: consumer cooperatives, owned by consumers, and generally indirectly governed by consumers who elect the board of directors; credit cooperatives (typically called credit unions), formally governed by their members; producer cooperatives, owned and governed by privately owned firms which join together for purposes of distribution and marketing; housing cooperatives, including communal housing, co-housing, and various other forms; solidarity cooperatives, governed by elected boards of stakeholders; and worker-owned cooperatives, owned by workers and governed on a one-person-one-vote basis. All of these are relevant to building a cooperative market economy.

Within this array of cooperative forms, worker-owned cooperatives are especially important in imagining a future in which capitalism no longer dominates economic life and in which the heart of the economic system is organized on the basis of democratic, egalitarian, and solidaristic principles. Two issues are at play here. First, worker cooperatives constitute a direct transformation of the social relations within firms. Workers are now owners, elect the management of firms on an egalitarian one-person-one-vote basis, control the surpluses generated by the firm, and are involved in setting the basic strategic priorities of firms. While worker cooperatives generally produce for the market, they are organized around values very different from capitalist firms: solidarity, equality, democratic governance, dignity of work, community development. To the extent that the firms that populate a market are organized in this way, that market will be less capitalistic.

Still, worker cooperatives are producing for a market and thus are competing with other firms, and such competition imposes external constraints on their priorities. Like all market-oriented firms, worker cooperatives need to make profits to stay alive. Won't this simply lead them to behave like capitalist firms? Won't they still set investment priorities based on self-interested profits, ignoring issues of positive or negative externalities or other social objectives? As Paul Samuelson once claimed, "it doesn't really matter who hires whom: so have labor hire capital" (1957: 894); will worker-owned firms still behave the same way?

This brings us to the second way that worker cooperatives could play a critical role in an overall democratization of the economy. Two of the central obstacles to effective democratic regulation of capitalist markets are the concentration of power of wealthy owners of capitalist corporations and the ease of capital mobility to escape regulation. Both of these obstacles are significantly reduced with worker-owned cooperatives. Worker-owners, even in highly successful cooperatives, will not accumulate the fortunes that would enable them to wield the kind of political power that owners of capitalist corporations do. Perhaps even more significantly, worker cooperatives are rooted in particular places. Such firms constitute geographical anchors for investment, thus rendering capital less footloose. This makes them intrinsically easier to regulate. Thus, even though the firms of a cooperative market economy would still be profit-oriented, a cooperative market economy would more easily be subordinated to democratically determined priorities. Unlike markets dominated by capitalist firms, it would be a democracy-conforming market.

In existing capitalist economies, worker cooperatives generally occupy relatively marginal niches within the overall economic ecosystem and generally do not figure as central components of the political programs of anti-capitalist movements. This was not always the case. At times in the nineteenth century, there were significant currents within anti-capitalist movements that saw cooperatives as potentially replacing capitalism altogether. This was at the heart of the famous debate between Proudhon and Marx. At a minimum, cooperativists hoped that even if worker cooperatives did not displace capitalist firms entirely, they could nevertheless eventually constitute a significant sector within market economies, offering workers an alternative to capitalist employment. Marx was skeptical that worker cooperatives could ever reach a scale sufficient to challenge capitalism, though in the course of his life he became much more appreciative of the symbolic value of cooperatives as a visible demonstration that workers didn't need capitalists. The historical record is much more consistent with Marx's prediction than Proudhon's vision.

The relative marginality of worker-owned firms in contemporary capitalist economies poses a serious puzzle: if worker cooperatives in fact offer a desirable alternative to capitalist employment, why are they largely confined to niches on the margins of contemporary economies? Some people argue that the transaction costs of running a firm democratically place them at a competitive disadvantage once a firm gets above a relatively small size, both because the tasks of running the firm become more complex and because the labor force of the firm becomes more heterogeneous, making decision-making more difficult (Hansmann 2000). Others argue that the understandable risk-aversion of workers means that few are willing to put whatever savings they have into a cooperative. Furthermore, when worker cooperatives do become successful, there is a strong temptation for the original members of the firm to begin hiring employees and ultimately convert the firm to an ordinary capitalist enterprise.

Supporters of worker cooperatives argue that the existing empirical distribution of capitalist and non-capitalist firms in the market is heavily conditioned by the nature of the institutional environment in which firms are incubated, developed, and sustained. Credit markets, government programs to encourage local economic development, and management training programs in universities are all heavily oriented to ordinary capitalist firms. We simply don't know what the potential economic space for worker cooperatives, as well as the broader array of cooperatives, would look like if public policy were systematically oriented toward fostering a cooperative market economy. A number of changes in the rules of the game could facilitate the building of a cooperative market economy:

1. *Conversions of capitalist firms into cooperatives.* The conversion of existing capitalist firms into cooperatives is especially relevant in contexts where small- to medium-sized enterprises are owned by a family in which no adult children are interested in running the firm, and thus there is a succession problem when the existing owner dies or wishes to retire. Straightforward worker buy-outs are generally difficult, since workers lack the capital for such an investment, and even if they can get loans from the ordinary credit market, this is likely to create a debt burden on the firm that would undermine its viability for the future. A public policy to subsidize the conversion of firms into worker cooperatives could remove this obstacle. In the United States today, there already exists a mechanism, called an ESOP (employee stock ownership plan), which facilitates employees owning some or all of the stock in a capitalist firm. Such firms are still governed by a one-share-one-vote principle, so generally management has much more voting power than ordinary workers, and in any case in most ESOPs employees own only a minority of the shares. If the democratic governance of firms were seen as an important value, then there could be additional subsidies to underwrite the conversion of firms into fully democratic cooperatives.

2. *Worker take-overs of firms in contexts of bankruptcy.* In various places around the world, workers have taken over enterprises when those enterprises were facing bankruptcy. In recent years, the most striking instance of such worker take-overs were the *empresas recuperadas* (recovered enterprises) in Argentina, beginning in the severe financial crisis of 2001, but continuing afterwards during the economic recovery as well. Several hundred firms were occupied by their employees, who continued to operate the firms, producing goods and services for the market. These firms were generally terribly undercapitalized, and in the conditions of the crisis it was difficult for the workers running the firms to get needed capital from any source (Rebón 2007; Itzigsohn and Rebón 2016). Nevertheless, many survived.

Worker take-overs of enterprises typically occur under desperate conditions, hardly the optimal situation for creating worker cooperatives. Nevertheless, there are a number of public policies which could be used in these cases which could significantly facilitate the conversion of failing capitalist firms into worker cooperatives. Bankruptcy laws could be changed to give the workers in a firm the right to state-supported buy-outs with favorable loans and grants from the state. In cases where enterprises are abandoned by their owners – as was the case in the Argentinian crisis – the right of eminent domain could be used to initially transfer property rights to the state (Rannis 2016). This would create the breathing room needed to plan a proper conversion.

3. *Management training and technical support for cooperatives.* Management of cooperative enterprises is not the same as management of ordinary firms. One of the reasons why the cooperatives in the Mondragon cooperative group in Spain have been so successful is the existence of systematic programs for training people in how to work in and manage cooperative firms. The Mondragon group also has a range of research and technical support organizations to help individual cooperatives with various planning and innovation tasks. These organizations are themselves organized as cooperatives. The result is a dense network of specialized cooperatives in the service of the Mondragon cooperative market economy. In order to facilitate the development and sustainability of a cooperative market sector, the state needs to play a role in developing comparable institutions elsewhere.

4. *Credit institutions for a cooperative market.* Credit markets are not well-suited for a cooperative market sector. The risk profile of small firms in general makes it difficult for them to get loans, but this is especially the case for worker-owned firms. Subsidized access to capital – in the form of both credit and grants – is essential if there is to be a vibrant cooperative market sector and eventually a cooperative market economy. An objection to such subsidy is that it would give cooperatives an "unfair" advantage over conventional capitalist firms in market competition. But once it is recognized that enhanced democracy is a positive externality of cooperatives and a cooperative market economy is a key part of a more democratic economy, then a significantly subsidized credit market specifically designed for cooperatives is justified.

21.5.1.2 Democratizing the Large Capitalist Corporation

It is well and good to imagine a more democratic economy with a substantial sector organized through cooperatives of various sorts. But worker-owned cooperatives are nearly always very small firms. Even the largest industrial cooperatives in the Mondragon group have only a few thousand members. Can one really imagine General Motors or Exxon being organized as a worker-owned cooperative? The large corporation owned by outside investors is at the very heart of the capitalist economy. What would it mean to "democratize" the large multinational corporation?

Isabelle Ferreras has proposed an institutional design for governing the capitalist firm that answers this question (Ferreras 2017). She calls the model "Economic Bicameralism." She develops the idea through an analogy with the development of bicameral legislatures in the early modern state. A stylized characterization of the development of British parliamentary democracy would note that the pre-modern state consisted of a king in political dialogue with a chamber of great landed magnates. In the late fourteenth century a second chamber, the House of Commons, was added, although it took several more centuries before this rudimentary form developed into a fully empowered bicameral parliamentary democracy. This two-house parliament, in Ferreras's words, "expresses a dualist ontology of society with land-owners on one side and the people (or at least their representatives) on the other" (2017: 122).

Now think of the modern corporation. The largest of these firms generate more income annually than most countries in the world. They have a chief executive officer, analogous to a king, who is accountable to a chamber of wealthy investors, analogous to the House of Lords. These massive organizations are political entities insofar as they have the capacity to command massive resources for various purposes and control the activities of tens of thousands of people. And yet the ruler of such organizations is only accountable to one kind of person: the investors of capital. Ferreras proposes the creation of a second chamber of the board of directors representing the investors of labor in the firm. This "House of Labor Investors" would have co-equal powers to the "House of Capital Investors," creating the kind of balance of power found in bicameral parliamentary systems:

> The essential – and sought-after – effect of economic bicam-eralism is to allow all of the firm's investors, through the representatives they elected to the Capital and Labor Investors' Chambers, to participate in decisions about all issues affecting the life of the firm, without exception … That both Chambers must participate in all decisions should be reiterated here: reserving certain issues for one Chamber alone would create an incomplete form of bicameralism, and reproduce the power imbalances that characterize firms' current unicameral system, which has caused the illegitimate, unreasonable and unintelligent governance now all too common in the contemporary business world, with the dire consequences we know today. (Ferreras 2017: 132–133)

A corporation with a bicameral governance structure would still produce for the market and would still have to contend with competitive pressures, but it would no longer be governed by the single imperative of maximizing the returns on capital invested. It would be a hybrid form forced to seek compromises between the priorities of capital investors and those of labor investors in the firm.

21.5.1.3   Universal Basic Income

Universal basic income (UBI) is a proposal to give every legal resident of a territory an income sufficient to live above the poverty line without any work requirement or other conditions.[16] Taxes are raised to pay for the UBI, so even though everyone gets the income, high-income earners would be net contributors (their increases in taxes would be larger than the UBI they received). Existing public programs of income support would be eliminated, except for those connected to special needs (e.g. disabilities that require extra income). Minimum wage laws would also be eliminated, since there would no longer be any reason to prohibit low-wage voluntary contracts once a person's basic needs were not contingent on that wage. The UBI for children would be calibrated at some appropriate level compared to that for adults.

UBI opens up a wide array of new possibilities for people. It guarantees that any young person can do an unpaid internship, not just those who have affluent parents who are prepared to subsidize them. Market-oriented worker cooperatives would become much more viable, since meeting the basic needs of the worker-owners would not depend on the income generated by the enterprise. This would also mean worker cooperatives would be better credit risks to banks, making it easier for cooperatives to get loans. UBI would constitute a massive transfer of resources to the arts, enabling people to opt for a life centered around creative activity rather than market-generated income. The social and solidarity economy would be invigorated, including new forms of care-giving cooperatives. UBI would also be a way of supporting people who provide care work for family members outside of the market. UBI, if it could be instituted at a relatively generous level, would move us significantly toward the egalitarian principle of giving everyone equal access to the material conditions to live a flourishing life.[17]

Most defenses of UBI revolve around ways in which a basic income would eliminate poverty and reduce inequality. These are, of course, important issues. Insofar as UBI reduces poverty, it would itself directly contribute to social progress. But in the present context, there is an additional important consequence of UBI for social progress: in a world with UBI people could much more easily choose to engage in initiatives to build new forms of economic and social relations.[18]

---

[16]   See Van Parijs and Vanderborght (2017) for a detailed discussion of the arguments for and against universal basic income.

[17]   It is important to stress that UBI by itself is not a cure-all for the social impediments to human flourishing in contemporary society. For example, people also have needs for meaningful productive activities, and there is no guarantee that UBI would expand the opportunities for this. What UBI would accomplish is a more favorable economic terrain for efforts at expanding such opportunities.

[18]   While a generous, above-poverty-level basic income has the potential to open up new dynamic possibilities for non-capitalist economic development, there are also libertarian proposals which advocate introducing a basic income and then scrapping not only existing income support programs, but also virtually all public provision of services to meet human needs (i.e. education, health care, etc.). People would then have to purchase these services on the market without further subsidy. The best known advocate this position is Charles Murray (2006).

Insofar as social progress depends on the creativity and energy of activism in civil society, UBI would increase the capacity of people to dedicate themselves to these goals.

Universal basic income is not simply a proposal for rich countries that already have expansive programs of income redistribution. Because the standard of living that would be considered a dignified minimum is much lower in poor countries, the actual cost of a meaningful UBI would not necessarily take a larger share of national income. A basic income that would be below a culturally acceptable level in a rich country could still make a tremendous difference in the lives and opportunities of people in poor countries. Indeed, because households in poor countries often involve much wider kin networks, even if the individual UBI was small, there would be the possibility of pooling basic incomes to generate significant collective assets for the household. There is at least some evidence from basic income experiments in the global South that this happens.[19]

There are, of course, many objections to UBI, even from people who might share its egalitarian objectives. Three issues stand out. First there is the practical problem of affordability: is it really possible to give everyone, unconditionally, a stipend above the poverty line? While there are many technical difficulties in answering this question, in those countries with a highly developed redistributive welfare state it is already the case that through a patchwork of programs – means-tested income transfers, unemployment payments, disability payments, social security, child allowances, and so on – poverty is nearly eliminated. A generous UBI would eliminate most of these income support programs and would be administratively much cheaper, since it virtually eliminates monitoring costs. This means that in an already generous welfare state, most people would not experience a dramatic increase in their tax payments.

The second objection is that UBI is unfair to employed, hardworking people: a recipient of a basic income who then refuses to contribute to society is being supported by those who do. Some form of reciprocity is a very strong normative principle. While there are sophisticated arguments by philosophers about why it is just for "surfers to be fed" (to use a metaphor of Philippe van Parijs), nevertheless many – perhaps most – people are likely to feel strongly that recipients of basic income should be required to contribute something to society (Atkinson 2015). This need not take the form of working in the market for pay – unpaid care work for family members would count as a contribution to society, as would all sorts of other forms of unpaid volunteer activity. But many people might regard a person who is supported by UBI and makes no contribution as a parasite. Should making a contribution be monitored? Would this undermine the principle of UBI that people should be enabled to find their own way to contribute? There are always trade-offs in any social policy, and defenders of the reciprocity principle may still decide on practical grounds as well as principle that reciprocity-enforcement is not worth the cost. Whether or not support for a UBI would be sustained over time would then depend, in part, on the number of people who violate norms of reciprocity.

A final objection sometimes raised against UBI is that it is a highly individualistic policy, enhancing the freedom of many people to make separate choices about their lives, but doing nothing to foster conditions for solidarity and community, so critical for human flourishing. Indeed, by not requiring any contribution from recipients, UBI could further undermine the values of caring and reciprocity that are already precarious in highly competitive, individualistic market economies. It is just as plausible, however, that by giving individuals more autonomy and control over their life plans, UBI would foster not just the ability but the willingness of many people to leave the competitive individualism of the capitalist labor market to participate in collaborative, socially constructive projects of all sorts.

21.5.1.4   Universal Care Services

To live, people need not only need money and the goods money can buy. They also need care, that is, help with the activities of everyday living that many people can do for themselves for much of their lives, but may need help to do when they are young, disabled, or becoming frail as they age. While UBI would give everyone enough money to cover their material needs, it would not give them the care they may also need. This leaves a huge source of inequality in terms of peoples' ability to live a fulfilled life. It also leaves people vulnerable to unexpected care needs that they may not be able to meet on their own either by buying care on the market or relying on family and friends willing to devote time to their care.

The need for care also generates huge inequalities between those who devote time to the care of others and those who do not. Since gender norms tend to allocate care responsibilities primarily to women, this inequality is a gendered one, which UBI would also not tackle. UBI would liberate people without care responsibilities to do worthwhile and creative things. However, for those with full-time care responsibilities, UBI would give them something to live on, but not the opportunity to do anything else with their lives.

A proposal that would tackle this problem is a Universal Care Service (UCS), free at the point of need. This could be a complement to UBI, but is also a standalone proposal. It would give high-quality care to everyone who needs it, rectifying inequalities in the life chances of both those who need care and those who take responsibility for their care.

Of course, much unpaid informal care would still go on. The giving and receiving of care is one of those spaces in which people escape those pressures of capitalism to turn every minute into money. It is a positive activity, provided the care is of high quality, willingly given, and does not put obstacles in the way of a fulfilling life for both care receiver and caregiver. The problem arises when the demands on caregivers are very high and leave them with time to do little else. Society should share the responsibility for care, by providing a UCS.

It could be argued that, rather than providing care directly, it would be better to provide those with care needs – or, for children, their parents – with extra money to buy their own care. The problem with this proposal is that care provided by for-profit firms tends to be of poor quality. This is because the dynamic of competition requires firms to continually seek to cut costs, unless they can offer better quality than their competitors. However, good-quality care is notoriously difficult to judge because it depends so much on unquantifiable, and often unobservable, aspects of the relationship between care workers and their clients. Further, purchasers tend to be income-constrained. These factors together result in a market in which competition tends to be over costs, not quality. But care is a highly labor-intensive activity, so the only way to cut costs is to cut staff or hire cheaper, less well-qualified staff, both of which reduce the quality of care provided.

Better quality care therefore tends to be provided by those who work directly in the public or voluntary sectors, where profit-making is not the goal. A UCS delivered by these sectors could be not simply a service for those who currently need care, but also a focal point for communities.

For example, family centers could not only provide child care, but offer opportunities for families to meet, older children to play after school, and parents and others to learn skills to help them get more out of their lives. In England, there are Sure Start centers in the most deprived areas, which provide child care as well as help and advice on child and family health, parenting, training, and employment. Although the funding of these centers has not been adequate to fulfill their early promise, they could, if rolled out to every community, provide the basis for a system of family centers providing universal services.

In France, many residential care homes for the elderly also provide day centers and domiciliary care services for those who need assistance in their own homes. As a result, when those who are cared for in their own homes need extra help, they can move temporarily or permanently into the residential center and be cared for by staff with whom they are familiar. Such residential care homes could also become centers for the community, involving people of all ages and allowing generations to mix. Indeed, why not merge them with the family centers discussed above?

As capitalism has developed, the increased productivity of factory methods of production has rendered it more economical for households to earn the money to buy many of the necessities of life rather than produce them themselves. This has not been an uncontested process. For example, in the nineteenth century there were many protests about the adulteration of commercially bought food, contrasting the uncertainty of the quality of what could be bought in the shops with the known quality of home-produced food. In the most industrialized economies of today, care is effectively the last remaining home-produced good, or at least the last one that seriously limits what else people can do with their lives. But, many remain unwilling to turn care into a commodity, because the quality of care is so fundamental to people's lives and the market cannot be relied upon to produce good-quality care.

But how would such a UCS be paid for? It would not be cheap, but its net cost to the state might well be a small ratio of its gross cost. This is because revenue would be raised from the increased taxes and reduced benefits of those who previously could not take up employment because of caring responsibilities but now choose to do so. The exact costs would depend on the mix of types of care provided and a

country's tax and benefit system, but for England it has been estimated that the state would recoup between 89 percent and 95 percent of the gross cost of providing universal high-quality free child care (De Henau 2017).

21.5.2 Naming and Changing the Powerful and the Privileged

While they are key approaches to social progress, neither a UBI nor a UCS necessarily addresses some wider aspects of (in)equality, privilege, and citizenship. Citizenship has historically often been framed in neutral terms, but in practice has often reproduced a male, heterosexual, raced, and classed citizenry. In the light of the historical exclusion and marginalization of women, people of color, and further subordinated groupings, full citizenship requires addressing wide-ranging structures of inequality through policy intervention on such questions as democratic representation, work, and care in and across public and private spheres.

1. *Naming the powerful in institutions and policy development.* Confronting inequality certainly involves pursuing egalitarian agendas, but this does not only involve the inclusion of those excluded, marginalized, and subordinated. The other side of the coin is the naming of the powerful, the privileged, the superordinate, those already included, as defined by age, class, ethnicity, gender, or another social dimension (Pease 2010) or institutional position. Recognizing privilege is a key step in policy development, whether at the local or the organizational level; in societal transformations, for example, the complex transition to post-apartheid South Africa; or in policy responses to growing concentrations of power in the hands of the largely male, transnational capitalist class (Sklair 2001; Donaldson and Poynting 2006; Carroll 2010). Naming the powerful can encourage resistance to their influence.

2. *Developing institutional policies and practices for changing the powerful: the case of men and masculinities.* Naming the powerful and privileged can be a prelude to policy action. This applies at different institutional levels and takes many forms, for example, developing anti-racist, ethnically sensitive educational policy and workplace practices in moving toward ethnic and racial justice, anti-ageism training in working for intergenerational solidarity, or zero tolerance for bullying and harassment within institutions.

    Changing men and dominant masculinities in supporting gender justice is an exemplar of policy processes directed at the more powerful. Policies for changing men and dominant masculinities have become much more widespread in recent years, and have entered mainstream agendas, such as those of the UN, the EU, the Council of Europe, and OSCE. For example, the EU report *The Role of Men in Gender Equality* (2013) addressed policies for men's involvement in gender equality, with the promotion of caring masculinities as a central theme. Examples of such policy action include: education and training programs for less dominating and destructive forms of masculinity; promotion of men's health and healthy lifestyles; violence prevention and anti-violence work; targets and quotas limiting men's dominance in organizations; training for more egalitarian leadership and management; expanding sexuality and gender-diversity rights; promotion of men's and boys' engagement in paid and unpaid care, family, and fatherhood, and reconciliation of care, home, and work; and changing so-called "macho" work cultures to promote safety and reduce accidents at work.

3. *Building transnational, inter-organizational alliances for policy development: learning from the global South.* What is of special interest in such interventions and initiatives is that much of the most active work around men and boys is taking place in the global South, through major policy alliances. This demands new, creative, inter-organizational, transnational forms of policy development, as illustrated by the work of the global MenEngage Alliance, an umbrella organization of activists, NGOs, projects, and policy actors (http://menengage.org/), on gender justice, with over 700, mainly group, members, and national networks in Africa (17), the Caribbean (5), Europe (16), Latin America (10), North America (2), and South Asia (5). The Alliance's policy focus includes: gender-based violence; violence in armed conflict; caregiving and fatherhood; global political economy; sexual and reproductive health and rights; men's and boys' gender vulnerabilities and health needs; sexual exploitation; HIV and AIDS; and environment and sustainability. The 2014 Delhi Declaration on men's relation to global gender justice serves as a model for changing the powerful in desirable and viable ways (www.menengagedilli2014.net/delhi-declaration-and-call-to-action.html); the global North can learn much from the global South.[20]

4. *Extending equality agendas into "unmarked" and transnational policy arenas.* Similarly, strategies for changing the powerful need to extend beyond policy arenas explicitly labeled as "equal opportunities," "gender equality," or "diversity issues." This means thinking of equality/inequality agendas more broadly in "unmarked" arenas, such as trade, transport, foreign, and security policy. Thus, while policy around interpersonal violence is well recognized as part of gender-aware policy, this is much less so for terrorism, racist violence, state violence, and militarism. Having said that, explicit policy on the privileged, when developed, is often framed within local or national contexts rather than transnationally, in terms of, say, global finance or the environment. Analyzing and changing policy in transnational directions demands transnational social science and policy collaborations.

21.5.3   Democratizing Democracy

At the center of the idea of fighting current inequalities is the problem of democracy. This means both democratizing the power relations within the economy and deepening the democratic character of the state. These two dimensions of democratization work together: without advances in democracy within the state, it is unlikely that the necessary policies to facilitate economic democracy would be enacted; without advances in economic democracy, it is unlikely that a more deeply democratic state could be sustained.

The democratic vitality of political institutions in Western democracies has significantly eroded in recent decades. Trust in politicians and governmental institutions has declined to historic lows in many countries. In part this is due to the character of the problems democratic institutions confront: globalization and financialization of capital have undermined the autonomy and power of most national states, making it more difficult for them to effectively regulate their own economic conditions, and this in turn means that citizens have less confidence that their elected governments will be able to solve pressing problems.[21] Widespread cynicism about political institutions develops from the sense that the political process and elected officials fail to represent the interests of ordinary people. To many people, the feeling is that democracy itself is failing, not simply that the specific policies of the state need changing. What follows are two examples of institutional innovations that could contribute to a renewed, deepened democracy.

21.5.3.1   Randomly Selected Citizen Legislatures

The ideal of democratic government is often characterized as government *of* the people, *by* the people, and *for* the people. The standard institutional design for achieving this ideal is electoral democracy: citizens choose their political leaders through electoral competition, typically organized through political parties. The *by the people* element is supposed to be insured by elections; the *for the people* is insured by competition among politicians, so that if elected representatives fail to legislate in the interests of the people, they can be replaced in subsequent elections; and *of the people* is enabled by the principle that any citizen above a certain age can run for office. Those are the principles.

In practice, existing systems of electoral democracy fail to realize any of these ideals. While citizens certainly do vote, government *by the people* is blunted by the role of money in elections and the structure of political parties. *For the people* is undermined by the multiple pressures on politicians, regardless of political ideology, to cater to the interests of elites. And *of the people* is blocked by the deep inequalities in the real capacities to run for office and get elected of people from different social and demographic groups. The result is that nowhere does the distribution of economic and social attributes among legislators reflect that of voters.

There are many kinds of proposals for dealing with these democratic deficits, including, among other things: changes in the rules of electoral representation; new forms of campaign financing; shifts in the responsibilities of centralized and decentralized units of government; changes in the way citizens get information about political choices; reserved seats for people with particular demographic characteristics; and so on. Which of these sorts of reforms would be most important for improving democracy varies from place to place. But what virtually all proposals have in common is the reliance on elections as the pivotal way that the preferences of citizens get aggregated into political representation.

---

[20]   For further information on relevant resources, see, for example, www.genderjustice.org.za/, http://promundoglobal.org/ and www.xyonline.net/.

[21]   For a strong argument that democratic states have exhausted their capacity to regulate capitalism, and as a result democracy itself has eroded, see Wolfgang Streeck (2016).

There is an alternative to elections that has an ancient pedigree: selection of public officials for a legislature by random selection. This is sometimes referred to as a *sortition* legislature.[22] This was the way legislators were chosen in ancient Athens, albeit within very exclusionary definitions of citizens. And in many countries today, this is the way juries are selected in courts. Could random selection be adapted to legislatures in liberal democracies? And in what ways might this enhance democracy?

Here is a sketch of the design of a possible sortition legislature. The legislature would consist of two chambers. In the first, members would be elected in a conventional manner; in the second – the *sortition chamber* – members would consist of randomly selected citizens. Depending on the political and cultural context, the sample could be stratified on various dimensions to ensure that it reflected the salient demographic and social characteristics of the population.

The sortition chamber would have the same powers and responsibilities as the elected chamber, including budgetary authority and the opportunity to draft, debate, and vote on laws. Sortition legislators would serve sufficiently long terms to gain experience, for example four-year terms, with one quarter being replaced each year. The pay would be generous – say twice the median annual earnings – making the job an attractive one financially for most people. The chamber would have substantial staff support to provide initial training to newly selected sortition legislators, to organize a wide range of information services for the chamber, and to facilitate deliberation on proposed legislation (Gastil and Wright, forthcoming).

There are a variety of ways in which a sortition legislature would potentially deepen democracy. By enabling a sample of ordinary citizens to directly exercise legislative power, the new chamber would strengthen the idea of government "of the people," a government in which decision-makers are recruited not from elites but from the lay public. Since sortition legislators are randomly selected, they would not in any way be beholden to wealthy contributors to election campaigns. It would be easier to insulate a sortition chamber than an elected chamber from the political influence of money. The discussion of legislation within a sortition chamber would be more likely than that in an elected chamber to involve real deliberation, seeking common ground in the effort to solve problems.

What is more, in the sortition chamber the selection of problems to be solved through legislation is likely to be much more in tune with the needs and difficulties of ordinary people than is the case of legislation initiated by the elected chamber. As a result, a sortition assembly is not simply *of the people*; it would also enhance *for the people*.

21.5.3.2   Participatory Budgeting

A sortition legislature may embody the principle of government of the people, but by its very nature most people would not be selected. The only form of active political participation available to most people would remain voting for candidates for the elected chamber. A citizen observing the sortition assembly might say, it is people just like me that are making these decisions, and thus there is a kind of vicarious participation. But vicarious participation is not the same as direct participation.

There is another aspect of democratic ideals, therefore, which is missed by both elections and sortition: the idea that ordinary citizens should be able to actively participate in the direct exercise of political power, in making the decisions which affect their lives. This is sometimes referred to as "direct democracy" or "participatory democracy." Even though a core value of democracy is expressed in the idea of rule by the people, for practical reasons, the argument goes, in modern society this means rule by the freely chosen representatives of the people. The conventional wisdom is that direct citizen involvement in political decisions is hopelessly impractical in a complex modern society.

The development of what has come to be known as "participatory budgeting" is a sharp challenge to that conventional wisdom.[23] Participatory budgeting was invented almost by accident in the city of Porto Alegre, Brazil, in 1989. Porto Alegre is a city of around one and a half million inhabitants in the southeast corner of the country. In late 1988, after long years of military dictatorship and a period of transition to democracy, a left-wing party – the Workers Party (the PT) – won the mayoral election in the city. The PT had not expected to win, but the more conservative traditional parties split the conservative vote, and the PT's candidate for mayor won with a plurality of the vote. The party, however, did not control the city council, and thus faced the prospect of having four years in office without being able to do much to advance its progressive political program.

Faced with this situation, the activists in the party asked the classic question: what is to be done? Their answer was a remarkable institutional innovation: the participatory budget. Basically the PT decided to create a kind of parallel city government around the city budget that could effectively neutralize the power of the city council. As in most cities with an elected mayor and city council, the mayor's office is responsible for developing a city budget and presenting it to the city council for ratification. The charter of the city of Porto Alegre, however, did not specify how the mayor was to produce the numbers in the budget. The standard procedure, of course, is for technocrats in the mayor's office – economists, city planners, engineers – to produce the budget in consultation with politicians and various elites, but this was not mandated by the official "rules of the game." What the Mayor and the activists in the PT did, then, was to create a novel budget-making system anchored in the direct participation of ordinary citizens. Initially the process was pretty chaotic, but in a spirit of democratic experimentalism, the procedures were refined over time until eventually a coherent institutional model was achieved.

Instead of the city budget being formulated from the top down, Porto Alegre was divided into regions each of which had a participatory budget assembly. There were also a number of city-wide budget assemblies on various themes of interest to the entire municipality – cultural

---

[22]   For a discussion of the history of sortition legislatures, see Sintomer (2011).
[23]   Some of this discussion of participatory budgeting is taken from Erik Olin Wright (2011). See also Chapter 14.

festivals, for example, or public transportation. The mandate for each of these participatory budget assemblies was to formulate concrete budget proposals, particularly for infrastructure projects of one sort or another. Any resident of the city could participate in these assemblies and vote on the proposals. After ratifying these regional and thematic budgets, the assemblies chose delegates to participate in a city-wide budget council for a few months until a coherent, consolidated city budget was adopted.

In the years since the invention of the participatory budget in Porto Alegre, there have been hundreds of cities around the world in which some form of participatory budgeting has been tried. As the participatory budget idea has traveled around the world it has developed into a menu of institutional designs rather than a single model. In many cities, the use of PB is restricted to a very narrow range of city spending, rather than the more expansive scope of its original form in Porto Alegre. In some cities, final projects are approved through a popular vote rather than by an assembly of budget delegates. In some cities, the process has functioned more like a new form of patronage, controlled by political machines; in others, it has contributed to popular power and mobilization. One thing is clear: it is not enough to simply adopt the formal design of participatory budgeting for it to contribute to a process of deepening democracy. What matters is how this design intersects social movements, secondary associations, and grassroots activism. But when this intersection occurs, participatory budgeting opens up an arena of direct democracy.

The proposals we have discussed, if instituted, would significantly reduce the obstacles to social progress. Many more ideas could be added to this list. If one could snap one's fingers and implement such proposals, the world would be a better place. But of course, snapping fingers won't do the trick. To overcome the obstacles to social progress requires more than good ideas about what needs to be done; it requires mobilizing the social and political forces capable of translating those ideas into actual social changes. And for that, enlightenment is not enough.

21.5.4   Unanswered Questions

There are important aspects of the obstacles to social progress for which we do not know of compelling solutions. Six issues seem especially important:

1. What policies could robustly subordinate the capitalist market economy to democratic constraints in a globalized context? A global superordinate democratic state seems completely out of reach, and in any case, there are no serious models for how this could work. The answer probably involves resolving collective-action problems among states more than simply increasing the capacity of individual states to control their own economies. But when many of the critical states involved are not themselves democratic, and when even the democratic states operate in a political environment of large inequalities of power, it is not at all obvious that in practice successful solutions to coordination problems among states will have a democratic character. And if the solution to coordination problems is fundamentally undemocratic, then it is not at all clear that such a solution would open more space for social progress.

2. What politically achievable mechanisms would generate meaningful global redistribution, especially in the face of global environmental injustice? Stark differences in international living standards are the legacy of uneven economic development. The global economic system does an extremely poor job of protecting poorer countries from the actions of affluent countries (in the areas of financial policies, trade restrictions, or global investment and tax regimes), depriving them of much-needed resources and imposing huge costs in the form of capital volatility and climate change. As the Maastricht principles make clear, the promise of rich countries to provide 0.7 percent of GDP as aid to developing countries – met by only a handful of states – is inadequate to address these historical and structural inequalities.[24] All of the proposals outlined above are framed on the national level, and would do little to reduce international inequalities. At best, they might provide a model for more egalitarian and sustainable economic development.

3. Other legacy effects include inequalities based on ethnicity, race, gender, and other dimensions of social identity that would affect the functioning of any alternative economic system. These include major differences in the distribution of financial and human capital – both wealth and education. Some of the identity-based collective conflict we observe in the world is undoubtedly a displacement of underlying economic grievances, and if those grievances were resolved then many distributional conflicts would diminish (Stewart 2008). But some forms of identity-based collective conflict do not simply reflect underlying economic interests and what it would take to fully resolve these identity-based collective conflicts would mean further ethnic, racial, and gender transformations.

4. How should family and community life be integrated into the larger economic system in ways that promote real gender equality and human flourishing? Greater provision of public goods, including a basic minimum income and good-quality, publicly provided care centers, would improve the position of unpaid caregivers. Policies such as paid paternity leave from work – in "use-it-or-lose-it" form – could encourage more participation by fathers. Cultural renegotiation of care responsibilities could challenge constrictive definitions of both femininity and masculinity.

5. How can we improve, and perhaps modify the relationship between, material and subjective wellbeing? Whatever the limits of a happiness metric, the relationship between economic living standards and human satisfaction is far more complex than previously realized. The assumption that "more is always better" programmed into global norms has proved both deceptive and dysfunctional. Yet the desire to improve our position relative to others seems deeply embedded and difficult to change. Within wealthy countries, "voluntary simplicity" and non-consumerist lifestyles are essential for long-term environmental sustainability,

---

[24] Maastricht Principles on Extraterritorial Obligations of States in the Area of Economic, Social and Cultural Rights. www.ilsa.org/jessup/jessup17/Batch%202/Maastricht%20 Principles%20on%20Extraterritorial%20Obligations%20of%20States%20in%20the%20Area%20of%20Economic,%20Social%20and%20Cultural%20Rights.pdf.

but what kinds of achievable policies could robustly move us in this direction? Is it possible to have a stable market economy without consumerism?

6.   What practical strategies can help forge the collective agents necessary for sustainable social progress? The persistence, and sometimes intensification, of identity-based cleavages, especially as these intersect and interact with complex forms of class divisions, makes it very difficult to assemble social forces capable of sustained collective action. This is an urgent problem, not simply because future social progress depends on collective action, but because in the twenty-first century we face a real prospect of catastrophic social regress. In an earlier era, it was thought that the trajectory of social change was producing ever more homogeneous material conditions of life for the vast majority of people, and thus the task of creating collective actors for struggle would become easier over time. Instead, this task has become more difficult. However insightful are the discussions of intersectionality and heterogeneity of multiple forms of oppression, they do not provide clear answers to the vexing problem of how to overcome these divisions in a robust way. It is easy enough to proclaim the need for a democratic egalitarian coalition for collective action among people with cross-cutting, intersectional identities; it is quite another thing to figure out how to do so.

These are difficult questions. Some of them may, in fact, be unanswerable. Social sciences have proven quite successful in the diagnosis and critique of the world as it is. We know a great deal about the ways in which existing structures and practices generate harms in the world and generate obstacles to social improvement. And we also know a fair amount, with some important gaps, about what kinds of changes, if they could be instituted, would make things better. What is much more difficult is understanding how to get from here to there. This is like a doctor that has diagnosed an illness and identified the cure, but cannot get the patient to do what is needed to turn the cure on paper into a cure in reality. Perhaps the patient lacks willpower, or just doesn't have the material resources needed to follow through with the doctor's recommendations. A critical task for social science in the twenty-first century is helping to figure out how to actually implement the social, economic, and political changes needed for sustainable social progress into the future.

References

Acemoglu, Daron, and James A. Robinson. 2012. *Why Nations Fail*. New York: Crown Books.

Adam, Barbara, and Chris Groves. 2007. *Future Matters*. Amsterdam: Brill.

Alesina, Alberto, Reza Baqir, and William Easterly. 1999. "Public Goods and Ethnic Divisions." *Quarterly Journal of Economics* 114/4: 1243–1284.

Alic, J.A. 2007. *Trillions for Military Technology: How the Pentagon Innovates and Why It Costs So Much*. New York: Palgrave MacMillan.

Allan, S., B. Adam, and C. Carter. (eds.) 1999. *Environmental Risks and the Media*. London: Routledge.

Allen, R., 1992. *Waste Not, Want Not: The Production and Dumping of Toxic Waste*. London: Earthscan.

Arthur, W. Brian. 2013. "Complexity Economics: A Different Framework for Economic Thought." Working Paper 2013-04-012. Santa Fe, NM: Santa Fe Institute. http://tuvalu.santafe.edu/~wbarthur/Papers/Comp.Econ.SFI.pdf.

Atkinson, Anthony B. 2015. *Inequality. What Can Be Done?* Cambridge, MA: Harvard University Press.

Axelrod, Robert. 1997. *The Complexity of Cooperation: Agent-Based Models of Competition and Collaboration*. Princeton, NY: Princeton University Press.

Barboza, David. 2016. "How China Built Iphone City." *The New York Times*, December 29. www.nytimes.com/2016/12/29/technology/apple-iphone-china-foxconn.html.

Bargawi, Hannah, Giovanni Cozzi, and Susan Himmelweit. (eds.) 2017. *Economics and Austerity in Europe: Gendered Impacts and Sustainable Alternatives*. New York: Routledge.

Barro, Robert. 1994. "Democracy: A Recipe for Growth?" *The Wall Street Journal*, December 1.

Beddington, J., 2009. *Food, Energy, Water and the Climate: A Perfect Storm of Global Events?* London: Government Office for Science.

Beeson, M., 2010. "The Coming of Environmental Authoritarianism." *Environmental Politics* 19/2: 276–294.

Bengtson, Vern L., and Petrice S. Oyama. 2007. *Intergenerational Solidarity: Strengthening Economic and Social Ties*. New York: Department of Economic and Social Affairs Division for Social Policy and Development, UN. www.un.org/esa/socdev/unyin/documents/egm_unhq_oct07_bengtson.pdf.

Bhambra, Gurminder K., and Boaventura de Sousa Santos. (eds.) 2016. "Global Futures and Epistemologies of the South: New Challenges for Sociology." Special issue, *Sociology* 51/1: 3–10.

Bloom, A., and W. Breines. (eds.) 2003. *"Takin' it to the Streets": A Sixties Reader*. Oxford: Oxford University Press.

Brady, David, and Hang Young Lee. 2014. "The Rise and Fall of Government Spending in Affluent Democracies, 1971–2008." *Journal of European Social Policy* 24/1: 56–79.

Broers, A., 2005. *The Triumph of Technology*. Cambridge: Cambridge University Press.

Burda, Michael, Daniel S. Hamermesh, and Philippe Weil. 2013. "Total Work and Gender: Facts and Possible Explanations." *Journal of Population Economics* 26: 239–261.

Burke, L., K. Reytar, M. Spalding, and A. Perry. 2011. *Reefs at Risk Revisited*. Washington, DC: World Resources Institute.

Carroll, W.K. 2010. *The Making of a Transnational Capitalist Class: Corporate Power in the 21st Century*. London: Zed Books.

Castree, N., and B. Braun. (eds.) 2001. *Social Nature: Theory, Practice and Politics*. Oxford: Blackwell.

Charles, Maria, and David B. Grusky. 2004. *Occupational Ghettos: The Worldwide Segregation of Women and Men*. Stanford, CA: Stanford University Press.

Chesbrough, H. 2003. "The Governance and Performance of Xerox's Technology Spin-off Companies." *Research Policy* 32: 403–421.

Chou, C., and Shy, O., 2013. "The Crowding-Out Effects of Long Duration of Patents." *The RAND Journal of Economics* 24/2: 304–312.

Christophers, B., 2009. *Envisioning Media Power: On Capital and Geographies of Television*. Lanham, MD: Lexington Books.

Chua, Amy. 2004. *Worlds on Fire. How Exporting Free Market Democracy Breeds Ethnic Hatred and Global Instability*. New York: Anchor.

Cohen, Patricia. 2016. "A Bigger Economic Pie but a Smaller Slice for Half of the U.S." *The New York Times*, December 6. www.nytimes.com/2016/12/06/business/economy/a-bigger-economic-pie-but-a-smaller-slice-for-half-of-the-us.html.

Collingridge, D., 1983. "Hedging and Flexing: Two Ways of Choosing under Ignorance." *Technology Forecasting and Social Change* 23: 161–172.

Connell, Raewyn. 2014. "Margin becoming Centre: For a World-Centred Rethinking of Masculinities. *NORMA: International Journal for Masculinity Studies* 9/4: 217–231.

Connell, Raewyn, Fran Collyer, João Maia, and Robert Morrell. 2017. "Toward a Global Sociology of Knowledge: Post-colonial Realities and Intellectual Practices." *International Sociology* 32/1: 21–37.

Cowen, Tyler. 2013. *Average is Over: Powering America beyond the Age of the Great Stagnation*. New York: Dutton.

CPRE. 2013. *Going, Going, Gone? England's Disappearing Landscapes*. London: CPRE.

Cranor, C.F., 2011. *Legally Poisoned: How the Law Puts Us at Risk from Toxicants*. Cambridge, MA: Harvard University Press.

Crenshaw, Kimberlé. 1989. "Demarginalizing the Intersection of Race and Sex: A Black Feminist Critique of Antidiscrimination Doctrine, Feminist Theory and Antiracist Politics." *University of Chicago Legal Forum* 1/8: 139–167.

Curran, J. 2002. *Media and Power*. London: Routledge.

Dator, J.A., J.A. Sweeney, and A.M. Yee. 2015. *Mutative Media: Communication Technologies and Power Relations in the Past, Present, and Futures*. Berlin: Springer.

Davala, Sarath, Renana Jhabvala, Guy Standing, and Soumya Kapoor Mehta. 2015. *Basic Income: A Transformative Policy for India*. London: Bloomsbury.

De Henau, Jerome. 2017. "Costing and Funding Free Universal Childcare of High Quality." Women's Budget Group. https://wbg.org.uk/wp-content/uploads/2016/11/De_Henau_WBG_childcare_briefing3_2017_02_20-1.pdf.

Dewey, J. 1935. "The Future of Liberalism." *The Journal of Philosophy* 32/9: 225–230.

Doherty, B., and M. De Geus. (eds.) 1996. *Democracy and Green Political Thought: Sustainability, Rights and Citizenship*. London: Routledge.

Donaldson, Mike, and Scott Poynting. 2006. *Ruling Class Men: Money, Sex, Power*. Bern: Peter Lang.

Dosi, G., and R.R. Nelson. 1994. "An Introduction to Evolutionary Theories in Economics." *Journal of Evolutionary Economics* 4: 153–172.

Duggan, Lisa. 2003. *The Twilight of Equality? Neoliberalism, Cultural Politics, and the Attack on Democracy*. Boston: Beacon.

Edwards, D. and D. Cromwell. 2006. *Guardians of Power: The Myth of the Liberal Media*. London: Pluto Press.

Elborgh-Woytek, Monique Newiak, Kalpana Kochbar, Stefania Fabrizio, and Phillipe Wingender. 2013. "Women, Work, and the Economy; Macroeconomic Gains from Gender Equity." IMF Staff Discussion Notes 13/10. Washington, DC: IMF. http://econpapers.repec.org/paper/imfimfsdn/13_2f10.htm.

Elias, N. 1996. *Du Temps, traduit de l'allemand par Michèle Hulin*. Paris: Fayard.

Elster, J. 1985. *Making Sense of Marx*. New York: Cambridge University Press.

Eurobarometer. 2005. *Population Innovation Readiness*. Brussels: Eurobarometer.

Fagerberg, J. 2003. "Schumpeter and the Revival of Evolutionary Economics: An Appraisal of the Literature." *Journal of Evolutionary Economics* 13/2: 125–159.

FAIC. 2012. *The Fukushima Nuclear Accident Independent Investigation Commission*. Tokyo: FAIC.

FAO and WWC. 2015. *Towards a Water and Food Secure Future: Critical Perspectives for Policy-Makers*. Rome: FAO.

Felt, U., and B. Wynne. (eds.) 2008. *Taking European Knowledge Society Seriously: Report of the Expert Group on Science and Governance to the Science, Economy and Society Directorate, Directorate-General for Research, European Commission*. Brussels: European Commission.

Felt, U., D. Barben, A. Irwin, et al. 2013. *Science in Society: Caring for Our Futures in Turbulent Times*. Strasbourg: European Science Foundation.

Ferreras, Isabelle. 2017. *Firms as Political Entities. Saving Democracy through Economic Bicameralism*. New York: Cambridge University Press.

Fiske, Susan. 2012. *Envy Up, Scorn Down: How Status Divides Us*. New York: Russell Sage Foundation.

Fligstein, N., and D. McAdam. 2011. "Toward a General Theory of Strategic Action Fields." *Sociological Theory* 29: 1–26.

Folbre, Nancy. 2008. *Valuing Children: Rethinking the Economics of the Family*. Cambridge, MA: Harvard University Press.

Folbre, Nancy. 2013. "The Rise and Decline of Patriarchal Capitalism," in Robert Pollin and Jeannette Wicks-Lim (eds.), *Capitalism on Trial: Explorations in the Tradition of Thomas E. Weisskopf*. Cheltenham, Gloucestershire: Edward Elgar.

Folbre, Nancy. 2016. "Just Deserts? Earnings Inequality and Bargaining Power in the U.S. Economy." Working Paper. Washington, DC: Washington Center for Equitable Growth. http://equitablegrowth.org/working-papers/earnings-inequality-and-bargaining-power/.

Frank, Andre Gunder. 1967. *Capitalism and Underdevelopment in Latin America*. New York: Monthly Review Press.

Freire, P., 2001. *Pedagogy of Freedom: Ethics, Democracy and Civic Courage*. Lanham, MA: Rowman & Littlefield Publishers.

Gastil, John, and Erik Olin Wright. Forthcoming. *Legislature by Lot*. London: Verso.

Geels, F.W. 2006. "The Hygienic Transition from Cesspools to Sewer Systems (1840–1930): The Dynamics of Regime Rransformation." *Research Policy* 35/7: 1069–1082.

Gibson-Graham, J.K. 1996. *The End of Capitalism (as We Knew It)*. Ann Arbor: University of Michigan Press.

Gloor, P.A. 2006. *Swarm Creativity: Competitive Advantage through Collaborative Innovation Networks*. Oxford: Oxford University Press.

Goldman, M., and Schurman, R.A. 2000. "Closing the 'Great Divide': New Social Theory on Society and Nature." *Annual Review of Sociology* 26: 563–584.

Government Office for Science. 2014a. *Innovation: Managing Risk, Not Avoiding It – Evidence and Case Studies (Annual Report of the Government Chief Scientific Adviser 2014) – Report Overview*. London: Government Office for Science.

Government Office for Science. 2014b. *Innovation: Managing Risk, Not Avoiding It – Evidence and Case Studies (Annual Report of the Government Chief Scientific Adviser 2014)*. London: Government Office for Science.

Graham, Mark, S.A. Hale, and M. Stephens. 2011. *Geographies of the World's Knowledge*. London, Convoco! Edition. www.oii.ox.ac.uk/archive/downloads/publications/convoco_geographies_en.pdf.

Grieder, William. 1997. *One World, Ready or Not*. New York: Simon and Schuster.

Grossman, E. 2006. *High Tech Trash: Digital Devices, Hidden Toxics, and Human Health*. Washington, DC: Island Press.

Grove, R.H. 1995. *Green Imperialism: Colonial Expansion, Tropical Island Edens and the Origins of Environmentalism*. Cambridge: Cambridge University Press.

Hajer, M., M. Nilsson, K. Raworth, et al. 2015. "Beyond Cockpit-ism: Four Insights to Enhance the Transformative Potential of the Sustainable Development Goals." *Sustainability* 7: 1651–1660.

Hamilton, C., C. Bonneuil, and F. Gemenne. (eds.) 2015. *The Anthropocene and the Global Environmental Crisis: Rethinking Modernity in a New Epoch*. London: Routledge.

Hansmann, Henry. 2000. *The Ownership of Enterprise*. Cambridge, MA: Harvard University Press.

Harremoës, P., D. Gee, M. McGarvin, et al. (ed.) 2002. *The Precautionary Principle in the Twentieth Century: Late Lessons from Early Warnings*. London: Earthscan.

Hearn, Jeff. 1999. "Ageism, Violence and Abuse: Theoretical and Practical Perspectives on the Links between Child Abuse and Elder Abuse," in The Violence against Children Study Group (ed.), *Children, Child Abuse and Child Protection: Placing Children Centrally*. London: John Wiley.

Hearn, Jeff. 2015. *Men of the World: Genders, Globalizations, Transnational Times*. London: SAGE.

Hearn, Jeff, and Liisa Husu. 2016. "Gender Equality," in N. Naples et al. (eds.), *The Wiley-Blackwell Encyclopedia of Gender and Sexuality Studies*. Oxford: Wiley-Blackwell.

Hess, D.J. 2016. *Undone Science: Social Movements, Mobilized Publics, and Industrial Transitions*. Cambridge, MA: MIT Press.

Hess, S., and M. Kalb. (eds.) 2003. *The Media and the War on Terrorism*. Washington, DC: Brookings Institution.

Hickman, L. 2010. "James Lovelock: Humans Are Too Stupid to Prevent Climate Change." *Guardian*, 29 March: 2–5.

Hilgartner, S. 2009. "Intellectual Property and the Politics of Emerging Technology: Inventors, Citizens, and Powers to Shape the Future." *Chicago-Kent Law Review* 81/1: 197–224.

Hills, John. 2014. *Good Times, Bad Times: The Welfare Myth of Them and Us*. Bristol: Policy Press.

Holter, Øystein Gullvåg. 2014. "'What's in It for Men?' Old Question, New Data." *Men and Masculinities* 17/5: 515–548.

Hountondji, Paulin J. 1997. "Introduction: Recentring Africa," in P.J. Hountondji (ed.), *Endogenous Knowledge: Research Trails*. Dakar: CODESRIA.

Huesemann, M.H. 2003. "The Limits of Technological Solutions to Sustainable Development." *Clean Technology and Environment Policy* 5: 21–34.

IAASTD. 2009. *Agriculture at a Crossroads: International Assessment of Agricultural Knowledge Science and Technology for Development (IAASTD)*. Washington, DC: Island Press.

International Resource Panel. 2014. *Assessing Global Land Use: Balancing Consumption with Sustainable Supply*. New York: UN Environment Programme.

IPCC. 2015. *Climate Change 2014 – Synthesis Report*. Geneva: IPCC.

Itzigsohn, José, and Julián Rebón. 2016. The Recuperation of Enterprises: Defending Workers' Lifeworld, Creating New Tools of Contention." *Latin American Research Review* 50/4: 178–196.

Joergensen, U., and P. Karnoe. 1991. "The Danish Wind Turbine Story – Technical Solutions to Political Visions?" in A., Rip, J. Mise, and J. Schot (eds.), *Managing Technology in Society: The Approach of Constructive Technology Assessment*. London: Pinter Publishers.

Jonas, O.B. 2013. *Pandemic Risk*. Washington, DC: World Bank.

Kalleberg, Arne. 2011. *Good Jobs, Bad Jobs: The Rise of Polarized and Precarious Employment Systems in the United States, 1970s to 2000s*. New York: Russell Sage Foundation.

21

Kaplinsky, R. 2000. "Globalisation and Unequalisation: What Can Be Learned from Value Chain Analysis?" *Journal of Development Studies* 37/2: 117–146.

Kennedy, J., R.C. Eberhart, and Y. Shi. 2001. *Swarm Intelligence*. San Francisco: Morgan Kaufman.

Koselleck, R. (2004). *Futures Past: On the Semantics of Historical Time*. New York: Columbia University Press.

La Porte, T.R. (ed.) 1991. *Social Responses to Large Technical Systems: Control or Anticipation*. Dordrecht: Kluwer Academic Publishers.

Le, E. 2010. *Editorials and the Power of the Media*. Amsterdam: John Benjamins Publishing.

Leach, M., I. Scoones, and A. Stirling. 2010. *Dynamic Sustainabilities: Technology, Environment, Social Justice*. London: Routledge.

Lin, Ken-Hou, and Donald Tomaskovic-Devey. 2013. "Financialization and U.S. Income Inequality, 1970–2008." *American Journal of Sociology* 118/5: 1284–1329.

Lindert, Peter H. 2004. *Growing Public*, vols. I and II. New York: Cambridge University Press.

Luhmann, N. 1995. *Social Systems*. Stanford, CA: Stanford University Press.

Mankiw, N. Gregory. 2013. "Defending the One Percent." *Journal of Economic Perspectives* 27/3: 21–34.

Marshall, T.H. 1950. *Citizenship and Social Class, and other Essays*. Cambridge: Cambridge University Press.

Mbembe, Achille. 2001. *On the Postcolony*. Berkeley: University of California Press.

MEA. 2008. *Ecosystems and Human Well-Being – Volume 3: Policy Responses*. New York: Island Press.

Meadows, D.H., J. Randers, and D.L. Meadows. 2005. *The Limits to Growth: The 30-Year Update*. London: Earthscan.

Mies, Maria. 1999. *Patriarchy and Accumulation on a World Scale: Women in the International Division of Labour*. London: Zed Books.

Milanovic, Branko. 2012. *The Haves and the Have-Nots*. New York: Basic Books.

Mills, Charles W. 1999. *The Racial Contract*. Ithaca, NY: Cornell University Press.

Morel, Nathalie, Bruno Palier, and Joakim Palme. (eds.) 2012. *Towards a Social Investment Welfare State? Ideas, Policies and Challenges*. Chicago: Policy Press.

Muñoz-Erickson, T.A., and B.B. Cutts. 2016. "Structural Dimensions of Knowledge-Action Networks for Sustainability." *Current Opinion in Environmental Sustainability* 18: 56–64.

Murray, Charles. 2006. *In Our Hands: A Plan to Replace the Welfare State*. Washington, DC: AEI Press.

Neill, J., 2016. *Tackling Drug-Resistant Infections Globally: Final Report and Recommendations of the Review on Antimicrobial Resistance*. London: AMR Review.

Nelson, R.R., and S.G. Winter. 1977. "In Search of a Useful Theory of Innovation." *Research Policy* 6: 36–76.

Neumayer, E. 2011. *Sustainability and Inequality in Human Development*. Human Development Reports, Research Paper 2011/04. New York: UNDP.

Norgaard, R.B. 1994. *Development Betrayed: The End of Progress and a Coevolutionary Revisioning of the Future*. London: Routledge.

OECD 2010. *The OECD Innovation Strategy: Getting a Head Start on Tomorrow – Executive Summary*. Paris: OECD.

OECD. 2012. *Environmental Outlook to 2050*. Paris: OECD.

OECD. 2013. *Main Science and Technology Indicators*, volume 2013/1. Paris: OECD.

Oleksy, Elzbieta, Jeff Hearn, and Dorota Golanska. (eds.) 2011. *The Limits of Gendered Citizenship: Contexts and Contradictions*. New York: Routledge.

Ophuls, W., 1997. *Requiem for Modern Politics: The Tragedy of the Enlightenment and the Challenge of the New Millennium*. Boulder, CO: Westview.

Orenstein, Mitchell. 2008. "Post-Communist Welfare States." *Journal of Democracy* 19: 80–94.

OTA. 1979. *The Effects of Nuclear War*. Washington, DC: US Congress Office of Technology Assessment.

Paxton, Robert O. 2004. *The Anatomy of Fascism*. New York: Knopf.

Pease, Bob. 2010. *Undoing Privilege: Unearned Advantage in a Divided World*. London: Zed Books.

Pellizzoni, L. 2004. "Responsibility and Environmental Governance." *Environmental Politics* 13/3: 541–565.

Perreaul, T., G. Bridge, and J. McCarthy. (eds.) 2015. *The Routledge Handbook of Political Ecology*. London: Routledge.

Petmesidou, Maria, and Ana M. Guillén. 2014. "Can the Welfare State as We Know It Survive? A View from the Crisis-Ridden South European Periphery." *South European Society and Politics* 19/3: 295–307.

Petras, James. 2012. "The Western Welfare State: Its Rise and Demise and the Soviet Bloc." Global Research, July 4. www.globalresearch.ca/the-western-welfare-state-its-rise-and-demise-and-the-soviet-bloc/31753.

Phaal, R., C.J.P. Farrukh, and D.R. Probert. 2004. "Technology Roadmapping – A Planning Framework for Evolution and Revolution. *Technology Forecasting and Social Change* 71: 5–26.

Piketty, Thomas. 2014. *Capital in the Twenty-First Century*. Cambridge, MA: Harvard University Press.

Pope, Kenneth S. 2015. "Are the American Psychological Association's Detainee Interrogation Policies Ethical and Effective?" *Zeitschrift für Psychologie* 219/3: 150–158.

Puar, Jasbir. 2007. *Terrorist Assemblages: Homonationalism in Queer Times*. Durham, NC: Duke University Press.

Rannis, Peter. 2016. *Cooperatives Confront Capitalism*. London: Zed Books.

Rebón, Julian. 2007. *La Empresa de la Autonomía. Trabajadores Recuperando la Producción*. Buenos Aires: Colectivo Ediciones-Ediciones PICASO.

Redclift, M., 1987. *Sustainable Development: Exploring the Contradictions*. London: Routledge.

Rockström, J., W. Steffen, K. Noone, et al. 2009. "A Safe Operating Space for Humanity." *Nature* 461: 472–475.

Roy, Arundhati. 2004. *An Ordinary Person's Guide to Empire*. Cambridge, MA: South End Press.

Said, Edward. 1978. *Orientalism*. New York: Pantheon.

Samuelson, Paul. 1957. "Wages and Interest: A Modern Dissection of Marxian Economic Models." *American Economic Review* 47/6: 884–912.

Santos, Boaventura de Sousa. 2014. *Epistemologies of the South*. Boulder.

Shepherd, J., K. Caldeira, P. Cox, et al. 2009. *Geoengineering the Climate: Science, Governance and Uncertainty*. London: The Royal Society.

Singer, P. 2002. *Animal Liberation*. London: Harper Collins.

Sintomer, Y. 2011. *Petite Histoire de L'expérimentation Démocratique: Tirage au Sort et Politique d'Athènes à nos Jours*. Paris: La Découverte.

Sklair, Leslie. 2001. *The Transnational Capitalist Class*. Oxford: Blackwell.

Smith, A., M. Fressoli, D. Abrol, E. Arund, and A. Ely. 2016. *Grassroots Innovation Movements*. London: Routledge/Earthscan.

Spade, Dean. 2011. *Normal Life: Administrative Violence, Critical Trans Politics and the Limits of Law*. Cambridge, MA: South End.

Spivak, Gayatri Chakravorty. 1987. *In Other Worlds: Essays in Cultural Politics*. New York: Methuen.

Standing, Guy. 1999. "Global Feminization through Flexible Labor: A Theme Revisited." *World Development* 27/3: 583–602.

Standing, Guy. 2011. *The Precariat: The New Dangerous Class*. London: Bloomsbury Academic.

Steans, Jill. 2013. *Gender and International Relations*, third edition. Cambridge: Polity Press.

Stewart, Frances. (ed.) 2008. *Horizontal Inequalities and Conflict*. New York: Palgrave.

Stirling, A. 2008. "'Opening Up' and 'Closing Down': Power, Participation, and Pluralism in the Social Appraisal of Technology." *Science, Technology and Human Values* 23/2: 262–294.

Stirling, A. 2010. "From Enlightenment to Enablement: Opening Up Choices for Innovation," in A. Lopez-Claros (ed.), *The Innovation for Development Report*. Basingstoke: Palgrave Macmillan.

Stirling, A. 2011. "Pluralising Progress: From Integrative Transitions to Transformative Diversity." *Environmental Innovation and Societal Transitions* 1/1: 82–88.

Stirling, A. 2012. "Opening Up the Politics of Knowledge and Power in Bioscience." *PLoS Biology* 10/1: e1001233.

Stirling, A. 2014a. "Towards Innovation Democracy: Participation, Responsibility and Precaution in Innovation Governance," in Government Office for Science, *Innovation: Managing Risk, Not Avoiding It – Evidence and Case Studies (Annual Report of the Government Chief Scientific Adviser 2014)*. London: Government Office for Science. www.gov.uk/government/uploads/system/uploads/attachment_data/file/376505/14.

Stirling, A. 2014b. "Transforming Power: Social Science and the Politics of Energy Choices." *Energy Research and Social Science* 1: 83–95.

Stirling, A. 2015. "Emancipating Transformations: From Controlling 'the Transition' to Culturing Plural Radical Progress," in I. Scoones, M. Leach, and P. Newell (eds.), *The Politics of Green Transformations*. Abingdon, Oxfordshire: Routledge.

Stirling, A. 2016. "Knowing Doing Governing: Realizing Heterodyne Democracies," in J.-P. Voß and R. Freeman (eds.), *Knowing Governance: The Epistemic Construction of Political Order*. Basingstoke, Hampshire: Palgrave Macmillan.

Streeck, Wolfgang. 2016. *How Will Capitalism End?* New York: Verso.

Sveiby, Karl-Erik, Pernilla Gripenberg, and Beata Segercrantz. (eds.) 2012. *Challenging the Innovation Paradigm*. New York: Routledge.

Thompson, E.P. 1978. *The Poverty of Theory and Other Essays*. New York: New York University Press.

Tronto, Joan. 2013. *Caring Democracy: Markets, Equality and Justice*. New York: NYU Press.

UN. 2015a. *Transforming Our World: The 2030 Agenda for Sustainable Development*. New York: UN. https://sustainabledevelopment.un.org.

UN. 2015b. *World Population Prospects: Key Findings and Advance Tables*. New York: UN.

UNCTAD and CGIAR. 2013. *Wake Up before It Is Too Late! Make Agriculture Truly Sustainable for Food Security in a Changing Climate*. Geneva: UNCTAD.

UNDESA. 2015a. *Addis Ababa Action Agenda of the Third International Conference on Financing for Development*. New York: UNDESA. www.un.org/esa/ffd/wp-content/uploads/2015/08/AAAA_Outcome.pdf.

UNDESA. 2015b. *World Urbanization Prospects – the 2014 revision*. New York: UNDESA.

UNRISD (UN Research Institute for Social Development). 2010. *Combating Poverty and Inequality: Structural Change, Social Policy and Politics*. Geneva: UNRISD.

UNRISD. 2016. *Understanding Transformation for Sustainable Development*. Geneva: UNRISD.

UNSCEAR. 2017. *UNSCEAR 2016 Report: Sources, Effects, and Risks of Ionizing Radiation: Report to the General Assembly*. New York: UN.

Van Parijs, Philippe, and Yannick Vanderborght. 2017. *Basic Income: A Radical Proposal for a Free Society and a Sane Economy*. Cambridge, MA: Harvard University Press.

Veld, R.J. (ed.) 2010. *Knowledge Democracy: Consequences for Science, Politics and the Media*. Heidelberg: Springer.

Verloo, Mieke. 2006. "Multiple Inequalities, Intersectionality and the European Union." *European Journal of Women's Studies* 13/3: 211–228.

WEF, D. Waughray, and J.G. Workman. 2014. "Water Security: The Water-Food-Energy-Climate Nexus." *Igarss 2014* 1: 1–5.

Weil, David N. 2015. "Capital and Wealth in the Twenty-First Century." *American Economic Review* 105/5: 34–37.

WHO. 2015. *WHO Estimates of the Global Burden of Foodborne Diseases*. Rome: World Health Organization.

Wilkinson, Richard G., and Kate. Pickett. 2009. *The Spirit Level: Why Greater Equality Makes Societies Stronger*. London: Allen Lane.

Williams, R., and D. Edge. 1996. "The Social Shaping of Technology." *Research Policy* 25/6: 865–899.

Wilson, William J. 2012. *The Declining Significance of Race: Blacks and Changing American Institutions*, third edition. Chicago: University of Chicago Press.

World Bank. 2007. "World Development Indicators." http://data.worldbank.org/products/data-books/WDI-2007.

Wright, Erik Olin. 1998. *Classes*. New York: Verso.

Wright, Erik Olin. 2010. *Envisioning Real Utopias*. New York: Verso.

Wright, Erik Olin. 2011. "Real Utopias." *Contexts*, Spring: 37–42.

Young, Brigitte, Isabel Bakker, and Diane Elson. (eds.) 2011. *Questioning Financial Governance from a Feminist Perspective*. London: Routledge.

Zuboff, Shoshana. 2015. "Big Other: Surveillance Capitalism and the Prospects of an Information Civilization." *Journal of Information Technology* 30: 75–89.

Zucman, Gabriel. 2014. "Taxing across Borders: Tracking Personal Wealth and Corporate Profits." *Journal of Economic Perspectives* 28/4: 121–148.

21

22

The Contribution of the Social Sciences to Policy and Institutional Change

Coordinating Lead Authors:[1]
Matthew Adler, Helga Nowotny

Lead Authors:[2]
Cary Coglianese, Sheila Jasanoff, Ravi Kanbur, Brian Levy, Ole F. Norheim, Johan Schot, Simon Schwartzman, Christiane Spiel, Shana Starobin

[1]   Affiliations: MA: Duke University, USA; HN: ETH Zurich, Switzerland.
[2]   Affilitions: CC: University of Pennsylvania Law School, USA; SJ: Harvard University, USA; RK: Cornell University, USA; BL: Johns Hopkins University, USA; ON: University of Bergen, Norway; JS: University of Sussex, UK; SSchwartzman: Institute for Studies on Labor and Society, Brazil; CS: University of Vienna, Austria; SStarobin: Bowdoin College, USA.

Summary

This chapter engages the contributions of the social sciences to policy and institutional change. The chapter is organized as follows. The first six sections of the chapter cover six policy domains: economics (Section 22.2); education (Section 22.3); environmental protection (Section 22.4); health care (Section 22.5); development (Section 22.6); and science and technology (Section 22.7). A concluding section (Section 22.8) offers an overarching historical perspective on the societal role of the social sciences, and then outlines some critical challenges that must be met if the social sciences are, in the future, to function as a force for progress.

It would be absurd to aim here at a comprehensive accounting of the social science/policy nexus. However, in selecting six distinct and important policy domains to be reviewed in the chapter, we have tried to achieve coverage sufficiently wide that the emerging themes and lessons will not be seen as idiosyncratic to a particular area of policy choice.

Each of the six sections addresses the social science/policy nexus by addressing one or both of the following questions. First, how does social science help explain the process of policy development in the covered domain? (This first question takes policy and institutions as features of the social world that can be illuminated using the tools of social science.) Second, how has social science influenced policy development there?

With respect to this second question, two modes of influence might be delineated. One is direct. Social scientists transmit their research findings directly to policy-makers, or indeed play an official role (as policy-makers or civil servants) in governmental bodies or NGOs. A second, indirect mode of influence occurs in the elaboration of models and tools that help shape how policy-makers think about their choices.

On balance, the reviews of the six policy areas vindicate the importance of social science to policy and institutional change, both in explaining these features of social systems, and in (directly or indirectly) influencing policy choices and institutional design.

What, now, are some key themes that emerge from the six sections? One concerns the role of markets. The "laissez-faire" (or neoliberal) view of good policy says that the fundamental goal of government should be to safeguard the conditions for a free market: strong property and contracts, robust competition in markets for goods and labor, all secured by an impartial judiciary. The laissez-faire view is hotly contested, not merely between economics and other social sciences, but within economics itself. Many economists would endorse a "market failure" framework for policy design: policies should redress shortcomings in the free market. "Laissez-faire" is, then, the position that market failures are infrequent. But are they? A debate about the scope and extent of market failures occurs in all the policy domains covered by this chapter.

A second theme is that a healthy social science may be characterized by substantial internal debate. This is true of the physical sciences, and it's no less true of social sciences. There can be strong disagreement about which models best approximate social processes; about the appropriate methodologies for confirming, falsifying, or calibrating a given model; and about what current evidence suggests about the parameters of a given model. These familiar substantive and methodological debates within an academic community of social scientists then give rise to parallel disputes about appropriate governmental policy and institutions – when the learning of that community is deployed to give policy advice.

A third theme is the inevitable tension that arises when no accepted social-scientific model accounts for some of the policy-relevant mechanisms in the context at hand. The social scientist then faces a trade-off – either (a) rely on the models, and thereby give advice that ignores some of the real-world factors that are actually in play; or (b) take account of those factors, via a more holistic approach to policy advice that uses the models only as a jumping-off point, and then be vulnerable to complaints that the advice is ad hoc and lacks firm scientific foundations.

A final theme is the recurrent question of inequality. Although global income and wealth inequality has declined in recent decades with economic growth in China, India, Africa, and elsewhere, income and wealth inequality within developed countries has increased. Within-country inequality is both politically destabilizing (as in the Trump election or Brexit), and intrinsically ethically problematic, at least to the extent that it can be redressed without shifting costs onto those who are globally less well-off. How, then, should policy advice take account of inequality? A traditional view within economics counsels the separation of "efficiency" and "equity." Supposedly, equity concerns can be handled by the tax-and-transfer system; policy advice in other areas can ignore equity considerations. However, this view is hotly disputed by other approaches in economics (Section 22.2), and indeed cannot be sustained when we turn to specific policy domains such as education (Section 22.3), environmental protection (Section 22.4), or health and safety (Section 22.5). Social scientists must, therefore, grapple with giving policy advice that takes account of distributional concerns, rather than seeing inequality as a separable problem that can be hived off to a specialized set of policy instruments.

As already mentioned, Section 22.8 discusses challenges going forward. Perhaps the key challenge is this. The influence of social science on policy formation often comes in a technocratic mode – by way of communications with government officials or civil servants, or the formation of their conceptual frameworks – and not in conversation with the electorate. Social scientists need to think carefully about how to enter democratic discourse – a discourse that is anything but calm, with electorates roiled by the real and perceived harms of globalization and of rapid technological change. Moreover, in working to craft better policies, social scientists should also pay closer attention to the design of democratic institutions themselves. Explaining the workings of democracy, providing advice about how to craft participatory institutions, and taking part in public debate should be – even more than in the past – tasks that social scientists undertake.

22

22.1 Introduction

This chapter engages the contributions of the social sciences to policy and institutional change. The chapter is organized as follows. The first six sections of the chapter cover six policy domains: economics (Section 22.2); education (Section 22.3); environmental protection (Section 22.4); health care (Section 22.5); development (Section 22.6); and science and technology (Section 22.7). A concluding section (Section 22.8), entitled "It Could Be Otherwise … Normativity in the Social Sciences," steps away from specific policy domains. This concluding section offers an overarching historical perspective on the societal role of the social sciences, and then outlines some critical challenges that must be met if the social sciences are, in the future, to function as a force for progress.

The contributions of the natural sciences to societal change are obvious, to experts and laypeople alike. We live in an age where technology permeates the daily lives of many (increasingly even the poor), and in which the pace of technological development is evident.

The role of the social sciences is subtler. This is true, certainly, at the level of popular awareness, and even for experts. Social scientists themselves will be steeped in the knowledge base and theoretical paradigms constitutive of their discipline, but may not be personally engaged in giving policy advice or otherwise deeply aware of the linkages from the discipline itself to government and society. The aim of the chapter is, therefore, to review how the social sciences have shaped policy. This chapter forms the conclusion of the report of the International Panel on Social Progress – whose very ambition is to marshal the learning of hundreds of contemporary social scientists (and academics from other disciplines too) as a force for good. The chapter reflects on the enterprise of the IPSP, by discussing generally whether the social sciences have had the kind of influence that the IPSP hopes to have.

It would be absurd to aim here at a comprehensive accounting of the social science/policy nexus. However, in selecting six distinct and important policy domains to be reviewed by the chapter, we have tried to achieve coverage sufficiently wide that the emerging themes and lessons will not be seen as idiosyncratic to a particular area of policy choice.

Each of the six sections addresses the social science/policy nexus by addressing one or both of the following questions. First, how does social science help explain the process of policy development in the covered domain? Second, how has social science influenced policy development there?

The first question takes policy and institutions as features of the social world that can be illuminated using the tools of social science. Section 22.7 ("Science and Technology") provides an exemplary treatment of this first, explanatory, question. Three models of the social impact of technological innovations are surveyed: (a) "actor-network theory," a bottom-up model that stresses the role of individual innovators and the networks of researchers in which these individuals are embedded; (b) top-down "structuralist" models that point to the needs of the state and of corporations; and (c) "interactive" explanations that highlight the ways in which both market and state structures, and the agency of individual innovators, interact with shared understanding regarding the normative purposes of innovation.

Mainly, however, the chapter focuses on the second question. How have the social sciences influenced policy and institutional change?

Two modes of influence might be delineated. One is direct. Social scientists transmit their research findings directly to policy-makers, or indeed play an official role (as policy-makers or civil servants) in governmental bodies or NGOs. For example, the direct influence of the discipline of economics on macroeconomic policy (Section 22.2) is pervasive. Economists serve in key positions at central banks, as well as within treasury offices and on the staff of presidents and prime ministers. Legislative and bureaucratic choices regarding fiscal and monetary policy are directly shaped by the findings and contestation about these matters within academic economics.

Similarly, development policy (Section 22.6) has been substantially shaped by the World Bank, which in turn both employs numerous economists, and more generally has been responsive to the advice of economists regarding the importance for development of a "level playing field" and "good governance." Public health scholars have influenced policy choices about health care priority-setting and allocation (Section 22.5), both in direct conversation with national governments, and by virtue of their influence on these matters at the United Nations, World Health Organization, and the World Bank. The massive "Global Burden of Disease" study (IMHE 2016) has had, and will undoubtedly continue to have, a major role in guiding priority-setting.

Note that this direct influence is not equally strong across policy domains. One of the findings of the review of education policy (Section 22.3) is that although "[r]esearch in education provides an ample understanding of the role of education in different societies and of the impact of specific institutional arrangements and practices in students' outcomes" and "rigorous, randomized experiments are increasingly being used, making these findings more reliable and consistent," it is nonetheless the case that "education policies and practices are seldom directly based on evidence provided by research." The lack of direct social science influence on education policy is, in substantial part, a result of the fragmented structure for setting policy in this domain. Powerful centralized bodies that could "give voice" to social scientists are less common here.

A second, more indirect mode of influence from the social sciences to policy-making can also be delineated. This is in the elaboration of models and tools that help to shape how policy-makers think about their choices. To be sure, the line between the "direct" and "indirect" channels is fuzzy. But it does seem useful to differentiate between, on the one hand, social scientists giving advice on specific policy issues; and, on the other, the background – but potentially quite potent – function of social scientists in supplying the concepts that structure policy discussion.

Here are a few illustrative examples of the more indirect mode of influence, described in detail below. In the case of environmental policy (Section 22.4), economists and political scientists have played a central role in developing both an understanding of the justification for governmental interventions (in particular externalities and commons problems), and a typology of interventions to mitigate environmental harm (ex-post liability, means-based regulation, performance-based regulation, market instruments, and others).

In the case of health policy (Section 22.5), the concept of life expectancy is central both in assessing societal condition (for example, determining the current life expectancy in a given society of individuals depending on age, gender, socio-economic status, etc.), and in evaluating governmental interventions to improve health. The life expectancy concept and its refinements and cognate concepts (such as the "disability-adjusted life year," or DALY), as well as measurement techniques, derive from academic work. In economic policy (Section 22.2), the legacy of Keynes (the views of Keynes himself and his successor Keynesians, and the challenges to Keynesianism by leading scholars such as Milton Friedman) is the intellectual matrix within which political debate about fiscal and monetary choices occurs.

What, now, are some key themes that emerge from the six sections? One concerns the role of markets. The "laissez-faire" (or neoliberal) view of good policy says that the fundamental goal of government should be to safeguard the conditions for a free market: strong property and contracts, robust competition in markets for goods and labor, all secured by an impartial judiciary. The laissez-faire view is hotly contested, not merely between economics and other social sciences, but within economics itself. Many economists would endorse a "market failure" framework for policy design: policies should redress shortcomings in the free market. "Laissez-faire" is, then, the position that market failures are infrequent. But are they? For example, a free market for health insurance seems unworkable (Section 22.7). "Three factors – moral hazard, decisions under conditions of uncertainty, and asymmetrical information between the actors – are likely to cause market failure in the health insurance market. Voluntary health insurance will lead to adverse selection so that the young and healthy will get lower premiums and those with pre-existing conditions or the elderly at higher risk will be excluded or get higher premiums. In the absence of collective risk-pooling, premiums for low-risk patients will remain low, while premiums for those who really need health care will increase to the point where market failure and inefficiencies will occur. The state must, therefore, regulate this market and make risk-pooling mandatory." Analogous discussion of the scope and extent of market failures occurs in all the policy domains covered by this chapter.

A second theme is that a healthy social science may be characterized by substantial internal debate. This is true of the natural sciences, and it's no less true of social sciences. There can be strong disagreement about which models best approximate social processes; about the appropriate methodologies for confirming, falsifying, or calibrating a given model; and about what current evidence suggests about the parameters of a given model. These familiar substantive and methodological debates within an academic community of social scientists then give rise to parallel disputes about appropriate governmental policy and institutions – when the learning of that community is deployed to give policy advice.

A third theme is the inevitable tension that arises when no accepted social-scientific model accounts for some of the policy-relevant mechanisms in the context at hand. The social scientist then faces a trade-off – either (a) rely on the models, and thereby give advice that ignores some of the real-world factors that are actually in play; or (b) take account of those factors, via a more holistic approach to policy advice that uses the models only as a jumping-off point, and then be vulnerable to complaints that the advice is ad hoc and lacks firm scientific foundations. For example, the section on development (Section 22.6) describes a process "in which a dominant paradigm takes hold, in a way that goes beyond the evidence, and then pushes back against efforts to add complexity, to soften the edges of certainty, to open up room for exploration. The forces that drive this process seem general – so the likelihood is high that it will repeat itself well beyond the two examples that are the focus here, and be evident across a wide variety of areas of development discourse." (The dominant paradigms there described are the models that predict economic development to follow readily upon the introduction of free market and "good governance" institutions, ignoring the messy realities of existing social norms, networks, and culture in developing countries.) Similarly, neoclassical economic models fail to account for irrational behavioral forces that help to explain the financial crash of 2008 (Section 22.2).

A final theme is the recurrent question of inequality. Although global income and wealth inequality has declined in recent decades with economic growth in China, India, Africa, and elsewhere (Milanovic 2016), income and wealth inequality within developed countries has increased – as famously documented by the work of Thomas Piketty (2014). Within-country inequality can be both politically destabilizing (as may be illustrated in the Trump election or Brexit), and intrinsically ethically problematic, at least to the extent that it can be redressed without shifting costs onto those who are globally less well-off. How, then, should policy advice take account of inequality? A traditional view within economics counsels the separation of "efficiency" and "equity." Supposedly, equity concerns can be handled by the tax-and-transfer system; policy advice in other areas can ignore equity considerations. However, this view is hotly disputed by other approaches in economics (Section 22.2), and indeed cannot be sustained when we turn to specific policy domains such as education (Section 22.3), environmental protection (Section 22.4), or health care (Section 22.5).

Individuals can be expected to benefit from a market in goods and labor (using wealth as adjusted by government taxes and transfers), rather than being exploited by other market actors, only if they have sufficient skills and are sufficiently well informed. Issues of educational equity should, therefore, be seen as a key component of education policy, even for those whose basic policy commitments are laissez-faire (let alone for others). Inequalities of health and life expectancy raise ethical concerns, not merely inequalities of income and wealth. But it is hard to see how the tax-and-transfer system alone is sufficient to redress these. (For example, taxes based on health status or risk exposure would be difficult to implement, in part because of asymmetric information.)

Social scientists must, therefore, grapple with giving policy advice that takes account of distributional concerns, rather than seeing inequality as a separable problem that can be hived off to a specialized set of policy instruments.

This introduction has, thus far, reviewed the first six sections of this chapter, describing key questions and themes. As already mentioned, Section 22.8 discusses challenges going forward. Some of the challenges have been alluded to here, but Section 22.8 offers a more synoptic treatment, and the reader is encouraged to engage with this section closely. Perhaps the key challenge is this. The influence of social science on policy formation often comes in a technocratic mode – by way of communications with government officials or civil servants, or the formation of their conceptual frameworks – and not in conversation with the electorate. Social scientists need to think carefully about how to enter democratic discourse – a discourse that is anything but calm, with electorates roiled by the real and perceived harms of globalization and rapid technological change. Moreover, in working to craft better policies, social scientists should also pay closer attention to the design of democratic institutions themselves. Explaining the workings of democracy, providing advice about how to craft participatory institutions, and taking part in public debate should be – even more than in the past – tasks that social scientists undertake.

22.2 Economic Policy

22.2.1 Introduction: Two Axes

The emergence of economics as a self-standing discipline relatively independent of moral philosophy is commonly dated to the publication of Adam Smith's *Wealth of Nations* in 1776. In this founding tract, and in the subsequent quarter millennium of disciplinary discourse, economics has rarely been far from policy-making. Economic frameworks have influenced economic policy-making, and policy dilemmas have shaped the discipline. It is this interplay between the discipline and the policy arena which this contribution attempts to explore. The exploration is perforce limited given the space constraint and vast terrain to be covered. The approach taken here is to illustrate the interaction through a small number of key issues and players over this period.

There are two fundamental questions which run right through these two and a half centuries of economics and economic policy. First, what is the appropriate way to capture the workings of the economy, at the micro and at the macro level? Second, what is the appropriate way to evaluate economic outcomes? Among the issues raised by the first question are how best to describe the economic behavior of individuals and groups of individuals, and how best to describe the workings of economic markets. Among the issues raised by the second are the trade-off between total national income (or its growth) and its distribution among individuals and classes, and indeed whether economic policy-making should take into account non-economic outcomes in its design and assessment. These issues and their close cousins structure the discourse in this section as we look at the interactions between analysis and policy through the writings of a selection of great economists grappling with the big questions of their time.

22.2.2 Adam Smith, the Corn Laws, and the Compensation Principle

To begin at the beginning:

> As every individual, therefore, endeavours … to direct that industry that its produce may be of the greatest value, every individual necessarily labours to render the annual revenue of the society as great as he can. He generally, indeed, neither intends to promote the public interest, nor knows how much he is promoting it … he intends only his own gain, and he is in this, as in many other cases, led by an invisible hand to promote an end which was no part of his intention. (Smith 1776: book IV, chapter II, paragraph IX)

This paragraph, much quoted, much admired, and much reviled, captures the core of a particular line of economic argument. Individuals, acting in markets with free competition and no economic power, will in an uncoordinated fashion promote "the public interest," which, from the context and its economic setting, in effect means the general economic wellbeing, or the "size of the economic pie." It took two centuries for economists to refine and make precise this proposition, setting out the conditions under which it holds, now referred to in standard textbooks as "The Fundamental Theorems of Welfare Economics."

But these very theorems, because they set out the conditions under which the proposition holds, also highlight its limited direct applicability in the real world. Nobel prizes in the modern era have been awarded to economists such as Joseph Stiglitz (2002b) for advancing understanding of a world in which these conditions, of a free market, full information, and so on, are not met. But, despite this, the invisible-hand metaphor continues to frame the instincts of economic policy-makers – at least those who have been schooled in economics as a discipline.

The invisible-hand proposition also holds in abeyance the distributional question – who gains or who loses from economic policy? Here policy-makers have always been ahead of economists since they cannot afford to ignore distributional outcomes in the political arena. As a result, economists have struggled mightily to square the distributional circle. In the great Corn Laws debate of the 1830s and 1840s, those in favor of the repeal of tariffs on the import of corn certainly appealed to the invisible-hand proposition. The magazine *The Economist* was founded in 1843 to make the case for removing this interference in the market mechanism. But at its heart, the issue was one of distribution. The Corn Laws benefited the landed classes, which the Anti-Corn Law League described as a "bread-taxing oligarchy, unprincipled, unfeeling, rapacious and plundering" (Briggs 1959: 314).

But how can economics, if it is to be value-free, weigh the gains of one individual or one group of individuals against the losses of another? The "Pareto principle," according to which economists can pronounce an improvement only if no one has been harmed and at least one person has benefited, is a recipe for policy impotence, since most policy changes would surely entail winners and losers. In the 1930s, a series of debates between the giants of that time – Harrod

(1938), Robbins (1938), Kaldor (1939), and others – tried to resolve this through the "compensation principle," which states that a policy change can be pronounced an improvement if the gainers *could* compensate the losers and still have some surplus left over. But no actual payment was required by this principle, which, therefore, embodied a value judgment that gave distribution no weight whatsoever. It took the post-war work of Atkinson (1970) and others to establish that distributional value judgments will always be involved in economic policy-making, and that it is best to be explicit about these.

22.2.3 Keynes, Laissez-Faire, and the Treasury View

With the repeal of the Corn Laws, economic policy in Britain and perhaps in Europe settled into a long period of laissez-faire liberalism where the core of economic analysis was governed by a framework of markets in which no agent held economic power, and economic policy matched this analytical construct. The dominant text of the latter part of this period was Alfred Marshall's *Principles of Economics*, first published in 1890. The Royal Economic Society was also founded in 1890, the American Economic Association in 1885, and Marshall succeeded, against considerable opposition, in founding a separate degree in economics at the University of Cambridge in 1903.

It is perhaps ironic, then, that it was Marshall's student, John Maynard Keynes, who issued in 1926 a clarion call against laissez-faire liberalism. In his brilliant essay *The End of Laissez-Faire*, Keynes excoriated the foundations of the doctrine:

> Let us clear from the ground the metaphysical or general principles upon which, from time to time, *laissez-faire* has been founded. It is *not* true that individuals possess a prescriptive "natural liberty" in their economic activities. There is *no* "compact" conferring perpetual rights on those who Have or on those who Acquire. The world is *not* so governed from above that private and social interest always coincide. It is *not* so managed here below that in practice they coincide. It is *not* a correct deduction from the principles of economics that enlightened self-interest always operates in the public interest. (Keynes 1926: 287–288)

The above was of course only one salvo in Keynes's long battle against economic orthodoxy which he waged throughout the 1920s and the 1930s. As unemployment climbed dramatically, Keynes railed against the so-called "Treasury View," stated by the Chancellor of the Exchequer Winston Churchill in his 1929 budget speech as follows: "The orthodox Treasury view … is that when the Government borrow[s] in the money market it becomes a new competitor with industry and engrosses to itself resources which would otherwise have been employed by private enterprise, and in the process raises the rent of money to all who have need of it."

This proclamation of the impotence of fiscal policy in the face of massively underused labor and capital was the policy spur for Keynes (1936) to develop the arguments crystallized in his *General Theory of Employment, Interest and Money*, ushering in, analytically at least, the era of Keynesian economics.

And yet, for Keynes, the object was not to destroy markets and capitalism, but to save them from themselves. The easy association of Keynes with policy interventionism belies his conservatism once what he saw as the major market failures were addressed by government policy:

> We cannot therefore settle on abstract grounds, but must handle on its merits in detail what Burke termed "one of the finest problems in legislation, namely, to determine what the State ought to take upon itself to direct by the public wisdom, and what it ought to leave, with as little interference as possible, to individual exertion" … The important thing for government is not to do things which individuals are doing already, and to do them a little better or a little worse; but to do those things which at present are not done at all. (Keynes 1926: 287–291)

This tension between fixing market failures one by one or questioning the market system wholesale is one which runs through economics even today as it interacts with economic policy.

22.2.4 The Post-War Consensus in Macroeconomics and Its Breakdown

The "Keynesian revolution" is perhaps an apt description for the change in economics and economic policy, especially in the domain of macroeconomics, from the mid-1930s onwards. Young economists of the time took up Keynesianism with great fervor, including Paul Samuelson in the USA, whose best-selling textbook *Economics* spread the vision to a generation of students the world over. The basic economic policies pursued by post-war governments were also Keynesian, using fiscal policy to regulate the economy, and especially to keep unemployment low. Right through the 1960s and into the 1970s, these models and policies ruled the roost.

An iconic analytical construct of this time with enormous policy impact was the "Phillips curve," named after A.W. Phillips, an academic economist who posited that the lower the rate of unemployment, the higher the rate of inflation (Phillips 1958). Economic analysis thus seemed to have quantified a key trade-off for economic policy-makers. Given their preferences between unemployment and inflation, they could locate themselves as they wished along the Phillips curve. However, as the long post-war boom came to an end with the OPEC-driven oil price increases of the mid-1970s, the empirical foundations of the Phillips curve were beginning to be questioned. It came to be argued, a quarter century after the end of the war and the triumph of Keynesian doctrine, that in the macroeconomic arena there was, in fact, no stable Phillips curve, and a little less unemployment could not be purchased at the cost of a little more inflation – the cornerstone of post-war Keynesian economic policy-making. As famously stated by Milton Friedman in his Presidential Address to the American Economic Association: "At any moment of time, there is some level of unemployment which has the property that it is consistent with equilibrium in the structure of real wages … The 'natural rate of unemployment' … is the level that would be ground out by the … system of general equilibrium equations" (Friedman 1968: 8).

Friedman, of course, went on to win the Nobel Prize in Economics, in 1976. This shift in economic theorizing coincided with a corresponding move away from an interventionist stance in economic policy-making, in macroeconomics and as well as at the micro and structural levels regarding the operation of markets. In the "Reagan-Thatcher-Kohl" years of the 1980s, there was a decided shift toward free market orthodoxy of the laissez-faire era. But in the post-war years this long-running battle between laissez-faire and interventionism also played out in developing countries. We now turn to this story, told through the eyes of a giant of development economics, W. Arthur Lewis.

22.2.5 W. Arthur Lewis, Economics, and Economic Development Policy

W. Arthur Lewis, born in the West Indies, was a student and then a teacher at the London School of Economics in the 1930s. In the 1950s, Lewis became deeply involved in economic policy-making in Ghana, the first independent nation in black Africa, as an economic adviser to Ghana's charismatic leader, Kwame Nkrumah. How did this coming together of economic analysis and economic policy work out?

Arthur Lewis received an invitation to advise the soon-to-be-independent nation of Ghana in 1952 when it was still the colony of the Gold Coast, and he was asked to write a report on industrialization. At that time, Lewis was developing his famous theory of "economic development with unlimited supplies of labor" (Lewis 1954), for which he would win the Nobel Prize in Economics in 1979. His framing was with reference to the development of countries like India and Egypt. He characterized these countries as having surplus labor in agriculture and traditional activities, so that the path to growth was through industrialization, which would draw on the pool of labor. To the extent that this industrialization was being held back by failures of the market, Lewis advocated intervention and government support to build up manufacturing.

With this background, the radical policy interventionists in Ghana were expecting support from the eminent economist Lewis for their plans for government-subsidized manufacturing. However, Lewis disappointed them. His analysis of the situation was that in Africa, unlike in Asia, there was labor shortage, not labor surplus. The constraint to growth and development was not manufacturing growth but low agricultural productivity. The focus on market failures should thus be in agriculture and not in manufacturing: "Number one priority is therefore a concentrated attack on the system of growing food in the Gold Coast, so as to set in motion an ever increasing productivity" (Lewis 1953: paragraph 253). This line of reasoning continued into Lewis's period as resident economic adviser in Ghana during 1957–58 and eventually led to a break with Kwame Nkrumah.

The break itself came over the five-year plan, in which Lewis felt that many "white elephant projects" were being promoted for political reasons. Nkrumah, who is famously reported to have said, "seek ye the political kingdom first," responded as might be expected: "The advice you have given me, sound though it may be, is essentially from the economic point of view … I cannot always follow this advice as

I am a politician and must gamble on the future" (quoted in Tignor 2006: 173).

This gulf between "sound" economic advice and the political reality of economic policy-making continued to be a theme in Lewis's later writings even after he had left Ghana and returned to the safety of academic economics at Princeton University (Lewis 1965). But Lewis's careful, market-by-market analysis of market failure highlights a strand in policy analysis carried out by economists which does not always sit well with policy-makers or social theorists looking for "big" answers to "big" policy problems (Kanbur 2016c).

22.2.6 The Washington Consensus and the End of History

The laissez-faire liberalism of the late nineteenth and early twentieth centuries gave way to Keynesian interventionism in the 1940s and 1950s, and this transition was reflected in policy-making in developing countries as well, as shown in Kwame Nkrumah's predilection for government-subsidized efforts at industrialization. The Indian five-year plans of the 1950s and into the 1960s and 1970s were all supportive of industrialization through import substitution (Kanbur 2009). However, by the 1970s and 1980s doubts had set in about this "inward-oriented" strategy. The seeds of questioning are to be found, for example, in the Oxford economics doctoral thesis of Manmohan Singh, later finance minister and prime minister of India (Singh 1964), and in Bhagwati (1970).

Of course, this move in India came at a momentous time in global politics and at the time of crystallization of certain tendencies in thinking. The "Reagan-Thatcher-Kohl" decade ended with the fall of the Berlin Wall in 1989. In the same year, John Williamson (1989) coined the term "The Washington Consensus," which came to capture a neoliberal economic stance in policy-making, and Francis Fukuyama (1989) famously proclaimed "the end of history."

As we now know, "The end of history lasted for such a short time" (Kanbur 2001). Fukuyama (2014a) has himself reconsidered the finality of his proclamation in the political realm. In any event, the economic liberalizations of the 1980s and 1990s either had mixed results (for example the "lost decade" of low economic growth in Latin America and Africa) or, when there was success (for example in China), there is debate about how true economic policies were to laissez-faire liberalism in these countries. Further, the sharp rise in inequality in many countries (Kanbur 2014) raised the question of the connection between liberalization and the inclusivity of economic growth.

Thus, even before the financial crisis of 2008, the swing toward laissez-faire liberalism in development economics and development economic policy had abated. The report of the Growth Commission, chaired by Nobel prize winner Michael Spence, with leading economists and leading economic policy-makers as members, reflected well a balanced view on the debates of the previous two decades:

> governments should not try to do too much, replacing markets or closing the economy off from the rest of the world. But we believe this prescription defines the role of government too narrowly.

Just because governments are sometimes clumsy and sometimes errant, does not mean they should be written out of the script. On the contrary, as the economy grows and develops, active, pragmatic governments have crucial roles to play. (Commission on Growth and Development 2008: 4)

But then the financial crisis struck and the economics of laissez-faire liberalism was questioned even further.

22.2.7   Economics and the Financial Crisis of 2008

A decade before the great financial crisis of 2008, there was the Asian financial crisis of 1997. The debates which followed pitted proponents of setting markets free in cross-border capital flows against those who warned that such liberalization would lead to instability and crisis. A leading example of the critics is Joseph Stiglitz, who sees a direct link between his Nobel prize-winning research in the operation of markets with imperfect information (Stiglitz 2002b), and a range of policy issues, including capital controls (Stiglitz 2002a).

But it seemed that the lessons of the crisis of 1997 were never learned, or were forgotten, as the financial boom of the early 2000s took hold, driven by the development of financial derivative instruments which had themselves been facilitated by financial deregulatory policies in the 1980s, 1990s, and 2000s. This led eventually to the deepest and broadest economic crisis since the Great Depression of the 1930s. Economic analysis was implicated in the development of the crisis and the policy responses to it.

Famously, the Queen of England asked economists why nobody had seen the crisis coming, and the British Academy (2009) responded with a letter which concluded as follows:

> The failure was to see how collectively this added up to a series of interconnected imbalances over which no single authority had jurisdiction. Individual risks may rightly have been viewed as small, but the risk to the system as a whole was vast.

It is interesting to note the ancestry of this assessment, in Keynes's indictment of laissez-faire quoted earlier: "It is *not* a correct deduction from the principles of economics that enlightened self-interest always operates in the public interest" (Keynes 1926: 287–288).

The response to the crisis reignited many of the debates of the 1930s on the use of monetary policy and fiscal policy. The chairman of the United States Federal Reserve Board, Benjamin Bernanke, is a renowned scholar of the Great Depression, and used the monetary policy instruments at his disposal to shore up the economy, as did central banks around the world (Bernanke 2015). But the failures came on the side of fiscal policy, where a modern version of the "Treasury View" that Keynes railed against seemed to prevail. Fears of the consequences of a high level of public debt (for example, Reinhart and Rogoff 2011) were set against the Keynesian instinct to expand public expenditure at times of severe unemployment of labor and capital (for example, Krugman 2013).

It is fair to say that the "Treasury View" won in the fiscal battle, leaving a more depressed global economy for longer than necessary. Policymakers appear not to have been responsive to mismatches between large savings, especially in Asia, and great infrastructure needs the world over (Spence et al. 2015). The debate continues, and the interactions between economic analysis and economic policy remain as involved and as intricate as ever.

22.2.8   Rising Inequality: Economic Analysis and Policy Concerns

An excellent example of the coming together of academic analysis and popular and public concern is the phenomenal success of the book by Thomas Piketty (2014), *Capital in the Twenty-First Century*. It reached number one on the *New York Times* bestseller list for hardcover nonfiction. That an 800-page economics book with charts and graphs, and even an equation or two, should sell so well to the general public shows how it captured the Zeitgeist, also marked by the "Occupy Wall Street" movement and the immediate popular recognition of the "1 percent versus 99 percent" distinction.

In fact, Piketty (2014) was the culmination of two decades of detailed empirical work by economists documenting the rise of inequality and its causes (see the discussion in Atkinson 2015). Piketty's (2014) powerful thesis is that rising inequality is the natural tendency of capitalism and needs to be mitigated through active economic policy. Indeed, inequality has actually fallen in Latin America in the 1990s, 2000s, and 2010s. This has been put down to proactive policy on the part of Latin American governments to counteract the global forces of technical change, which are tending to displace basic labor and increase demand for skilled labor and capital (Kanbur 2014).

It is often argued by social scientists that economists ignore distributional considerations and are only concerned about "efficiency." However, the instincts of economics as a discipline are marked not so much by a neglect of distribution and a focus on efficiency, but a deep-seated drive to *separate out* efficiency from equity, especially in the policy arena (Kanbur 2001). Thus, James Meade, who won the 1977 Nobel Prize in Economics and was known as a prominent egalitarian, nevertheless wrote the following in his *The Intelligent Radical's Guide to Economics*: "In general … the intelligent radical will advocate more direct general measures for the redistribution of income and properties in preference to particular interventions in particular markets for this purpose" (Meade 1975: 73). It is this separation of efficiency from equity which has been questioned by other Nobel prize-winning economists such as Sen (1999) and Stiglitz (2012).

Economics as a discipline, and as an engine for policy analysis, is a battleground between these pulls, to separate out efficiency from equity on the one hand, and to view them as an integrated whole on the other. The strong empirical trends identified in the work of Piketty (2014) and others have also spurred new theorizing on how the working of markets needs to be conceptualized differently from the standard laissez-faire framework if we are to explain the stylized distributional facts of the past two decades (Kanbur and Stiglitz 2015).

22

22.2.9 Conclusion: The Two Axes Again

This quick run through the history of economics and economic policy-making highlights the two fundamental questions which face economics as a discipline. First, what is the appropriate way to capture the workings of the economy, at the micro and at the macro level? Second, what is the appropriate way to evaluate economic outcomes? Laissez-faire liberalism embodies a view of markets as functioning well, without impediments of imperfect information or concentrations of economic power. The analytical foundations of this perspective, or rather the conditions under which it has credence, also rationalize a tendency to be found in many strands of economic policy-making, namely the separation of efficiency considerations from distributional ones. Thus, those who find themselves at opposite ends of these two axes will generally differ in their policy recommendations and have done so throughout history.

The two axes also explain the cycles and swings of seeming consensus on economic policy – from market orientation to state interventionism and back again. Keynes, despite his searing critique of laissez-faire liberalism, agreed that "the chief task of economists at this hour is to distinguish afresh the *Agenda* of government from the *Non Agenda*" (Keynes 1926: 287–291). This is indeed the question of every hour; it is the eternal question of political economy, posed and formulated by each generation in its own terms and in its own context. Since the policy question is constant and the analytical axes are well set, it is perhaps not surprising then that the answers themselves have cycled, and will cycle, with some regularity (Kanbur 2016c).

22.3 Education Policy

22.3.1 The Purposes of Education

Education, broadly understood as the process of transmission of skills, values, beliefs, information, and habits between generations and individuals, is one of the central features of human societies, and a major subject for social research. In today's world, all persons are expected to spend a significant part of their life attending learning institutions, which are organized in complex systems of (pre-)schools, universities, and online and other types of learning organizations, staffed by many education professionals and fueled by vast amounts of public and private money.

Most societies place very high expectations on education, considering it a key mechanism for social progress in different dimensions: economic, by developing individual competencies to participate in the labor market, increasing productivity, and providing better living conditions for individuals and societies; civic, strengthening the values of social cohesion and participation; as an instrument for social equity, by overcoming socially ascribed differences and expanding opportunities for social mobility; and for the enhancement of the fullest array of human talents, knowledge, and interests through research and the cultivation of the arts and humanities.

The contents of education, beyond basic literacy and numeracy skills, have always included moral, cultural, and intellectual dimensions. The

traditional liberal arts curriculum was meant to provide students with the scientific and humanistic traditions and repertoires of their times; and higher education, beyond preparation for the professions, sought to enhance the values of intellectual curiosity and the expansion of knowledge through scholarship and research. These expectations remain in most general and higher education systems today.

For the modern nation-states, public education was considered a tool for social cohesion and citizenship, and a means to develop the human resources necessary for running the state and enhancing the economy. Religious organizations and churches have always participated strongly in education, sometimes in partnership and sometimes in dispute with the nation-states. More recently, business sectors have also got involved, either creating their own systems of vocational education or participating in the shaping of education policies.

The main role of schools in modern societies, as expressed early in the twentieth century by Émile Durkheim in France, was to make students understand their country and time and prepare them to take part in their collective tasks as citizens, providing the link between private life in the family and public life in society. For Durkheim, a fully educated citizen should be disciplined, attached to his social group, and endowed with autonomy and self-determination, provided by rationality (Durkheim 1922; Nisbet 1965; Wesselingh 2002). Reactions to the conservative tone of the Durkheimian tradition, in the context of a changing world, led to alternative approaches putting more emphasis on critical thinking, communitarian values, and individual self-determination (Freire 1970; Apple 1996; Benson, Harkavy, and Puckett 2007; Peterson 2011; Biesta, De Bie, and Wildemeersch 2014; Dalton and Welzel 2014). The notion that more education leads to more democracy has been a central assumption of the social sciences, since at least the pioneering writings of John Dewey (1916) and, more recently, has been linked to the concept of social capital and social cohesion (Coleman 1988; Fukuyama 2000; Putnam 2002).

The way these ideas were included in school curricula, were absorbed by the students, and had the desired effects, varied enormously in different times and societies, and are difficult to ascertain. It depended on countries' changing political climate, teachers' prevailing ideologies, the way they were taught, and students' socio-economic and cultural backgrounds. Empirical evidence and the historical record, however, have shown that these links cannot be taken for granted (Ringer 1979, 1990; Acemoglu et al. 2005).

22.3.2 Education Research and Policy

Most education research deals with these expectations and the ways they can be fulfilled. Research on education brings together skills and traditions of education scientists, psychologists, sociologists, political scientists, neuroscientists, historians, economists, and philosophers, with no established frontiers between these specialties. Research areas include the ways learning takes place in the human mind; the interactions between biological development and the social context; the impact of different pedagogical approaches and institutional arrangements on the student's achievement; the links between modalities of education and a person's lifelong productivity and wellbeing;

the effects of education on economic development and social equity; and the links between education, social cohesion, and values.

Research in education provides ample understanding of the role of education in different societies and the impact of specific institutional arrangements and practices in students' outcomes; rigorous, randomized experiments are increasingly being used, making these findings more reliable and consistent. However, education policies and practices are seldom directly based on evidence provided by research, in contrast, for instance, with health and medical practice (Slavin 2002; Nutley, Walter, and Davies 2007). Among the reasons for this are that in medical research, the effectiveness of science-based practice is much easier to see, there is a clear alignment between research outcomes and profit in the private sector, and the amount of resources invested in research, both public and private, is much larger. Also, without downplaying the complexity of biological research, brains are still much less understood than bodies, and the great variability of institutional arrangements and cultural contexts in which education takes place makes generalizations and the *ceteris paribus* condition difficult to obtain. The process of implementation is today a research field by itself, but the recommendations derived from implementation research are still not widely recognized in policy and practice (Meyers, Durlak, and Wandersmann 2012; Forman et al. 2013; Ogden and Fixsen 2014; Century and Cassata 2016; Spiel, Schober, and Strohmeier 2016); one reason is that implementation is too complex or strongly disputed by different sectors in the education establishment (Cerych, Sabatier, and European Institute of Education and Social Policy 1986; Clark 1987; Stevenson 2006; Olsen 2007). The expectation is that, with the growing accumulation of solid evidence from research and the dissemination of its conclusions to the education community, education practices and policies could become more efficient in the attainment of their goals.

23.3.3   Historical and Comparative Research on Education and Society

Today, most persons take for granted that formal education occurs in specialized institutions and is provided sequentially to groups of students organized per their ages. Comparative and historical studies, however, show that this arrangement is linked to a peculiar development of Western societies, which was later disseminated, with different arrangements, to the rest of the world. Education institutions and practices are strongly related to the social structure and stratification of different societies, reinforcing existing value and belief systems and the social standing of specific groups, leading to theories that stress the role of education in the reproduction of social stratification and credentials (Bourdieu and Passeron 1970; Bowles and Gintis 1973; Collins 1979). At the same time, education is often sought by specific groups in society to enhance their social standing and lead to social change, and the expansion of education and modern science in Western Europe has been interpreted, in the analytical perspective inaugurated by Max Weber, as part of the broad process of rationalization and individualism associated with the Protestant Reformation and the rise of capitalism (Merton 1938; Ben-David 1965, 1977; Archer 1979).

22.3.4   The Expansion of Education

The expansion of formal education is related to the emergence of the nation-states and the modern economy. The notion that all persons should be able to read the sacred books was part of the Jewish, Christian, and Muslim traditions, but was never fully practiced and was mostly limited to men (Gawthrop and Strauss 1984; Hanna 2007; Botticini and Eckstein 2012). This notion was adopted and spread out by the modern, industrialized Western nation-states, and exported to some degree to their colonies and areas of influence.

Access to formal education expanded dramatically after World War II and has continued to grow ever since. In 1950, about 47 percent of children aged 5–14 in the world were enrolled in some kind of school. In 2010, 89.1 percent of children were (Benavot and Riddle 1988). Secondary education, which used to be mostly a preparatory stage for universities, became part of the regular school system, starting with the "high school movement" in the United States and spreading later to Western Europe and other countries. Worldwide, the number of secondary school students went from 187 to 545 million between 1970 and 2010, a threefold growth to 63 percent of the relevant age group worldwide. Higher education, which used to be limited to a handful of elite universities, became a mass phenomenon in the 1970s and almost universal in several developed economies, reaching 32 million students worldwide in 1970 and 182 million in 2010 (Goldin and Katz 1997; Trow 2000; Schofer and Meyer 2005; Schwartzman, Pinheiro, and Pillay 2015; World Bank 2015).

22.3.5   Education and Economic Productivity

Economic research assumes that investments in human capital are rational responses to a calculus of expected costs and benefits. Empirical research shows that individual investments in education lead to higher income and that countries that expand and improve the quality of education are more likely to develop their economy (Mincer 1958, 1974; Schultz 1970; Becker 1973). Research on the economic dimensions of education seeks to explain the logic behind the individual and collective investments in education, the productivity of these investments at different moments of the life-cycle, the rates of return of these investments in different countries and for different levels of education, the transitions between school and the workplace, and the mechanisms that explain the differences in productivity of different types of educational institutions and practices, not only in economic terms, but also in terms of impact on social equity and other goals such as crime, health, and civic values (Hanushek, Machin, and Wössmann 2011–16).

22.3.6   Education and Equity

The expansion of education was also a response to growing aspirations for social mobility. Education came to be perceived as a social right, expected to pave the way for different forms of participation, including the benefits of individual choice, good employment and income, and social prestige. After World War II, the right to education was enshrined in Article 26 of the Universal Declaration of Human Rights, and embodied in the work of international organizations such as UNESCO, which not only spread the gospel of expanding education, but also helped countries organize their school systems. In 1990, the Jomtien World Conference on Education for All set the target to provide free and compulsory primary education for all children in the world, with the financial and technical support of public and private donors. This was enforced through UN Millennium Development Goal 2, which aimed to achieve universal completion of a full cycle of primary education by 2015, and by the new Sustainable Development Goal 4, with the headline "Ensure inclusive and equitable quality education and promote lifelong learning opportunities for all."

The links between education and equity have been approached at different levels, from the impact of individual differences on school achievement and social mobility to the equity issues related to stratified education systems. At the micro level, there is a large and controversial literature on the relative effect of inherited vs. acquired intelligence and learning capabilities on educational achievement, and, particularly in the United States, on the impact of race differences (Jencks and Phillips 1998; Knudsen et al. 2006). At the macro level, a central issue is the impact of differentiated vs. more homogeneous education systems on social equity (Teese 2011). A central issue regarding equity is the effects of affirmative action policies in access to education to compensate for the inequalities associated with meritocracy (Darity Jr. 2005; Sowell 2004). The prevailing consensus is that social and economic conditions, and the quality of the education provided, are the main determinants of educational equity; and that education systems that provide more choices and opportunities according to the student's abilities, interests, and social conditions tend to be more equitable than those that do not take these preconditions into account.

Some countries have developed highly differentiated systems, with general and vocation and university and non-university institutions. There are very different expectations and predictions about the effects of Vocational and Educational Training (VET) on inequality. On the one hand, for many, VET provides practical and useful skills and facilitates the transition from school to work; on the other hand, it may help to maintain social differentiation (Shavit and Muller 2000). The limitations of vocational education, associated with the dominance of general education and growing aspirations for higher education degrees, raise the issue of how to deal with the large number of students that, in most countries, never acquire the minimum competencies required by compulsory education, which, according to a recent OECD report, affects one in four 15-year-old students in the OECD countries (OECD 2016). The situation in low-income societies is much worse. There are many strategies to make education more attractive, meaningful, and accessible for the students, but the fact remains that millions of students, some in rich but mostly in low-income countries, go through school without learning to read and understand a simple text or to solve a simple arithmetic problem, or gaining a grasp of very simple scientific facts.

22.3.7 Assessing and Explaining the Effectiveness of Education

A large part of the research effort on education is dedicated to measuring its effectiveness in terms of its broad goals and explaining the reasons for the observed effects. Issues surrounding education as human capital include the effect of education on economic productivity, the study of education-related wage differentials, the mismatch and patterns of transition between school and work, and the relative economic returns of different levels and types of education, as well as all the factors that can lead to these different outcomes, at both the individual and the institutional levels.

Educational institutions have always assessed the extent to which students learn what they are supposed to at different stages of their student life. An important development of the last decades has been the development of large-scale, standardized assessments of student achievement, both within countries (such as the National Assessment of Educational Progress in the United States) and internationally, with comparative assessments such as the Trends in International Mathematics and Science Study (TIMSS), OECD's Program for International Student Assessment (PISA), and those from UNESCO's Latin American Laboratory for Assessment of the Quality of Education. These assessments have been criticized on different grounds, as being Eurocentric, as neglecting other more qualitative dimensions of education, and as leading schools to teach to the test. At the same time, they have generated large depositories of information on the characteristics of students, their families, their schools, and their practices, which are being widely used to learn about the different individual and school characteristics and practices that can lead to better outcomes.

There is today a clear consensus that early childhood education and care, if of good quality, brings a wide range of benefits, including better child wellbeing and learning outcomes, more equitable outcomes and reduction of poverty, increased intergenerational social mobility, higher levels of female labor market participation and gender equality, and better social and economic development for society as a whole (Kamerman 2000; Campbell et al. 2002; Clarke-Stewart and Allhusen 2005; Cunha et al. 2005; Cunha and Heckman 2007). Exposure to high-quality care appears especially important for at-risk children's later school success (Rolnick and Grunewald 2003; Early et al. 2007). The literature clearly shows that money, when properly invested in early childhood development and education, yields extraordinary public returns. Governments are increasingly working to assist families and support children. Between 1998 and 2011, public expenditure on young children in the form of child care and preschool increased 55 percent on average across OECD countries. However, there are large differences in the percentage of GDP that these countries spent on child care and preschool.

The second consensus is around the crucial role of teachers. Teachers are not just carriers of knowledge and information. They have a significant impact on children's quality of life – including their relationships with peers and adults, and their dispositions toward learning and life more generally. They are role models and conveyors of implicit values and modes of behavior which cannot be codified in books or transmitted through new technologies. Besides, teachers and professors are not just school or university employees, but members of established professions and unions that often make the difference on whether education policies succeed or fail (Sachs 2003).

Clearly, not all teachers are effective, not all teachers are experts, and not all teachers have powerful effects on students (Rivkin, Hanushek, and Kain 2005; Hanushek and Rivkin 2006; Hattie 2008). The IEA Teacher Education and Development Study in Mathematics (TEDS-M) showed considerable variation in national policies related to quality assurance, entry requirements, program length, and opportunities to learn, as well as differences in the organization and types of teacher education programs within and across the participating countries. Countries with programs providing the most comprehensive opportunities to learn university- and school-level mathematics tended to have higher scores on the TEDS-M tests. The data further indicated a positive relationship between the strength of quality-assurance arrangements and future teachers' mathematics and pedagogy knowledge (Ingvarson et al. 2013).

22.3.8   The Challenges for the Twenty-First Century

A crucial challenge for the twenty-first century is to increase the quality and scope of education research and to consider the large variability of educational policies and governance. There is no "one-size-fits-all" model of educational governance that could be transferred from one country to another. At the same time, international comparisons show that some countries are better than others at using their resources to provide better education to their citizens, and there is an intense flow of information, communication, and debates about these findings, fostered to some extent by international and multilateral institutions. The transferability of positive experiences, however, is limited by the fact that education systems are part of broad institutional settings, characterized by shared ideas and values supported by established social structures, which restrain the ability of governments and education authorities to manage them at will (Benavot 1997).

A further big challenge for the twenty-first century is the role technology can and should have in education. The most dramatic change over the past generation in the lives of both teachers and students is the explosion of information and communication technologies, affecting both the way education is provided and its contents. It has been widely suggested that online technologies can help address issues of educational equity and social exclusion and expand access to educational opportunities; but there is growing evidence that technologies by themselves cannot replace the presence of well-qualified teachers, supported by solidly based teaching methodologies, who can prepare students to find their way in the flood of information that is now available (Fu 2013; Voogt et al. 2013). The implications of the changes that new technologies are bringing to labor markets, destroying traditional professions and making competencies such as problem-solving and social interaction more crucial than the sheer accumulation of information, are still to be fully realized by education systems anywhere (Autor, Levy, and Murnane 2003; Levy and Murnane 2013; OECD 2016).

22.4   Environmental Protection

The contributions of the natural sciences to environmental policy have been key to understanding of the chemical, biological, and ecological causes and consequences of environmental problems. The social sciences have likewise made many contributions to identifying the behavioral sources of environmental problems and understanding how laws and other institutions can help solve these problems. In this section, we distill major contributions of the social sciences – notably economics, political science, psychology, and sociology – in understanding environmental problems and their solutions.

22.4.1   Understanding Environmental Problems

By environmental problems, we mean primarily the negative by-products of economic activity – pollution – and other unintended consequences which entail risks to human health, loss of environmental amenities, damage to ecosystems, or resource-based reductions in quality of human life. Environmental problems have been closely associated with aspirations for sustainable development, famously defined as "development which meets the needs of current generations without compromising the ability of future generations to meet their own needs" (World Commission on Environment and Development 1987). Whether understood in terms of the ill effects of pollution and resource depletion or in terms of sustainability, it is clear that environmental problems do not emerge in a vacuum. They manifest from the interaction of humans with the environment, often arising from very complex, dynamic systems of economic and social behavior (Matson, Clark, and Andersson 2016).

22.4.1.1   Externalities

Economists' conceptualization of environmental problems as a form of market failure has become widely accepted. Although markets in principle allocate goods and services efficiently, market failures can arise when transactions do not accurately reflect the full value of goods and services either to the parties to those transactions or to third parties affected by them. Environmental problems take the form of market failures known as "negative externalities" – the imposition of harmful effects to third parties from market activity. These externalities, or spillovers, are not reflected in the price of goods and services, and hence the relevant goods and services are oversupplied in the market from the standpoint of society.

22.4.1.2   Transaction Costs

At a micro level, externalities can be understood by reference to economist Ronald Coase's well-known parable of a farmer and a rancher – a puzzle depicting a conflict between two neighbors which provides a metaphor and analytic framework for understanding all problems of negative externalities (Coase 1960). The Coase Theorem suggests that markets fail in the face of externalities largely due to the existence of transaction costs (Zerbe and McCurdy 1999), for if transaction costs did not exist, the relevant parties could achieve an efficient allocation of resources (Coase 1960; Ellickson 1986). In a Coasian world without transaction costs, the farmer and rancher would bargain between

22

themselves to minimize the sum of both the damages from cattle straying into the farmer's crops and the costs of damage avoidance, such as building a fence. In reality, of course, as Coase himself understood, very real transaction costs are associated with gathering information, negotiating agreements, and resolving disputes over pollution and the use of natural resources. The existence of these transaction costs means that negative spillovers will occur because it is too costly for the affected parties – often many thousands upon thousands of people, not just an individual farmer and rancher – to negotiate "win–win" agreements.

22.4.1.3   Public Goods and Commons Problems

The impact of any single polluting source on any single individual within a large affected population may only be modest, even if in the aggregate, across all affected individuals, these impacts are quite large. The asymmetry between the individual and collective impact of many environmental harms gives rise to the well-known problem of collective action (Olson 1965; Hardin 1982). This problem arises when each member of an affected group does not have enough at stake relative to the costs of avoiding the externality (or of mobilizing pressure to have a polluting source move or invest in avoidance). It is often rational under such circumstances for individuals to free-ride on the efforts of others. Collective-action problems derive from the fact that many environmental amenities are public goods: that is, they are non-rivalrous (use by one person does deplete from others) and non-excludable (cannot be kept from those who do not contribute to or pay for them). Environmental quality often possesses the characteristics of a public good; everyone can breathe clean air without having paid for it.

The public-goods nature of natural resources can lead to the "tragedy of the commons" (Hardin 1968). Many commons problems arise from the attributes of a common pool resource being non-excludable but rivalrous in consumption – meaning that use by one person makes that same resource unavailable to another (or potentially diminishes the overall quality of the resource) (Ostrom 1990, 2008). Open ocean fisheries are a classic example of a common pool resource; boats "race to fish" to catch as many fish as possible, fish taken by one vessel leaves the fish stock depleted for subsequent fishing boats in the area, and it is challenging, if not impossible, to exclude boats from fishing in open waters.

22.4.1.4   Environmental Equity

The principal concern with market failures lies with the overall social costs of economic activity; when externalities exist, pollution becomes overproduced (or natural resources become overexploited). But environmental problems also raise distributional or fairness concerns, as the negative impacts of economic activity are not equally borne by everyone in society. Especially palpable concerns have arisen over racial disparities in the imposition of environmental harms – concerns that have been reflected in an "environmental justice" movement in the United States and elsewhere (Cole and Foster 2001).

22.4.2   Solving Environmental Problems

The general solution to environmental problems as market failures lies in finding ways to ensure that individuals and businesses internalize their externalities. Although such a solution seems straightforward in concept, determining how best to motivate the internalization of externalities raises challenging policy issues: (1) the identification of the criteria against which solutions should be chosen or assessed; (2) the general advantages and disadvantages of different environmental policy instruments; and (3) choices about what entities – local, national, or international – should seek to implement solutions and how policy choices should be made.

22.4.2.1   Criteria and Values

A perennial question in environmental policy decision-making is, "How safe is safe?" In recent years, scholars and policy-makers have renewed this question by advocating a "risk-based" approach to regulation (Black 2008; Bounds 2010; Wiener 2010), with the implication being that policy decisions can automatically follow from a clear and rigorous scientific understanding of effects on human health or ecological viability. But natural science by itself cannot determine how (or how stringently) environmental policy should be made, as policy determinations call for making normative judgments in addition to gathering scientific information (Coglianese and Marchant 2004). To be coherent, any risk-based approach to environmental regulation needs to be grounded in a clear articulation of policy criteria (Finkel and Golding 1995; Rothstein et al. 2006; Paoli and Wiles 2015). Principled environmental decision-making depends on value choices about how much pollution should be deemed acceptable – or, more generally, by what criteria environmental policy should be guided. A variety of potential criteria can be discerned throughout the policy-relevant social science literature, although any thorough consideration of them requires exploration of moral or political theory.

One well-accepted criterion derives from standard welfare economics: *efficiency*. Efficiency not only takes into account the benefits of environmental policy in terms of reductions in harm, but also factors in those benefits and seeks to balance them with the costs of achieving them. The concept of Pareto efficiency demands that a policy make at least some individual better off without making any individual worse off. Another test of efficiency is known as Kaldor-Hicks efficiency, which accepts as efficient any option where the "winners" under a policy (say, those whose water source becomes cleaner) reap aggregate benefits in an amount greater than the costs the policy will impose on the "losers" (say, those businesses that must pay to install equipment to reduce their water pollution). Kaldor-Hicks efficiency leads to the estimation of *net* benefits (Gramlich 1990).

The application of an efficiency test raises a host of analytical and methodological challenges. The underlying risks to be addressed must first be identified and characterized. The enterprise of risk assessment has been largely driven by natural sciences – but not exclusively so (Jasanoff 1987; Stern and Fineberg 1996). It also raises normative questions which hold implications either more narrowly for various methodological choices or more broadly about whether to use benefit–cost analysis at all (Kelman 1981; Ackerman and Heinzerling 2005; Adler and Posner 2006; Bronsteen, Buccafusco, and Masur 2013).

Other applicable policy criteria avoid some of the contested valuation judgments involved when benefits must be monetized for purposes of applying a benefit–cost test. One alternative is *cost-effectiveness*, which also accounts for the costs of a policy but does not call for balancing those costs against benefits, and thus does not necessitate any attempt to monetize benefits such as avoided mortality or morbidity or environmental amenities. The cost-effectiveness criterion would point decision-makers toward policies that can achieve the desired level of environmental or health improvement for the lowest cost.

Others have proposed using *feasibility* as a policy criterion, seeking to maximize environmental protection within the constraint of what is feasible (Driesen 2005; but see Masur and Posner 2010). The feasibility criterion is a close cousin to the *precautionary principle*, which has been widely urged as the better way to make policy decisions about environmental risk (Freestone and Hey 1996). In general, the precautionary principle shifts the burden of proof onto those who create potential externalities – for example, those who create new products or processes that could harm the environment or human health. It forbids economic activities until they can be shown to impose no externalities. Although the precautionary principle possesses considerable appeal to policy-makers and members of the public, some scholars have questioned its coherence (Sunstein 2005).

22.4.2.2   Policy Instruments

Policy criteria can be used to inform decisions about a variety of possible policy instruments. In this section, we review key findings from social science research on the major tools available to the environmental policy-maker (Richards 2000). The tools discussed have been adopted and implemented by national governmental bodies, even though several of the instruments discussed here could be applied by other decision-makers, whether private or public, international or local.

Ex-Post Liability

One policy instrument involves imposing liability on polluters after they cause harm to others. Sometimes referred to as the "polluter pays" principle, ex-post liability could, at least in theory, provide a deterrent effect that leads polluters to adopt preventive measures. Although ex-post liability may be deemed appropriate for special types of environmental concerns or as a general backstop to other options, such liability by itself is generally thought to be insufficient as a principal means of addressing environmental concerns, mainly for the very same kinds of reasons that environmental problems arise in the first place: transaction costs and the problems of collective action.

Means-Based Regulation

Proactive regulation can take a variety of forms. One form consists of rules directing regulated entities (e.g. business firms) to use particular means of pollution control or to take other specific action to reduce environmental problems. Sometimes characterized as technology or specification standards, "means standards" include requirements for the installation of catalytic converters on automobiles and the operation of emissions scrubbers on factory smokestacks. This type of regulation is not uncommon in environmental policy. Means standards generally offer greater certainty that regulated firms will take the desired environmentally protective action, and they may also be easier for regulatory officials to enforce. Despite these advantages, means standards will often be less cost-effective than other forms of regulation because they mandate the same "one-size-fits-all" action for every regulated firm.

Performance-Based Regulation

Regulation can also mandate the attainment or avoidance of certain outcomes – setting a goal of "what" to achieve but not specifying "how" to achieve it. All that firms must do is deliver on the outcome (Coglianese, Nash, and Olmstead 2003; May 2011). An emissions limit is a common example of a performance standard.

By specifying requirements in terms of outcomes and giving firms flexibility in meeting those outcomes, performance standards can overcome the one-size-fits-all disadvantage of means standards. Performance standards can also better allow for innovation to occur (Jaffe, Newell, and Stavins 2004). For these reasons, many social scientists recommend performance standards as more cost-effective regulatory instruments.

Yet performance standards are not without their disadvantages (Coglianese 2017). Sometimes, measurement of outcomes can be difficult with respect to environmental standards. Furthermore, performance standards can be susceptible to a type of gaming known as "teaching to the test," which occurs when regulated firms find ways to meet the required outcome but in ways that work to the detriment of the larger purpose of the regulation. Performance standards may also be somewhat more prone to the incidence of unintended consequences as firms use their flexibility in creative ways that produce new, unanticipated problems (May 2003).

Market Instruments

Although performance standards can prove more cost-effective than means standards, they still can be less cost-effective than market-based regulatory instruments. This is because performance standards require uniform levels of emissions control even when the marginal costs for controlling those emissions can vary across different firms. Rather than demanding every firm meet the same emissions limit, market instruments allow for – and even provide incentives for – firms to choose their own level of emissions. Market instruments operate either by setting a per-unit tax on emissions or by establishing a system of tradable emissions permits (Tietenberg 1985).

Emissions trading – or "cap and trade" – can provide greater certainty about the overall level of pollution reductions. Under a cap-and-trade system, an overall desired level of emissions is established and a number of aggregate emissions "credits" are issued that total the desired level. Each individual firm then receives credits equaling a portion of the overall emissions level; they must keep their emissions below the amount allowed by the permits they possess – much like with any performance standard. But, unlike with uniform performance standards, firms can exchange credits under cap and trade, thus varying the level of control each firm must achieve. Those firms with lower marginal costs of control can free up emissions credits by reducing pollution more than required and selling excess credits to other firms with higher marginal costs of control, ultimately achieving the same overall level of pollution reductions but at a lower cost (Cropper and Oates 1992; Stavins 2007).

Management-Based Regulation

Management-based regulation does not require firms meet a targeted outcome or even adopt any direct means that aim toward a desired outcome, but instead mandates that firms collect information, develop internal plans and procedures, and engage in other management-related actions that aim indirectly toward reducing environmental problems (Coglianese and Lazer 2003; Bennear 2006). Some laws direct companies using toxic chemicals to engage in pollution prevention planning to try to reduce their use of toxics, even without requiring those companies to take any specific pollution prevention or control measures – or sometimes without even demanding that they carry out their required plans. In short, management-based regulation aims to solve environmental problems by spurring improvements in private-sector environmental management (Coglianese and Nash 2006).

Empirical evidence shows that these regulations can lead to improvements in some measures of environmental quality (Coglianese and Lazer 2003; Bennear 2006, 2007). However, research also indicates that improvements induced by management-based regulations may not be long-lived, as over time the required planning appears to become more routinized and environmental improvements diminish.

Information Disclosure

Another regulatory approach requires not just the gathering of information for internal planning purposes, but the affirmative public disclosure of certain kinds of information (Tietenberg 1998; Sunstein 1999). The US Toxics Releases Inventory (TRI) regulation serves as a prominent example of this policy instrument. TRI requires certain industrial facilities to disclose to the public the volume of toxic chemicals they release into the environment. Some researchers have attributed the decline over time in chemicals reported under TRI as a sign of the policy's success (Fung and O'Rourke 2000; Thaler and Sunstein 2008). Others have shown that observed reductions can be explained instead by other, more traditional forms of regulation operating in the background or by factors other than real improvements in environmental performance (Poje and Horowitz 1990; Natan Jr. and Miller 1998; de Marchi and Hamilton 2006; Bennear 2008).

Although the precise effects of the TRI law are not known (Hamilton 2005), other research has shown that information disclosure can sometimes contribute to some modest environmental improvement (Bennear and Olmstead 2008). Researchers theorize that information disclosure can reinforce various other legal, market, and social pressures for companies to reduce pollution (Hamilton 1995; Konar and Cohen 1997; Khanna, Quimio, and Bojilova 1998). Furthermore, if the aphorism that "what gets measured, gets managed" is true, then information disclosure may operate essentially as a form of management-based regulation (Karkkainen 2001).

Voluntary Programs

A related approach is to reward firms that voluntarily adopt environmentally responsible actions or achieve high levels of environmental performance. Through so-called voluntary environmental programs, governments sometimes offer qualifying firms technical assistance, awards and public recognition, special eco-labels, or specified forms of regulatory relief (Coglianese and Nash 2014).

22.4.3   Choices About Sectors, Scale, and Processes

Just as social science has helped identify and evaluate different policy instruments for addressing environmental problems, it has also clarified several other important, policy-relevant choices. These include choices about who should bear the primary responsibility for addressing environmental problems – specifically, the public or private sector – as well as about the appropriate scale of policy responses – top-down versus bottom-up. In addition, social science research about policy decision-making more generally has made contributions to the design of processes used to make and enforce environmental policy.

22.4.3.1   Public versus Private

Although governments are major sources of environmental policy, a variety of non-governmental actors fulfill governance roles. Especially in societies lacking in state capacity or for problems that governments are unable or unwilling to address, private third parties can serve as surrogates for (or supplements to) governmental actors (Büthe 2010). Sometimes called "private regulators," business associations or NGOs operating in this capacity derive their authority more through moral persuasion and market power than coercion (Cashore, Auld, and Newsom 2004; Green 2013). For example, a variety of privately created labeling and certification schemes have emerged to provide global consumers and businesses credible information and assurances related to niche preferences for more sustainable or ethical forms of agriculture and manufacturing (Prakash and Potoski 2006; Starobin and Weinthal 2010). These non-state schemes can impose means or performance standards – or any other types of rule – but they lack the ability to mandate compliance with the threat of state-imposed sanctions. As a result, private forms of environmental governance will bear many similarities to voluntary programs adopted by governments. That said, the market pressures available to business associations, NGOs, and even multinational corporations like Wal-Mart can sometimes create incentives for compliance that rival those provided by state authority (Starobin 2013).

22.4.3.2   Top-Down versus Bottom-Up

A perennial issue concerns the scale at which environmental solutions should be sought (Young 2002). Except problems with highly localized impacts, environmental problems often transcend political boundaries, raising the question of whether the responsibility for addressing them should be assumed by national bodies or devolved to lower levels of scale. The choice between a top-down and a bottom-up set of solutions assumes particular significance for transnational environmental problems, such as climate change.

Top-down approaches have generated concerns not only about effectiveness but also about global equity, as top-down treaties may reflect the preferences of the developed countries whose industrialization and development have fueled accelerated environmental degradation, to the exclusion of developing and emerging economies, many of which face more of the negative consequences of environmental problems (Baland and Platteau 1996). The most negatively affected individuals and communities – those at the bottom of the global economic pyramid – may not have their interests and concerns reflected in top-down policy discussions.

Although bottom-up approaches to environmental governance may ameliorate disadvantages of top-down approaches, when problems transcend a smaller scale, a bottom-up approach may not be up to the task (Keohane and Ostrom 1994). Furthermore, when governance is devolved to lower scales, a concern arises about a "race-to-the-bottom" effect, as local jurisdictions may have an incentive to compete for business activity through less stringent policy measures.

22.4.3.3   Policy Processes

Much social science research has sought to understand the processes and politics of how environmental policy choices are made and implemented. Relevant issues have included the role of experts (Jasanoff 2009), consensus-building (Coglianese 2003), public participation (Tyler and Markell 2008), and enforcement (Bardach and Kagan 1982; Ayres and Braithwaite 1995).

22.4.4   Conclusion

In this section, we have endeavored to illuminate principal contributions from social sciences to the understanding of environmental problems and to the design of policies to change individual and collective behavior in ways that enhance environmental quality. To solve environmental problems, governments, businesses, and global civil society not only need sound natural scientific information but must confront key social science questions as well.

22.5   Health Care

22.5.1   Introduction

In the earlier history of medicine and public health, statisticians and epidemiologists had a well-documented and prominent role (Ackerknecht 1982). In the twentieth century, demography, social epidemiology, economics, and political science increasingly contributed to the improvement of population health.

One of the early pioneers in this history of health improvement was the physician and epidemiologist John Snow, who contributed to a better understanding of a cholera outbreak in London in 1854. By mapping cases and using statistical methods he was able to identify a water pump in Broad Street as the most likely source of the recent outbreak. With this evidence in hand, he was able to convince local authorities to implement a simple measure that led to the control of the epidemic: the removal of the handle to the water pump (Porter 1991).

Public health policies to improve health care are not always this simple; other contributions have included vaccinations, better housing and better hygiene, reduction of poverty, and improved surgical techniques and anesthesia. The twentieth-century public health achievements include widespread immunization and control of infectious diseases, workplace safety, safer births, contraception and family planning, fluoridation of drinking water, safer and healthier food, motor-vehicle safety measures, tobacco control and taxations, and prevention and treatment of heart disease and stroke. The rise and fall of tobacco-related deaths documented by Doll and Peto should especially be mentioned here (Doll 1994). Finally, health systems started to develop, first with social health insurance for the few, later expanding to universal health coverage in country after country throughout the century. The establishment of the NHS in the UK in 1948 was one milestone, and the Affordable Care Act in the US in 2010 was another long overdue achievement. Yet, more than 50 countries fail to offer true universal health coverage (UHC), leading the World Health Organization in 2010 to advocate for UHC worldwide and in 2012 to declare that UHC is the single most powerful concept that public health has to offer (WHO 2010). In 2015, all countries in the world signed up to Sustainable Development Goal 3 (Health and Wellbeing), in which UHC is an important sub-target (Summers on behalf of 267 signatories 2015; UN 2015).

Medical knowledge, medicine, technology, and improvements in living standards undoubtedly contributed to the rapid improvements in health and longevity we have witnessed in the last half century. This story is convincingly told in Angus Deaton's book *The Great Escape: Health, Wealth, and the Origins of Inequality* (Deaton 2013). However, the contributions of the social sciences – such as statistics, demography, social epidemiology, economics, and political science – to health care are perhaps less well known and documented. Modern medicine and health policy are unique in the sense that they are evidence-based, or at least evidence-informed. This reliance on science made possible the influence of the social sciences and the interaction between disciplines. There are also large inequalities in health and longevity, and the social sciences have much to offer in terms of diagnosing the challenges, identifying gaps in knowledge, producing relevant new evidence, providing critical perspectives, and suggesting improved health policies on the path to social progress in health and health care.

The following sections offer a brief sketch of some contributions from the social sciences to better understanding changes and proposing improvements in health care.

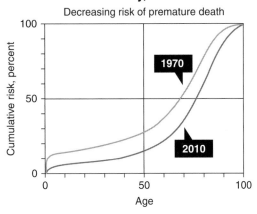

Figure 22.1 | Risk of premature death, world, 1970 and 2010.
Source: Peto, Lopes, and Norheim (2014).

22.5.2 Improved Life Expectancy and Reduced Mortality

The story of social progress in health is, unlike in many other sectors, predominantly positive. The world has seen a remarkable improvement in life expectancy at birth, from on average 48 years for both sexes in 1955 to above 71 years in 2015 (UNPD 2015; see also Chapter 18). This is an increase of 23 years over a time span of 60 years or, put differently, more than four months of increase per year. By also taking chronic disease and morbidity into account, healthy life expectancy at birth (HALE) is measured by a more recently developed summary measure of population health. As part of the Global Burden of Disease study, Salomon et al. found that in 1990, global healthy life expectancy at birth was 55 years for men and 59 for women, while by 2015 it had increased to 61 years for men and 65 years for women (GBD 2015 DALYs and HALE Collaborators 2016).

Another way to look at progress in health is by age-specific mortality. The worldwide cumulative risk of death before the age of 50 years almost halved between 1970 and 2010 (from 28 percent to 15 percent; see Figure 22.1).

The risk of premature death (before age 70) has decreased substantially worldwide and for all World Bank income groupings of countries (see Figure 22.2). Globally, the risk fell by a third (54 percent to 36 percent) (Norheim et al. 2015). If we look at cumulative risk of death in the age group 0 to 4, we see that the absolute reduction was largest for low-income countries (with highest initial mortality), while the relative reduction was more rapid for the highest income countries (with lowest initial mortality).

Similar positive reductions are seen for all the other age groups represented in Figure 22.2, except for some increase in mortality for the age range 5–49 years in low-income countries due to the HIV/AIDS epidemic. These changes in age-specific mortality explain the rapid improvement of life expectancy almost all over the world.

22.5.3 Inequalities in Health

Average life expectancy or healthy life expectancy is not the only measure of population health that matters; the distribution around this average is also important. According to the UN Population Division (2015 revision), estimated life expectancy at birth for both sexes for the period 2010–15 in low-income countries was 60.3, in lower-middle-income countries it was 66.3, in upper-middle-income countries 73.8, and in high-income countries 78.8 years (UNPD 2015). The gap between the worst-performing country (Swaziland, 49.2 years) and the best-performing country (Japan, 83.3) was 34.1 years. Although these inequalities have declined during the last decades, large inequalities in life expectancy between countries remain.

In addition to looking at between-country inequalities in life expectancy at birth, it is also possible to measure within-country inequality in premature death. One group of demographers has developed an overall measure of health inequality called life disparity. Life disparity is a measure of how much lifespans differ among *individuals* and is calculated from life tables. Vaupel et al. found that there are still substantial inequalities in life disparity, but that they have decreased substantially. Increases in life expectancy are highly correlated with decreases in overall inequality in life disparity, and this study concludes that: "Greater longevity and greater equality of individuals' lifespans are not incompatible goals. Countries can achieve both by reducing premature deaths" (Vaupel, Zhang, and van Raalte 2011). The overall picture regarding improvements in and reduction of inequalities in longevity is, therefore, one of clear social progress, although the best-off countries improved faster than the worse-off.

Yet, the picture should be further nuanced. Social epidemiologists, such as Michael Marmot and others, are less concerned about overall health inequalities, and more concerned about social *group* inequalities in health. Social justice should worry about whether unfairly distributed social determinants of health – such as social status, income, and level of education – translate into unequal and unfair health outcomes. These *inequities* in health, defined as *unfair and avoidable inequalities* in health, are now well documented, from the first Whitehall studies in London (Marmot et al. 1991), to the World Health Organization's 2008 global report *Closing the Gap in a Generation* (WHO 2008), to studies of inequality in life expectancy between social groups in the US. In the US, the gap in life expectancy between the richest 1 percent and poorest 1 percent of individuals was 14.6 years (Chetty et al. 2016). In the UK, differences in life expectancy between neighborhoods with high and low incomes have been found to be around ten years (Marmot et al. 2010). In many countries, *relative* social group inequities in age-specific mortality are increasing. While most people live longer and better lives, the rate of change is faster among the well-off than the worst-off.

22.5.4 Disease and Poverty

In addition to inequalities in health outcomes, social group inequalities in access to health services are also well documented, and especially so in low-income countries through Demographic Health Surveys and

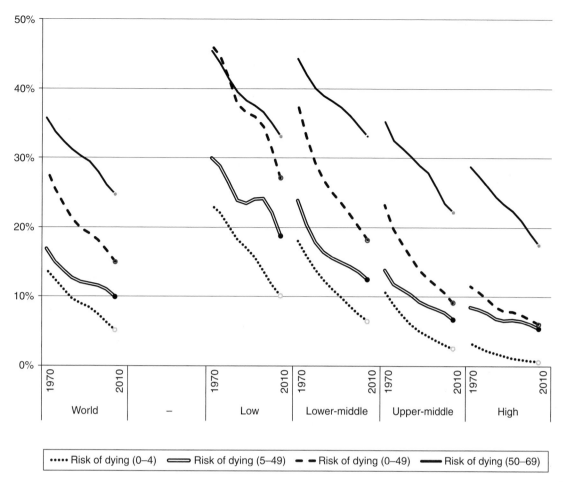

Figure 22.2 | Risk of dying in selected age ranges for the world and four World Bank income groupings of countries, 1970–2010.
Source: Norheim et al. (2015).

Multiple Indicator Cluster Surveys (World Bank 2012). For example, Cesar Victora et al. provide a useful overview of inequalities in access to maternal and child health services, or service coverage, in 35 low- and middle-income countries (Victora et al. 2012). This study found prevalent pro-rich inequalities in coverage, but with average coverage increasing for most indicators, and inequalities by socio-economic quintile decreasing.

Impoverishment from disease and out-of-pocket expenditures for health services have also been documented (Xu et al. 2003). The World Health Report of 2010 found that direct out-of-pocket payments represented more than 50 percent of total health expenditures in 2007 in the worst-performing 33 countries (WHO 2010). Individuals and households resort to a variety of strategies to cope with illness-related bills, such as borrowing money from peers or selling assets. Without pre-existing financing arrangements, like social health insurance, household medical expenditures can sometimes be catastrophic.

The threat from climate change to health, especially for the global poor, should also be mentioned. Tackling climate change could be the greatest global health opportunity of the twenty-first century (Watts et al. 2015).

Summing up so far, people all over the world are living longer and better lives on average; inequalities around these averages are decreasing substantially, while some countries and social groups within each country are falling behind. Lack of universal public financing of health systems also pushes people into poverty or catastrophic health expenditures. Many countries have achieved universal health coverage, but for those that have not, health care financing reform is today seen as the strongest concept public health has to offer to improve health and protect against health-related poverty (Chan 2016). The threat from climate change is another challenge. With existing effective medical technologies, we have enough knowledge to vastly improve global health, yet the health systems, their organization, and their financing leave much to be improved. This is where social science can contribute to health care. Countries not only need doctors and nurses; health policy today is increasingly being developed by insights from demographers, economists, social epidemiologists, statisticians, and political scientists.

22.5.5 The Role of Markets and the State

Most developed countries, and all OECD countries, now have universal health coverage (WHO 2010). The level of care varies, and health systems are organized and financed in different ways, but common to all countries is that they provide essential health services to all citizens free of charge or with relatively small co-payments (Chisholm and Evans 2010). Financing of services comes from pooled resources, financed either through tax revenue as in single payer systems such as the NHS in the UK or through compulsory health insurance as in Germany, the Netherlands, or the USA. Many of these countries also have private health insurance and private providers of services, but payment for services comes primarily from pooled resources. If direct out-of-pocket health expenditures exceed 20–30 percent of total health expenditures, countries will hardly qualify as having universal health coverage (WHO 2010).

It is important to note that universal health coverage systems are fundamentally meant to be redistributive. Prepayment mechanisms have the potential to address many of the shortcomings associated with out-of-pocket payments, thus promoting both access to services and financial risk protection. This is primarily because such mechanisms allow for pooling of funds and consequently pooling of risk. Evidence at all national income levels shows that mandatory contribution mechanisms (taxation or mandatory social health insurance) are more efficient than voluntary mechanisms (WHO 2010; Cotlear et al. 2015). UHC will normally require a degree of financial subsidy not only from the better-off to the worse-off but also from the young and healthy to the elderly and ill.

Thus, the state has a fundamental role in securing universal health coverage, even in systems with mixed private and public financing and service provision. This view is now fairly well established (although still a matter of debate in some parts of academia) and in 2005, all member states of the WHO endorsed UHC as a central goal (WHO 2005).

This emerging consensus is supported by two fundamentally different arguments from the social sciences that both reinforce each other. The first is an economic argument about failure in health insurance markets; the second is an argument from political theory about the moral right to health and health care.

In a seminal paper, the economist Kenneth Arrow demonstrated how health insurance behaves differently from other goods normally distributed in the market (Arrow 1963). This argument has now become widely accepted, with some variations, in standard textbooks in health economics. The market for health services involves three principal actors: the patient, the doctor, and third-party payers. Three factors – moral hazard, decisions under conditions of uncertainty, and asymmetrical information between the actors – are likely to cause market failure in the health insurance market. Voluntary health insurance will lead to adverse selection, so that the young and healthy will get lower premiums and those with pre-existing conditions or the elderly at higher risk will be excluded or get higher premiums. In the absence of collective risk-pooling, premiums for low-risk patients will remain low, while premiums for those who really need health care will increase to the point where market failure and inefficiencies will occur. The state must, therefore, regulate this market and make risk-pooling mandatory. The upshot is that medical need should determine health benefits, not risk or ability to pay.

The argument for a moral right to health and health services arrives at the same conclusion, namely that access to health services should be allocated according to need and not ability to pay, but from a different direction. The arguments have been presented by many, but perhaps most effectively by political theorists in the social justice tradition such as Norman Daniels and Amartya Sen. Building on the work of John Rawls, but extending his theory, Daniels has argued that health and health care are special goods and that normal health is a necessary, if not sufficient, condition for citizens to achieve equality of opportunity to develop and fulfill a rational life plan. Citizens, therefore, have a moral right to health and, insofar as health services contribute to equality of opportunity, a right to health care (Daniels 1985). For Sen, good health and avoidance of premature mortality are key human capabilities that everyone has reason to want and are hence fundamental to achieving freedom. Health has both intrinsic and instrumental value (Sen 2002).

For both, it should be noted, the importance of health equity not only justifies a right to health care but also includes a concern for fair distribution of the social determinants of health. Their definitions of fairness also include fair process (Sen 2002, 2009; Daniels and Sabin 2008). Health is an important element of equality of opportunities and freedoms, and if the market fails to distribute health fairly, social justice requires that society's basic institutions and their governance contribute to that goal.

22.5.6 Constructive Contributions from the Social Sciences

Previous sections have already discussed major findings by demographers and statisticians; their analytic tools, such as life tables, are used for the estimation of life expectancy and inequalities in mortality. Two other important contributions demonstrate how they have helped to shape health policies toward social progress.

According to the UN Population Division's 2015 medium estimate of population growth, the world population will grow to 8.5 billion people by 2030, and to 9.7 billion people by the year 2050 (UNPD 2015). Especially in Sub-Saharan Africa, fertility rates are still very high; the average woman has more than five children over her lifetime (UNPD 2015). Fertility can be reduced by two types of policies: first, by educating women and girls and providing access to modern contraceptives; second, all the evidence demonstrates that reduced child mortality is followed by reduced fertility rates (Preston, Heuveline, and Guillot 2000; UNPD 2015). The latter insight has been influential in shaping global health policies.

The demographic dividend is another key concept of high relevance for national health policy (Bloom and Canning 2000). Countries with a high ratio of working populations to dependent populations (children and the elderly) can benefit from the demographic dividend. Countries with a high proportion of children will, after they experience falling fertility rates, see a demographic shift, with a higher proportion of people of working age and still a low proportion of elderly people. If countries invest well in health care for their children, and education and employment opportunities for the young, there is a window of opportunity for harnessing the benefits of the demographic dividend. This positive development can be hampered or missed through inappropriate policies. Poverty and income affect health, but investing wisely in health can also affect income, growth, and prosperity (Sachs 2015).

In the last 25 years, the contributions from economists have been substantial, not only through the World Bank and IMF's influence on cutting public expenditures, which was deeply felt in the health sectors of low-income countries in the 1990s, leading to increased reliance on user fees and in some countries deteriorating health systems, but also through the shaping of health reforms such as experiments on quasi-markets in the British NHS, New Zealand, and other countries in the early 1990s. But economists have also made some remarkable and constructive contributions to health.

In a famous interview in *The New Yorker*, Bill Gates told the story of what influenced him the most when deciding how to spend his wealth when moving into philanthropy (Specter 2005). It was a small report from the World Bank called *Investing in Health* (World Bank 1993), commissioned by chief economist Lawrence H. Summers and written by a team that included a young doctor and health economist, Chris Murray, and economist Dean Jamison as senior lead author. This small report has been hugely influential, also beyond the Gates Foundation, perhaps because it tried to answer three questions of great concern for global and national health policies: (1) How can the burden of disease in a country and the world be measured? (2) Why should finance ministers invest in the health sector? (3) How should the resources within the sector be allocated?

The burden of disease can be measured by disability-adjusted life years (DALYs) lost, the report suggested, measured against a norm defined by what the best-performing country at that time, Japan, had achieved. The DALY captures not only life years lost from disease, but also morbidity such as living with depression or a lost limb. Today, the Global Burden of Disease Project has become one of the key starting points for nearly all discussions of health policy (IHME 2016): which conditions and risk factors are associated with the largest disease burden?

Second, the report provided a convincing analysis that investing in health could yield substantial economic returns. Health care is not only an expenditure for the ministries of finance. If resources are invested wisely, the population can live longer and more productive lives. Healthy children learn better, malaria prevention reduces absenteeism and increases productivity, and public finance protects against catastrophic health expenditures.

Third, resource allocation within the health sector should aim at health maximization, the report suggested, and the best tool for identifying which interventions and policies to invest in is cost-effectiveness analysis. By modeling the cost per DALY averted, the most efficient ranking of services can be determined. The report also proposed that countries should invest in packages of essential public health interventions and clinical services that would yield the maximum health benefit.

In 2013, 20 years later, Larry Summers and Dean Jamison were asked to revisit the analysis and formed the Lancet Commission on Investing in Health. Their report, *Global Health 2035*, had four conclusions that are relevant for social progress (Jamison et al. 2013). First, a "grand convergence" in mortality associated with reproductive, child, maternal, and infectious conditions is achievable by 2035. Second, the returns to investment in health are even greater than originally estimated. By using the full-income account and by combining demographic estimates of increasing life expectancy with the value of a statistical life, they estimated that for every dollar invested in essential interventions for child, maternal, and infectious conditions, the economic benefits are 9 to 20 times higher. Third, they proposed a package of essential interventions of cost-effective, clinical interventions for NCDs and injuries, and, fourth, public policy instruments such as increasing taxes on tobacco and alcohol and reducing subsidies on items such as fossil fuels (which produce air pollutants that cause NCDs).

22.5.7 Distributive Issues and Governance for Better Health Care

The contributions from demographers, social epidemiologists, and economists have been supplemented by those of philosophers and human rights advocates trained in the traditions of political theory. Building on a good understanding of what is known about the major trends in health and its distribution, a key issue is how to allocate scarce resources for health services in a fair and efficient way. While the WHO and the World Bank had earlier championed cost-effectiveness as a key criterion for global and national resource allocation (World Bank 1993; WHO 2012), philosophers and others in the social justice tradition have argued that this approach is insensitive to the distributional aspects of priority-setting (Daniels 2008; Norheim 2016). Health policy needs to go beyond cost-effectiveness and set priorities also with regard for the worse-off (in terms of health and poverty) and for financial risk protection (WHO 2014).

Some even argue that all substantive criteria for priority-setting, and especially cost-effectiveness, are so contested that they should be replaced by a fair and legitimate process (Holm 1998). Others hold that both process and substantive judgments are important (Daniels and Sabin 2008).

The broader democratic processes include better governance for health and public participation. Governments and other relevant institutions can be held accountable for ensuring that proper participatory processes are in place (Potts 2008; Yamin 2008). Yet, few countries have really succeeded in going beyond technocratic approaches to inclusive health policy development. The "political determinants" of health and barriers to global governance, such as power structures and unfair trade agreements, can also hamper social progress (Ottersen et al. 2014).

Better results have been achieved in the area of monitoring and evaluation. Such systems are needed to promote accountability and participation. Several monitoring systems were put in place for the MDGs for health, financial accountability can be improved through National Health Accounts, the Global Burden of Disease is and will be a good source for data monitoring progress toward the SDG for health

(Murray 2015), and the UN system and the World Bank are working together on new monitoring frameworks for health (WHO and World Bank 2015). Countries must follow up and improve their national monitoring systems.

22.5.8 Lessons Learned

As mentioned above, modern medicine and health policy are unique in the sense that they are evidence-based, or at least evidence-informed. Although economic growth and better living standards have substantially improved health, making use of evidence – also from the social sciences – may also have contributed. There has been a clear demand for evidence from the policy arena, and this has enabled legal regulation, pooled resource financing, active governmental agencies, and insurance companies to draw on knowledge, assessments, and proposals for policies from the different social science disciplines.

22.5.9 Conclusion

Demographers have documented substantial improvements in life expectancy and reductions in inequality in longevity, although some countries and social groups within each country are falling behind. The threat from climate change to health, especially for the global poor, could be a challenge for further reductions in health inequality. Resilient health systems may be part of the answer. Global public finance of progressive universal health coverage is justified on both economic and ethical grounds, and economists and ethicists agree that fair and efficient resource allocation is essential to achieve this goal. So are, as political scientists have reminded us, fair process and better governance.

22.6   Development Policy

For the past 40 years the field of economic development has been dominated by the intellectual hegemony of the "Washington Consensus" paradigm – first in a narrower, and then in an expanded version (Williamson 1989; Rodrik 2006). The broader political and social drivers of this hegemony were the loss of credibility of central planning as a mode of economic organization, the success of pro-market political movements (with Thatcherism and Reaganism as early examples and, later, the extraordinary economic success of "Dengism" in China), the fall of the Soviet Union, and the "third wave" of democratization of the 1990s. An added driver has been the central role, over the past half century, of the World Bank, the International Monetary Fund, and some other official multilateral and bilateral institutions in shaping both development thinking and practice; this dual role provided sustained, ongoing momentum for translating the Washington Consensus paradigm into an agenda for action. Riding these waves of history, neoclassical economics and democratic constitutionalism became the dominant frameworks for development scholars and practitioners alike.

But the trouble with intellectual hegemony is that it airbrushes out complexity. In contrast to the Washington Consensus, an alternative view is that development gains come from engaging with developing countries' messy realities, not from seeking to override them with blueprints of best practice (Levy 2014[3]). How has the tension played out in practice between those scholars and practitioners who embrace the dominant development paradigm and those who contest some of its key tenets? Why? This section explores these questions, using the evolving discourses on industrial policy and on "good governance" as illustrative cases.

22.6.1   Industrial Policy: The Level Playing Field Meets the East Asian Miracle

The Washington Consensus was unequivocal that the business environment most conducive to development was one which was "market-friendly" – that provided a "level playing field" for private firms operating within competitive markets, moderate and uniform external tariffs, flexible markets, and light regulation. These elements became a staple of many of the World Bank's structural adjustment programs.

There was, however, a problem. From the 1960s onwards, the stellar development performers were the East Asian tigers. And, as a growing literature explored in depth, the policies which these countries championed could not easily be reconciled with the nostrums of a "level playing field" (Johnson 1982; Wade 1990; Amsden 1992; Chang 1993; Kohli 2004).

Take the example of Korea. Between 1961 and 1987 Korea grew at an average real annual rate of over 6 percent per annum. In the early 1960s, over half the population lived below a minimum threshold of absolute poverty; by the mid-1990s, the proportion had fallen below 4 percent (World Bank 1994). Contrary to the logic of "market-friendliness," during this period the Korean government used top-down political levers to override markets and private decisions in highly targeted discretionary ways.

At the heart of Korea's development success was the relationship between a dominant leader, General Park Chung Hee, and the country's leading private firms, the *chaebol*. In a classic book written in the late 1970s, Leroy Jones and Sakong Il described the relationship as one of "partial mutuality," where one actor (i.e. business) undertakes an action in order either to win goodwill, or to forestall an action by the other participant (i.e. government) which would inflict an even greater loss.[4] As they put it, "In Korea, the dominant partner is unequivocally the government … The success of government requires the success of business … [but] the Korean government can ensure the failure of any businessman, should it care to do so" (Jones and Sakong 1980: 66–68). Control over credit was the "fulcrum … the knowledge that the government can cut off the credit tap at any time is sufficient for the operation of partial mutuality. The threat need only be carried out occasionally" (Jones and Sakong 1980: 109).

---

[3]   This section draws extensively on Levy (2014).

[4]   For a more recent analysis of Korea during the Park period which adds some complexity to the story, even as its central features remain similar, see Kim and Vogel (2011).

The origin of Korea's world-beating shipbuilding industry offers an especially vivid example of how this worked:

> One of the more impressive entrepreneurial feats in Korea was the creation of a world-class shipbuilding firm by Hyundai … International financiers and shipbuilders were no doubt bemused at the pretensions of someone soliciting funds with little more to show than a picture of a lovely sandy beach where the proposed Hyundai dry dock was to be built … Hyundai Chairman Chong persevered only because of the urgings of President Park [who encouraged him by saying "if you only want to do what is easy you'll get no help from me"]. (Jones and Sakong 1980: 357–358)

Among champions of a market-friendly worldview, one initial response was to try and reframe the East Asian approaches in ways that minimized the inconsistencies with "level playing field" nostrums by emphasizing the widely accepted conventional neoclassical economics distinctions between private and public goods, and the role of government in addressing the latter.[5] Gradually, though, the paradigm seemed to move.

In 1994, the World Bank issued a widely-read report on *The East Asian Miracle*. For all its limitations (highlighted by Wade 1996), the report went further than the organization had previously gone in coming to grips with the reality that the successes of at least some East Asian countries' policies were attributable, in part, to the ways in which they overrode markets. At the time, *The East Asian Miracle* seemed to be a landmark – an illustration of the power of sustained efforts on the part of social scientists to bring evidence to bear in a way capable of moving a dominant paradigm. But that was not the end of the story.

In 1997, a financial crisis engulfed Korea along with other East Asian economies. The crisis brought to the light of day corrupt self-dealing among Korea's *chaebol*, banks, politicians, and public officials – thereby exposing a downside of discretionary policies. As it happened, the Korean economy turned around very rapidly, continuing its rapid growth. But the damage had been done.

Over the subsequent decade, the discourse surrounding proactive industrial policy largely disappeared from the mainstream development discourse. The "market-friendly" paradigm enjoyed a renewed reign. The flagship product became the World Bank's Doing Business indicators.[6] Introduced in 2003, these globally comparable measures redirected attention to regulatory rigidities and market-friendly regulatory reforms as the way to accelerate private-sector development. Though often criticized,[7] since their introduction these indicators have taken center stage in dialogue on private-sector development between donors and development policy-makers.

In the wake of the global financial crisis of 2008 (and the appointment of Chinese economist Justin Lin as chief economist of the World Bank) some revisionist thinking vis-à-vis market-friendliness began to resurface. But, to those familiar with the earlier round of the discourse, there was a sad sense of déjà-vu – with the contestation of ideas starting at almost the same place as in the earlier round, and no ground won from earlier battles.

22.6.2   "Good Governance Is Necessary for Development"

Even as the effort to contest the dominant paradigm of a "level playing field" was contained, a broader wave of change swept through the development discourse. During the Cold War era, the discourse surrounding aid was framed exclusively in economic terms – the combination of money, good technical advice, and evident goodwill would provide a sufficient platform for development. Failures in the ways in which governments used aid were not to be spoken about directly. With the fall of the Berlin Wall, these strictures were eased and governance became part of the discourse.

The intellectual ground for such a shift seemingly had been well laid, not only among political economists (who had long focused on structural variables) but within mainstream economic thought. Going back to the 1970s and earlier, there had been a major revival of work on the institutional and political underpinnings of development. Major contributors to the "new institutional economics" included five Nobel prize winners: Douglass North (1982), Elinor Ostrom (1990, 2005), Herbert Simon, Ronald Coase (1937), and Oliver Williamson (1985, 2000). A variety of scholars built on the insights of the new institutional economists to explore how institutions, politics, and economic policy interacted with one another (Acemoglu et al. 2001; North, Wallis, and Weingast 2009; Acemoglu and Robinson 2012; Fukuyama 2012, 2014b).

But these contributions generally took a long-run view. The challenge for practitioners was to translate these insights into practical programs of action.

Three distinct approaches vied for supremacy. The first two fit comfortably with prevailing currents of thinking in the Western development and aid communities. The third, as it turned out, less so.

The approach that posed the least threat to established ways of doing things was a focus on "building state capacity" through training, reform of organizational systems, and the like. But intellectually it was the least defensible. As the World Bank's 2004 World Development Report put it: "If organizational failures are the result of deeper weaknesses in institutional arrangements (weak political commitment, unclear objectives, no enforceability), direct attacks on the proximate

---

5   Robert Wade (1996) explored in depth how the World Bank's analytical work responded to the East Asian experience, including a detailed examination of the analytical choices made in the World Bank (1994) study.

6   Details of the Doing Business indicators, including links to a variety of research papers underlying the methodology and published in academic journals, are available at www.doingbusiness.org/methodology.

7   One common criticism is of the way in which the indicators seemingly conflate light regulation with better development policy; a second criticism is of their focus on de jure regulation rather than how regulations are experienced de facto by firms.

determinants will fail" (World Bank 2004: 58). Notwithstanding this conclusion, technocratic programs of capacity building continue to be widely supported by donors (World Bank 2008).

The second approach was especially well aligned with the tenor of the times in the aftermath of the Cold War. This approach comprised the embrace of the notion that good governance was necessary for development. In their widely read book *Why Nations Fail*, Daron Acemoglu and James Robinson argued (notwithstanding the "short-term" realities of East Asian authoritarian development) that the historical evidence signaled that sustainable development needed democracy. As they put it:

> It is the societies with inclusive institutions that have grown over the past 300 years and have become relatively rich today … Nations can take steps toward prosperity by transforming their institutions from extractive to inclusive … Authoritarian growth is neither desirable nor viable in the long run, and thus should not receive the endorsement of the international community as a template for nations in LAC, Asia and Africa … Attempting to engineer prosperity without confronting the root cause of the problems – extractive institutions and the politics that keeps them in place – is unlikely to bear fruit. (Acemoglu and Robinson 2012: 436, 444, 446, 450)

The World Bank's 2004 World Development Report translated generalized advocacy of "good governance" into a detailed set of micro-level prescriptions. Its point of departure was the logic of hierarchy – a logic in which "principals" set goals to be implemented by "agents," with the principal–agent relationships organized to assure alignment of the actions of the agents with the goals of the principals. The 2004 report laid out in detail the logic of a "long route of accountability" – an impersonal, institutionally robust chain of authority and delegation between successive "principals" and "agents" – as the pathway for achieving development results. The long route of good governance generally incorporated the following:

- An enabling environment that protects human rights, as well as rights to property, via the rule of law;
- Political leaders who take hold of the reins of executive authority, and translate their general vision for the country into a strategy for action and allocation of public resources;
- Capable bureaucracies, staffed by public officials committed to the achievement of social goals, with well-defined roles and responsibilities, and transparent and predictable decision-making – plus robust internal arrangements for monitoring how effectively resources are used;
- Front-line service providers (public, NGO, or private) who take responsibility for delivering on these priorities;
- Accountability of public officials and politicians to the citizens that they are intended to serve through electoral and other

oversight arrangements – at national and local levels, and at the service-provision front line;
- Keeping corruption to a minimum – and, when it is discovered, meeting it with the sanction of law;
- Most broadly, assurance that the overall public order is broadly accepted as "legitimate" by the vast majority of society.

The above translated seamlessly into an ambitious program of action which, especially in the aftermath of the Cold War, aligned well with prevailing conceptions of how polities and bureaucracies should be organized: foster democratic accountability; construct a clear division of labor between politicians responsible for goal-setting and bureaucracies responsible for implementation; build efficient bureaucracies along hierarchical lines codified in the early twentieth century by Max Weber (combined, some argued, with the more high-powered incentives for performance associated with the "new public management" (Pollitt and Bouckaert 2011); and strengthen the justice system and other checks-and-balances institutions. Insofar as a chain is only as strong as its weakest link, simultaneous action was called for on multiple fronts.

Other researchers, however, drew very different implications from a long-run view of history than the nostrum that "good governance is necessary for development" – namely that weaknesses in formal governance institutions are part of the reality of underdevelopment, and that institutional improvements come slowly (North, Wallis, and Weingast 2009; North et al. 2013).[8] The development journey is one not only from low income to high income but from weak to progressively stronger institutions. As Douglass North, and co-authors John Wallis and Barry Weingast put it:

> Societies do not jump directly from personal to impersonal relationships; rather, it is a long process … Transplanting institutions and policies cannot produce economic development. Indeed, to the extent that these institutions are forced onto societies by international or domestic pressure but do not conform to existing beliefs about economic, political, social and cultural systems, the new institutions are likely to work less well than the ones they replace. Worse, if these institutions undermine the political arrangements maintaining political stability, these new institutions may unleash disorder, making the society significantly worse off. (North et al. 2009: 32, 264–265)

Consistent with these latter insights, the third approach to integrating governance and development used the new openness to institutional analysis to call for "politically smart," problem-driven approaches to development – to explicitly incorporate political and institutional constraints into the design and implementation of development policies. There have been multiple contributions (Pritchett, Woolcock, and Andrews 2010; Andrews 2013; Booth and Cammack 2013; Fritz, Levy, and Ort 2014; Levy 2014).[9] While they differ in their emphases, all share the following features:

---

[8]   Fukuyama (2012, 2014) and Pritchett and de Weijer (2010) calculated that even if one assumed the most rapid rates of institutional improvement that have ever been observed historically, it would take over two decades for low-income and fragile Sierra Leone to reach levels of institutional capability approximating those of less-low-income but nonetheless institutionally imperfect Ghana.

[9]   All of these are in the spirit of the path-breaking earlier effort by Hausmann, Rodrik, and Velasco (2008). For an example of an earlier generation of work which made a parallel argument to some of the recent contributions, see Lindblom (1959).

- An insistence that the appropriate point of departure for engagement is the way things actually are on the ground – not some normative vision of how they should be;
- A focus on working to solve very specific development problems – moving away from a preoccupation with longer-term reforms of broader systems and processes, where results are long in coming and hard to discern, and where the risks are high of altering only formal, de jure structures, with little effect on de facto realities;
- An emphasis on ongoing learning – in recognition that no blueprint can adequately capture the complex reality of a specific setting, and thus that implementation must inevitably involve a process of iterative adaptation.

It would be nice to be able to report that scholarly input has been helpful in resolving the contestation among these distinct approaches. But, as of this writing, this has not happened. Instead, each continues to operate in its own parallel universe: on the one hand, a sweeping, triumphalist, bracingly straightforward, and (at least for some) ideologically comfortable set of prescriptions; on the other, an embrace of messiness, historical contingency, and an ongoing search for ways forward across a variety of distinct contexts.

22.6.3   What Accounts for These Patterns?

The industrial policy and good governance discourses share a common pattern. In both, the discourse quickly (and in ways that were premature in light of the weight of evidence) locked into a dominant narrative which then turned out to be difficult to dislodge – even in the face of evidence to the contrary. The reasons for this are multiple – some good, some less so.

The good reasons for this pattern of discourse can be summarized by the aphorism that "if you don't know where you are going, you will never get there." "Good governance" and a "level playing field business environment" are normatively valued descriptors of how, at their best, high-income economies function. (Note, though, that a "level playing field" need not imply limited regulation.) Viewed through such a lens, descriptions of "best practices" thus function as guideposts on a journey – supporting navigation in ways akin to the North Star, as useful points of reference, if only of limited relevance in addressing immediate challenges. (For many practitioners, a further strength of advocating this route is that it seemingly avoids some especially dangerous hazards of predation and capture, associated with discretionary policies of a kind that can be introduced under the cover of "East Asian Miracle"-style activism.)

But "best practice" approaches can be abused. They risk locking in narrow ways of seeing – a preoccupation with technical ("engineering") conceptions to the neglect of more complex systems ("evolutionary") approaches to thinking of change as an adaptive process. If abused, they can be an invitation to arrogance – certainty as to what should be done, and judgmentalism when things do not work out as intended, rather than reflection as to the reasons why they did not.

"Best practices" thinking also privileges a role for global experts, their specialist skills, and their prescriptions. Moreover, much of this global expertise is housed within international organizations, which are constrained in their analyses and prescriptions by the political positions of their member countries. As noted in the introduction, these global experts and the international organizations within which they work are influential in shaping the development discourse. Insofar as they are resistant to change, this risks slowing the broader evolution of the development discourse in response to the accumulation of evidence.

In their book *Development Aid Confronts Politics*, suggestively subtitled *The Almost Revolution*, Tom Carothers and Diane de Gramont (2013) reviewed in detail the track record of efforts to introduce "politically smart" approaches into the toolkit of development agencies. They concluded that:

> Politically informed methods imply a whole set of operational characteristics – such as flexibility, open-endedness, toleration of uncertainty, labor intensiveness, significant investments in preparatory analysis, and devolution of control – that cut directly against many of the central imperatives and habits of mainstream aid organizations … The established edifice of institutional mindsets and mechanisms that control how aid is carried out has considerable staying power … It tends to dilute what new methods are put in place, leading, for example to superficial political economy analyses or the reduction of bottom-up assistance into technocratic exercises that avoid core political obstacles. (Carothers and Gramont 2013: 264)

Perhaps even more fundamentally, both the "market-friendly" and the "good governance" discourses support a preoccupation with challenges of improving economic efficiency, moving to the back-burner concerns about the relationship between equity and development (Kanbur 2016a). This affinity is obvious vis-à-vis "market-friendliness." But there is more to be said as to how the affinity plays out vis-à-vis "good governance."

On its surface, the good governance discourse is an uplifting one, an affirmation of the deepest values of the Western Enlightenment. But, depending on how it is used, it could become a basis for opposing proactive policies in a way that obscures any ideological preconception that might be at work. Evidence of complexity could be interpreted not as a reflection of the inevitable messiness of fostering change, but as the basis for a "disappointed" conclusion that government failure is inevitable, so ambitious reforms should not be attempted. (Perhaps this was why "good governance" was embraced so wholeheartedly by America's so-called neoconservatives.)

To be sure, governments can fail, sometimes disastrously so – and sometimes, indeed, by being destroyed from within by predatory kleptocrats. But there is a vast gray area between, at one end of the spectrum, idealized notions of good governance and, at the other, predatory kleptocracy. A preoccupation with institutional reforms that foster "good governance" risks shutting down the space between the extremes – and with it the encouragement to explore creative approaches through which government and society might address some of development's knottiest challenges.

22.6.4   "Possibilism" versus the Rhetoric of Intransigence

Both of the examples considered in this section describe a process in which a dominant paradigm takes hold, in a way that goes beyond the evidence, and then pushes back against efforts to add complexity, to soften the edges of certainty, to open up room for exploration. The forces that drive this process seem general – so the likelihood is high that it will repeat itself well beyond the two examples that are the focus here, and will be evident across a wide variety of areas of development discourse. What broader lessons can we draw from this process as to how social science engages with the development discourse? Albert Hirschman, the great twentieth-century development economist, identified two distinct modes of engagement.

One mode is to reinforce the dominant paradigm with what Hirschman called "the rhetoric of intransigence."[10] Insofar as the dominant paradigm contains more than an element of truth (indeed may reflect a central tendency along some important dimensions), research can provide a powerful buttress for the dominant views. Hirschman identifies three characteristic rhetorical devices that can be used to shut down space for contestation, and that can be implicit in programs of research: the "perversity thesis" (wherein "any purposive action to improve some feature of the political, social or economic order only serves to exacerbate the condition one wishes to remedy"); the "futility thesis" (wherein "attempts at social transformation will be unavailing … will fail to 'make a dent' "); and the "jeopardy thesis" (wherein "the proposed change endangers some previous, precious accomplishment") (Hirschman 1991: 7). Much social science research over the past four decades (especially among neoclassically trained economists) has functioned in one of these three ways. An alternative mode is in the spirit of what Hirschman described as "possibilism":

> Most social scientists conceive it as their exclusive task to discover and stress regularities, stable relationships, and uniform sequences. This is obviously an essential search … But there is a special room for the opposite type of endeavor … To perceive an entirely new way of turning a historical corner … to widen the limits of what is or is perceived to be possible … figuring out avenues of escape from exaggerated notions of absolute obstacles, imaginary dilemmas and one-way sequences. (Hirschman 1971)

The two examples in this section suggest that, for almost four decades, the first of Hirschman's two modes – that is, the rhetoric of intransigence – has held sway. To be sure, clarity can be bracing; arguably, the Washington Consensus prescriptions have yielded substantial gains for global development. But the development (and global) challenges that increasingly are coming to the forefront are ones for which the "rhetoric of intransigence" is unhelpful: fostering inclusive economies, facilitating collective action to provide public goods, and protecting the collective commons. Perhaps coming decades will be a time for Hirschman's second mode of discourse, for "a more democracy-friendly kind of dialogue … to move public discourse beyond extreme, intransigent postures … with the hope that in the process …

participants engage in meaningful discussion, ready to modify initially held opinions in the light of other arguments and new information" (Hirschman 1991: 167–170).

22.7   Science and Technology

Change for the good is often thought to begin with making something new, and in this respect innovation is a starting motor of progress. Technological change is central to innovation, although perceptive observers have long noted that innovation does not necessarily begin in the technical sphere. In his influential theory of the "cultural lag," the sociologist William Ogburn (1957: 171) noted that the variable precipitating a lag could be "technological, economic, political, ideological, or anything else." Ogburn's thinking on the subject dates from the 1920s. Yet, science and technology continue to maintain a privileged position in common-sense understandings of innovation – so much so that, as observed by the anthropologist Andrew Barry (1999), invention is usually regarded as synonymous with *technical* invention, whereas society is seen as a source of inertia.

Basic indicators of social progress appear to confirm the conventional wisdom. During and after the Industrial Revolution, discoveries about nature's workings, translated into industry and commerce, liberated human lives from the condition that Thomas Hobbes (1996 [1651]) memorably deplored as "solitary, poor, nasty, brutish and short." The long, pleasurable, and on the whole productive lives led by the more fortunate members of today's global societies are usually attributed to the technological breakthroughs of the past two hundred years: the steam engine, electrification, the internal combustion engine, antibiotics, pesticides, transistors, the contraceptive pill, the Green Revolution, genetic engineering, and personal computing. In all of these cases, innovation seems to have followed a linear trajectory, from a flash of scientific insight to transformative technological applications to products that reach and materially aid millions, even billions, of people.

Investigations of the practices of science and technology over the past 50 years, however, have complicated that linear model of innovation. First, the progression from idea to application to distribution and uptake is far from simple or smooth. In place of linearity, researchers uncovered more complex webs of interaction that require scientists and engineers to engage with a wide variety of social institutions and actors whose contributions also shape the courses of innovation. Second, socially beneficial innovations do not necessarily originate at the laboratory bench, and the hypothesis that scientific knowledge is the only kind of knowledge that gives rise to progressive innovation has been repeatedly refuted. Third, from the standpoint of social progress, not all that is scientifically or technologically new has proved to be beneficial; nor, given competing technological solutions for a social problem, does the best option always win out in the marketplace. A homely example is the QWERTY typewriter keyboard (David 1985), which persists although its arrangement of letters does not maximize the speed or comfort of typing. Social analysis has illuminated some of

---

10   This, according to Hirschman's biographer, Jeremy Adelman (2013: 632) was the title Hirschman wanted to use for one of his last books; his editor, however, persuaded him to maintain the original title, *The Rhetoric of Reaction* (1991).

the reasons for such suboptimal results, and policies for how to make innovation more socially responsible have developed from that work. This section provides a brief overview of relevant literature from one branch of social science research – specifically, science and technology studies (STS) – on each of these points.

22.7.1   Theorizing Innovation

Like other research on innovation,[11] STS scholarship confirms that, contrary to the premise of the linear model, even path-breaking scientific ideas do not directly reshape society. Innovation involves a multiplicity of actors, institutions, materialities, and norms. But how do these elements come together, why do some combinations gain ground more readily than others, and how do the observed dynamics of bringing new socio-technical arrangements into being fit with classical social science theories about structure and agency? Furthermore, under what conditions does innovation lead to social progress as commonly understood? Three broad schools of thought may be discerned within STS: those favoring agency, especially of inventors, users, and policy-makers; those favoring structure, especially pre-established relations between states and markets; and those concerned with ways in which both structure and agency interact with the normative goals of innovation.

These theoretical orientations correlate with well-known views about the dynamics of policy and power. Agent-centered theorists tend to focus on openings for bottom-up action, granting actors from outside official institutions significant power over the direction of innovation. Structuralists, by contrast, see innovation as occurring mainly top-down, under the aegis of already authoritative institutions that should make choices about how to steer science and technology. Interactionists for their part emphasize the interplay of structure and agency in the performance of background norms that should be assessed for their capacity to foster or hinder progressive social innovation.

22.7.2   Innovation from Below

Over the past few decades, evidence has accumulated that innovation is a dispersed and multi-site process requiring the alignment of many actors, institutions, and work routines to change ways of life on a mass scale. Innovative ideas, as ethnographers have shown, often grow out of "technoscientific imaginaries," or beliefs and commitments that contain more than just the germ of a breakthrough scientific discovery (Marcus 1995; also MacKenzie 1998). Different scientific fields, moreover, have their own "epistemic cultures" (Knorr Cetina 1999), marked by distinctive relationships among co-workers and objects of investigation.

Furthermore, the reward structures of science reflect social and political presuppositions that influence the recognition and progress of discovery. Thus, politics routinely intervenes in the selection of Nobel prize winners, introducing subjective elements into the determination of

which discoveries "confer the greatest benefit on mankind" (Friedman 2001). The prize itself ostensibly acknowledges individual brilliance. Thus, a single scientist, Kary Mullis, was recognized as the brain behind polymerase chain reaction (PCR), a technique that revolutionized modern biotechnology by enabling millions of copies of a string of genetic material to be made in a short period of time. Yet, as Paul Rabinow (1997) showed, "making PCR" became possible only by marrying idea with practice and engaging an entire cohort of actors, including private firms, none of whom shared the official scientific glory.

Actor-network theory (ANT) influentially generalizes from case-specific ethnographic studies of individual inventions to paint innovation as a process of building durable networks. Far from bringing worlds into alignment through the force of an idea, ANT depicts a process in which painstaking negotiation and struggle is the rule at every node of the network (Callon 1986). Only through such interactions do innovators achieve the translations that ensure the spread of ideas and practices throughout the network. ANT amplifies on classical sociological accounts of innovation by casting non-human entities, or *actants*, as symmetrically engaged in the production of novelty. Analytically path-breaking in that it expands the range of entities subject to sociological analysis, this move also carries important implications for social policy: it calls attention to the central, though unevenly distributed, role of material resources, such as venture capital and state-of-the-art biomaterials or lab instruments, in enabling innovations that remake society.

Like more traditional theories of innovation, however, ANT still accords a position of crucial importance to the laboratory, not simply as an originator of ideas but as the site where ideas and their material realizations most forcefully join together. Thus, in Bruno Latour's well-known telling, a revolutionary public health technique, the pasteurization of milk, spread throughout France because Pasteur brought the disease-causing microbes into his laboratory, disciplined them, and transformed them into a vaccine that won wide social acceptance (Latour 1988). The lab, in this analysis, was the locus of an innovation that enrolled disparate actors – microbes, cattle, dairy farmers – into a new approach to curing an old problem.

In ANT accounts, scientific and technological actors responsible for putting together the networks of innovation also determine which inventions are most worth pursuing. But inventing can be initiated from below, or perhaps more accurately from the side, by members of a technological workforce operating as active agents and not mere cogs in the system of production. Engineering innovation is rarely a product of individual scientific inspiration, but rather is a result of sustained teamwork in hospitable circumstances, as at the historic Bell Labs, the cradle of many breakthrough technologies grounded in the physical sciences (Narayanamurti and Odumosu 2016). Medical innovation may begin with the discovery of an active molecule but is carried forward by physicians who observe and direct its use in patients. New lines of treatment emerge from off-license prescription by physicians or experimentation by patients who discover unexpected benefits from using licensed drugs for unlicensed purposes. Technology transfer can

---

[11]   This section explicitly does not deal with economic analyses of innovation or the broader body of work in innovation studies. It is limited to literature typically found under the rubric of STS.

become a further motor of innovation if the design of the original systems and devices is "fluid" enough to permit adaptation for local use (de Laet and Law 2000).

In translating ideas from discovery to use, technical innovators may alter their perception of society's needs and, consequently, their research and development priorities. Patient groups, for example, helped transform how French clinical researchers thought about improved treatments for cystic fibrosis (Rabeharisoa and Callon 2004). More generally, patient activists with rare genetic diseases have placed their concerns on the research agenda through strategic enrollment of scientists and even companies, reversing the conventionally imagined direction of innovation from science to capital to society (Stockdale and Terry 2002). In turn, by engaging with new scientific discoveries, social actors may sort themselves into groups that become interactive in the sense proposed by Ian Hacking (1999). For example, as genetic knowledge has advanced, humans' understandings of themselves as genetic beings have begun to loop back and inform, indeed activate, new modes of "biological citizenship" (Rose 2007), with citizens assuming more active responsibility for their bodies.

Technological systems are constructed not only by the supply of ideas and techniques but also, and equally, by the demand side of technology's supply–demand dynamic (Bijker et al. 1987; Bijker 1997). Design choices emerge not simply from the minds of inventors and innovators but in constant interaction with the needs and preferences of those who use the novelties that scientists and engineers produce. Like ANT researchers, investigators of the social construction of technological systems (SCOT) recognize that categories such as "users" or "concerned social groups" may not remain constant throughout the innovation process (Oudshoorn and Pinch 2003). Preferences shift as products acquire new characteristics, partly in response to disaffected customers who demand design changes. Indeed, users can most powerfully shape technology by resisting it, whether the mechanical looms of eighteenth century that the Luddites destroyed or such contested technologies as childhood vaccines, genetically modified (GM) crops, and social media such as Twitter or Facebook.

22.7.3   Innovation from Above

Structuralist accounts of innovation most often originate with historians and sociologists concerned with alliances between capital and government. The state-supported "military-industrial complex" (so designated by US President Dwight D. Eisenhower) has been a major source of innovation, consuming vast amounts of public resources while pursuing a "secluded science" (Callon, Lascoumes, and Barthe 2009), largely shielded from public attention and scholarly critique. Military spending has a pervasive influence on the nature of scientific and technological innovation (Edgerton 2006; Oreskes and Krige 2014). Scientists themselves function sometimes as a "reserve labor force" (Mukerji 1989), supported with public funds so long as they stand by, like the Manhattan Project physicists, to be of service in times of national need. In the computer age, state ambitions of prediction and control shaped the discourses and the subjectivities of scientists engaged in statist projects (Edwards 1996). State interests in having effective military machines may demand additional technical

inventiveness, such as how to measure a weapon's accuracy without using it in practice (MacKenzie 1990). But national interest may blind high-tech organizations from taking a critical look at their own weaknesses, as demonstrated by the tragic explosion of the space shuttle Challenger in 1986 (Vaughan 1996).

If states dominate the world of military innovation, capital enjoys relatively freer rein in the manufacture of new consumer commodities. Even large corporations and global multinationals, however, are constrained by social norms. Historians of technology have long noted that what gets invented often reflects prior orderings of power in society, for example the dynamics of race, class, and gender. The technological artifacts of the modern world "have politics," the political scientist Langdon Winner argued, either because their design solves social problems or because they mirror existing regimes of dominance (Winner 1986). Feminist studies of technology have noted the migration of gender biases into biomedical invention, especially those related to sexuality and reproduction (Oudshoorn 2003; Thompson 2007). Gendered social relations permeate innovation more broadly, through women's representation – or underrepresentation – in the labor force. Thus, many modern inventions that simplified housework easier also heightened expectations of domestic cleanliness and efficiency, making "more work for mother" (Cowan 1985).

Capital's drive to seek out new forms of commodification forces innovation by turning things that were not previously in exchange systems into things that can be bought and sold. The important point for social progress is that the power of commodification is not equally distributed among human societies. Corporate-driven innovation may exacerbate rather than ameliorate inequality (Jasanoff 2016).

The forms of extraction and manipulation associated with recent advances in biological knowledge and technique have aroused particular anxiety about who governs human bodies and selves. The discovery of the structure of DNA, and the industrialization of genetic technologies in agriculture and biomedicine, have underscored unequal power relations in the development of biocapital (Sunder Rajan 2006, 2012; Skloot 2010). First-movers, usually in Northern countries, enjoy distinct advantages in shaping bio-innovation trajectories, from setting research priorities to enrolling populations in poorer countries as research subjects (Petryna 2009). Power imbalances exist even within wealthy states, as exemplified by the contested and ultimately unsuccessful effort by a state-corporate alliance to create the Icelandic Health Sector Database (Rose 2001; Fortun 2008). Biomedical innovation threatens to perpetuate stigmatized categories of race and gender, even though the discourse of genetic discovery claims to have eliminated the basis for such invidious distinctions (Reardon 2004; Epstein 2007; Kahn 2012). Even moves intended to benefit less advantaged societies, such as nutritionally enhanced Golden Rice (Smith 2009), may narrow both the pathways and the opportunities for innovation from the bottom up (Scoones 2006).

Capital's innovative force manifests itself not only in the extraction of new resources, such as human biological materials, but in the extension of the market into areas thought to lie outside commerce and commodification. Many see as progressive the extension of market principles to forms of environmental behavior historically treated as externalities. That policy move, enabled by the burgeoning fields of environmental and ecological economics (Costanza et al. 1997), made it possible to create new markets in chemical and carbon emissions, permitting exchanges among entities not previously deemed commensurable, such as trees and human-built water cooling plants. Exchanges between those who produce "too much" and "too little" of environmental burdens make it possible in theory to reduce the total volume of undesirable by-products such as chemical pollutants and carbon emissions. However, there can be fictions or flaws that enter into the calculations underlying such market-making (MacKenzie 2007). At their limit, economic models operate not as reflections of a real world but as instruments that make the very realities they presume to represent. Market devices are in this special sense "performative" (MacKenzie, Muniesa, and Siu 2008; see also Callon 1998).

In the era of climate change, there is rising demand for innovation in the ways we use and depend on earth systems for our livelihoods and the health of the planet. Whether through a "moonshot" that solves the global energy problems without compromising economic growth,[12] or through countless smaller innovations that may lead to more sustainable ways of living on the earth, the idea of the "technological fix" – or solving society's problems by technological means – has gained a new hold on scientific, engineering, and policy imaginations. STS analysis, however, calls for caution, especially in the design and adoption of one-size-fits-all solutions at a planetary scale.

One strand of the literature focuses on the contingency of models and experiments that underpin forecasts of climate impacts and the unavoidable indeterminacy of what is known (Jasanoff and Wynne 1998). These observations suggest that massive engineering solutions, such as solar radiation management, should be approached with care if not reluctance (Hulme 2014; Stilgoe 2015). Another strand stresses the need for governance structures and processes that allow for ethical deliberation in making large-scale decisions on climate change (Newig, Voss, and Monstadts 2008; Rayner et al. 2013).

22.7.4   Interactive Innovation: The Role of Norms

Agency-based and structure-based theories of scientific and technological innovation have one thing in common. Both presume that innovation's purposes are unproblematic or self-evidently good, such as the need to combat disease and hunger, extend human life, enhance cognitive or physical faculties, and protect people against attacks on their security and wellbeing. Sad, unfortunate, even disastrous outcomes of technological projects are seen, in the light of this assumption, as "unintended consequences" of a trajectory of development whose inbuilt drives are beneficial and thus not open to ethical or moral questioning.

This relatively comfortable understanding of technological change ignores the institutionalized patterns of belief and practices that inscribe norms and values into innovation. STS research has shown that entrenched power structures and belief systems exert a profound influence on the directions of technological innovation. Equally and symmetrically, technological innovation can underwrite and indeed legitimate the structures that define society. This mutual interplay of the social, the scientific, and the material is best described in the idiom of co-production (Jasanoff 2004). That lens for analyzing the world brings to light the normative foundations of technological change, showing how collective imaginations of desirable and undesirable futures – or "sociotechnical imaginaries" (Jasanoff and Kim 2015) – leave their imprint on processes of innovation.

To begin with, the ideas of "innovation" and the "market" are far from neutral. Attempts to realize them naturalize particular definitions and accompanying values, which resist being rethought (Mirowski 2013). Silicon Valley, for example, has lent new luster to "disruptive innovation," an idea conventionally traced back to Joseph Schumpeter's notion of creative destruction. Detached from context, the term sounds like a force of nature that simply rejuvenates, replacing old, worn, and presumably no longer useful or efficient things with newer, improved substitutes. However, examinations of the production of newness offer a constant reminder that disruption, too, is a complex social process, with political implications, such as producing winners and losers, people who gain and people who suffer. Making markets, too, involves, at its core, making things commensurable, hence calculable and exchangeable, and this likewise is far from a value-neutral process (Espeland 1998). Thus, the market that permits trading in carbon was seen by its creators as an ingenious technical solution to climate change. But critics in developing countries saw the like treatment of all emitted carbon as deeply political in that it erased the histories by which some countries became higher emitters, as well as the social inequalities between the poor who generate greenhouse gases through subsistence activities such as farming, and the rich who raise emissions through luxuries such as flying (Agarwal and Narain 1991).

Viewed through the lenses of co-production and socio-technical imaginaries, neither agency nor structure look like independent variables or primary drivers of change. Rather, each is embedded in deep-seated ways of thinking about how things hang together in a given society and how they could be transformed to make the world a better place. Imaginaries, for example, incorporate particular understandings of government's appropriate role and capabilities. Thus, a comparative study of nuclear power in the United States and Korea revealed that the two nations' policies rest on different compacts between state and society (Jasanoff and Kim 2009). In its early, defining years, US nuclear energy policy followed an imaginary of containment premised on expert control of atomic risks; public skepticism, however, led to a de facto moratorium on development after the 1979 Three Mile Island accident. By contrast, South Korea, under the banners of developmental nationalism and technological competitiveness, continued to build power plants even after Chernobyl and eventually positioned itself as a leading exporter of nuclear technology and know-how. Similarly, divergent responses to agricultural and biomedical biotechnologies in the United States, Britain, and Germany reflect cross-cultural differences in public expectations concerning the

---

[12]   For insights into the ways that today's high-tech capitalists conceive of world-changing innovations, see Andrew Revkin's interview with Bill Gates (Revkin 2016).

state's handling of risks and construction of policy-relevant evidence and reason (Jasanoff 2005).

Era-defining ideologies, such as deregulation, privatization, neo-liberalism, or sustainability, can cut across national specificities and create convergences across geopolitical boundaries. For example, the rise of genetics and genomics, coinciding with a global turn toward neoliberal policies, arguably increased worldwide demand for personalized data and individually tailored precision medicine, along with expectations that genetically informed citizens would assume more responsibility for their own health (Rose 2001; 2007). The targeting of the human brain as a major object of research in Europe and the United States in the past decade or two illustrates similar convergences. The imaginary of a zero-carbon future is fueling worldwide investment in renewable energy sources, new modes of transportation, and "smart cities." Yet, socio-technical imaginaries operating at regional, national, and subnational levels keep tempering these global trends and introduce localized differences in research, development priorities, and technological applications (Jasanoff 2005; Jasanoff and Kim 2009, 2015).

22.7.5 Conclusion

Social analysis of science and technology contributes to understanding innovation in two ways: first, by offering a thicker description of all that is involved when one technological order displaces another; second, by problematizing the very concept of novelty, asking for whose purposes and to whose benefit the new order is built. The first line of inquiry focuses attention on the machinery of innovation, drawing attention to its material, economic, and institutional supports. Actor-centered accounts stress the creativity, but also the resistances, involved in pulling together these heterogeneous elements to produce durable innovations that are widely taken up by society. Structuralist analysis, by contrast, emphasizes the durable infrastructures of physical environments, capital, or law that can promote and shore up innovation without remedying underlying imbalances of wealth and power. According to these accounts, innovation steered from the top down mostly tends to perpetuate older topographies of power, such as the gravitational pull of state sovereignty and corporate capital. Both lines of work warn against being too sanguine about the reformist potential of innovation, although actor-centered accounts do suggest that ideas and influence can originate from any point in the networks of production, and therefore favor policies for empowering consumers, users, and workers.

The third STS approach places the purposes of innovation at the center of the analytic lens. Stressing the co-production of epistemic, material, and normative arrangements, this body of work illuminates the shared imaginaries of desired, or undesired, futures whose attainment, or prevention, supplies the impetus for innovation. This inquiry suggests that profound changes in society's visions for itself may change the direction of innovation, perhaps to the point of rendering some imaginable technological pathways (germline gene engineering, nuclear weapons) out of bounds for society. It offers in this way a prescription for aligning innovation more securely with the positive ideals of social progress, by inviting citizens to build and implement socio-technical imaginaries of just, inclusive, and sustainable futures.

22.8 It Could Be Otherwise… Normativity in the Social Sciences

22.8.1 Social Progress and the Rise of the Social Sciences

The idea of social progress is inextricably intertwined with the origins of early modern science, although not in a straightforward way. Progress never was linear. Among historians of science, the genesis of what came to be known as *The Scientific Revolution* and its impact on the birth of the modern world remains a contested topic (Shapin 1996; Orthia 2016). Shunning accounts of the achievements of great scientists in the last decades opened the way for approaches and methods that emphasize contextual factors and the actual practice of science, which emerges as an eminently social undertaking. The striving to uncover the secrets of nature is seen as intermixed with mundane and practical concerns. The image of the lonely genius is replaced by the often dense and heterogeneous global networks that allowed for the exchange of ideas, people, and practices (Mokyr 2016).

Instead of seeing the future predetermined by fate, the radically novel idea became accepted that it could be otherwise. By extending the time horizon, it also became conceivable that the future was open to human intervention. For the first time, the idea of human betterment – including a wide range of material conditions – entered the realm of feasibility through a combination of a better understanding of how nature works and practical know-how applied toward easing the burdens of everyday life. It was the *belief in progress* that kept the enterprise of modern science going. It was the forward-looking, future-oriented project, shared among a distinct minority of scientists, natural philosophers, artisans and craftsman, notaries, apothecaries, and other largely urban dignitaries. They also got the material support of rulers and governments who had been persuaded that they had something to gain. The basis was the shared belief that a systematic exploration of the natural world would yield tangible, material benefits (Roberts 2012). The Baconian program of modern science, with its emphasis on practical utility, was never far away from the sense of awe and wonder that modern science continued to elicit.

The belief in scientific progress, central to the Enlightenment, included the belief that it would also lead toward moral progress (Ferrone 2015; Robertson 2015). In the *Encyclopédie*, D'Alembert offered a historical account of progress – le progrès – of knowledge and human understanding. The idea of *Aufklärung* reached a much broader scope through Kant's famous definition as the freedom to make public use of one's reason with the goal of liberating mankind from its self-imposed immaturity. Human betterment would be achievable through the use of reason. The core idea of the ability of *Rational Man* (yes, mainly men) to solve problems through rational discussion persisted far into the nineteenth century. It was core to liberalism and also the establishment of nation-states as imagined communities of rational people. And it became embedded in international organizations, many of which were founded during the second half of the nineteenth century and led to thinking that wars could be overcome through rational decision-making (Kaiser and Schot 2014). This was one reason World War I turned out to be such a shock.

Les sciences morales, conceived in the eighteenth century, were intended to be equivalent to the natural sciences. The *split* between what was to become the natural sciences and the social sciences was by no means a foregone conclusion (Heilbron 1991). Besides the many other factors accounting for the split, it might well be that the development of the concept of technology turned out to be the dividing wedge. Technology came to be understood as applied science, excluding social and economic aspects, and escaping moral judgment. Technology was believed to be a neutral irresistible force bringing about social progress. The handling of this force was delegated to experts. This may explain why this conception of technology underpinned all major ideologies of the twentieth century, from Marxism to fascism and liberalism, and why technocracy could attach itself to all three, leading to a shared legacy which shaped in a deep way the development of nation-states, international organizations, and their social progress agenda.

In a technocratic framework, the production of scientific knowledge and the making of technology are disconnected from the negative impacts they might generate. The technosciences are to be set free and protected, like the goose whose golden eggs are desired, while it is left to the state (helped by the social sciences) to manage impact and to mediate unwanted consequences. Progress became predominantly equated with *technological* progress – highly visible and tangible. Technological progress would chart the route toward modernization, and social progress would follow in its wake. Negative impacts persisted in the shadow of technological progress as an irritating reminder that neither technology nor technological fixes could solve all social problems. As a consequence, the discussion was no longer whether specific technological options should be promoted (as was still the case with the Luddites, who opposed de-skilling innovation, but certainly not all innovation) but how to use technology for modernizing purposes. More technology simply meant "progress of society." Technology became the measure of men (Adas 1989). This was by no means confined to the Western world. This idea circulated across the globe, and colonizers working with local elites used the colonies as testbeds and laboratories for experimenting with technology and the social progress it would bring (Diogo and van Laak 2016).

Following social progress through measurement and comparison has always kept some affinity with the natural sciences. From what was termed *social physics* by Quetelet to statistics as a well-equipped arm and instrument of the state, the information and knowledge thus gained was predominantly collected in the service of the state and processed to enable it to control its population. Beginning with regular measurements of the height of young men for army recruitment, a host of indicators followed to keep track of almost everything the state was interested in and capable of measuring. Statistics were used to measure the wealth of nations and to quantify people (Hacking 1986; Porter 1995; Scott 1998). Behind the numbers and advances in quantification techniques, serious social-scientific arguments began to lay the theoretical and methodological foundations of some social science disciplines. Economics, originally conceived as political economy, became the dominant social science (even if, at times, it does not want to see itself as a *social* science). The measurements economists use, especially GDP, still function as the dominant yardsticks despite the many objections that have been raised. Criticisms include that value is allocated only to

certain activities, while others, like the costs of pollution, informal care work, but also digitally delivered services, are eliminated completely However, social progress has not only been measured through the economic lens (Stiglitz, Sen, and Fitoussi 2009). Other societally desirable goals and yardsticks continued to be articulated by reformers, political activists, social scientists and engineers, and social movements. One of the latest manifestations are the 17 Sustainable Development Goals (SDGs), agreed upon by the United Nations in 2015. They form part of a wide variety of efforts at the national and international level to employ concepts and instruments that enable collective action with the explicit aim of producing better outcomes for the huge variety of present-day challenges.

Other branches of the social sciences, especially sociology and political science, also became engaged in describing, measuring, analyzing, and proposing policy measures to alleviate the massive fall-out and widely felt consequences of the Industrial Revolution. This epochal transformation which led, in Marx's formulation, to "everything solid melt[ing] into air" spawned waves of social surveys undertaken by doctors, epidemiologists, sociologists, statisticians, and others to find out empirically how the industrial working class was living and working, crowded in rapidly growing dense urban conglomerates. Amid this social turmoil, the shaping of social science disciplines took place (Wagner, Wittrock, and Whitley 1991). At the center was what became known as "the social question," fueled by the fear of the bourgeoisie that the underlying conditions could induce massive and violent uprisings. Eventually, and facilitated by a number of truly remarkable social innovations, such as a comprehensive social insurance system, what was widely perceived and experienced as social progress took form: the rise of the welfare state.

A complement to the idea that negative impacts of science and technology, such as safety, unemployment, or health risks, are not the problem of those who produce them is the assumption that in the end the overall balance will be positive and everyone will benefit. Schumpeter (1942) famously defined innovation as "creative destruction" and rightly saw it as a double-edged sword. But neither he nor his followers went further to ask *who* would end up on the destructed side or which destructions would be shifted to other parts of the world. For Schumpeter, the creative element outweighed the destructive one. Arguably, we can ask the question whether this is still the case. Perhaps the destructive elements of technical change have begun to overshoot the constructive ones (Soete 2013). The immense challenges humanity faces today, including climate change, loss of diversity, nuclear disaster, and deep inequality, carry the danger of massive and irreversible destruction, revolt, and ultimately war, which is highly unlikely to be countered by relying solely on science and technology promoting economic growth and national state inventions. New ways of measuring social progress are badly needed which can account also for longer-term impact and are explicitly inclusive, as well as new practices for incorporating the results into the very process of science and technology development, redirecting it to respond to the SDGs, and by doing so avoiding ex ante some of the negative impacts to emerge.

Historically speaking, the social sciences grew up in Europe in the shadow of the nineteenth-century nation-state. Although the natural

22

sciences also enjoyed a close relationship with the state, especially through their military-industrial connections, the dependence of the social sciences upon the state has always been much stronger, mainly due to the kind of problems they study. However, social scientists also often worked with civil society, social actors, and social movements. The resulting double, and often contradictory, allegiance produced fertile ground for contestation. It continues to foster critical analysis. To this day, taking a critical stand based on tacitly assumed or explicitly expressed values and norms forms part of the identity and self-image of the social sciences. However, since World War II the ongoing professionalization of the social sciences (and humanities) has also led to a greater distance from the state and to a more distanced stance from the idea of practical relevance to societal concerns. This tendency has been exacerbated by the narrowing of "impact" and its academic measurement toward the business-friendly introduction of rankings and citation measures focused solely on scientific excellence.

The upshot of our argument is that if the social sciences are to become more deeply engaged again with enabling social progress, they will also have to engage with science and technology, and innovation, working in close alignment with the natural sciences and engineering disciplines. They will need to convince their colleagues that social progress cannot be disentangled from technological progress, that social progress is built in the choices made for certain technological options, and that questions about potential impact and consequences of a wide and diverse range of possibilities must be injected upstream in a collaborative way. It is in this area that the field of science and technologies studies (STS) has made its greatest contributions: making visible the relationships between and co-construction of the social and the technical and, more recently, nature too. As a consequence, it calls for a democratization of science and technology and new ways of relating democracy to technocracy.

The problems the social sciences face in the twenty-first century are formidable and discussed extensively in the various sections of this chapter: climate change, massive inequalities, global migration, digitalization, transnational workflows, and other factors marking a shift in power between globally operating corporations and the capabilities of traditional national institutions to cope with these challenges. Yet, there is another challenge. Modernization has created a set of socio-technical systems for the provision of energy, mobility, food, health care, water, and more, which have reached certain limits of what they can deliver in a globalized world. Equal access to the services and provisions these systems provide demands a deep transition of the material backbone of our current civilization (Schot and Kanger 2018). This entails moving away from systems built upon abundant availability of fossil fuels.

One main question is who will be responding to this world in transition. The altered relationship between the state and the market has catapulted problems of *governance* to the fore. Many institutions operating today were designed in the past to confront other problems and perform other functions. Their adaptation is slow, and tested knowledge of how to design new institutions, better fitted to resonate with problems of a more intricate and interconnected nature, is in short supply. As governance cannot simply be ordered from above, new alignments among the various stakeholders are needed. It is doubtful,

however, whether the current relationships between state, industry, and civil society mediated by various kinds of scientific-technological experts are sufficiently inclusive, calling again for experiments with novel forms of governance.

The social sciences also have yet to fully come to terms with this world in transition. For example, they will have to develop new concepts which are less state-centric, assuming the nation-state as the natural unit of analysis. This process is well underway. However, they also need to keep up with their empirical database under conditions which have changed dramatically in the era of "big data." Information and empirical data that once were within the tutelage of the state, and hence at the service of the social sciences, have partly, or largely, shifted under the private ownership and control of large corporations like Google and Amazon. Access to an expanding and ever more relevant database, tracking facets of social behavior, that was unavailable before, has come under unexpected restrictions, although not only for the social sciences. Also for this reason, it will be important to forge new alliances with the natural sciences beyond instrumental-utilitarian considerations. As algorithms and computation are rapidly altering our views of how complex systems evolve and function, the social sciences will not remain untouched by these advances. An algorithm reconfigures and adapts to changes in a system that it has created. Algorithms can be very useful in constructing alternatives and opening up to socio-technical imaginaries (Jasanoff and Kim 2015). Social systems as complex adaptive systems cannot be left to the natural sciences alone.

We can summarize this impressionistic account by arguing that a major challenge ahead is the development of a productive close interaction between the social world and the science-based technologies. This calls for a much deeper understanding of the forceful role of science and technology in shaping the present world, while equally understanding how *we*, the social world, create, shape, select, and embed scientific knowledge and technological artifacts into the socio-technical systems in which we live and work. One of the urgent challenges ahead is therefore how to overcome the current split between the social and the natural sciences and reach better alignments across different disciplines and practices. STS have a crucial role to play in this. To succeed, STS will have to address issues of social progress head on and STS scholars will have to become reflexive constructivists engaged in constructing a new world, using the tools developed in their field, but moving beyond a deconstructivist reflex.

22.8.2 Where to Go from Here

As the winds of neoliberalism blow across much of the globe, a new hierarchical split occurs which manifests itself in a horizontal way. It is exemplified by the emergence of an interconnected, highly educated professional elite who have adopted a cosmopolitan lifestyle and easily move across the globe. Their influence extends to policy-making in areas where their interests are involved. The split manifests itself in the growing gap between these elites and all those who claim that they have no say. A growing number of people, including those in the middle class, feel that they have been left behind. They voice their anger and frustration in giving support to populist, right-wing, and nationalistic movements in many countries and, increasingly, also across countries. The "disconnect" between the elites and those who claim to be "the people" has many unforeseen consequences. One is that it has led to a marked decline in the value attached to expertise – be it professional and scientific or simply observing the standards that previously prevailed in public argumentation. The decline in expertise goes far beyond the loss of trust in science which has been deplored for some time. It amounts to the devaluation of the main currency of modernization. It has far-reaching implications for policy advice everywhere. It transcends legitimate questions like "Whose voice is being heard?" or "Whose evidence is being invoked?" in public discussion of policies under contestation. It goes to the heart of the ways in which novel and still precarious forms of governance can be designed and experimented with. Without legitimacy, there can be no institution-building and no institutionalization. The outright and wholesale denigration of expertise represents a serious threat to reshaping policies so that they can meet new challenges. While there is a growing realization that expertise is ubiquitous, the time has come to rethink its role, especially in mediating between knowledge production and application, taking context into account. Empirically, science has a limited function in providing reliable knowledge for practical political purposes. There is a recurrent need to embed the decision-making processes within stakeholders groups originating from outside science (Grundmann 2016).

One of the most pressing concerns for the social sciences is therefore to devise ways in which the legitimate concerns of citizens can enter the various policy arenas. Policies can be fiendishly technical. They are usually framed in complex legal language and regulatory arrangements. The task appears even more overwhelming when citizens are to be invited to inject their socio-technical imaginaries and values into processes and procedures that have not – yet – been designed to incorporate them. These processes are now separated from the development of science and technology itself, as they are part of managing impact. Once more, new ways of developing socio-technical solutions to the problems we face are needed, which reach out and include citizens and social movements. Values frame and inform which options and pieces of information are to be considered or ignored. As public controversies concerning scientific-technological developments have made abundantly clear, contested values cannot be adjudicated by appealing to science either, nor can they be separated from their incorporation into scientific and technological developments. Values are already embedded into choices that have been made and will continue to influence choices to be made in the future. Social scientists are very much aware and self-conscious about projecting their own values into research. Some take pride and even see it as their professional obligation "to be normative." Elaborate methodologies have evolved to straddle the thin line separating professional and ethical standards from personal conviction and advocacy. There are occasions when taking a normative stand and positioning one's advocacy are considered not only legitimate, but necessary. There is also agreement that scientific knowledge, either in the natural sciences or in the social sciences, is not and can never be value-free. There is widespread allegiance to a mutual reinforcement of science and democracy that provides sufficient space for values shared in liberal democracies to enter, inform, and shape scientific discourse (Rosanvallon 2014).

So, are we back to the Enlightenment ideals of rational discourse between engaged citizens or do we have other observations and proposals to add? Citizens are currently included in the making of new technologies and scientific advances in quite unexpected ways. These are the mostly well-educated citizens who have seized the opportunities offered by the thriving ICT sector. On a voluntary basis, they provide data on almost every aspect of interactive social behavior, collective moods, and individual sentiments, together with data on their health, mobility, and consumer habits. The large corporations of GAFA (Google, Amazon, Facebook, Apple) use them for predictive analytics when designing their products. This kind of "engagement" of citizens on a profit-oriented basis, allegedly conducted in their interest, has led to concerns about privacy and surveillance, questions about ownership, access, and the right "to be forgotten." As we noted before, the data are typically proprietary and cannot be accessed by social scientists as of right.

But there also exists a large number of citizens who are excluded or deprived of voicing their concerns, which go beyond a digital divide. They feel evicted by the society they knew. This brings us back to the question of values. In times of disorientation, values often are presented as the only firm anchoring points. Yet, rationales often do not match, and a plurality of values pervades our societies. This needs to be acknowledged if institutions designed for mutual learning and bridging are to be built. One of them could be the new practice of *responsible research and innovation* (Stilgoe, Owen, and Macnaghten 2013); others could build on movements for *open access* and *open innovation*, and, more generally, *citizen science*.

The work of IPSP has been inspired by a belief in value pluralism. There are many plural ways toward achieving social progress and advancing social justice. However, when it comes to the articulation of concrete policies, some areas seem to be legal-technical minefields, underpinned by the vested interests of governments, corporations, and other powerful actors. It is not easy to see how values and norms can be introduced and upheld beyond professing general principles. The test, as always, comes through contestation. Therefore, the work done by courts and a well-functioning legal system is equally crucial, and all the more so at international or transnational level, where the law is "soft" and many policy areas are shrouded in an undefined gray zone.

The overall picture that emerges from analyzing the contributions from the social sciences to policy-making and action is, therefore, one in which their contributions continue to be solid and strong, even if they are not always visible and appreciated. They take place within and are constrained by the specific institutional framework of the policy field in which they operate. As always, context matters. The distribution of social science knowledge in each field also varies considerably. It influences not only the overall balance or lack of power, but also future prospects for the social sciences to "be normative." In other words, the specific situatedness of social scientists in the policy field in which they operate matters. Simultaneously, they work within a given institutional policy context as well as outside and against it. In some fields, and depending on how welcome the incorporation of more normative content is, this leads to open contestation. The appeal to "evidence-based" policies, whether mere rhetoric or seriously intended, cannot and will not provide a solution accepted by all. The questions of who provides evidence and legitimacy, and under which conditions, remain important.

In what turned out to be his last lecture given at the Collège de France, the eminent sociologist Pierre Bourdieu gave a moving testimony of the place of reflexivity in the social sciences, ending with a sketch of "auto-socioanalysis." The social sciences, he argued, enjoy only weak autonomy. They are under greater pressure from outside, and the conditions for their inner autonomy are less favorable. Practical or reformist reflexivity, in contrast to narcissistic reflexivity, consists in "objectifying" the social conditions of possibilities that enable and limit the actual work of the social sciences. In detailed analysis, he exemplified how critical reflexivity proceeds, showing how his own lifelong scientific work – normative by any standard – was fashioned, enabled, and constrained by the structure of the scientific field and the hierarchies as they existed in France at the time. He highlighted the epistemological and practice-oriented differences between points of view, visions, and taking a normative stand. He left space for intuition, the "creative imagination" which arises from social experience that has been subjected to critical analysis. In the end, however, reflexivity only gains effectiveness if it takes root in the collectivities that practice it. In any research group, collective censure is strong, but it can also be liberating – liberating each participant from the "bias" linked to their positions and dispositions (Bourdieu 2001).

In the search for the right kind of governance and ways of being that are more inclusive, to give citizens a chance not only to voice their grievances but to become actively involved, it is worth re-reading Albert O. Hirschman's magistral *Exit, Voice, Loyalty* (Hirschman 1970). We have recently seen unprecedented waves of a kind of *super exit*. It is not only about Brexit. It reveals itself in many places in the frenetic and chaotic desire to escape, a genuine flight from reality toward an undefined, imagined nowhere, colored by nostalgia for a past that never was and seeking certainties that simply do not exist. It can take on more sinister and violent forms when it mixes with political extremism and religious fundamentalism.

One of the main – and decidedly normative – tasks of the social sciences has always been, and is even more so now, to open up toward the realm of possibilities, to show in scientifically plausible ways that *it could be otherwise* (Nowotny 2015). This is a task that goes beyond the technocratic policy options that experts prepare for policy-makers to choose from. It originates from tapping into one's own creative imagination and into collective socio-technical imaginaries. It comes from doing research using scientific methods, and building models when the assumptions on which they are based are critically reflected. It draws from many sources that the social sciences have creatively used in the past and which they continue to interrogate, adapt, and expand.

But this is not sufficient. To open up toward the realm of the possible, the social sciences must stimulate public debate, making room for multiple perspectives, allowing for contestation. What is needed is nothing less than to redefine *voice* in ways that can strongly resonate with and within the diverse and complex policy landscapes. The ultimate goal, however, will be to rearticulate what Hirschman meant by *loyalty* as

the basis for communal identities, solidarity, and action. It is no longer sufficient to express loyalty to a political party, a social group, or the nation-state. This kind of loyalty has been eroded through processes of individualization, marketization, and globalization, reinforced through the effects of social media. What can it be replaced with? Loyalty to whom and to what? This will be an important question for the future and will shape definitions of social progress.

In the nineteenth century, the overriding question for the social sciences was how there could be social order when faced with the economic turmoil following the Industrial Revolution and the political upheavals that gave birth to liberal democracies. In the twenty-first century, any social order must come to terms with globalization and its discontent, with the major ongoing geopolitical shifts and the grappling efforts to avert a further depletion of natural resources for a still-growing world population and their rising aspirations. It is intrinsically intertwined in ever closer processes of co-production with the amazing advances of possibilities offered by science and technology – possibilities that far outnumber what can actually be realized. The challenge for the social sciences consists in imagining, conceptualizing, and designing feasible and effective processes of selection and social shaping that are more inclusive and driven by a commitment to social justice for all. One of the challenges of the twenty-first century for the social sciences will be to redefine *exit*, *voice*, and *loyalty* within a space of possibilities firmly anchored in the normative belief that *it can be otherwise*.

References

Acemoglu, D., and J. Robinson. 2012. *Why Nations Fail*. New York: Crown Books.

Acemoglu, D., S. Johnson, and J. Robinson. 2001. "The Colonial Origins of Comparative Development: An Empirical Investigation." *American Economic Review* 91/5: 1369–1401.

Acemoglu, D., S. Johnson, J. Robinson, and P. Yared. 2005. "Income and Democracy." NBER Working Paper 11205. Cambridge, MA: National Bureau of Economic Research.

Ackerknecht, E.H. 1982. *A Short History of Medicine*. Baltimore, MD: Johns Hopkins University Press.

Ackerman, F., and L. Heinzerling. 2005. *Priceless: On Knowing the Price of Everything and the Value of Nothing*. New York: The New Press.

Adas, Michael. 1989. *Machines as the Measure of Men. Science, Technology and Ideologies of Western Dominance*. Ithaca, NY: Cornell University Press.

Adelman, J. 2013. *Worldly Philosopher: The Odyssey of Albert O. Hirschman*. Princeton, NJ: Princeton University Press.

Adler, M.D., and E.A. Posner. 2006. *New Foundations of Cost–Benefit Analysis*. Cambridge, MA: Harvard University Press.

Agarwal, A., and S. Narain. 1991. *Global Warming in an Unequal World: A Case of Environmental Colonialism*. New Delhi: Centre for Science and Environment.

Amsden, A. 1992. *Asia's Next Giant: South Korea and Late Industrialization*. New York: Oxford University Press.

Andrews, M. 2013. *The Limits of Institutional Reform in Development: Changing Rules for Realistic Institutions*. New York: Cambridge University Press.

Apple, M.W. 1996. *Cultural Politics and Education, The John Dewey Lecture*. New York: Teachers College Press.

Archer, M.S. 1979. *Social Origins of Educational Systems*. London and Beverly Hills, CA: SAGE.

Arrow, K.J. 1963. "Uncertainty and the Welfare Economics of Medical Care." *American Economic Review* 53/5: 941–973.

Atkinson, A.B. 1970. "On the Measurement of Inequality." *Journal of Economic Theory* 2: 244–263.

Atkinson, A.B. 2015. *Inequality: What Can Be Done?* Cambridge, MA: Harvard University Press.

Autor, D., F. Levy, and R. Murnane. 2003. "The Skill Content of Recent Technological Change: An Empirical Exploration." *Quarterly Journal of Economics* 118/4: 1279–1333.

Ayres, I., and J. Braithwaite. 1995. *Responsive Regulation: Transcending the Deregulation Debate*. Oxford: Oxford University Press.

Baland, J.M., and J.P. Platteau. 1996. *Halting Degradation of Natural Resources: Is There a Role for Rural Communities?* Rome: FAO.

Bardach, E., and R.A. Kagan. 1982. *Going by the Book: The Problem of Regulatory Unreasonableness*. Philadelphia: Temple University Press.

Barry, A. 1999. Invention and Inertia. *Cambridge Anthropology* 21/3 : 62–70.

Becker, Gary Stanley. 1973. *Human Capital: A Theoretical and Empirical Analysis, with Special Reference to Education*, third edition. Chicago and London: The University of Chicago Press.

Benavot, A. 1997. "Institutional Approach to the Study of Education," in L. Saha (ed.), *International Encyclopedia of the Sociology of Education*. Oxford: Elsevier Science.

Benavot, A., and P. Riddle. 1988. "The Expansion of Primary Education, 1870–1940: Trends and Issues." *Sociology of Education* 61: 191–210.

Ben-David, J. 1965. "The Scientific Role: The Conditions of its Establishment in Europe." *Minerva* 4/1: 15–54.

Ben-David, J. 1977. *Centers of Learning: Britain, France, Germany, United States: An Essay*. New York: McGraw-Hill.

Bennear, L.S. 2006. "Evaluating Management-Based Regulation: A Valuable Tool in the Regulatory Toolbox?" in C. Coglianese and J. Nash (eds.), *Leveraging the Private Sector: Management-Based Strategies for Improving Environmental Performance*. Washington, DC: Resources for the Future Press.

Bennear, L.S. 2007. "Are Management-Based Regulations Effective? Evidence from State Pollution Prevention Programs." *Journal of Policy Analysis and Management* 26/2: 327–348.

Bennear, L.S. 2008. "What Do We Really Know? The Effect of Reporting Thresholds on Inferences using Environmental Right-to-Know Data." *Regulation & Governance* 2/3: 293–315.

Bennear, L.S., and S.M. Olmstead. 2008. "The Impacts of the 'Right to Know': Information Disclosure and the Violation of Drinking Water Standards." *Journal of Environmental Economics and Management* 56/2: 117–130.

Benson, L., I.R. Harkavy, and J.L. Puckett. 2007. *Dewey's Dream: Universities and Democracies in an Age of Education Reform: Civil Society, Public Schools, and Democratic Citizenship*. Philadelphia: Temple University Press.

Bernanke, B. 2015. *The Courage to Act: A Memoir of a Crisis and Its Aftermath*. New York and London: W.W. Norton & Company.

Bhagwati, J. 1970. *India: Planning for Industrialization: Industrialization and trade policies since 1951*. Oxford: Oxford University Press.

Biesta, G., M. De Bie, and D. Wildemeersch. 2014. *Civic Learning, Democratic Citizenship and the Public Sphere*. Dordrecht: Springer.

Bijker, W. 1997. *Of Bicycles, Bakelites, and Bulbs: Toward a Theory of Sociotechnical Change*. Cambridge, MA: MIT Press.

Bijker, W., T. Pinch, and T. Hughes. (eds.) 1987. *The Social Construction of Technological Systems*. Cambridge, MA: MIT Press.

Black, J. 2008. *Risk-Based Regulation: Choices, Practices and Lessons being Learned*. Paris: OECD.

Bloom, D.E., and D. Canning. 2000. "The Health and Wealth of Nations." *Science* 287: 1207–1209.

Booth, D., and D. Cammack. 2013. *Governance for Development in Africa: Solving Collective Action Problems*. London: Zed Books.

Botticini, M., and Z. Eckstein. 2012. *The Chosen Few*. Princeton, NJ: Princeton University Press.

Bounds, G. 2010. "Challenges to Designing Regulatory Policy Frameworks to Manage Risks," in *Risks and Regulatory Policy: Improving the Governance of Risk*. Paris: OECD.

Bourdieu, P. 2001. *Science de la science et réflexivité*. Paris: Raisons d'agir éditions.

Bourdieu, P., and J.C. Passeron. 1970. *La reproduction; éléments pour une théorie du système d'enseignement*. Paris: éditions de Minuit.

Bowles, F.H., and H. Gintis. 1973. *Schooling in Capitalist America*. New York: Basic Books.

Briggs, A. 1959. *The Making of Modern England 1783–1867: The Age of Improvement*. New York: Harper & Row Torchbooks.

British Academy. 2009. "Letter to Her Majesty the Queen." www.britac.ac.uk/news/newsrelease-economy.cfm.

Bronsteen, J., C. Buccafusco, and J.S. Masur. 2013. "Well-Being Analysis vs. Cost–Benefit Analysis." *Duke Law Journal* 62: 1603–1689.

Büthe, T. 2010. "Private Regulation in the Global Economy: A (P)review." *Business and Politics* 12/3: 1–38.

Callon, M. 1986. "Some Elements of a Sociology of Translation: Domestication of the Scallops and the Fishermen of St. Brieuc Bay," in J. Law (ed.), *Power, Action, and Belief: A New Sociology of Knowledge?* London: Routledge and Kegan Paul.

Callon, M. (ed.) 1998. *The Laws of the Markets*. Oxford: Blackwell.

Callon, M., P. Lascoumes, and Y. Barthe. 2009. *Acting in an Uncertain World: An Essay on Technical Democracy*. Cambridge, MA: MIT Press.

Campbell, F. A., C. T. Ramey, E. Pungello, J. Sparling, and S. Miller-Johnson. 2002. "Early Childhood Education: Young Adult Outcomes from the Abecedarian Project." *Applied Developmental Science* 6/1: 42–57.

Carothers, T., and D. de Gramont. 2013. *Development Aid Confronts Politics: The Almost Revolution*. Washington, DC: Carnegie Endowment for International Peace.

Cashore, B.W., G. Auld, and G.D. Newsom. 2004. *Governing through Markets: Forest Certification and the Emergence of Non-state Authority*. New Haven, CT: Yale University Press.

Century, J., and A. Cassata. 2016. "Implementation Research: Finding Common Ground on What, How, Why, Where and Who." *Review on Research in Education* 40/1: 170–215.

Cerych, L., P.A. Sabatier, and European Institute of Education and Social Policy. 1986. *Great Expectations and Mixed Performance: The Implementation of Higher Education Reforms in Europe*. Stoke-on-Trent: Trentham.

Chan, M. 2016. "Making Fair Choices on the Path to Universal Health Coverage." *Health Systems & Reform* 2/1: 5–7.

Chang, H.-J. 1993. "The Political Economy of Industrial Policy in Korea." *Cambridge Journal of Economics* 17/2: 131–157.

Chetty, R., M. Stepner, S. Abraham, et al. 2016. "The Association between Income and Life Expectancy in the United States, 2001–2014." *JAMA* 315/16: 1750–1766.

Chisholm, D., and D. Evans. 2010. "Improving Health System Efficiency as a Means of Moving towards Universal Coverage." Background paper 28 to World Health Report 2010, *Health System Financing: The Path to Universal Coverage*. Geneva: WHO.

Churchill, W. 1929. House of Commons, 227 HC Deb., Hansard.

Clark, B.R. 1987. *The Problem of Complexity in Modern Higher Education*. Los Angeles: Graduate School of Education, University of California, Los Angeles.

Clarke-Stewart, A., and V.D. Allhusen. 2005. *What We Know About Childcare*. Cambridge, MA: Harvard University Press.

Coase, R.H 1937. "The Nature of the Firm." *Economica* 4/16: 386–405.

Coase, R.H. 1960. "The Problem of Social Cost," in C. Gopalkrishnan (ed.), 2000, *Classic Papers in Natural Resource Economics*. Houndmills, Hampshire: Palgrave Macmillan.

Coglianese, C. 2003. "Is Satisfaction Success? Evaluating Public Participation in Regulatory Policymaking," in R. O'Leary and L. Bingham (eds.), *The Promise and Performance of Environmental Conflict Resolution*. Washington, DC: Resources for the Future.

Coglianese, C. 2017. "The Limits of Performance-Based Regulation." *Michigan Journal of Law Reform* 50: 525–563.

Coglianese, C., and D. Lazer. 2003. "Management-Based Regulation: Prescribing Private Management to Achieve Public Goals." *Law & Society Review* 37/4: 691–730.

Coglianese, C., and G.E. Marchant. 2004. "Shifting Sands: The Limits of Science in Setting Risk Standards." *University of Pennsylvania Law Review* 152/4: 1255–1360.

Coglianese, C., and J. Nash. 2014. "Performance Track's Postmortem: Lessons from the Rise and Fall of EPA's 'Flagship' Voluntary Program." *Harvard Environmental Law Review* 38: 14–18.

Coglianese, C., J. Nash, and T. Olmstead. 2003. "Performance-Based Regulation: Prospects and Limitations in Health, Safety, and Environmental Protection." *Administrative Law Review* 55: 705–729.

Cole, L.W., and S.R. Foster. 2001. *From the Ground Up: Environmental Racism and the Rise of the Environmental Justice Movement*. New York: NYU Press.

Coleman, J.S. 1988. "Social Capital in the Creation of Human Capital." *The American Journal of Sociology* 94 (Supplement: Organizations and

Institutions: Sociological and Economic Approaches to the Analysis of Social Structure): S95–S120.

Collins, R. 1979. *The Credential Society*. New York: Academic Press.

Commission on Growth and Development. 2008. *The Growth Report*. http://wayback.archive-it.org/2180/20101029231255/www.growthcommission.org/index.php?option=com_content&task=view&id=96&Itemid=169.

Costanza, R., R. d'Arge, R. de Groot, et al. 1997. "The Value of the World's Ecosystem Services and Natural Capital." *Nature* 387: 253–260.

Cotlear, D., S. Nagpal, O.K. Smith, A. Tandon, and R. Cortez. 2015. *Going Universal. How 24 Developing Countries Are Implementing Universal Health Coverage Reforms from the Bottom Up*. Washington, DC: World Bank.

Cowan, R.S. 1985. *More Work for Mother: The Ironies Of Household Technology from the Open Hearth to The Microwave*. New York: Basic Books.

Cropper, M.L., and W.E. Oates. 1992. "Environmental Economics: A Survey." *Journal of Economic Literature* 30/2: 675–740.

Cunha, F., and J.J. Heckman. 2007. "The Technology of Skill Formation." NBER Working Paper 12840. Cambridge, MA: National Bureau of Economic Research.

Cunha, F., J.J. Heckman, L. Lochner, D.V. Masterov, and H. School. 2005. "Interpreting the Evidence on Life Cycle Skill Formation," in E. Hanushek and F. Welch (eds.), *Handbook of the Economics of Education*. Amsterdam: Elsevier.

Dalton, R.J., and C. Welzel. 2014. *The Civic Culture Transformed: From Allegiant to Assertive Citizens*. Cambridge: Cambridge University Press.

Daniels, N. 1985. *Just Health Care*. New York: Cambridge University Press.

Daniels, N. 2008. *Just Health: Meeting Health Needs Fairly*. Cambridge: Cambridge University Press.

Daniels, N., and J.E. Sabin. 2008. *Setting Limits Fairly: Learning to Share Resources for Health*. Oxford: Oxford University Press.

Darity Jr., W. 2005. *Affirmative Action in Comparative Perspective: Strategies to Combat Ethnic and Racial Exclusion Internationally*. Durham, NC: Sanford Institute of Public Policy, Duke University.

David, P.A. 1985. "Clio and the Economics of QWERTY." *American Economic Review* 75/2: 332–337.

de Laet, M., and A. Mol. 2000. "The Zimbabwe Bush Pump: Mechanics of a Fluid Technology." *Social Studies of Science* 30/2: 225–263.

de Marchi, S., and J.T. Hamilton. 2006. "Assessing the Accuracy of Self-Reported Data: An Evaluation of the Toxics Release Inventory." *Journal of Risk and Uncertainty* 32/1: 57–76.

Deaton, A. 2013. *The Great Escape: Health, Wealth, and the Origins of Inequality*. Princeton, NJ: Princeton University Press.

Dewey, J. 1916. *Democracy and Education: An Introduction to the Philosophy of Education*. New York: The Macmillan Company.

Diogo, M., and D. van Laak. 2016. "Europeans Globalizing," in J. Schot and P. Scranton (eds.), *Making Europe*. London: Palgrave Macmillan.

Doll, R. 1994. "Foreword," in R. Peto, A.D. Lopez, J. Boreham, M. Thun, and C. Heath Jr. (eds.), *Mortality from Smoking in Developed Countries 1950–2000*. Oxford: Oxford University Press.

Driesen, D. 2005. "Distributing the Cost of Environmental, Health, and Safety Protection: The Feasibility Principle, Cost–Benefit Analysis, and Regulatory Reform." *Boston College Environmental Affairs Law Review* 32/1: 34–38.

Durkheim, Émile. 1922. *Éducation et Sociologie*. Edited by Jean-Marie Tremblay. Les Classiques des Sciences Sociales. Chicoutimi: Université du Québec à Chicoutimi.

Early, D.M., K.L. Maxwell, M. Burchinal, et al. 2007. "Teachers' Education, Classroom Quality, and Young Children's Academic Skills: Results from Seven Studies of Preschool Programs." *Child Development* 78/2: 558–580.

Edgerton, D. 2006. *Warfare State: Britain, 1920–1970*. Cambridge: Cambridge University Press.

Edwards, P. 1996. *The Closed World: Computers and the Politics of Discourse in Cold War America*. Cambridge, MA: MIT Press.

Ellickson, R.C. 1986. "Of Coase and Cattle: Dispute Resolution Among Neighbors in Shasta County." *Stanford Law Review* 38: 623–687.

Epstein, S. 2007. *Inclusion: The Politics of Difference in Medical Research*. Chicago: University of Chicago Press.

Espeland, W.N. 1998. *The Struggle for Water: Politics, Rationality, and Identity in the American Southwest*. Chicago: University of Chicago Press.

Ferrone, V. 2015. *The Enlightenment: History of an Idea*. Princeton, NJ: Princeton University Press.

Finkel, A.M., and D. Golding. 1995. *Worst Things First? The Debate over Risk-Based National Environmental Priorities*. Washington, DC: Resources for the Future Press.

Forman, S.G., E.S. Shapiro, R.S. Codding, et al. 2013. "Implementation Science and School Psychology." *School Psychology Quarterly* 28/2: 77–100.

Fortun, M. 2008. *Promising Genomics: Iceland and deCODE Genetics in a World of Speculation*. Berkeley: University of California Press.

Freestone, D., and E. Hey. 1996. "Origins and Development of the Precautionary Principle," in D. Freestone and E. Hey (eds.), *The Precautionary Principle and International Law*. The Hague: Kluwer Law International.

Freire, P. 1970. *Pedagogy of the Oppressed*. New York: Herder and Herder.

Friedman, M. 1968. "The Role of Monetary Policy." *American Economic Review* 58/1: 1–17.

Friedman, R.M. 2001. *The Politics of Excellence: Behind the Nobel Prize in Science*. New York: Henry Holt.

Fritz, V., B. Levy, and R. Ort (eds.). 2014. *Problem-Driven Political Economy Analysis: The World Bank's Experience*. Washington, DC: World Bank.

Fu, J.S. 2013. "ICT in Education: A Critical Literature Review and Its Implications." *International Journal of Education and Development using Information and Communication Technology* 9/1: 112–112.

Fukuyama, F. 1989. "The End of History?" *The National Interest* 16: 3–18.

Fukuyama, F. 2012. *The Origins of Political Order*. New York: Farrar, Straus and Giroux.

Fukuyama, F. 2000. *Social Capital and Civil Society*. Washington, DC: International Monetary Fund Institute.

Fukuyama, F. 2014a. "At the 'End of History' Still Stands Democracy." *The Wall Street Journal*, June 6.

Fukuyama, F. 2014b. *Political Order and Political Decay*. New York: Farrar, Straus and Giroux.

Fung, A., and D. O'Rourke. 2000. "Reinventing Environmental Regulation from the Grassroots Up: Explaining and Expanding the Success of the Toxics Release Inventory." *Environmental Management* 25/2: 115–127.

Gawthrop, R., and G. Strauss. 1984. "Protestantism and Literacy in Early Modern Germany." *Past and Present* 104: 31–55.

GBD 2015 DALYs and HALE Collaborators. 2016. "Global, Regional, and National Disability-Adjusted Life-Years (DALYs) for 315 Diseases and Injuries and Healthy Life Expectancy (HALE), 1990–2015: A Systematic Analysis for the Global Burden of Disease Study 2015." *The Lancet* 388/10053: 1603–1658.

Goldin, C., and L.F. Katz. 1997. "Why the United States Led in Education: Lessons from Secondary School Expansion, 1910 to 1940." *National Bureau of Economic Research* w6144: 683–723.

Gramlich, E. 1990. *A Guide to Benefit-Cost Analysis*, second edition. Long Grove, IL: Waveland Press.

Green, J.F. 2013. *Rethinking Private Authority: Agents and Entrepreneurs in Global Environmental Governance*. Princeton, NJ: Princeton University Press.

Grundmann, R. 2016. "The Problem of Expertise in Knowledge Societies." *Minerva* 55/1: 25–48.

Hacking, I. 1986 "Making Up People," in T. Heller, M. Sosna, and D. Wellbery (eds.), *Reconstructing Individualism*. Stanford, CA: Stanford University Press.

Hacking, I. 1999. "Kind-Making: The Case of Child Abuse," in *The Social Construction of What?* Cambridge, MA: Harvard University Press.

Hamilton, J.T. 1995. "Pollution as News: Media and Stock Market Reactions to the Toxics Release Inventory Data." *Journal of Environmental Economics and Management* 28/1: 98–113.

Hamilton, J.T. 2005. *Regulation through Revelation: The Origin, Politics and Impacts of the Toxics Release Inventory Program*. New York: Cambridge University Press.

Hanna, N. 2007. "Literacy and the 'Great Divide' in the Islamic World, 1300–1800." *Journal of Global History* 2/02: 175–193.

Hanushek, E.A., and S.G. Rivkin. 2006. "Teacher Quality," in E.A. Hanushek and F. Welch (eds.), *Handbook of the Economics of Education*, vol. 2. Amsterdam: Elsevier.

Hanushek, E.A., S. Machin, and L. Wössmann. 2011–16. *Handbook of the Economics of Education*, vols. 1–5. Amsterdam: Elsevier.

Hardin, G. 1968. "The Tragedy of the Commons." *Science* 162: 1243–1248.

Hardin, R. 1982. *Collective Action*. Baltimore, MD: Johns Hopkins University Press.

Harrod, R.F. 1938. "Scope and Method of Economics." *Economic Journal* 48/191: 383–412.

22

Hattie, J. 2008. *Visible Learning: A Synthesis of Over 800 Meta-analyses Relating to Achievement*. Abingdon, Oxfordshire: Routledge.

Hausmann, R., D. Rodrik, and A. Velasco. 2008. "Growth Diagnostics," in N. Serra and J. Stiglitz (eds.), *The Washington Consensus Reconsidered: Towards a New Global Governance*. Oxford: Oxford University Press.

Heilbron, J. 1991. "The Tripartite Division of French Social Science: A Long-Term Perspective," in P. Wagner, B. Wittorck, and R. Whitley (eds.), *Discourses on Society. The Shaping of the Social Science Disciplines*. Dordrecht: Kluwer Academic Publishers.

Hirschman, A.O. 1970. *Exit, Voice and Loyalty: Responses to Decline in Firms, Organisations, and States*. Cambridge MA: Harvard University Press.

Hirschman, A.O. 1971. "Political Economics and Possibilism," in *A Bias for Hope*. New Haven, CT: Yale University Press.

Hirschman, A.O. 1991. *The Rhetoric of Reaction*. Cambridge, MA: Harvard University Press.

Hobbes, T. 1996 [1651]. *Leviathan*. Cambridge: Cambridge University Press.

Holm, S. 1998. "Goodbye to the Simple Solutions: The Second Phase of Priority Setting in Health Care." *British Medical Journal* 317: 1000–1002.

Hulme, M. 2014. *Can Science Fix Climate Change? A Case Against Climate Engineering*. Cambridge: Polity Press.

IHME. 2016. "Institute of Health Metrics and Evaluation." www.healthdata.org/.

Ingvarson, L., J. Schwille, M. T. Tatto, et al. 2013. *An Analysis of Teacher Education Context, Structure, and Quality-Assurance Arrangements in TEDS-M Countries: Findings from the IEA Teacher Education and Development Study in Mathematics*. Amsterdam: IEA.

Jaffe, A.B., R.G. Newell, and R.N. Stavins. 2004. "Technology Policy for Energy and the Environment," in A.B. Jaffe, J. Lerner, and S. Stern (eds.), *Innovation Policy and the Economy*, vol. 4. Cambridge, MA: MIT Press.

Jamison, D.T., L.H. Summers, G. Alleyne, et al. 2013. "Global Health 2035: A World Converging Within a Generation." *The Lancet* 382/9908: 1898–1955.

Jasanoff, S.S. 1987. "Contested Boundaries in Policy-Relevant Science." *Social Studies of Science* 17: 195–230.

Jasanoff, S. 2005. *Designs on Nature: Science and Democracy in Europe and the United States*. Princeton, NJ: Princeton University Press.

Jasanoff, S., 2009. *The Fifth Branch: Science Advisers as Policymakers*. Cambridge, MA: Harvard University Press.

Jasanoff, S. 2016. *The Ethics of Invention*. New York: W.W. Norton.

Jasanoff, S. (ed.) 2004. *States of Knowledge: The Co-production of Science and Social Order*. London: Routledge.

Jasanoff, S., and S.-H. Kim. 2009. "Containing the Atom: Sociotechnical Imaginaries and Nuclear Regulation in the U.S. and South Korea." *Minerva* 47/2: 119–146.

Jasanoff, S., and B. Wynne (with contributing authors). 1998. "Science and Decisionmaking," in Steve Rayner and Elizabeth L. Malone (eds.), *Human Choice and Climate Change*. Washington, DC: Battelle Press.

Jasanoff, S., and S.-H. Kim (eds.). 2015. *Dreamscapes of Modernity: Sociotechnical Imaginaries and the Fabrication of Power*. Chicago: University of Chicago Press.

Jencks, C., and M. Phillips. 1998. *The Black-White Test Score Gap*. Washington, DC: Brookings Institution Press.

Johnson C. 1982. *MITI and the Japanese Miracle*. Stanford, CA: Stanford University Press.

Jones L.P., and I. Sakong. 1980. *Business, Government and Entrepreneurship: The Korean Case*. Cambridge, MA: Harvard University Press for Harvard Institute for International Development.

Kaiser, W., and J. Schot. 2014. *Writing the Rules for Europe. Experts, Cartels and International Organizations*. Houndmills, Hampshire: Palgrave Macmillan.

Kahn, Jonathan. 2012. *Race in a Bottle: The Story of BiDil and Racialized Medicine in a Post Genomic Age*. New York: Columbia University Press.

Kaldor, N. 1939.' "Welfare Propositions of Economics and Interpersonal Comparisons of Utility." *Economic Journal* 49/195: 549–552.

Kamerman, S.B. 2000. "Early Childhood Education and Care: An Overview of Developments in the OECD Countries." *International Journal of Educational Research* 33/1: 7–29.

Kanbur, R. 2001. "Economic Policy, Distribution and Poverty: The Nature of Disagreements." *World Development* 29/6: 1083–1094.

Kanbur, R. 2009. "The Co-Evolution of the Washington Consensus and the Economic Development Discourse," *Macalester International* 24: 33–57.

Kanbur, R. 2014. "Globalization and Inequality," in A.B. Atkinson and F. Bourguignon (eds.), *Handbook of Income Distribution. Volume 2B*. Amsterdam: Elsevier.

Kanbur R. 2016a. "Economics and Economic Policy." Paper prepared for International Panel on Social Progress.

Kanbur, R. 2016b. "The End of Laissez-Faire, the End of History, and the Structure of Scientific Revolutions." *Challenge* 59/1: 35–46.

Kanbur, R. 2016c. "W. Arthur Lewis and the Roots of Ghanaian Economic Policy," in R. Kanbur and E. Aryeetey (eds.), *The Economy of Ghana Sixty Years After Independence*. Oxford: Oxford University Press.

Kanbur, R., and J. Stiglitz. 2015. "Wealth and Income Distribution: New Theories Needed for a New Era." VoxEU, 18 August. www.voxeu.org/article/wealth-and-income-distribution-new-theories-needed-new-era.

Karkkainen, B.C. 2001. "Information as Environmental Regulation: TRI and Performance Benchmarking, Precursor to a New Paradigm?" *Georgetown Law Journal* 89: 257–370.

Kelman, S. 1981. "Cost–Benefit Analysis: An Ethical Critique." *Regulation* 5: 33–40.

Keohane, R.O., and E. Ostrom. (eds.) 1994. *Local Commons and Global Interdependence*. London: SAGE.

Keynes, J.M. 1926. "The End of Laissez-Faire," in *The Collected Writings of John Maynard Keynes, Volume IX, Essays in Persuasion*. London: Royal Economic Society, Palgrave MacMillan, 1972.

Keynes, J.M. 1936. "The General Theory of Employment Interest and Money," in *The Collected Writings of John Maynard Keynes, Volume VII*. London: Royal Economic Society, Palgrave MacMillan, 1972.

Khanna, M., W.R.H. Quimio, and D. Bojilova. 1998. "Toxics Release Information: A Policy Tool for Environmental Protection." *Journal of Environmental Economics and Management* 36/3: 243–266.

Kim, B., and E. Vogel (eds.). 2011. *The Park Chung Hee Era: The Transformation of South Korea*. Cambridge, MA: Harvard University Press.

Knorr Cetina, K. 1999. *Epistemic Cultures: How the Sciences Make Knowledge*. Cambridge, MA: Harvard University Press.

Knudsen, E.I., J.J. Heckman, J.L. Cameron, and J.P. Shonkoff. 2006. "Economic, Neurobiological, and Behavioral Perspectives on Building America's Future Workforce." *PNAS* 103/27: 10155–10162.

Kohli, A. 2004. *State-Directed Development: Political Power and Industrialization in the Global Periphery*. New York: Cambridge University Press.

Konar, S., and M.A. Cohen. 1997. "Information as Regulation: The Effect of Community Right to Know Laws on Toxic Emissions." *Journal of Environmental Economics and Management* 32/1: 109–124.

Krugman, P. 2013. *End This Depression Now!* New York: W.W. Norton & Company.

Latour, B. 1988. *The Pasteurization of France*, transl. A. Sheridan and J. Law. Cambridge, MA: Harvard University Press.

Levy, B. 2014. *Working with the Grain: Integrating Governance and Growth in Development Strategies*. New York: Oxford University Press.

Levy, F., and R. Murnane. 2013. *Dancing with Robots: Human Skills for Computerized Work*. Washington, DC: Third Way NEXT.

Lewis, W.A. 1953. *Report on Industrialization of the Gold Coast*. Accra: Government Print Department.

Lewis, W.A. 1954. "Economic Development with Unlimited Supplies of Labour." *Manchester School* 22/2: 139–191.

Lewis, W.A. 1965. *Politics in West Africa*. Oxford: Oxford University Press.

Lindblom, C. 1959. "The Science of Muddling Through." *Public Administration Review* 19/2: 79–88.

MacKenzie, D. 1990. *Inventing Accuracy: A Historical Sociology of Nuclear Missile Guidance*. Cambridge, MA: MIT Press.

MacKenzie, D. 1998. *Knowing Machines: Essays on Technical Change*. Cambridge, MA: MIT Press.

MacKenzie, D. 2007. "The Political Economy of Carbon Trading." *London Review of Books* 29/7: 29–31.

MacKenzie, D., F. Muniesa, and L. Siu. (eds.) 2008. *Do Economists Make Markets? On the Performativity of Economics*. Princeton, NJ: Princeton University Press.

Marcus, G. 1995. *Technoscientific Imaginaries: Conversations, Profiles and Memories*. Chicago: University of Chicago Press.

Marmot, M., J. Allen, P. Goldblatt, et al. 2010. *Fair Society, Healthy Lives: The Marmot Review*. London: Ministry of Health.

Marmot, M.G., S. Stansfeld, C. Patel, et al. 1991. "Health Inequalities among British Civil Servants: The Whitehall II Study." *The Lancet* 337/8754: 1387–1393.

Marshall, Alfred. 1890. *Principles of Economics*. www.econlib.org/library/Marshall/marP.html.

Masur, J., and E. Posner. 2010. "Against Feasibility Analysis." *The University of Chicago Law Review* 77: 657–716.

Matson, P., W.C. Clark, and K. Andersson. 2016. *Pursuing Sustainability: A Guide to the Science and Practice*. Princeton, NJ: Princeton University Press.

May, P.J. 2003. "Performance-Based Regulation and Regulatory Regimes: The Saga of Leaky Buildings." *Law and Policy* 25/4: 381–401.

May, P.J. 2011. "Performance-Based Regulation," in D. Levi-Faur (ed.), *Handbook on the Politics of Regulation*. Northampton, MA: Edward Elgar.

Meade, J. 1975. *The Intelligent Radical's Guide to Economic Policy: The Mixed Economy*. London: George Allen and Unwin.

Merton, R.K. 1938. *Science, Technology and Society in Seventeenth Century England*. Bruges: Saint Catherine Press.

Meyers, D.C., J.A. Durlak, and A. Wandersmann. 2012. "The Quality Implementation Framework: A Synthesis of Critical Steps in the Implementation Process." *American Journal of Community Psychology* 50/3: 462–480.

Milanovic, B. 2016. *Global Inequality: A New Approach for the Age of Globalization*. Cambridge, MA: Harvard University Press.

Mincer, J. 1958. "Investment in Human Capital and Personal Income Distribution." *The Journal of Political Economy* 66/4: 281–302.

Mincer, J. 1974. *Schooling, Experience, and Earnings. Human Behavior and Social Institutions, 2*. New York: National Bureau of Economic Research, distributed by Columbia University Press.

Mirowski, P. 2013. *Never Let a Serious Crisis Go to Waste: How Neoliberalism Survived the Financial Meltdown*. London: Verso.

Mokyr, J. 2016. *A Culture of Growth: The Origins of the Modern Economy*. Princeton, NJ: Princeton University Press.

Mukerji, C. 1989. *A Fragile Power: Scientists and the State*. Princeton, NJ: Princeton University Press.

Murray, C.J. 2015. Choosing Indicators for the Health-Related SDG Targets." *The Lancet* 386/10001: 1314–1317.

Narayanamurti, V., and T. Odumosu. 2016. *Cycles of Invention and Discovery: Rethinking the Endless Frontier*. Cambridge, MA: Harvard University Press.

Natan T.E., Jr., and C.G. Miller. 1998. "Are Toxics Release Inventory Reductions Real?" *Environmental Science & Technology* 32/15: 368A–374A.

Newig, J., J. Voss, and J. Monstadts. 2008. *Governance for Sustainable Development*. Abingdon, Oxfordshire: Routledge.

Nisbet, R.A. 1965. *Makers of Modern Social Science: Émile Durkheim*. Upper Saddle River, NJ: Prentice-Hall.

Norheim, O.F. 2016. "Ethical Priority Setting for Universal Health Coverage: Challenges in Deciding upon Fair Distribution of Health Services." *BMC Medicine* 14/1: 75.

Norheim, O. F., P. Jha, K. Admasu, et al. 2015. "Avoiding 40% of the Premature Deaths in Each Country, 2010–30: Review of National Mortality Trends to Help Quantify the UN Sustainable Development Goal for Health." *The Lancet* 385: 239–252.

North, D. 1982. *Structure and Change in Economic History*. New York: W.W. Norton.

North, D.W., J. Wallis, and B. Weingast. 2009. *Violence and Social Orders*. Cambridge: Cambridge University Press.

North, D.W., J. Wallis, S.B. Webb, and B. Weingast. 2013. *In the Shadow of Violence*. Cambridge: Cambridge University Press.

Nowotny, H. 2015. *The Cunning of Uncertainty*. Cambridge: Polity Press.

Nutley, S.M., I. Walter, and H.T.O. Davies. 2007. *Using Evidence. How Research can Inform Public Service*. Bristol: The Policy Press.

OECD. 2016. *Skills Matter: Further Results from the Survey of Adult Skills*. Paris: OECD.

Ogburn, W.F. 1957. "Cultural Lag as Theory." *Sociology and Social Research* 41/3: 167–175.

Ogden, T., and Fixsen, D.L. 2014. "Implementation Science: A Brief Overview and a Look Ahead." *Zeitschrift für Psychologie* 22/1: 4–11.

Olsen, J.P. 2007. "The Institutional Dynamics of the European University," in P. Maasen and J. P. Olsen (eds.), *University Dynamics and European Intgrattion*. Amsterdam: Springer.

Olson, M. 1965. *The Logic of Collective Action: Public Goods and the Theory of Groups*. Cambridge, MA: Harvard University Press.

Oreskes, N. and J. Krige. (eds.) 2014. *Science and Technology in the Global Cold War*. Cambridge, MA: MIT Press.

Orthia, L.A. 2016. "What's Wrong with Talking about the Scientific Revolution? Applying Lessons from History of Science to Applied Fields of Science Studies." *Minerva* 54: 353–373.

Ostrom, E. 1990. *Governing the Commons*. New York: Cambridge University Press.

Ostrom, E. 2005. *Understanding Institutional Diversity*. New York: Cambridge University Press.

Ostrom, E., 2008. "The Challenge of Common-Pool Resources." *Environment: Science and Policy for Sustainable Development* 50/4: 8–21.

Ottersen, O.P., J. Dasgupta, C. Blouin, et al. 2014. "The Political Origins of Health Inequity: Prospects for Change." *The Lancet* 9917: 630–667.

Oudshoorn, N. 2003. *The Male Pill: A Biography of a Technology in the Making*. Durham, NC: Duke University Press.

Oudshoorn, N., and T. Pinch. 2003. *How Users Matter: The Co-construction of Users and Technology*. Cambridge, MA: MIT Press.

Paoli, G., and A. Wiles. 2015. "Key Analytical Capabilities of a Best-in-Class Regulator." Research paper prepared for the Penn Program on Regulation's Best-in-Class Regulator Initiative, University of Pennsylvania.

Peterson, A. 2011. *Civic Republicanism and Civic Education: The Education of Citizens*. Houndmills, Hampshire: Palgrave Macmillan.

Peto, R., A.D. Lopes, and O.F. Norheim. 2014. "Halving Premature Death." *Science* 345/6202: 1272–1272.

Petryna, A. 2009. *When Experiments Travel: Clinical Trials and the Global Search for Human Subjects*. Princeton, NJ: Princeton University Press.

Phillips, A.W. 1958. "The Relationship between Unemployment and the Rate of Change of Money Wages in the United Kingdom 1861–1957." *Economica* 25/100: 283–299.

Piketty, T. 2014. *Capital in the Twenty-First Century*. Cambridge, MA: Harvard University Press.

Poje, G.V., and D.M. Horowitz. 1990. *Phantom Reductions: Tracking Toxic Trends*. Washington, DC: National Wildlife Federation.

Pollitt, C., and G. Bouckaert. 2011. *Public Management Reform: A Comparative Analysis*. Oxford: Oxford University Press.

Porter, R. 1991. "Cleaning Up the Great Wen: Public Health in Eighteenth-Century London." *Medical History* 35/S11: 61–75.

Porter, T.M. 1995. *Trust in Numbers: The Pursuit of Objectivity in Science and Public Life*. Princeton, NJ: Princeton University Press.

Potts, H. 2008. *Accountability and the Right to the Highest Attainable Standard of Health*. Colchester: University of Essex.

Prakash, A., and M. Potoski. 2006. *The Voluntary Environmentalists: Green Clubs, ISO 14001, and Voluntary Environmental Regulations*. Cambridge: Cambridge University Press.

Preston, S., P. Heuveline, and M. Guillot 2000. *Demography: Measuring and Modeling Population Processes*. New York: Wiley.

Pritchett, L., and F. de Weijer. 2010. "Fragile States: Stuck in a Capability Trap." World Development Report 2011 Background Paper. Geneva: World Bank.

Pritchett, L., M. Woolcock, and M. Andrews. 2010. "Capability Traps? The Mechanisms of Persistent Implementation Failure." Working Paper 234. Washington, DC: Center for Global Development.

Putnam, R. D. 2002. *Democracies in Flux: The Evolution of Social Capital in Contemporary Society*. Oxford and New York: Oxford University Press.

Rabeharisoa, V., and M. Callon. 2004. "The Involvement of Patients in Research Activities Supported by the French Muscular Dystrophy Association," in Sheila Jasanoff (ed.), *States of Knowledge: The Co-production of Science and Social Order*. London: Routledge.

Rabinow, P. 1997. *Making PCR: A Story of Biotechnology*. Chicago: University of Chicago Press.

Rayner, S., C. Heyward, T. Kruger, N. Pidgeon, C. Redgwell, and J. Savulescu. 2013. "The Oxford Principles." *Climatic Change* 121/3: 499–512.

Reardon, J. 2004. *Race to the Finish: Identity and Governance in an Age of Genomics*. Princeton, NJ: Princeton University Press.

Reinhart, C., and K. Rogoff. 2011. *This Time Is Different: Eight Centuries of Financial Folly*. Princeton, NJ: Princeton University Press.

Revkin, Andrew. 2016. "Bill Gates, the 'Impatient Optimist,' Lays Out his Clean-Energy Innovation Agenda." Dot Earth: *New York Times* Blog, February 23. http://dotearth.blogs.nytimes.com/2016/02/23/bill-gates-the-impatient-optimist-lays-out-his-clean-energy-innovation-agenda/.

Richards, K.R. 2000. "Framing Environmental Policy Instrument Choice." *Duke Environmental Law & Policy Forum* 10: 221–285.

Ringer, F.K. 1979. *Education and Society in Modern Europe*. Bloomington: Indiana University Press.

Ringer, F.K. 1990. *The Decline of the German Mandarins: the German Academic Community, 1890–1933*. Hanover: University Press of New England.

Rivkin, S.G., E.A. Hanushek, and J.F. Kain. 2005. "Teachers, Schools, and Academic Achievement." *Econometrica* 73/2: 417–458.

Robbins, L. 1938. "Interpersonal Comparisons of Utility: A Comment." *Economic Journal* 48/192: 635–641.

Roberts, L.L. 2012. "The Circulation of Knowledge in Early Modern Europe: Embodiment, Mobility, Learning and Knowing." *History of Technology* 31: 47–68.

Robertson, J. 2015. *The Enlightenment. A Very Short Introduction*. Oxford: Oxford University Press.

Rodrik, D. 2006. "Goodbye Washington Consensus, Hello Washington Confusion." *Journal of Economic Literature* 44/4: 973–987.

Rolnick, A., and R. Grunewald. 2003. "Early Childhood Development: Economic Development with a High Public Return." *The Region* 17/4: 6–12.

Rosanvallon, P. (ed.) 2014. *Science et démocratie*. Paris: Odile Jacob.

Rose, H. 2001. *The Commodification of Bioinformation: The Icelandic Health Sector Database*. London: Wellcome Trust.

Rose, N. 2007. *The Politics of Life Itself*. Princeton, NJ: Princeton University Press.

Rothstein, H., P. Irving, T. Walden, and R. Yearsley. 2006. "The Risks of Risk-Based Regulation: Insights from the Environmental Policy Domain." *Environment International* 32/8: 1056–1065.

Sachs, Jeffrey D. 2003. "Institutions Matter, but Not for Everything." *Finance & Development*, June.

Sachs, J.D. 2015. *The Age of Sustainable Development*. New York: Columbia University Press.

Schofer, E. and J.W. Meyer. 2005. "The Worldwide Expansion of Higher Education in the Twentieth Century." *American Sociological Review* 70/6: 898–920.

Schot, J., and L. Kanger. 2018. "Deep Transitions: Emergence, Acceleration, Stabilization and Directionality." Working Paper. Brighton: Science Policy Research Unit.

Schultz, T.W. 1970. *Investment in Human Capital: the Role of Education and of Research*. New York: Free Press.

Schumpeter, J.A. 1942. *Capitalism, Socialism, and Democracy*. New York and London: Harper and Brothers.

Schwartzman, S., R. Pinheiro, and P. Pillay. (eds.) 2015. *Higher Education in the BRICS Countries – Investigating the Pact between Higher Education and Society*. Dordrecht: Springer.

Scoones, I. 2006. *Science, Agriculture and the Politics of Policy: The Case of Biotechnology in India*. Hyderabad: Orient Longman.

Scott, James C. 1998. *Seeing Like a State: How Certain Schemes to Improve the Human Condition Failed*. New Haven, CT: Yale University Press.

Sen, A. 1999. *Development as Freedom*. New York: Alfred Knopf.

Sen, A. 2002. "Why Health Equity?" *Health Economics* 11: 659–666.

Sen, A. 2009. *The Idea of Justice*. London: Allen Lane/Penguin.

Shapin, S. 1996. *The Scientific Revolution*. Chicago: University of Chicago Press.

Shavit, Y., and W. Muller. 2000. "Vocational Secondary Education – Where Diversion and Where Safety Net?" *European Societies* 2/1: 29–50.

Singh, M. 1964. *India's Export Trends and Prospects for Self-Sustained Growth*. Oxford: Clarendon Press.

Skloot, R. 2010. *The Immortal Life of Henrietta Lacks*. New York: Crown Books.

Slavin, R.E. 2002. "Evidence-Based Education Policies: Transforming Educational Practice and Research." *Educational Researcher* 31/7: 15–21.

Smith, A. 1776. *An Inquiry into the Nature and Causes of the Wealth of Nations*. www.econlib.org/library/Smith/smWN.html.

Smith, E. 2009. "Imaginaries of Development: The Rockefeller Foundation and Rice Research." *Science as Culture* 18/4: 461–482.

Soete, L. 2013. "Is Innovation Always Good?" in J. Fagerberg, B. Martin, and E.S. Andersen (eds.), *Innovation Studies: Evolution and Future Challenges*. Oxford: Oxford University Press.

Sowell, T. 2004. *Affirmative Action Around the World: An Empirical Study*. New Haven, CT: Yale University Press.

Specter, M. 2005. "What Money Can Buy," *The New Yorker*, October 24.

Spence, M., D. Leipziger, J. Manyika, and R. Kanbur. 2015. "Restarting the Global Economy: Three Mismatches that Need Concerted PUblic action." VoxEU, November 4. www.voxeu.org/article/restarting-global-economy.

Spiel, C., B. Schober, and D. Strohmeier. 2016. "Implementing Intervention Research into Public Policy – the 'I3-Approach'." *Prevention Science*, February 27: e-publication ahead of print.

Starobin, S. 2013. "Global Companies as Agents of Globalization," in J. Mikler (ed.), *The Handbook of Global Companies*. Oxford: John Wiley & Sons.

Starobin, S., and E. Weinthal. 2010. "The Search for Credible Information in Social and Environmental Global Governance: The Kosher Label." *Business and Politics* 12/3: 1–35.

Stavins, R.N. 2007. "Market-Based Environmental Policies: What Can We Learn from U.S. Experience (and Related Research)?" in J. Freeman and C.D. Kolstad (eds.), *Moving to Markets in Environmental Regulation: Lessons from Twenty Years of Experience*. New York: Oxford University Press.

Stern, P.C., and H.V. Fineberg (eds.), 1996. *Understanding Risk: Informing Decisions in a Democratic Society*. Washington, DC: National Academies Press.

Stevenson, D.L. 2006. "The Fit and Misfit of Sociological Research and Educational Policy," in Maureen T. Hallinan (ed.), *Handbook of the Sociology of Education*. New York: Springer Verlag.

Stiglitz, J. 2002a. *Globalization and Its Discontents*. New York: W.W. Norton & Company.

Stiglitz, J. 2002b. "Information and the Change in the Paradigm in Economics," abbreviated version of Nobel lecture. *American Economic Review* 92/3: 460–501.

Stiglitz, J. 2012. *The Price of Inequality: How Today's Divided Society Endangers Our Future*. New York: W.W. Norton.

Stiglitz, J., A. Sen, and J.P. Fitoussi. 2009. *Report by the Commission on the Measurement of Economic Performance and Social Progress*. www.insee.fr/fr/publications-et-services/dossiers_web/stiglitz/doc-commission/RAPPORT_anglais.pdf.

Stilgoe, J. 2015. *Experiment Earth: Responsible Innovation in Geoengineering*. Abingdon, Oxfordshire: Routledge/Earthscan.

Stilgoe, J, R. Owen, and P. Macnaghten. 2013. "Developing a Framework for Responsible Innovation." *Research Policy* 42: 1568–1580.

Stockdale, A., and S.F. Terry. 2002. "Advocacy Groups and the New Genetics." In J.S. Alper, C. Ard, A. Asch, J. Beckwith, P. Conrad, and L.N. Geller (eds.), *The Double-Edged Helix: Social Implications of Genetics in A Diverse Society*. Baltimore, MD: Johns Hopkins University Press.

Summers, L.H., on behalf of 267 signatories. 2015. "Economists' Declaration on Universal Health Coverage." *The Lancet* 386: 2112–2113.

Sunder Rajan, K. 2006. *Biocapital: The Constitution of Post-Genomic Life*. Durham: Duke University Press.

Sunder Rajan, K. (ed.) 2012. *Lively Capital: Biotechnologies, Ethics, and Governance in Global Markets*. Durham, NC: Duke University Press.

Sunstein, C.R. 1999. "Informational Regulation and Informational Standing: Akins and beyond." *University of Pennsylvania Law Review* 147: 613–675.

Sunstein, C.R. 2005. *Laws of Fear: Beyond the Precautionary Principle*. Cambridge: Cambridge University Press.

Teese, R. 2011. "Vocational Education and Training in France and Germany: Friend or Foe of the Educationally Disadvantaged?" in S. Lamb, E. Markussen, R. Teese, N. Sandberg, and J. Polesel (eds.), *School Dropout and Completion*. Dordrecht: Springer.

Thaler, R.H., and C.R. Sunstein. 2008. *Nudge: Improving Decisions About Health, Wealth, and Happiness*. New Haven, CT: Yale University Press.

Thompson, C. 2007. *Making Parents: The Ontological Choreography of Reproductive Technologies*. Cambridge, MA: MIT Press.

Tietenberg, T.H. 1985. *Emissions Trading: An Exercise in Reforming Pollution Policy*. Washington, DC: Resources for the Future Press.

Tietenberg, T.H. 1998. "Disclosure Strategies for Pollution Control." *Environmental & Resource Economics* 11/3: 587–602.

Tignor, R.L. 2006. *W. Arthur Lewis and the Birth of Development Economics*. Princeton, NJ: Princeton University Press.

Trow, M. 2000. "From Mass Higher Education to Universal Access: The American Advantage." *Minerva* 37/4: 303–328.

Tyler, T., and D.L. Markell. 2008. "Using Empirical Research to Design Government Citizen Participation Processes: A Case Study of Citizens' Roles in Environmental Compliance and Enforcement." *Kansas Law Review* 57/1: 7–14.

UN. 2015. *Transforming Our World: The 2030 Agenda for Sustainable Development*. New York: UN.

UNPD. 2015. *World Population Prospects: The 2015 Revision*. http://esa.un.org/unpd/wpp/Excel-Data/population.htm.

Vaughan, D. 1996. *The Challenger Launch Decision. Risky Technology, Culture, and Deviance at NASA*. Chicago: University of Chicago Press.

Vaupel, J., Z. Zhang, and A. van Raalte. 2011. "Life Expectancy and Disparity: An International Comparison of Life Table Data." *BMJ Open* 1/1: 000128.

22

Victora, C., A. Barros, H. Axelson, et al. 2012. "How Changes in Coverage Affect Equity in Maternal and Child Health Interventions in 35 Countdown to 2015 Countries: An Analysis of National Surveys." *The Lancet* 380: 1149–1156.

Voogt, J., G. Knezek, M. Cox, D. Knezek, and A. ten Brummelhuis. 2013. "Under Which Conditions Does ICT Have a Positive Effect on Teaching and Learning? A Call to Action." *Journal of Computer Assisted Learning* 29/1: 4–14.

Wade, R. 1990. *Economic Theory and the Role of Government in East Asian Industrialization*. Princeton, NJ: Princeton University Press.

Wade, R. 1996. "Japan, the World Bank, and the Art of Paradigm Maintenance: 'The East Asian Miracle' in Political Perspective." *New Left Review* 217: 3–36.

Wagner, P., B. Wittrock, and R. Whitley. 1991. *Discourses on Society – The Shaping of the Social Science Disciplines*. Dordrecht: Kluwer Academic Publishers.

Watts, N., W.N. Adger, P. Agnolucci, et al. 2015. "Health and Climate Change: Policy Responses to Protect Public Health." *The Lancet* 386/10006: 1861–1914.

Wesselingh, A.A. 2002. "Durkheim, Citizenship and Modern Education," in W.S.F Pickering and G. Walford (eds.), *Durkheim and Modern Education*. Abingdon, Oxfordshire: Routledge.

WHO. 2005. *Sustainable Health Financing, Universal Coverage and Social Health Insurance*. Geneva: WHO.

WHO. 2008. *Closing the Gap in a Generation. Health Equity through Action on the Social Determinants of Health*. Geneva: WHO.

WHO. 2010. *World Health Report. Health Systems Financing: The Path to Universal Coverage*. Geneva: WHO.

WHO. 2012. *Choosing Interventions that Are Cost Effective (WHO-CHOICE)*. www.who.int/choice/en/.

WHO. 2014. *Making Fair Choices on the Path to Universal Health Coverage. Final Report of the WHO Consultative Group on Equity and Universal Health Coverage*. Geneva: WHO.

WHO and World Bank. 2015. *Tracking Universal Health Coverage: First Global Monitoring Report. Joint WHO/World Bank Group Report, June 2015*. Geneva: World Bank.

Wiener, J. 2010. "Risk Regulation and Governance Institutions," in *Risks and Regulatory Policy: Improving the Governance of Risk*. Paris: OECD.

Williamson, John. 1989. "What Washington Means by Policy Reform," in J. Williamson (ed.), *Latin American Readjustment: How Much Has Happened*. Washington, DC: Institute for International Economics.

Williamson, O.E. 1985. *The Economic Institutions of Capitalism*. New York: The Free Press.

Williamson, O.E. 2000. "The New Institutional Economics: Taking Stock, Looking Ahead." *Journal of Economic Literature* 38/3: 595–613.

Winner, Langdon. 1986. *The Whale and the Reactor: A Search for Limits in an Age of High Technology*. Chicago: University of Chicago Press.

World Bank. 1993. *Investing in Health. World Development Report 1993*. Oxford: Oxford University Press.

World Bank. 1994. *The East Asian Miracle. A World Bank Policy Research Report*. Oxford: Oxford University Press.

World Bank. 2004. *Making Services Work for Poor People*. World Development Report 2004. Washington, DC: World Bank and Oxford University Press.

World Bank. 2008. *Public Sector Reform: What Works and Why*. Washington, DC: Independent Evaluation Group.

World Bank. 2012. *Health Equity and Financial Protection Datasheet*. Washington, DC: World Bank.

World Bank. 2015. "World DataBank – Education Statistics – All Indicators." http://databank.worldbank.org/data/reports.aspx?source=education-statistics-~-all-indicators.

World Commission on Environment and Development. 1987. *Our Common Future: Report of the World Commission on Environment and Development*. UN Documents (online).

Xu, K., D.B. Evans, K. Kawabata, R. Zeramdini, J. Klavus, and C.J. Murray. 2003. "Household Catastrophic Health Expenditure: A Multicountry Analysis." *The Lancet* 362/9378: 111–117.

Yamin, A.E. 2008. "Beyond Compassion: The Central Role of Accountability in Applying a Human Rights Framework to Health." *Health and Human Rights* 10/2: 1–20.

Young, O.R., 2002. *The Institutional Dimensions of Environmental Change: Fit, Interplay, and Scale*. Cambridge, MA: MIT Press.

Zerbe, R.O., and H.E. McCurdy. 1999. "The Failure of Market Failure." *Journal of Policy Analysis and Management* 18/4: 558–578.

22

Volume **3**

Authors

Introduction

Olivier Bouin, RFIEA
Marie-Laure Djelic, Sciences Po
Marc Fleurbaey, Princeton University
Ravi Kanbur, Cornell University
Elisa Reis, Federal University of Rio de Janeiro

Chapter 15

Coordinating Lead Authors:
John Bowen, Anthropology, Washington University in St. Louis, USA
Will Kymlicka, Philosophy, Queen's University, Kingston, Canada

Lead Authors:
Martin Hopenhayn, Instituto de Humanidades, Universidad Diego Portales, Chile
Takyiwaa Manuh, United Nations Economic Commission for Africa, Ethiopia
Abdul Raufu Mustapha, Centre for African Studies, University of Oxford, UK

Contributing Authors:
Faisal Garba, Sociology, University of Cape Town, South Africa
Jan Willem Duyvendak, Sociology, University of Amsterdam, Netherlands

Chapter 16

Coordinating Lead Authors:
Grace Davie, University of Exeter, UK
Nancy T. Ammerman, Boston University, USA

Lead Authors:
Samia Huq, BRAC University, Dhaka, Bangladesh
Lucian N. Leustean, Aston University, UK
Tarek Masoud, Harvard University, Kennedy School of Government, USA
Suzanne Moon, University of Oklahoma, USA
Jacob K. Olupona, Harvard Divinity School, USA
Vineeta Sinha, National University of Singapore
David A. Smilde, Tulane University, USA
Linda Woodhead, Lancaster University, UK
Fenggang Yang, Purdue University, USA

Contributing Author:
Gina Zurlo, Boston University, USA

Chapter 17

Coordinating Lead Authors:
Merike Blofield, University of Miami, USA
Fernando Filgueira, CIESU, Uruguay

Lead Authors:
Carmen Diana Deere, University of Florida, USA
Maxine Eichner, University of North Carolina, USA
Guðný Björk Eydal, University of Iceland
Rhacel Parreñas, University of South California, USA
Neetha Pillai, Centre for Women's Development Studies, India
Frances Rosenbluth, Yale University, USA
Tine Rostgaard, KORA, Denmark
Lynn Welchman, University of London, UK

Contributing Authors:
Annabelle Hutchinson, Yale University, USA
William McGrew, Yale University, USA
Tee Zhuo, Yale University, USA

Chapter 18

Coordinating Lead Authors:
Ama de-Graft Aikins, University of Ghana, Ghana
Dan Wikler, Harvard University, USA

Lead Authors:
Pascale Allotey, Monash University and United Nations University-International Institute for Global Health (UNU-IIGH), Malaysia
Uli Beisel, University of Bayreuth, Germany
Melinda Cooper, University of Sydney, Australia
Nir Eyal, Harvard University, USA
Dan Hausman, University of Wisconsin-Madison, USA
Wolfgang Lutz, IIASA, Austria
Ole F. Norheim, University of Bergen, Norway
Elizabeth Roberts, University of Michigan, USA
Denny Vågerö, Stockholm University, Sweden

Contributing Authors:
Karim Jebari, Institute for Futures Studies, Sweden

Chapter 19

Coordinating Lead Authors:
Christiane Spiel, University of Vienna, Austria
Simon Schwartzman, Institute for Studies on Labor and Society, Brazil

Lead Authors:
Marius Busemeyer, University of Konstanz, Germany
Nico Cloete, CHET, South Africa
Gili Drori, Hebrew University of Jerusalem, Israel
Lorenz Lassnigg, Institute for Advanced Studies, IHS Vienna, Austria
Barbara Schober, University of Vienna, Austria
Michele Schweisfurth, University of Glasgow, UK
Suman Verma, Panjab University, India

Contributing Authors:
Bilal Bakarat, IIASA, Austria
Peter Maassen, University of Oslo, Norway
Rob Reich, Stanford University, USA

Chapter 20

Coordinating Lead Authors:
Akeel Bilgrami, Columbia University, USA
Prabhat Patnaik, Jawaharlal Nehru University, India

Lead Authors:
Faisal Devji, University of Oxford, UK
Michele Lamont, Harvard University, USA
Ernesto Ottone, University Diego Portales, Chile
James Tully, University of Victoria, Canada
Nira Wickramasinghe, University of Leiden, Netherlands
Sue Wright, Portsmouth University, UK

Chapter 21

Coordinating Lead Authors:
Nancy Folbre, University of Massachusetts, Amherst, USA
Erik Olin Wright, University of Wisconsin-Madison, USA

Lead Authors:
Jenny Andersson, Sciences Po, France
Jeff Hearn, University of Huddersfield, UK
Susan Himmelweit, Open University, UK
Andrew Stirling, University of Sussex, UK

Chapter 22

Coordinating Lead Authors:
Matthew Adler, Duke University, USA
Helga Nowotny, ETH Zurich, Switzerland

Lead Authors:
Cary Coglianese, University of Pennsylvania Law School, USA
Sheila Jasanoff, Harvard University, USA
Ravi Kanbur, Cornell University, USA
Brian Levy, Johns Hopkins University, USA
Ole F. Norheim, University of Bergen, Norway
Johan Schot, University of Sussex, UK
Simon Schwartzman, Institute for Studies on Labor and Society, Brazil
Christiane Spiel, University of Vienna, Austria
Shana Starobin, Bowdoin College, USA

Index